D1155000

Jesus the Sage

BEN WITHERINGTON, III

Jesus the Sage
The Pilgrimage of Wisdom

FORTRESS PRESS MINNEAPOLIS

JESUS THE SAGE

The Pilgrimage of Wisdom

Witherington. Ben. 1951-
Jesus the sage : the pilgrimage of wisdom / Ben Witherington III.
p. cm.
Includes bibliographical references and indexes.
ISBN 0-8006-2711-3
1. Wisdom literature—Criticism, Interpretation, etc. 2. Jesus Christ—History of doctrines—Early church. ca. 30-600. 3. Bible. N.T.—Relation to the Old Testament. 4. Wisdom (Biblical personification) I. Title.
BS1455.W57 1994
223'.06—dc20
93-28174
CIP

AF 1-2711
98 97 96 95 94 1 2 3 4 5 6 7 8 9 10

Beginning of the teaching for life,
The instructions for well-being...
Give your ears, hear the sayings,
Give your heart to understand them;
It profits to put them in your heart,
Woe to him who neglects them!
Let them rest in the casket of your belly,
May they be bolted in your heart;
When there arises a whirlwind of words,
They'll be a mooring post for your tongue,
If you make your life with these in your heart,
You will find it a success;
You will find my words a storehouse for life,
Your being will prosper upon earth.

—The Instruction of Amenemope, Prologue and Chapter One, (excerpts)*

*Translated by C. Fontaine, *Traditional Sayings in the Old Testament: A Contextual Study* (Sheffield: Almond Press, 1982), pp. 140–41.

Contents

PART TWO: FROM JESUS TO THE CHURCH

Preface

This book is yet another example of the fact that not many people have heeded the sagacious warning of the final redactor of Ecclesiastes about the production of books (Eccles. 12.12). When I began this study I had no idea of the enormity of the task I was setting for myself. As a New Testament scholar I had assumed that Wisdom literature, being a subject widely neglected in many if not most scholarly circles until about twenty-five years ago, would be a manageable topic for a monograph, especially since my concern was with some specific matters such as how Wisdom literature developed over time and the degree of indebtedness of portions of the New Testament to sapiential material and ways of thinking. I was especially interested in the degree of indebtedness of early Jewish–Christian thinking about Jesus as the Christ to Wisdom ideas. Once I began to study in earnest, however, it became clear to me that a mastery of just the secondary literature on the subject, much less of Wisdom literature itself, was quite beyond the realm of possibility in a few years' span. It is no accident that those who are leaders in this field on the American scene, and I am thinking in particular of R. E. Murphy and J. L. Crenshaw, have spent virtually their entire scholarly careers ruminating and writing on Wisdom literature. The primary dividends come only after long reflection on this intriguing, figurative, and often enigmatic literature. Thus, when I went outside my area of particular expertise, I relied heavily on scholars like Murphy and Crenshaw, or M. V. Fox and N. Habel, or C. Camp and C. Fontaine, or B. Lang and G. von Rad.

To those whose expertise is in Wisdom material, either in the Hebrew Scriptures or in Sirach or the Wisdom of Solomon, much of what I say in the first two chapters will seem rudimentary and all too familiar. I was not concerned in these chapters to offer bold new theories or ideas, but rather to collect and summarize the best insights of those who have gone before me in order to provide the necessary and proper foundation for the discussion in the remaining seven chapters.

I am especially indebted to R. E. Murphy for critiquing the early drafts of the first two chapters. Whatever merits they may have are owed to his wise counsel, but the defects must be attributed to me. I should also like to thank W. Brosend for allowing me to read his dissertation while still in progress and to my colleague D. W. Baker for his critique of the Old Testament material.

A special thanks goes to Marshall Johnson and other editors at Fortress Press for their editorial supervision. I wish also to thank Robinson College, Cambridge University for electing me a Bye Fellow for 1992 which coupled with my half-sabbatical from Ashland Theological Seminary made possible the completion of this manuscript.

It has been my own experience that New Testament scholars too often approach the study of Wisdom literature as if it were a fishing expedition – one is after something in particular and only stays with the project until one catches the desired object. This leads to any number of distortions, even if one is merely trying to show the *background* of New Testament sapiential material. Wisdom literature deserves to be treated as a subject in itself, and especially books like Job and Ecclesiastes need to be heard on their own terms and not merely used as gold mines or foils for the study of some New Testament subject. To this end I have spent the last two years studying and even teaching an introductory course in Wisdom literature to make sure I had listened carefully to the voices of the Jewish sages who produced this marvelous literature. It is evident to me that I still have much to learn, "miles to go before I sleep."

This book has arisen in part out of my concern that biblical studies has increasingly become a series of exercises in specialty studies. In part this is a good thing which the Society of Biblical Literature has rightly fostered and nurtured. Everyone has his or her own baileywick and normally keeps carefully within its confines. This sort of approach, however, leads to depth but not breadth of vision which is just as often needed. For example, what does one do when one discovers that the teachings of Jesus reflect the influence not only of Wisdom forms and ideas but also of prophetic, especially late prophetic, forms and ideas? I suspect that the tendency to try and too rigidly compartmentalize Jesus or Q is because the specialty approach coupled with the legacy of form criticism encourages us to think in discrete categories when in fact we should have been observing how forms and ideas have cross-fertilized across the boundaries of our categories and the limitations of particular literary genres. The parables of Jesus are a perfect example of what I mean. They are a form of Wisdom literature, but it appears they developed only when Jewish prophets adopted and adapted Wisdom forms to serve narrative purposes. This is why, before the time of Jesus, we find no real parables in Hebrew Wisdom literature, but rather only in the Old Testament prophetic material. It then becomes obvious that it is not enough to say Jesus is a sage; one must ask what kind of sage. I will be arguing that he was and would have been seen to be a Jewish prophetic sage whose teaching and style primarily reflected, as did Ben Sira's or Pseudo-Solomon's before him, the confluence of Hebrew sapiential and prophetic forms and ideas, and to a much lesser degree revealed traces of Hellenistic influence.

There is a need for general practitioners as well as specialists, and in the realm of biblical Wisdom literature I am seeking to be the former, not the latter. I do so precisely because some rather exaggerated claims continue to be made on the basis of narrow specialty studies or special interest approaches to Wisdom literature about subjects as varied as the personification of Wisdom, the character of Jesus' teaching and lifestyle, the development of Wisdom Christology, or the modern appropriation of biblical Wisdom literature to mention but four complex matters. It is my hope that by exposing the reader to a wide range of Wisdom material and seeking to trace the development of Jewish and then Jewish–Christian Wisdom literature, a framework for evaluating particular and specialist interests will be provided.

This book then is not only about the pilgrimage of Wisdom but also about Jesus the sage as one who contributed to the growth and development of Jewish Wisdom and, for the community of his own followers, charted a course that they would follow in further developing Wisdom ideas and forms. Jesus stands at the center or heart of this book for he is the pivotal figure who not merely mirrors previous developments in sapiential thinking and the creation of Wisdom material, but also charts some new courses which left an indelible impression on the compiler(s) of Q, on James, on the creators of the christological hymns, on Paul, and finally on the Gospel writers, in particular the first evangelist.

This preface then must serve as an invitation to come on a journey, the pilgrimage of Wisdom. I am convinced that through carefully studying the material in chronological order one can learn how biblical Wisdom developed and changed over the course of time and have a framework for answering a panoply of particular questions that we bring to the texts from other quarters. Jesus Ben Sira reminds us,

> An educated person knows many things,
> and one with much experience knows
> what he is talking about. An inexperienced
> person knows few things, but *one that has traveled*
> acquires much sagacity.
>
> Sir. 34.9–11.

Ben Witherington, III

PART ONE
FROM SOLOMON TO JESUS

1

Beginning the Journey: Drinking from the Fount

STUDYING Wisdom literature requires patience and time. Since so much of Wisdom literature involves indirect speech (metaphors, similes, figures, images, and riddles) rather than straight-forward propositions or normal discourse, one is obligated not merely to read the Wisdom material but also to ruminate upon it. It is the sort of literature that more often than not seeks to persuade by causing the audience to think, rather than simply demanding assent to its world-view. If one takes the further step of not only studying Wisdom literature but also trying to trace some of the ways in which the corpus of biblical Wisdom material developed over the period between about 960 B.C. to A.D. 100, then one must begin at the beginning, at the font of biblical Wisdom, and then journey chronologically. This will entail, after a brief discussion of what sages and Wisdom literature are, an examination of some of the earliest forms, themes, and trends in biblical Wisdom literature as we find them in Proverbs, followed by a discussion of some of the crucial material in Ecclesiastes. In Chapter 2, a discussion of Ben Sira and the Wisdom of Solomon will be undertaken before we turn to the material in the New Testament.[1]

[1] The latter two works, of course, are not included in the Protestant canon, but they deserve our close attention both to show how the Wisdom tradition found in the Hebrew Scriptures continued to develop, and because these works also had an impact on various New Testament figures and authors.

A. BACKGROUND AND FOREGROUND

1. *DEFINITIONS AND DISTINCTIONS*

The term *hakam* means wise, *hokmah* wisdom, but these are not by any means technical terms for a specific kind of information or literature. The terms themselves are frequently found in the Hebrew Scriptures in tandem with other similar terms such as *yada* (to know), *da'at* (knowledge), or *bin* and *bina* (understanding). These terms overlap in meaning to a significant degree. Wisdom in the Hebrew Scriptures can refer to a variety of things: (1) political *savoir faire* (worldly wisdom), i.e., knowing what the politic thing to do in a particular situation would be (1 Kgs. 5.21); (2) encyclopedic knowledge of nature (1 Kgs. 4.33); (3) the gift of discernment, of knowing the right thing to do, or how to judge and evaluate various options presented to one (e.g. 1 Kgs. 3.16–28); (4) a saying, riddle, or proverb that reveals a *secret* about life that gives one true insight into how things really are, allowing one to look at life from the proper perspective. Here Wisdom literature overlaps to a certain extent with apocalyptic and eschatological material. Finally, there is a more basic use of the term *hokmah* to mean (5) skill, expertise, or artisanship (*hakam* then means one who has such skills, cf. 1 Chron. 22.15; 2 Chron. 2.7).[2] Often in the Hebrew Scriptures, particularly in Proverbs, Wisdom refers to the third meaning presented above, though frequently it simply has the more general meaning of knowing how to read the ways and the moral structure of the world and live according to them so that one not only copes with life but also lives well and in an upright manner.

Was there a class of "sages" that paralleled prophets and priests in ancient Israel? At least by 700 B.C. if not before the answer seems to be yes, for we hear in Prov. 25.1 that there were those who collected Wisdom material for Hezekiah.[3] While the collectors may not have been sages, their activity suggests a group of people who had produced a body of oral or written Wisdom material. One could also point to a text that comes from about 100 years after Hezekiah, Jer. 18.18, where we read of the instructions that come from priests, counsel that comes from "the wise" and the "word" which comes from a

[2] Cf. A. de Pury, "Sagesse et Révélation dans l'Ancien Testament," 3ff.

[3] Cf. R. B. Y. Scott, "Solomon and the Beginnings of Wisdom in Israel," in *Wisdom in Israel and the Ancient Near East*, 273: "Since no tendentious purpose can be suspected in the mention of the otherwise unknown 'men of Hezekiah', this is first-rate evidence that an organized literary wisdom movement existed at Hezekiah's court and under his patronage. The king's men *transcribed, published*, or *carried forward from tradition* a collection of maxims which, *in this late editorial title*, are designated 'proverbs of Solomon'." The arguments of R. N. Whybray, *The Intellectual Tradition in the Old Testament*, 15ff. are only partially convincing. That there was not a "professional" class of sages who were royal counselors may well be so at least up to the time of Hezekiah, but this does not rule out the existence of sages in other settings. Too much weight is put on the word "professional". Kings may well have consulted sages, whose main provenance was not the court, much like they consulted prophets.

prophet. What may be in view here, however, is a group of counselors, not sages, to the king who gave advice about how the king should act.[4]

There is evidence that probably as early as David and certainly in the time of Solomon, Israelite kings had such counselors (cf. 2 Sam. 16.23; 1 Kgs.4.1–19; 10.1). The sort of wisdom such counselors would offer would mainly be category (1) listed above, not (3) or (4).

Yet on closer scrutiny this does not provide us with a full clue as to who was likely to have produced the Wisdom material that found its way into the Hebrew Scriptures. Only a small amount of the material we find in Proverbs could be called advice to a ruler in regard to the politically astute thing to do. Prov. 22.17 and 24.23 indicates that the wise one is the author of *meshalim* (figurative sayings such as proverbs or parables). Proverbs 1.6 divides the output of the wise person into *mashal, melitsah* (taunt), words of wisdom, and finally *hiddah* (riddle), such as those Samson offered. This suggests that we cannot look simply to a class of court counselors as the producers of Wisdom literature. Indeed, when we read Proverbs various sayings suggest that some of this material arose in the home or clan, not in the royal court. There is only a minority of this material that *clearly* betrays a courtly origin.[5]

Yet we must not be too hasty to discard the court setting especially if we are concerned about who and where biblical Wisdom *literature* was produced and how it was transmitted through the ages. Here the suggestions of G. von Rad and E. W. Heaton, among others, require close scrutiny.[6] They point to the scribal schools in Egypt and argue for the likelihood that as early as Solomon's time the Jewish monarch had such scribes for the production and transmission of various sorts of documents. The Egyptian scribes were noted for compiling and/or copying all sorts of material including what we find in the *Instructions of Amenemope.*[7] The fact that we find significant portions of this Egyptian material in the book of Proverbs *may* suggest that at an early date, at least as early as the time of Hezekiah but perhaps already during the reign of Solomon, there were court scribes in Israel like the scribes in Egypt copying such documents. D. W. Jamieson-Drake warns, however, that we have no certain epigraphical or archeological evidence in Israel for schools prior to the eighth century at the earliest, and cross-cultural analogies must be used with great caution. In fact, he is willing to suggest that there is precious little evidence of

---

[4] I do not rule out that some sages may have been court counselors and vice versa.

[5] Cf R. H. Whybray, "The Sage in the Israelite Royal Court," in *The Sage in Israel and the Ancient Near East*, 138: "A large proportion of Proverbs is concerned with matters of interest to the agriculturalist rather than the courtier." This is true; however, as G. E. Bryce has shown in *A Legacy of Wisdom. The Egyptian Contribution to the Wisdom of Israel*, 135ff., material likely from a court setting predominates especally in Proverbs 22–25, and reflects the attempt to adapt and assimilate material from Egyptian Wisdom collections.

[6] Cf. G. von Rad, *Wisdom in Israel*, 15ff.; E. W. Heaton, *Solomon's New Men. The Emergence of Ancient Israel as a National State*, 101ff., especially 121ff.

[7] Cf. A. Alt, "Zur Literarischen Analyse der Weisheit des Amenemope," in *Wisdom in Israel and the Ancient Near East*, 16–25.

even much literacy prior to the eighth century in Israel, and even less evidence of scribal schools.[8] Most scholars would say that the first clear evidence of a *bet midrash* comes in Ben Sira (cf. Sir. 51.23).

Mass literacy is a modern phenomenon. Writing materials in antiquity were often cumbersome and always expensive. Surveys of as literate a culture as ancient Egypt suggest only about a 1–10% degree of literacy. Education was for the well-to-do, and was not cost effective, for most trades required apprenticeship but not book learning.[9] This means one of two things – either the Wisdom material comes to us from the royal courts and the wealthy landed folk who had the leisure time and money for education, or a significant portion of this material was once oral, but was collected and written down by those who were literate and had the time and financial support to produce such documents. It does not follow from the lack of evidence for royal schools in Israel in the early monarchical period that education was not going on in that age. Perhaps, however, the *primary* venue for education was the home, and parents were involved in teaching their children a wide variety of things, even if most of the teaching was oral and the learning was a matter of listening and reciting rather than writing. I agree with J. Crenshaw that the "primary sense of father and son within Proverbs must surely reflect a family setting, and the occasional reference to mother cannot be rightly attributed to the demands of parallelism."[10]

Since sages can be characterized as "wide of ear" as well as "broad of heart" one may suspect that a goodly portion of Wisdom material began as oral sayings and only later was set down in writing. This would open the door to a variety of sources of Wisdom material, rich and poor, family, clan, and court. The preservers of this tradition were very likely found in the court setting for in Prov. 25.1 we hear of the officials of Hezekiah who copied proverbs of Solomon (Hezekiah reigned 716–686 B.C.). This suggests that the conservers and writers of this sort of material were court officials who could have gathered this material not only from the king but also from a wide variety of other sources.

I am suggesting that there is a distinction between *sages*, those who coined proverbs or offered various sorts of oral teaching that could be called wisdom, and *scribes* of the court and later of the school who put such material

---

[8] Cf. D. W. Jamieson-Drake, *Scribes and Schools in Monarchic Judah. A Socio-Archeological Approach,* 143ff. Even the texts in Proverbs which may suggest schools, are all found in Proverbs 1–9, with the exception of Prov. 17:16. This paucity does not inspire great confidence that there were already schools in the 10th century B.C. of the sort possibly evidenced in the appendix to Ecclesiastes, or more certainly in Ben Sira.

[9] This was rightly stressed by J. Crenshaw in his Nov. 1990 lecture at the national SBL meeting, offering a "Retrospective and Prospective on Wisdom."

[10] J. Crenshaw, "Education in Ancient Israel," 614. I agree that ancient Israelite education should not be seen as confined to the home. Nevertheless, the argument that the instructional material found in Proverbs 1–9 comes from the family setting seems very likely, and the family must be seen as *a* if not *the* primary venue in the earliest part of the monarchical period.

in writing and so preserved it for later audiences. A further distinction is required in regard to the king's counselors (and courtiers) for they could have fallen into the categories of sage or scribe or both (cf. the story of Daniel). It is likely that being a sage involved more than just what the king's counselors did, and there were probably counselors who coined no proverbs, riddles, or other forms of wisdom speech. In short, some sages may have been counselors in the court and some counselors may have been sages but the two categories could be distinguished. R. N. Whybray is right to caution,

> although the advisers of foreign kings are occasionally called "wise men" (e.g. Isa. 19.11–12), no passage in the Old Testament unequivocally uses the term wise to describe persons serving Israelite kings. The supposition, for example, that the wise men condemned by Isaiah were royal counselors is purely inferential. No class of Israelite court officials bore the title wise men or sages.[11]

Scribes could probably be distinguished in almost all cases from both these groups. Scholars will no doubt continue to debate whether Israel's sages were a distinct class of people, and if so whether they occupied a particular social class or station in society and operated out of a particular setting (the home? a teaching house as was later the case with Ben Sira? the court?). Certainly, it is significant that the ethos that Proverbs exudes is that of relative prosperity.[12] Job also was portrayed as extremely wealthy, and even the author of Ecclesiastes suggests enjoying pleasure and prosperity, but one must have such things to enjoy them. This suggests an upper class ethos as the setting for the final writing and editing of Israelite Wisdom *literature*. Here the detailed work of R. Gordis on the social background of Wisdom literature is of great value. His own conclusion is that

> Wisdom literature... was fundamentally the product of the upper classes in society, who lived principally in the capital, Jerusalem. Some of them were engaged in large scale foreign trade... Most were supported by the income of their country estates which were tilled either by slaves, or by tenant farmers, who might have once owned the very fields they now worked as tenants. This patrician group was allied by marriage with the high-priestly families and the higher government officials, who represented the foreign suzerain, Persian, Ptolemaic, or Seleucid....

---

[11] Whybray, "The Sage in the Israelite Royal Court," 134.

[12] One must be able to distinguish between the sage who offered proverbs and the later redactors of the Wisdom material who wrote such proverbs down. R. N. Whybray may be right that the sages themselves who coined the many sayings about wealth and poverty in Proverbs very likely stood somewhere between wealth and poverty and considered either a real possibility for themselves, living in a precarious world. However, it seems likely that those who wrote down and edited the sayings were from or supported by the upper class. Cf. R. N. Whybray, *Wealth and Poverty in the Book of Proverbs*, 60-61.

> As is to be expected, the upper classes were conservative in their outlook, basically satisfied with the status quo and opposed to change. Their conservatism extended to every sphere of life, and permeated their religious ideas, as well as their social, economic and political attitudes. What is most striking is that this *basic conservatism is to be found among the unconventional Wisdom teachers as well* [e.g. Qoheleth].[13]

Account must also be taken of the insights from cultural anthropology that suggest the material we find in Proverbs is written by people for whom the group is more primary in shaping one's sense of identity than one's individuality. Collective wisdom takes precedent and indeed shapes individual insight. In Israelite society, as in many other Ancient Near East cultures, individuals manifest what is called dyadic personality, and thus what is most crucial and what determines one's self image is how others view a person. Such a person is concerned not so much with guilt but with maintaining honor and avoiding shame in the eyes of the group. In this sort of culture, in order to be human one must live out the expectations of significant others in one's life, such as one's parents, the sage in the village, one's king.[14] This is why it is so significant when we move from Proverbs to Qoheleth in the post-exilic period and hear an individual, albeit anonymous, voice (or at least an individual interpretation of the collective voice of wisdom) which is highly critical of the received wisdom. The sense of group wisdom, like the sense of group identity was breaking down in Qoheleth's day, as we will discuss in the second major part of this chapter.

The ending of the book of Ecclesiastes helps us to see how we came to have Wisdom literature (cf. Eccles. 12.9–11). The material began its life as oral tradition in a variety of settings, including the home and the court, and in due course was collected and set down in writing by literate and reasonably well-to-do people like Qoheleth, by court scribes and counselors, and perhaps by others we cannot name at this juncture.[15] If scribal practices in Israel were like those in Egypt, the scribal transmission of Wisdom material entailed rote memorization and word-for-word copying of previous manuscripts.[16] It was

---

[13] R. Gordis, "The Social Background of Wisdom Literature," 81–82. This essay still deserves close scrutiny. De Pury, "Sagesse et Révélation," 18ff., rightly stresses that Job and Qoheleth are protesting against a dogmatic or doctrinaire form of sapiential thinking, perhaps like that exhibited by Job's comforters, not against Wisdom thinking *in toto*.

[14] For illumination about all of this one should compare B. Malina, *The New Testament World; Insights from Cultural Anthropology*, 53ff. Actually, Malina's work is even more insightful for its understanding of pre-Hellenized and pre-individualized Jewish culture than it is for its understanding of the New Testament world.

[15] Whybray, *The Intellectual Tradition*,. 47ff., wants to drive a wedge between the fact that Qoheleth is called a sage and the fact that he taught, based on a certain reading of Eccles. 12:9a (but this sounds like special pleading).

[16] Cf. J. Crenshaw, "The Acquisition of Knowledge in Israelite Wisdom Literature," 247. This may provide some clues about the transmission of Jesus' Wisdom teachings, if the Wisdom material had come to have a particular way in Israel of being preserved and transmitted over the centuries.

very likely scribes that produced most of the genre of literature called Wisdom literature. It will be well to stop now to define more clearly what is meant by Wisdom literature. J. Crenshaw offers the following helpful definition:

> Formally wisdom consists of proverbial sentence or instruction, debate, intellectual reflection; thematically wisdom comprises self-evident intuitions about mastering life for human betterment, groping after life's secrets with regard to innocent suffering, grappling with finitude, and quest for truth concealed in the created order and manifested in Dame Wisdom. When a marriage between form and content exists, there is wisdom literature. Lacking such oneness, a given text participates in biblical wisdom to a greater or lesser extent.[17]

This definition suggests that while some Psalms or the Joseph cycle may reflect wisdom ideas and concepts about the nature of life, they are not Wisdom literature *per se*; they merely reflect a wisdom view of the world. Another helpful definition of the most common form of wisdom teaching is that a proverb is a short sentence founded upon long experience containing a truth.[18] It appears that "gnomic apperception endeavored to capture insights from experience and to clothe them in clever statements that could easily be committed to memory."[19]

In this book I will be following J. G. Williams' distinction between proverb and aphorism. The former is described above. Since proverbs are the crystallization of the wisdom of the ages, they are usually anonymous. Aphorisms, by contrast, provide not the wisdom of the collective group, or the apt summary of many similar experiences, but rather the unique insight of a creative individual, such as a Qoheleth or a Jesus. Williams puts it this way: "The attribution of specific authorship to aphorism, and of popular origins and appeal to proverb are useful but not decisive characteristics. What is decisive... is the difference between a *collective* voice and an *individual* voice." The aphorist is one who reacts against "the timeless types of traditional order...", attempting to articulate instead some kind of counter order which provides "insights into an ideal forming of life, whether this be a principle of the order of creation, of primary experiences, of God's new domain, or of the world of thought and imagination."[20] In the main, proverbs and aphorisms differ not so much in their form as in their purpose and use. Both proverbs and aphorisms are short pithy sayings, often involving analogy and vivid imagery.

One thing that characterizes Wisdom literature, at least until one reaches parts of the writings of Ben Sira, is that it deals with experiences that are common to humanity, not with particular and distinct historical events that are

---

[17] J. L. Crenshaw, *Old Testament Wisdom. an Introduction*, 19.
[18] Crenshaw, *Old Testament Wisdom*, 67.
[19] Crenshaw, "Acquisition of Knowledge," 246.
[20] J. G. Williams, *Those Who Ponder Proverbs*, 80, 81, 83.

unrepeated and unrepeatable.[21] This means that early Israelite Wisdom literature deals with a different sort of human experience than a good deal of the rest of the Hebrew Scriptures. It focuses on the common or mundane, on daily life and recurring experiences.

The sages dealt with and drew deductions from the repeatable patterns and moral order of ordinary life, both of human life and the life of the larger natural world. For the most part they were trying to explain how God's people should live when God is not presently intervening and when there is no late and particular oracle from God to draw on. Jewish sages often had a more general audience in mind than those who wrote much of the Egyptian Wisdom literature in order to prepare a group of civil servants for a particular vocation.[22] The teaching of a sage was meant to be a form of persuasion, encouraging someone to pursue a particular course of life. It did not usually resort to simple commands, or to some sort of oracular formula to indicate its authority. As R. E. Murphy says, "The proverbial sayings do not advertise their authority. This is presumed to lie in the teacher, or to be intrinsic to the experience and tradition that is expressed in the saying..."[23]

Like the prophets, the sages were also concerned to provide an alternative, not to Yahwism but to a religion based on the cycles of nature. In short, it seems likely that they spoke, and in due course wrote, with one eye on Yahwism's chief competition, the pagan fertility religions. This may partially explain why in biblical Wisdom literature there is considerable warning about the "stranger" (in particular, foreign women) and sexual immorality, as well as why *hokmah* is placed clearly within a context where it is seen as at most a personification of an attribute of God or perhaps of God's creation.

The biblical sages accomplished their aims by offering a theology of creation and creation order that de-divinized nature and continued to inculcate respect and reverence for Yahweh, who was to be seen not only as a

---

[21] Ben Sira seems to have been the first to deliberately link the traditional faith story about Israel's salvation history with Wisdom's generalizations. As we shall see, there is a gradual particularizing of the tradition. Not only do generalizing proverbs give way in Qoheleth to more specific aphorisms, but also Woman Wisdom goes from being a personification of a divine attribute to being closely identified with the Mosaic law. This particularizing trend continues in the teaching of Jesus. While Qoheleth does indeed provide us with individual insight, which distinguishes it from the largely anonymous character of previous Israelite Wisdom, it is insight into a general human condition when one lives in a world gone wrong and God doesn't seem willing to intervene and correct things. Qoheleth's skepticism is expressed because of a general human malaise that many were experiencing, but which he articulated in a unique way.

[22] Cf. O. Plöger, *Sprüche Salomos (Proverbia)*, XXXIII. This is not to deny that some of the material in Proverbs may well have been used for such purposes, but only that most of this Jewish Wisdom material was probably not generated for such a narrow purpose.

[23] R. E. Murphy, "The Faces of Wisdom in the Book of Proverbs," in *Mélanges bibliques et orientaux en l'honneur de M. Henri Cazelles*, 339. He is right, however, that the issue of authority is addressed somewhat differently in Proverbs 1–9. There the approach is much more didactic, and less a matter of stating observations as facts.

redeemer God, but also as a creator God.[24] These sages knew that ordinary daily experience could be either good or bad, either pleasurable or painful. They were not naive optimists, not even in the case of those who coined various of the earliest sayings now enshrined in Proverbs. Their teachings, however, had definite limitations because they were based on *generalizations* about nature or human nature.

A generalization is by definition something that has been shown to be usually, often, or under normal circumstances true, but it is not *always* true or applicable. "As limited generalizations, then, proverbs might be more appropriately described as paradigms than as laws.... Since proverbs are not universally valid laws but admit of exceptions, their application depends on the identification of the right time."[25] The Book of Proverbs for the most part does not try to deal with the exceptional individual or situation. Ecclesiastes, like Job though in a different manner, sets about to make good this lack, while still largely maintaining the framework of a Wisdom world view. As K. A. Farmer reminds us, "Those who spoke to a stable, settled, and orderly society might make observations about reality that would not hold true for those who lived in troubled or chaotic times."[26] It was the task of a sage to find a "word in season" that would fit the situation he was addressing.[27] Even a generalization was only applicable in a certain *sort* or class of circumstances.[28]

2. HEBREW WISDOM: SACRED OR SECULAR, NATIONAL OR INTERNATIONAL?

Discerning the origins of Wisdom thinking in Israel is difficult and much disputed. It seems, once one has examined the Wisdom corpus in detail, that by and large true wisdom was thought to come not merely from human experience or the observation of human and animal nature or the material creation but ultimately from God, or in a non-Israelite setting from the gods, even if it came through these other means. The sage reflected on what the world and

[24] I find the suggestion that the phrase "the fear of Yahweh" was something that was only appended to the Wisdom corpus as a late afterthought most unlikely. Yahwism had existed for a considerable period of time before there was ever any Wisdom *literature* in Israel. The fact that this phrase or its equivalent is found in a whole variety of strains of Wisdom literature should be given more attention, especially since we are repeatedly told that reverence for Yahweh is either the beginning or the very essence of Israelite Wisdom.

[25] J. J. Collins, "Proverbial Wisdom and the Yahwist Vision," in *Gnomic Wisdom*, 6, 12.

[26] K. A. Farmer, *Proverbs and Ecclesiastes. Who Knows What is Good?*, 5.

[27] One should keep steadily in view the difference between a generalization based on the observation of how certain causes lead to certain effects in a set of repeatable circumstances (e.g., "if a person jumps off a tall building, s/he will get hurt"), and a universal truth, something that is always and everywhere true without exception (e.g. "human beings all die eventually").

[28] There are at least two further sorts of limitations one can find in Wisdom literature. It is limited because it is admittedly usually a matter of human insight rather than direct divine revelation (one may see the figure of personified Wisdom as an attempt to overcome this limitation). There is a further sociological limitation in that, at least in the case of the early Jewish sages that came before Qoheleth, there is a presupposition about their *Sitz im Leben*, namely, that they are experiencing "normal circumstances".

ordinary human and animal affairs can reveal about God but especially about how as a human being one ought to live in order to rightly express reverence for God in accord with the moral structure of the universe God set up in the first place. Wisdom transcended mere knowledge in that it entailed the capacity of knowing or discerning how to use information for human good.[29]

There were at least three ways to gain wisdom according to the Hebrew sages: (1) the careful scrutiny of nature and human nature; (2) learning from the traditions of one's elders, the accumulated wisdom of previous generations; and (3) through encounter with God or a special revelation that came to a person through such an encounter (e.g., Prov. 8 and Job 40–41).[30] If one is asking about the starting point or ultimate source of Wisdom, however, the main answer offered by the Hebrew Scriptures has to do with the third of these sources. P. Craigie put it this way:

> Hebrew wisdom, though it sought to develop both the reason and the intellect as did the Greeks, could start only with God. The mind and its capacities were God-given; thus however secular in appearance the wisdom of the Hebrews might seem, it had God as its starting point. The reverence of God, namely the acknowledgment that God existed, created, and was important in human life lay behind all the developments in Hebrew wisdom.[31]

Craigie is also right to say that the wisdom enshrined in Proverbs had its weakness – it was subject to the attack of skepticism and this is what we find in Ecclesiastes. It was also subject to the attack of those who experienced extreme suffering, such as we find in Job. Under such exceptional circumstances, proverbial wisdom and common sense did not work and proverbs looked like mere platitudes.

In international Wisdom literature as well, whether one is thinking of Egyptian or Babylonian literature for instance, there was a close connection between wisdom and the divine, as people sought help from a higher power to cope with life. Of course, the divine was sometimes seen in impersonal terms, for instance, in some of the Egyptian treatments of *Ma'at* as a divine ordering principle rather than an ordering Person. Nevertheless, wisdom and the divine were integrally linked throughout the Anient Near East. This may explain why it is that in various international courts the sages were in fact astrologers, magicians, or even dream interpreters (e.g., Daniel) who sought by consulting the divine to gain insight into the real nature of things and even of the future for the benefit and aid of the king.

It is a mistake to impose on ancient literature modern notions which sharply distinquish the sacred from the secular, whether one is talking about

---

[29] So Crenshaw, "Acquisition of Knowledge," 247.

[30] Crenshaw, "Acquisition of Knowledge," 251.

[31] P. Craigie, "Wisdom Literature," *Baker Encyclopedia*, Vol. 2, 2149.

ancient world views or ancient literature. W. Brueggemann puts it this way:

> It is not at all necessary to suggest that such wisdom is secular (as opposed to sacral)... It is now readily agreed that wisdom is "creation theology," which means not only that it is a study of creation ("nature") but that wisdom in this context is a disciplined marvelling at the order of the world by God. That is, these teachers can be grateful to the creator, astonished at the delicate and resilient order of the world, but nonetheless deeply curious about how this order works.[32]

In Israel, as throughout the Ancient New East, religion and world view, and also religion and literature, were ever intertwined even in regard to the most seemingly mundane of matters.[33] The evidence is strong, even in the case of a person like Qoheleth, that the ancient person was essentially *homo religiosus*.[34] Furthermore, as R. N. Whybray stresses:

> the concept of wisdom as a divine gift was a very ancient one ... Moreover, the support and protection given to Jeremiah by the powerful scribal family of Shaphan, Josiah's "Secretary of State" (Jer. 25.24; 29.3 ...), and other officials (*sarim* in 26.16; 36.19) shows that the wisdom of some of the royal scribes was of an intensely religious and moral character.[35]

It is thus doubtful that biblical Wisdom literature should be read as a non-supernatural and humanistic alternative to the sort of literature we find elsewhere in the Old Testament.[36] Such a suggestion is only partially plausible

---

[32] W. Brueggemann, "The Social Significance of Solomon as a Patron of Wisdom," in *The Sage in Israel and the Ancient Near East*, 126.

[33] This has been pointed out in regard to traditional wisdom sayings found outside the Wisdom corpus by C. Fontaine, *Traditional Sayings in the Old Testament. A Contextual Study*, 152–53: "the realm of divine–human interactions is not excluded from encapsulation in the images and messages of the traditional saying.... The experience of the Holy, the paradoxical and often frightening ambiguity of events, are all part of daily life, and as such, are just as much 'proper' content for the traditional saying as agricultural or mundane observations."

[34] Cf. R. E. Murphy, "The Faith of Qoheleth," 253–60.

[35] Whybray, "The Sage in the Israelite Court," 139.

[36] Cf. Plöger, *Sprüche Salomos*, XXIV–XXV. In more recent articles, J. L. Crenshaw seems to have moderated some of his earlier suggestions, e.g., "The Sage in Proverbs," in *The Sage in Israel and the Ancient Near East*, 205–216. On the one hand Crenshaw says, "Israelite instructions are profoundly religious. Were they pious from the beginning, or did a later reading of this literature infuse it with religious conviction?" (referring to material such as we find in Proverbs 1–9). On the other hand in the same article he says, "In due time, religious instruction seized the lion's share of attention, and professional teachers consciously interpreted sacred traditions" (209). Crenshaw also suggests that Egyptian literature followed a definite development from secular to sacral ("pious fatalism", 212). I am convinced he has misread this data. What can be said is that a particular kind of religious fatalism comes to the fore in the later Egyptian literature, but it was religious all along (cf. below pp. 20ff and the evidence presented by G. von Rad and E. W. Heaton).

in the case of certain parts of Ecclesiastes, and even there it does not give a fully satisfactory account of what Qoheleth is trying to accomplish.

The sages of Israel then were probably not offering an alternate world view to Yahwism. It is more likely that they were offering a corrective to two errors that were apparently prevalent in Israelite society: (1) a God of the gaps approach to religion; and (2) a tendency to rely on fertility religions in regard to everyday life, in particular, everyday agricultural life. Yahwism, if misunderstood and misappropriated, could and apparently did lead to both of these errors. Thus, the sages were trying to fill in the gaps and orient God's people in regard to everyday living, within a Yahwistic framework or world view.[37] In a helpful study, J. J. Collins has pointed out that

> while proverbial wisdom is primarily constructive, and cannot be compared directly to either prophecy or parables, it is thoroughly comparable with the historical traditions which were basic to Yahwism... . The affinities between proverbial wisdom and the Yahwistic vision... show that the familiar dichotomy between wisdom and biblical history cannot be maintained.[38]

Wisdom literature not only reveals a great deal about how some early Jews viewed everyday life and sought to live it well, it also reveals the extent to which Israel was willing to draw on the wisdom of other Ancient Near East cultures to help them understand and cope with life's vicissitudes. Nowhere is this more evident than in the close parallels between various verses in Prov. 22.17 — 23.11 (except verses 19, 23, 26–27) and the Egyptian Instruction of Amenemope written somewhere between 1550 and 1069 B.C. during the New Kingdom. J. H. Walton has assembled the relevant data in the following helpful form:[39]

Proverbs	**Amenemope**
Pay attention and listen to the sayings of the wise; apply your heart to what I teach, for it is pleasing when you keep them in your heart and have all of them ready on your lips. Have I not written thirty sayings for you, sayings of counsel and knowledge, teaching you true and reliable words, so that you can give sound answers to him who sent you? Do	Give your ears, listen to the things which are spoken; Give your mind to interpret them. It is profitable to put them in your heart; They will act as a mooring post to your tongue. See for yourself these thirty chapters. They are pleasant, they educate. To know how to rebut an accusation to the one who makes it. To return a charge to the one who made it. Guard

[37] Cf. Plöger, *Sprüche Salomos*, XXXV–XXXVII.

[38] Collins, "Proverbial Wisdom," 14. On this showing what Ben Sira attempts is not such a radical departure from earlier Wisdom material, but rather a making explicit of the implicit connections between Wisdom and the Yahwist vision.

[39] J. H. Walton, *Ancient Israelite Literature in its Cultural Context*, 192-93.

not exploit the poor because they are poor and do not crush the needy in court. Do not make friends with a hot-tempered man, do not associate with one easily angered, or you may learn his ways and get yourself ensnared. Do you see a man skilled in his work? He will serve before kings; he will not serve before obscure men. When you sit to dine with a ruler, note well what is before you, and put a knife to your throat if you are given to gluttony. Do not crave his delicacies, for that food is deceptive. Do not wear yourself out to get rich; have the wisdom to show restraint. Cast but a glance at riches, and they are gone, for they will surely sprout wings and fly off to the sky like an eagle. Do not eat the food of a stingy man, don't crave his delicacies; for he is the kind of man who is always thinking about the cost. "Eat and drink," he says to you, but his heart is not with you. You will vomit up the little you have eaten and will have wasted your compliments. Do not move an ancient boundary stone set up by your forefathers (2:28). Do not move an ancient boundary stone or encroach on the fields of the fatherless, for their Defender is strong; he will take up their case against you. (NIV)

yourself from robbing the poor, from being violent to the weak. Do not associate with the rash man nor approach him in conversation... when he makes a statement to snare you and you may be released by your answer. As for the scribe who is experienced in his office, he will find himself worthy of being a courtier. Do not eat food in the presence of a noble or cram your mouth in front of him. If you are satisfied pretend to chew. It is pleasant in your saliva. Look at the cup in front of you and let it serve your need. Do not strain to seek excess when your possessions are secure. If riches are brought to you by robbery,they will not stay the night in your possession. When the day dawns they are no longer in your house. Their place can be seen but they are no longer there. The earth opened its mouth to crush and swallow them and plunged them in the dust. They make themselves a great hole, as large as they are and sink themselves in the underworld. They make themselves wings like geese and fly to heaven. Do not covet the property of a poor man lest you hunger for his bread. As for the property of a poor man it obstructs the throat and wounds the gullet... Do not remove...the boundary of the widow lest a dread thing carry you off.

This Egyptian material is in all likelihood from a considerably earlier period than the parallel Proverb material and so it appears that the final editor of Proverbs has drawn on an Egyptian source here.[40] Sometimes there is evidence

---

40 Even though, as Walton says (*Ancient Israelite Literature*, pp. 193–95), the material has been rearranged so as to highlight the parallels, and thus this form of the material is an artificial creation, nonetheless the parallels are too numerous to be simply a matter of coincidence. It is also important to stress that some of the material in Amenemope is also found in even earlier Egyptian wisdom material. There is certainly no likelihood of the Egyptian material being indebted to the later Israelite material.

of a rather simple adaptation of Egyptian material, sometimes evidence of a more thorough assimilation and even integration of the material, as G. E. Bryce has shown.[41] Such borrowing, if it really is that, is hardly a surprise as Wisdom literature in general is less ethnic or culture specific than much of the rest of the Old Testament material. It has a much more international flavor and applicability.

1 Kgs. 5.9–14 says that during the monarchical period, and in particular during the reign of Solomon, there was much contact between Israelites and other Ancient Near East cultures, and Solomon's wisdom was being compared to and said to exceed that of other nearby famous sages — "his fame was in all the surrounding nations." Solomon very likely drew on international resources for the building of the temple and intermarried with other near-eastern royal families, so that an influx of international Wisdom material into Jerusalem, which would perhaps be coupled with and shaped by Solomonic Wisdom material is very believable. The editors of the Wisdom material in the Hebrew Scriptures, however, have made such international material their own and used it for their own purposes in furthering an Israelite view of life which includes a belief in and reverence for the one God, Yahweh.

THE WISDOM OF SOLOMON

When dealing with the question of Solomon's connection to biblical Wisdom literature several important things must be pointed out. First, it is quite possible and believable that he was a patron of the arts and a collector of such material from various other cultures and countries.[42] This would not distinguish him from other ancient potentates. But was he also a contributor as well as a collector of this material? Second, 1 Kgs. 5.9–14 mentions that he spoke proverbs (*meshalim*) but it then goes on to list what may be called nature wisdom, or encyclopedic knowledge about nature. Few if any of the proverbs in the biblical book of Proverbs fit this description. One may conclude from this that much of the Solomonic contribution to Wisdom literature has been lost, or at least the sort of wisdom this writer thought most characterized Solomon's contribution. This does not rule out that some proverbs from the two oldest collections in the book of Proverbs may well go back to Solomon, or at least to

---

[41] Bryce, *A Legacy of Wisdom*, 39ff. He also makes clear that the historical evidence provides no encouragement to the now largely abandoned theory that Amenemope may have been borrowing from Hebrew Wisdom.

[42] Brueggemann, "Social Significance," 131, cautiously puts it this way: "I therefore conclude it is sociologically probable that Solomon was a patron of a wisdom that was at once emancipatory and ideological. Only such a conclusion can explain the *canonical memory* of Solomon, both as the one who embraced creation with joy (Song of Solomon), and as the one who also knew despair about the failure of the system of creation (Ecclesiastes). More skeptical is Scott, "Solomon and the Beginnings of Wisdom in Israel," 262–79, but even he admits that "general historical considerations do not preclude, but rather favor, the connection with Solomon of the origins of literary wisdom in Israel..."(279).

his court.[43] Third, it is clear from a remark like that in Prov. 25.1 that Proverbs was collected and edited considerably *later* than the time of Solomon who reigned from about 970 to 930 B.C. Hezekiah was more than two hundred years later (716–686 B.C.). Fourth, the beginning and the end of Ecclesiastes refer to one "Qoheleth" which very likely means "Assembler" or "Collector" from *qahal* (cf. 1.1, 12 and 12.9, the latter by a later editor). Nowhere is the author called Solomon. He is said to be a ruler in Jerusalem and a son of David. Most scholars would take this to be a literary fiction – someone who knew that Solomon was the font of Wisdom literature in Israel was laying claim to write following in his footsteps. This is possible, but what we find in Ecclesiastes except perhaps for the first few verses of Eccles. 2, hardly matches up with what we can deduce about Solomon and his approach to life in the Historical books.

Most importantly, as even so conservative a commentator as D. Kidner admits, the Hebrew in Ecclesiastes is late Hebrew, probably with some Hellenistic influence and thus it is entirely unlikely Solomon wrote this.[44] It is not totally impossible that one of the later kings of Israel was responsible, such as a Hezekiah, or less likely an Ezra or Nehemiah. Perhaps Eccles. 12.9ff, clearly written by a later editor, gives the clue that Qoheleth was a teacher of wisdom in Jerusalem and is called a Son of David and ruler in Jerusalem because of this – he had a spiritual kinship with Solomon the great prototype of Wisdom. Eccles.12.11 suggests he was one who shepherded God's people by wise teachings.

The upshot of all this is that one very likely should not attribute Ecclesiastes to either Solomon or the early monarchical period in Israel. The fragment of this document from Qumran that dates to 150 B.C. shows it already existed then but how much earlier is only a matter of conjecture. I suspect, due to its Hellenistic flavor and its rather fatalistic world view, that it comes from a time near to or after the Alexandrian conquest of Palestine (after 333 B.C.) making it possibly the last Wisdom book in the Old Testament to be written, though it may be earlier than Job.

Putting all these considerations together, the probability seems good that Solomon was a patron of Wisdom and an initial catalyst for its production in Israel, but he is not likely the author of any of the wisdom books in the Hebrew Scriptures as we now have them. The evidence from the Egyptian sources may provide a parallel at this point as well. As G. E. Bryce points out, Wisdom literature in the Ancient Near East was traditionally associated with the kings, "whether it is actually written by them (Merikare, Ammenemes I), addressed to them (*Advice to a Prince*), admonishing their support (Sehetepibre), or advising royal personnel (...Ptahotep, Khety, Amenemope...)."[45]

---

[43] Cf. Plöger, *Sprüche Salomos*, XIV–XV.

[44] Cf. D. A. Kidner, *The Wisdom of Proverbs, Job and Ecclesiastes*, 105.

[45] Bryce, *A Legacy of Wisdom*, 150.

Nevertheless, the real possibility that some of Solomon's own wisdom teaching is enshrined in the two old collections of maxims in Proverbs should not be ruled out.[46]

THE TRAJECTORY OF EARLY HEBREW WISDOM THINKING

There seems to be a certain development or shift in biblical Wisdom thinking about key matters which can be traced from Proverbs to Ecclesiastes and even beyond to Ben Sira and the Wisdom of Solomon. Proverbs reflects two fundamental assumptions – that the universe is basically harmonious and that it has a moral structure, in particular a structure of retribution. The good and just are rewarded or at least their deeds naturally lead to health and well being if not prosperity, the bad or evil are punished or their deeds result in disaster. As Walton says,

> In pre-exilic Israel, besides the lack of any text that would confirm hope or belief in the righteous or wicked receiving the fruits of their deeds as a result of judgment after death, there are several passages that make it clear that the biblical authors expect that judgment needs to take place in the temporal sphere (Pss. 27.13, 119.84; Prov. 11.31).[47]

Job, however, especially in the dialogue portion (3ff) makes clear that this view cannot be universalized. It will not explain the day to day fortunes and destinies of all the good and wicked. Job suffered as an innocent, as the prologue in Job 1–2 makes clear. It should be seen that the philosophy enshrined in Prov. 11.31 is predicated on the assumption that there is no judgment or reversal of fortunes after death, so God must be seen to be just on earth and in this life. It would appear that both the author of Job and of Ecclesiastes begin to grope toward a doctrine of an afterlife in order to cope with the lack of full justice or retribution in this life.

Besides the theology of retribution and justice in this lifetime which is found in Proverbs (perhaps with the proviso usually or normally) but is challenged in both Job and Ecclesiastes, all three books reflect a theology of creation. Wisdom is inherent in creation, and, as even Eccles. 10.7 suggests, so is beauty. Therefore creation is to be reflected upon and its lessons learned. Interestingly, biblical Wisdom reflects very little on inanimate nature, but mainly on living things whether human or animal. For the most part it draws

[46] In part this judgment depends on what one takes to amount to "nature Wisdom". For instance, many of the sayings in Proverbs 25–26 are based on analogies with phenomena in nature ("like snow in summer," "like a fluttering sparrow", "a whip for a horse"). Similar things can be found in the collection that begins in Proverbs 10, e.g., "No bull, empty crib..." (14:4).

[47] Walton, *Ancient Israelite Literature*, 182.

its lessons from the human sphere, and only secondarily from the realm of other creatures. What may be learned from the examination of creation in Proverbs, Job, and Ecclesiastes is human limits – it makes clear how little we know. This is surely one of the functions of God's rhetorical question-laden reply to Job (Job 38). It makes clear that humans are unable to see the larger design of God, though one does get some glimmerings or inklings of a moral order, an order of that which is good, true, and beautiful encoded into creation. This order leads to negative consequences if violated. Dangerous and harmful things normally hurt or have disastrous consequences.

It is to this general moral structure of the animate world that the sages point, though to a lesser or greater degree they recognize that not all experiences can be explained by an appeal to this sort of theology of creation and its retributive side. Such a theology presupposes that the faculty of human conscience can be appealed to, and that human reasoning can discern the good, and that human beings can, by and large, be expected to make rational and moral choices about how they will live and cope with life. What is called "folly" shows that it is possible to do otherwise as well. These major themes or ideas which underlie much of Wisdom literature must be kept in mind. It is to this world of moral discourse that this study must now turn, looking at some of the forms, themes, and key passages in Proverbs.

B. THE BOOK OF *MESHALIM*—THE FOUNTAINHEAD

1. *PRELIMINARY CONSIDERATIONS*

The title "Proverbs" is an English rendering of the Hebrew word *meshalim* which in turn is translated "*parabolos*" in the New Testament. The meaning of this Hebrew word is disputed but it seems probable that it derives from the Hebrew word for "to be like" rather than the word for "to rule," though either is possible.[48] The title suggests some form of metaphorical or figurative speech.

The term *mashal* is a broad one which includes everything from one liners to riddles to full-fledged parables. There are none of the latter in the book of Proverbs, and very little of what could be called riddles (*hidoth*). Mainly one finds what can be called general instructions on the one hand, or proverbs (one or two line sayings often in some kind of parallelism) on the other. It is not possible to make a hard and fast form critical distinction between these two forms of wisdom because often proverbs are cited in the course of the instructions (e.g. Prov. 6.6). Crenshaw mentions in passing the interesting possibility that the instruction form, such as we find in Proverbs 1–9, was chiefly used for those just beginning as disciples of the sages, while the proverb, which simply states a truth, was the form in which teaching was conveyed to the more

[48] Kidner, *Wisdom of Proverbs, Job, and Ecclesiastes*, 28 and n. 1.

advanced.[49] The *Sitz im Leben* out of which the material in Proverbs 1–9 arose may be debated. Much depends on whether the instructions in Proverbs 1–9 were from scribe to pupil, or from father to son.

The Book of Proverbs, like Psalms, is not penned by a single author, but is rather a collection of collections. As the Law is traced back to Moses, though not all in the Pentateuch goes back to him, and the Psalms are especially associated with David, though other authors such as the sons of Korah crop up in that collection, so here Solomon, who was apparently at an early date recognized as the font and fountainhead of Israelite Wisdom, is given pride of place by putting his name at the beginning of the document. This follows a practice of labeling a document by means of its most famous source, contributor, or perhaps patron.

Yet this book clearly derives from a variety of sources for one finds in it: (1) sayings of the unnamed sages (22:17 — 24:22) and another anonymous collection at 24:23–34 (the former group is based in part on *The Instructions of Amenemope* from the first millenium B.C.); (2) the sayings of Agur (30:1–4); (3) the sayings of Lemuel (31:1–9); and (4) the *meshalim* of Solomon which make up the two largest collections in Prov. 10:1 — 22:16 (375 proverbs) and in Prov. 25–29 (128 proverbs).

In view of Prov. 25:1, this material cannot have reached its final form any earlier than 715 B.C. and was probably finally assembled even later than that. As Crenshaw points out, however, most scholars are convinced that the proverbs at least arose during or in some cases even before the monarchical period.[50] It follows from this that the oldest Wisdom material we have in the Bible very likely comes in Proverbs 10ff. and it will be appropriate to look at some of the proverbs in that collection first.[51]

If one studies carefully the material found in *The Instructions of Ptahhotep, The Instructions of Ani,* and *The Instructions of Amenemope,* the latter of which was certainly used by Jewish sages early on, one important lesson stands out: there is no clear-cut division between sacred and secular wisdom in the Egyptian sources, these sources are frequently and often profoundly religious in character. To the degree that Israelite Wisdom was initially drawing on Egyptian material one should not expect it to be any different. This makes suspect the suggestion that motifs like "the fear of Yahweh" are later theological addenda to a basically secular corpus of material in Proverbs, the earliest Hebrew Wisdom collection.[52] C. Camp also warns us against such an assump-

[49] Crenshaw, "Acquisition of Knowledge," 248.

[50] Cf. Crenshaw, *Old Testament Wisdom*, 45.

[51] I agree with N. Shupak, "The *Sitz im Leben* of Proverbs in the Light of a Comparison of Biblical and Egyptian Wisdom," 117, that it is probable that a good deal of the material in the oldest collection of proverbs not only goes back to the Solomonic era in its oral form, but may even have been first written down then as well.

[52] Compare the careful refutation of the secular to sacred thesis of the development of Israelite wisdom by F. M. Wilson, "Sacred or Profane? The Yahwistic Redaction of Proverbs Reconsidered," in *The Listening Heart. Essays in Wisdom and the Psalms in Honour of R. E.*

tion on another basis, "The concerns voiced by the wise women reveal they were active tradents of the Yahwistic covenantal values of land and inheritance (2 Sam. 14.16, 20.19). This latter point should caution against an arbitrary division of a so-called secular wisdom tradition from 'religious' Yahwism."[53]

It is much more probable that when Egyptian or other sorts of international Wisdom material were used by Jewish sages, one of the first editorial activities was to make the material serviceable in an environment where Yahwistic monotheism was the dominant sanctioned religious orientation.[54] One would also expect Jewish sages, when they coined their own *meshalim*, to draw on their own theological reserves as their Egyptian counterparts had done. As F. M. Wilson says, "those sayings in Proverbs which make Yahweh the supreme possessor of wisdom ... need not be construed as repudiating mundane wisdom. What they do reject is a misconception of wisdom thinking as an autonomous human endeavor."[55]

In Proverbs 1–9 there is a rather sophisticated concept of Wisdom including reflections on the personification Woman Wisdom, which may in part be based on the Egyptian reflections about *Ma'at* (which meant either "justice" or "order" and was spoken of in much the same terms as we find Wisdom spoken of here).[56] While this may point to the international character of Wisdom literature, this literature should not be labeled secular, for even in non-Israelite wisdom, wisdom was a divine gift and closely associated with a religious world view.[57] The view of W. McKane that the theological or religious orientation was later tacked on to Wisdom sayings and then to the Book of Proverbs is unlikely at best.[58]

Though the structure of Proverbs tells us little about individual sayings, nevertheless it tells us something about how the final editors viewed the overall function of this material. It appears that Proverbs 1–9 serves as an

---

Murphy, 313–34, particularly in the form that it takes in McKane's commentary but also in the writings of H. Preus. Even Crenshaw, *Old Testament Wisdom*, 92, admits that while the editors of Proverbs had religious agendas, "this editing process must surely have found a kindred base upon which to work. It follows that wisdom contained a religious element from the beginning." The argument of a development from secular to sacred wisdom seems especially strange in view of the fact that a book like Qoheleth, which is surely from a later era than the material in the oldest collections in Proverbs, appears *more* secular and *less* Yahwistic than Proverbs.

[53] C. Camp, "The Female Sage in the Biblical Wisdom Literature," in *The Sage in Israel*, 189.

[54] Camp, "The Female Sage," 122ff.

[55] Wilson, "Sacred or Profane?" 323.

[56] B. Lang, *Die weisheitliche Lehrrede. Eine Untersuchung von Spruche 1–7*, 27ff., reveals the problems with taking Proverbs 1–9 as a unity.

[57] Cf above p. 13, the remark of Whybray.

[58] Contrast W. McKane, *Proverbs*, 1–22, with B. S. Childs, *Introduction to the Old Testament as Scripture*, 556ff. The Israelite sages, while using international Wisdom as well as that which arose on Israelite soil, have made all of it their own and oriented it to serve the end of, and ultimately to be seen as deriving from their covenant God-Yahweh, hence the recurring phrase "the fear of the Lord". What we do not find in this material is a clear association of Wisdom with Torah.

introduction or prologue to and hermeneutical key for all that follows.[59] R. C. van Leeuwen has argued that the root metaphors that underlie the material in Proverbs 1–9 are not the notion of the two ways, or Woman Wisdom, but rather the polarities of Wisdom/Folly, good/wicked, life/death, which reflect the limits Yahweh has set on life.[60] There is also an epilogue in Prov. 31:10–31 which is an acrostic poem about the good wife or possibly about Woman Wisdom. In between these two ends of the book are various collections, and often there seems to be little rhyme or reason why certain sayings appear grouped with certain sayings, though there are some thematic collections and collections based on a catchword. At this point a glance at the outline of the book's structure as delineated by R. E. Murphy helps one to see how the material is arranged.[61]

I.	Title, "the proverbs of Solomon"	1:1
II.	Introduction	1:2–7
	A. Purpose	1:2–6
	B. Programmatic saying	1:7
III.	Series of instructions and speeches by Wisdom (Wisdom's speeches found at 1:20–33, 8:1–36)	1:8–9:18
IV.	Collection of "proverbs of Solomon"	10:1–22.16
V.	Collection of "words of the wise" (restored title)	22:17–24:22
VI.	Collection of "words of the wise"	24:23–34
VII.	Collection of "proverbs of Solomon" (men of Hezekiah)	25:1 – 29:27
VIII.	Collection of "the words of Agur"	30:1–9
IX.	Collection of mostly numerical sayings	30:10–33
X.	Collection of "the words of Lemuel"	31:1–9
XI.	An acrostic poem on the ideal housewife/Woman Wisdom	31:10–31

The Book of Proverbs includes some notable paradoxes. On the one hand, one learns in the prologue that the purpose of this book is that human beings may know wisdom and receive instruction in wise dealings. On the other hand wisdom, in the persona of Woman Wisdom, is said to be seeking humankind. On the one hand, wisdom seems to involve the investigation of natural and human phenomena and deducing practical lessons from them, but on the other hand, wisdom is something that God must reveal if anyone is to know it. Wisdom is on the one hand a challenge to the listener, and in other contexts the required response of that same listener.

These two perspectives are brought together by two considerations: (1) G. von Rad has pointed out that at least *part* of the discussion about Woman

[59] Cf. C. Camp, *Wisdom and the Feminine in the Book of Proverbs*, 186ff.

[60] There is considerable merit in his argument; cf. Van Leeuwen, "Liminality and Worldview in Proverbs 1–9," in *Semeia 50: Parenesis: Act and Form*, 111–44.

[61] R. E. Murphy, *The Forms of Old Testament Literature*. Vol. XIII *Wisdom Literature*, 49.

Wisdom implies that wisdom is inherent in creation, as a sort of ordering principle or pattern;[62] (2) this being so the human scrutiny of the human and natural world amounts to an encounter with what may be called general revelation – the voice of God in both nature and ordinary human affairs. In any case the final editor makes quite clear in 1.7 that the beginning of being wise entails proper respect for, trust in, and commitment to Yahweh. If one does not start there, one is lost in any case. B. Childs points out that in Proverbs 10ff. "wisdom is a human, indeed rational process of intellectual activity, which sought to discern patterns of truth within experience circumscribed by God" while in Proverbs 1–9 wisdom is above all seen as a gift from God.[63]

In examining Proverbs the reader must keep in mind that while a good deal of this material could be called ethics, it is not the same sort of material as the imperatives believed to have been given by special revelation in the Pentateuch (e.g. the Ten Commandments). Here intellectual and experiential activity are coupled with religious behavior to provide a guide for living well and living properly. Wise behavior is not grounded here in the Mosaic law, but in what may be called spiritual good sense and a sagacious reading of the world and its realities.

THE CHARACTER, VALUES, AND FORMS OF EARLY HEBREW PROVERBS

It is striking how unedited collections like those in Proverbs 10ff. and 25:1ff seem to be. There is no attempt to rewrite this material and conform it to some of the later views on Wisdom expressed in Proverbs 1–9. The collections seem piecemeal, sometimes presenting a group of proverbs in antithetical parallelism and sometimes not. This leads one to think that this material has been passed down very much in the form in which it was originally transmitted during the early monarchical period.

In various cases there are sayings paired together that seem almost flat contradictions of one another ("do not speak to a fool in his folly", followed by "speak to a fool in his folly" Prov. 26:4–5). This raises the question of whether the author or editors saw this material as timeless truth, or whether such sayings placed in tandem were intended to have a dialogical rather than a didactic function. That is, rather than trying to offer Truth with a capital T, perhaps in some cases the function of a proverb was either to provide a general rule of thumb, not an exclusive rule, or the maxims were meant to aid the listener to discern the proper context in which to illuminate the human situation. Perhaps the function of Prov. 26:4–5 is to show that either piece of advice might be appropriate in a given situation.

---

[62] Cf. G. von Rad, *Wisdom in Israel*, 144ff.

[63] Childs, *Introduction to the OT as Scripture*, 554.

Not all the Wisdom material is presented in such antithetical pairs, and so this observation cannot apply to all wisdom sayings. "When the wisdom teacher challenged his pupil to pursue wisdom, it involved not only moral decision in respect to right behavior, but was an intellectual and highly pragmatic activity as well which sought to encompass the totality of experience,"[64] or at least ordinary human experience.

The values inculcated in Proverbs are much the same as those urged in the Pentateuch, e.g., commitment to God and God's divine order, love, justice, and honesty, caring for the poor and the needy, accepting life as a gift from God, despising and avoiding what is wicked or evil. This intimates that the sages discovered that the truth one can derive from human scrutiny of life and its general revelation is little different from the revealed truth in Torah.

Though there is no overall structure to the oldest collection of Israelite proverbs, there are connections from one couplet to another in various places by means of a catchword. For example, Prov. 10:24–5 and 27–32 are bound together by the catchwords "wicked/righteous", a frequent antinomy in sayings that have antithetical parallelism. In fact, all the sayings in Prov. 10:1 — 22:16 reflect either synonymous or antithetical parallelism as they are all either comparative or contrastive couplets (with the exception of 19.7b where a line seems to be lost). It seems reasonably clear that the sages who put this material together understood that these sayings were only true within a limited field of applicability. They could not be universalized to fit every possible situation; rather they dealt with a particular type of situation. These are truisms that are valid under a certain set of circumstances.

Here again Prov. 26:4–5 is a good example. Each saying will stand on its own, but one cannot apply them both at once, nor should one be dismissed and the other accepted, nor one interpreted so as to explain away the other. Proverbs 10ff. is basically a collection of two liners each of which stands on its own and has no real context except the Israelite ethos of the audience which is presupposed by the author.

When one reads this material in the Hebrew, one notes the various poetic qualities it has – alliteration, word plays, onomatapoeia, paronomasia, rhetorical questions, even occasional end rhyme. Especially in the antithetical couplets there is an attempt to say something true by contrasting extremes – wisdom and folly, the righteous and the wicked, the rich and the poor. There are hardly any shades of gray here and nuanced sayings are in a minority.

Here are some examples to illustrate the formal features of this material. First, of 183 verses in Proverbs 10–15, 163 use antithetical parallelism (e.g., "a wise child is a father's joy [but] a foolish child is a mother's grief", 10:1). In the second part of this collection from 16:1 — 22:16, one finds fifty-two examples of synonymous parallelism, forty-seven of antithetical, and thirty-seven of

---

[64] Childs, *Introduction to the OT as Scripture*, 558.

synthetic. An example of synonymous parallelism is Prov. 16.11 where both lines are two slightly different ways of saying the same thing or at least making the same point: "The balance and true scales are Yahweh's, all the weights in the bag are his work." Or consider Prov. 19.5: "A false witness will not go unpunished, and he who utters lies will not escape." Synthetic parallelism involves a saying that is neither a simple comparison between the two lines or a simple synonym but the second line gives a further development of the first line (cf. Prov. 16.31: "Grey hair is a splendid crown; it is acquired in the way of righteousness").

Second, in some sayings there are simple juxtapositions of ideas without any action or verbs connecting the clauses (e.g., Prov. 13.12: "Hope deferred, a sick heart, and a tree of life, desire fulfilled"). This entails a chiastic ABBA pattern, where the first and last clauses contrast as do the two middle clauses. Third, comparisons are normally indicated by the use of the particle *ke* (like) or *ken* (so); e.g., Prov. 26:1: "Like a bird that is far from its nest, so is a man who is far from home." Another way of forming a comparison is by the use of *tob min* (better than) or simply *min*; e.g., Prov. 22:1: "A good name is to be chosen rather than great riches, and favor is better than silver or gold" (cf. also Prov. 16:8).

Fourth, other sayings that also convey value judgments directly are the so-called "good" sayings; e.g., "Without knowledge, even zeal is not good" (Prov. 19:2; cf. 17:26a; 18:5a; 20:23b). Fifth, in regard to catchword connection of originally isolated sayings, compare 10:16–17 where the catchword is life, or 13:2–4 where the catchword is *nephes* (meaning life, or desire), or 15:13–15 where *lev* (heart) is the catchword, which attracted the editor to put these sayings together. It seems probable the catchword connection was used not due to similar themes, for often the sayings are quite different, but rather as a device to aid memorizing and transmission of these sayings.

Sixth, alliteration (repetition of consonants) is another device used to make a saying memorable and memorizable. Unless one reads Hebrew one misses all this (e.g., 10:9a has *"holek battom yelek betah"* or 11:2a has *"ba zadon wayyabo qalon"*).

Seventh, as an example of word play we may point to 21:23 where the word *smr* "keep" is used in two different ways in the same couplet. Eighth, onomatopoeia (something that sounds like what it is trying to convey) may also be noted in 20:11a (*yitnakker/na'ar*).

The above eight examples should give us a feeling for the form of this material. It was meant to be striking to the hearer, for it was originally given orally to an oral culture, and a good deal of it depends on its oral effect, which one misses by just reading it in a translation. Since some of this material is playing for rhetorical and dramatic effect it sometimes uses the device of exaggeration or hyperbole to get its point across.

Finally, Bryce reminds us that the sages showed some concern for the aesthetics involved in speaking, so that sound and sense would comport with one another in a given saying. There was apparently some interest in showing that beauty was a facet of truth, or at least that they belonged together.[65] It is time to consider a small sampling of the more interesting isolated sayings in this collection, focusing first on a few examples from Proverbs10.[66]

EARLY PROVERBS ASSOCIATED WITH SOLOMON – PROV. 10:1 – 22.6

Proverbs 10:4 is very characteristic of so many of these *meshalim* – diligence is rewarded by prosperity, indolence by poverty. There are other sayings which speak of the wicked or the foolish having wealth which make clear that this rule does not always apply, as in fact hardly any of these proverbs do. Notice that the way "virtue" is inculcated in most of these sayings is not by direct command or imperative but rather by setting examples before the listeners' ears and letting them discern and decide which examples to shun and which to follow. Proverbs are basically a form of moral persuasion, not authoritative command. This saying, like the next one to be examined, however, presupposes that there is a moral structure to life so that certain kinds of actions normally have certain kinds of consequences.

Proverbs 10:9 makes the act–consequence idea plain. It has a near twin in 28.18. There are many doublets and repetitions in these collections (e.g., 14.12 = 16.25) which again suggests that the material has been gathered but not carefully edited by the copiers and editors. The point of Prov. 10.9 is that true security on the road of life is afforded by integrity or sincerity (*tom*). By contrast, the person who follows crooked or devious ways has no security or integrity and is eventually revealed for what s/he is.

At Prov. 10.16 "life" is juxtaposed with sin to show where two different lifestyles lead. Here "sin" would seem to imply the result of sin as well – punishment and death. It is proper to ask what "life" means here. In most of these sorts of statements it is reasonably clear that a happy and prosperous, trouble free and long life in this world is envisioned, not eternal life. The Hebrew beliefs about the afterlife in the monarchical period will be discussed when I examine a saying about Sheol. Prov. 10:16 does seem to envision two persons both of whom have money, hence the use of the terms wage and earn. Most of these sayings seem to be advice or truisms for those who have property and the real prospect of prosperity, not for the indigent or slave. This supports the supposition of an upper class *Sitz im Leben* for many if not most of these proverbs.

In Prov. 10:17 as in 10:16 life is not merely the state of existing but a particular quality or kind of life is envisioned. Here we have a contrast between keeping and forsaking instruction. It is possible to translate this saying as the

---

[65] Bryce, *A Legacy of Wisdom*, 150ff. Bryce especially associates this with the concerns of the court about matters of good "form" as well as godly content, and he contrasts it with the often "vulgar" images used in the prophetic tradition.

[66] On all this cf. Murphy, *Forms of Old Testament Literature*, 63–68.

NIV does: "He who heeds discipline shows the way to life, but whoever ignores correction leads others astray", or one could follow the NRSV: "Whoever heeds instruction is on the path to life, but one who rejects a rebuke goes astray." In the former translation the saying is talking about the effect of one's behavior on others; in the latter its effect on self. If the latter is correct, a specific kind and quality of life which is helpful to self and pleasing to God is seen as a goal, not something one has inherently (i.e., the good life). Notice too the contrast between true life and going astray. Clearly life here has a moral quality to it, not merely a physical one.

One of the frequent character types discussed in the Book of Proverbs is the "sluggard". He may be found in 10:26, but he is also referred to in 6:6–8; 10:4; 12:24, 27; 19:15; 21:25. Such sayings about the problems caused by laziness presume a situation where a hard-working person can make a good life for himself or herself. That is, these sayings assume a situation where a nation is at peace, where there is not a famine or economic crisis in the land, where one is not in exile, in some foreign land, or in jail. In short, these sayings and many others presume "normal circumstances" for such a deduction to be often true. In Prov. 10:26 the sluggard is a dawdling messenger who is as irritating as smoke is to the eyes or vinegar is to the teeth. One is meant to think of a person entrusted with a mission who lacks any drive or desire to bring it to a swift and successful conclusion. This is a straight simile with an analogy being drawn between three things that are otherwise dissimilar using the particle *ke*.

It is possible to draw up a character profile of the sluggard if one takes the various sluggard sayings together, as Kidner does.[67] He is a very lazy person; he is not merely anchored to his bed, he is hinged to it (Prov. 26:14)! He makes ridiculous excuses for not doing things, e.g., "there's a lion outside" (Prov. 22:13, 26:13). Here is a person who puts off beginning things, but he also puts off finishing things! Consequently as in a saying like 12.27 he goes without, even without food. Here is a person who also will not face facts or his real character – he's heavily into denial and fantasy. He thinks he is smarter than others (cf. 26:14ff.) This person is, as Kidner says, "restless, helpless, and useless".[68] Yet he is surprised when poverty comes upon him like an armed man. The sluggard is not an incapable person but one who makes too many excuses. For him the chief good in life is relaxing and sleeping; he has no goals or plans to achieve things. Life is just too much effort, too hard, and too frightening. This sort of person comes in only for scorn in a book which often touts the merits and benefits of hard work.

Prov. 10.27 is one of the crucial "fear of Yahweh" sayings.[69] The phrase in question very likely refers to proper reverence for God and commitment to

---

[67] D. Kidner, *Proverbs*, 42–3.

[68] Kidner, *Proverbs*, 43.

[69] It is important to note that Yahweh clauses are found not only in proverbs but also in the instructions. In view of the lack of evidence for heavy handed final editing in Proverbs that imposes a consistent pattern on the whole corpus, this suggests that possibly two different

and trust in him, not abject terror. The outcome of such an attitude and commitment is that one's life in this world is extended and one lives long enough to see the fruits of a life of long labor and see one's progeny and grandchildren begin to make their way in the world. By contrast, the wicked person's life will be cut short. No doubt the author knew there were various exceptions to this saying. Sometimes the good and righteous die young. The point here is that long life is a blessing and gift from God that he *often* gives to those who love him, whereas the wicked, by their very course of life often don't live so long because they are caught in a crime, or killed for one reason or another. This amounts to saying, keep your nose clean and things are likely to lead to a long happy life.

Proverbs 10:28 follows naturally from 10:27. Both the righteous and the wicked have expectations and hopes in life. An Egyptian saying puts it this way: "Wrongdoing has never brought its undertaking into port."[70] Life is seen as teliological; humans have goals that can either be realized in space and time or not. The righteous can generally expect their good plans to come to fruition and so to rejoice. By contrast, whatever hopes the wicked may have, they will be dashed.

Chapter 11 of Proverbs begins with the issue of honesty or justice. Yahweh hates cheating, and in this case cheating that would deprive someone of some degree of good or product they might need to live. As Kidner points out, the Law (Lev. 19.35–6) the Prophets (Mic. 6.10–11, Amos 8.5) and the Wisdom writings (cf. Prov. 20.10, 23) all agree in condemning dishonesty because there is a God and God cares about such things for God is just.[71] There is a close parallel in Deut. 25:15–6. One should also note that such warnings are also found in the teachings of Amenemope 17:8 — 19:9: "Make not for yourself a bushel measure of two capacities." This is said to be "perversion before the God." Or again, "The bushel is the eye of Ra; its abomination is he who gives short measure." Such calls for honesty in commercial dealings are common both in international Wisdom literature and in other sorts of literature.

The Hebrew word *to'eba* ("abomination") occurs regularly in Proverbs (cf. 3:32; 6:16; 8:7; 11:1, 20; 15:8ff., 16:5; 17:15; 20:10, 23) and may be contrasted to the sayings which speak of blessedness (*beraka*) the so called beatitudes (cf. Prov. 3:13; 8:32, 34, 14:21; 16:20; 20:7; 28:14; 29:18). The language of abomination, like the language of sacrifice and offering, crops up from time to time in the Proverbs showing that the sage is cognizant that there is a larger world on which he is basically not commenting. The sage is not addressing matters of cultic religion or salvation history but rather ordinary life. The language of sacral religion, however, drifts over into the sage's conversation.

---

sorts and sources of material bear witness that the Yahwistic emphasis was present early on in Israelite Wisdom material.

[70] ANET, 412b, from the *Teaching of Ptahhotep*, c. 2450.

[71] Kidner, *Proverbs*, 90.

J. M. Thompson is right to say, "First of all, we do not see the wise man at any point standing deliberately against the cult or sacred history. As von Rad has pointed out, these matters were simply not his primary concern."[72] Gordis argues that the sages, being part of or attached to the upper class, believed in upholding the temple ritual though they show no great enthusiasm for it, and in general their whole approach to the cult as well as other matters affecting the status quo foreshadows the views of the Sadducees.[73]

In Prov. 11:4 one hears about the *Yom Yahweh* which the prophets so often spoke of – the day of God, the day of wrath or retribution where one is recompensed for what one has done during life in this world. While riches might buy protection from harm in this life, when one comes into the presence of God at the day of judgment righteousness will be the only possible armor. The sage is convinced that righteousness delivers from death. The terms death and die are used between twenty and thirty times in Proverbs. There are an additional twelve references to Sheol, the land of the dead (cf. 1:12; 5:5; 7:27; 9:18; 15:11, 24; 23:14; 27:20; 30:16); Abaddon, which means destruction (15:11, 27:20); the pit (1:12, 28:17) and also the *rephaim* ("shades", 2:18, 9:18, 21:16).

In these proverbs, death is basically seen as something active. It is a realm which is in conflict with life, and refers to more than just the literal physical event of death. What is beyond death is said to be Sheol, Abaddon, the deep abode of dead persons. But death also casts its shadow over the living, so that a person who goes astray is in fact already experiencing a taste of death (Prov. 5.23) which will very likely lead to physical death. As Prov. 9.16–17 make clear, a person who wanders into the house of Dame Folly is keeping company with those who are already in the shadows of Sheol, already in a real sense dead. Thus, there are those who are the living dead and those who have experienced physical death already. Life after death in any full sense is not envisioned in Proverbs, (that idea was to develop in later Israelite literature), but there does seem to be the first glimmerings of the idea that there is an afterlife to be shunned.

One may compare Prov. 14:32, which should probably read "but the righteous person seeks safety [in God] in his death" (following the Masoretic Text and not the LXX which reads here "in his integrity"). The image here seems to be one of exoneration rather than judgment being experienced at death, or at the *Yom Yahweh*. This may reflect the start of a positive view of the afterlife, even if undeveloped. The sages may have been groping in this direction precisely because they realized that the wicked do not always get their just desserts in this life, nor the righteous theirs.

Returning to Prov. 11.4 a moment, the NJB reads it to mean that when a natural or human calamity comes, the righteous will be delivered from death

---

[72] J.M. Thompson, *The Form and Function of Proverbs in Ancient Israel*, 99; cf. von Rad, *Old Testament Theology I*, 435.

[73] Gordis, "Social Background of Wisdom Literature," 110.

but the rich will not be able to hide behind their riches. The problem with this reading is that the second line reads, "seeks safety at/in his death."

Prov. 11:13 involves a different sort of saying. Here the issue is respecting confidences. There is a connection between gossip and disloyalty on the one hand, and closed lips and integrity on the other. This is one of many sayings in Proverbs about guarding one's tongue or what comes from one's lips. Silence then can be an expression of loyalty and maintaining a trust. The person here is called a talebearer. Kidner points out that such a person is seen as malicious and not just indiscreet.[74]

There are about sixty sayings in the Solomonic collections about proper speech and the following judgments are made about it: (1) it is precious and is compared to silver and gold (10:20, 20:15); (2) it is expressed with grace and eloquence (15:2, 16:21, 23, 22:11, 25:11); (3) it is beneficial and kind (16:24, 15:26, 12:25); (4) it is gentle (15:1, 25:15); (5) it is just and open and includes a just rebuke (16:13, 10:10, 25:12); (6) it is honest and reliable (12:19, 22; 14:5, 25); (7) it is spoken at the appropriate time (15:23); (8) it brings good to others, acting as a fount of life (10:11, 13:14) or even a means of deliverance (11:9).

Proverbs 11:14 is the sort of saying one might expect to arise from a court setting. The Hebrew word *tahbulot* literally means the steering of a ship and in a derived sense refers to giving guidance, in this case political advice to the king. Verse 14b expresses confidence that "several heads are better than one" in making policy. Here is perhaps some justification for the view that Wisdom material arose from and/or was collected by political counselors of the king. Good and wise policy results in the *tesua* (safety) of the community. It may be that safety through a military victory is in view.

One of the more famous of the proverbs is found in 11:22: "Like a gold ring in a pig's snout is a lovely woman who lacks or shows no discretion/good sense." This is another simile out of which parables very likely grew in due course, starting with *ki* (like). This particular saying reminds us that Wisdom literature, like the rest of the Old Testament, is largely androcentric and sometimes clearly patriarchal as well. It views the world from a man's point of view. A patriarchal text would be one that not merely assumes such a world view as an androcentric one does, but actually promotes, enforces, or encourages it. This androcentricity is especially clear in Proverbs 1–9 where advice from a father to a son gives warning against temptresses, strong drink, bad company and the like.

Prov. 11.22 is meant to present us with a monstrosity, bearing in mind especially that pigs were not kosher food and so were already taboo and abhorrent to Jews. The nose ring was a common piece of near eastern jewelry and still is today. The point is that beauty is wasted on such a person because though she looks beautiful she does not act in accord with her looks; her actions

[74] Kidner, *Proverbs*, 91.

are anything but lovely. The subject of the *isshah zara*, or strange woman, will be addressed shortly.

We may see the personification of Woman Wisdom and Dame Folly at Prov. 14.1. In favor of this conclusion is 9.1 which speaks of Woman Wisdom building a house. The alternative is to understand this saying as does Kidner and translate, "Womanly wisdom builds a home, folly (abstract noun) pulls it down" or perhaps following the Masoretic Text as it is now vocalized, "The wisest of women builds..."[75] I tend to favor the first suggested reading with McKane.[76] Folly has no constructive task; its only role is to destroy what Wisdom has created. Here as elsewhere in the Old Testament the "fool" (from the *nbl* radical) refers not to a simpleton but to a person with no spiritual insight, no wisdom. Sometimes it can even mean not merely a person who is blind to wisdom but also positively destructive and wicked, as here. We will have a good deal more to say about the personification Lady Wisdom when we get to Proverbs 1–9.

In 14.4 we see a proverb in its most compact form, without verbs. "No oxen, empty manger, strong bull, much cash" as the NJB puts it. McKane suggests we must take the Masoretic Text at face value and see its meaning as, "Where there is no ox, there is a crib of grain [uneaten], but crops are increased by the strength of an ox."[77] As Kidner points out the sense seems to be as follows: While it is true that it is less work and mess without an ox, for then one doesn't have to keep cleaning up and refilling the corn crib, nevertheless there is greater gain with an ox because it can increase the crop many fold.[78] There is debate over whether *bar* means empty or pure (hence clean).

There is a second way to understand 4b, namely, that a strong bull which can sire many young will produce much cash. The point then would be that to make money there are necessary sacrifices and investments that need to be made. While there is less work without an ox, the gains of having a good ox or bull far outweigh the cost of providing for it. This is the sort of proverb which would very likely have come from the clan or family circles.

In Prov. 14:9 we are led into the temple and the realm of sacrifices. *Asam* refers to the guilt offering. The text very likely should be translated, "Every fool [plural subject, singular verb] scoffs at the guilt offering, but favor resides among the upright (or honest)." In view of the cultic thrust of the first line, *rason* in the second line, translated here "favor" or "acceptance," probably also has a cultic sense.

Various scholars object to the cultic reference here thinking that sages operated with a world view that had no place for matters of sin, guilt, sacrifice. Israel's world, however, was a place where the cultic, the sagacious, and the

---

[75] Kidner, *Proverbs*, 105–6.
[76] McKane, *Proverbs*, 472.
[77] McKane, *Proverbs*, 470.
[78] Kidner, *Proverbs*, 106.

prophetic overlapped to mention but three factors.[79] R. E. Clements, besides noting this fact, also points out that the sages tend to moralize or spiritualize cultic ideas or commands, thereby applying ideas about sacrifice, guilt, purity and the like to everyday life apart from the temple.[80]

I take Prov. 14:9 to mean that the fool does not think it necessary or beneficial to atone through sacrifice. To the contrary says the sage, God's favor resides on the upright who do such things, thus proving the value of such procedures. This conclusion does not prevent the sage from criticizing a sacrifice offered without repentance (15:8) nor does it prevent him from making the same sort of critique that the prophets did in 21:3; doing *seddiqa* is more pleasing to God than just sacrifice, though sacrifice has its place and value.

One of the undergirding principles of all the proverbs is expressed in 15:33. It is a variant of the theme announced in 1:7 (which says piety is the beginning of wisdom, here the school or foundation of it). Piety, the proper trust in and respect for Yahweh, is the foundation or school of wisdom. Notice that piety is associated with humility, which does not mean feelings of inferiority, but rather a true grasp of one's place in things. Only God is God. This does mean a recognition of one's limits and relationship to the creator of all. But when one has these things in right order, in right relationship, there can be *kabod* glory, or here it may mean status or significance. One's significance can only be seen and appreciated when one first sees and recognizes God's *kabod* or weightiness (the word literally means heaviness).

All the sayings in Prov. 16:1–7 are Yahweh sayings of some sort. At 16:1 we may find a variant: humans propose but God disposes. It reads, "The plans of the mind/heart belong to human beings, but the answer of the tongue is from Yahweh." One may wish to compare the somewhat similar saying from Ahikar 8:115: "If he were beloved of the gods, they would put something good in his palate to speak." From Amenemope 19:16f. we have, "One thing are the words that humans say, another is that which the god does." This is perhaps closer to Prov. 16:9. In any case both 16.1 and 9 indicate that ultimately God settles matters whatever one may plan. Yet if one takes the wording of 16:1 literally it might be understood to mean that while a person thinks up various plans, God puts the right words on the tongue, God gives a person the answers

[79] There is a considerable danger, as H. C. Kee reminds us, in assuming that the different genre of biblical literature were ever immune to influences from other genres. Material that originated from different social settings interacted, precisely because sages, like prophets, priests, and others, lived in a world that involved them in a variety of activities including the cultic. There is no evidence of a group of sages in Israel creating a type of literature in isolation from various other sorts of traditions. It is also debatable that the sages were creating a literature intended to be in competition with cultic or prophetic literature. Cf. Kee, "Jewish Wisdom/Apocalyptic and Greco-Roman Stoicism," delivered at the SBL meeting in Kansas City (Nov. 1991).

[80] R. E. Clements, *Wisdom for a Changing World. Wisdom in Old Testament Theology*, 31–35.

to speak. This is how von Rad takes it and probably he is right.[81] The New Testament variant of this would be the promise that the Spirit will give one the right words when one is taken before a court and has to testify.

The investigation of the oldest Israelite Wisdom collection will be concluded by examining three important proverbs. Prov. 21.30 says that wisdom, understanding, and advice do not exist in the presence of Yahweh. This is a critique of human wisdom and its limitations. That it is found here in the Wisdom literature is probably not due to a later critique of Wisdom but reflects the fact that the sages knew their limits. Wisdom, if it does not come from or comport with Yahweh and his wisdom, evaporates in God's presence. It is worthless.

Proverbs 21:31 sounds like an old theocratic saying: "If God is for us..." Trust in Yahweh is the first rule of Israelite warfare, which may be compared to the more cynical modern proverb "Praise the Lord and pass the ammunition." All Israel's wars were to be holy wars in which the people relied on God not on their own strength for victory, which meant they would fight but trust Yahweh with the results. Reliance on human strength alone will not avail.

Proverbs 22:6 is a general maxim about the value of moral training of children. "Give a child training on the mouth or entrance of his way (or on the way he ought to go) and even when old he will not go back on it." The stress here is on parental opportunity and duty. Usually such training will stick with the child into adulthood and they will continue on the right road or way. But this saying as well is not without exceptions. Like almost all these Wisdom utterances they describe a usual and prevalent outcome, not a universal one.

Several important matters have come to light through this examination of a few of the earliest of the proverbs. First, various of these sayings support the suggestion that the teaching of the sages was oral before it was written. We have seen material that very likely originally came from the family, from clan wisdom, and some also from the court, though it was probably first put into writing in the setting of the court. Second, the subjects covered in these proverbs pertain to matters of everyday life in one setting or another, and more importantly they are generalizations about everyday life. The juxtaposition of seemingly contradictory proverbs shows that the sages knew that a given proverb always had exceptions, and that different sorts of sayings would speak to different sorts of situations. Third, the act–consequence idea seems evident and widely upheld. The sages seemed confident that righteous living regularly leads to prosperity and long life. These early sages did not look for, or were only beginning to grope towards the idea of a correction of wrong or a rewarding of righteous deeds in some sort of afterlife. Fourth, the androcentric character of this material is evident at various points. These sages looked at everyday life from a man's point of view. Finally, even in the earliest collection of proverbs,

[81] Von Rad, *Wisdom*, 99–100.

there already appears to be the beginnings of reflection on the idea of the personification of Wisdom (cf. Prov. 14:1ff). For the fuller treatment of that subject one must look elsewhere, possibly in Proverbs 31, and certainly in Proverbs 1–9, and so I now turn to these much disputed texts.

THE GOOD WIFE OR WOMAN WISDOM IN PROVERBS 31?

Proverbs 31:10–31 is an acrostic poem. Precisely because of the vast array and perfection of things done in this description many are open to the suggestion that this passage is not really about a wife, but rather another portrait of Wisdom, the true bride of the sage.[82] There is, however, another way of looking at this text. The finding of the right wife (a woman of strength, substance, or valour (*hayil*)), has already been said in 18:22 to amount to finding both happiness and the favor of God. In short the finding of the right wife is the ultimate test and proof of having *hokmah* in a society where the family is the very focus and fabric of that society. Thus one's life partner is all important. At 12:4 such a woman is called the crown of her husband. This poem may be an expansion on 12:4a or at least on the idea expressed there.[83]

This woman is indeed the very embodiment of Wisdom and its various virtues. Like Wisdom she is priceless, worth far more than expensive pearls (cf. 3:15, 8:11). Gordis reminds us that "one characteristic of Hebrew Wisdom, lacking in Oriental Wisdom generally, is the stress upon piety as a womanly virtue (Prov. 31:30…)."[84] As Kidner points out the picture here is not just of any woman but a woman not only of great character and industry but also of material prosperity (said to be the reward for being wise in this book).[85] This is a portrait of a woman with unusual gifts and resources, as is especially clear from the mention of the serving girls in v 15 (if this is not a later addition). The acrostic device causes a certain lack of logical flow to the text; it jumps from one activity or virtue to the next, but its overall effect is powerful. We might call this the picture of the strong and invaluable wife from A to Z.

The husband trusts his wife in her dealings, and he himself derives good from her. She makes clothes, brings in the food to the house, prepares the food, rises early to order the household affairs for the day; she is also a business woman making deals, and a farmer planting a vineyard. She works wholeheartedly at her task and is physically strong. She knows how things are going, very likely because she stays up at night taking full stock of things. She spins and provides warm woolen clothes for the winter, but she also gives to the poor

---

[82] Cf. R. E. Murphy, *The Tree of Life*, 27.

[83] Cf. Plöger, *Sprüche Salomos*, 376: "Es bleibt eine leichte Resignation, vergleichbar jener Skepsis, die angesichts der (personifizierten) Weisheit anklingt: Die Wesiheit-woher kommt sie? (Hi 28,20)….Die Frau is keine Idealgestalt, sondern eine Realität, aber sie zu finden ist das Problem."

[84] Gordis, "Social Background," 112.

[85] Kidner, *Proverbs*, 183–84.

and needy, showing a concern for the larger community. She dresses well, even to wearing the royal purple. Her husband is a well-respected man giving judgments in the city gates, where such judgments would be given. It may even be suggested he is a sage.

This wife also sells clothing items for extra resources. She has both strength and dignity and so she looks to the future with confidence; indeed, she even laughs at the time to come. Her words are laced with wisdom and kindness; she is industrious, not wasting time ("eating the bread of idleness"). She is praised by the whole family. She is indeed priceless not because of her beauty or charm, though she may not lack these things, but because she is a "God-revering woman". As such she is Wisdom truly embodied. Verse 31 ends by saying that she should get some of the benefit of her vast work, and her praise should ring out in the city gate, which very likely means her husband should praise her there.

The first verse has warned us that finding such a person is difficult for they are rare and precious, but this is not merely starry-eyed idealism. The sage has seen at least a few exceptional women of faith who sat for this portrait. It is noteworthy that this poem assumes that a woman's place is not just in the home, but also in the fields and in the marketplace, and in dealing with human problems like poverty. In other words it has a broader view of women's roles than was the case in some quarters in early Judaism.[86]

There are some interesting images in this poem. For instance, in v 25 the picture is of a woman who has gathered up her dress, girded it about her loins, so she can do hard manual labor. Also the profit from her garment-making is reinvested in the planting of a vineyard. Verse 25 suggests that she can laugh at the future because like a Joseph she is in charge of it and has built up ample reserves for the lean times. No tide of adversity will be able to swamp her.[87] Verses 26ff. indicate she is equally adept at instruction and management. Verse 26b may also be speaking not just of ordinary kindness but perhaps of covenant love and loyalty since *hesed* is used there. This seems to suggest that she teaches her children wisdom and covenant loyalty.

The family was certainly one venue in which Wisdom was taught and passed on and here is a clue that women were transmitters of it. Here the suggestions of C. Camp and others about female sages in Israel seem to find a basis.[88] This woman then may also be an educated person. This chapter also gives credence to the suggestion that Wisdom arose out of the context of well-to-do families who had time for such higher pursuits as seeking Wisdom. This woman, however, seems to have no idle moments. In any case she deserves high praise not only from her family but also in the community. The poem is written from the vantage point of a man, but nonetheless it is remarkable for

---

[86] Cf. B. Witherington, *Women in the Ministry of Jesus*, 1ff.

[87] McKane, *Proverbs*, p. 669.

[88] Camp, "The Female Sage," 185–204.

its somewhat enlightened view of women and its ample extolling of women's abilities and intelligence.[89]

PROVERBS 1-9 AND WOMAN WISDOM

Proverbs 1–9 provide the reader with a literary and religious context in which what follows can and should be understood. This material may be called a prologue, but in any case it may well be the latest and last material to be added to the *meshalim*. Nevertheless, as Camp points out, in view of the fact that there is little here to suggest an exilic or post-exilic provenance for this material (i.e., evidence of theodicy, anxiety, despair, evidence of an author or audience in distress), it may well date to the monarchical period.[90] B. Lang rightly notes that there is no hard evidence of specifically post-exilic vocabulary in Proverbs 1–9.[91] The prologue seeks to make clear that the purpose of the Wisdom material included in the book is not merely to intrigue or entertain but for "training in righteousness," to give guidance on how a life well lived should look, and what sort of commitments, actions, and attitudes should be endorsed and undertaken.

Proverbs 1:5 says that the key to understanding the book is that it intends to provide "steering" (*tahbulot*). R. E. Murphy rightly stresses that the writer of these lines "did not distinguish between the secular and religious in the way we do. All the so-called secular advice that is given in the course of the thirty-one chapters belongs to training in wisdom that is essentially religious."[92] Knowledge is not pursued for its own sake, but for the purpose of giving insight into how to live "in the fear of Yahweh," how to live well and right in the light of the existence of a sovereign God. All of the material in the book, whatever its original source and provenance, even if it came from Egypt or Mesopotamia, has now been retooled and incorporated into a new corpus to serve the purpose of Israel's faith. Thus, this material is now being presented and used as Israel's Wisdom, Wisdom in the tradition of the archetypal wisdom figure during the monarchical period – Solomon.

Proverbs 1:7 then provides a sort of motto for the book or, as von Rad says, it "contains in a nutshell the whole Israelite theory of knowledge."[93] A profound and abiding commitment to Yahweh is the basis of and the starting point for obtaining *hokmah*. This verse is then echoed in 9:10, 15:33, Job 28:28 and even Ps. 111:10 in various ways. What the person gains from listening to

---

[89] There are several factors which count against taking this passage as simply dealing with the personification of Woman Wisdom – for example the way her *husband* is discussed, and also the lack of stress on her educative tasks.

[90] Camp, *Wisdom and the Feminine*, 53, rightly critiquing the assumptions of B. Mack, "Wisdom, Myth and Mythology," 46–60.

[91] Cf. B. Lang, *Frau Weisheit. Deutung einer biblischer Gestalt*, 46ff with Lang, *Wisdom and the Book of Proverbs. A Hebrew Goddess Redefined*, 4, 157.

[92] Murphy, *Tree of Life*, 16.

[93] Von Rad, *Wisdom*, 67.

the sages is "the art of steering," a proper and successful course through life that leads not to an early grave but to a long and satisfying existence with many accomplishments and perhaps even some prosperity. Yahweh is said to be the one who is the ultimate giver of wisdom (2:6ff.), even though the proximate giver may be a parent or teacher (the reference to "son" might suggest either). While there are many passages one could examine in Proverbs 1–9, this study will look briefly at a few key verses that do not have to do with personified Wisdom but will concentrate on the crucial passages where Wisdom is personified in 1:20ff, 3:13ff., 4:5ff., 7:4–5, 8:1ff., and 9:1–6.

Proverbs 5 is a long discussion, probably from a father to an adolescent son, about staying away from an *isshah zara*, a loose woman, *or* it may mean a foreign or strange woman, an outsider, as K. A. Farmer has urged.[94] Farmer also suggests that the *isshah zara* is a figure meant to stand for the allurement of foreign culture and even foreign religion. If so, one may need to see this material as connected with the passages about Dame Folly as the antithesis of Woman Wisdom. The negative warning comes first and it is followed by the positive advice to confine oneself to one's own cistern, one's own wife.

The latter half of Proverbs 5 is much like the sexually explicit love poetry of Song of Songs (cf. S of S. 4:5ff.). The basic advice here recognizes that while the initial taste of sin may seem pleasurable, its consequences are not. Nevertheless, in the positive advice that follows sexual delight is seen as a good thing in the right context. It is not seen in the Bible as a sin, but rather a danger if it is shared with a non-marital partner.

If *isshah zara* does refer to a foreign woman then there may be an ethnic thrust to this teaching as well. It seems more likely, however, that this term means a woman who is beyond the pale. "Strange" here would then connote estranged from the proper flow of society, an outcast.[95] In that case what is meant is a prostitute. What tips the balance in favor of this explanation are the parallels with international Wisdom material.

The warning against the seductive and alluring prostitute or loose woman is stock Wisdom material (cf. Babylonian *Counsels of Wisdom, Ahikar*, and the Egyptian literature as well). Notice how this chapter initially begins by talking about lips – the lips of the son which must guard knowledge, be discreet and then the lips of the loose woman which are a temptation. The first contrast then is between proper and improper speech (e.g., her speech is smoother than oil). The initial taste is like honey, but in the end it leaves the flavor of wormwood in one's mouth, the taste of death. This woman leads one where she is already going – to Sheol, the grave, the land of the dead.

In view of the complex nature of the debate about Woman Wisdom it is necessary to define terms first. By personification I mean the assigning of

---

[94] K. A. Farmer, *Proverbs and Ecclesiastes. Who Knows What is Good?*, 41ff. For an examination of the view that the "strange woman" is a reference to a woman, possibly a cult prostitute involved in some sort of non-Israelite religion, cf. Lang, *Die weisheitliche Lehrrede*, pp. 87–96.

[95] McKane, *Proverbs*, 285.

human or divine qualities, abilities, or actions to a non-personal entity or thing, whether it is an attribute (e.g., righteousness), some other sort of abstraction (e.g., Truth), or a thing (e.g., a tree). By hypostasis I mean some sort of power or lesser divinity that is an extension or agent of a greater god, or comes forth from a higher divine being and takes on something of a life of its own. The terms personification and hypostasis have too often been confused or used almost interchangeably in the discussion of Woman Wisdom. For the sake of clarity, it is necessary to state conclusions in advance of the discussion. It appears that personification best describes the Woman Wisdom material in Proverbs, Job, and Sirach, though in the Wisdom of Solomon the author *may* have progressed to the stage of the hypostasization of Wisdom.[96]

When one considers Woman Wisdom in Proverbs it is well to keep in mind the warnings of H. Ringgren that "in Israelite religion and in Islam the strict monotheistic belief did not allow the hypostases [or the personifications] to become real deities. In other religions, where this obstacle is not extant, nothing prevents the creation of new gods in this way."[97] He thus concludes that what we are dealing with is a quasi-personification of one of God's attributes. Such a practice was widely known in antiquity.[98]

More to the point the evidence for the use of personification is plentiful in the Old Testament, including Proverbs.[99] "Languages whose grammatical structures give male or female gender to 'things' invite personification.... In addition the Hebrew language has a stylistic preference for nominative construction and tends to link abstract concepts to action verbs."[100] For example, in Job 11:14 one hears, "Do not let wickedness dwell in your tents." Or in Prov. 20:1 the sage says, "Wine is a good for nothing, strong drink a brawler." In Prov. 30:15–16 Sheol, fire, the earth, and the barren womb are all personified as thirsty creatures who are never satisfied. Or again in Ps. 96:11–12 earth and sky can be said to have the qualities of rejoicing or being glad. In Ps. 85:13 one hears of righteousness going before God and preparing God's way. Sometimes personification can take a more extended form and become a fable such as in Judg. 9:8ff. Over the course of time, the Hebrew use of the personification of Wisdom came to have what amounted to almost a full storyline.[101]

---

[96] Cf. Lang, *Wisdom and the Book of Proverbs*, 140: "In the Book of Proverbs, Wisdom neither represents an aspect of a deity of higher rank nor does she mediate between Creator and creation."

[97] H. Ringgren, *Word and Wisdom. Studies in the Hypostatization of Divine Qualities and Functions in the Ancient Near East*, 192.

[98] Cf. K. A. Kitchen, "Some Egyptian Background to the OT," 4ff.

[99] Cf. Lang, *Frau Weisheit*, 164ff.

[100] Lang, *Wisdom and the Book of Proverbs*, 132.

[101] Lang, *Wisdom and the Book of Proverbs*, p. 142, is right to stress that there was in all likelihood no pre-existing Wisdom myth which was simply adapted and adopted by Israelite sages. Rather, the most one can say is that some of the characterizations of *Ma'at* in the earlier period, and perhaps of Isis, are also, by the time we get to Pseudo-Solomon (or Sirach?), used of personified Wisdom in Hebrew Wisdom literature. On the possible influence of *Ma'at* material on Proverbs 8, cf. C. Kayatz, *Studien zu Proverbien 1–9*, 76ff.

There is, however, a big difference between personifying *one* attribute of a deity, and talking about God in all God's attributes. The material in Proverbs is not close to being language about a goddess or about goddess worship because the sage makes clear in numerous ways that s/he is talking about *one* attribute of God, a character trait if you will, not God as a personal entity or God in all God's attributes.[102] Even when it appears the sage is talking about creation rather than the Creator, he is only talking about *an* aspect of creation, not creation as a whole.[103] Later this study will examine Ben Sira's use of the personification of Wisdom to talk about essential attributes or qualities of Torah.[104]

Murphy objects to the idea that in Prov. 3:6, 18, 7:4, or 8:31 we are merely dealing with a personification of a divine attribute, on the grounds that divine attributes cannot be said to be a gift or to play before God or delight to be with humans (but cf. Prov. 3:19).[105] He is right, for what one is dealing with is a complex phenomenon. Wisdom in some cases is an attribute of God, in some cases an attribute God has bestowed on creation, and in some cases a gift that God can give to human beings that they are called upon to embrace and live with. When creation and/or the human creature reflect the quality of *hokmah* they are reflecting an aspect of God's character in which God takes special delight. In all cases, however, one is talking about *an attribute*, or *a quality*, or *an abstraction* that has been personified. The possible analogy with *Ma'at* does not

[102] Lang, *Wisdom and the Book of Proverbs*, 6ff., argues that the personification of Wisdom in Proverbs amounts to an elegant redefinition of an early Hebrew or Semitic goddess *Hokmah* by those who were monotheists. This is possible, but one may require the scholar to produce evidence for such a claim that comes from Palestine, and not from a papyrus that was found in Elephantine which included an Aramaic version of the Assyrian story of Ahiqar (*Ahiq*. 94–95)! It is clear that the ones who produced that document were polytheists, but the evidence that they came from "polytheistic (i.e. non-converted) Jewish circles" is lacking (cf. Lang 130-31). On Lang's own showing the attempt to use Proverbs 1–9 to find traces of early goddess worship in Israel must fail for as Lang himself admits, "the canon of sacred literature that emerged gradually after the exile does not contain anything of the polytheistic literature that must have existed. It is completely lost" (126). In short, if there was such goddess worship of an early Jewish goddess, all traces of it have been expunged from Proverbs and other books. Thus, to argue for such goddess worship of a Hokmah figure is an argument from silence if one takes the canonical books as one's evidence, or an argument from evidence from a foreign place and milieu, if one starts with the Elephantine papyrus, or other Egyptian texts.

[103] Thus the suggestions of Camp and others (cf. her article "Woman Wisdom as Root Metaphor: A Theological Consideration" in *The Listening Heart. Essays in Wisdom and the Psalms in Honour of R. E. Murphy*, 45–76, especially 66ff.) that we take Woman Wisdom as a precedent or root metaphor that justifies embracing a relationship with God as Goddess flies in the face of the historical evidence itself. The sage uses the material in a way that does not justify such a development. Indeed it is possible that this personification arose in the first place as a means of co-opting or ruling out goddess worship in Israel by attributing to Yahweh the very attributes that others were finding in pagan goddesses (cf. below pp. 45ff.). The search for the feminine attributes or traits of God, as they are expressed in the biblical literature is a worthwhile endeavor, but it is not well served by ignoring or dismissing the way the personification Woman Wisdom is in fact used in its original historical and literary context.

[104] Cf. below pp. 92ff.

[105] Murphy, "Faces of Wisdom in the Book of Proverbs," 341.

encourage one to think otherwise. After a detailed study, C. Camp rightly stresses

> the obvious difficulty in envisioning personified Wisdom as a goddess or, at least, as a self-existent being beside Yahweh. The burden rests with those scholars who hold such a view of the Wisdom figure to explain her role in the normative monolatry of Israel, and this has not been done. There is no compelling reason to accept the hypothesis that Israel understood this figure as anything more substantial than the product of poetic imagination, in spite of the tendencies of its neighbors. Indeed, the bulk of the biblical material would suggest quite the contrary, and eloquently bespeaks Israel's ability to transform utterly whatever technique or content of "thought and imagination" it may have borrowed.[106]

Ma'at seems to mean order or justice, not wisdom, though like Woman Wisdom it is referring to an aspect or attribute of something, not a personal being.[107] There are some texts which speak of *Ma'at* as created before the creatures and before the sky. Ptah-hotep describes *Ma'at* as follows: "*Ma'at* is great, and its appropriateness is lasting; it has not been disturbed since the time of him who made it ... It is the path before him who knows nothing ... The strength of *Ma'at* is that it lasts."[108]

There seems then to be good reason to suggest that there has been some influence of this figure *Ma'at* on the depiction of personified Wisdom in Proverbs 1–9, though they are not identical any more than the broader concept of order/justice in Egypt is identical with the idea of Wisdom which comes from Yahweh.[109] Some similar values may be noted, i.e., the following of the right path and the emphasis on the good life. *Ma'at* and Wisdom are also seen as the givers or dispensers of life, and in both cases the respective concepts are seen as the foundation of royal rule that is going to be good and equitable. One notable difference is that *Ma'at* is always talked about but never speaks in the Egyptian literature, unlike the figure in Proverbs 1–9.[110] Furthermore, as B. Mack points out, *Ma'at* lacks the sexual dimension and any sort of fully

[106] Camp, *Wisdom and the Feminine in the Book of Proverbs*, 36. This judgment, which is so clearly on target, makes her later willingness to speak of finding the goddess in and behind this material very puzzling.

[107] Cf. Lang, *Wisdom and the Book of Proverbs*, 144.

[108] ANET, 412; AEL, 2, 64; LAE, p. 162.

[109] I am not convinced that there is much compelling evidence of Isis influence on the personified Wisdom material in Proverbs 1–9. Even the "I" style can be explained on other grounds. The influence of the Isis material, if it exists at all, is very slight. It must be borne in mind that "the hellenized Isis cult revitalized during the second century B.C." not earlier, and it would be very difficult to date this material that late, especially in view of Ben Sira's knowledge of it. The influence of the Isis material on Sirach or Pseudo-Solomon is another question. The above quoted phrase is from J. M. Reese, *Hellenistic Influence on the Book of Wisdom and its Consequences*, 36.

[110] Murphy, *Tree of Life*, 160–63.

developed mythology surrounding it.[111] One must then conclude that the evidence for influence here is somewhat strong, but *Ma'at* cannot simply be identified with Woman Wisdom.[112] The biblical writer has used ideas and incorporated them into a new Yahwistic framework. It is important to add, however, that the connection of Israelite and Egyptian Wisdom at this point may suggest that the personification first arose in Israel during the monarchical period when Egyptian influence and cross-fertilization were apparently considerable.[113]

Von Rad has disputed that in Proverbs 1–9 we are dealing with the personification of a divine attribute. He sees wisdom as something immanent in creation, yet not to be simply identified with that creation. Rather, he calls it the meaning or divine mystery of creation which one must seek out in creation. Later he calls it the order or ordering principle given to creation. It is hard to doubt that this conclusion has in part been arrived at because of the association of Wisdom with *Ma'at* in the literature.[114] But is von Rad right that we are *simply* dealing here with an attribute of the world, something immanent in creation rather than an attribute of God?[115] Can it not be that we are dealing with something that existed before creation and had an effect on the creation in accord with God's design?

Von Rad's view requires that we deny that various passages speak of *hokmah* pre-existing. Prov. 3:19–20 especially comes to mind. Here we are told that God laid out creation's foundations in (or by) Wisdom, and "in (or by) his knowledge, the depths were cleft open". This suggests more the idea of something that exists prior to creation, namely, God's wisdom and knowledge that were used in the creating of the universe. It is true that since creation was founded in Wisdom, the creation to a certain extent reflects a moral ordering principle. This is why humans can scrutinize creation and learn something of the creator's design and purpose in it all. But Woman Wisdom is not to be identified with her effects, but rather with the *hokmah* or knowledge in the mind of God. As Job 28:23–27 so eloquently puts it, when God created things he gave

---

[111] B. Mack, *Logos und Sophia. Untersuchungen zur Weisheitstheologie im hellenistischen Judentum*, 38ff. He then wishes to argue that Isis is a more appropriate parallel to the material in Proverbs 8. This in part depends on when one dates the material in Proverbs 1–9. A better case can be made for the influence of Isis material on Sirach (cf. pp. 100ff. below). Even if Proverbs 1–9 should prove to be not from the monarchical period, it is noteworthy that we find nothing like the mythology of Isis and Horus developed in the biblical material. Personified Wisdom is basically *not* depicted in the same sort of maternal terms as Isis.

[112] Cf. the conclusions of Kayatz, *Studien zu Proverbien 1–9*, 135–39.

[113] This point must count against the argument of those who want to see the personification of Woman Wisdom arising in a post-monarchical period. Even Camp, "Female Sage," 190, n. 18 accepts that at least Proverbs 8 probably comes from the Solomonic era. I agree, but the final redaction of Proverbs as a whole including Proverbs 1–9 must be dated later. Analogies between material in Proverbs and Isis material are more remote but cf. H. Conzelmann, "Die Mutter der Weisheit," in *Zeit und Geschichte*, 223ff.

[114] Von Rad, *Wisdom*, 147-8.

[115] Von Rad, *Wisdom*, 156.

Wisdom a visible setting. Wisdom could be seen and appraised in such a setting, but it was not to be simply identified with the setting, or even an ordering principle in the setting. To be sure Wisdom and her effects can be seen "in the world" but she is not ultimately "of the world" – she existed before it. Plöger puts it this way: "Die Weisheit ist nicht schöpfungsimmanent, sie kann aber in ihrer Herleitung von Jahwe ein 'kreatürliches' Element nicht völlig abstreifen."[116]

Certainly one of the earliest interpreters of this tradition saw it as described above, for in Sirach 1:3–10 Wisdom is said to be created before all things (v 4). She is then poured forth on all God's created works. Again then Wisdom is not simply immanent in creation, though she may be found there as well. Murphy is right to stress, however, the direct connection of Wisdom not just with an order in creation but also with God.

> It appears then that Wisdom is the peculiar quality of God that is manifest in creation because he has lavished it upon his works. Unless human beings have this perspective they cannot find Wisdom. If they fail to find Wisdom's divine affiliation they will not find her. She is the divine secret in the created world. One cannot predicate Wisdom of an individual work of creation. The heavens are not wise, the earth is not wise, but Wisdom is present in God's creation.[117]

All this is true but one must bear in mind that Wisdom was transcendent before its effects were ever immanent, and after becoming immanent it still remains a quality of God. More importantly it is an attribute of God that addresses God's people both in his word as well as in his world. The striking contrast between *Ma'at* as a mute ordering rule or principle and *hokmah* in Proverbs as a personification is that *hokmah* even has the human quality of directly addressing humankind. This should have warned scholars against reducing Wisdom to nothing more than a mute principle of order in creation. It is also critical that one see Woman Wisdom in the same sort of way as her negative counterpart, Dame Folly. Both are cases of personification, the difference being that Wisdom is a personification of an attribute of God or creation or even a human being, while Folly is the personification of the attribute of unwise human beings.[118]

---

[116] Plöger, *Sprüche Salomos*, 93.

[117] Murphy, *Tree of Life*, 135.

[118] Van Leeuwen, "Liminality and Worldview in Proverbs 1–9," p. 112 is quite right to sharply criticize Camp's attempt to merge these two opposite personifications into yet another figure "Woman Language." Cf. Camp, "Woman Wisdom as Root Metaphor," 45–76. Even more disturbing and non-historical in methodology is Camp's admission that this is a purposeful misreading of the author's or editor's intent (cf. 62–63). Camp's work is very valuable but she allows certain agendas from radical feminist theology to skew her use of the data, and thus violate the historical thrust of the material.

In an important article E. A. Johnson has argued that while the creator(s) of this personification have drawn on extra-biblical sources that do deal with goddesses for some of the traits of Woman Wisdom, nevertheless, "the biblical writers, in consciously assimilating religious tradition outside of their own, were not drawing the same conclusions for worship and practice as the devotees whose tradition they borrowed: there were no priests or temples of Sophia."[119] Nevertheless, she goes on to argue that Woman Wisdom is *not* a personification of a divine attribute, but rather a personification of God's own self in God's creating and saving involvement with the world.[120]

This approach, however, has two major flaws. First, it fails to take into consideration the antithesis of Dame Folly to Woman Wisdom. What one says about the latter one must also be prepared to say about the former, at least to some degree. It is quite clear that Dame Folly is an abstraction, not a real person, and this must count against seeing her counterpart as more than a personified quality or attribute.[121] Second, and more importantly, in the text of Prov. 8 clear distinctions are made between God and Wisdom. The latter is said to be created by the former. Prov. 8:22 is hardly arguing that God created God! One must attend to the way Wisdom and God are distinguished in the text as well as the ways they are identified. The identification comes, it appears, at the level of creating and redeeming *functions*, not at the ontological level.

If one looks at other texts where the Wisdom personification may be found, such as Job 28 or Sirach 24, one hears of God searching for Wisdom (which did not amount to searching for God's own self), or of Wisdom coming forth from God's mouth. None of these other texts encourage one to think the authors had straightforward identification of God and Wisdom in mind. Lang is right to finally conclude, "[a]n identification of Wisdom with Yahweh, however subtly explained, is not borne out by the poems."[122] R. Marcus has suggested in his critique of Ringgren's theories that because "*Hokmah* was not only a divine quality but also the ideal of a human quality, which was to be realized in practical form, it never became sufficiently detached from either God or the Torah to become a concrete hypostasis and the occasion of a polytheistic development."[123] Consideration to some details of the Woman Wisdom material must now be given.

In several ways Prov. 8:22–29 reminds the listener that the origin of Wisdom is from before the beginning of creation. If one starts with Prov. 8:22 one reads, "Yahweh procreated me the first-born (or first-fruits) of his way." The verb *qanani* can mean "acquire" and thus we might translate, "Yahweh

---

[119] E. A. Johnson, "Jesus the Wisdom of God. A Biblical Basis for a Non-Androcentric Christology," 271.

[120] Johnson, "Jesus, the Wisdom of God," 273.

[121] One may wish to compare at this point 1 Enoch 42 where the personification of Wisdom and Iniquity are contrasted.

[122] Lang, *Wisdom and the Book of Proverbs*, 140; cf. J. Cranford, "Wisdom Personified," 39.

[123] R. Marcus, "On Biblical Hypostases of Wisdom," 170.

acquired me" (so Aquila, Symmachus, Theodot, and Jerome), but this hardly suits the context here where one expects to hear something about the origin of Woman Wisdom. As Ringgren points out in Gen. 14:19, 22 the meaning of the radical must be "creator" and in Gen. 4:1 "to bear". In Ps. 139:13 as well it is properly rendered, "For you have *formed/created* my inward parts."[124] Thus it is possible to translate *qanani* as either create or procreate, i.e., either "to fashion" or "to beget" (the Greek, Syriac and Targum suggest "create")[125]. In favor of the latter meaning are vv 24–25 which speak of Wisdom being brought forth. M. Gilbert makes clear the structure of this entire passage and the logic of its development. The passage moves from the procreation of Wisdom (v 22), to the forming of her parts in the womb (v 23) to her infancy existing before the creation of the world (vv 24–26), to her assisting in the creation of the world (vv 27–30a), and then finally she is seen as the link or bond between Yahweh and human beings (vv 30b–31).[126] Thus it is very plausible that this is a poetic description of the birth of Wisdom, and this may connect nicely with what one finds in 8:30–31: "I was beside him as an *amon*, I was delight day by day, playing before him all the time, playing on the surface of his earth, and my delight (was) with humankind."[127]

A third possible way to translate *qanani* is "possessed me", which as K. A. Farmer says, "leaves open the possibility that Wisdom should be understood here as a personification of an attribute of God."[128] In favor of such a rendering is that in the twelve other passages in Proverbs (e.g., 4:5–7) where we find *qanah* it very likely means either "acquire" *or* "possess".[129] Perhaps more importantly it makes sense of a passage like Prov. 1.5 and comports with the idea expressed in Prov. 3.19. The much disputed word *amon* can mean craftswoman, in which case the passage envisions Wisdom playing a role in the creating activities, but if it is taken to mean "nursling" or "small child" then the image is simply of a child playing.[130]

If one takes a cue from Jer. 52:16 then the meaning artisan/ craftsman is likely. Also, in Wis. 7:22 and 8.6, one of the earliest interpretations of this material, "craftswoman" is very likely in view (there called a *technitis*). In any event, there is evidence in Prov. 8:22ff. that the author sees Wisdom as pre-existing and probably as having an active role in the work of creation.[131] Unlike

---

[124] Ringgren, *Word and Wisdom*, 101. He proposes that the connection between the two major sorts of meanings of this word is that while it is right to say that *QNH* has as its fundamental meaning "acquiring" something not previously possessed, this may be accomplished by either buying it, or making/creating it. In short, the context must determine the proper nuance in a given instance.

[125] Cf. B. Gemser, *Sprüche Salomos*, 46.

[126] M. Gilbert, "Le Discours de la Sagesse en Proverbes 8," in *La Sagesse de l'Ancien Testament*, 214–15.

[127] Here following Murphy, *Tree of Life*, 136

[128] Farmer, *Proverbs and Ecclesiastes*, 54.

[129] Cf. R. B. Y. Scott, *Proverbs–Ecclesiastes*, 71.

[130] Cf. the arguments of Plöger, *Sprüche Salomos*, 95–96.

[131] Cf. Ringgren, *Word and Wisdom*, 102–03.

that creation, Woman Wisdom was begotten, not made or, if "possess" is the right translation, then always existed, even before creation. She comes forth from God directly or is possessed by God, and yet here is not identified with or as God, but rather as a personified attribute of God, and then once the universe is made, of God's creation. Some more details about Woman Wisdom must now be considered.

Woman Wisdom is introduced in Prov. 1:20ff. as a messenger who cries aloud in the streets and the public squares and at the city gates. She cries out over the noise of the marketplace. The image is of a town crier going through the village calling out to a large group of people. Yet she is not one who simply calls; she has a message to deliver. She does not merely call to the sage or educated but to the untutored youth (*peti*), the mockers, even the fools. The audience she seeks is everyone, for her concern is with the business of daily living, not with some esoteric scholarly pursuit of wisdom.[132]

It is not impossible that the image here is drawn from the actual practice of sages who taught in the city gate and called out to draw a crowd.[133] Her message has to do with knowledge and the fear of the Lord (cf. v 29) and how to live a particular way of life which is different from their chosen course (cf. v 31). Those who do not listen to her commit errors which lead to death, but those who do listen "may live secure, will have quiet, fearing no mischance" (v 33). Most striking of all, Lady Wisdom offers life (9:6).

There is an urgency about the address here and an indictment is offered because people had "turned away from" (*tasubu*) "wisdom" while it was being offered. Thus, the day will come when they will seek and not find it. While Wisdom is depicted as a preacher here, her style is that of the sage. She speaks authoritatively but there is no "thus saith the Lord." As McKane stresses, she demands attention, obedience, recognition, but there is no mention of sorrow or repentance unlike the case with the prophets.[134] This may lead to R. E. Murphy's conclusion that "nowhere in vv. 22–33 does Wisdom invite the audience to conversion. She simply proclaims the punishment of those who reject her. Verses 24–33 constitute an unremitting, ineluctable condemnation which is hardly softened by the alternative of 'one who hears' in the final verse."[135] Wisdom then has been rejected by some if not many, for Prov. 1:24ff.

---

[132] Cf. Kidner, *Proverbs*, 39.

[133] McKane, *Proverbs*, 273. This may indeed raise, however obliquely, the question of whether there were women sages performing such tasks in the city gates. Cf. S. Amsler, "La sagesse de la femme," in *La Sagesse de l'Ancien Testament*, 112–16. The woman of Tekoa makes an allusion possible (cf. 2 Sam. 14.2ff), but the subject matter is still divine Wisdom. The point would be to draw an analogy – like a woman sage crying out in the city gate, so Wisdom calls to God's people.

[134] McKane, *Proverbs*, 275–6.

[135] R. E. Murphy, "Wisdom's Song: Proverbs 1:20–33," 456–460. It is possible that we should see vv 23–31 as a discourse for the future to be proclaimed *if* the current audience doesn't hear and heed Wisdom now. Cf. Murphy, 458, n. 6.

speaks of that rejection, and in fact says "no one has taken notice." This accounts for the negative tone of the speech.

The writer is not talking about a divine being separate from Yahweh, for he can turn around and say essentially the same things without the personification. Thus in Prov. 2:6ff we read, "For Yahweh himself is the giver of wisdom, from his mouth issue knowledge and understanding. He reserves his advice for the honest" (JB).

Moving along to Prov. 3:13–20 one hears that those who discover Wisdom are blessed. As McKane says, this passage is rather hymnic in tone for it addresses no one directly and it makes no direct demands.[136] There is a dialectic between Wisdom who seeks God's people and now here the reverse of that. Crenshaw, with his usual penetrating insight, suggests that this view of Wisdom as a revealer comes out of the setting, not of the scrutiny of nature or human nature, but of belief in direct encounter with God, and thus with the mind of God.[137] This in turn leads to an understanding of at least some aspects of Wisdom as hidden unless she is revealed in such an encounter. This helps to explain the stress placed here on the preciousness of Wisdom, worth a great deal more than great riches. Yet among her benefits are length of days, riches, and honor, delight, contentment.

The hiddenness of at least some wisdom is a theme found throughout the Wisdom corpus and the way it develops is striking. Proverbs 25:2 speaks of this hiddenness and the duty of the king, the human intermediary between God and his people, to seek it out. The personified Wisdom material in Proverbs 1–9 also encourages humans to seek out and listen to wisdom. By the time one gets to the hymn in Job 28 wisdom is still hidden, but now no one is being urged to seek it out, least of all the king.[138] In fact it is God who searches it out and understands it, but it is hidden from "the eyes of all living". This teaching, however, is given in the context in which God still speaks to his people, thus the hymn ends with God telling the listener what is wisdom for human beings. In Ecclesiastes, Qoheleth may be willing to allow true wisdom is hidden, but he gives little hope of God revealing it to us. The personification of Wisdom is notably absent from his book. Thus, God's wisdom becomes basically inscrutable, past finding out (but cf. Eccles. 2:26).[139]

---

[136] McKane, *Proverbs*, 294ff.

[137] Crenshaw, "The Acquisition of Knowledge," in *Word and World*, 251: "In these appeals to direct encounter with the Most High, a decisive step is taken that opens the door to elaborate theories about communication between creator and creature. The first impressive figure to walk through this door was a woman who identified herself as Wisdom.... The imagery seems at first to be purely metaphorical, but eventually it signified an actual divine attribute. Egyptian influence is evident at the beginning, Greek at the end. Antedating creation, Wisdom assisted the creator and later came to earth in order to communicate the deity's thoughts to all creatures."

[138] This in itself may favor the view that Job is from the post-monarchical period.

[139] As Bryce, *Legacy of Wisdom*, 154 says, at the end of the day even von Rad had to admit that Wisdom does to some extent deal with a hidden order of and in things that needs searching out. This is so even in some of the earliest sayings of Israelite wisdom (e.g. Prov. 25:2).

The word translated honor in Prov. 3:16 is *kabod*, which means literally weightiness or heaviness and thus importance or significance. Thus McKane remarks, "This is what Wisdom does for a man; he becomes a weighty person in his community, a man of substance who exercises power and influence and commands respect."[140] These, however, are the by-products of the quest to seek and live by Wisdom. The metaphor about Wisdom as a tree of life means perhaps both that length of days are given to those who pursue the path of Wisdom, and also that the quality of life is improved as well for 3.18 says that those who hold fast to her live happy lives.

Proverbs 4.5–9 provides the instruction of a father to his children to "get Wisdom" and keep her and never deviate from her instruction. Here we learn that the first principle or beginning of wisdom is to acquire Wisdom. There is a certain paradoxical quality to this advice since presumably one must to some extent be wise enough to recognize wisdom to acquire it. Kidner, however, points out that what one is being exhorted to do here is get wisdom, which requires a decision, not brains.[141] This passage also suggests the idea of Wisdom as a sort of patroness from whom one can get preferred treatment if one will adhere closely to her.[142] One should also compare 7.4–5 where the listener is exhorted to call Wisdom his sister to save himself from the peril of the *isshah zara*.

More detailed consideration must now be given to Prov. 8. Verses 1–11 basically reiterate the calling out of Wisdom in the streets we heard about in Prov. 1. In vv 12ff. some new thoughts come to the surface. In this section one sees Wisdom speak emphatically. In vv 14–17a, "I", "me", and "mine" are emphatic. The focus here is on Wisdom herself, not her benefits. Here Wisdom is seen as *savoir-faire*, that is, political astuteness or prudence or shrewdness (*sekenti*). McKane makes the point that Wisdom here speaks like a stateswoman or counselor to a king, or perhaps even a queen.[143] Yet she offers more than just advice. At her disposal is not only good advice, but perception and power. By Wisdom, kings rule and rulers make just laws. "Wisdom is envisaged as framing and executing policies in the highest circles of government." [144]

One must always bear in mind that *hokmah*, as was said earlier in this chapter, can mean a variety of things, including political astuteness, being worldly-wise and knowing how to deal in public affairs. This meaning is especially in evidence in royal contexts, since the king was the ultimate arbiter of power, and one sees this idea in the monarchical material on Solomon in 1 Kings 10ff. It is not necessary to divide up the kinds of wisdom on some sort of chronological timeline, since the term *hokmah* refers to a variety of concepts.

---

140 McKane, *Proverbs*, 296.
141 Kidner, *Proverbs*, 67.
142 McKane, *Proverbs*, 305-6.
143 McKane, *Proverbs*, 346ff.
144 McKane, *Proverbs*, 348.

It may be that Wisdom is modeled on *Ma'at* in vv 17–21, for she is depicted as both lover and beloved.

In Prov. 9.1ff. Wisdom is presented as the hostess. She does not invite the well-to-do to her banquet, however, though she is presented as a wealthy householder who has built a perfect house with an interior courtyard with seven columns.[145] If a temple is in view then there may be some justice to the suggestion that Wisdom is here depicted as a sort of alternative to the goddess of love in a pagan setting like the temple to Aphrodite on Cyprus which was named by the Roman pro-consul, "The Holy Place of the Seven within the Stelae". If the analogy is with a temple then the meal depicted here may be seen as a cultic meal.

R. J. Clifford has noted numerous parallels between the personification in Proverbs 9 and an important Ugaritic text from the fourteenth century B.C. The Canaanite goddess Anat is involved and she cries out:

> "Eat of food, ho! Drink of the liquor of wine, ho!"...She raises her voice and cries "Hear, O Aqht the hero, Ask silver and I will give it to you, Gold and I will bestow it on you. Only give your bow to Anat...Ask for life, O Aqht the hero, Ask for life and I will give it to you, Not-dying and I will grant it to you...For Ball, when he gives life, gives a feast. For the one brought to life he gives a feast and makes him drink."[146]

What is striking about this parallel, besides the similarity in language and content, is that here the figure in question speaks to the youth, unlike the mute *Ma'at*. Clifford also notes how Anat laughs in scorn of human folly, like what we find in Proverbs. W. F. Albright pointed out that there were numerous "Canaanitisms" in Prov. 8–9 not the least of which is the use of *hokmot* instead of the Hebrew *hokmah*.[147] The arguments of both these scholars must be taken seriously, and what they suggest, as do the parallels with Egyptian wisdom material is a monarchical not post-exilic point of origin for this personification of Wisdom. The Canaanite parallels support the view that the sages in the Wisdom they promulgated were offering alternative ways of looking at ordinary life to the world view provided by the fertility religions of the region. In this case they would be suggesting that all that one actually sought from these other religions was to be had from Yahweh, whose attribute it was not merely to have Wisdom and life, but to bestow it on his creation and creatures. It is striking how the personification in Proverbs 8–9 fits in with the view that Wisdom theology is a form of creation theology.

---

[145] Seven represents perfection. There are as many guesses as exegetes as to what the seven columns might stand for, but it is best to see here the simple idea of Wisdom building the perfect house or home.

[146] R. J. Clifford, "Proverbs IX: A Suggested Ugaritic Parallel," 300–303.

[147] W. F. Albright, "Some Canaanite-Phoenician Sources of Hebrew Wisdom," in *Wisdom and the Ancient Near East*, 7–9.

Wisdom invites the untutored youth and even the fool. In a sense she is calling out to the least, the last, and the lost. Notice she sends out her maidservants, not manservants, to do this task. The only qualification for coming to the banquet is the deficiency of those called.[148] She calls them to forsake fools, not folly. This passage is not just about a new attitude, but also about a new way of life (no longer keeping company with fools).

Proverbs 9:1–6 must be contrasted with the feast of Dame Folly in 9:13–18. Wisdom offers at her banquet a rare and luxurious commodity – meat. The point is that Wisdom offers one only the best. The wine also is the best, the sort mixed with honey and spices. If a sacramental meal is in mind this might comport better with the idea of Wisdom providing religious and spiritual nourishment, as well as material well-being and nourishment.[149]

CONCLUSIONS

Wisdom, which begins with the idea of reverence for Yahweh, is seen as the key to the good life. Wisdom teaches the art of steering through life's difficulties and how to live long, live well, and live in an upright fashion. The material in Proverbs may be called generalizations, things usually true under normal circumstances. It deals with everyday life quite apart from salvific and crisis experiences when God intervenes.

As I have suggested, the sages may well be providing an alternative to reverting to Canaanite fertility religion and faith in the cycle of the seasons, by making trust in Yahweh an everyday necessity and the key to prosperity and blessing in daily affairs. I make this suggestion because it seems to have been a problem for Israelite faith that their God was a God of history, one who from time to time intervened in human affairs. This raised the question of where God and God's guidance may be found during the course of ordinary day to day life. Perhaps the sages sought to fill the void left when one was not involved with or celebrating the activities of the God of salvation history.

Yet the sages were well aware that there were also crisis experiences of a negative sort – extreme suffering or systemic failure of a society's vision and world view. The other two major Wisdom books in the Old Testament, Job and Ecclesiastes, the latter of which will be discussed next, either critique or attempt to accommodate a Wisdom view of life so as to deal with life's abnormalities and irregularities, what may be called its exceptional, but still common, aberrations.

Several further notable conclusions can be drawn from this investigation of Proverbs. First, the degree of indebtedness of early Israelite Wisdom to

---

[148] Kidner, *Proverbs*, 81ff.

[149] Cf. the conclusion of Gemser, *Sprüche Salomos*, p. 48 about the personification of Wisdom in Proverbs 9: "Es ist also kein Grund vorhanden, hier den Anfang der späteren jüdisch-hellenistischen Hypostasenlehre... oder der späteren christlichen Logosspekulation zu suchen."

international Wisdom and particularly Egyptian Wisdom is notable. This is so not only in the proverbs, but also in the instructions, and possibly also in the personification of Woman Wisdom. Second, some of the material in Proverbs seems to have arisen in a family or clan setting, particularly some of the material in Proverbs 1–9, but there is also considerable evidence that some of this material arose in a court setting, whether being written for courtiers or in other cases for royalty. There is little or no compelling evidence at this stage that any of this material arose from a school setting, if by that one means a house of learning like that to which Ben Sira bears witness. It seems likely that scribes or others in the context of the court collected, transcribed, and edited this material, at least as early as the time of Hezekiah, but perhaps earlier.

Another important point is that this wisdom seems in large part to be wisdom from above, that is, wisdom produced either by and/or for the well-to-do, those who had time to be educated and reflect on the meaning of life, and in some cases the royal well- to-do in particular. This will stand in contrast then to some of the wisdom material in the Jesus tradition which is clearly "from below", a wisdom from and especially concerned about the underclass of society.

The very character of the collections of proverbs suggests that the sages were aware of the usefulness but also the limitations of such generalizations. This is why one has various sayings which come close to finding their antithesis in the same corpus. These proverbs, like the instructions found in Proverbs 1–9, by and large seem to presuppose a normal state of affairs both in an individual's life, and also in the life of the culture or nation. In such circumstances sages were willing to talk about a moral act–consequence structure to reality in everyday affairs. There are a few inklings in this material of a larger vision that not only allows for exceptional situations but also comes to grips with the fact that justice is not always done in this lifetime. Occasionally one sees some groping towards a positive as well as a punitive view of the afterlife, beyond the traditional ideas about Sheol. Clearly, however, these ideas have not yet come to full fruition.

The importance of the personification of Wisdom cannot be overemphasized. It is an idea that, once introduced into the biblical Wisdom tradition, took on a life of its own and grew in importance, in complexity, and in depth as time went on. In due course it would come not only to represent an attribute of God or God's creation, but also to be used as a way of talking about what later became the central focus of Israelite faith – Torah. Then, in an even more striking move, Wisdom became a way of talking about the central figure of Christian faith, Jesus, both in some Gospel traditions and in the Christological hymns. If it is true that Woman Wisdom is drawn in part from the portrait painted in Egyptian Wisdom of *Ma'at,* clearly the Israelite sage or sages who first presented this personification have done so in a way that comports with Israelite faith, adopting and adapting their source(s). Woman Wisdom does not seem to be presented or used *primarily* as a tool for polemics against other forms of international Wisdom or polytheistic faith, but rather as an aesthetic device meant to stress the moral beauty and personal character of God's wisdom as opposed to other kinds of so-called worldly wisdom which might allure or attract one's attention as a way of life or living. Probably Crenshaw is right that, "[b]ecause students almost without exception were males, wisdom was described as a beautiful bride, and folly was depicted as a harlot enticing young men to destruction. In this way language became highly explosive, and the quest for Wisdom took on erotic dimensions."[150]

The androcentric quality of the book of Proverbs should not be underemphasized, but very little of it, least of all Proverbs 31, seems to be intended as a means of putting women in their place. To the contrary, some of it, including the personification and Proverbs 31, may reflect the influence of wise women who contributed to Israelite Wisdom and saw a woman's contribution to the moral and intellectual life of Israel as important (cf. Prov. 31:1–9 and 31:10ff).

In some cases negative conclusions are as important as positive ones. One finds nothing in this whole book that even remotely resembles the parables of Jesus; one must look elsewhere for the source of the narrative *meshalim*. In particular, it appears to be at the juncture where Wisdom, the prophetic tradition (2 Sam. 12:1–15), and later the prophetic apocalyptic tradition (cf. Ezekiel 31) cross-fertilize that one finds the wellsprings of narrative *meshalim* in Israel.[151] Furthermore, narrative *meshalim* are also absent from Job, Ecclesiastes, Ben Sira and the Wisdom of Solomon. None of these sources provide any real evidence that the sages were producing parables. As will be discussed further in a later chapter, it would appear likely that Jesus drew on a variety of Israelite traditions in his teaching so that he was equally at home with either aphorisms or narrative *meshalim*, and he felt free to mix Wisdom forms (and content) with prophetic, eschatological, or on occasion even apocalyptic forms and content.[152] But this is getting ahead of the story. For

---

150 Crenshaw, "Acquisition of Knowledge," 246–7.

151 The only possible exception to this observation is the material we find in 2 Samuel 14 (cf. 2 Samuel 20), where a wise woman seems to be involved in what may be called an enacted parable. This would provide some connection between the Hebrew Wisdom tradition and parables but caution is in order on three fronts. According to the story in 2 Samuel 14, the actual source of this symbolic action is Joab, one of David's henchmen, and certainly no sage, unless by that one simply means one of the King's advisers or authorities. Secondly, is this actually an acted parable, or is it just a symbolic act? Thirdly, and perhaps most importantly, there is no connection here with the telling of *meshalim*, much less the writing down of narrative *meshalim*. The parallels from the prophetic corpus are much closer on this score.

152 We should remind ourselves that just as Wisdom literature is hard to pin down in a form critical sense, so too is the role and function of a sage. As Camp, "The Female Sage," says (186): "the rather amorphous role of the sage sometimes overlaps with other, more recognizable roles." Thompson, *Form and Function*, 102–3, stresses that there is considerable evidence for the influence of the wisdom tradition on the prophetic tradition. Besides the possibility of listing numerous aphorisms quoted in the prophetic corpus (e.g., Isa. 1:3, 22; Jer. 13:23; 17:11; Ezek. 11:3;16:44; Hos. 8:7; Amos 3:3–6) which suggest that Wisdom traditions were already extant and influential in Israel before the exilic period, it may be that the narrative *mashal* is

the second step in the pilgrimage of Israelite wisdom one must consider one of the earliest if not the earliest examples in the Hebrew Scriptures of counter order wisdom – Ecclesiastes.

ECCLESIASTES: A PUBLIC MALAISE

1. BACKGROUND

The journey of life can have many twists and turns, and sometimes the wisdom one has long relied upon becomes insufficient if one is to complete the journey. It is critical to examine the relevant data that reveals something about the pilgrimage of Wisdom as it develops in the context of the community of believers in the biblical God. Especially relevant are the points on the journey where the audience is being told that the old maps are not always sufficient to chart the course one ought to take. There are two possible examples one could turn to to see the beginnings of a counter order Wisdom in early Judaism – Job and Ecclesiastes. Because of the suprising lack of influence of the former of these two works on the later developments in Wisdom literature in the Intertestamental and New Testament era, and because Job primarily deals with the exceptional suffering of a particular individual, we will concentrate our attentions on perhaps the clearest full-fledged example of counter order Wisdom in the Hebrew Scriptures – Ecclesiastes.

While the Book of Job challenges the ability of a Wisdom approach to life to deal adequately with life's extreme situations of suffering, Ecclesiastes offers an even broader and more telling critique. In Ecclesiastes it is not just that someone's individual boat seems to have unfairly sunk; rather, the whole ocean has become so turbulent that no one's boat seems safe on the water. The view seemingly espoused in Ecclesiastes challenges the adequacy of most basic Wisdom assumptions about even normal everyday life. Yet even if it was recognized in early Judaism that Ecclesiastes was a serious challenge to such an approach to life, the epilogue of the book, written after the time of Qoheleth, makes clear that Qoheleth was still seen as a sage who stood within the Wisdom tradition, even if as the "loyal opposition" he offered a fundamental rethinking of various Wisdom generalizations about life.[153]

---

a new creation resulting from the confluence of the prophetic and wisdom tradition. It may have arisen because the prophetic corpus has an interest in narrative, both historical and otherwise, and the Wisdom corpus expresses itself in the form of metaphors and similes. Both traditions share an interest in what can broadly be called ethics. When these forms and interests come together we have a narrative *mashal*.

[153] I am aware of M. V. Fox's contention in "Frame-Narrative and Composition in the Book of Qohelet," 100–03 that the epilogist *is* Qoheleth, or to put it another way, Qoheleth is but a persona to protect the epilogist from criticism for some of his radical ideas. This view seems unlikely, not least because the Epilogue deliberately qualifies the more radical Wisdom found earlier in Ecclesiastes. Cf. Fox, *Qoheleth and his Contradictions*, 315–18.

The title "Ecclesiastes" comes from the LXX and then the Vulgate. The word in classical Greek means one who sits and speaks in the *ekklesia*, or assembly, and as such it is an adequate description of the role of a *hakam* who sat and gave counsel in the city gate where people gathered (cf. Job, revered in the city gate).

Scholars, including conservative ones, are almost universally agreed that this book was not written by Solomon, who is in any case not named directly by the book. The point of the superscript "the words of Qoheleth, the son of David, king over Jerusalem" is probably to establish that the author stands in the line and tradition of Solomonic (i.e., Israelite) Wisdom and therefore should be given a hearing by fellow Jews.[154] It may also be right to say that Ecclesiastes, like Job, was written by a "unique and somewhat unorthodox individual."[155] Both works, though in different ways, confront the ideology of retribution or act–consequence that stands behind much of Proverbs.[156]

The word *qoheleth* is a feminine singular *qal* participle from the verb *qahal* which means "assembling" or "gathering together" of a community. *Qoheleth* then is not a proper name for it is given with the definite article in Eccles. 7:27 and 12:8 – "the *Qoheleth*". This suggests that the term refers to some sort of office or function the author of the book had.[157] While Luther translated the word "the preacher", it is better to translate it the "gatherer" or "assembler."[158]

Perhaps Eccles. 9:13–16 can be seen as autobiographical. It tells of a poor *hakam* who saved a city from a threatening foe by his wisdom, but afterwards no one remembered or thanked the poor wise man. This might explain the tone of this book – being a *hakam* could be a thankless task, like being a prophet.

Several factors favor a rather late date for this book: (1) its tone seems definitely post-exilic, when pessimism and even cynicism had set in in some quarters (cf. Ezra–Nehemiah, Malachi); (2) the Hebrew of this book is much more like later Hebrew, even Mishnaic Hebrew, and has various Aramaisms; (3) various scholars have pointed out the evidence that the author had been influenced both in tone and content by Hellenistic thinking.[159] Some have even suggested that Qoheleth is interacting with various Stoic ideas.[160] Perhaps

---

[154] H. L. Ginsberg, "The Structure and Contents of the Book of Qohelet," in *Wisdom in Israel and in the Ancient Near East*, 138–49, even suggests that one take *mlk* to mean owner, not ruler, in 1.12, and in 2.12 the verbal form means "to own". This raises the question of whether 1.1 might not also mean something more general like authority over/in Jerusalem, for the expression "king in Jerusalem" is peculiar. On authorship, cf. pp. 53–54.

[155] Cf. Clines, *Job 1–20*, lxi.

[156] I suspect that Murphy, "The Sage in Ecclesiastes and Qoheleth the Sage," in *The Sage in Israel and the Ancient Near East*, 263-71, is right in saying that Qoheleth was not as shocking in his own day as he seems to us (265). Perhaps the final editors of the Hebrew Scriptures saw the function of this book as attempting to keep Wisdom honest (271).

[157] Childs, *Introduction*, pp. 583-84.

[158] Cf. Crenshaw, *OT Wisdom*, 148.

[159] Cf. M. Hengel, *Judaism and Hellenism I*, 109–10.

[160] Cf. J. G. Gammie, "Stoicism and Anti-Stoicism in Qoheleth," 169–87.

more telling is the evidence presented by A. Schoors on Qoheleth's style, in particular his use of pronouns which leads to the conclusion that "the language of Qoheleth seems to belong to a late stage of development, one under Aramaic influence and already close to MH."[161] Furthermore, the individualism of the book points to its lateness, and may reflect the effect of Hellenism. In particular, Qoheleth's focus on the achievement of happiness in an indifferent or malevolent world, and his use of sensory experience as the ultimate arbiter of what is real and true seem rather similar to Epicurean perspectives.[162] On the whole then the book has various factors which suggest its lateness, though doubtless it includes various earlier Wisdom traditions which the gatherer has collected, sifted and presented.

The Epilogue in 12:9–10 tells us that Qoheleth was a sage who imparted knowledge to people. He pondered, searched out, and "set in order" many *meshalim*. He searched for just the right words to say. This sounds like the voice of one of Qoheleth's disciples bearing testimony, as the final editor of his sayings. One may set a *terminus ad quem* for this book sometime before 150 B.C. since fragments of it have been found at Qumran.

F. Crüsemann has plausibly demonstrated the sort of malaise or crisis to which Qoheleth is reacting. On the one hand it is clear that he is well enough off to have time, opportunity, and resources to make a test of pleasure, among other things, and perhaps also to have servants (cf. 7:21). It thus seems unlikely that Ecclesiastes is manifesting a purely private and personal crisis. Rather,

> the landowning classes are now among the immensely rich...The social and political balance between the free peasantry and the monarchy that was characteristic of pre-exilic Judah has ceased to exist. Taxes and duties are levied by outside forces, bringing heavy burdens and serious causes of insecurity. The pressure is intensified by the fact that the economy is increasingly based on money and then on coinage, and the self-sufficiency of the individual farm and village is significantly undermined. Increasing pressure for productivity leads to the conversion of farmland to olive orchards and vineyards, which are geared to export....Especially for the aristocratic class, a segmentary solidarity with poorer relations becomes a chancy matter.... But the decisive factor was that this aristocracy became involved in the state system of taxes...as a lessee of the state. In so doing it came to represent objectively the interests of foreign rulers. This meant in turn its inevitable alienation from the other groups in Judah, and finally, the open conflict that broke out under Antiochus IV....The growing economic inequality within kinship groups undermined both the structures and the ethic.[163]

---

[161] A. Schoors, "The Pronouns in Qoheleth," 71–87. The repeated use by Qoheleth of 'I', making clear he speaks as an individual and on his own authority in itself probably points to its lateness.

[162] So Fox, *Qoheleth*, 16.

[163] F. Crüsemann, "The Unchangeable World: The 'Crisis of Wisdom' in Koheleth," in *God of the Lowly. Socio-Historical Intepretations of the Bible*, 62–63.

It is no accident that Qoheleth speaks in this book about what amounts to "gain" (*yitron*), which normally means net gain from an economic transaction, and about the protection of wisdom being like the protection of money (7.12). He lives in an age where it appears that money, not the act–consequence schema, and not kinship is the primary determining factor in regard to whether things go well or ill for someone. "If you see in a province the poor oppressed and justice and right violently taken away, do not be amazed at the matter" (Eccles. 5:8; cf. 4:1). Eccles. 10:20 suggests that Qoheleth lives in a society where rulers must resort to spies and informants to keep the people in line, rather than relying on loyalty earned by leaders who are trusted because they are just and honest.[164] While Qoheleth admits that rulers can make mistakes (10:5) his advice is still to keep the words of the ruler and not to curse him (8:2–5; 10:20). In short, Qoheleth lives in an age where oppression seems to be structured into the very fabric of society, and thus everyone must look out for themselves. Qoheleth's individualism is in part a reflection of the state of the society in which he lives.

J. Loader has pointed out that Qoheleth seems to have deliberately set up various antinomies or polar opposites.[165] There is some evidence from other Ancient Near East texts that it was common procedure to offer a generally recognized truism as a sort of foil for one's own view which critiques that truism. Qoheleth juxtaposes something good and something bad and states the good in such a way as to show its basic flaws.[166] It has also been noticed that the antinomies are set together by a "yes ... but" kind of structure. For example in 3:16–17 the latter verse affirms divine justice as if to qualify the statement in 3.16 about the existence of injustice (similarly in 8:11–13 about the sinner).

There is no general agreement on the structure of Ecclesiastes. On the one hand, because of its similarities to Proverbs (especially Eccles. 7:1ff. and 10:1ff), it seems to be a collection of disparate items.[167] This would explain the abrupt shifts in the book. There are, however, as in Proverbs, some extended sections of discusssion on one topic (cf. 6:10 – 7:14 or 11:9 – 12:7). It is possible to argue that there are two major parts to the book, 1:12 – 6:9 and 6:10 – 11:6, which are preceded and followed by a poem in 1:2–11 and 11:7 – 12:8).[168] Apart from various maxims or aphorisms, and admonitions/commands/prohibitions which are also find in Proverbs, the one new literary form one finds in Ecclesiastes is what Murphy calls the Reflection. This form is characterized by observation and a meditation on the meaning or lack thereof of things. It has

[164] Cf. Crüsemann, "Unchangeable World," 70–71.

[165] J. A. Loader, *Polar Opposites in the Book of Qohelet*.

[166] Cf. Crenshaw, "The Wisdom Literature," *The Hebrew Bible and its Modern Interpreters*, 378.

[167] Ginsberg, "The Structure and Contents of the Book of Koheleth," 138–49, believes the book can be divided into four major divisions but one must accept 4.9 — 5.8 as a set of digressions. This leaves too much of the book in the category of digression.

[168] Murphy, *Forms of Old Testament Literature*, 128–9.

a loose structure and may include rhetorical questions and various other genre (cf. e.g. 1:16 – 17; 2:14, 24).

The book has 222 verses of which over a third are in poetry. There are twenty-seven words that are the author's favorites and they make up a full one-fifth of the whole book![169] Some of the oft repeated ones are: (1) absurd / vanity / futility / emptiness / profitless / a mere breath, which are the proposed meanings of *hbl* which occurs thirty-seven times in the book and is perhaps *the* major theme; (2) key phrases such as "pursuit after wind", "under the sun" "eat and drink"; (3) key words or word pairs such as do / deed; wise / wisdom; know / knowledge; time; good / evil; toil; fool / folly; rejoice, profit; wind / breath (*ruach*); die / death; sin / sinner; justice / just; power; remember / memory; portion; vexation; affair / matter (*hps*); skill (*ksr*). It appears that the key phrases "absurdity of absurdities" and "he cannot find it out" may provide a structural unity to the book.[170] Paranomasia is found various times (absurdity of absurdities, the toil at which I toiled, 2.11, 18, 22), as is word play which is lost in translation (cf. 7.1, *tob sem missemen tob*).

If one puts all of this together it seems that the author is concerned to repudiate or severely qualify various Wisdom maxims about: (1) the law of retribution; (2) the value and meaningfulness of the work and accomplishments of humans in this life; (3) the ability to discern God's plan or hand or action in this life. At the same time, the author strongly stresses the sovereignty of God so this is no atheistic tract. Rather it is a trenchant critique of a Wisdom approach to life. It is not that he does not think there is value in a Wisdom approach to life, it is just that from Qoheleth's perspective such a life strategy does not seem to be properly compensated or rewarded.[171]

It would seem too that one must take 12:13–14 as a later editorial addition meant to offer a corrective to Qoheleth, and point the reader in the direction that Ben Sira and the Wisdom of Solomon would pursue in Wisdom literature, i.e., the locating of Wisdom in Torah, in particular in the keeping of God's commandments. This latter theme is absent from the body of Ecclesiastes, as is any real reference to covenants or salvation history.[172]

The author has concentrated on everyday experience which was the usual provenance of sages in all Ancient Near East cultures. In fact, M. V. Fox singles him out as one whose epistemology is essentially empirical – his primary source of solid knowledge about the world is not Wisdom traditions

[169] Cf. O. Loretz, *Qohelet und der Alte Orient*, 167-73.

[170] Cf. A. Wright, "The Riddle of the Sphinx: The Structure of the Book of Qoheleth," 313–34; and *idem* "The Riddle of the Sphinx Revisited: Numerical Patterns in the Book of Qoheleth," 38–51.

[171] R. E. Murphy, "Qohelet's Quarrel with the Fathers," in *From Faith to Faith. Essays for D. Miller*, 235–45, "Qohelet complains that human wisdom is not achieving the goals she should. This is not so much a rejection of wisdom, as a complaint about the failure of wisdom to deliver" (237).

[172] Cf. Murphy, "The Sage in Ecclesiastes," 265–66.

or maxims but his own experience.[173] He often offers one-line maxims as his comments (cf. 1:13b, 15, 18; 2:14a; 4:4–5; 5:2; 6:9a; 7:1–12; 8:1; 9:18 — 10:4; 10:8–9, 12–13; 11:1–2 and contrast the two liners in Proverbs).

Death hangs over this book like a shroud. "The book has indeed the smell of the tomb about it."[174] The author from time to time seems to see death and Sheol as casting a shadow of absurdity on all that humans do in this life, making it pointless and profitless. The wise man dies as does the fool (2.16). This at times seems to reduce Qoheleth to a *carpe diem* kind of life philosophy. One should enjoy the day while one has it, and especially while one is young (cf. 11:9; 9:10).

The author even resorts to a form of picture language in his justly famous portrayal of death in 12:1–7 which shows how preoccupied he is with the terminus of life. Partly this is because the author does not believe one can figure out "the work of God," i.e., God's design in creation and for his creatures. Though God has placed *ha olam* in our hearts one cannot discern the scope of the divine work and its purpose or meaning (cf. below on 3:11). One may perhaps wish in the end to see Qoheleth as one who is given a place in the Wisdom corpus because, as Murphy suggests, he is keeping Wisdom honest.[175]

There is a certain modernity to this work for the author seems very alone and lonely in the universe and he is introspective about all of this. His "introspective reporting has no good parallels in other Wisdom literature."[176] The book is pervaded with a sense of loss and futility. Both God and human community and companionship seem absent or distant. It is not surprising that this book has proved a favorite for existentialists, and for some modern Old Testament scholars like Crenshaw who lauds what seems a secular point of view here.[177] Yet it is not true that Qoheleth is an atheist or even an agnostic.

It would be better to say that Qoheleth is encouraging an honest facing of the dark side of life. These facts are so troubling precisely because Qoheleth *is* a theist.[178] The evidence of his theism is found not only in the fact that he mentions God some forty times in this book, but also in one of his most typical phrases which is spread evenly throughout the book – "all is in / from the hands of God" (cf. 2:24; 3:10, 13; 5:18, 19; 6:1, 2; 7:15; 9:1, 7, 9; 11:9).[179]

Qoheleth has provided a great service by showing the hopelessness of such a view of life. Qoheleth stands at the ragged edge of a world gone wrong and sees it for what it is. A Wisdom philosophy under such circumstances, especially if there is suffering, persecution, oppression, and poverty is frankly

---

173 M. V. Fox, "Qohelet's Epistemology," 37–55.

174 H. Wheeler Robinson, *Inspiration and Revelation in the Old Testament*, 258.

175 Murphy, *Tree of Life*, 59–60.

176 Fox, "Qohelet's Epistemology," 148.

177 Cf. J. L. Crenshaw, *Ecclesiastes*, 23ff.

178 Cf. Murphy, "The Faith of Qoheleth," 253–60: "He took God on God's terms. And God's terms were most mysterious for him."

179 Cf. M. Laumann, "Qoheleth and Time," 308.

inadequate and this book proves it, however accurate certain maxims may be under certain limited good circumstances.

Qoheleth is weary of battling the world. He does not sally forth against it as do the prophets, but he sees the future as something that happens to one, not something that one shapes. In short he sees life as a sort of victim. Von Rad explains:

> What is new and also alarming is his opinion of the relationship of [humankind] to ...the continuing divine activity...it is completely beyond [human] perception and comprehension and that [humankind] therefore is also incapable of adapting *himself* to it. The consequences of this conviction...are catastrophic. The strong urge to master life – a main characteristic of old wisdom – has been broken. [Humankind] has lost contact with events in the outside world. Although continually permeated by God, the world has become silent for *him*...."That which happens is far off, deep, very deep; who can find out?" (7.24).[180]

Thus von Rad characterizes this author as a lonely rebel and outsider. In such a world view, Qoheleth as it were "spies out" (the verb *tur* in 1.13, 2.3, 7.25 means this) what good is left if one accepts his premises. This good amounts to "enjoy it while you can, for even this too will pass". He is not a mere hedonist for he knows the limitations of that view as well. Childs sums up as follows:

> Koheleth's sayings arose in reaction to an assumed body of Wisdom tradition. Therefore, almost every topic within the traditional teachings of the sages is touched upon in Ecclesiastes; God rewards the righteous and punishes the wicked; an act and its consequence is inextricably linked; life is the highest gift of God and death is a threat; diligence brings its reward and slothfulness its toll. At times Koheleth flatly rejects the tradition, while at other times he modifies or affirms it. That there are contradictions within the book arises from the shifting contexts to which he speaks and from his critical judgment against traditional Wisdom which would lay claim to greater human understanding than Koheleth would grant.[181]

If Qoheleth had any sort of view of a moral division of the good and the evil in the next life and/or a view of a rectifying of matters there (or after the *Yom Yahweh*) so that the good are blessed and the wicked are cursed, this book would not have the thrust and poignancy that it does. The developing Jewish and early Christian view of the afterlife and final judgment drastically changed how people of faith evaluate this life and its inequities. The need for all to be rectified and shown to be right in this life is set aside in favor of eventual

[180] Von Rad, *Wisdom in Israel*, 232.
[181] Childs, *Introduction to the Old Testament*, 587.

rectification in God's own time and place. This proves to be one of the salient differences between, for example, the Wisdom material in the Jesus tradition and the Wisdom material in some parts of Proverbs.

J. G. Williams helps the reader to see what is distinctive about Qoheleth. He is not opposed to all wisdom, but seeks to expand the category of what amounts to Wisdom on the basis of his own empirical tests and insights. "Koheleth breaks away from the ancient collective voice. For him the limited wisdom that human beings can attain is drawn from the experience of the individual."[182] What this amounts to time and again is the qualifying and sometimes even the contravening of the collective with insights from individual experience. A classic example of this is Eccles. 7:1. First Qoheleth quotes the old wisdom, "A good name is better than precious ointment," then he offers his rejoinder or qualifier, "and the day of death, than the day of birth." Here is someone in dialogue with traditional wisdom, who feels and knows its inadequacies personally. "His primary literary mode of representing the paradox of the human situation is the citation of contrasting proverbs, some of which may be his own aphorisms, in order to contradict traditional wisdom."[183]

I believe Williams is right in seeing Proverbs and Ben Sira as essentially reflecting the views of advocates of the traditional order, while Ecclesiastes and the Jesus tradition offer aphorisms of counter order. Qoheleth seems to believe that there is a place and time for a sage who practices both tearing down and building up, both planting and supplanting of old Wisdom.[184] Yet all of this material may be called Wisdom material. This shows the flexibility of the genre.

2. *ECCLESIASTES 1–4*

The Book of Ecclesiastes begins and ends its basic argument in the same way, with the cry *hebel, hebel* (cf. 1:2 and 12:8). This word which derives from a root that means a breath or vapor tends to have two sorts of nuances: (1) temporal, in which cases it means something like transitory, ephemeral, and so insubstantial; and (2) it can mean something existential, such as absurd, meaningless, empty, futility. The superlative *habel habilim* means either absolutely futile/useless, completely ephemeral, or totally absurd. This is the leitmotif of the book and needs to be examined closely.

In view of the numerous references to time which follow and the reference to chasing after or herding wind it can be argued that the meaning is likely to be a temporal one, i.e., absolutely nothing lasts, completely ephemeral or insubstantial. Everything is like a breath or puff of smoke, here and then

---

[182] Williams, *Those Who Ponder*, 27.
[183] Williams, *Those Who Ponder*, 60.
[184] Laumann, "Qoheleth and Time," 306.

gone. As will become clear, the reason why Qoheleth renders this judgment is because of the relativizing shadow of death. Fox, however, has made a very strong case for taking the meaning of *hebel* to be absurd/absurdity.[185] That Qoheleth is capable of saying that all is *hebel* suggests that this term should be seen to have a common meaning throughout the book, otherwise it cannot act as the book's leitmotif. The point is not just that things are ephemeral, ironic, inefficacious, or incongruous but that since the moral order encapsulated in the act–consequence idea is shown by Qoheleth's experience *not* to be in effect, everything is absurd and hence without much significance or meaning. This includes human toil, pleasure, Wisdom, and even life itself. Without act–consequence, life and its occurrences are ridiculous. This is a problem for Qoheleth precisely because he is a theist. The whole structure of his culture, the very system of life he is a part of, seems ridiculous without justice or fairness. Fox puts it this way:

> When...we believe that an action is in principle morally good,or at least neutral, and yet find that it does not yield what we consider proper results, then it is not essentially the action that is absurd but rather the *fact* that there is a disparity between rational expectations and the actual consequences....Wisdom literature insisted that God's behavior is rational and that rationality is perceptible in the bond between deed and consequence. For Qohelet the reliability of the causal nexus fails, leaving only fragmented sequences of events which, though divinely determined, must be judged random from human perspective. Awareness of the absurdity of life fills the human heart with "evil and madness" (9:3). The vision of the absurd is quite literally, demoralizing.[186]

Various commentators have pointed out that this book has echoes from Genesis, and one may say that it is a look at life in the light of the fallenness of everything and everyone except God. Qoheleth lives in a world of built-in obsolescence to be sure, but perhaps even worse he also lives in a world of oppression, poverty, and absolute egocentrism. It sounds all too strikingly familiar.

In 1:3–4 Qoheleth raises a question that he only later answers: What does a person gain/profit (*yitron*) from all his or her *hamal* (toil/ or trouble) "under the sun"? The basic answer appears to be little or nothing. Human generations come and go but only the earth remains forever. Verses 4ff. strike at the heart of the matter; life, including human life, is cyclical, not linear. Hence there is nothing new under the sun, everything has existed or happened before. It sounds rather clearly like Qoheleth has capitulated to the prevailing cyclical view of human life, based on analogy with the cycles of nature, which so

---

[185] Cf. M. V. Fox, "The Meaning of *Hebel* for Qohelet," 409–27.
[186] Fox, "Meaning of Hebel," 426–27.

dominated extra-biblical religion in that region (especially fertility cults that focused on the dying and rising of the crops). Yet the only thing of permanence or of lasting quality seems to be the earth itself. Qoheleth says it lasts *ha olam*.

The meaning of this phrase has been endlessly debated. The basic options are: (1) time from now on, i.e., forever (a prospective use); or (2) or all time up to now (retrospective); or (3) "that which is hidden".[187] It does not seem to mean eternity but rather can mean all of time, past, present, and future. Thus the point here would be that the earth lasts until the end of time or at least as Crenshaw says as far into the future as the mind can project.[188] Qoheleth seems to lack totally any teliological sense of time. Rather he sees time as ongoing, but going nowhere so far as a purpose or goal is concerned. This being so, one is not surprised at what 1.14 says: having surveyed everything under the sun, Qoheleth has concluded that everything is either ephemeral (of no lasting value) or worthless/useless. Whatever one does, it's still a chasing after or herding of wind, a project with no lasting or tangible outcome or results.

Qoheleth, in the guise of the king,[189] says that indeed he had increased greatly in wisdom and knowledge, but it did not bring the expected result. What it brought was insight into the fallenness and transitory character of everything, and so he moans "with much *hokmah* comes much sorrow; the more knowledge, the more grief." This does not mean he does not think that wisdom is better than folly (cf. 2.13). But perhaps, unlike various sages, he was under no delusion that greater wisdom would bring greater happiness, or necessarily bring greater prosperity and longer life, i.e., the things promised in Proverbs. "Qohelet's great increase in wisdom brings a surplus of trouble as well."[190]

Ecclesiastes 2 consists of three examples of what may be called test (*anassekah*) cases: (1) pleasure (*simhah*) or joy which has meanings ranging from religious ecstasy to sexual excess; (2) the pursuit of wisdom; and (3) work. Qoheleth's conclusion in each case is that though each may provide temporary satisfaction of a sort, in the end it was all *hebel*, either insubstantial, not lasting, or futile/worthless. In 2:10ff. one learns that Qoheleth went all out in the pursuit of pleasure; he denied himself nothing that eyes or heart desired. One might wish to read Song of Songs at this point. He says in 2:3 that he determined to "spy out" (*tur*) what was worthwhile for humans to do in their few days on earth. Though pleasurable, such pursuits finally gain one nothing of lasting value; it's like trying to herd the wind.

Test case (2) was Wisdom and folly. The former is decidedly better, for the fool is like one stumbling around in the dark; the wise at least has eyes in his head and can see what is coming. But then Qoheleth in effect says "so what",

---

[187] R. B. Y. Scott, *The Way of Wisdom in the Old Testament*, 182.
[188] Crenshaw, *Ecclesiastes*, 63.
[189] It is possible that he was of Davidic descent.
[190] Crenshaw, *Ecclesiastes*, 76.

both the wise man and the fool have the same *miqreh* (one of Qoheleth's favorite terms, cf. 2:14, 15; 3:19; 9:2, 3; the verbal form in 2:14–15 and 9:11). The term does not refer to an impersonal or even malign force called Fate that destines one for some end. It means something more like what chances to happen, what befalls one. In the end the same thing befalls both the wise and the foolish – death.

Adding insult to injury, Qoheleth disputes one of the usual dictums of wisdom literature (Prov. 10:7) that a wise person will be long remembered. He says that at least eventually ("in days to come" which does not necessarily mean immediately after death) even the wise will be forgotten. It will be noted, as Crenshaw points out, that in 2.17ff. we have a totally egocentric perspective.[191] Qoheleth is upset because someone else is going to get the fruit of his labor when he dies. There is little or no sense of community or self-sacrifice here, no joy here about giving to others or leaving an inheritance for others. Even more shocking from a *hakam* is 2:17 which indicates that Qoheleth hates life, the usual desideratum of all wisdom literature (cf. Prov. 8:35). Eccles. 2:23 says that work brings pain and grief continually. Perhaps because this person has a restless and ambitious nature "his mind does not go to bed." Qoheleth thus comes to a preliminary conclusion not about what is *good* in a fallen world when all equally must go down to Sheol, but rather what is *better* than the alternative. It is *better* to eat and drink and find some satisfaction in one's work. Verse 24b says that the ability to enjoy life is a gift from God in the end. Also wisdom (in v 25a) and knowledge with happiness comes from God. These are not achieved but received from God. It may be that the satisfaction Qoheleth has in mind is not that which comes from a frantic pursuit of wealth or pleasure, but that which comes from knowing one has enough to provide for one's needs, as 4:6 says clearly, "better one handful with tranquility than two with toil/ trouble and chasing after wind."

Eccles. 3:1–8 might be titled "Timing is everything." The sages did indeed believe there was a right time and a wrong time for everything, and these verses may be a quote from traditional wisdom which is then critiqued in vv 9ff. The Hebrew word *et* while it can mean simply the moment of a particular occasion can also mean the appropriate or "right" time (cf. Jer. 8.7) and this seems likely to be the meaning here. Qoheleth, however, in his qualification of this dictum will say in v 11 that while this is true, yet one cannot fathom what God has done from beginning to end. That is, one cannot seek out or discover this "right" time, one can only receive it when it happens. Qoheleth is counseling a philosophy of life that is not an active one; his is not a "make things happen" philosophy, but rather "take it as it comes" and seize one's opportunities when they arise.

Eccles. 3:1–8 is meant to be all encompassing and involves a series of merisms (speaking of the totality of a set by mentioning its extreme members) notably being born and dying, and war and peace. It includes both things that

---

[191] Crenshaw, *Ecclesiastes*, 88.

happen and things humans do. Verse 7 refers to mourning, the rending of garments. In v 11 it is said that God has made everything *yapeh* in its time. This may mean fitting or appropriate, or perhaps it means beautiful. It is, however, a time bound beauty, like when a rose comes to full flower. God has set *ha olam* in human minds. This is taken to mean eternity by the LXX and so by many translations, but more likely it means something which begins here and now and lasts into the seemingly endless future. Thus, it may mean forever. The point is that human beings have a longing for forever, for something that lasts, but they live in a world where things are only in bloom in season, where the motto of the world is "nothing lasts forever". Though God has placed the idea of something more than the mere transitoriness of life in a human mind, yet one is unable to fathom what God has wrought from beginning to end – it is beyond human understanding. Under such circumstances, one should be satisfied to be happy, do good while one lives, and eat and drink and derive satisfaction from one's work, though even this is a gift from God.

Eccles. 3:16ff indicates that Qoheleth is deeply disturbed because the much vaunted law of retribution does not seem to work. Rather, wickedness has shown up even in the courts, the place of judgment! In a world of wickedness and oppression, human beings truly are little better than animals, and in some cases worse. God tests humankind to show them how much like the animals they are. Both live and die, and God gives the same life force or breath or animating principle to both. All bodies of all creatures crumble into dust, but what of the human spirit? *Ruach* in v 21 would seem to mean more than breath, though it means only breath in v 19. Qoheleth entertains the possibility that the human spirit might rise up (to God) while that of the animal goes down (into the earth), but he is far from sure. He simply says, Who knows if this is so? It is thus pointless to speculate about immortality. Perhaps Qoheleth knows of the idea of a positive afterlife that is more than just Sheol, similar to that which is found in other late Jewish documents (cf. Dan. 12:2–3; Wis. 3:1–8). Even if this is so, he hardly puts any confidence in such a notion.

Ecclesiastes 4 continues with the theme of oppression and the horrors of being alone in the world. Qoheleth becomes poignant. It is obvious he cares, though he does not offer any sage advice about how to remedy these problems. "I saw the tears of the oppressed and they have no comforter; power was on the side of their oppressors." In 4:1 he says he saw *all* the oppression – this conveys a sense of a pervasive condition. It would seem that Qoheleth lived in dark days that went well beyond an isolated case of severe suffering as was true in Job.[192] So much is this so, that Qoheleth is even willing to say in 4:3 that those who have never been born are better off than either the living or dead for they at least have never seen the evil that exists under the sun. Eccles. 4:4 states a principle,

[192] The conclusion of Scott, *Way of Wisdom*, 188, that Qoheleth lived in a stable society must be rejected. The problem is not just that he lives in a stratified society, but in a very unstable one. Thus Qoheleth's wisdom rightly should be seen as the sort of survival tactics one would expect from an underdog in a culture where oppression is the norm.

literally, "And I saw that all the toil and all skillful activity is one person's jealousy of another."[193] Human efforts grow out of envy and rivalry and even jealousy. As Whybray puts it, the meaning seems to be that competition and rivalry are inseparable from work and striving for success.[194] Qoheleth for his part would like to avoid both the Scylla of a life of idleness (v 5a) which leads to ruin and the Charybdis of striving after too much and so living in constant anxiety with too much toil/trouble. Qoheleth's view is "be satisfied with what amounts to enough." In v 8ff. Qoheleth lauds the virtues of companionship and family. The passage ends with an analogy between a rope with three strands which is not quickly broken and the human situation where the more hands the better return for one's labor. Though Qoheleth may indeed be a loner, he knows the value of not being in such a condition.

3. ECCLESIASTES 5-8

Chapter 5 begins with a discussion of cultic matters, in particular, sacrifices, prayer, and vows. This immediately raises the question of whether Qoheleth lived during a time when there was a holy place for sacrifices. If the answer is yes, then this material may have arisen as early as the time of Ezra–Nehemiah. It is also possible that the author is commenting on hypothetical things, but this seems unlikely. Probably he lived in Judea in or near Jerusalem during a time when there was still sacrificing.

There is nothing here which suggests Qoheleth disapproves of cultic worship, but he advises one to approach the matter with caution.[195] Inappropriate behavior in the holy place could arouse God's anger. The first verse says literally, "watch your foot when you go to God's house." This is rather conventional wisdom advice about watching one's conduct and being circumspect in one's speech (cf. Prov. 1:15, 3:26, 4:27). Qoheleth says one should go to listen, and not to offer the sacrifice of fools. Here as elsewhere in the Hebrew Scriptures it is affirmed that one cannot offer an acceptable sacrifice unless there is also the right intention and contrition accompanying it. The view here seems to be that the foolish person is one who comes and offers a sacrifice assuming that it will right him with God, without amendment of life. Prov. 15:8 says that offering an unworthy sacrifice is a positive evil, not merely useless. The fool does not know this, or even that sacrifices do not achieve their results *ex opere operato*. The proof that fools are morally dense is that "they have no awareness of doing evil" (v 1b). Verse 2 is about prayer and not offering it without sufficient reflection first. A few well chosen words are better than many hasty ones (cf. Matt. 6.7).

---

[193] Crenshaw, *Ecclesiastes*, 107–8.
[194] R. N. Whybray, *Ecclesiastes*, 83–84.
[195] So Scott, *Way of Wisdom*, 187.

Verses 4ff. are about vows. When one has vowed something to God one had better fulfill it with dispatch. Here too caution is in order; better no vow than a hasty one that leads to sin. Literally v 6a reads, "do not let your mouth bring guilt upon your flesh." The word *segagah* in 6b means an unintentional sin, a mistake (cf. Leviticus 4–5) which could be atoned for by confession to the priest (Lev. 5:5) and a guilt offering. The scenario seems to be that one makes an intentional vow, and then tells the Temple messenger (the priest, some of the priest's entourage?) that it was a mistake. If one has a proper awe, reverence or even fear of a God who can judge, then one will be careful to avoid such blunders and sins.

Beginning in Eccles. 5:10ff. the author carries on with further comments on the absurdity of human greed. Verse 10 reminds one that the person who loves wealth for its own sake, has an addictive disease. The person who loves money is insatiable; s/he can never get enough. What verses 10–17 will affirm is, as Whybray shows: (1) wealth only creates restlessness, not satisfaction in its holders; (2) it brings no enduring benefit, and on the debit side it attracts sycophants and parasites; (3) it brings no peace of mind, only worries that lead to sleeplessness; (4) there is no guarantee it will protect one from disaster – fortunes come and go; and (5) no one can take it or its benefits with them (a non-Egyptian viewpoint).[196] Thus one should simply accept and enjoy whatever God gives without cultivating the acquiring instinct.

Since there are various Wisdom traditions in Proverbs that suggest that wealth is a sign of divine favor which brings a sense of well-being, Qoheleth is here countering any such naive one-sided viewpoint. Wealth can bring unhappiness and worry; the poor who do not have to worry about losing possessions sleep better (v 12).

Verse 15 speaks of a universal condition – a person brings nothing into the world and can take nothing from life's work upon leaving the world. This implies that whatever one has or earns in this life is only of value in this lifetime. It may also imply that humans do not really own anything; they are only stewards of what they hold temporarily while they live. Job 1:21 is essentially the same sort of observation.

Eccles. 5:19–20 seems to say that there is no positive correlation between industry and prosperity, between hard work and wealth. Rather wealth is a gift from God as is the ability to enjoy what one has and take pleasure in one's work. These things do not come automatically. Qoheleth advises in v 20 not to do too much reflecting, but to simply enjoy and appreciate what one has. Eccles. 6:1ff. seem to directly contradict what has just been said. Probably we should see 6:1ff as a qualification of what precedes it, i.e., Qoheleth has observed wealthy people to whom God has not given the gift of the ability to enjoy what they have. Instead, some stranger ends up enjoying it. This may suggest the wealthy

---

[196] Whybray, *Ecclesiastes*, 98ff.

person has no heirs, or Qoheleth may be referring to non-Jewish invaders or overlords who end up with the benefit of someone else's hard work.

Eccles. 6:3ff. seems to refer to a different case – the wealthy man who has no ability to enjoy his wealth, *and* no one gives him honorable or proper burial, even though he has various children and has lived a long life. This last responsibility was considered one of the foremost duties of a child to his parents. With acidity Qoheleth says a stillborn child is better off than this man! The usual blessings of long life and many children do not necessarily lead to blessed treatment when one dies.

Eccles. 6:7 has been read one of two ways: all human effort/toil is for Sheol's appetite (death and the underworld were seen as a ravenous never sated creature);[197] more likely is the translation "all human toil is for one's mouth, and yet one's appetite is never satisfied." This echoes the observation of Prov. 16:26 with a slightly different twist. Here the idea is that one's hunger and desire to eat impels one to work ceaselessly. In the end this craving can never be finally satisfied.

Moving on to Ecclesiastes 7, Qoheleth takes another Wisdom maxim and gives it a jolting rejoinder: "a good name is better than precious oil, and the day of death better than the day of birth." The first line of this couplet is very likely a quote from traditional Wisdom (note its poetic form *tob shem missemen tob*). It plays on two meanings of the word *tob*: good in the first case and precious in the second.[198] Prov. 22:1 had touted the virtues of a good name. By contrast are those whose names stank or were offensive (Job 30:8). This reflection on the "odor" of one's name leads to a comparison with precious fragrant oil or perfume. One's reputation or at least the deeds which build it are completed at one's death. Once one is dead one cannot spoil that reputation, and thus there is a sense in which the day of death is preferable to the day of birth.

Ecclesiastes 7:14 reiterates Qoheleth's basic belief that the future is unknowable; God has made both the good times and the bad times so one cannot tell what is coming. This leads to an "enjoy the good times while they're here" philosophy coupled with a "be reflective in the bad times about the divine mystery of it all" attitude. "Both the good and the evil that God sends conceal any pattern or any trend useful for predicting the future." [199].

Eccles. 7:23–24 returns to the theme of making a test of things by Wisdom or perhaps making a test of (conventional) Wisdom. He was determined to be wise, but unfortunately Wisdom was unattainable and so he could not measure all things by it. This may echo the inaccessibility theme in the wisdom poem of Job 28 (cf. Prov. 30:1–4). Crenshaw makes the observation that Qoheleth has in mind God's wisdom, not mere practical knowledge, which Qoheleth be-

[197] Perhaps drawing on the idea of Mot.
[198] Cf. Murphy, *Forms of OT Literature*, 130.
[199] Crenshaw, *Ecclesiastes*, 139.

lieves one can have.[200] This mysterious wisdom is *rahoq* which means distant (*rahoq* is emphatic here). No one can reach out far enough in their minds to grasp true wisdom. Verse 24 reads literally, "Whatever Wisdom is, it is deep deep," i.e., impenetrable. Thus conventional Wisdom fails the test; it does not unveil this deeper wisdom that explains life and God's ways.

It is striking that there is no reference in this book to Woman Wisdom, *à la* Proverbs 8, who there is said to reveal the secrets of God. Qoheleth shows no acquaintance with this Woman. He does know of another sort of woman, the temptress, who leads one into sin – she is more bitter than death. The one who pleases God will escape her, but not so the sinner.

We have noticed that Qoheleth obviously takes an independent attitude toward Wisdom: sometimes he affirms conventional wisdom, sometimes he qualifies it, sometimes he rejects it. Eccles. 7:29 exonerates God from the trouble humans are in; God made all *yasar* (upright, straight). Humans have made themselves crooked. They have gone in search of *hissebonot* which means something like devices or intrigues. It means the results of human ingenuity (cf. 2 Chron. 26:15 on the other use of this word in the Old Testament). This may be a comment on the human refusal to simply follow and obey God and God's will. It may refer to the mental devices or corruptions one uses to get around things or overcome the limitations God has put on humankind. These sorts of things have made humans crooked.

Chapter 8 talks about obedience to the king. This once again raises the question of this book's *Sitz im Leben*. Could it really have been written at the end of the Judean monarchy or is the author just quoting and critiquing traditional Wisdom here? Here he counsels obedience to the king, and such a person will come to no harm. The wise person knows the proper way and timing to make a request or get what he wants from the king. Eccles. 8:2 may mean an oath before God and to the king, or possibly God's oath or promise to the King. Wisdom literature seems in the main to be written by and for people in the upper echelon of society, in this case people who have dealings with kings. Eccles. 8:5 may be advice to courtiers, in any case this is an example of Wisdom that is for the courts if not from the courts. One could translate 8:2 "observe the king's face," i.e., decide whether or not to speak by reading his mood.

It is very difficult to reconcile Eccles. 8:12–13 with chapters 6–7. On the one hand, Qoheleth recognizes that a wicked person may live a long time. Yet he thinks it will go better with the one who fears God. The wicked's days will not lengthen like a shadow. Crenshaw sees here a refusal by Qoheleth to completely give up on traditional Wisdom.[201] This is very likely correct. In an unjust world it is truly everyone for him or herself, for the world is morally upside down.

---

[200] Crenshaw, *Ecclesiastes*, 144ff.

[201] Crenshaw, *Ecclesiastes*, 155–57.

Once again Qoheleth commends enjoying life – eat, drink and be glad he says (8:15). There could be some contact here with Epicurean or Stoic ideas. Whybray notes that each time that enjoyment is commended it is commended with increasing vigor and emphasis.[202] Even the wise should follow this procedure for in Qoheleth's view at the end of chapter 8 "even if a wise man claims he knows, he can't really comprehend it"

4. ECCLESIASTES 9–12 AND THE END OF THE LINE

In chapter 9 Qoheleth reflects once again on death as the great leveler of humanity. It is interesting to compare this section to 4:2–3 where death is seen to be preferable to life. Here Qoheleth says the opposite. This raises the question of the function of a Wisdom discourse like this. Is it simply to state the truth, or is it to prompt in-depth reflection about life's complexities? Perhaps Qoheleth is using a dialectical form of discourse which is meant to force one to ponder the apparent contradictions in life. Perhaps like a marksman we may see a wise man firing arrows towards a target called "truth." Perhaps Qoheleth is saying that when one considers all sides of the issue, somewhere within this range is the truth. The sayings would then function not merely to force reflection but as aids for the listener to zero in on the bull's eye, which represents the truth about reality. Some of this may be said for the sake of argument, or even as a way of playing the Adversary's advocate in order to force people to abandon living by platitudes that do not suit life's extraordinary occasions.

It is striking that in the first epilogue to this book in 12:9–11, one who is apparently a student or colleague of Qoheleth commends the sayings of Qoheleth as an imparting of knowledge to the people, as a writing of what was upright and true. Anyone who saw this book so full of tensions in that light must surely have had a broader vision of truth, or at least of a *hakam*'s way of getting at truth than a modern person normally does. If one is indeed to take all he says as *meshalim*, as 12.9 says, then this is some kind of figurative or metaphorical speech or speech that uses analogies to make its point. It uses approximations even juxtaposing apparent contradictions, to force one to get at the heart of the matter.

Despite some things Qoheleth says in 9:1–2, he ranks the righteous with the wise, and then parallels the righteous, the good, the clean, and those who offer sacrifices in contrast to their opposite counterparts. There is no evidence that Qoheleth disparages the cultic part of Israel's life; rather, he assumes its rightful ongoing existence. Had he thought otherwise this cynical tongue surely would not have refrained from saying so! The first verse, though it states that the righteous and wise are in God's hands, also states that the proximate

---

[202] Cf. Whybray, *Ecclesiastes*, 138 ; on the connection of this document with Greek and specifically Stoic ideas cf. Scott, *Way of Wisdom*, 177.

future is unknowable (whether it involves love or hate or neither). The Hebrew reads literally "neither love nor hate". The ultimate future is the same for both good and wicked – both will die. Against Crenshaw, the author does not say that God treats all exactly the same in regard to length of life or in all regards.[203] What it says is that there is no *necessary* correlation between righteousness, longevity and prosperity. This latter is Qoheleth's view. Thus, he is combating making this connection between these three things universal.

Eccles. 9:4 contrasts one of the most despised with one of the most prized animals in the Ancient Near East – the dog was not a household pet in this era. The *keleb* was seen as a scavenger, a wild animal like the vulture who feasted on the death and misery of other creatures. The lion by contrast was seen as the king of beasts. Yet Qoheleth says, better to be a live dog than a dead lion. Whoever is living still has a chance for their life circumstances to change. Not so the dead. Verse 5 states a rather common view of Sheol – the dead know nothing, they get no further reward than they got in this life and their memory is soon forgotten, contrary to what some *hakamim* apparently thought. This verse involves a notable wordplay between *zeker* (memory) and *sakar* (reward). This leads Qoheleth to encourage the listener in verses 7–8 to enjoy life now. Some of these verses have interesting parallels in the Gilgamesh Epic.[204] White clothes were festal garments and anointing with oil was a sign of a time of joy. Eccles. 9:10 says emphatically that in Sheol there is no knowledge, no wisdom, no planning, indeed no consciousness, and hardly what one would normally call *being* in any real sense. It seems to be a state of oblivion and not bliss.[205]

Chapter 10 turns to the subject of folly, which usually means not just the action of the ignorant but the action of the morally obtuse or even the wicked. The problem, as the first graphic metaphor suggests in 10.1, is that a little folly can undo a whole lot of Wisdom, for instance, when someone leaks a secret that ruins a planned attack. Here the analogy is with a "fly in the ointment." A dead fly in ointment or perfume causes a scum on the top of it and ruins the whole bottle. The Hebrew reads literally "fly of death" so it may even envision a poisonous fly. The point is, an ounce of folly can ruin a pound of Wisdom.[206]

Ecclesiastes 10:6–7 would suggest that Qoheleth knew what it meant to live in a world turned upside down, where the fool rules while the rich and royal are debased. Verse 7 speaks of the reversal of roles between a slave and a prince. Clearly Qoheleth does not see this as a good thing. *Hakamim* were apparently upholders of the royal *status quo*, perhaps because they had been incorporated into the system as counselors to kings and had vested interests.

Chapter 11 starts with a much debated saying in 11:1–2: "Cast your *lehem* upon the waters, for after many days you will find it again." The word *lehem*

[203] Crenshaw, *Ecclesiastes*, p. 160.
[204] Cf. ANET, 90.
[205] Cf. the negative portrayal of Sheol in Is. 14:9–11; and Ezek. 32:18–32.
[206] Crenshaw, *Ecclesiastes*, 169.

can mean either grain, or the product of grain, bread. It has been thought that this saying refers to a commercial venture, i.e., sending grain overseas. Verse 2 then would be about distributing it amongst various ships to be sure that some of it makes the trip successfully.[207] Another possibility would be that the reference is to some sort of ritual act, like perhaps hanging out a fleece. A third possibility, and one that is more likely, is that one should take seriously the parallel from the Egyptian *Instructions of Onkhsheshonqy* 19.10 which reads, "do a good deed and throw it in the water; when it dries you will find it." One may also wish to compare the Arab proverb, "Do good, cast thy bread upon the waters, and one day thou shalt be rewarded." These sayings would suggest that the Ecclesiastes saying has to do with taking a risk of faith and doing something, perhaps a charitable act or good deed. The point would be that it would not go unrewarded.[208] Verse 2 then would be about sharing with others, for in a time of disaster one may never know when one needs a friend and some help from those one has once helped.

Eccles. 11:5 may refer to two unexplainable things (the path of the wind and the formation of the fetus in the womb), or possibly only one, "the mysterious way the life-breath functions within the pregnant womb."[209] The conclusion of the saying reiterates the earlier point that the work of God, like God, is impossible to understand – it too is a mystery.

The end of the material that is clearly from Qoheleth comes in 12:2–5. This material could be seen as a description of the deterioration and ruin of a household. The alternative is to see this as a sort of allegory about old age. Whybray favors the latter view and interprets it as follows:[210] (1) the house is one's body; (2) the keepers of the house are the hands which may tremble when one gets old; (3) the strong men bending would seem to refer to bent legs; (4) the grinders are the teeth which cease working because they are few; (5) those who look through the windows are surely the eyes which grow dim with age; (6) the doors to the street closing would seem to refer either to the ears or possibly to the eyelids; (7) then it refers to men who rise at the sound of birds, i.e., old men who are light sleepers and awake at dawn with the birds; (8) the daughters of song are also brought low (this might mean the vocal cords, and so the loss of the ability to sing).

If one follows Whybray's view, v 5a is about the old being afraid of heights and being ambushed in the street due to their feebleness. Verse 5b would seem to be a reference to the blossoming of white hair on the head. The question is, what is meant by "and the grasshopper drags himself along?" This in part depends on what one makes of "and *abiyyonah* fails." This word seems to mean the caper or caperberry used to spice up food and stimulate the appetite. The Targum and *B.T. Shab.* 152a see this as a reference to sexual desire,

[207] Farmer, *Proverbs and Ecclesiastes*, pp. 190ff.
[208] Cf. Crenshaw, *Ecclesiastes*, 178–79.
[209] Crenshaw, *Ecclesiastes*, 180.
[210] Whybray, *Ecclesiastes*, 163ff.

and so it is translated desire in various English translations (NIV, NRSV, but not the NJB).

The image could refer to when the insect is gorged or sated, so much so that it must drag its belly along. It cannot even be enticed to eat by spices like the caper. This would be a comment on loss of appetite in old age. The alternative is to see the grasshopper as a euphemism for the penis; it hangs limp and desire no longer stirs it. This is how the Talmud understands this verse. The conclusion of the analogy then is that when one loses either one's appetite or perhaps sexual appetite then death is at the door.[211] The Egyptians, as here, referred to the grave as an eternal home. This was sometimes called the house of eternity (cf. Tobit 3:6).[212]

There is some debate as to what to make of 12:7. It may simply say the body crumbles into dust, and the breath God breathed returns to God. Or is *ruach* a reference to the human personality or spirit? Gen. 2:7 and 3:19 seem to be in the background here. In view of Eccles. 3:21, one should not rule out a reference to the human spirit rather than just the life breath. The author obviously believes that something survives death and goes to Sheol. Eccles. 12:8 ends Qoheleth's contribution and reiterates the original leitmotif – all is completely ephemeral/transitory/absurd.

While the old allegorical way of interpreting this text is plausible, M. V. Fox has offered an alternative that both makes sense and provides some hints about the *Sitz im Leben* of the book.[213] The book has the shadow of death, not age or aging, constantly lurking in the background. It would be only appropriate then if Qoheleth's contributions in this book finished with a meditation on death. It may be that we should see 12:1 as a description of old age, but thereafter the text can be seen to be discussing death. The poem is meant to make the hearer see his or her death from the viewpoint of an outside observer. What is described then is death followed by a funeral and mourning. Examination of texts from Jer. 25:10–11 and Ezek. 32:7–8 suggest that v 2 must be seen as a description of death – the day the lights go out. This in turn is followed in v 3 by mourning by those in the house (the keepers of the house and powerful men are involved). During a period of mourning the normal daily activities cease, such as grinding at the mill (vv 3–4). All humans if they are not mourning are silent in the presence of death; only the birds and nature in general do not know to be sorrowful (v 4b–5). Then one is told explicitly that the person in question has died (v 5b), and that the funeral procession has begun (v 5c). Graphic images of death follow (v 6, a smashed bowl, a jar is thrown into a pit, not unlike a broken body placed in the ground). What follows is that the dust returns to the earth and the human spirit or life-breath returns to God (v 7). If all this striving ends in death, life is indeed totally absurd (v 8). Thus, the

[211] Obviously, this is an androcentric way of viewing the matter.

[212] Cf. Crenshaw, *Ecclesiastes*, 188.

[213] M. V. Fox, "Aging and Death in Qohelet 12," 55–77.

primary subject of the poem here is death, not aging or old age, though it begins by a mention of old age.

As Fox says, this is no ordinary reflection on death and a funeral. Qoheleth has brought in vivid images from the prophetic corpus that are used to speak of eschatological catastrophe, and national destruction at or before the *Yom Yahweh*. The depiction of a community at mourning is not just about the death of one individual. Such a death hardly causes the sun to go dark or the light of the moon to fail. The imagery suggests "a disaster of cosmic magnitude."[214] Inactivity at daily chores can also be caused by depopulation following a national disaster, and note that even the strong men in the village are gripped with terror, something considered shocking in Jer. 30:6. This individual death is part and symptomatic of the larger cultural malaise. Qoheleth reveals no positive consciousness of being part of a community or nation, but here surely he reveals a negative consciousness of it. The sense of group identity has broken down, leaving Qoheleth to his own personal introspection and devices.[215]

This strongly suggests a time in Israel's history not only when individualism was possible but also when group identity had not been able to be effectively re-established after the return from exile. This places this material before the reawakening of nationalism in the Maccabean period (175–130 B.C.) but well after the initial attempt to build Israel anew recorded in Ezra–Nehemiah, and after at least the first wave of Hellenism. Then too there is some evidence that Ben Sira knew this book.[216] In short, the book is best dated somewhere in the third century B.C. perhaps toward the middle of that century once Hellenism had had time to take considerable effect even in Jerusalem.

Eccles. 12:9–10 comes from some colleague or more likely a student of Qoheleth who admired him. Probably v 11 comes from the same hand while vv 12–14 comes from another and later editor. Qoheleth is said to have been wise and have taught the people knowledge. This was the duty of the *hakam* (cf. Sir. 37:22–26).

Qoheleth weighed (assessed, tried out), studied (*hqr* means to explore or examine or perhaps most likely compose) and arranged (*tqn*) or set in order or established *meshalim*. This may refer to the three stages of literary composition – experimenting with, refining, and arranging in a collection or shaping proverbs. This reading suggests that some of the things Qoheleth said were meant for effect or as experiments, things he was trying out. The term *meshalim* does not just mean an aphorism or one liner but can refer to all sorts of proverbial speech including the story in 9.13ff. or parables. [217] Eccles. 12:10

---

[214] Ibid., p. 64.

[215] Here I depart from Fox. It is true that Qoheleth's values are solitary, but this text seems to suggests that his plight reflects the larger malaise of his community.

[216] Cf. Crenshaw, *Ecclesiastes*, 50.

[217] Cf. Ps. 49:3–4 where it parallels the word for riddle *hiddah*. In Ps. 78.2 it refers to the utterance of hidden things, things from of old. It can refer to all sorts of wise sayings or even stories.

suggests that Qoheleth searched and expressed himself with care and with elegance of expression.[218] One may think of a saying like 7:1. The student says that what Qoheleth spoke was trustworthy words.

Eccles. 12:11 describes metaphorically two characteristics of such teaching. First, they can be like cattle prods (a goad); they prod one into taking a certain path or course or direction. They are meant to prompt activity or action, or a course of living. Second, they are said to be like planted or firmly embedded nails (*samek*). This would seem to mean that the teaching of the wise provides something that helps you hold things together in life, to get a firm grip on things.[219] It is said that Wisdom ultimately goes back to the one Shepherd.

Eccles. 12:12ff would seem to be a further addition first warning students (only here in Ecclesiastes called "my son") against adding anything to the teaching of the wise, or perhaps especially of this book. Verse 12b would seem to go with 12a and means, Do not try adding to the sayings of the wise – it would be superfluous and weary further students with more study. Verse 13 has been thought to reflect the later view of post canonical Wisdom that connects fear of God and keeping God's commandments which grew out of the assumption that Torah is the sole source and expression of Wisdom. There are some hints in this direction in Proverbs, though it becomes more pronounced in Sirach, for example. The book concludes with a warning about the judgment of God perhaps in relation to the comment about adding to the Wisdom books. It is interesting that the Masoretes did not like to close a book of Scripture on a negative note and so, as they did with Isaiah, Lamentations and the minor prophets, they reversed the last two verses.

CONCLUSIONS

There are many conclusions that one could draw from a close analysis of Ecclesiastes. Certainly it is clear that while still drawing on the Wisdom genre and Wisdom ideas, its author is concerned to show that a traditional or purely Wisdom approach to life is insufficient to deal with all of life's vicissitudes. Sometimes one can encounter personal tragedy that cannot be explained by the act–consequence schema. Sometimes there are such systemic problems in the culture that Wisdom assumptions about how things happen under normal circumstances do not apply precisely because one is experiencing abnormal circumstances in general. The presumptions or presuppositions required for a Wisdom view as espoused in Proverbs to work include: (1) that one has some

---

[218] *Dibre hepes* means "words of delight" and is measuring the teaching by aesthetic standards.

[219] Fox, "Frame-Narrative and Composition in Qohelet," 102–03, suggests that both metaphors are about goading or stinging the hearer into action, like the saying of R. Eliezer, "Warm yourself before the fire of the wise, but be careful not to get burned by their coals, for their bite is the bite of a jackal, and their sting is the sting of a scorpion" (*M. Aboth* 2.10).

control over one's work, one's life, one's family; (2) that systemic problems are not so severe that there is no possibility of a person becoming healthy, wealthy and wise; (3) that there is a moral structure to reality which usually rewards the righteous and punishes the wicked.

It is intriguing to note the alternative world view offered in Ecclesiastes to a strictly Wisdom approach to life. Qoheleth encourages one to enjoy this ephemeral life while one can, and perhaps not to expect too much out of it. While admirably showing the real limitations of a Wisdom approach to life in a situation where the whole world seems to have gone wrong, in the end he offers very little beyond resignation and a *carpe diem* philosophy to aid one in coping with such a situation. He still believes in God, but he does not seem to share the faith of the author of Job that God both can and will intervene to set things right. Doubtless, this somewhat gloomy perspective is intentionally redirected in the appendix, perhaps by a disciple of Qoheleth. The redirection amounts to a closer connection of Wisdom with Torah in order to understand the ways and will of God as well as the ways of the world. This redirection is developed further in the work of both Ben Sira and the author of the Wisdom of Solomon and to them this study now turns.

2

Wisdom at a Turning Point: From Ben Sira to the Wisdom of Solomon

WHEN one has reached Qoheleth, one may be forgiven for asking, Is this all there is, is this where Wisdom's journey ends? In Qoheleth's musings it seems that the act–consequence idea has been decisively smashed on the hard rocks of reality, i.e., both the good and the wicked in the end endure the same fate, death. Furthermore, in this lifetime the wicked often prosper and the righteous often suffer. Even more strikingly, the voice of personified Wisdom has been silenced altogether. Qoheleth reflects not even a passing acquaintance with this Woman. Clearly, Wisdom stands at a turning point, having reached Qoheleth's cul de sac. Under such circumstances, it seemed to at least one sage, Jesus Ben Sira, that the only way forward for Wisdom was in part to go back and recover some of her heritage and then to go on in a fresh direction, not previously attempted in any serious way in the earlier stages of Wisdom's pilgrimage.

In the study of Qoheleth's wisdom, the rise of a new phenomenon was noted, i.e., a person speaking as an individual and thus with a particular voice, even if anonymously. When one turns to Sirach one finds a different sort of particularism. The sage speaks in his own name, something Qoheleth did not do, but he speaks as one deeply indebted to Israel's wealth not only of Wisdom traditions, but also of prophetic and legal traditions as well. Ben Sira is also bold enough to go beyond the collective Wisdom of the past and make his own contributions. One of these contributions involves a hermeneutical particularism, for in Ben Sira's writings Wisdom traditions and Torah are wed, or at least Wisdom, by means of an arranged marriage, has become engaged to Torah in a way not seen in earlier Wisdom material.[1]

[1] J. Blenkinsopp, *Wisdom and Law in the Old Testament*, 130ff., wishes to argue that it is when Wisdom comes together with the legal traditions in Ben Sira, that wisdom "entered the

A. WISDOM GAINS A NAME: THE CONTRIBUTIONS OF BEN SIRA

1. BACKGROUND

The study of the Wisdom of Ben Sira is bedeviled by a complex set of problems caused by the various manuscripts in Greek, Hebrew, Latin and other languages.[2] At the end of the 19th century a large portion of the book was found in the Cairo Genizah, a storeroom in a synagogue. In 1952 a small portion of the book (6:20–31) was found at Qumran, and in 1956 a revision of 51:13–19, 30 was discovered there. Then in 1965 Y. Yadin found fragments of 39:27–32 and 40:10–44. At present slightly over two thirds of the book is available in its original language. The question then had to be raised whether the large portions found in Cairo were copies of the Hebrew original or retroversions of the Greek translation of Ben Sira's grandson, which had its own special shortcomings.[3] The general opinion of scholars today is that they are *not* retroversions, but copies of the Hebrew original.[4] The issue is not settled, however. Thus, it appears that an eclectic procedure (drawing now from one manuscript, now from another, to recover the original text) is required, not least because there are long and short recensions of the Hebrew text in the Cairo manuscripts, as well as long and short versions of the Greek text.[5] What the complex textual history of this book reveals is that Ben Sira's writings were very popular in early Judaism and later in the early Church. The popularity of

---

mainstream of Israelite religion." This conclusion, I fear, is another testimony to the long held false assumption that Wisdom literature was somehow *out* of the mainstream in Israel. One must ask, is Ben Sira's aim to promote or even to rescue a Torah-centric orientation for his audience by closely connecting it with Wisdom, or is his aim to domesticate Wisdom and place it in the mainstream? It looks like the former rather than the later more nearly expresses his agenda.

[2] For an interesting comparison of the Syriac version of the Wisdom of Ben Sira with the Greek and Hebrew versions see M. D. Nelson, *The Syriac Version of the Wisdom of Ben Sira compared to the Greek and Hebrew Materials*. Besides arguing that the Syriac version draws on a Hebrew version more primitive than that found in the Cairo Genizah, Nelson (p. 132) has also pointed out that later recensions of the Syriac version by Christians somewhere before the middle of the fifth century A.D. led to the following interesting alterations: (1) passages which suggested no belief in a positive afterlife were omitted (cf. also the changes made in the later recensions of the Hebrew and Greek texts of the book); (2) passages implying that Wisdom (now understood to mean Christ) was created were altered; (3) immodest passages or those derogatory towards women are omitted or altered!; (4) many references made to the Jewish Fathers are left out; (5) passages extolling poverty are enhanced. This simply shows the ongoing impact of Ben Sira on the Christian church, and suggests one should consider more seriously whether or not it had an impact on Jesus and the earliest Jewish Christians.

[3] On comparing the original Hebrew to the grandson's Greek translation, see H. J. Cadbury's helpful analysis, "The Grandson of Ben Sira," 219–25.

[4] Cf. Murphy, *Tree of Life*, 68–69; M. Gilbert, "The Book of Ben Sira; Implications for Jewish and Christian Traditions," *Jewish Civilization in the Hellenistic-Roman Period*, 81-91, especially 84.

[5] Cf. P. W. Skehan and A. A. Di Lella, *The Wisdom of Ben Sira*, 59–60. The longer recensions of both the Hebrew and also the Greek text are theologically tendentious as well for there is evidence of an attempt to add a belief in a positive afterlife into the text. Nevertheless, R. Smend, *Die Weisheit des Jesus Sirach. Hebräisch und Deutsch* still provides for most passages one of the most convenient available sources for examining the possible form of the original text.

the book and especially the finds at Qumran *and* at Masada suggest that it would be fruitful to explore the possibility of the influence of Ben Sira's work on the later Wisdom material found in the Jesus traditions.[6]

In regard to the literary forms that one finds in the Wisdom of Ben Sira, the previous forms that predominated, proverbs (e.g. in Proverbs 10ff.) and more extended discourses or meditations (e.g. in Proverbs 1–9), are clearly in evidence. There are also numerical proverbs (Sir. 25:2), and imagaic comparisons which begin with 'like' (cf. Sir. 19:12, 20:4).[7] Note also the use of the traditional pedagogical address, 'son' (Sir. 2:1; 3:12, 17; 4:1; 6:18, 32; 10:28; 11:10 *passim*). There are some new developments, however, and some further expansions of forms that are little in evidence in earlier Jewish Wisdom literature. For one thing, Ben Sira has composed some beautiful wisdom hymns, or one should perhaps call them poems with wisdom themes such as the praise of God's creation (cf. 16:24 — 18:14, 39:12–35, 42:15 — 43:33). For another thing one finds various sapiential beatitudes in this book (10 in 25:7 — 10, cf. 31:8). There is also a debate form of saying which begins with a rejoinder to one's opponents or to those who think it is not necessary to live a God-fearing life ('Say not. . .' [*al to mar*, cf. Sir. 5:1–6; 15:11–12; 16:17]). As J. Crenshaw has shown, this is an ancient form found at least once in Eccles 7:10 but more commonly in ancient Egyptian Wisdom material.[8]

Is there an overall literary structure to Ben Sira's book? W. Roth has suggested that Ben Sira's original book contained 1:1 — 23:27 and 51:1–30. To this Ben Sira is said to have added three sections (24:1 — 32:13; 32:14 — 38:23; and 38.24 — 50.29). Each of the four sections of the original book were prefaced by what may be called a prologue (1:1 — 2:18 as prologue to 2:19 — 4:10; 4:11–19 as prologue to 4:20 — 6:17; 6:18–37 as prologue to 6:19 — 14:19, and 14:20 — 15:10 as prologue to 15:11 — 23:27/51:10). When the three additional sections were added they also were prefaced with prologues in 24:1—29; 32:14 — 33:15, and 38:24 — 39:11. While in the original book the topics immediately follow the prologues, in the additional sections an autobiographical note comes between the prologue and the body of the section.[9] The additions were justified by claims in each case that God had given Ben Sira some new insights.

This theory has some merits but there is no general agreement on the structure or successive redactions of the book. Most scholars see Chapter 51 as an appendix, not an original part of the book, and have pointed out how Ben Sira has patterned many of his compositions after the longer meditations,

---

[6] On which cf. below pp. 143ff.

[7] On Ben Sira's numerical proverbs cf. W. C. Trenchard, *Ben Sira's View of Women: a Literary Analysis*, 175–78.

[8] Cf. *ANET*, pp. 420 and 423 for the relevant sayings of Ani and Amenemope; J. Crenshaw, "The Problem of Theodicy in Sirach: on Human Bondage," 48–49.

[9] Cf. W. Roth, "On the Gnomic-Discursive Wisdom of Jesus ben Sirach," in *Semeia* 17, *Gnomic Wisdom*, 60. He is largely following, with some modifications M. Z. Segal, *Seper Ben Sira' Hasalem*, a source not available to me.

discourses, or poems found in Proverbs 1–9.[10] Ben Sira's book does not appear like the rather random collection of proverbs in Proverbs 10ff. perhaps because he was an excellent editor and grouped proverbs together thematically (cf. Sir.13:1 — 14:2), although he did draw on isolated maxims to a great degree. It is interesting that Ben Sira tends to end a discourse with some sort of proverb or perhaps an admonition (cf. 7:36; 28:6–7; 35:12–13).[11]

By 180 B.C., which is the approximate time most scholars feel Ben Sira's Wisdom writings first came to light,[12] things seem to have been on a somewhat more solid footing than in Qoheleth's day. The second temple cultus was not only operating properly and well, but at least in Ben Sira's mind the High Priesthood had recently been well served by a godly, admirable man, Simeon II (219–196 B.C., cf. Sir. 50:1–21).[13] Simeon had repaired and refurbished both the temple and Jerusalem's defenses, and Ben Sira is positively gushing in his praise and description of the priest performing his offices. He is even willing to make this priest the climactic example in his long historical review in praise of the great fathers of the faith, which in some respects reflects the traits of the Greek encomium (cf. Sir. 44:1 — 50:21).[14]

This did not mean that all was necessarily well in Zion, for it is quite clear that one of the major purposes of the Wisdom of Ben Sira is to stress the need for both a more Torah-centric and temple-centric orientation among Jews, especially in view of the ever growing influence of Hellenism in Jewish culture.[15] This becomes especially evident when one notes the three major theological ideas of the book: Wisdom, Torah, and fear of the Lord. The key term *sophos/hokmah* is found more frequently than the other two, but all three come together in 19:20 where one hears 'the whole of Wisdom is fear of the Lord, and in all Wisdom there is the fulfillment of the Law.'[16]

---

[10] Cf. Murphy, *Tree of Life*, 70.

[11] So Murphy, *Tree of Life*, p. 70 following J. T. Sanders, *Ben Sira and Demotic Wisdom*, 15. This insight may be helpful in understanding Wisdom collections in Q and their closures (cf. below pp. 225ff.).

[12] Cf. Skehan and di Lella, *The Wisdom of Ben Sira*, 15; Murphy, *Tree of Life*, 65; Crenshaw, *Old Testament Wisdom*, 149ff; G. Boccaccini, *Middle Judaism. Jewish Thought 300 B.C.E. to 200 C.E.*, 77-78.

[13] Here and elsewhere in this study the numbering system for the Wisdom of Ben Sira found in the NRSV is followed.

[14] The term "fathers" is used advisedly, for Ben Sira was not merely androcentric but misogynist in his orientation and deliberately omitted any heroines of the faith in his list of worthies.

[15] Cf. T. Middendorp, *Die Stellung Jesu Ben Siras zwischen Judentum und Hellenismus*, 173: "Der Einfluss griechischer Bildung war auch in Palästina sehr stark." In such an environment, while Ben Sira's approach certainly does not amount to a total rejection of the dominant culture and its wisdom nonetheless Middendorp is right that one should not minimize the fundamental "antihellenistische Tendenz Ben Siras" (173).

[16] Here I follow the suggestion of P. C. Beentjes, "Full Wisdom is Fear of the Lord," 27–45, that we take *pasa sophia* as having an elative force, i.e., 'the whole of wisdom' rather than 'all wisdom.' This may also be the force of the phrase in Sir. 1:1: "The whole of Wisdom is from the Lord."

These emphases, when coupled with Ben Sira's reassertion of the act–consequence idea while eschewing any sort of the afterlife that went beyond the old Israelite concept of Sheol, show that Ben Sira was not just trying to reassert the old values of Wisdom thinking. He was also attempting to establish a new sort of conservatism among Jews, with Wisdom and Torah in tandem, that could withstand the challenges presented by Hellenism without giving up some benefits from and dialogue with Hellenism.[17] To this end he felt it necessary to ground Wisdom not just in creation but also in the history of Israel, and in particular to connect it with Torah. The balanced assessment of J. Marböck is worth repeating:

> Ben Sira steht in der Tradition der Weisheit Israels und führt die seit dem Deuteronomium sich anbahnende Verbindung mit der Torah zu einem ersten Abschluss ohne Enge und Exklusivität. Er ist aber auch an Vorabend der grossen Auseinandersetzung und Auseinander-entwicklung im Judentum einer der ersten, der unbefangen manche Formen hellenistischen Denkens und Lebens aufgreift, *ohne sich damit zu identifizieren.* [18]

Ben Sira was not wrong to be concerned about Hellenism, for had he lived until 174 B.C. he would very likely have been horrified at some of the steps the new High Priest Jason/Joshua was prepared to take to accommodate Judaism to Hellenism, including building a Greek gymnasium in Jerusalem. [19]

If there is a hint of Hellenism in Qoheleth's writing, in Ben Sira's there may be more than trace amounts to be found. Yet Ben Sira, whatever the forms of his Wisdom teaching, is not willing to appropriate Hellenistic or international Wisdom thought in any way that he sees as compromising or significantly altering what he takes to be the true and traditional Jewish faith. Crenshaw's assessment that Ben Sira "attempts a marriage between Hellenism and Hebraism, between Athens and Jerusalem, although he saw to it that Zion wore a chastity belt," although vivid, probably says too much.[20] It would be better to speak of a marriage of Wisdom and Torah, or Wisdom and the wider

---

[17] I do think that J. Marböck, *Weisheit im Wandel*, 175-76, is right to criticize the idea that Ben Sira is simply a reactionary. He offers both old and new things in his book and does not settle for merely reiterating what he had learned about the fear of the Lord from Proverbs and elsewhere. It is true, however, that the basic trajectory of his thought is in a more conservative direction as is shown both by his attempt to tie Wisdom to Torah, and to tie the present Jewish community to its priestly and prophetic past in Sirach 44–50.

[18] Marböck, *Weisheit in Wandel*, 176–77, emphasis mine.

[19] Scholars are right to suggest that the absence of any reference to Jason and his Hellenizing agenda in this book give us a rather clear date after which this book surely could not have been written.

[20] Crenshaw, "The Problem of Theodicy in Sirach," 57. His later assessment in *Old Testament Wisdom*, 159 is nearer the mark where he says that Ben Sira subjects what Hellenistic thought or forms he takes over to a thorough Hebraizing.

scope of sacred Jewish traditions, although one must admit that the bride occasionally appears to be wearing wedding clothes imported from Greece.

One must not underestimate what the Prologue to the Wisdom of Ben Sira, written by Ben Sira's grandson, suggests. It indicates that the sage knew and drew on what one might call a prototype of the canon of Hebrew Scriptures, for he speaks of Ben Sira's knowledge of and reflection on the Law, the Prophets, and the other books.[21] Perhaps even more importantly, Ben Sira seems to have seen himself as some sort of prophetic sage or, as O. Rickenbacker has suggested, some sort of successor to the prophets in an unsettled time.[22] The word 'prophet' and its cognates appear over twenty times in this book, in addition to which one must add the texts where Ben Sira claims inspiration for himself (e.g. 24:30–33). The idea of a prophetic sage or the combination of prophecy and Wisdom utterances has some precedent in Egyptian circles where "ist die Profetie Bestandteil der allgemein Weisheitslehre."[23]

Some evidence for the influence of Hellenism has been found in Sir. 44:1—51:10 known as "In Praise of the Fathers", which seems to be modeled on the encomium, drawing on Greek rhetoric. Part of the problem with this argument is that its effectiveness at the level of "form" depends in large measure on relying on the grandson's Greek translation, not on Ben Sira's Hebrew original. Nevertheless, making allowances for the differences in linguistic expression in Hebrew and Greek, it does seem that Sirach 44–50 owes something to the encomium form. B. Mack's argument that Sirach 44–50 should be seen as an epic modelled on Greek epics will not work, not least because it is not a long narrative poem about a particular heroic figure whose travels and exploits are traced.[25] Sirach 44–50 is closer to Hebrews 11 than it is to the *Odyssey, Iliad* or *Aeniad.* He may be right that the combination of an interest in authorship, scholarship, and instruction indicates some influence of Hellenism on Ben Sira.[26]

[21] So H. M. Orlinsky, "Some Terms in the Prologue to ben Sira and the Hebrew Canon," 483–490. B. L Mack, *Wisdom and the Hebrew Epic*, pp. 94ff. does not think Ben Sira was operating with some sort of closed canon, though he admits there is some trace of a canonicity idea here. He adds: "In Sirach, neither the term Torah nor 'the Book of the Covenant' can be taken definitely as a specific reference to the five books of Moses" (101). Within the larger context this view seems overly cautious. Ben Sira is surely trying to inculcate a Torah-centric approach, as is shown by, among other things, his interest in a priestly orientation and in Aaron about whom Ben Sira says more than about Moses (cf. Sirach 45)!

[22] O. Rickenbacher, *Weisheit Perikopen bei Ben Sira*, 170–71.

[23] Rickenbacher, *Weisheit Perikopen bei Ben Sira*, 170–71 points out that prophecy in Egypt amounted to a form of persuasion, not charismatic preaching, which used the recognizable patterns of history to convince the audience. Could this have some bearing on how one views the encomium in Sirach 44–50?

[24] Cf. T. R. Lee, *Studies in the Form of Sirach 44–50*, J. G. Gammie, "The Sage in Sirach" in *The Sage in Israel*, 355–71.

[25] Cf. B. Mack, *Wisdom and the Hebrew;* and the proper critique by Gammie, "The Sage in Sirach," 357, n. 9.

[26] Gammie, "The Sage in Sirach," 102.

More evidence of Hellenistic influence comes when one compares Ben Sira to the teachings of the Stoics about God, humankind, and the cosmos, as R. Pautrel has done.[27] When one comes across phrases like *to pantos estin autos* (cf. Hebrew *hu'hakol*) in Sir. 43:27, there seems to be some evidence of influence. Ben Sira uses this material in the service of his own form of Jewish monotheism, however; he does not simply take over Stoic thought without alteration.

J. G. Gammie asserts that Sir. 31:16 and 32:1 indicate that Ben Sira had "abandoned the line of separation [between Jews and Gentiles] insofar as the ingestion of food is concerned."[28] But these texts in themselves do not suggest such a conclusion. There is no evidence that Ben Sira is here discussing a banquet involving both Jews and Gentiles, or at least a banquet where Jews would be expected to eat unclean food. Rather, this is advice given to his Jewish students, the children of wealthy Jews in Jerusalem who would have been likely to host such a dinner at some point in their lives, or perhaps be invited to dine with a ruler on some occasion. One has to *assume* Chapter 31 is about behavior on the road while with *goyim* to reach the conclusion Gammie does. It is a conclusion that does not comport with what Ben Sira says elsewhere.

For instance, in Sir. 34:30 the sage asks what value there is in washing after touching a corpse if one then turns around and touches it again. This saying assumes that the Levitical laws about clean and unclean are still in effect and should be observed. To be sure, Ben Sira sees the sage as one who travels in foreign lands and appears before rulers (39:4), but there is nothing in that material which states or implies that one should eat ritually unclean food.

The most one can get out of texts like Sir. 31:16 and 32:1 is that well-to-do early Jews may have adopted some of the Hellenistic customs in regard to the *symposion*, a banquet involving food and wine. But Ben Sira also warns at various times against over-eating or over-drinking at such occasions (cf. 31:25), which shows that even if some Greek customs have been adopted, they have also been adapted so that Jewish moral sensibilities would not be offended.[29] W. Roth rightly points out that Ben Sira seems to be expanding on what was already said about such banquets in Prov. 23.1–3.[30]

As A. A. di Lella argues, Ben Sira's thought and approach is conservative, i.e., "characterized by a tendency to preserve or keep unchanged the truths or answers of the past because only these are adequate as solutions for present problems."[31] "The author's conservative viewpoint may be deduced from the fact that he wrote in Hebrew at a time when it was quite common for

---

[27] R. Pautrel, "Ben Sira et le Stoicisme," 535–49.

[28] Gammie, "The Sage in Sirach", 360–61.

[29] Cf. Skehan and di Lella, *Wisdom of Ben Sira*, 389ff.

[30] Roth, "On the Gnomic–Discursive Wisdom of Jesus ben Sirach," 73. Sir. 31-32 no more suggests the eating of unclean foods than the wedding feast at Cana, where there is also a master of ceremonies or toast master (John 2), or the feast in the house of Simon, where Jesus reclined at table (Luke 7).

[31] A. A. di Lella, "Conservative and Progressive Theology: Ben Sira and Wisdom," 139.

Jewish authors to seek a broader audience for their works by writing in Greek, the language of the dominant culture."[32] Furthermore, in the one section of the book where he clearly does deal with Gentiles, we have Ben Sira's one eschatological utterance where he calls down God's wrath on the Gentile nations (36:1–17).[33] This hardly seems like the attitude of one who balanced Judaism with "a decidely open stance toward Hellenistic culture, appropriating a great deal of its *paideia*."[34] Hengel rightly warns that we should not try to explain away Ben Sira's largely anti-Hellenistic stance.[35] It is true, as J. Marböck concludes, that Ben Sira's stance is not *simply* anti-Hellenistic, but the manner in which he uses Hellenistic ideas and forms shows that it is not his aim to encourage an appreciation of Hellenism's riches, or to remain neutral about Hellenism's influence on Judaism.[36]

A reasonable case can be made to suggest Ben Sira knew and drew on a Greek writer like Theognis.[37] But J. T. Sanders is surely right that if there is any dependency at all, it is first on earlier Jewish Wisdom sources, especially Proverbs, and second *possibly* on Egyptian Demotic Wisdom, not Greek Wisdom.[38] In fact, Sanders says that it is more probable that Ben Sira's Wisdom and that found in Papyrus Insinger show how Egyptian and Israelite Wisdom continued to develop along parallel tracks, without necessarily suggesting a specific or direct influence of one document on the other.[39] Finally, R. Murphy is perhaps right to ask how the Demotic material could have been known to Ben Sira, even though there are some interesting parallels in both form and content to the Jewish sage's work, since there is no evidence that it was ever translated into Hebrew or Greek during Ben Sira's age.[40] Should one think of international Wisdom traditions and ideas that circulated so widely in Egypt and Israel that they were known to both Ben Sira and the author of Papyrus Insinger?

Sanders has demonstrated at length on the one hand the extensive parallels between Proverbs and Ben Sira, and on the other hand how uncon-

---

[32] Blenkinsopp, *Wisdom and Law*, 40.

[33] Cf. E. P. Sanders, *Paul and Palestinian Judaism* 331.

[34] B. L. Mack, "Wisdom makes a Difference: Alternatives to Messianic Configurations," in *Judaism and their Messiahs at the Turn of the Christian Era*, 21.

[35] Hengel, *Judaism and Hellenism*, 150.

[36] Cf. Marböck, *Weisheit im Wandel*, 175.

[37] Cf. Middendorp, *Die Stellung Jesu Ben Siras zwischen Judentum und Hellenismus*. Note the probably correct conclusions of J. T. Sanders, "Ben Sira's Ethics of Caution," 95ff.: "Middendorp has not demonstrated that Ben Sira's shame-related ethics of caution has a Greek origin" (96). In fact Middendorp himself rightly admits that basically Ben Sira is trying to pick up and continue the agenda and themes found in Proverbs. In short, his major influence is biblical Wisdom literature. Probably Skehan's and di Lella's cautious approach is right to follow; at most Ben Sira seems to have known a few of Theognis' poems from Book 1 of his writings. Cf. Skehan and di Lella, *Wisdom of Ben Sira*, 48.

[38] Cf. the helpful study by J. T. Sanders, *Ben Sira and Demotic Wisdom*. In my judgment the Demotic material is much closer in substance to Ben Sira than the Hellenistic parallels, even including the Stoic ones, as Sanders shows at length.

[39] Sanders, "Ben Sira," 105-06.

[40] Murphy, *Tree of Life*, 174.

ventional Jewish Wisdom as it is found in Job and Ecclesiastes is *not* a significant influence on Ben Sira.[41] Nevertheless, Ben Sira in his conservatism does not simply recycle material from Proverbs but develops it in some new ways as well as reaffirming older ideas and values, including linking Wisdom with Torah. This linking of Torah with Wisdom does not amount to a subsuming of the latter under the heading of the former. "Ben Sira has not given up the traditional sage orientation of Judaic wisdom, for Torah is to be followed because it is sage, not sage advice because it [comports with Torah]."[42]

It is probably true that Ben Sira's wrestling with the freedom of the human will, all the while affirming God's complete foreknowledge (cf. 15:11–17, 16:17–23), bears witness to the penetration of Hellenistic ideas into Jewish culture.[43] But Ben Sira handles the issue in a way consonant with his Jewish faith.[44] He rejects notions either that God does not concern himself with the fate of an individual, or that God has pre-determined everything in a rigid fashion.[45] Again, in his doctrine of creation and his theodicy it is possible that he has been somewhat influenced by Greek thinking on such matters, but this indebtedness does not cause him to reject a traditional monotheistic approach to these issues (cf. Job).[46]

The influence of Hellenism could possibly be seen in Ben Sira's individualism. He is willing to speak in his own name and add new things to the store of Israelite Wisdom.[47] Yet if one looks carefully at what his purposes are, he is trying to encourage a more Torah-centric and temple-centric and androcentric orientation in his listeners. Some have thought that his ethic seems rather *eudaemonistic*, perhaps due to the influence of Hellenism, but here too, as Sanders has shown, Ben Sira's ethics about happiness are based on an ethic of caution lest one bring shame on one's self and one's family, or cause one's name to live on in infamy rather than in honor.[48] Occasionally in his ethical teaching

---

[41] Sanders, *Ben Sira and Demotic Wisdom*, 3–26. On the Old Testament influence on Ben Sira cf. also Middendorp, *Die Stellung*, 35–91.

[42] Sanders, *Ben Sira and Demotic Wisdom*, 16.

[43] Cf. Hengel, *Judaism and Hellenism* I, 140ff.

[44] Cf. Skehan and di Lella, *Wisdom of Ben Sira*, 50: "though Ben Sira used foreign authors, what he writes comes out as something completely his own, something thoroughly Jewish and compatible with earlier biblical thought and sentiment."

[45] Perhaps he is reacting as much to Qoheleth's determinism as to various Greek ideas floating around in the larger cultural environment; cf. Hengel, *Judaism and Hellenism* I, 141.

[46] Hengel, *Judaism and Hellenism* I, 147–48. Boccaccini, *Middle Judaism*, encourages us to see Ben Sira as not merely a representative of conservative old style Judaism, especially because "the problems and tensions he interprets are the same ones around which the confrontation will develop in the following three centuries" (125). This is a good point, but I would maintain that while Hellenism is to a real degree shaping what questions Ben Sira deals with, and occasionally but rarely how he responds, the vast majority of the content of his answer to Hellenism is not deeply indebted to Greek thought, but rather to traditional Jewish thought, especially Wisdom thought.

[47] Cf. Crenshaw, *Old Testament Wisdom*, 159.

[48] Sanders, "Ben Sira's Ethics of Caution," 73–106.

a note that sounds Greek appears, however: "In everything you do be moderate; and no sickness will overtake you" (Sir. 31:22b).

More attention should be paid to the extensive amount of honor–shame language, and teachings inculcating a world view that nurtures dyadic personality in Ben Sira's writings. Crenshaw is right that if the basic goal and prize in Proverbs was life, in particular long life well-lived, in Ben Sira it would seem that the basic goal is in having and preserving an honorable name, one that will outlast one's days (Sir. 41:12–13).[49] This might explain not only why Ben Sira names himself in this book, but why he offers an encomium to the heroes of Jewish faith who preserved a good name, and unlike Pseudo-Solomon mentions them *by name*.[50] On all these counts what we find in Ben Sira goes beyond anything we find in Proverbs or other earlier Jewish Wisdom literature. Cultural anthropologists would stress that this book is striving to inculcate strong boundaries between Jews and the outside world by means of honor–shame language, by means of male–female role stereotyping, and by means of stressing the traditional values of the group as the values which should dictate the values of the individual.[51] To this one must add Ben Sira's clear affirmation of the election of Israel (cf. Sir. 24:12, 36:13) coupled with his distaste for some of Israel's traditional enemies (Sir. 50:26). Sanders is right that "Ben Sirach seeks a fruitful theological harmonization which maintains the value of the wisdom tradition but which sets it within the framework of the election of Israel and the divine law given to Israel through Moses."[52] This is not to minimize Ben Sira's indebtedness to international Wisdom, but it should be seen that the goal even in his use of such material is to inculcate a more Torah-centric and temple-centric orientation in his hearers. Doubtless his hearers were those who had *already* been affected and to some degree impressed by the riches of Hellenism, and so Ben Sira attempts to build a bridge between where

[49] Crenshaw, *Wisdom*, 62, 153.

[50] Sanders, *Ben Sira and Demotic Wisdom*, 105, finally concludes that Ben Sira got this orientation from reading and adopting the basic orientation towards life found in Papyrus Insinger (Phibis), and except for Proverbs shares more in common with that collection of Wisdom sayings than any other.

[51] A dyadic person is one who derives his or her sense of identity from what others say about them. In such a culture the group or clan or family values take precedence over individual values, if there are any of the latter, and there is a great concern about family/clan honor and gaining or saving face for the group. A fool in such a society is a person who gives honor or respect to someone or something to which they ought not to give honor to – i.e. a person who is not discerning enough to reflect the moral distinctions and pecking order preferred by the group. Ben Sira's misogynism is in large measure a result not of his appropriation of material from Proverbs which is androcentric but not specifically inculcating misogyny, but of his agenda to inculcate or further reinforce an honor–shame culture among Jerusalem Jews in order that they might have their own culture and survive as a people. Cf. Malina, *The New Testament World*, especially 55–70 on all the above, and the chart of honor-shame and its effect on male–female roles and values on 45.

[52] Sanders, *Paul and Palestinian Judaism*, 333. One must still ask, however, whether the aim of this move is to place non-mainstream Wisdom into the mainstream or to promote a more Torah-centric orientation among those likely to listen to Wisdom? I think the latter is the case.

his listeners are and a more Torah-centric approach to life, without simply dismissing the riches of non-Hebrew sapiential material.[53]

In the Wisdom of Ben Sira we are able to have greater clarity on several issues of importance that were discussed in the examination of Proverbs. For example, it is rather certain from Sir. 51.23 that at least by Ben Sira's day there were houses of instruction where well-to-do young Jewish boys were instructed in the ways of Wisdom, and perhaps other matters as well. If the Wisdom of Ben Sira is any indication, however, these other subjects such as the Law were viewed and explained from a Wisdom point of view.

In Ben Sira it also appears clear that the upper class ethos, which is suggested by a good deal of earlier Wisdom literature, is confirmed for at least this point in time in Jewish history. Ben Sira say that 'the wisdom of the *soper* depends on the opportunity of leisure;' only the one who has little business can become wise (Sir. 38.24). Furthermore, his extensive warnings about the dangers of greed and wealth, about being concerned for one's good name which outlives its owner, coupled with advice on how to behave if one is made master of the feast at large banquets or in the presence of rulers, and the need to keep one's wife from parading her beauty in public or from becoming jealous of a rival, or the dangers of seeking high office, surely all indicate that his audience included well-to-do youth who might have occasion to face such challenges (cf. Sir. 7:4–6; 11:18–19; 26:6; 29:22; 30:14–15; 31:8; 32:1–2; 40:18; 41:12; 42:12–13). The Wisdom of Ben Sira also suggests that at this juncture in time the equation *soper* = *hakam* = king's counselor is a correct one, although the first two parts of the equation are more certain than the third (cf. Sir. 8:8; 10:1–3; 20:7; 24:31–34; 33:16–19; 34:12–13; 38:24–25; 39:1–5; 51:13–30).

A few words of explanation about the relationship of Wisdom and Torah in Ben Sira is in order. Sanders is right that it is too simple to say that Ben Sira thinks the Wisdom tradition is subsumed by or fully identified with the Torah,[54] or that Torah is somehow part of the Wisdom tradition. There is some sort of dialectical relationship going on here.[55] One is not simply identified with the other, as is clear from the content of the teaching in Ben Sira's book. Nor is this book an example of *halakah*. But at the very heart and root of Wisdom is the fear of the Lord, and this is also at the heart of the Deuteronomistic approach

[53] Middendorp, *Die Stellung Jesu Ben Siras zwischen Judentum und Hellenismus*, concludes that Ben Sira is building a bridge "zwischen griechischer Bildung und alttestamentlich-jüdischer Überlieferung" (174). More specifically he is trying to build a bridge on which his Hellenized audience can come *back* to a more conventionally Jewish approach to life, without dismissing that there is gain to be had from appropriating the insights of international Wisdom.

[54] Contra von Rad, *Wisdom in Israel*, 245.

[55] Sanders, *Paul and Palestinian Judaism*: "It is neither the case that Torah overwhelms wisdom, nor that Torah is simply legitimatized and interpreted 'from the realm of understanding characteristic of wisdom'. The relationship is dialectical, and neither subordinates the other" (332).

to *Torah.* One could say that Torah then is "the manifestation of wisdom in history".[56]

Following Wisdom teaching in the end leads to the same goal, and is based on the same principle of reverence for the biblical God that one finds in Torah. For good measure Ben Sira has taken matters a step further by saying that all Wisdom entails fulfilling what the law requires (19:20), in addition to heeding the *other* admonitions of the sage. Furthermore, keeping the commandments leads to wisdom (15:1). Then, finally, personified Wisdom is either identified with the Mosaic law or, better said, the benefits Wisdom has and gives are the benefits the Law provides (Sir. 24:23) because the Law is a written embodiment of Wisdom. Later when Sirach 24 is exegeted in detail, it will appear that Ben Sira first identifies Wisdom with God's oral word, which spoke the universe into being and ordered it, and then suggests that God's Wisdom has taken up particular location in Zion in the form of the Book of the Covenant, God's written word. This means that while Torah expresses Wisdom for Israel, *it does not exhaust it.* One might almost speak of Wisdom becoming concrete or even incarnate in Torah in the theology of Ben Sira. This is a striking new development, for in Proverbs 8, on which Sirach 24 is partly modeled, while Wisdom stands at the crossroads and calls to God's people, or in Proverbs 9 builds a temple and invites Israel to a feast, it is not suggested that the host or even the main course *is* Torah, the law of Moses. Thus we must speak of a further particularization of Wisdom in Ben Sira.[57]

2. *BEN SIRA'S WISDOM*

As this study has already pointed out, one of the key indicators that helps one understand the character of Wisdom in a particular sapiential book is how the act–consequence idea is handled. Though some have tried to suggest that there is evidence in Ben Sira for a belief in some sort of afterlife that sets things right, in particular by means of resurrection, this conclusion, based on Sir. 46:12, 48:11, 13 and 49:10, is very doubtful.[58] As 46.12b makes clear the only sort of immortality Ben Sira affirms is name immortality.[59]

A clearer indication of how Ben Sira views the afterlife can be obtained by examining the passages where he mentions Sheol. For example in Sir. 17:27–30 we hear very clearly, "Who will sing praises to the Most High in Sheol in place of the living who give thanks? From the dead, as from one who does not exist thanksgiving has ceased;... human beings are not immortal." In regard to mourning for the dead, Ben Sira stresses: "Do not forget there is no coming

---

[56] Boccaccini, *Middle Judaism*, 94.

[57] Cf. above pp. 38ff. on Proverbs, and especially pp. 64ff. on Qoheleth.

[58] Cf. V. Hamp, "Zukunft und Jenseits im Buche Sirach," in *AT Studien, Festschrift Nötscher*, 86–97.

[59] Cf. Skehan and di Lella, *Wisdom of Ben Sira*, 86, and the exegesis of these particular verses.

back; you do the dead no good, and you injure yourself… When the dead is at rest, let his remembrance rest too, and be comforted for him when his spirit has departed" (Sir. 38:21–23). Or again, "Whether life lasts for ten years or a hundred or a thousand, there are no questions asked in Sheol" (Sir. 41:4). Sounding a bit like Qoheleth he urges, "Give, and take, and indulge yourself, because in Sheol one cannot look for luxury" (Sir. 14:16). However, unlike Qoheleth, Ben Sira reasserts the act-consequence concept with a new modification.

Ben Sira is very firm in asserting that the wicked and the righteous both get their just due (cf. Sir. 2:7–11; 7:1; 27:26–27). Sometimes he even affirms that retribution does not delay (Sir. 7:16). However, Ben Sira is well aware that just recompense is not always immediate and sometimes not apparent at all. How then was one to explain an apparent delay in or absence of justice without resorting to a theory of a settling of accounts in an afterlife? Ben Sira's response is twofold. First, justice or vindication may be deferred but it will not in the end be denied, hence his exhortation to wait for it (Sir. 2.7). Sir. 51.30, the concluding verse of the entire book exhorts "Do your work in good time, and *in his own time* God will give you your reward." Thus, the first solution to the apparent failure of the act–consequence theory, is that God has his own timing for these things. Sometimes from a human point of view justice may *seem* to be delayed, but if one is patient and faithful it will come. In his second response to this dilemma Ben Sira comes up with an even more original idea: "It is easy for the Lord on the day of death to reward individuals according to their conduct. An hour's misery makes one forget past delights, and at the close of one's life one's deeds are revealed. Call no one happy before his death; by how he ends, a person becomes known" (Sir. 11:26–28).

There are several ideas being expressed here. The first is that even if accounts have not been settled before death, at the point of death justice will finally be done. Secondly, one will be able to tell whether a life was good or not by its end. A person's true character will be revealed by how he or she dies. What is interesting about this is that it is not death *per se*, which happens to all, but rather *how* one dies that settles accounts. Crenshaw is right to suggest that here Ben Sira resorts to a sort of psychological compensation theory. If one dies *in misery*, one is compensated for a wicked life (Sir. 3:26). If one dies peacefully one is rewarded for a good life (Sir. 1:13).[60] In fact Ben Sira goes one step further in a psychological direction by affirming that wicked and guilty people have nightmares (Sir. 40:1–11; cf. 34:1–8).

One could add two more collateral points that flesh out the scope of Ben Sira's thinking on this subject. The first of these is that if one reflects on the history of God's dealings with the world and in particular his own people, no one who has trusted in the Lord has been disappointed (cf. Sir. 2:10). This may

[60] Cf. Crenshaw, "The Problem of Theodicy in Sirach," 58–59.

explain part of the reason why this book closes with the "Praises of Fathers," i.e., they are the evidence that Ben Sira is right in his views on the act–consequence idea (cf. 44:1—50:24). B. Mack has conjectured that theodicy was the formative influence that led to the creation of the personification of Wisdom.[61] I would say it was *an* important and formative influence but not the only one.[62] It appears that some of the factors mentioned in the discussion of Proverbs 8 were also involved.[63] Then too, it may be that the sages were simply grasping for images large enough to convey their own experience of the grandeur and scope of God's Wisdom and its reflection in creation. Hengel is very likely right that for Ben Sira act–consequence is not a wooden moral principle structured into the universe, but rather a matter of God intervening to right wrongs.[64] Retribution in Ben Sira's view is personal, not the effect of some impersonal principle or Greek idea of 'fate', even if it does not come until the moment of death.

From the Wisdom hymn in Sirach 24 one learns that God's creation was infused with wisdom from the start. Does this mean that into creation was structured a moral order that involves both justice and mercy (cf. Sirach 18)? "[T]he essential point Sirach wishes to make is that *in the creative act* God brought into being a universe that encourages virtue and punishes vice."[65] It is intriguing that at one point Ben Sira asserts that God, who has created everything (18:1), distinguished between the righteous and the wicked and appointed different ways for each, one a way of blessing the other a way of curse (Sir. 33.10–15). He is willing to reckon with a theory that God created polar opposites in the universe.[66] His point seems to be that just as God has created opposites such as day and night, life and death, we should not be surprised that human moral behavior reflects a pattern of polar opposites, which is in some ways like the very fabric of material creation.[67]

Yet elsewhere Ben Sira is very clear in avoiding the impression of determinism, strongly asserting free will and responsibility for one's actions (cf. Sir. 15:11–20; 5:1ff.). Furthermore, one may argue that Ben Sira sees retribution as personal not impersonal.[68] The point is that Ben Sira is willing to contemplate both free will and divine ordering at once without feeling compelled to show how the the two can be reconciled. This tension between God's sovereignty and free will is preserved in later Pharisaic teaching as well. One

---

[61] Cf. Mack, "Wisdom Myth and Mythology,", 46–60.

[62] Were it the decisive factor, it is hard to understand why there is no reflection on personified Wisdom in Qoheleth.

[63] Cf. pp. 38ff. above.

[64] Hengel, *Judaism and Hellenism*, 143.

[65] Crenshaw, "The Problem of Theodicy," 59.

[66] Cf. above pp. 55ff. on the theory of polar opposites in Wisdom literature.

[67] It is not clear that he is suggesting that God is the author of evil or wickedness. In view of Sir. 39:33–34 which asserts that all of God's works are good, and prove to be good in their appointed time, this is unlikely.

[68] Cf. pp. 89ff.

must also keep steadily in view that in Proverbs a willingness to pass on pairs of maxims that cannot both be true in the same way and at the same time has already been seen.[69]

Ben Sira also does not want his disciples to confuse God's mercy or slowness to anger (Sir. 5:4) with a failure ultimately to do justice, as God's punishment of sinners in the past shows (Sirach 16). Thus creation, salvation history, and general human experience are all called upon to bear witness to the validity of the act–consequence concept.

Ben Sira's work is an interesting reassertion of old Wisdom ideas mixed in with some new and original thoughts. Of the latter sort is Ben Sira's claim to offer new revelation. Thus he claims that he was "the last to keep vigil" (Sir. 33.16). He is aware that he is drawing on the riches of previous Wisdom, but by God's providence while he expected to be a mere gleaner who comes after the grape pickers to gather up what is left, he actually arrived before the grape pickers and so gathered an abundant harvest of Wisdom. One cannot help but notice that Ben Sira is surprised at this turn of events. He had modest expectations of the contribution he would make, perhaps like a canal transporting water from the river of Wisdom to his own dry garden. But as things turned out, his canal became a river and then a sea (Sir. 24:30–34), and he makes the disclaimer that he did not do this just for himself but for all who seek Wisdom.

More intriguing is his claim that "I will again pour out teaching like prophecy, and leave it to all future generations" (Sir. 24.33). This seems to mean he, like the prophets, claims inspiration from God, not that he sees his work as prophecy.[70] Nonetheless, 39:1–5 makes clear that he will certainly study prophecies as well as traditional Wisdom lore, and 39:6ff. seems to suggest once again that God inspires the sage so that he may both understand what he meditates on from the sources he studies, but also that "he will pour forth words of wisdom of his own" (39:6). Here is a claim that suggests Ben Sira saw his role as more than that of a gleaner or even a grapepicker in someone else's vineyard. "Ben Sira regards wisdom as belonging to the divine world and available to humankind only as a gift. There is therefore a close parallelism between wisdom and the Spirit, and correspondingly, between one endowed with wisdom and the prophet."[71] There is a clear testimony to the accuracy of this observation in the poem/hymn on Wisdom in Sirach 24.

Equally important is the way Ben Sira draws on cultic, historical, and even prophetic ideas and forms to make his case. It is not a new thing in Jewish

---

[69] Cf. pp. 23ff. above.

[70] Skehan and Di Lella, *Wisdom of Ben Sira*, 338. Contra Von Rad's assertion in *Wisdom in Israel*, 254 that Ben Sira sees his teaching as just human instruction, not divine command. It is intriguing that *B.T. Babba Batra* 12a says that God took prophecy from the prophets and gave it to the sages. This claim to inspiration by a sage sheds fresh light on the Jesus tradition (cf. e.g, Sir. 39:6–8 and Mt. 11:25–27 with Wis. Sol. 10:21: "for Wisdom opened the mouths of those who were mute, and made the tongues of infants speak clearly").

[71] Blenkinsopp, *Wisdom and Law*, 141.

Wisdom literature for Ben Sira to speak of the fear of the Lord or to reflect on cultic matters. We have seen these concerns already present in Proverbs, and Ecclesiastes.[72] What is new is both the amount of attention Ben Sira gives to such matters, and also what may be called his historical consciousness, like that found in a variety of places in the Hebrew Scriptures. Ben Sira affirms the value of the sacrificial system and the second temple (Sir. 38:11; 50:1ff.), but he also evidences the prophetic concern that sacrifices be offered with a sincere heart, and that those which are not offered with the right attitude of the giver, or out of a life generally characterized by moral integrity are not acceptable to God (cf. Sir. 35:1–13). Even beyond this, Ben Sira believes that certain good deeds, quite apart from sacrifices of animals, make atonement for sin. For instance, in Sir. 3:3 he says honoring parents atones for sins, and at Sir. 3:30 he says that almsgiving produces the same result. Or again, the one who keeps the commandments or returns a kindness or forsakes unrighteousness is making an offering or making atonement (Sir. 35:1–5).

One of the most important new developments in Ben Sira is his willingness to draw on traditional prophetic eschatology at one point (Sir. 35:21 — 36:22). The material draws on ideas and phrases from some of the later major prophets (Isaiah, Jeremiah, Ezekiel) and some of the lament Psalms.[73] The eschatology in 35:21ff. in part reflects Ben Sira's historical consciousness (cf. Sir. 16:7ff. and 44:1ff). He is one who stands in a long line of those who have spoken inspired words for and about God and God's dealing in creation, especially in human history. Since he believes God is just, and that the idea of act–consequence will in the end be shown to be a correct assessment of life even if on occasion in the present God's justice seems absent or delayed, it is natural for him to reflect on the ultimate resolution of such moral dilemmas.

J. D. Martin has suggested that in his interest in history, its periodicity, the order immanent in the cosmos or created world, and in matters astronomical, Ben Sira shows affinities with those prophetic figures who produced Jewish apocalyptic literature.[74] This is so, and I would suggest it is because he already lived in an age where there was considerable overlap between prophetic, apocalyptic, and sapiential ideas and forms.

There was also a more pressing problem that Ben Sira was aware of – ever since the battle of Panium in 198 B.C. the Seleucids had been in charge of Israel. Thus Ben Sira's prayer for deliverance is probably not a mere echoing of general prophetic sentiments, but reflects a passionate desire of the sage in view of the current situation of his people. It is possible that *goyim* in 36:2 should be translated Gentiles and so be a direct reference to the Seleucids.[75] But

[72] Cf. above pp. 11ff. and pp. 64ff.

[73] Cf. Skehan and di Lella, *Wisdom of Ben Sira*, 420–22.

[74] J. D. Martin, "Ben Sira – a Child of His Time," in *A Word in Season. Essays in Honour of William McKane*, 143–61.

[75] Cf. Skehan and di Lella, *Wisdom of Ben Sira*, 421.

Ben Sira is not just praying for divine intervention so that Israel may be rid of its present oppressors, but also for the return of Diaspora Jews to the Holy Land (36:13–16). This material envisions a this-worldly resolution of all these matters in keeping with Ben Sira's lack of belief in a positive afterlife. Here is a sage who spoke on more than just mundane matters, or the routines of daily life.

Nevertheless, the vast majority of the Wisdom of Ben Sira is about the usual variety of subjects on which Jewish sages discoursed: (1) knowing when to speak and when to be silent (i.e., the matter of being wise about 'timing'); (2) proper advice about honoring parents, marriage, family life, the raising of children; (3) appropriate behavior towards one's neighbors, friends, and strangers; (4) the value but also the dangers of riches; (5) specifically religious duties such as prayer, fasting, almsgiving, sacrifices; (6) how to relate to one's social superiors, and when to seek or avoid seeking high offices of various sorts; (7) care in choosing one's friends and associates; (8) the usual negative evaluations of the fool and the sluggard or idler; (9) honesty in business dealings and other settings as well; (10) the value of health and physicians; and (11) the duties of hospitality. Though there is much that could be said on all these topics, most of Ben Sira's advice reproduces or simply spells out further the advice of earlier sages.[76]

Something must be said about Ben Sira's negative remarks about women. It is not enough to say, as Gordis does, that Ben Sira's attitude toward women is characteristic of what can be found in Proverbs, where women are stereotyped as either temptresses, quarrelsome wives, or ideal wives (or possibly women of valor).[77] Rather, it must be admitted that at times in the writings of Ben Sira androcentricism becomes outright misogyny. Not only does Ben Sira, in the space he allots to discussing women, spend more time on bad wives than any other single sort of woman having especially negative things to say about bad daughters,[78] but when one reads Sir. 42:12–14 one has gone beyond a mere androcentric orientation: "Do not let her parade her beauty before any man, or spend her time among married women; for from garments comes the moth, and from a woman comes woman's wickedness. Better is the wickedness of a man than a woman who does good; it is woman who brings shame and disgrace." Part of this no doubt is due to Ben Sira's great concern to preserve Jewish culture intact from non-Jewish, particularly Hellenistic, influences, but such remarks cannot be justified even on that basis.[79]

It is possible that, as J. Levison argues, Sir. 25:24 is not blaming Eve for the origin of sin, but rather the evil wife as the origin of sin and trouble for a

---

[76] Ben Sira does not see wealth as an unqualified good. Indeed, he sees greed, the desire to accumulate, as a serious sin. He is also cognizant of the possibility of ill-gotten gains. Thus Ben Sira tempers some of the more unrestrained affirmations of wealth as simply a blessing from God.

[77] Gordis, "Social Background," 111.

[78] Cf. Trenchard, *Ben Sira's View of Women*, 169.

[79] Trenchard, *Ben Sira's View of Women*, 172.

husband.[80] This explanation makes better sense of its immediate context.[81] Even so, one still must contend with Sir. 42:12–14 and also parts of 25:13–26.

While it is true that even more misogynous things were said by other ancient male writers,[82] this does not exonerate Ben Sira. On the other hand, in view of the words of praise Ben Sira has for women whom he does not consider immoral (cf. Sir.3:1–6; 26:1ff), it is probably wrong to argue, as W. C. Trenchard does, that "Ben Sira wrote about women as he did, because he was motivated by a personal, negative bias against them."[83] Ben Sira does not blame all of society's ills on women.

It would be better to say that Ben Sira was caught up in and was trying to inculcate a highly patriarchal honor–shame type of culture. In such a culture, women were often stereotyped as either saints or sinners, and were thought to be mainly responsible for the sexual purity or impurity of the society. Proper blame for male sexual aggression was usually not placed where it ought to have been placed in an honor–shame culture. Ben Sira does not escape from stereotyping women, often seeing them chiefly as temptresses. He should not be defended in this matter, regardless of how highly one may esteem other things about his Wisdom teaching. Furthermore, this attitude cannot be explained away as simply an inevitable by-product of ancient patriarchal Jewish culture, since not all Jewish sages in antiquity reacted as Ben Sira did in regard to women, as I have shown elsewhere in regard to Jesus.[84]

3. *WISDOM AND HER MARRIAGE TO TORAH*

According to Skehan and di Lella, the Wisdom hymn / poem in Sirach 24 begins the second half of the book, just as a similar poem began the first half.[85] The personification of Wisdom is found in a variety of texts (e.g., Sir. 1:4–20; 4:11–19; 6:18–31; 15:1–8; 24:1–29). That one is dealing with a personification in Sirach is suggested by both the immediate context and what Wisdom is compared and contrasted with in that context. For example, M. Gilbert is right that the terms *sophia*, *sunesis*, and *paideia* are likely synonyms in Sir. 24:25–27.[86] He has also

---

[80] J. Levison, "Is Eve to Blame? A Contextual Analysis of Sir. 25.24," 617-23 wants to argue that the text is about the evil wife and so translates it "From the [evil] wife is the beginning of sin, and because of her we [husbands] die." Contrast the conclusion of Trenchard, *Ben Sira's View of Women*, 170.

[81] Cf. Skehan and di Lella, *Wisdom of Ben Sira*, 348–49, who argue that in view of 2 Cor. 11:3 and 1 Tim. 2:14 the argument used by Levison may be wrong.

[82] Cf. B. Witherington, *Women and the Genesis of Christianity*, 1ff; and M. R. Lefkowitz and M. B. Fant, *Women in Greece and Rome*, 15ff.

[83] Trenchard, *Ben Sira's View of Women*, 7.

[84] Cf. Witherington, *Women in the Ministry of Jesus*, chapters 2 and following. Never once do we find any negative remarks about women that reflect gender stereotyping on the lips of Jesus.

[85] Skehan and di Lella, *Wisdom of Ben Sira*, 331.

[86] Cf. also Rickenbacher, *Weisheit Perikopen*, 128.

pointed out the similarity of Sir. 24:20 to 23:26.[87] In Sir. 23:22ff Ben Sira has warned his audience against an adulterous wife whose sexual misadventures will bear no good fruit; rather, 'she will leave behind an accursed memory' (23:25–26). This is to be contrasted with the sweetness of heeding God's commandments (23:27). The theme of 23:27 is then expanded upon in 24:19 where Ben Sira uses sexual imagery to speak of the invitation of Wisdom to her listeners: 'eat your fill of my fruits, for the memory of me is sweeter than honey' (24:19, 20).[88] In view of Ben Sira's view of sexual ethics and of women it is hardly plausible that what one finds in Sirach 24 is anything other than a personification of Wisdom, which is closely identified with the commandments of God. Ben Sira would hardly have used this sort of sexual imagery if he believed he would be understood to be describing not just an attribute of God, or the alluring character of God's Word, but God in God's personal being. Ben Sira was interested in inculcating a traditional androcentric approach to his faith (cf. his use of father language in 23:1, 51:10), not encouraging his audience to think of God as a being rather like Isis.[89] The really striking thing is how, despite his conservatism, Ben Sira appears willing to draw on the Isis aretologies to inculcate a very different sort of faith.[90]

Turning to the crucial hymn/poem in Sirach 24, in terms of structure as well as content this is not simply Ben Sira's version of the similar material in Proverbs 8.[91] As P. W. Skehan has shown, while the hymn/poem in Proverbs 8 has seven rather uniform stanzas, Sir. 24 has uneven stanzas, and it may be that the latter poem reflects the putting together of three related themes (in vv 1–22, 23–29, and 30–33) while Proverbs 8 is a single draft composition.[92] More significantly Skehan argues that while the whole poem is thirty-five lines long in Proverbs 8, the speech Wisdom delivers in Sirach 24 is twenty-two lines long, like the alphabet acrostics (cf. Prov. 31:10ff). This is not unusual for Ben Sira for there are also twenty-two line speeches in 1:11–30, 6:18–37 (which both involve personified Wisdom), and 51:13–30.

As a good example of the similarities and differences between Sirach 24 and Proverbs 8, in both poems one hears that Wisdom opens her mouth to speak and the first and last stanzas of each poem begins with this 'I'(*ani*), but

---

[87] M. Gilbert, "L'Éloge de la Sagesse, (Siracide 24)," 335–38.

[88] Cf. Marböck, *Weisheit im Wandel*, 42ff.

[89] On E. A. Johnson's thesis, cf. above pp. 43ff. My point *here* is about the historical probabilities of what Ben Sira's view was, not about the merits of the current debate about the use of goddess language in the synagogue or church.

[90] Cf. Marböck, *Weisheit in Wandel*, 49ff. for a thorough discussion of the Isis material and its possible bearing on Sirach 24. In view of the close connection of Wisdom with Torah one cannot speak of a mere light retouching of Isis aretological material in Sirach 24. His essential orientation is biblical or, as Marböck (95–96) would put it, his Wisdom theology is grounded in a Deuteronomistic outlook.

[91] For a thorough overview of the German discussion of this hymn up to 1972 cf. Rickenbacher, *Weisheit Perikopen*, 111ff.

[92] Cf. P. W. Skehan, "Structures in Poems on Wisdom: Proverbs 8 and Sirach 24," 365–79.

only in Sirach 24 does one also hear that Wisdom came forth from the mouth of the Most High.

As was already suggested, it is a fundamental mistake to simply identify Wisdom and Torah, even in view of Sir. 24:23. E. J. Schnabel, while arguing for both a formal and material identity between Wisdom and Torah in the writings of Ben Sira, says that the consequences of this close identification were that "the universalistic tendency of wisdom was limited, profane wisdom was excluded, and the law acquired a universalistic dimension as comprehensive order for the relationship between God, creation, and man."[93] This judgment is in part based on the faulty assumption that originally even Israelite Wisdom was profane rather than religious in character.[94] Further, the *content* of Ben Sira's book does not suggest that the sage had ceased to draw on traditional Wisdom in favor of a Wisdom drawn from, much less limited to, Torah (cf. 39:1–3). Rather, to the old source Ben Sira has simply added further new sources of Wisdom including especially Torah, but also the prophets and other sacred traditions. Much nearer the mark is Boccacini's observation that Torah is seen as a manifestation of Wisdom, indeed the special and unique gift of Wisdom to Israel: "the law is the historical manifestation in Israel of a pre-temporal wisdom."[95] That Wisdom is embodied or expressed in Torah does not mean it is exhausted thereby.

One of the most helpful detailed studies of Sirach 24 is found in G. T. Sheppard's *Wisdom as a Hermeneutical Construct*.[96] He rightly talks about the sapientializing of other sacred Hebrew traditions in Ben Sira. This is particularly evident in Sirach 24. Ben Sira comes at the Law, the Prophets, and the other books from a Wisdom perspective and draws freely from all of them to make the points he wishes to make about Wisdom. It is true that this leads to a more Torah-centric approach to life, but this is achieved by Ben Sira's using Wisdom, and a Wisdom hermeneutic, to achieve that end. In Sirach 24 we hear Wisdom endorse Torah, by claiming that Torah embodies all the traits and positive attributes of Wisdom.

The hymn/poem may be outlined in regard to content as follows: (1) Wisdom's origin (v 3); (2) Wisdom's search for rest and inheritance (vv 4–7); (3) God's command to settle (vv 8–9); (4) Wisdom's settlement and subsequent growth (vv 10–17); and (5) Wisdom's appeal to the listeners based on all the above (vv 18–22).[97] Sir. 24.23–29 then should be seen as commentary on what has been said in the hymn/poem.

H. Conzelmann, among others, has suggested that in this hymn/poem one sees a clear dependence on an Isis aretology, especially in 24:5–6, in view

---

[93] E. J. Schnabel, *Law and Wisdom from Ben Sira to Paul*, 90–91.

[94] Cf. above pp.12ff. on the problems with this view.

[95] Boccaccini, *Middle Judaism*, 88–89; cf. the heading in Blenkinsopp, *Wisdom and Law*, 40: "Torah assimilated to Wisdom". This is much nearer the mark than Schnabel's view.

[96] Cf. G. T. Sheppard, *Wisdom as a Hermeneutical Construct*, 19–71.

[97] Here I am following Sheppard, *Wisdom*, 39.

of several key features in the hymn (e.g. Wisdom speaking in the first person, Wisdom as heavenly ruler and one who wanders the cosmos alone). His conclusion is that in this hymn there is nothing specifically Jewish.[98] As Sheppard has shown, all of these features can be explained by means of Ben Sira's "anthological style of biblical interpretation." In regard to vv 5–6 in particular, it appears more likely that Ben Sira is synthesizing ideas found in Job 9:8, 22:14, and 38:14[99] than that he is appropriating ideas from an Isis hymn.[100] What is remarkable in this hymn is that Ben Sira alternates applying statements to Wisdom that are elsewhere in the Hebrew Scriptures applied to God, with statements that are elsewhere made of Israel. Thus, for example, while Wisdom, like Yahweh, is involved in the event of creation (24:3),[101] on the other hand Wisdom is also said to be like Israel wandering in the wilderness looking for a promised land to inhabit, a place in which one could rest (24:7). Wisdom's taking up residence in Zion is an expression of the divine presence with Israel, but it is also an expression of God's specially revealed will for Israel since "all this is the book of the covenant." "While the transcendental character of Wisdom has been sustained by the adaptation for her of God language found outside the traditional wisdom literature, events in her history are borrowed from the narrative tradition of Israel's pilgrimage to a Promised Land."[102]

The hymn/poem begins with Wisdom singing her own praises before the heavenly hosts, for she has a rightful place beside God in heaven. She is so identified with God that in the place where only the praise of God should be heard, now Wisdom's praise is heard. It is not clear whether one should see vv 1–2 as strictly parallel or not. Are Wisdom's people in v 1 the same as the heavenly host in v 2? Perhaps not, as Skehan and di Lella suggest, for surely Ben Sira intends this poem to be directed to God's people.[103] The point is rather that Wisdom's self-praise may be heard in heaven and on earth.

Wisdom is clearly seen in this hymn/poem as a created being, for not only do we hear that she comes forth from the mouth of the Most High, but also in vv 8–9 she is said to have been created, though created 'before the ages'. She comes forth from God and is of God, and divine qualities may be attributed to her, but her subordination to the Most High is clear. Verses 8–9 echo what has already been said in Prov. 8:22–30.[104]

---

[98] Cf. H. Conzelmann, "Die Mutter der Weisheit," 228 with Hengel, *Judaism and Hellenism*, 158–59. Even if it does prove to be the case that some ideas have been borrowed from an Isis liturgy, it is done to supplant any such pagan deity and redirect the listener to the worship of the Jewish God, cf. Hengel, 162.

[99] Cf. Sheppard, *Wisdom as a Hermeneutical Construct*, 34–37.

[100] Cf. also Lang, *Frau Weisheit*, 152–54.

[101] Cf. Ringgren, *Word and Wisdom*, pp. 108-09.

[102] Sheppard, *Wisdom as a Hermeneutical Construct*, p. 30.

[103] Skehan and di Lella, *Wisdom of Ben Sira*, p. 331.

[104] Cf. Gilbert, "L'Éloge de la Sagesse," 341. On whether Wisdom had a role in creating that which came after her, cf. 344ff.

One may ask, what sort of created being? Careful attention to vv 3–4 suggests that Wisdom is like a spirit, or perhaps *the ruach* of God for in those verses she is described in terms reminiscent of Gen. 1:1–2 where first darkness and then a *ruach* from God swept over the face of the waters (cf. Prov. 8:23–24).[105] This allusion very likely reveals the beginnings of what was to become very important in the later development of Wisdom literature particularly in the Wisdom of Solomon where Wisdom is more clearly connected with (if not identified with) God's Spirit.

The distinction between God and Wisdom can be seen in that while God dwells on high, Wisdom camps there and then looks for a dwelling place elsewhere.[106] Verse 6 is of great importance. It reads that Wisdom took/gained a possession in every land, or perhaps more likely it held sway over every nation.[107] In view of Prov. 8:15–16, which seems to stand in the background here, the point is that Wisdom has an international character, ruling in every land, guiding minds everywhere. This truth is not negated by the later statement that Wisdom took up residence in Jerusalem. Verse 6a is an indicator that Ben Sira does not have in mind an exclusive identification of Wisdom with Torah in this poem.[108]

It was God who commanded Wisdom to take up residence among the tribes of Jacob, otherwise she might have continued to wander over the face of the earth. But lest someone should think that Wisdom is thereby confined to dwell in Zion and in Torah, and thus located in space and time, it is immediately added that Wisdom is eternal – she was created before the ages and will outlast them. Here is no mere time-bound Word or just a special revelation of God for a special occasion. The special embodiment of Wisdom in Torah does not exclude her presence elsewhere. While Torah is indeed all the good things that can be said about Wisdom, since she resides therein, Wisdom is not confined to the Torah.

One could argue that what is being described is the increasing particularization of Wisdom. What begins as an attribute of God becomes an attribute of creation and thus available to all creatures everywhere, and then finally becomes an attribute of Torah. This means that God's wisdom may be found not merely by examining creation or the behavior of creatures, but by consult-

---

[105] Cf. Skehan and di Lella, *Wisdom of Ben Sira*, 332. The parallel with Prov. 8.23 depends on how one translates the crucial verb there.

[106] Cf. Sheppard, *Wisdom as a Hermeneutical Construct*, 30.

[107] There is a textual problem here, and the translation depends on which version of the text one follows. Sheppard, *Wisdom as a Hermeneutical Construct*, 33–34 and notes, prefers the former rendering, but I am following Skehan and di Lella, *Wisdom of Ben Sira*, 332 and Murphy, *Tree of Life*, 139.

[108] Or with God. Ringgren, *Word and Wisdom*, 110–11, goes too far in claiming that in 4.14 God and Wisdom are simply identified. Rather, agency language is used so that the one who serves Wisdom thereby serves God as well. Marcus, "On Biblical Hypostases," 166–67, rightly rejects Ringgren's interpretation of this text. "The author of Sirach is merely saying that Wisdom is the channel through which God and man [sic] come into relation as master and servant" (167).

ing his written revelation to his special people. But none of this negates that Wisdom may be found beyond Torah as well, for Ben Sira has not given up the creation theology of the sage, as is clear from the beautiful hymn of thanksgiving in Sir. 39:12–35. Wisdom then endures forever and may be found everywhere, though it has established its *legal* and indeed permanent residence in Jacob, in Jerusalem, in Torah. Sirach 24 may well have been the spark that fueled later rabbinic speculation about the eternality of Torah, but Ben Sira is not arguing for that in this poem.[109]

In v 10 a rather surprising new twist to the argument is taken up. Ben Sira is not merely going to locate Wisdom in Zion and in Torah, but particularly in the priestly service in the Tent of Meeting. Ben Sira has a very high view of the Temple cultus (cf. Sir. 45:6–14 with 50:1–21). Sheppard has shown that the imagery that Ben Sira uses of Wisdom growing and flourishing in Zion (vv 13–17), especially in the Tent of Meeting (where one finds the divine presence, the book of the covenant, and various priestly activities), is imagery associated elsewhere with priests and their ministry. For instance, the flora comparisons here are also found repeated in a very similar fashion in the praise of Aaron in Sir. 45:6–22.[110] This is very striking indeed and amounts to a sapientializing of priestly traditions.

Rather than a wooden joining of the two traditions, Ben Sira is looking at legal and especially priestly traditions through Wisdom's eyes, as he does elsewhere with the prophetic tradition (Sirach 48). Ben Sira is one so enraptured by the moral beauty of Wisdom that he sees her in all things that are good and true and beautiful, and he believes God has spread her blessings throughout the corpus of Israel's sacred traditions. Wisdom took root amongst God's chosen people, and in a chosen place, in Torah, and even more particularly in the priestly service.

That Ben Sira had great hopes for the priesthood, in view of the record of Simeon II, is clear from Sirach 50, but these hopes were to be dashed in the person of Jason, presumably shortly after the sage had died. Later, the Qumran community and then, post-A.D. 70 Pharisaism were to become more Torah-centered rather than temple-centered, partly because of what was seen as the notable corruption involved in recent Jewish attempts at a temple-centered religion. It may be, especially in view of the presence of Ben Sira's book at Qumran and Masada, that such communities saw in Ben Sira a way forward by means of a Torah-centered approach. If this is so two important factors should not be forgotten: (1) that Ben Sira's basic orientation was sapiential and that all else was viewed through that filter; (2) that Ben Sira was urging not merely Torah-centrism, but within that focus on Torah a stress on the temple cultus and priesthood.

---

[109] Cf. Sheppard, *Wisdom as a Hermeneutical Construct*, 46, n. 69.
[110] Cf. Sheppard, *Wisdom as a Hermeneutical Construct*, 54–55.

Those who try to insist on too exclusive an identification of Wisdom with Torah in Ben Sira's writings[111] have not fully taken the measure of a sage who could say in the very first chapter of his work that God poured out Wisdom "upon all his works, upon all the living according to his gift; he lavished her on those who love him" (Sir. 1:9–10). Clearly, "all flesh" includes not only Jews but also Gentiles (cf. Prov. 8:15–16).[112] The point then will be that God has granted Wisdom in greater measure or with further specificity to Jews, and in particular to Jews who obey God's word (cf. Sir.24:7–12).

But receiving Wisdom is not something which simply happens because one has Torah in one's midst. Ben Sira stresses that it requires discipline to acquire Wisdom. When one first sets out to obtain her it is like one who plows and sows but must wait for the harvest (Sir. 6:19). But soon enough this toil will bear fruit, *if one is disciplined*. To the undisciplined, or to the morally obtuse (i.e., the *nabal*) she seems harsh, like a heavy stone that cannot be carried for long once one picks it up (6:20–21), 'for Wisdom is like her name: she is not readily perceived by many" (6:22).

This Wisdom then is not something that is *obvious* to all, even to all Jews. It requires diligent study and discipline, a devoting of one's whole heart to the task beginning in youth to obtain it (6:23ff.). It is like taking a yoke upon one's shoulders, but in the end Wisdom will bring both rest and joy to the laborer in her vineyard.

The discourse in Sir. 4:11ff. suggests similar things. "For at first she will walk with them on tortuous paths, she will bring fear and dread upon them, and will torment them by her discipline" (4:17). If one continues in her discipline, she will eventually bring the person joy and life; they may inherit glory (4:12–13), eloquence in the assembly (15:5), and finally preferment in important roles such as that of judge or ruler(4:15–16). Sir. 4:17 is an important verse for it makes clear that Wisdom must reveal her secrets (cf. 39:3, 7b; 51:19–20). Wisdom is hidden unless diligently sought and finally revealed and received.[113] This is true even though Israel has been given the objective repository of Wisdom called Torah.

Thus Ben Sira continues the traditional idea that Wisdom is hidden until revealed, and revelation comes not merely by the possession of the Torah, but rather also by the subjective understanding and living out of Wisdom through diligent and disciplined study of Torah and other sources of Wisdom.

> In Qohelet, wisdom is a human faculty, the cognitive tool used to investigate reality... (1:13). For Ben Sira, however, wisdom as a deep and universal knowledge of things, is not of humankind but of God. Only God can properly be defined as "wise"... Humankind can acquire wisdom, but only as a gift from God.[114]

[111] E.g., Schnabel, *Law and Wisdom*, pp. 8ff.
[112] So Skehan and di Lella, *Wisdom of Ben Sira*, 139.
[113] Cf. Skehan and di Lella, *Wisdom of Ben Sira*, 172.

This sort of approach to Wisdom was to characterize later developments in Wisdom literature as well.

Ben Sira is rather like the one referred to in Matt 13:52: "Therefore every scribe who has been trained for the kingdom of heaven is like the master of a household who brings out of his treasure what is new and what is old." In some ways Ben Sira's work represents the apex of the development of the Hebrew Wisdom tradition prior to the time of Jesus. But it is well to say in closing that Ben Sira was no Gnostic; he did not affirm that knowledge was the way to salvation. In fact, surprisingly, he affirms, "He who finds wisdom is great indeed, but not greater than he who fears the Lord. Fear of the Lord surpasses all else" (Sir. 25:10–11). Thus while being a sage is a very desirable goal it was only obtainable by a few, especially the few who had the time, education and wealth for such a profession. Ben Sira knew this, and so he stressed that obeying the Lord and living in a way that pleases God is the most critical thing of all. One more work deserves close scrutiny at this juncture, and so this study turns to the Wisdom of Solomon.[115]

B. SPIRIT OF WISDOM/WISDOM AS SPIRIT: *THE WISDOM OF SOLOMON*

Ben Sira was interested in creating or encouraging a social order in which he believed Wisdom could make sense again.[116] "With Ben Sira we stand at the headwaters of that period of Jewish history in which politics and religion clashed, models and institutions failed to mesh, and ideal figures were imagined dislodged from their rightful place in the center of things."[117] In such an environment where could Wisdom go? The answer in the Wisdom of Solomon seems to be on the one hand forward to an otherworldly future (and to the Day of Judgment), and on the other back to the past. But this is not all, for in the Wisdom of Solomon one also finally sees what a substantive interaction of Judaism and Hellenism looks like.

---

[114] Boccaccini, *Middle Judaism*, p. 82, cf. p. 83: "Ben Sira seems to be obliged to align himself with the apocalyptic idea of knowledge as illumination granted to an 'elect'."

[115] Since this is a study of canonical and deutero-canonical Wisdom material, I will not be investigating Philo in this study, though it is obvious he too draws on Wisdom material. If one wants to see what a strong marriage of Hellenistic and Hebrew thought really looks like, one should look at Philo, not Ben Sira. It is my judgment that Philo, under ongoing Alexandrian influence, represents a step *away* from the mainstream of Jewish Wisdom thought. In Philo, Greek ways of thinking often become the *determining* factors in how he expresses himself *and* in what he actually says. Philo is in some ways also a step away from the mainstream of the Jewish Wisdom that was appropriated by early Jewish Christians. It may be argued that Philo shows the ultimate outcome of what pursuing a Hellenizing path does to Jewish thinking. The Wisdom of Solomon seems also to be headed down the road towards Philo's position, but is still in closer contact with the earlier traditions.

[116] Cf. Mack, "Wisdom Makes a Difference," 24.

[117] Mack, "Wisdom Makes a Difference," 25. I would differ from Mack in saying that Ben Sira stood just before those headwaters.

1. BACKGROUND

In this work a sage once again speaks using the persona of Solomon and speaks as if addressing other monarchs. Yet this sage, unlike a Qoheleth or a Ben Sira, does not generally distill his wisdom into proverbs or aphorisms. Rather, he offers an extended exhortation in discourse form (*logos protreptikos*).[118] The sage who produced this document, like Ben Sira, also chose to offer something of a historical review. Unlike the optimism of Ben Sira, this review (which begins with Adam in Chapter 10 and ends in the Promised Land in Chapter 12, only to double back to the wilderness wandering period in chapters 15–16, 18:20ff., to the Passover event in chapter 17–18, and finally to the Red Sea crossing in chapter 19) does not begin to suggest that this anonymous sage's own time is in direct continuity with those ancient ages in which divine intervention for God's people was both possible and evident. Rather, this book was clearly written when the times were out of joint, and the only real hope seemed either in the distant past, in the afterlife, or possibly at the eschatological Day of Judgment. Thus, no contemporary figure is set up as the crowning example for the sage's audience but rather Solomon is summoned back from the dead ostensibly to lecture current monarchs about righteous deeds and the value of Wisdom. In part, this may be because the author did not see either virtue being exhibited in the monarchs of his day and age.

But when was this sage's time? Most scholars would argue that this book should be dated to the period of Roman rule in Egypt, probably sometime after 30 B.C. following the Roman conquest of Alexandria.[119] Certainly it must be dated after the appearance of the LXX, since it appears to use it (alluding to Isa. 3:10 LXX in 2:12; cf. also Wis. 15:10 which seems to draw on Isa. 44:20 LXX). This means it cannot be earlier than 200 B.C. The author has chosen not to write in the style of the LXX, for he uses some 335 words never found in the LXX.[120]

There are further clues about the date and provenance of this book. First, there is the remarkable and well documented degree of affinity between this book and the writings of Philo, although the direction of the influence can be debated. For example, the view that Wisdom is, or can be virtually identified with, the divine and holy spirit of God is an idea we find in Wisdom literature for the first time in the Wisdom of Solomon, but this idea is also found in

---

[118] Mack, "Wisdom Makes a Difference," rightly stresses that this should not lead to the conclusion that this book is an attempt to recommend Judaism to the Hellenistic world. "Hellenistic logic and genres have been marshalled, but the issues addressed are thoroughly Jewish concerns. And the argumentations that are set forth are certainly matters that pertain to a debate internal to the Judaisms of the time" (29).

[119] Cf. D. Winston, *The Wisdom of Solomon*, 3; Mack, "Wisdom Makes a Difference," 25; Murphy, *Tree of Life*, p. 83.

[120] J. M. Reese, *Hellenistic Influence on the Book of Wisdom and its Consequences*, 3–25, 153.

[121] Cf. Winston, *Wisdom of Solomon*, 59–63; and Winston, "Sage as Mystic," in *The Sage in Israel*, 387.

Philo.[122] D. Winston urges that the Wisdom of Solomon should be dated as late as the time of Caligula and the persecution of Jews that ensued in Alexandria under that emperor's reign (*c.* A.D. 37–41).[123] If this is correct, then Philo may have influenced the Wisdom of Solomon.

It does not seem necessary to date the book that late. Josephus speaks of attacks against the Jews by *Egyptians* (*Apion* 2:69–70), and one need not correlate the obvious evidence of persecution in the book with a specific persecution instigated by *Romans*. Except for periods when the Jews' special status as resident aliens was withdrawn, surely the chief social tension that existed in Egypt under Roman rule was between Egyptians and Jews, the two underclasses both jockeying for position and protected privileges from their overlords. Furthermore, apart from a vague reference to distant authorities, probably Roman (Wis. 14:17), the sage focuses his hostility on the Egyptians who are alluded to repeatedly and their demise celebrated especially at the close of the book (Wis. 19:13ff., cf. Wisdom 17–18). Thus, any time after the rule of the distant monarchs began (i.e., 30 B.C.), is possible for the date of this book.

Other clues to the provenance of this book include its rather clear reflection of Stoic and Middle Platonic ideas and terms (cf. "the knowledge of existent being" in 7:17; the list of the four virtues in 8:7; pre-existence of the soul in 8:20; the all pervading immortal spirit of God in 12:1 or of Wisdom in 7:24; the treatment of the knowledge of God in 13:1–9).[124] A further clue is its apparent indebtedness to Isis aretologies, especially considering their connection with the question of royal rule and the conduct of monarchs.[125] The most likely place where a Jew would have been in contact with this collocation of ideas is Egypt and in particular Alexandria. The connections with the earlier LXX coupled with the high degree of parallels with Philo also point in this direction.

The sage who wrote this book was capable of writing very elegant Greek (cf. 12:27; 13:11–15) using all the devices of good Greek style ranging from chiasmus, to hyperbaton, to *sorites* (cf. 6:17–20), to *litotes*, assonance, alliteration, and anaphora (cf. Chapter 10). It is very difficult to believe that this book is a Greek translation of an originally Hebrew or Aramaic work.[126]

---

[122] Cf. Blenkinsopp, *Wisdom and Law*, 149; Philo's dates are from *c.* 20 B.C. to *c.* A.D. 50. If the affinities between his writings and our book are any clue, it is likely it also came from this period and locale.

[123] Blenkinsopp, *Wisdom and Law*, 59.

[124] Cf. E. de Places, "Le Livre de la Sagesse et les influences grecques," 536–42.

[125] Mack, *Logos und Sophia*, 38ff.; J. S. Kloppenborg, "Isis and Sophia in the Book of Wisdom," 57–84; Reese, *Hellenistic Influence*, 46–49.

[126] F. Zimmermann, "The Book of Wisdom: Its Language and Character," 1–27, 101–35, cf. especially 127, wishes to argue for an Aramaic original, on the basis of occasional clumsy Greek and the presence of Semitisms. But the latter can as easily be explained by the author's knowledge of the Hebrew Scriptures, which he alludes to regularly. As to the former they are few in number compared to the considerable evidence marshalled by Winston, *Wisdom of Solomon*, 14ff., not merely for a Greek original but for skill in writing Greek. Zimmermann's retroversions into Aramaic are often speculative at best, and most scholars have not been convinced by them. Using Zimmermann's method of arguing one could just as well urge that there were Aramaic originals of Paul's letters, based on the well known Greek malapropisms and Semitisms in his writings.

In view of the evidence of uniformity of Greek style and vocabulary throughout the work, most scholars have accepted the work as a unity composed by one author.[127] The structure of the Wisdom of Solomon has been highly debated. In regard to the smaller units of material in the book, one is helped by the evidence that the author used the rhetorical device of *inclusio* (cf. e.g. 1:1–15 with *dikaiosune* forming an *inclusio*). The major debate is over whether Wis. 10:1–11:1 goes with what precedes or with what follows.[128]

Some scholars wish to argue for a break after 11:1 with a new major section beginning at 11:2.[129] The difficulty with this argument is two fold: (1) the prayer of Solomon seems to end at 9:18; and (2) 10:1, like 11:1, begins with the anaphoric "she" referring to personified Wisdom, and Chapters 10–11 look to be part of a larger unit explaining the saving acts of Wisdom which continues on into Chapter 12. In terms of both form and content, the most natural break is after 9:18, not 10:21 or 11:1, with the reference to those saved by Wisdom in 9:18 being the signal that the author will be giving some historical examples in what follows.[130]

More importantly, Winston appears to be right that in the historical review there is a series of antitheses, which often involve the idea that the natural elements which brought judgment on the Egyptians brought redemption to the Israelites (e.g., the Red Sea, cf. 19:1–9). There are, however, already several antitheses in Chapter 10 where the historical review begins: (1) Adam is contrasted with Cain in 10:1–3; (2) Abraham is contrasted with those who built the Tower of Babel in 10:5; (3) Lot is contrasted with the ungodly in the five cities which were destroyed in 10:6–7; (4) in 10:10ff it is Jacob being rescued from his counterpart Esau; and (5) in 10:13ff. it is Joseph being preserved by Wisdom from his enemies. Thus, although the antitheses in Wis. 11.1ff. begin to focus more on the same natural element having two different effects on two different peoples due to the guiding hand of Wisdom, the use of the antithesis format is already in evidence in Chapter 10. As M. J. Suggs puts it, "The idea of Wisdom's repeated efforts among men through her envoys, is elaborated in Wisdom 10–11 into a new interpretation of *Heilsgeschichte*, in which Israel's history is seen as determined by Sophia's providential guidance of the people

[127] Cf. Winston, *Wisdom of Solomon*, 12–14.

[128] Cf. Winston, *Wisdom of Solomon*, 9–12; J. M. Reese, "Plan and Structure in the Book of Wisdom," 391–99; A. W. Wright, "The Structure of Wisdom 11-19," 28–34.

[129] Cf. Winston, *Wisdom of Solomon*, pp. 10-11; Reese, "Plan and Structure," 392.

[130] It should also be noted that while in 11:1 the subject is probably "she" (depending on whether one takes *eudoō* as a transitive or an intransitive verb) and in 11:2 "they", 11:1 prepares us for the change in subject with the reference to "their works". Thus, there is a natural antecedent in 11:1 for the new subject of the verb at the beginning of 11:2. If one chooses to divide matters after 10:21 (so Winston *Wisdom of Solomon*, 225–26 though not without reservations), one cuts off the natural conclusion of 10:21 in 11:1. The reference to 'their works' is surely a reference back to what is mentioned especially in 10:17 (the labors), and 10:20–21. I thus conclude that a much more natural place to divide the material is after Chapter 9.

through chosen vessels in each generation."[131] This strongly suggests one should not separate Chapter 10 from Chapter 11 too sharply, even though there may be the change in subject from "she" to "they" between 11:1 and 11:2, and even though it may be correct to say that while the theme of Wis. 10.1ff is simply that Wisdom saves her own, in 11.5 we hear a new development in the theme of salvation by Wisdom. That which rescued Israel, punished their enemies.[132]

In any case, the author's real concern and focus, beginning with 10:13ff., is on the events of the Exodus and the wilderness wandering period. There are, however, two major excurses that interrupt the flow of the discussion of saving events: (1) one on Divine Mercy being extended to all in 11:15 – 12:22; and (2) one on the perils of idolatry in 13.1 – 15.19.[133] At least part of the function of these excurses seems to be to show that God's concern extends beyond God's own chosen people, God cares about all the human race.

Though the book *appears* to be addressed to monarchs, in view of the author's allusive style, relying as he does on his audience's knowledge of Jewish history and the Torah, it is more likely this document is addressed to Hellenized Jews in Egypt whom the author fears are in danger of completely giving up their faith due to persecution and cultural pressure. The address to monarchs is part of the literary strategy that comes with adopting the fiction of Solomon as the one giving this exhortation.[134]

The author is attempting to forge a new but risky marriage of mainly Jewish ideas with some Greek ones (such as the idea of body–soul dualism or of immortality), in order to show his audience that whatever is really of worth that they might be seeking in Hellenistic religion or culture can in fact be found in Judaism. This strategy suggests that the author is not arguing for his audience to give up entirely social interaction with the dominant culture. The point is rather that at the substantive level, whatever Isis or Hellenistic philosophy and culture in general may offer, *Sophia* in fact can deliver. J. Kloppenborg puts it well when he says:

> The newly formed similarities between Isis and Sophia were the expression of the desire of Jews for less restricted social intercourse. In effect, Pseudo-Solomon asserted that Jewish theology corresponded significantly with Hellenistic Isis beliefs. This assertion provided the symbolic basis for enhanced social contact. At the same time, the differences between the two figures aimed at the preservation of social and religious boundary.[135]

---

[131] M. J. Suggs, *Wisdom, Christology, and Law in Matthew's Gospel*, 21.

[132] Cf. Wright, "Structure of Wisdom 11–19," 29. My point is that 11.5 does *not* enunciate a new theme, but rather a new development within the continuing theme of Wisdom saving her own.

[133] Cf. Winston, *Wisdom of Solomon*, 11. There is some debate as to what to do with the transitional material in 12:23–27.

[134] Cf. di Lella, "Conservative and Progressive Theology," 147; Mack, "Wisdom Makes a Difference," 29-30.

[135] Kloppenborg, "Isis and Sophia", 84.

2. *PSEUDO-SOLOMON'S WISDOM*

As previously stressed, how a sage handles the act–consequence idea is a telling indicator of his overall perspective on what amounts to Wisdom and how it works. Our author does not hold the conviction that all wrongs will be righted in the lifetime of the individual involved, although he does adopt Ben Sira's last gasp expedient of suggesting some sort of compensation in the way someone dies or at the point of death. Nor does he give way to the pessimism or *carpe diem* sort of approach of a Qoheleth. In fact, it looks like our author considers the answers of Qoheleth, and some things said in Job as well, *not* as God's wisdom but as the views of those who oppose the righteous. Consider some of what the *ungodly* say in the diatribe in Wis. 2:1ff.:

> Short and sorrowful is our life, and there is no remedy when a life comes to its end, and no one has been known to return from Hades....hereafter we shall be as though we had never been, for the breath in our nostrils is smoke...when it is extinguished the body will return to ashes and the spirit will dissolve like empty air. Our name will be forgotten in time, and no one will remember our works; our life will pass away like the traces of a cloud....For our allotted time is the passing of a shadow, and there is no return from our death....Come therefore, let us enjoy the good things that exist, and make use of the creation to the full as in youth. Let us take our fill of costly wine and perfumes, and let no flower of spring pass us by.

Even a cursory comparison of Wisdom 2 and Ecclesiastes, especially Eccles. 2:15–24; 3:9–22; 9:1–12; 11:7–10 shows a striking similarity not just in both sources' assertion that the act–consequence idea is seen to be falsified by human experience, but also in the advice given as a result of the breakdown in the moral order – *carpe diem*.[136] Both sources also stress the ideas of the allotted time, and the ephemerality and absurdity of life in the light of the finality of death. Parallels can also be pointed to between Wisdom 2 and Job 7:9–10, 10:20, and 14:1–2.

These parallels suggest that this diatribe is a way for the author to set up an intramural debate between two different voices in Judaism over what amounts to Wisdom in this life. The ungodly, reflecting as they do some of the material in Ecclesiastes and Job, represent one extreme in the Jewish Wisdom debate, and this author is trying to steer his audience in a different direction.[137] He believes that the outcome of following a certain interpretation of Qoheleth's philosophy leads not merely to enjoying things while one can but to actual unrighteousness. Thus Wisdom 2 continues with the arguments of the ungodly

[136] These parallels with Ecclesiastes have also been noticed by Crüsemann, "Unchangeable World," 73.

[137] It is not likely that the ungodly represent the Egyptians here, for there had long been a widespread belief in an afterlife in Egypt.

that in view of what has been said in 2:1–10 might makes right (2:11). Counsel is then given to lie in wait for the righteous person and test him with insult and torture, and then condemn him to a shameful death (2:12–20). It is this sort of outcome that our author seeks to avoid.

But how will he accomplish his aims? The surprising answer is, by drawing on certain Hellenistic ideas, particularly body–soul dualism and immortality, to explain how in the end all will be well indeed. In addition to this there is some appropriation of Jewish eschatological ideas, in a fashion not unlike what Ben Sira attempts. These ideas entail the vindication of the righteous over the wicked at a judgment day scene (cf. 3:8–9; 5:1–23), but just how and where this final resolution will happen is not made clear. It is also not clear that our author affirms the idea of bodily resurrection, though 5:1ff suggests this.[139]

Especially crucial is Wis. 8:19–20 where one not only sees the idea of body–soul dualism enunciated but probably also the idea of the pre-existence of the soul. Solomon says that he, in the form of his soul, "being good entered an undefiled body."[140] But it will be seen that this author is not stressing the natural immortality of the soul in his work, but rather the 'good' immortality that comes to the righteous. Fundamentally the kind of immortality he is *commending* to his audience is "Immortality . . . not rooted in the human makeup, but in one's relationship to God."[141] Wis. 3:4 seems to make this clear for it speaks of the *hope* of immortality and 'who hopes for what they already have?' Also, Wis. 1.4 states that Wisdom will not enter a 'soul' that is deceitful, nor dwell in a body in the bondage of sin (cf. 1:5). Further. in Wis. 8:13 immortality is seen as a gift given by God to Solomon because of Wisdom. Most striking of all is Wis. 1:15 where it is affirmed that "righteousness is undying."[142] God is the powerful one who can convey the ultimate good that overcomes or even reverses death's power – a blessed immortality. But this is conferred on those rightly related to God (Wis. 15:3).[143] Pseudo-Solomon believes there is a great prize for "blameless souls" (Wis. 1:22). Reese stresses that in the Wisdom of Solomon for the first time among the books of the Old

[138] Cf. P. Grelot, "L'Eschatologie de la Sagesse et les Apocalypses Juives," in *A la Recontre de Dieu. Memorial Albert Gelin*, 165–78.

[139] But cf. P. Beauchamp, "Le salut corporel des justes et la conclusion du livre de la Sagesse," 491–526 and C. Larcher, *Études sur le Livre de la Sagesse*, 321ff.

[140] Contrast Larcher, *Études sur le Livre de la Sagesse*, 273–74 to Winston, *Wisdom of Solomon*, 26.

[141] Rightly, Reese, *Hellenistic Influence*: "the Sage does not look upon immortality as a metaphysical entity. For him it is not the inherent indestructibility of the soul, as Platonic tradition conceived it, but rather a state of eternal, blessed communion with God and his saints" (62). Cf. Murphy, *Tree of Life*, 86. It is as important to stress *how* the sage uses Greek ideas as to stress *that* he does so.

[142] Cf. Murphy, *Tree of Life*, 86.

[143] Murphy, "To Know Your Might is the Root of Immortality, (Wis. 15.3)," 88–93, is surely right that the link in this verse between God's power and immortality is that God has death-destroying power.

Testament one finds the future life and an other-worldly future clearly and categorically stressed as the goal of human life.[144] The body–soul dualism is also clear in this book, but the mere fact of having a soul is no guarantee of a blessed life or a good immortality.[145] Rather, righteousness and Wisdom must be pursued and God must be obeyed. God's design for all humans is life not death (1:13–14). Life like the afterlife has an ethical quality to it – either good or bad. Thus, the link between conduct and eternal destiny is preserved in the Wisdom of Solomon. Here is one of the first attempts in any full sense in early Judaism to combine both the idea of a blessed and peaceful immortality directly after death for the righteous (3:1–4) with the idea of an historical day of reckoning for both the just and the wicked (5.1ff). This foreshadows later developments both in the Jesus tradition and in the teaching of Paul.[146]

There is also an interesting development of a compensation or reversal theory. The sage, perhaps drawing on material from Isaiah, pronounces a blessing on the barren woman and the eunuch (cf. Isa. 54:1ff; 56:4ff); both will gain "fruit" and "blessing" "when God examines souls." In the sage's mind, childlessness with virtue or short life with virtue, is to be preferred to profligacy and long life (Wis. 4:1–10). The sage seems to be considerably qualifying or even correcting the earlier dictums of Jewish Wisdom about long life and plentiful progeny being the reward of the righteous. Here too some of the developments of the Gospel tradition are foreshadowed (cf. Matt 19:11–12; Luke 11:27).

One further development that will become of enormous significance later is the fact that three of the very few occurrences where one finds God addressed as Father in pre-Christian Jewish literature are to be found in Sir. 23:1, in Sir. 51:10 in prayer, *and* in Wis. 14:3 in direct address ('O Father'). The only other example which is very likely earlier than these is found in Isa. 64:8.[147] What this may suggest is that this sort of address first came to prominence in Wisdom literature.

D. Winston has seen in some of the material in the Wisdom of Solomon, coupled with the lack of any exhortations to enjoy life, wine, music and banquets which is evident in Ben Sira (cf. Sir. 30:21–25; 31:12–32:13), the

---

[144] Reese, *Hellenistic Influence*, 62.

[145] Two of the clearest signs of Hellenistic influence on this book are the use of the term *athanasia* and its cognates (immortality, 3:4; 8:13, 17; 15:3) and the term *aphtharsia* and its cognates (incorruption, 2:23; 6:18, 19; 12:1; 18:4). Reese (*Hellenistic Influence*) concludes: "The principle areas of hellenistic culture that have influenced the Sage are Epicurean speculation on immortality and its nature, popular religion of hellenized Egypt as exercised in the Isis cult, and anthropological and ethical teachings found in the treatises on kingship" (89).

[146] Cf. below. and B. Witherington, *Jesus, Paul, and the End of the World,* 184ff. on Jesus' and Paul's views of the resurrection and the afterlife.

[147] Cf. Crenshaw, *Old Testament Wisdom*, 176. One may also wish to point to 3 Macc. 6:3 "O Father"; and Tob. 13:4 "our Father" but not in direct address; and to *Apocalypse of Moses* 35:3. In regard to the possible Qumran references cf. B. Witherington, *Christology of Jesus*, 217.

beginnings of a Jewish ascetical and mystical approach to God.[148] He also suggests that the reason this sage eschews the use of proverbial wisdom is because he believes that the experience of Wisdom is open to *all*, and so the appropriate thing to do is to exhort all to seek after and embrace her, not to transmit the distilled Wisdom of previous generations in the form of proverbs or maxims.[149] This may also explain why it is that this author offers very little reflection on what a class of sages might do, as opposed to the role of a monarch on the one hand or all the devout and righteous believers on the other. It is not some class of sages in particular or the disciples of sages who are exhorted in this book. Rather, Pseudo-Solomon says, "if *anyone* loves righteousness, her labors are virtues; for she teaches self-control and prudence, justice and courage" (Wis. 8:7). Doubtless he especially means all Jews.[150] The fact that the author in his use of the historical traditions of the Jewish faith mentions none of the key figures (e.g., Moses) by name also suggests an attempt to universalize his material.[151]

As B. Mack has pointed out, when one reads carefully Wisdom 10–19 what comes to light is the fact that this author not only believes that Wisdom has saved and providentially guided God's people throughout their history, but that "secret wisdom" is to be discerned by a careful re-reading of Torah. Thus, as was the case with Ben Sira, "again it is a correlation of Torah, wisdom, and society that has made the study possible..."[152] Yet the sage who wrote the Wisdom of Solomon does not make the relationship or correlation of Torah and Wisdom as clear as Ben Sira did. In fact, as Blenkinsopp points out, our author hardly ever refers directly to the law, usually at most only alluding to it (cf. 2:12; 6:4; 16:6). Most striking of all he does not mention it at all when he refers to Moses (in 11:1 he is called prophet not law giver) nor when he refers to Moses' leadership of Israel in the wilderness (10:15–11:14).[153] The law he does refer to in Wis. 6:17–20 is "her law," i.e., Wisdom's![154] What then does our sage say directly about this Sophia who has her own law?

---

[148] Winston, "The Sage as Mystic in the Wisdom of Solomon," 383–97. On the possible relationship of this supposed ascetical tendency and the bride of Wisdom motif, cf. P. Beauchamp, "Épouser la Sagesse – ou n'épouser qu'elle? Une énigme du Livre de la Sagesse," in *La Sagesse de l'Ancien Testament*, 347–369

[149] Winston, "The Sage as Mystic in the Wisdom of Solomon," 395.

[150] It is a fault in an otherwise fine article that Winston, "The Sage as Mystic in the Wisdom of Solomon," 384, interprets Wis. 8:7 to refer to what Wisdom bestows on sages.

[151] It would also suggest that his audience is a group of educated Jews familiar with both the narratives of the Jewish faith and with Hellenistic philosophy, religion, and culture. It is intriguing how Pseudo-Solomon is able to use Hellenistic or Greek ideas in the service of a basically Jewish faith. For example, his use of the term *ambrosios* (19.21), traditionally the food of the Greek gods, to describe the manna that came to God's people from heaven. Cf. Reese, *Hellenistic Influence*: "His use of Hellenism, therefore, is primarily strategic; it serves as an effective means of building a bridge between received biblical faith and the contemporary situation of his readers" (156).

[152] Mack, "Wisdom Makes a Difference," 31.

[153] Blenkinsopp, *Wisdom and Law*, 147.

[154] This may have some relevance when Paul's letters are examined for Wisdom influence, since Paul identifies Christ with Wisdom, and speaks of the law of Christ.

SOPHIA *AS BOTH CREATOR AND SAVIOR*

More detailed consideration must now be given to what is said about Sophia in Wisdom 1, 6–9, and several isolated verses in 10–19. It is instructive to note not only the ways the sage is indebted to previous Wisdom hymns, and perhaps also to ideas found in Isis aretologies, but the ways he *modifies* his sources. For example, on the one hand this sage, like the one who wrote Prov. 8, or Sir. 24, affirms Wisdom's role in creation. Wisdom was the "fashioner of all things" (cf. Wis. 7:22).[155] On the other hand there is a new stress on Wisdom as the savior of God's people throughout Israel's history (cf. 9:18 with 10:1 — 19:12). "The similarity with Isis is here inescapable. She is frequently called *soter*, *soteria*, and *pansoteria* and numerous dedications recall her saving deeds."[156] In addition, many of the qualities or attributes or even names Sophia is called in the Wisdom of Solomon had been used already in a similar way of Isis (e.g., emanation of God, her radiance brighter than the sun, craftswoman, guide, throne partner of God, bride, penetrates all by her purity, taught the "constitution of the world" [Wis. 7:17 cf. *Kore Kosmou*, 52], teaches about nature and plants). These parallels are so substantial that any partially alert listener who had grown up in a environment where the cult of Isis was flourishing would have heard the echoes of the Isis aretologies.[157]

Yet *Sophia* is neither identified with God, nor is she said to be the mother of a divine being such as Horus.[158] In Wis. 9:17–18 we hear that God sends Wisdom from on high. Here and elsewhere she is seen as subordinate to the biblical God. In a new development she is identified as "a holy and disciplined spirit" (1:5, cf. v.4) or we hear "Wisdom is a kindly spirit" (1:6). The two parallel phrases in 9:17 also suggest that Wisdom is being identified with God's holy Spirit.[159] Thus while she is sent from heaven, and even from or from beside God's glorious throne (9:4, 10) she is not simply identical with the Almighty who still dwells in heaven once Wisdom has been sent. She is the one who lives with God and is loved by God (8:3).[160] She can also be spoken of in the same breath with God's *logos* in 9:1–2, as the means by which God fashioned humankind, a development which is to be made a great deal of in the *logos* hymn in John 1.[161] Yet she is more than an abstract Stoic ordering principle pervading all things. She pre-existed that cosmos and helped in its creation (cf. 6:22, 8:1, 8:6).

---

[155] Here *technitis* surely means craftswoman or fashioner, and as such seems to be this sage's exegesis of what Prov. 8:30's *amon* means.

[156] Kloppenborg, "Isis and Sophia," 67 and nn. 40–41.

[157] Cf. the charts of parallels in Reese, *Hellenistic Influence*, 46ff.

[158] She is said to be the mother of the benefits she conveys in Wis. 7:12.

[159] Cf. Larcher, *Etudes*, 411ff.

[160] In 9:5 she seems to be called God's serving girl, and there may be cause for saying that Wisdom is portrayed as God's bride in 8:3; however, 8:2 mentions her as the bride Solomon sought.

[161] Cf. Schnabel, *Law and Wisdom*, 131 and pp. 287ff. below.

This sage is even willing to go so far as to say that Wisdom is a "breath of the power of God, a pure emanation of the glory of the Almighty; . . . and an image of his goodness. . . In every generation she passes into holy souls" (7:25–27). This is a truly remarkable series of statements for a monotheistic Jew. Here one sees the beginnings of a groping beyond just personification of an attribute of God to a hypostasis. It may be as Murphy avers that the author is here speaking of "the ways in which God is present to the world and to humans."[162] On the one hand Wisdom can be distinguished from creation, for creation is something she helped fashion, but on the other hand the sage can say that she penetrates both all spirits (7:23) and all things (7:24). That is, she comes from the very being of the Creator as spirit, light, glory and penetrates the very being of creation and creature. It is because of her purity that she is able to relate to both Creator and creature in this way. There is an undefined interplay between Wisdom being a spirit, and having a holy spirit (cf. 7:7, 9:17 to 7:22–23).

One gets a sense from reading through all the passages on personified Wisdom in this book that here one is talking about something that is much greater, because she is more powerful, than one god in a pantheon of deities, and yet she is less than an exhaustive description of the one true God. H. Ringgren's assessment is that "It is apparent that the author's doctrine of wisdom is no carefully prepared and non-contradictory philosophic doctrine. Wisdom has an obscure position between personal being and principle. She is both, and she is neither the one nor the other."[163] For this reason some have spoken of a hypostasis of Wisdom in the Wisdom of Solomon.[164] For the sake of clarity, I will call what is being expressed in the Wisdom of Solomon an hypostasis, not merely a personification of an attribute, because it now entails the new element of Wisdom emanating from God.[165] This idea is closely linked with the idea of Wisdom as light or even more radiant than mere light (cf. Wis. 7:10).[166] It is wise to be cautious at this juncture because the author did not want to say anything that would compromise his monotheism, and this may account for the deliberate ambiguity of some of this material. It may be the case that there is an element of polemic against the cult of Isis in this portrayal, which is conveyed by assigning Isis' attributes as savior and guide to Wisdom. Certainly, the author is not trying to encourage polytheism, for that would work at cross purposes with the whole aim of this book which is to encourage

---

[162] Murphy, *Tree of Life*, 143.

[163] H. Ringgren, *Word and Wisdom*, 119.

[164] Cf. R. Marcus, "On Biblical Hypostases of Wisdom," 157–71, following Oesterley and Mowinckel in defining hypostasis as "a quasi-personification of certain attributes proper to God, occupying an intermediate position between personalities and abstract beings" (159).

[165] Crenshaw, *Old Testament Wisdom*, says: "Here Wisdom goes beyond personification to hypostasis: she becomes a manifestation of God to human beings, an emanation of divine attributes" (176). Mack, *Logos und Sophia*, 67ff. may be right in seeing this as the result of the author drawing on Isis material.

[166] Mack, *Logos und Sophia*, 65ff., sees this concept, and also the idea of Wisdom coming out of God's mouth, as possibly reflecting an appropriation of some of Isis' attributes or story.

Hellenized Jews in the Diaspora to maintain their Jewish faith and identity, while not abandoning dialogue with the larger world.[167] Mack is right to point out that while one may talk of an hypostasis, in the light of Wis. 9:3ff. where Wisdom is seen as a throne partner of God, one cannot even in this book talk about a simple identification of God with Wisdom.[168]

Wisdom, in 6:12ff. is seen as something which should be sought, but also she is readily found – she hastens to make herself known to the true devotee (6.13). Verse 14 is interesting because it suggests she will be found in the utterances of the sages in the city gates.[169] It is also striking that in 6.17 one learns that the beginning of Wisdom is in the desire for instruction (cf. Proverbs 1) but also that love for her is shown by keeping *her* laws (6:18). Here Wisdom does not just point to Torah; she has her own commandments. In addition, Wisdom is said to provide the cornucopia of benefits usually said to be the result of living wisely – wealth, friendship with God (7:11–14), encyclopedic knowledge of all sorts of subjects including cosmology, zoology, and more (7:17–22, cf. 1 Kgs. 4:29–34), knowledge of riddles, signs and wonders (8:8), even salvation now (9:18), and immortality hereafter (6:18–19). She is also said to be the *apaugasma* (either reflection or, more likely, radiance) of everlasting light.[170]

Furthermore, when Wisdom enters holy souls she makes them not only friends of God but also prophets (7.27)! It is important to bear in mind that already with Ben Sira there was the beginnings of the sapientializing of the prophetic corpus, and what this sage is suggesting here is a similar development. When one obtains Wisdom, one obtains the key to right understanding of both Torah and the Prophets. This sapientializing process is in evidence in this work at various points. For example in Wis. 2:10 — 5:1 there are considerable echoes of the Fourth Servant Song, as M. J. Suggs has shown.[171]

Another new note is the idea that through Wisdom there is continual creating or renewing of creation (7:27), even to the point when we are told that in the Red Sea crossing, "the whole creation in its nature was fashioned anew, complying with your commands so that your servants might be kept unharmed" (19:6). As di Lella says, our author is a progressive, willing to interact meaningfully with Stoic and Platonic ideas, and with popular religion in the form of the Isis cult, and use these ideas in the service of the biblical God and God's Wisdom.[172] He has sapientialized not only the Hebrew Scriptures, but all of the sources he draws on. They have all been transfigured in the light of his understanding of Wisdom.

---

[167] On which cf. p. 71ff. above.

[168] Mack, *Logos und Sophia*, 67. If he is right that the relationship of Wisdom and God is modeled somewhat on that of Isis and Osiris here, then again one cannot speak of Wisdom being simply equivalent to God, or God's alter ego without remainder.

[169] This is perhaps the only place in the book where one may find some allusion to the specific function of a sage in this setting.

[170] Cf. Ringgren, *Word and Wisdom*, 116 and below pp. 277ff. on Heb. 1:3.

[171] M. J. Suggs, "Wisdom of Solomon 2.10-51.: A Homily Based on the Fourth Servant Song," 26-33; cf. also pp. 100ff. above.

[172] Di Lella, "Conservative and Progressive Theology," 146ff.

Pseudo-Solomon is no mere gleaner of domesticated grapes, for he has both picked and consumed various of the wild grapes as well. The end result is an intriguing marriage of Jewish and Hellenistic ideas, though clearly the former predominate, and the latter (such as body–soul dualism or immortality) are used in the service of those Jewish ideas. The author sees no contradiction in combining or adapting Greek ideas about the afterlife with early Jewish eschatological notions – "pour l'essentiel son eschatologie ne differe pas de celle de l'apocalyptic juive. Comme elle, elle est individuelle et trans-historique..." (cf. Wis. 2:22–3:13, 4:20–5:23).[173]

The creativity and daring of this Jewish sage goes well beyond anything examined up to this point in this study. Various Jewish rabbis after A.D. 70, for whom Torah and its oral interpretations had become almost the sole field of focus, were to take a dim view of the writings of Ben Sira or Pseudo-Solomon. It was felt that these writings compromised too much with Hellenism, or were written after the period of inspiration was over (cf. *Tos. Yadaim* 2.13).[174] The material studied in this chapter raises the question of where subsequent Jewish sages such as a Jesus, or a Paul, or a James, or the composers of the early Christological hymns might go from here. The answers to these and other questions will be pursued in subsequent chapters.

CONCLUSIONS

In the first two chapters of this book the remarkable development of early Jewish Wisdom has been traced, a development that involved the evolution and creation of a variety of forms as well as the development and genesis of new ideas. It could be said, by way of generalization, that 'in the beginning was the proverb,' the distillation of collective wisdom into, usually, a two-line form of expression, which was then passed on orally at first and finally collected and grouped by catchwords, at least as early as the time of Hezekiah's scribes.

Subsequent developments in the realm of form are the meditation or discourse (cf. e.g. Proverbs 1–9), the aphorism (Qoheleth), the sapiential hymn (Job 28, Ben Sira), the full scale beatitude (Ben Sira), and finally the exhortation (Wisdom of Solomon). To be sure, probably none of these forms are without precedent in the wider corpus of international Wisdom literature and/or other forms of international literature. This study's concern, however, is with the appearance of these forms in the development of Jewish Wisdom. Notable by

[173] Grelot, "L'Eschatologie de la Sagesse," 176.

[174] Cf. Gordis, "Social Background," 117 and n. 85. Indeed the later rabbinic Jewish authorities were to call Ecclesiastes, Job, and even Proverbs into question in regard to their sacred worth (cf. *B. T. Shab.* 30a,b). *Aboth of R. Nathan* 1 calls Proverbs mere sayings not Scripture; Qoheleth is said to suffer from contradictions, it was the Wisdom of Solomon not of God (*B. T. Shab.* 30a,b); *Mish. Sot.* 5.5 queries whether Job served God from motives of love or of fear.

its *absence*, in light of subsequent developments in the Jesus tradition, is the evidence of any sort of narrative *meshalim*. It will be argued later that this form arose as a result of the prophetic appropriation of the *mashal*, expanding it from a simple one or two line comparison to a comparison of some length, often taking the form of a brief story. It appears that sometime shortly after the turn of the era this became an extremely popular form of prophetic–wisdom utterance. From the start it was a hybrid form bearing witness to the cross-fertilization of various sorts of early Jewish traditions. Such a development is no surprise in the light of the trend seen in both Ben Sira and the Wisdom of Solomon of the sapientializing of prophetic, and in Ben Sira even legal, traditions. Doubtless, the influence flowed in both directions on various occasions.

But it has also been seen that if one wishes to speak of cross-fertilization when the topic is early Jewish Wisdom one must also reckon with the impact of international Wisdom especially in its Egyptian form, on even the earliest forms of biblical Wisdom, and, increasingly from the time of Qoheleth on with the effect of Hellenistic ideas and forms. It was not until very near the turn of the era, in the Wisdom of Solomon, that any sort of profound interaction or marriage between Judaism and Hellenism could be noted. It is also the case that one always had to reckon in Judaism with a conservative backlash against Hellenization, something which is particularly evident in Ben Sira's book.

The profoundly religious character of Jewish Wisdom was also stressed, and one may also add in general its mundane character – by and large it deals with the commonplaces of everyday life (e.g. work, marriage, family, social interaction of the daily sort). The sages do not seem to have been offering an alternate world view to that of the prophets or priests or kings, but rather were concerned to infuse a religious orientation into everyday life. Their goal was probably not to supplant other forms of Jewish tradition, but rather to supplement them. This may have been partially in response to the considerable appeal that a wide variety of pagan religions had in Israel, since they focused on everyday matters such as the fertility of the soil.

Wisdom thought in its Jewish form can be said to be a form of creation theology. The sages believed that life was good and that there was a moral structure to creation, creature, and indeed the universe in general. This moral structure normally encouraged good and punished evil. This belief amounts to an affirmation that all actions have moral consequences (the act–consequence concept). This sort of creation theology, with its moral component, was never, except possibly in the writings of Qoheleth, entirely abandoned but it was significantly modified in a variety of ways in Job, the Wisdom of Ben Sira, and finally the Wisdom of Solomon.

The fear of Yahweh in Wisdom literature was not just an attitude appropriate for occasional cultic ceremonies but rather was the wise attitude to take towards life in general – it led to respect for neighbor, honesty in business, right choices in family dealings. This orientation towards life inculcated by the sages was in turn believed, at least in the early stages of Jewish Wisdom thinking, to lead to health, wealth, happiness, long life on the earth and the like.

But the act–consequence concept was vulnerable in at least two ways: (1) it was subject to the criticism that sometimes bad things do happen to good individuals (Job); and (2) sometimes the whole social system goes awry (Qoheleth). In the latter case, there is a general malaise and the moral order is not upheld in such an oppressive situation.

The response to these sort of objections also came in two forms. In Ben Sira it was reasserted that right would prevail either in this life, or possibly at the point of death, or finally at an eschatological Day of Judgment. It will be noted, however, that Ben Sira affirms this not in an abstract way, but concretely by saying that God will intervene and make things right. In the Wisdom of Solomon the stage for the morality play was widened considerably because the author now affirmed an afterlife, and in particular a positive and blessed afterlife for those who live rightly and wisely in this life. Facilitating this argument is the notion of a soul separable from the body. But it is striking that even in the Wisdom of Solomon an historical resolution and righting of all wrongs is not entirely abandoned. Even this sage affirmed, albeit vaguely, the concept of a final day of reckoning when the righteous and wicked would see each other and the former would be vindicated in the presence and sight of the latter.

It appears that Wisdom traditions and then Wisdom literature were produced by sages, most of whom very likely came from and spoke to those who were well off. Certainly arguments about working hard and gaining wealth, or studying hard and gaining preferment in royal circles, are arguments for those who can be upwardly mobile, who have time and leisure for education, who are literate. It follows that by and large this literature was produced for the small educated minority in Jewish society. This is evident not just in Proverbs but especially in sophisticated works like Job or Ecclesiastes or Ben Sira and the Wisdom of Solomon. The latter two clearly rely on considerable biblical knowledge on the part of the hearer/reader as well as knowledge of the surrounding intellectual environment.

This is not to say that Wisdom thinking and Wisdom traditions in oral form could not have often originated from the family or clan and influenced those same groups. If, however, one is talking about the transmission of Wisdom traditions in writing and then the creating of Wisdom literature one should look for their points of origin first to the courts with their scribes, and then at least by the time of Ben Sira to the houses of instruction. In Ben Sira we have seen that the equation of sage = scribe = counselor seems quite clear. Though there are also hints in this direction in earlier Wisdom literature as well, the equation is less certain in the earlier period. Even in Qoheleth one hears about leaders who do not take the counsel of their sages and so things go wrong for a city (cf. Eccles. 9:14–16), but there the sage is said to be poor.

From the appendix to Qoheleth as well as from Ben Sira, it is surely warranted to talk about a class of people who could be called sages or, alternately scribes. Yet in the Wisdom of Solomon the author wants to suggest that Wisdom is not only for everyone but should be sought by everyone. In short, there are still a variety of uncertainties about these matters.

There are many surprises as the Jewish Wisdom tradition developed over time. After studying Proverbs, with its air of optimism one could hardly have been prepared either for the suffering sage of Job (cf. the suffering servant in the Wisdom of Solomon), or the somber tone and aphorisms of counter order of Qoheleth. The disappearance of both proverbs and aphorisms in the Wisdom of Solomon in favor of the exhortation and diatribe form signals a new stage of things, where Hellenism and Judaism are openly conjoined. But surely nothing could be more surprising or significant than the way the personification of Wisdom grows and develops from Proverbs through Job to Ben Sira and finally to the Wisdom of Solomon.

As this cursory summation of Jewish pre-Christian Wisdom literature is concluded, it is of critical importance that we bring together in the form of a composite profile the threads of what has been said about the personification or, in the Wisdom of Solomon possibly the hypostasis, of Wisdom. Though no one source includes all the data collected here, the vast majority of it is found in more than one source, and more importantly it shows the range of attributes, associations, and actions that could be predicated of personified or hypostasized Wisdom. Table 1 is, with minor alterations, R. Murphy's summary of the evidence.[175]

TABLE 1

THE PROFILE AND PILGRIMAGE OF WISDOM

(cf. Proverbs 1; 8; 9; Job 28; Sir. 1:9–10; 4:11–19; 6:18–31; 14:20 — 15:8; 51:13–21; Bar. 3:9 — 4:4; Wisd. 6:12 — 11:1)

(1) Wisdom has her origin in God (Prov. 8:22; Sir. 24:3, 9; Wis. 7:25–26)

(2) Wisdom pre-existed and very likely has a role in the work of creation (cf. Prov. 3:19; 8:22–29, 24:3; Sir. 1:4, 9–10; Sir. 16:24 — 17:7; Wis. 7:22, 8:4–6; 9:2, 9)

(3) Wisdom is infused in creation, accounting for its coherence and endurance (cf. Wis. 1:7, 7:24, 27, 8:1, 11:25)

(4) Wisdom is identified with the divine spirit (Wis. 1:7, 9:17, 12:1) and in some sense is immanent in the world (Wis. 7:24; 8:1)

[175] Murphy, *Tree of Life*, 145–46.

(5) Wisdom comes to the human world with a distinctive mission (Prov. 8:4, 31–36; Sir. 24:7,12, 19–22; Wis. 7:27–28, 8:2–3)

a. the mission entails personally addressing the world (Prov. 1, 8, 9; Sir. 24:19–22; Wis.6.12–16;7: 22a; 8:7–9; 9:10–16)

b. to her devotees Wisdom offers life, sometimes prosperity, and a panoply of other blessings (Prov. 1:32, 3:13–18, 8:1–5, 35; 9:1–6; Sir. 1:14–20; 6:18–31; 15:1–8; 24:19–33; Wis. 7:7–14)

(6) Wisdom is especially associated with Israel

a. by divine order she dwells in Israel (Sir. 24:8–12)

b. Wisdom can be identified with Torah (Sir. 24:23; cf. 1:25–27; 6:37; 15:1; 19:20; 33:2–3; Bar.4:1)

c. Wisdom was at work in Israel's history (Wis. 10:1–21)

(7) Wisdom while a gift from God (Prov. 2:6; Sir.1:9-10, 26; 6:37; Wis. 7:7; 9:4) is associated with disciplined effort to obtain her (Prov. 4:10–27; 6:6; Sir. 4:17; 6:18–36; Wis. 1:5; 7:14).

The further development of this personification or hypostasis can be found in other early Jewish literature, notably in 1 Enoch. In 1 Enoch 42:1–3, which can be dated at least as early as the first century A.D.,[176] one finds one further step in the pilgrimage of wisdom – she returns to heaven because she found no dwelling place on earth and resumes her rightful place, sitting down amongst the angels. The relevant material in 1 Enoch 42, which appears to be part of an early hymn to Wisdom reads:

> Wisdom could not find a place in which she could dwell; but a place was found (for her) in the heavens. Then Wisdom went out to dwell with the children of the people, but she found no dwelling place. (So) Wisdom returned to her place and she became settled among the angels. [177]

Once one has examined all the relevant data on the personification of Wisdom in early Judaism one can only say that Murphy is right to stress the malleability of this personification – "defined anew in successive generations."[178]

It is clear from the flexibility of what is predicated of Wisdom in all this material that the sages are not dealing with a person and certainly not with a goddess, but with the personification of an idea, concept, attribute, or quality

---

[176] Cf. Witherington, *Christology of Jesus*, 234–35, on dating the material in the parables of Enoch.

[177] I am following the translation in *OT Pseudepigrapha I*, p. 33, with minor modifications.

[178] Murphy, *Tree of Life*, 146.

that was seen as desirable for humans to obtain and was already something that characterized God and God's orderly creation. Nevertheless, a certain particularization of the tradition has been detected as the personification develops so that Wisdom obtains names. She can be identified with, or as, Torah in Sirach or Baruch, or as God's spirit in the Wisdom of Solomon. It may be that in the Wisdom of Solomon there is a hypostasis of Wisdom. It is striking that what happens to personified Wisdom is what happens in general in Ben Sira's book and the Wisdom of Solomon, for in both these books one sees a drawing on the particularistic traditions of Israel's history and a focus on God's elect people and their future direction. This trend of particularization takes a further and dramatic step in the New Testament Wisdom material.

3

Hokmah Meets Sophia: Jesus the Cynic?

SOMETIMES there is a tendency in biblical scholarship, perhaps caused by the ever present urge to say something new without reflecting on whether it is true, to neglect to fully explore old paths that are often well trod. The path that Wisdom has been seen to follow is one of increasing particularism in the use of personification on the one hand, and increasing variety in form and in the sources drawn on for Wisdom on the other. In Ben Sira we have seen the remarkable development not only of the close correlation of Wisdom with Torah, but also of a sage who draws on eschatological traditions, Deuteronomistic themes, the story of Israel's salvation history, prophetic assessments of cultic worship, and expresses his wisdom even in hymns and beatitudes. In some of these matters one finds an important pointer to where Wisdom might go next. Indeed, I am prepared to argue that in the Jesus tradition one finds the further development of the Wisdom tradition, drawing on all of it but especially on Ben Sira and, to a lesser but significant degree on the Wisdom of Solomon and Qoheleth.

In the Gospels one hears a sage who expressed himself primarily in Wisdom forms of utterance or in the sapiential *adaptation* of eschatological and legal forms of utterance, or finally in the prophetic adaptation of the Wisdom form *mashal*. Such cross-fertilization of traditions in the Gospels is precisely what one would expect in the light of the Wisdom of Ben Sira and the Wisdom of Solomon. In the Gospels, as in those two earlier Wisdom books, there is one who spoke with authority and Wisdom, believing he was inspired by God and was revealing new things, and yet he did not use the prophetic formula, "Thus saith Yahweh."

But what of the union of Judaism with Hellenism seen in the Wisdom of Solomon? Is such a development also evident in the Jesus traditions? Even more importantly, does Hellenism become the dominant partner if there is such a union in the Jesus traditions? These matters will be addressed in the following two chapters, with this chapter being devoted to the discussion of the degree of Hellenistic influence evidenced in Jesus' environment, teaching, and lifestyle. In particular, the degree of possible influence on Jesus of Hellenistic philosophy and culture, especially the possible influence of the Cynic traditions, must be considered.

The undergirding thesis of this chapter and the next has been stated in the first two paragraphs of this chapter but the discussion of the positive side of it must be deferred until Chapter 5 so that consideration can be given to two related challenges to the view that Jesus was a thoroughly Jewish prophetic sage. The first is the idea that Palestinian Judaism in Jesus' day was *so* Hellenized at all levels of society that it is no longer adequate to look at the Jesus tradition in the light of mainly Jewish sources. Rather one must rely *primarily* on Greek resources to make sense of the Jesus material. The second challenge is the idea that Jesus himself and his teaching must be seen in light of a very specific sort of Greek tradition – namely the Cynic tradition. In short, Jesus may have presented himself and have been seen as a traveling Cynic preacher and teacher.

A. THE LEGACY OF ALEXANDER IN THE HOLY LAND

1. THE "HARVEST OF HELLENISM"

The term "Hellenization" is a chimera. It can appear to mean one thing in one context, but another in a different setting. To be clear, when the term Hellenization is used in this study, it refers to the effects of Greek language, Greek lifestyle, education, philosophy, religion, technology, and a host of other factors on a culture that was not indigenously Greek prior to its being "Hellenized." Broadly speaking Hellenization refers to the degree to which a culture, in this case a Jewish culture, has been socialized in a Greek way as a result of the various conquests of Alexander the Great and his successors from the fourth century B.C. onwards. The issue of the degree of Hellenization of first century Palestine is a complex one and calls for a cautious assessment of all the data both for and against significant Hellenization of Palestine, and in particular of Galilee.

M. Hengel stresses that the Greek language and Hellenization had

> penetrated Judea from the second half of the third century on, and in 175 B.C. this development reached its first climax with the construction of a gymnasium in

---

[1]Borrowing the title of F. E. Peters' classic survey, *The Harvest of Hellenism. A History of the Near East from Alexander the Great to the Triumph of Christianity.*

> Jerusalem by the high priest Jason. The process of Hellenization in the *Jewish upper class* then entered an acute phase, the aim of which was the complete assimilation of Judaism into the Hellenistic environment.[2]

Though there was a significant attempt during the Maccabean era to eliminate most of the effects of the Ptolemaic and Seleucid program of Hellenization on the Jewish people, this effort was far from completely successful. Indeed, by the first century A.D. it appears that the trend, at least in the upper echelon of society, was going in the opposite direction. Herod the Great and his sons (especially Antipas) engaged in massive building programs that furthered various Greek ideals of society. "In essence Herod [the Great] merely developed consistently a tendency which was already visible among the Hasmoneans, but in a new situation, i.e., in a form appropriate to the rule of the Roman principate. He saw himself in absolutely every respect as a Hellenistic ruler."[3] The numismatic and epigraphical in addition to the archeological evidence bears witness to this deliberate further effort at Hellenization in the Herodean era.

One must never forget, however, that there is *also* evidence of strong resistance in various ways and places in Palestinian Judaism to some forms of Hellenization, even well after the Maccabean period. Josephus makes evident that there was fierce opposition to Herod introducing pagan athletic contests and spectacles in either a theater or an amphitheater (cf. *Ant.* 15:267–291). The reaction against images seems to have been even stronger (*Ant.* 17:149–154, *Ant.* 18:55–59). Indeed, the palace of Herod Antipas in Tiberias was destroyed in A.D. 66 precisely because it contained representations of animals in it (*Life* 66–67). It is impressive that in Galilee there is little or no archeological evidence of the influence of the Greek style of architecture on ordinary houses.[4]

One needs to distinguish levels or degrees of Hellenization, and also to distinguish what conclusions are and are not warranted on the basis of a particular type of evidence. For example, while there is widespread evidence of the commercial use of the Greek language, the use of coins with Greek inscriptions, and the use of Greek in funeral inscriptions in Palestine, including lower Galilee, this does not demonstrate that the influence had become profound at the level of Jewish education, philosophy, or religion. Nor does the extant evidence suggest that *ordinary* Jews were condoning or practicing to any significant degree intermarriage with thoroughly Hellenized individuals. Indeed what evidence there is from both early Jewish, New Testamental, and even pagan sources suggests otherwise. Tacitus, for example, remarks on the absence of images from Jewish cities and temples as something that distinguishes early Judaism (*Histories* 5:5.4).

---

[2]Hengel, *Judaism and Hellenism*, I, 102.

[3]M. Hengel, *The Hellenization of Judea in the First Century after Christ*, 33.

[4]On all of the above one should consult the helpful study by L. H. Feldmann, "How Much Hellenism in Jewish Palestine?" 102–3.

Luke 7:36–50 (and par.). may suggest that a Pharisee or even Jesus might recline at table, following Greco-Roman customs,[5] but the Pharisee also reflects very traditional views about clean and unclean in this same story. One may also wish to stress that this is a story about a rather well-to-do person capable of hosting such a banquet. G. H. R. Horsley urges scholars not to underplay the significance of the Gospel data reflecting Hellenistic dining conventions.

> The NT uses a number of verbs which sometimes denote reclining at a meal: *anakeimai* (Mt. 26:20; Mk. 14:18; Lk. 22:27; Jn. 13:23,28 [cf. v. 25 for the close proximity of the diners to one another]); *katakeimai* (Mk. 14:3; Lk. 5:29; 7:37; 1 Cor. 8:10); *anaklino* (Mt. 8:11 = Lk. 13:29; Lk. 12:37); *kataklino* (Lk. 7:36, 14:8, 24:30...)....Now, the most arresting aspect about this list of references is that all but one of the examples comes from the gospels; all but one deal with Palestine. This evidence accords very well with the visual evidence collected by Dentzer. For if the custom of the *kline* was pre-eminently a Greek style of banqueting, it has made its appearance in a thoroughgoing manner in first-century Palestine, and that not merely in the cities. As with the the introduction of the fashion to Egypt under the Ptolemies, so we have evidence from Palestine for the ubiqitous spread of Hellenism... So typical must the *kline* have been that parables can be told in which this fashion is alluded to (Lk. 12:37; 14:7ff). Even the heavenely Banquet at which patriarchs will be in attendance is conceived in these terms (Mt. 8:11 = Lk.13:29).[6]

The evidence just reviewed suggests that one must take a balanced approach to the question of Hellenization, Palestine, and the Jesus tradition. It is as unwise to *overestimate* the influence of Hellenism on early Judaism in general and the Jesus tradition in particular as it is to *underestimate* its effect. The effect of Hellenization seems to have been *widespread* in various regards, without necessarily being *deep*, at least if one is discussing an ordinary Jew's piety and religion. In the only documented cases where Hellenization seems to have had a *thoroughgoing* effect even at the level of education, life philosophy, or religion, one is talking about a very few, very wealthy and highly educated people most of whom either ruled the land, or were close associates with the Herods or Roman rulers.[7] There is no evidence that Jesus was wealthy or that he regularly kept company with royalty and their sycophants. To this conclusion one may now add the voice of J. P. Meier, who rightly stresses:

> But if even the gifted Jerusalemite intellectual Josephus was not totally at home in Greek after years of writing in it while living in Rome, and if in A.D. 70 he had found it necessary or at least advisable to address his fellow Jews in Jerusalem in Aramaic rather than Greek, the chances of a Galilean peasant knowing enough

[5]On this story cf. Witherington, *Women in the Ministry of Jesus*, 53–57.
[6]G. H. R. Horsley, *New Documents Illustrating Early Christianity*, (1984) 9.
[7]So W. Jaeger, *Early Christianity and Greek Paideia*, 107–8, n. 7.

> Greek to become a successful teacher and preacher who regularly delivered his discourses in Greek seem slim. Especially if scholars like Sean Freyne are correct about the basic conservative nature of the Judaism of Galilean peasants, the citizens of Nazareth and other villages of the Galilean countryside may have consciously avoided the use of Greek whenever they could....In his woodworking establishment Jesus may have had occasion to pick up enough Greek to strike bargains and write receipts....But without formal education in Greek it is highly unlikely that Jesus ever attained "scribal literacy" – or even enough command of and fluency in Greek to teach at length in it with his striking verbal artistry.[8]

Meier is referring to the passage where Josephus admits he needed help with his Greek not only with pronunciation but also in writing (cf. *Against Apion* 1:50; cf. *Ant.* 20:263). When Titus asks Josephus to go and speak to the Jews of Jerusalem in order to ask them to surrender, he sends Josephus not least because he needed someone to speak to them "in their ancestral language" (probably Aramaic – *War* 5:361; cf. Acts 21:40, 22:2).[9] If one was to find significant evidence that suggested the influence of Hellenism on ordinary Palestinian Jewish views (including those of Jesus) about matters such as Torah, temple, territory, monotheism, or history and its purpose and goal, then one might be entitled to talk about Hellenism's influence being *deep* at all levels of society.

The concrete evidence suggests that Hellenization had *primarily* affected the 1%–5% of Jewish society that might be called upper class. This included the wealthy landowners, various of the Sadducees, members of the priestly hierarchy, and *also* those who had received educational training beyond what one received in the home or synagogue. Even Hillel can be cited as an example by Hengel of one who seems to have been influenced by "Socratic humanism".[10] But there is no hard evidence to suggest that Jesus studied in Jerusalem or in some school (in Sepphoris?) where he might have received the sort of education a Hillel did.

It is unwise, however, to completely dismiss the trickle-down effect of Hellenization even on ordinary Jews. Not only the political leaders and the wealthy, but also those who received educational training in Jerusalem, including religious training like Hillel received, would have been subject to learning Greek and various Greek ideas. Pharisees especially were not only a key link with common folk in Jewish society but they themselves often came from such families. Religious leaders who interacted on a daily basis with ordinary Jews in many cases would have been products of educational training that had been affected by Hellenization. They in turn passed such learning on

---

[8] J. Meier, *A Marginal Jew. Rethinking the Historical Jesus*, Vol. I, 261–62. The picture then of Jesus reading Meleager is very likely far–fetched.

[9] Cf. the discussion in Feldmann, "How much Hellenism" 92. Then, too, the much discussed scandalous *graffito* involving a love poem from one Marisa appears to be Sidonian, not Jewish in origin.

[10] M. Hengel, *The "Hellenization" of Judaea*, 52.

to ordinary Jews and it must have had at least *some* impact. It would be a mistake then to assume that *only* the upper class had felt the effects of Hellenization.

In *The Christology of Jesus* I argued that Greek had penetrated to some degree all layers of Palestinian society and that

> The evidence...is sufficient to show that Jesus grew up in the most developed area in both Galilees. Furthermore, Jesus' ministry seems to have been largely confined to lower Galilee, yet a survey of the Gospels shows him avoiding (deliberately?) the major cities of the region such as Sepphoris and Tiberias. His ministry seems directed primarily to the small towns and villages, especially around the Sea of Galilee, with Capernaum as his base of operations. Jesus, then, lived in a region where there was a more cosmopolitan and open environment than was true in upper Galilee and the evidence supports the view that lower Galilee, while maintaining Aramaic as its main spoken language at least among the Jews dwelling there, had a substantial Greek component in its linguistic character, in contrast to upper Galilee. This strongly suggests that in terms of culture and cultural attitudes, lower Galilee was more Hellenized than either upper Galilee or the Transjordan region....[11]

The question then of whether and to what degree Jesus might be seen as a Hellenized Jewish sage is one which cannot be ignored. The larger cities of Galilee were significantly Hellenized (there were Greek schools in Tiberias and Sepphoris),[12] and some degree of Greek speaking is evident not only in the upper echelon of society but also among the working class, for whom Koine Greek had become the language of commerce.[13] Then, too, early Jews seem to have placed a considerable stress on education. Even if the Gospel evidence does not encourage one to think of a Jesus who read Greek literature, perhaps through oral communication he may have acquired some knowledge of Hellenistic thinking and sayings. These factors, among others, have led F. G. Downing and others to argue that there seems to be a definite relationship between the proclamations of Jesus in the Synoptics and Greek gnomic wisdom, especially Cynic wisdom.[14] Why should not the craftsman Jesus, who grew up in the neighborhood of Sepphoris, have made contact with Cynic itinerant preachers, especially as he himself spoke some Greek?[15]

---

[11] Witherington, *Christology*, 89.

[12] On Sepphoris, and Jesus' possible involvement in that city as an artisan during the stages in which the Hellenistic city was being constructed, cf. R. A. Batey, *Jesus and the Forgotten City*, especially 29–104.

[13] Cf. Hengel, *The Hellenization of Judaea*, 7ff.; S. Freyne, *Galilee, Jesus and the Gospels*, 135ff.

[14] Cf. F. G. Downing, especially *Christ and the Cynics: Jesus and Other Radicals in First Century Traditions.*

[15] Hengel, *Hellenization of Judaea*, 44.

One must be cautious, however, for the attempt to argue for a specifically *Cynic* influence on the Jesus tradition is taking the Hellenization argument a step further. General evidence for the influence of Hellenism in lower Galilee does not prove an influence of a specifically Cynic sort. It is also possible that whatever influence of Hellenism the Jesus tradition reflects is a result of the general influence of earlier partially Hellenized Jewish Wisdom material, not direct contact by Jesus with Cynic material or preachers. In order to make a strong case for Cynic influence on Jesus one must not only point out certain parallels at the level of linguistic phenomena or at the level of ideas, but one must also show that such traits are unique to or at least characteristic of the Cynic tradition, and not to other traditions to which Jesus might have been indebted.

Several scholars have now undertaken to compare in some detail both Jesus' style of ministry and his actual teaching with the corpus of Cynic material. Particularly important are the works of F. G. Downing, B. Mack, and J. D. Crossan.[16] It is Downing who has made the most thorough going attempt to make such a case, and this analysis will concentrate on his work.

2. A CYNIC JESUS?

At the outset two points deserve mentioning. First, a few examples of parallel phenomena in language usage or even at the level of thoughts expressed do not necessarily mean influence. One will have to provide a sufficient body of evidence or parallels striking enough [17] that the cumulative effect is the appearance of one specific sort of tradition influencing another. Second, one must bear in mind that Wisdom literature in general, including Greek gnomic wisdom, often focuses on universal themes – life and death, lessons to be learned from nature, work, the role and functions of humans in this world, the moral order that operates in this world, to mention but a few. Then, too, the apparatus of religion and religious conversion were to a large degree the same in many ancient religions in the Roman Empire, i.e., most of them involved priests, temples, sacrifices, and many of them had rites of conversion/initiation as well.

Diogenes of Sinope (*c.* 400–325 B.C.) is the person normally credited with the founding of the Cynic movement. It was thus a living philosophy and way of life well before the time of Jesus. One of the main things that seems to have characterized Diogenes' teaching or preaching was his stress on *autarkeia*, or self-sufficiency. This aim was to be accomplished by living simply (cf. Diogenes

[16] Cf. especially F. G. Downing, *Christ and the Cynics*, and his *Jesus and the Threat of Freedom*; B. Mack, *A Myth of Innocence*; V. K. Robbins, *Jesus the Teacher. A Socio-Rhetorical Interpretation of Mark*; J. D. Crossan, *The Historical Jesus. The Life of a Mediterranean Jewish Peasant*. We will be focusing especially on the first of these.

[17] As for example is the case with the Amenomope material and the material from Proverbs we referred to in Chapter 1.

Laertius *LEP* 6.37). A second important trait of Diogenes that was also to characterize other Cynics was *parresia*, or boldness and bluntness of speech. For example, there is the famous story of Diogenes sunning himself when the great Alexander came to visit him and asked if there was any boon he would ask of the great ruler. Diogenes' reply was "Stand out of my light" (Diogenes Laertius *Lives* 6.38). One may see in this same episode yet another trait of the Cynics, namely that they often showed or had little respect for authority figures or governmental institutions. Bear in mind that the movement got its name because Diogenes was apparently called Diogenes the 'Dog' (*kuon*), as a result of his shameless behavior in public (e.g., among other things he would defecate in public, and Diogenes, Crates, and Hipparchia flouted customs in regard to sexual modesty as well).[18] In due course, stories about Diogenes and other later Cynics such as Crates were written down and told in such a way as to teach a moral or *chreia*. This is very likely because the Cynics told such stories themselves to drive home a *chreia*.

Now immediately there are some points of contact with the Jesus tradition, but they ought not to be exaggerated. While Cynics may have stressed self-sufficiency by means of simple living, Jesus stressed God-dependency and so simple living (cf. below on Matt. 6:19–21, 6:25–34). The point is that even where the lifestyle or course of behavior seems sometimes similar between the Cynics and Jesus, *the motivation for the behavior is entirely different*. As one examines the Cynic corpus of literature, this important difference surfaces time and again. The philosophical or theological motivations for various actions or lifestyles diverge significantly between the Cynic tradition and the Jesus tradition.

It is also doubtful if one can find any incident in the Jesus tradition that suggests he engaged in public indecency or for that matter in totally anti-institutional behavior or rhetoric. Even the cleansing of the Temple should probably be seen as an effort at radical reform. As I have argued elsewhere "The most plausible interpretations of Jesus' action in the temple suggest that Jesus performed a prophetic sign that was meant either as a signal of coming judgment on the temple or more probably as a symbolic action of cleansing, perhaps like that of Nehemiah's (cf. Neh. 13:4–9, 12–13)."[19]

On the other hand Jesus was certainly a person, who like the Cynics, spoke with boldness, but then this was hardly a Cynic-specific trait. One needs look no farther than the Old Testament prophetic tradition for a precedent for this, and Jesus' *parresia* frankly sounds a good deal more like that of these Jewish prophetic figures or perhaps like the sages of early Judaism such as Qoheleth than it does the Cynics.

Cynics apparently were also noted for their ascetical practices. This hardly characterizes the reports of Jesus' behavior in the Jesus tradition. Indeed

---

18 Cf. Downing, *Jesus and the Threat of Freedom*, 129; *Christ and the Cynics*, 129–30.

19 Witherington, *Christology*, 115.

from what one can tell Jesus gained a reputation for being "a wine drinker and a friend of sinners". The Jesus tradition contrasts Jesus with John the Baptist precisely at the point of ascetical practices (cf. Mark 2:21–22).[20]

The Cynics *anaideia* (shamelessness) in public has already been mentioned, but it will be well to quote here an able summary statement about the Cynics from E. Ferguson on this matter.

> The Cynics carried to an extreme the Sophists' contrast between custom and nature.... They sought to free themselves from luxuries and so inure themselves to hardship by ascetic practices. In order to excite censure they exposed themselves to scorn by deliberately acting against the conventions of society: using violent and abusive language, wearing filthy garments, performing acts of nature (defecation, sex) in public, feigning madness.[21]

The goal of such behavior is summed up by the Cynic tradition itself: "But I deem it enough to live according to virtue and nature, and that is in our power" (Pseudo–Diogenes, *Epistle* 25).[22] The offensive public behavior was part of an attempt to 'live according to nature,' but also part of an attempt to shock the public into considering their lifestyle and changing it for one that was simpler and more natural. Again, the underlying motivations of Jesus' sometimes shocking language and behavior seem very different. His concern was to lead people back to God or, better said, to wake them up about the inbreaking reign of God, not to urge them to "live according to nature." It was what was in accord with God's activity and will that concerned him, not what was in accord with nature. The contrast in the Jesus tradition then is not between custom and nature, but rather between tradition and God's will and activity being presently revealed in Jesus' ministry.

In general, though some Cynics seem to have been monotheists, they rejected popular religion and dogma and urged that it was possible to live as a wise man quite apart from such things. Jesus on the other hand seems to have valued the heritage of his Jewish religion, as is shown by the various traditions that indicate that he went up to Jerusalem for the feasts (cf. Mark 11:1–11 and par.; Luke 2:41–52), and also by his very likely celebration of the Passover Seder with his disciples before he died (Mark 14:12ff. and par.). Though it is plausible that Jesus intended to be in various respects a radical reformer of early Judaism, a Jesus *totally* at odds with the religious life of early Judaism can not be ferreted out of the Synoptics, unless one so truncates the tradition to a very few aphorisms or parables that one conveniently leaves out all the evidence of Jesus' Jewishness.[23]

---

20 Cf. Witherington, *Christology*, 71–81.

21 E. Ferguson, *Backgrounds of Early Christianity*, 276.

22 Most conveniently found in A. Malherbe. *The Cynic Epistles*, 117.

23 On which one may now wish to consult the collection of essays in J. Charlesworth (ed.) *Jesus' Jewishness. Exploring the Place of Jesus in Early Judaism.*

While very little is known about the viability of the Cynic movement in the two centuries before Jesus was born, nonetheless "from the first century A.D. to the end of antiquity the Cynic beggar philosophers were a common feature in the cities of the Roman world."[24] The Cynics were apparently a somewhat identifiable lot.[25] They wore woolen cloaks, carried walking sticks, beggars' bags, and often wore long beards. On the surface of things, this description might seem to be a clear parallel to the so-called commissioning speeches of Jesus to his disciples during the course of the ministry (cf. Mark 6:7–13 and the Q version in Luke 10:1–17).

The similarities between the Jesus tradition and the description of the Cynics in these matters, which have been noted,[26] should nonetheless not be exaggerated. Cynics carried beggars' bags. In both the Markan and Q forms of the commissioning speech the disciples are told *not* to take a bag with them. Rather they are to rely on the system of standing hospitality when they go from town to town. This is rather different from a lifestyle of begging.

The carrying of a staff is hardly something that could be called a Cynic-specific trait, so that when Jesus urges the disciples to do so, it does not follow that he was indebted to Cynic practice at this point. In fact, there seems to have been a variety of peripatetic teachers wandering around the Mediterranean crescent in general and Palestine in particular offering their preaching or teaching. Josephus tells us that even some of the Essenes went around with no change of clothes or sandals and made their way into the homes of people whom they had never met before (cf. *War* 2:125–127). The point here is that the similarities between the Jesus traditions and the Cynic practices do not need to suggest influence in one direction or the other, not least because there were a variety of such teachers/preachers in antiquity, and their apparel and appearance would have been similar in some respects.

One might argue that the Cynics were distinguishable by their long beards, or perhaps also by some specific sort of cloak (a woolen one) that they wore. If so, it should be noted that the Gospel tradition does not suggest either that the disciples or Jesus wore long beards, or that (unlike the Baptist) they wore distinctive apparel. The Gospel tradition is silent at this point about what sort of cloaks they wore. Furthermore, associated with both versions of the commissioning speech is the fact that the disciples are said to have engaged in exorcisms (cf. Mark. 6.13; Luke. 10.17), something which does not characterize Cynic practices at all.

To sum up, the disciples in the Markan speech are simply urged to carry a staff, wear sandals, take no extra tunic, no bread, no bag and no money (Mark. 6:8–9). One is not told that they wore woolen cloaks or long beards. The

---

[24] Ferguson, *Backgrounds*, 279.

[25] This was not entirely the case for Lucian tells us of a Cynic who dressed himself in a bear skin; cf. *Demonax* 5 and 19.

[26] Downing, *Christ and the Cynics*, 46–47; Mack, *Myth of Innocence*, 53–77.

Lukan account is even less specific, and in fact says they are *not* to take sandals (Luke 10:4). One must conclude that neither in what they are said to take, nor in what they leave behind, nor in what they do is one encouraged to assume that either Jesus or his disciples were necessarily following some sort of Cynic model of behavior or appearance. If one is going to argue from parallels to make a case for influence, the parallels must be more circumstantial than this. There is no evidence of Cynic-*specific* traits that are also found in the Jesus tradition. There is thus no firm basis for Downing's conclusion that "a raggedy cloak and outspoken figure with no luggage and no money would not have just looked Cynic, he would obviously have wanted to."[27] This sort of conclusion far outreaches the degree of parallel one can actually find between Cynic practices and the mission speech in the Gospels. One could as well argue that Jesus was following Essene practices at this point.

Nevertheless, one must not too quickly dismiss the possibility of Cynic influence on either Jesus or his disciples in view of the fact that only six miles from the southern border of Galilee lay the city of Gadara, which Jesus may even have visited on one occasion (cf. Mark 5:1ff., but there is a textual problem involving this very matter). In Gadara dwelt Menippus, the inventor of satire in the fourth to third centuries B.C. and a pupil of the Cynic Metrocles. In Gadara one also finds Meleager, the founder of the Greek anthology in the second century B.C. Furthermore, in the first century A.D. Gadara also produced Theodorus and in the second century A.D. Oenomaus, a Cynic philosopher, lived there.[28] It remains now to examine the evidence of Cynic teaching when compared to the Jesus tradition to see if a cogent case can be made for Jesus or the Jesus tradition being influenced by the Cynics.

At the very outset one must note a crucial *non*-parallel. The Cynics (specifically Bion and Menippus) are credited with developing the diatribe style. This style involves a dialogue with an imaginary interlocutor who raises objections or draws faulty conclusions. The diatribe could involve direct address, quotations from poetry, and questions and answers among other traits.[29] A very good case can be made that we see this style of rhetoric in the New Testament at places like Romans 2–4, or James 2:14ff, but evidence that Jesus or his first disciples used such a technique from the arguably authentic Gospel material is not forthcoming.

F. G. Downing has provided the best set of detailed parallels between the Jesus tradition and the Cynic material and it will be necessary to examine samples of the most impressive parallels in a moment. It may be well to point out that these parallels almost without exception *post-date* the time of Jesus and in some cases even post-date the New Testament age.

---

27 Downing, *Christ and the Cynics*, vi.

28 On all this cf. Hengel, *The Hellenization of Judaea*, 20. Hengel is right to be cautious, however, especially since, as he says, Hellenized cities such as Sepphoris and Tiberias play no part in the Gospels (cf. 43).

29 Cf. S. K. Stowers, *The Diatribe and Paul's Letter to the Romans*.

For example the parallels from Dio of Prusa clearly post-date Jesus and probably also the composition of Mark and Q for Dio, as Downing admits,[30] was not born until about A.D. 40 and apparently was not converted to Cynic teaching until he met Musonius Rufus. Furthermore, he did not become a wandering Cynic teacher in the eastern part of the empire until he was exiled from Italy by the Emperor Trajan. Epictetus follows a similar path. He was born sometime in the middle of the first century A.D. (*c*. 55) and likewise studied with Musonius and was banished by Domitian. One may argue that both of these teachers drew on earlier Cynic material, and doubtless that is true, but the problem is that often one can not be sure which material was already extant in the time when Jesus spoke, or when Mark or Q were put together. This sort of data has to be used with some caution. This is all the more necessary in the case of Lucian of Samosata who did not write before the middle of the second century A.D. and Diogenes Laertius who wrote in the third century A.D. at the earliest. This leaves the following sources. First and most importantly the Cynic Epistles which are pseudonymous letters ascribed to early Cynic teachers, such as Diogenes, and others such as Socrates. It can be argued that the letters come from a widespread range of dates from before the time of Jesus to well into the second century A.D.; however, H. C. Kee has recently stressed that these letters were not available to either Jesus or Paul, for they seem to have first come to light during the reign of Vespasian.[31] Second, the writings of Musonius Rufus. Musonius also postdates Jesus, but since he lived and wrote in the middle of the century, it is possible that his material could have influenced the Gospel tradition before its final composition. Third, Plutarch was a contemporary of Dio and no Cynic. For this reason as well as his dates the Cynic anecdotes he tells must be used critically and with caution. Fourth and finally there is Seneca, who though he was not properly speaking a Cynic, was nonetheless influenced by the Cynic philosopher Demetrius who lived in his household. Seneca was the spiritual adviser to Nero, and again it is not impossible that some of the material he presents could have influenced the Gospel tradition.

In what follows only some of the best examples that Downing can produce of parallels with the Gospel traditions will be considered. There is no attempt here to argue for or against the historicity of the Jesus material used at this juncture. Of course, if some of this material does *not* go back to Jesus, then

---

30 Downing, *Christ and the Cynics*, 192.

31 H. C. Kee, "Jewish Wisdom/Apocalyptic and Greco–Roman Stoicism," given at the SBL meeting (Kansas City, Nov. 1991). In this same lecture he offers the following relevant observations: (1) Jesus' aphorisms and Wisdom sayings (e.g., the Beatitudes) must be denuded of their specific and often eschatological content in order to compare them meaningfully with the timeless aphorisms of the Cynics; (2) it would be an exaggeration to speak of a Cynic school, as a wide variety of thinkers are usually lumped together under the label Cynic; and (3) by the third century Stoicism distanced itself from Cynicism (citing D. Dudley, *History of Cynicism*).

it does not support a Cynic-influenced Jesus. For the sake of argument the more difficult position, that the Jesus material Downing cites *may* go back to Jesus in some form, will be assumed, in order to give him the full ability to make his case. To an extent this case rests on the cumulative effect of finding many parallels. The problem is that in numerous cases the degree of similarity is very slight, or is tangential to the actual substance or point of, or even assumptions behind, a particular saying, or there is in fact a contrast with the Gospel tradition.

Even more troubling is the fact that Downing takes little or no time to assess Jesus' indebtedness to the Old Testament and other early Jewish Wisdom material, apart from that found in his near contemporaries Josephus and Philo. This is disappointing because at many points the aphorisms he cites from the Jesus tradition are closer to the material in Proverbs or the teachings of Qoheleth than they are to the teachings found in the Cynic Epistles or other Cynic sources. Downing, however, at least tries to deal with all the relevant Synoptic data.

As an example of a non-parallel between Jesus and the Cynics that Downing in fact takes to be a parallel one may point to the beginning of Downing's work where he cites for us a saying of Dio: "I visited as many countries as I could... sometimes among Greeks and sometimes among barbarians... arriving in the Peloponnese, I stayed away from the towns, passing my time in the countryside" (*Dio* 1.50).[32] Frankly, there is a distinct lack of evidence that either Jesus or his followers during his earthly ministry were similarly well traveled, or dealt with Greeks or barbarians to any significant degree. The examples of the Roman centurion, or the Syro-Phoenician woman are very rare exceptions, as were apparently Jesus' infrequent trips to either the Decapolis or for that matter even to Samaria. Otherwise Jesus seems always to be dealing with Jews in Galilee or Judea or occasionally perhaps Samaritans.

Furthermore, it is very likely a mistake to overdo the idea of a bucolic Jesus. It appears that his ministry focused on cities and villages around the Sea of Galilee and elsewhere. This is precisely why the absence of any reference of Jesus having visited Sepphoris or Tiberias is so important. Jesus, like the early Christians such as Paul who followed him later, seems by and large to have had an urban (as opposed to rural) strategy of ministry. It is true that Jesus' teaching, like Cynic teaching, seems to have been primarily directed towards the masses,[33] but this was true of other ancient teachers as well. The Pharisees seem to have been especially concerned with common people as well. A similar choice of audience by Jesus and the Cynics is no proof of influence because it is not a Cynic-specific trait.

---

32 Downing, *Christ and the Cynics*, 3.

33 Cf. Downing, *Jesus and the Threat of Freedom*, 61.

It is more interesting that apparently some Cynics taught in parables, but: (1) there are no examples of close parallels to the Gospel narrative *meshalim*; and (2) when Dio (55.9, 11, 22) cites Greeks who told parables he cites Socrates and Homer and Aesop who were hardly Cynics, whatever may be said about a person like Antisthenes who has been linked to Socrates (but cf. 72:13).[34] That some Cynics used figurative speech, sometimes drawing on the likes of a Socrates or an Aesop, is not unimportant, but the fact remains that there is no clear evidence that Jesus ever told fables, and what evidence there is in regard to Jesus' parables reveals a much closer affinity to early Jewish parables as shall be shown in the next chapter, than to anything from the Cynics. It is not enough to note a parallel, one must assess the degree of affinity.

As an example of a parallel that does not suggest influence one may cite Downing's discussion of *metanoia*. The Q material in Luke 3:8/Matt. 3:8 does indeed talk about a change of mind and life. Such discussions were not the special province of early Jews or early Cynics. Changing one's life and converting to a new religion or philosophy was a widespread phenomenon in antiquity as A. D. Nock long ago pointed out.[35] Thus, one must ask not merely whether Jesus or Dio or others talked about repentance and life transformation but how they talked about it. The question is, from what was a Jesus or a Dio trying to convert people and to what alternative end? In general, the Cynic material is primarily interested in promoting virtue and curing people of wickedness. Thus, for instance, Dio argues, "There are two ways to cure wickedness or prevent it... One resembles dieting and drugs, the other is like cautery and surgery.... The task that really needs doing is the gentler one, to be performed by people able to sooth and reduce a soul's fever by persuasion and reason" (*Dio* 32:17–18). In the Jesus tradition repentance/conversion is associated with either one or the other of two eschatological ideas – "the wrath to come" or the inbreaking Dominion of God (cf. Luke 3:8 and par. to Mark 1:15). Repentance and/or conversion is seen as preparation for these inbreaking events. Sometimes it is associated with accepting some sort of *euangelion*. By contrast, the Cynic material is dealing pragmatically with attempts to improve human conduct in general. The motivations, inducements, and benefits are very different in the various Cynic examples that Downing cites. There are to a certain extent parallel discussions of religious and ethical change in human lives and lifestyles, but the differences are such that no influence should be posited, especially in view of how widespread the phenomenon of repentance/conversion was in antiquity.

One may also suggest that in some cases, if there is any influence it runs from early Judaism to Cynic thought. Consider for example *Epictetus* 2.9.20: "When someone is convinced and has made their choice and been baptized, then they are a Jew in reality as well as in name. We are 'pseudo-baptists', like

[34] Cf. Downing, *Jesus and the Threat of Freedom*, 63–4.

[35] A. D. Nock, *Conversion*.

make believe Jews, out of tune with the reason we lay claim to, miles from using the things we talk about." There are other places in Epictetus where he discusses the behavior of Galileans in particular (4:7.5–6), and reflects knowledge of the Jewish practice of not eating pork (1:22.4). Clearly, Epictetus knows something about Jews, their practices, and specifically how they approach conversion to Judaism which entailed baptism.[36] In short in some cases the influence, if it exists at all, may run in the other direction.

Downing also points to disturbing symbolic actions as a parallel between the Jesus tradition and the Cynics (cf. *Epictetus* I.2.29, *LEP* 6.41 – Diogenes lighting a lamp at midday and going around saying he is looking for a real human being).[37] More interesting is the material in *Diogenes Laertius LEP* 6:64 where one hears of Diogenes, while dining in a temple, arguing that nothing unclean must come in the temple, or in 6:45 where he comments about thievery in the temple on the part of temple officials.[38] These attitudes about the moral integrity of sacred precincts of the divine were surely widely held in antiquity. Furthermore, symbolic actions are not a Cynic-specific trait. One can just as well argue that Jesus when he cleanses the temple or curses the fig tree is standing in the tradition of the Old Testament prophets (cf. Ezek. 4 and 12, Jer. 13). The Old Testament parallels are actually closer in various regards, not least because they often have to do with judgment on Jerusalem or its environs. One will have to look elsewhere for convincing parallels with the Cynic corpus.

There are some cases where there are parallel ideas, though expressed in different words, for example, Jesus' teaching about not judging (Matt. 7:1–2; Luke 6:37) and about the speck in the brother's eye and the plank in one's own (Matt 7:3–5; Luke 6:41–42). This may fruitfully be compared to what Seneca says: "And you, are you at liberty to examine other's wickednesses, and pass judgment on anyone...? You take note of other's pimples when you yourselves are a mass of sores.... It's like someone covered in foul scabs laughing at the odd mole or wart on someone of real beauty" (*De Vita Beata* 27:4).[39] Seneca

[36] Some classics scholars (e.g. W. A. Oldfather in the Loeb edition) have taken these references to Jews, and to Galileans in particular as references to Christians. Cf. *Epictetus I and II* (London: Heinemann, 1926 [Vol. 1] and 1928 [Vol. 2]), xxviff. in Vol. 1 and 362, n. 1 in Vol. 2. I think this is likely to be an error on two grounds: (1) Epictetus refers to the practice of not eating pork; and (2) early Jews most certainly did practice prosleyte baptism. Cf. A. F. Segal, "The Cost of Proselytism and Conversion," 336–69. Furthermore, the Baptist sect that lived on after John's death was another Jewish sect which had such practices. Oldfather may also be incorrect in too quickly ruling out the possibility of Jewish and/or Christian influence on Epictetus. Downing's argument (*Jesus and the Threat of Freedom*, 89) takes some odd turns not the least of which is when in the midst of arguing for Cynic influence on Jesus he says in passing "There is of course no sign in the Jesus tradition of any awareness of a wider Greek culture."

[37] Downing, *Jesus and the Threat of Freedom*, 13.

[38] Cf. Downing, *Jesus and the Threat of Freedom*, 108.

[39] Here and elsewhere in this section I am following Downing's translation (here *Christ and the Cynics*, 30) to allow him to make his case as strong as possible with his own translation. Normally I would offer my own or draw on one of the standard translations such as those in the Loeb editions.

could not have influenced Jesus, and it seems unlikely that the influence goes the other way, though that cannot be entirely ruled out, especially in view of the growing presence of Christians in Rome even in Seneca's day. It would seem unlikely that this Seneca material could have influenced the compilers of the Q material either, since they were very likely doing their work before Seneca made this observation. More likely, these parallels reveal two different examples of two astute observers of human nature complaining about the general tendency to be more judgmental of others than of oneself. The point is expressed or driven home by means of a colorful, or even comical example. One of the great problems in dealing with Wisdom material in general is that it so often comments on common or characteristic human behavior or repeated phenomena in nature that it is very difficult to assess when and to what degree there might be borrowing. Here then there is a somewhat striking parallel, but it is difficult to argue that it amounts to a case of influence.

More striking is the parallel between Luke 7:24–6/Matt. 11:7–8 and what we find in *Dio* 33:1,13–14:

> I wonder what on earth you came expecting or hoping for, looking for someone like me to speak to you. Did you come expecting me to have a nice voice, to be easier to listen to than other people...like a songbird?... So, whenever you see someone who begins by flattering himself on everything he does, and courting favor with his dinners and his dress..."

Again, Dio is too late to have influenced either Jesus or, in all likelihood, even the Q or Synoptic material. One may argue that Dio is drawing on earlier Cynic ideas but this is very difficult to prove since he does not say so, and since his sources aren't available to be checked. In such circumstances we can only render the judgment of *non liquet*.

More promising is the parallel between the Son of Man saying about having nowhere to lay one's head unlike foxes and birds (Luke 9:58/Matt. 8:20) and the saying found in Epictetus, "I've no property, no house, no wife, no children, not even a straw mattress..." (4.8.31). Possibly an earlier form of this lament is found in LEP 6.38: "No city, no house, no fatherland, a wandering beggar, living a day at a time." This is the lament of one who is peripatetic and takes no resources with him. These sorts of difficulties would be characteristic of those who were traveling teachers and preachers. There are some distinguishing points here, however. There is no evidence of Jesus begging, indeed there is evidence in Luke 8:1-3[40] that women provided support and perhaps provisions when Jesus and his disciples were traveling, and in other cases (cf. Luke 10:38–42) he relies on the system of standing hospitality. It is the factor of

---

[40] Cf. Witherington, "On the Road with Mary Magdalene, Joanna, Susanna, and other disciples: Luke 8:1–3,", 242–48.

homelessness that provides the real element of parallel here. Homelessness was not a Cynic-specific trait. The evidence suggests it was the common plight of traveling preachers in antiquity when they were journeying. There is no compelling proof of influence here.

Sometimes one find examples of a common sense deduction in variant forms in both the Jesus tradition and the Cynic material. For instance, Dio Chrysostom says at one point: "A good physician goes to be helpful where there's most sickness..." (8:5). This is reminiscent of the Q saying of Jesus found in Matt. 9:12/Luke 5:31: "Those who are well have no need of a physician, but those who are sick." The similarity is not so much at the level of verbal expression as in the realm of ideas. When one is dealing with common sense deductions based on the observation of human life, it is not surprising that in the Wisdom material of the Jesus tradition there are similarities with gnomic sayings outside that tradition. It is not impossible that there is a case of influence here in one direction or another, but it is equally plausible that these sayings were formulated as the result of two parallel and independent reflections on life. The small degree of verbal similarity suggests this latter conclusion.

From Epictetus there is a partial parallel to the Q teaching found in Matt. 7:7–11/ Luke 11:9–13. In one place he says: "Seek and you will find" (1.28.20). In another we hear: "The door has been opened" (1.24.19; 3.13.14). In yet a third place we hear: "Work it all out with more care, 'know thyself', look for supernatural help in your questioning, don't start on the Cynic way without God" (3.22.53). What is clear is that both the Jesus and the Cynic traditions called people to search for answers and meaning in life, and to do so by relying on God. One has to be measured in this conclusion because only some of the Cynics were monotheists. It is possible that Jesus may at some point have heard some early first century Cynic preacher from Gadara urge this sort of quest, making these kinds of statements. Epictetus cannot have influenced Jesus and probably not the Jesus tradition either, but it is significant that his Greek is some of the closest to the Greek one finds in the New Testament, and Epictetus was apparently well-traveled. It is possible then that he himself, in his search for answers, had contact both with early Jews and perhaps even with early Christians. Here is a case where the influence could go in either direction. We must count this example as showing a *possible* influence of the Cynic tradition on Jesus, *if* this material antedates Epictetus and was circulating at the turn of the era.

Another example of a fairly close parallel comes from Musonius who says: "Suppose I have lots of children, where am I going to get food for them all? Well where do the little birds go to get food from to feed their young, though they're much worse off than you are – the swallows and nightingales and larks and blackbirds...? Do they store food away in safekeeping?" (15). Those familiar with the Jesus tradition will immediately think of Matt. 6:25–33/Luke 12:22–31.

These are two similar sounding observations, based on close analysis of what happens in the natural world. In both cases the sayings are attempting to combat anxiety about the ability to provide the necessities of life. Again one must say that such anxieties, and also such observations which urge one to learn from what is the case with lower life forms are common, especially in ancient Wisdom traditions. There are similar sorts of exhortations to learn from nature in Proverbs (e.g., 6.6).

In the case of the Cynic material there seems to be a different motivation for such an exhortation. The Cynic wants individuals to act according to nature, not according to custom, and act in such a way that they can be free of entanglements that prevent them from manifesting *autarkeia*. Jesus by contrast is urging God dependency. Thus, while there is here a significant cross over in the ideas expressed, and even in how they are expressed, the motivation and aims of such teaching seem to be rather different in each case. There *may* be a case of influence here, though not of Musonius on Jesus. Possibly the Q material was influenced by this Cynic material, but even that is uncertain, for it depends on how early the Q material was in a rather fixed form.

The next parallel at first sight seems more important than it in fact is. Epictetus remarks: "If you want to be crucified, just wait. The cross will come. If it seems reasonable to comply, and the circumstances are right, then its to be carried through and your integrity maintained" (2.2.20). This may be compared most fruitfully with Matt. 10:38/Luke 14:27: "and he who does not take up his cross and follow me is not worthy of me." In the latter saying the cross is used metaphorically to refer to the cost of discipleship. It looks like Epictetus is talking not simply about being a disciple, but martyrdom in particular, and about not provoking one's judges. His advice is not to seek crucifixion. If it comes, one should accept it if it's necessary to do so to maintain one's integrity. Crucifixions were not rare in the first century A.D. and it is hardly surprising that various people might see it as the 'extreme penalty' which someone might have to pay for something believed, said, or done. The difference in the way the cross is referred to in each saying makes it probable that they originated independently.

On occasion it seems that Jesus and the Cynics are at opposite ends of the spectrum in regard to disciples. Dio on the one hand says: "If someone starts following you, claiming to be your disciple, you must drive him away with your fists and clods of earth and stone: he's either a fool or a knave" (35.10). By contrast Jesus not only seeks out disciples but tells them he is going to teach them how to fish for human beings.[41] While the Cynics had disciples or followers, they apparently in most cases did not seek them out or encourage them, perhaps in part due to their teaching about *autarkeia*.[42]

---

[41] Cf. Witherington, *Christology*, 126–29.

[42] Downing, *Jesus and the Threat of Freedom*, 120 admits this issue is debated. There is an alternative tradition (cf. *Pseudo Diogenes* 9–38) which may suggest that at least Diogenes sought followers, and Epictetus seems to suggest one does not make oneself a disciple (3.3). However, this stands in contrast to what Dio (12.13, 35.10) clearly says and it contrasts with the data in LEP 6.21 and 87.96–97 as well.

Jesus and the Cynics seem to have shared similar disgust for those who parade their piety or beliefs in public for the sake of public recognition. Seneca remarks: "People who want their moral virtue advertised are not interested in virtue, but advertisement" (*EM* 113.32). Epictetus offers the following satirical comment: " 'Why do you walk around among us as though you had swallowed a roasting-spit?' 'I've been wanting everyone who met me to admire me, and follow me as I walk saying loudly, This is our great philosopher!'" (3.12.16).[43] This material bears some resemblance to what we find in Matt. 6:1–3, 5, 16–17. Deflating pomposity or hypocrisy is not a Cynic-specific trait. In non-biblical writers one may think of the satire of Lucian, but there are plenty of biblical writers who had no time for "the display of religion". What this shows is that both Jesus and the Cynics were indeed looking for earnestness, honesty, and perhaps also a proper sense of *humilitas* in human beings.

In Matt. 11:28–30 there is the familiar teaching about coming unto Jesus who will relieve them of their heavy burdens and in exchange offer a light yoke. This may be compared to what Epictetus says at 4.8.28–29.[44] However, Epictetus is ridiculing anyone who says: "Come unto me, anyone whose head is aching, who's got a fever, or who's lame, or blind, and see how healthy I am, nothing's wrong with me at all!" To this Epictetus replies: "That's a useless and insensitive thing to do – unless... you are someone like Asclepius, and can show them there and then how they can be restored there and then to good health..." The Jesus saying does not seem to be about matters of physical health,[45] but it looks from this saying as if Epictetus would have been skeptical about Jesus if he had made claims to heal people. Perhaps he had seen too many charlatans posing as miracle workers. In any event, this material is too late to have influenced Jesus and in view of its attitude probably didn't influence the Gospel tradition of Matthew either.

The parable of the sower in Mark 4 (and par). needs no rehearsing, but a similar saying from Seneca bears repeating at this point: "Divine seeds are sown in our human bodies. If a good farmer receives them, they spring up like the parent stock, and as good. But if the farmer's a bad one, and provides only barren or waterlogged ground, he kills off the divine seeds and raises only weeds, instead of any fruitful plants" (*EM* 73.16). In both cases a comparison or analogy is being drawn with the sowing of seeds. In the saying by Seneca he is apparently not talking about missionary work, but the reaction to planting

---

[43] Here and elsewhere one may take issue with Downing's translation. If one looks at the Loeb edition of this same passage 3.12.16 a more literal and correct rendering is offered (cf. *Epictetus II*, 86–87). I would render the relevant text, "but if they tend toward display, they are characteristic of a person who has turned toward the outside world, and is hunting for something other than the thing itself which he is doing, and is seeking those saying 'O what a great human being.'" A similar problem arises with Downing's rendering of 3.22.81 for the Greek does not include the word only; it reads *ei me gamesei e paidopoiesetai*, "if he will never marry or have children" (cf. *Epictetus II* 158–9).

[44] Cf. Downing, *Christ and the Cynics*, 99.

[45] Cf. below pp. 205ff.

and activity of the divine in humankind. The parable of the sower, by contrast seems to have originally been Jesus' comment on the response to his preaching and ministry, and in its present setting is very likely used to comment on what reactions disciples can expect to their own missionary endeavors. Again, Seneca is too late to have influenced Jesus, and while it is possible he might have influenced the author of the Gospel of Mark, the sayings and the purposes they serve are different enough to leave room for significant doubt on this point. Agricultural metaphors or analogies are rather common in Wisdom literature in any case.

Counterbalancing the parallels are the notable contrasts between the Cynic material and the Jesus traditions. For example Dio says: "How one can consider any supernatural power [daimon] evil, I just cannot say. But then, if you philosophers accept that a daimon is in fact divine, you've made any such adverse judgment quite impossible" (23.9). Elsewhere he adds: "the good and bad daimons do not come from outside us. Each person's mind is the 'daimon' that each one has" (4.80).[46] On the one hand Dio seems to deny the reality of the possibility of supernatural evil. If it is divine it must be good, seems to be his conclusion. On the other hand, he associates the human mind with the divine, and says that it is the source of one's daimons, whether good or evil. This certainly contrasts with the material both in Q and in Mark which suggests that Jesus believed in supernatural evil, including demons, that he practiced exorcism, and that he did not believe that such problems were simply a matter of some sort of mental illness or natural human affliction.

Another point in which there is an important contrast between the Jesus tradition and some Cynic teaching is on the issue of marriage. As I have argued,[47] Jesus affirms both the married and the single state for disciples, but he also warns that if there is division over being his disciple, then discipleship must take priority over family obligations. By contrast one may point to the following three sayings from the Cynic tradition. In the first Diogenes is giving his response as to when is the right age to get married. He says: "For young men, not yet, and for old men, never at all" (LEP 6.54). Similarly in *Pseudo-Diogenes* 47 one hears: "We should neither marry nor raise children. We're a sickly lot, and marriage and children weigh down this sickly humanity of ours with troubles." Finally, Epictetus says: "Only a Cynic will never marry or have children" (3.22.81). This attitude stands basically in contrast to various important pericopes in the Jesus tradition. It is a serious mistake to assume that Paul or other early Christians were anti-marriage either.[48] They did, however, appreciate and affirm the validity of remaining single, especially for the sake of one's religious service. The Cynic movement was by no means united on the issue of marriage, however. Musonius Rufus remarks on one occasion:

[46] Cf. Downing, *Christ and the Cynics*, 68.
[47] Cf. Witherington, *Women in the Ministry of Jesus*, 18–35.
[48] Cf. Witherington, *Women in the Earliest Churches*, 24ff.

> What was the Creator's purpose in originally dividing our human race in two and providing us with our respective genital organs, so we are male and female and then in building in a strong desire to share sexual union with each other, mixed with a deep yearning for each other's company...? Isn't it quite clear that he meant them to come together as a single unit, to live together, and to work hard to share a common livelihood together, and to procreate children and bring them up–and so perpetuate our human race?[49]

This teaching may fruitfully be compared to Mark 10:1–9 (and par). Jesus' teaching is clearly derived from Genesis, while Musonius' teaching would seem to be based on his own deductions from reflecting on the two genders of the human race and their behavior towards each other. What this parallel shows is that there were areas of ideas and teachings where the Jesus tradition and *some* Cynic material sounded similar. This may have led some in the second two thirds of the first century A.D. who heard Christian preaching or teaching to associate it with what they had heard from the Cynics. *Some* Christian teaching may well have sounded to some Gentiles like some of the Cynic teaching with which they were familiar. In the example cited above one cannot talk about influence of the Cynic tradition on Jesus, though some such influence on the writer of Mark's Gospel cannot be categorically ruled out. If he was in Rome he may have heard Musonius at some point. Again, however, the teaching is different enough and the Markan teaching so clearly built upon ideas in Genesis that one may say that there was probably no influence of Cynic teaching on the Gospel tradition at this point.[50]

A stronger case for some sort of relationship between Cynic teaching and the Jesus tradition can be made when one compares Mark 10:17–26 and the important parallel in *Epictetus* 2:14. 14,18–24 which reads in part:

> "Where then" asked the would-be student of philosophy, "...should I start?" "...You have come here to me like a man who thinks he has no real need. What could anyone possibly imagine you lacked? You're rich, you have children, even a wife still, lots of slaves, Caesar knows you, friends in Rome, you perform all recognized duties... What do you still lack? You don't know about God, you don't know about being human, you don't know about good or evil... But if I go on to tell you you don't understand your own self, how will you put up with me and my questions then? Will you stay? Not a chance! You'll go off at once...you whose concern is with property..."[51]

---

49 Musonius Rufus, *Discourse* 14.

50 On this Markan material and its grounding in Genesis cf. Witherington, *Women in the Ministry of Jesus*, 25ff.

51 Downing, *Christ and the Cynics*, viii. One may wish to compare the more detailed treatment of some aspects of the Jesus tradition in Downing, *Jesus and the Threat of Freedom*, 126–60.

In general there is a certain similarity between the teaching found in the Jesus tradition on riches and that found in passages like this one. Both sets of traditions see wealth as a hindrance or even an obstacle to pursuit of true religion, or in the case of Cynicism, true philosophy. What makes this passage even more significant is that it deals with the rather brusque exchange between a teacher and a prospective disciple who is wealthy, as does Mark 10:17–26. Note, however, that the actual response to the wealthy person differs in important ways. Jesus urges the wealthy person to do the one thing he has failed to do – sell all his possessions and come and follow Jesus. Epictetus' story, by contrast, simply states that the teacher spoke to the student in a dismissive way, saying in effect that he would never endure all his teaching. He did not give him something to do, and beckon him to come and follow thereafter.

Thus there is a parallel in views about wealth and how it can be an obstacle, but there is no parallel in the attitude towards the disciple. The Jesus tradition is not dismissive or sarcastic in the way that the story in Epictetus is. These two stories illustrate the fact that Jesus took a more positive attitude toward recruiting or keeping disciples than the Cynics often did. Here again there is no question of Epictetus having influenced Jesus or, in view of his dates, probably even the Markan tradition. This may be another case, however, where an outsider who was neither Cynic nor Christian might observe certain similarities in the two movements and their characteristic attitudes about things like wealth.

This sort of similarity in the two movements is further illustrated if one compares the parable of the rich fool found in Luke 12:16–20 and the words of Dio: "You fool! Even if everything turns out right, what assurance have you that you'll live to see tomorrow, and not be torn away from all the good things you expect to enjoy?" (16.8). Here the point of comparison is in regard to the contingency of life and the folly of relying on one's material goods to secure one's future. Clearly, there is a strikingly parallel attitude in the two traditions. While one cannot argue for the influence of Dio on Jesus or probably even on Luke, it is possible that if Dio is simply reflecting an earlier Cynic teaching there *may* have been some cross fertilization, possibly even at the stage of the *Sitz im Leben Jesu*.

One cannot, however, be at all sure of this since there is no apparent evidence that this teaching or something very much like it was either extant as early as Jesus, or was circulating perhaps from Gadara at that time. It may be, again, that the attitudes of both the Cynic and Jesus arose from independent reflection on life. There is the further point that if Jesus was influenced by the Old Testament Wisdom material, such as is found in Qoheleth, this in itself might explain the source of the ideas that appear in the Lukan parable, without any need to posit Cynic influence on Jesus (cf. Eccles. 5:13ff).

There is another, larger, more disturbing issue that arises not so much in the work of Downing, who accepts that there is a significant body of non-Cynic material in the Jesus tradition,[52] but in the work of B. Mack and others who follow his lead. In order to come up with a truly Cynic Jesus one must argue that basically Jesus said nothing on matters eschatological such as the Dominion of God, or else he meant something non-eschatological or non-apocalyptic by it. One must also argue that Jesus said nothing about the Danielic Son of Man and never drew on such apocalyptic traditions. In addition, one must deny that the miracle tradition about Jesus in any sense goes back to a *Sitz im Leben Jesu*, since the working of miracles is not a characteristic of those who took up the mantle of the Cynics. Further, one must also dispute or deny that Jesus engaged in disputes about the meaning of the Old Testament, or other uniquely Jewish phenomena such as the rules about Corban. Finally, one must deny any sort of discussion about messianic or Christological matters. In short, one must explain away a huge amount of the Synoptic Jesus material, and this includes many many traditions which pass even the most stringent tests of the criteria for authenticity.[53]

Consider, for example how Mack argues: "According to a recent listing of the authentic sayings of Jesus (not including parables), however, there are only three sayings among them that contain a reference to the kingdom of God (Luke 11:20; 17:20–21; Matt. 11:12)."[54] This list has been provided by scholars who seem already predisposed to deny any sort of eschatological dimension to Jesus' teaching, if it does not amount to some sort of realized eschatology, and as Mack admits it totally neglects the material in the parables. Mack goes on to argue: "One seeks in vain a direct engagement of specifically Jewish concerns. Neither is Jesus' critique directed specifically toward Jewish institutions, nor do his recommendations draw upon obviously Jewish concepts and authorities."[55] To draw this conclusion, Mack has to dismiss, without any real argument, such Synoptic material as Jesus' discussions about Corban, marriage, Levirate marriage, Messiah, clean and unclean, fasting, gleaning on the sabbath, any sort of critique of the temple, any sort of discussion about the messianic banquet, any sort of use of the Abraham traditions, and any sort of discussion about the twelve tribes of Israel and their future, to give but a few examples.

Frankly, this sort of heavy-handed and cavalier dismissal of the Jewish aspects of the Jesus tradition in favor of another hypothesis, which is only supported by a *certain interpretation* of a distinct minority of the possible data from or about Jesus comes across as transparently tendentious. Doubtless it is possible to come up with almost any sort of Jesus provided one's list of critically accepted *logia* is sufficiently small. By contrast, Downing's work is refreshing

---

52 As Downing (*Christ and the Cynics*, 36) rightly admits.

53 This same sort of complaint must now be registered against Crossan's pretentiously titled work *The Historical Jesus*.

54 Mack, *A Myth of Innocence*, 72 following here N. Perrin and D. Duling.

55 Mack, *A Myth of Innocence*, 73.

in his agreement that not all the data fits the picture of a Cynic Jesus, and that perhaps at most one can argue for some Cynic influence on *some* of Jesus' teaching. It is this latter hypothesis that deserves the sort of serious examination to which it has been subjected in this chapter.

A further and more telling critique of Mack's *A Myth of Innocence* has now been offered by J. A. Overman, a social historian who knows the archeological and historical situation of early first century Palestine. The following summarizes several of his main points. First, the selection of what amounts to authentic Jesus material "frequently seems arbitrary" relying largely as it does on a few of the Q Wisdom sayings, to the neglect of the eschatological material even in Q. Second, the aphoristic material in Q is simply assumed, without sufficient argument, to be the earliest layer of Q. Overman rightly asks, "Why is Q the bench mark against which all other recitals of the Jesus story are measured? Why are the Pauline traditions or other early Gospel traditions not given a similar place...?" Overman is very likely right that the answer is, Because Mack simply prefers the Greek philosophical tradition to the traditions of Israel. Third, is it really plausible that Meleager and the Hebrew Scriptures would have had equal influence on Jesus? Fourth, Mack's argument seems most peculiar. On the one hand he wants to argue for a thoroughly Hellenized Palestine. On the other hand, he wants to argue that Mark's myth of origins about a dying and rising saviour could only has arisen in Hellenistic Christ cults outside of Palestine, namely in northern Syria and beyond. As Overman says, "[m]ost of the influences and notions Mack associates with 'Hellenistic' groups could easily have been part of the social experience of the first followers of Jesus." Fifth, Mack's treatment involves a too ready dismissal of the Pauline evidence, in part so that the author can argue that Mark imposes an eschatological framework on the myth of origins about the dying and rising savior.[56] The Pauline evidence suggests, to the contrary, that an eschatological outlook characterized the Jesus movement and the Christian community that arose out of it (cf. 1 Thessalonians). Finally, Overman suggests rightly that the image Mack comes up with of Jesus is in fact a reflection of himself: "There is something disturbingly familiar about a mildly reforming, sagacious teacher, who is gifted at repartee, only utters things of this world, and does not use language and imagery that promises the reversal of the rulers of the world."[57] This process of re-creating Jesus in one's own image happens all too often when one works with an overly truncated corpus of Jesus' sayings.

Jesus was a much more complex figure than one sometimes imagines. That he often cast his teaching in Wisdom forms does not mean he always did so. It is the purpose of this study to show that *one crucial dimension*, perhaps the

[56] Mack like others also uses the term apocalyptic when in fact eschatological would have been appropriate. Cf. Witherington, *Jesus, Paul, and the End of the World*, Chapter 1.

[57] This and the above quotes come from A. Overman's helpful review "Deciphering the Origins of Christianity" 193–95.

most comprehensive dimension of Jesus' teaching, is the Wisdom dimension, and that therefore the best overall categorization of the man is that he was a sage. This is not to be seen as necessarily in competition with the other dimensions already explored in *The Christology of Jesus*. The real challenge is to imagine a Jesus complex enough that room is made for all the dimensions of who he was, what he said, and the way he acted, as it is revealed in that material from the Gospels that is arguably authentic.

In a lengthy monograph, J. D. Crossan argues that Jesus should be seen as "a peasant Jewish Cynic."[58] But one must ask how convincing this characterization really is when Crossan has to make qualifications like: "Greco–Roman Cynics, however, concentrated primarily on the marketplace rather than the farm, on the city dweller rather than the peasant. And they showed little sense of collective discipline, on the one hand or of communal action, on the other. Jesus and his followers do not fit well against *that* background."[59] In fact, in the end he says, "We are forced, then, by the primary stratum itself, to bring together two disparate elements: healer and Cynic..."[60]

But it is neither necessary nor sufficient to call Jesus a Cynic at all. On the one hand the influence of the Cynic tradition on his teaching does not seem to have been pervasive or profound. On the other hand, most of the alleged parallels with the Cynic tradition are better explained in light of the Jewish sapiential material. Too much of the arguably authentic Jesus tradition falls outside both the characterization healer/magician and the characterization "Cynic" for Crossan's argument to be persuasive, and some of the Cynic tradition positively clashes with the Jesus tradition. In the end, like the arguments of Mack, Crossan's presentation seems to be another over-reaction to the old Schweitzerian apocalyptic seer model of characterizing Jesus.

NON-CYNICAL CONCLUSIONS

A WANDERING CYNIC WAS NOT HIS FATHER

Having now come to the end of our survey of the parallels between the Jesus tradition and the Cynic material, some conclusions are in order. First, almost all the closer parallels that have been cited come from either Musonius Rufus, Epictetus, Seneca, or Dio. The Cynic Epistles provide a distinct minority of the relevant data. This is a significant fact and it means that it is simply not possible to come up with a Cynic Jesus, on the basis of such data. The problem of anachronism is a serious one and should not be lightly dismissed. It may be that

58 Crossan, *Historical Jesus*, 265ff.

59 Crossan, *Historical Jesus*, 421.

60 Ibid.

the ideas expressed by Dio or Epictetus or Musonius have a long pedigree, but this must be shown to be likely and not simply assumed. Otherwise one's case is based on an argument from silence. Secondly, even in the closest parallels there is no question of actually copying phrases or whole sentences. The parallels are at the level of ideas, where they exist at all. Thirdly, some traits which do seem to characterize the Cynic movement are nonetheless not Cynic specific traits. The example of the garb of the Cynics and what they carried with them is a case in point. There were other peripatetic teachers besides the Cynics in antiquity who took staffs, wore some kind of cloak and traveled light. This sort of parallel with the Jesus tradition really proves nothing.

In regard to more positive conclusions, one must allow that it is *possible* that at some points the Jesus tradition may have been affected by Cynic ideas. It is more likely that this happened while Q or Mark or Luke were being put together[61] than during the ministry of Jesus, but the possibility of influence on even Jesus cannot be *entirely* ruled out, especially due to the proximity of Jesus' ministry to places like Gadara, and the fact that his was a peripatetic ministry, and no doubt he was exposed to a variety of people in his travels. It is also possible that some of the wandering Cynics were influenced by traditions originating in early Judaism, and perhaps even in early Christianity (in the case of the later Cynics). Data in Epictetus may suggest that the influence might have gone in the opposite direction to that which Downing, Mack and Crossan would lead one to think. This is not to deny that the parallels cited above, especially the more striking ones, may have led some first century observers who were not *fully* informed about either the Cynic or Jesus traditions to wonder if the Jesus material was a form of Cynic teaching or had been influenced by Cynicism. Finally, even if Jesus was influenced by some Cynic ideas and attitudes and practices, the influence seems to have been *slight* in comparison to the profound impact that the Jewish Wisdom material had on both the style and substance of his teaching. In the end it may be that the only significant impact Hellenistic ideas had on Jesus was through the medium of the Jewish wisdom material on which he drew, which was already partially Hellenized, especially in the case of the material from Qoheleth, Ben Sira, and the Wisdom of Solomon. It will be worthwhile to conclude this section of discussion with a quote from B. B. Scott:

> Besides the obvious problems with wonder-working and eschatology, there are even more substantial grounds against a Cynic interpretation of Jesus. The primary *forms* of the synoptic and Thomas traditions are forms closely identified with the Jewish wisdom tradition....While short narratives have been found in Hellenistic literature, the parable is a form limited to the Jesus tradition and the

---

[61] On the influence of Hellenism on early Judaism and Christianity cf. W. Jaeger, *Early Christianity and Greek Paideia*, 6ff. and 107 n.7.

> rabbinic tradition. The clearest formal parallels to the Jesus parables are still the rabbinic parables. Second the *content* of these forms is Jewish. The debate issues are Jewish in their interest and background.[62]

This is so, and some of the aphorisms and narrative *meshalim* will be explored in the next chapter. The energy spent comparing the Jesus tradition to the Cynic tradition might have been better spent comparing the Jesus tradition to any of the Wisdom books in the Hebrew Scriptures, or perhaps even more tellingly with Ben Sira's book, as the following cursory examination shows.

FROM JESUS TO JESUS

There are some important parallels in both form and content between the Wisdom of Ben Sira and the Jesus tradition. The following highlights a few of these.
Sir. 11:18–19: "One becomes rich through diligence and self denial, and the reward allotted him is this: when he says 'I have found rest, and now I shall feast on my goods!' He does not know how long it will be until he leaves them to others and dies."

Luke 12:13–21, especially vv 18-20: "And [the rich man] said 'I will do this: I will pull down my barns, and build larger ones; and there I will store all my grain and my goods. And I will say to myself, Self you have ample goods laid up for many years; take your ease, eat drink, be merry.' But God said to him 'Fool! This night your life is required of you; and the things you have prepared, whose will they be?' So is he who lays up treasure for himself, and is not rich toward God."

Various of the speeches of or about personified Wisdom are relevant.
Sir. 24:19: "Come to me, you who desire me, and eat your fill of my fruits."

Sir. 6:19–31: "Come to her like one who plows and sows. Put your neck into her collar. Bend your shoulders and carry her…Come unto her with all your soul, and keep her ways with all your might.… For at last you will find the rest she gives...Then her fetters will become for you a strong defense, and her collar a glorious robe. Her yoke is a golden ornament…" (cf. Sir. 51.26).

Matt. 11:29-30: "Take my yoke upon you, and learn from me; for I am gentle and lowly in heart and you will find rest for your souls. For my yoke is easy and my burden is light."

---

[62] B. B. Scott, "Jesus as Sage: an Innovating Voice in Common Wisdom," in *The Sage in Israel*, 401.

Sir. 23:9: "Do not accustom your mouth to oaths, nor habitually utter the name of the Holy One."

Matt. 5.34: "But I say to you, Do not swear at all, either by heaven, for it is the throne of God, or by earth for it is his footstool..."

Sir. 28:3–4: "Does anyone harbor anger against another, and expect healing from the Lord? If one has no mercy toward another like himself, can he then seek pardon for his own sins?"

Mt. 5.22: "....everyone that is angry with his brother, shall be liable to judgment... whoever says 'you fool' shall be liable to the Gehenna of fire."

Sir. 29.11: "Lay up your treasure according to the commandments of the Most High, and it will profit you more than gold. Store up almsgiving in your treasury, and it will rescue you from every disaster."

Matt. 6.19: "Do not lay up for yourselves treasures on earth, where moth and rust consume... but lay up for yourselves treasure in heaven."

Sir. 32.1: "If they make you master of the feast, do not exalt yourself; be among them as one of their number."

Luke 22.26-27: "For which is greater, one who sits at table, or one who serves? But I am among you as one who serves."

Sir. 36.31: "So who will trust a man that has no nest, but lodges wherever night overtakes him?"

Luke 9:58: "Foxes have holes and birds of the air have nests; but the Son of man has nowhere to lay his head."

The beatitudes in Q (Matt. 5:1; Luke 6:20ff.) should also be compared to the form of Ben Sira's beatitudes, not only in Sir. 25:7–10 but consider the form of Sir. 31:8: "Blessed is the rich person who is found blameless, and who does not go after gold."

There are a great many more passages and themes that could be compared, but by now one has got the sense that there are some substantial parallels both in form and content between Ben Sira and the Jesus tradition that warrant further exploration, even though Ben Sira is not being directly quoted in the Jesus tradition. Often, in form, content, and intent these parallels are closer than the vast majority of those cited from the Cynic tradition. In part this is because Jesus, like Ben Sira was a Jewish sage who drew on the substantial and shared resources of the Jewish Wisdom tradition, but it may also suggest that the Jesus tradition, if not Jesus himself, drew on the riches found specifically in the Wisdom of Ben Sira. If so, then the differences are at least as important as the similarities, for at Matt. 11:29 it is Jesus, not Torah, that is identified or associated with the personification of Wisdom. But it is time to explore the aphorisms and narrative *meshalim* of Jesus the sage and the idea of Jesus as Wisdom.

4

Wisdom in Person: Jesus the Sage

WISDOM had traveled far and encountered many things along the way by A.D. 30. She had even visited foreign lands and had collected sayings and ideas from other cultures and religions. What new things would she say or do with her people chafing under the yoke of Roman rule in their own land for many years now? How could she minister to a people in pain with no evident signs of improvement on the horizon? Would Wisdom react to or interact with the world view of the rulers of the land or perhaps engage in some of both? In this chapter we intend to examine some of the Jesus tradition that reveals something about Jesus the sage's approach to life lived in Israel under the reign of the likes of Tiberius or, more locally, Herod Antipas. This will entail a study of some of his aphorisms of counter order, his narrative *meshalim*, and finally an examination of some of the evidence that Jesus presented himself as Wisdom in person. In order to make sense of some of this material, especially the narrative *meshalim*, in the light of the modern scholarly discussion, it will first be necessary to discuss briefly a theory of language and meaning. This is crucial in order to avoid imposing one's own epistemology and semantic theories on the relevant data, for the problem of anachronism is a serious one when one is dealing with Wisdom material.

THE NARRATIVE *MESHALIM* AND A THEORY OF LANGUAGE

THE CHARACTER OF COMMUNICATION

Whenever one is dealing with something as malleable and as variable as the narrative *meshalim* in particular but also with aphorisms, it is important to be clear about one's theory of language at the outset. In fact, it is just about impossible to be involved in the modern discussion of parables without also dealing with language theory. This issue comes into play especially in the case of parables because they are a form of narrative fiction. Clarity is necessary especially in parable interpretation because several schools of thought, in particular deconstructionism, poststructuralism, and also reader-response criticism, have raised serious questions about the traditional notion of authorial intention and its importance to interpretation, as well as the issue of whether or not language is referential .

In regard to the latter issue, J. D. Crossan has argued that language is essentially arbitrary, plurivalent, non-referential, with no particular meaning at its core.[1] In fact, Crossan contradicts himself on this very issue for in the same context he is willing to speak of Jesus' speech as directed toward a particular audience for the purposes of communication and persuasion.[2] As A. N. Wilder says, "The demands of intelligibility alone would have ruled out sheer enigma in his utterance, or total discontinuity with the language heritage of his auditor...the novelty of the Gospel could not mean a total subversion of the language of the past."[3]

More to the point, a purely non-referential view of language is inherently self-defeating. If the claim were true that language is inherently non-referential or at least that it can have no *particular* reference, one could not know it to be true since the words used to make this point would necessarily not be referential or at least would not have a clear and succinct meaning. One would not be able to talk about what the author meant by such words since the issues of reference and *particular* meaning are ruled out in advance. Thus, while it is true that in some cases Jesus' parables do involve paradox, and even subversion of conventional ideas and attitudes, this does not necessitate denying the normal assessment that, "Jesus' tales... 'said' and 'meant' what could only have had a distinctive and particular purport and were thus neither paradoxical in the sense of excluding understanding, nor open to gratuitous free play of signification."[4] Putting it slightly differently, "one does not have to accept the extreme position of some post-structuralists, that the text is an empty space made meaningful only by the act of reading, to grant that the process of reading is indeed a creative endeavor."[5]

---

[1] One may wish to consult especially Crossan's critique of A. N. Wilder in his *A Fragile Craft: The Work of Amos N. Wilder*. But cf. also his *Cliffs of Fall: Paradox and Polylvalence in the Parables of Jesus*. It does seem that he has backed off somewhat from his earlier stance on polyvalency; cf. Crossan, *The Historical Jesus*, xxvii–xxxiv.

[2] Cf. for instance the chapter in Crossan, *Cliffs of Fall*, on "Parable and Metaphor."

[3] A. N. Wilder, *The Bible and the Literary Critic*, 132.

[4] Wilder, *The Bible and the Literary Critic*, 130. B. B. Scott, *Hear Then the Parable. A Commentary on the Parables of Jesus*, 61, n. 232 is quite right to reject Crossan's idea that paradox is a *sine qua non* in Jesus' parables. Jesus does use paradox and reversal on various occasions in the parables, but this is not always so.

[5] M. A. Tolbert, *Sowing the Gospel*, 8. For a helpful overview of the more audience–oriented forms of literary criticism, cf. F. Lentricchia, *After the New Criticism*. Lentricchia also presents the various views about the matter of validity in interpretation (257–80).

At times it appears that the fact that a parable could be recycled or reapplied to a different situation by later tradents is being confused with the idea of polyvalency. For instance, B. B. Scott attempts to argue for the inherent polyvalency of certain rabbinic parables by demonstrating how in one context a particular rabbinic parable could be commenting on the impenetrable nature of the king of kings but in another it is used to allude to the impenetrable nature of the foundations of the universe.[6]

This is to confuse questions about the *nature* of a parable with questions about its various *applications*. It is perfectly plausible that a sage created a parable with a particular meaning in mind and also a particular application, but later it was adapted and adopted to serve another and different meaning and context. Indeed H. K. McArthur and R. M. Johnston have shown how recycling was a regular practice in the case of early Jewish parables.[7] Thus, it should surprise no one to find such a practice happening in the Gospels as well, since Jesus' parables initially arose out of basically the same milieu.

Further problems are caused by the attempt to define parable as metaphor using various modern notions of what amounts to a metaphor and how it functions. In the end this is an anachronistic enterprise for it does not take account of ancient perspectives on metaphor such as Aristotle's view that in a metaphor a single aspect of A is related to a single aspect of B (cf. *Art of Rhetoric* 2.20ff.).[8] Furthermore, it also fails to comport with the way metaphors are used in early Jewish and Jewish Christian literature where *tertia comparationis* are an issue.[9]

Sometimes a purely modern literary approach to the parables can even *in extremis* lead to the treating of a whole Gospel as a giant metaphor or at least a narrative *mashal*.[10] Consider for example Scott's conclusion: "The Gospels, as fictional redescriptions of the kingdom, are faithful to the parables' original hermeneutical horizon, and thus it is proper to state paradoxically that the parables generate the Gospels – they generate their own context."[11] Scott's view, relying as it does on P. Ricoeur's theories about hermeneutics, leads to the argument that the original handlers of Jesus' parables basically mishandled and distorted them.[12] This in turn supposedly provides the justification for taking the parables out of their historical matrix, so that they may be seen as something entirely different from the *meshalim* we find both in the Old

[6] Scott, *Hear Then the Parable*, 54.

[7] H. K. McArthur and R. M. Johnston, *They Also Taught in Parables*, 156ff.

[8] Cf. the analysis by G. Lakeoff and M. Johnson, *Metaphors We Live By*, 110ff.

[9] Cf. C. Westermann, *The Parables of Jesus in the Light of the Old Testament*.

[10] Mack, *A Myth of Innocence*, comes perilously close to this extreme. His actual position seems to be that the Gospel of Mark can be treated *essentially* as a work of narrative fiction, and thus treated like one would treat a *narrative mashal*.

[11] Scott, *Hear Then the Parable*, 55–56.

[12] Cf. Ricoeur, "Biblical Hermeneutics," 29–148, here 106: "The insertion of the parable into the Gospel–form is . . . the beginning of its misunderstanding. This is why we must interpret the parables both *with the help of and against the distortions* provided by the ultimate context."

Testament and in early rabbinic literature. It is true that Scott somewhat inconsistently draws back from the radical form of this approach to Jesus' *meshalim*, seeking to give some due to considerations about historical context and *Sitz im Leben*, but this should not cause one to ignore that his basic approach is one which involves the proposition: "The fictive, narrative quality of parable bestows on it an independence of its immediate *Sitz im Leben*: as narrative *with open meaning*, parable can be used in a variety of situations.... Situational meaning is the particular meaning that a given real hearer or reader *imparts* to the text depending on his or her situation and context."[13] This is a methodology that is an open invitation to remake the text in one's own image, and cause it to say whatever one would like it to say.

FALLACIES ABOUT AUTHORIAL INTENT

In regard to the matter of intentionality, while the theories of E. D. Hirsch and others are not without some difficulties and limitations, nevertheless the spectre of "the intentional fallacy" should not be allowed to distract one from affirming in principle the importance of seeking out an author's meaning.[14] Some practioners of reader-response criticism have acted as if texts are little more than literary ink blots into which one may read whatever meaning one sees there or finds viable.[15] For instance, S. Brown has argued that "meaning exists formally only in human beings. In the case of a human being who is also a reader, meaning is generated by a reader reading a text... rather than residing in the text...."[16]

Unfortunately such an approach, besides resting on a very dubious and radically subjective theory of language and meaning, shows little respect for important historical considerations and even less for the original author or authors of a document. It is much like the case of someone translating one's words into another language but the translator in question feeling under no obligation to try to convey the equivalent in the receiver language of what a person has said. Rather, the translator chooses to use another's words to convey his own meaning. In both cases there is little respect for what the original speaker was trying to say. When the reader of a text sets out to *tell* the

[13] Scott, *Hear Then the Parable*, 75, emphasis mine. Scott does go on to talk about a second level of meaning which involves textual structuring, presumably by the original author, but this second level is seen as supportive and the condition for the first level of meaning which clearly is seen as primary in this approach.

[14] I would distinguish between authorial intention and authorial meaning. The former one can only conjecture about on the basis of the text. The latter one can know without the author still being present or alive, if the author has adequately expressed his meaning in the words he has chosen.

[15] For an argument in favor of multiple interpretations from a reader–response viewpoint, cf. W. Iser, *The Act of Reading: A Theory of Aesthetic Response*, 163–231.

[16] S. Brown, "Reader Response: Demythologizing the Text,", 232–37, 232.

text what it means or even just to find a personal, subjective, unintended meaning in the text, the author seldom gets a word in edgewise.

Furthermore, "publicly accepted standards are available for evaluating the plethora of interpretations of a text."[17] Several basic criteria have been offered by M. A. Tolbert for adjudicating interpretations of texts. These are as follows:

> (1) An interpretation of a text should be in accord with the standards of intellectual discourse of its age. It should reflect the contemporary status of scientific and philosophical knowledge; (2) The more fully an interpretation can demonstrate its points from the text itself, the more convincing it becomes; (3) The more coherence an interpretation can disclose in a text, the more persuasive it becomes; (4) An interpretation should be cognizant of the general historical, literary, and sociological matrix out of which the text comes.[18]

As Tolbert points out, criteria (3) above presumes that a text is not random but intentional and coherent and in some sense a unit. F. Kermode rightly urges, "Our whole practice of reading is founded on such expectations."[19] It may well be true that a text can mean *more* than what the original author meant to say. Nevertheless, it cannot mean something that violates or contradicts or misrepresents what the original author meant to say. For example, "Blessed are the peacemakers" cannot be construed to mean "Blessed are the warmongers." In short, the meaning derived must be in continuity with, or pursuing the same path as the author's meaning. There must always be a line of continuity between the original intended authorial meaning, to the extent it can be discerned, and whatever meaning one may derive from the text. Otherwise the line of communication has been severed between the historical author and whoever is reading a text at a given moment. This means that historical study of a text and historical reconstruction is always necessary when one is asking about the meaning of a text, unless it can be shown that the author in question is deliberately trying to avoid conveying some meaning. Purely literary studies of ancient texts that have some historical substance and purpose to them are both valuable and necessary, but they can never be sufficient in themselves if one is asking the questions "what does this text mean?" or even "how does this text mean?"

The distinction of Hirsch deserves to be affirmed: "*Meaning* is that which is represented by a text; it is what an author meant by his use of a particular sign sequence: it is what the signs represent. *Significance*, on the other hand, names a relationship between that meaning and a person, or a conception, or a

[17] Tolbert, *Sowing the Gospel*, 10.

[18] These criteria and others are found in Tolbert, *Sowing the Gospel*, 10ff. The numbering in the quote is my own.

[19] F. Kermode, *The Genesis of Secrecy: On the Interpretation of Narrative*, 53.

situation..."[20] The significance of a work to an individual can and does involve what M. V. Fox calls "fruitful misunderstandings" as well as eisegesis.[21] But significance should not be confused with meaning. Furthermore, an author may say more or less than s/he means to say on various occasions. A reader may draw out something that was at most implicit in the author's mind when s/he wrote.

This means that both the writer and the reader play an *active* role in communication and the discernment of meaning. Of course, the reader is not simply a *tabula rasa* on which a writer's words are written, any more than the text is a *tabula rasa* on which the reader may write. The reader brings to the text a whole host of things, for example: (1) prior knowledge; (2) a certain level of attentiveness or care given to the reading; (3) some ideas as to what one hopes to gain by reading a particular text, to mention but three things.

None of this should lead one to minimize the importance of hearing an author out, and doing one's best to try to understand what s/he is trying to say. This is the very essence of good listening – listening that respects the speaker and tries to pay close enough attention to find out what s/he is intending to communicate. The theory of P. Ricoeur that once a person writes something this entails the "disconnection of the mental intention of the author from the verbal meaning of the text, of what the author meant and the text means" should be rejected. This view involves the fallacy of semantic autonomy, a fallacy unfortunately perpetuated in the otherwise helpful book by S. M. Schneiders, who follows Ricouer in arguing, "once speech is inscribed as text...the text now means whatever it can mean by virtue of the semantic range of its language and structures. The text is cut off from authorial intention and begins to live its own life as a medium of meaning....In short the semantic autonomy of the text grounds the surplus of meaning that makes multiple valid interpretations not only possible but inevitable, and, indeed desirable."[23]

It is important not to confuse intentions and actions. When authors write they are expressing their intentions in the form of words, phrases, sentences. These units of expression *have meaning* because the author has configured them in such a way to express her or his meaning. While texts, not being persons, can not have intentions, they most certainly can have or convey meaning or meanings, just as oral speeches have or convey meaning. The basic difference between oral and written communication is that with oral communication the creator is present and can be questioned about meaning and intent. With written communication this is not, or not usually so.

Basically, texts transmit meaning; they do not *have* meaning apart from the meaning an author or authors have given them, though they may have

[20] E. D. Hirsch, *Validity in Interpretation*, 8ff.
[21] Fox, "Job 38 and God's Rhetoric," 53.
[22] Ricouer, *Interpretation Theory: Discourse and the Surplus of Meaning*, 29–30.
[23] S. M. Schneiders, *The Revelatory Text*, 143, cf. 142–48.

significance beyond the author's intent. A random combination of words could be called a text, but it could not be called a communication because it has no meaning. This in turn is because meaning involves the purposeful choice and arrangement of words by an author or editor. As Fox says,

> No one would bother to write if he did not assume *his* meaning was conveyed by the text.... For most readers a text is a vehicle to an author's consciousness rather than a goal in itself, as is shown by the fact that a reader will commonly – and properly – ignore the text, even an autograph in favor of the authorial intention, when encountering a manifest typographical error.[24]

A radically subjective theory of meaning is, in the end, an anti-historical theory of meaning, for it cuts the reader off from the historical matrices and circumstances out of which the text originally arose. In doing this, it not only undercuts the very character and importance of historical–critical study of any ancient document, but also it cuts off the line of communication between the original author and the current reader. Literary criticism that seeks to short circuit historical inquiry will in the end not do justice to either the text being studied or the one who originally wrote it.

This is especially critical with the parables and aphorisms for they arose in a largely *oral* environment, an environment where most written documents are not to be seen as independent "texts" but as surrogates for or tools for oral communication. As P. Achtemeier has said, "Reading was therefore oral performance *whenever* it occurred and in whatever circumstances. Late antiquity knew nothing of the 'silent solitary reader'."[25] This is clearest in the case of Paul's letters where it is evident that the letters are not ends in themselves but part of an ongoing dialogue that also involves oral communication, and there are clear instructions that the letters are to be read aloud during the congregational meeting. It is equally clear, in the case of maxims like that in Prov. 10.9a (*"holek battom yelek betah"*), that originally this material was meant to be heard and perhaps recited, not merely read.

In recent years it has become increasingly accepted that the Gospels as well were documents that were meant to be read aloud in worship or whenever believers gathered. They were documents meant to be heard, and their literary devices were ear-catching, not eye-catching. It should not surprise us if these documents have kerygmatic among other possible functions.[26]

---

[24] Fox, "Job 38," 54.

[25] Achtemeir, "*Omne Verbum Sonat*: The New Testament and the Oral Environment of Late Western Antiquity," 17.

[26] A great weakness in Tolbert's, *Sowing the Gospel*, is that it avoids the difficult questions of historical substance in the Gospels. This avoidance is based on the assumption that at least in the case of Mark's Gospel the closest analogy in antiquity is the ancient novel rather than ancient historical biographies (cf. 55ff.). If it is really true that "Literary criticism understands

The Gospels, like the rest of the New Testament documents, are in the main prompts or aids for the living voice and its proclamation. If this is so, then to treat the Gospels simply as "texts" is to misunderstand not only their character but also their original function. As Tolbert puts it, "The Gospel of Mark, then like its counterparts up and down the aesthetic scale of Hellenistic literature, was an *aural text*, a spoken writing, a performed story."[27] Various forms of recent literary criticism rest on assumptions created by a long history of the production of documents meant for *reading*, not as tools for oral communication, and these assumptions do not suit the character of most if not all of the New Testament documents, nor do they suit the Old Testament Wisdom material. In conclusion a quote from F. Young and D. Ford aptly sums up some of the basic assumptions about language and the handling of texts that lie behind this study.

> If we only ever found in texts what we were looking for and never learned anything, there would be no point in reading them....The reader brings a good deal to the reading, but also takes something away. In fact there is a hermeneutical spiral, because consciously or unconsciously a kind of dialogue is going on between the text and the reader. The text is not a *tabula rasa* on which the reader can draw his own pictures unrestrained, but a communication to which the attentive reader has to pay attention. Furthermore, to deny all objectivity... fails to do justice to the fact that everything is not subjective, and that it is possible to acquire competence, and improve one's understanding. There is an external world and an external text that impinges upon us, and to which our models of understanding approximate. The approximation can always be improved. Furthermore, questions of meaning are not private but belong to the realm of the public domain, because language belongs to the public... humankind is not only a creator of significations, but significations are imposed upon human beings. In other words an author's creativity is constrained by the structures of the language being used, and the possibilities of meaning are limited by what the text actually says. Some debates about meaning are capable of being settled.... We refuse to accept that disciplined search for the meaning intended or assumed by the author is not the proper starting-point for exegesis... [However] It does not seem to us that taking the philological method seriously precludes the possibilities of mean-

---

the biblical text as *fiction*, the result of literary imagination, not of photographic recall" (25), then it would seem that meaningful discussion of other possibilities have been ruled out in advance of serious scrutiny of the issues involved. I have argued elsewhere that the ancient popular biography provides us with our closest analogies for the genre of the Gospels. Cf. Witherington, "Women and their Roles in the Gospels and Acts", Chapter 1. There are certainly many other options besides pure fiction and photographic recall. For instance, it is possible the Gospel writers have used material of some historical substance and a broad historical outline of the life of Jesus, coupled with their selection, editing, and arrangment of various pericopes according to their various theological purposes.

[27] Tolbert, *Sowing the Gospel*, 44. On the largely oral character of the environment of early Christianity, cf. the very helpful discussion in Achtemeir, "*Omne Verbum Sonat*," 19ff: "... to be understood, the NT must be understood as speech" (p. 19).

> ings beyond what the author intended. This is not... to give free rein to the subjectivity or vested interests of the interpreter(s). It is simply to acknowledge the possibility of latent meanings discernible only within a subsequent perspective, and to recognize the mutual interaction of worlds involved in reading and responding to a text.[28]

My only cavil with this quote is that when the authors talk about a meaning beyond that which an author or speaker intended, it would be better to talk about a personal significance that a text might have for a listener or reader, beyond anything the author or speaker may have imagined or intended. This study now turns to an examination of some of Jesus' aphorisms and parables examining them in the light of the Jewish Wisdom material discussed in Chapters 1–2 of this study, and in the light of the near parallels from early Judaism.

FIGURES OF SPEECH: JESUS' PARABLES AND APHORISMS

GENERAL CONSIDERATIONS

It is not difficult to demonstrate in a general way the degree of indebtedness of the Jesus material to Jewish Wisdom traditions.[29] For one thing, by far the majority of the arguably authentic Jesus material takes the form of either aphorisms, or narrative *meshalim* (i.e., parables). For another thing, one does not find Jesus using the classic prophetic formula, "thus says Yahweh". Indeed, the closest approximation of this formula in the Gospel is in the Q saying found in Luke 11:49 which is introduced by "Therefore the Wisdom of God says!" Jesus' main chosen way of public communication appears to have involved the art of persuasion by figurative or indirect speech, and thus it seems that he intended to be seen, at least in part, as some kind of sage.[30] It is also quite likely that Jesus was perceived to be some sort of sage by the part of his audience that was conversant with the world of Jewish Wisdom traditions.

Those who collected, edited, and passed on the Jesus tradition also seem to have gone out of their way to emphasize the Wisdom element in Jesus' teaching, for no other literary type receives anywhere near the representation in the teaching material in the Synoptics. By even a conservative estimate, at

[28] F. Young and D. F. Ford, *Meaning and Truth in 2 Corinthians*, 4–5.

[29] Cf. Scott, "Jesus as Sage: an Innovating Voice in Common Wisdom," 399–415, "... at the base of the early tradition as represented by Q, Thomas, Mark, Matthew, and Luke is the common Jewish wisdom tradition." For a survey of the variety of Wisdom forms used by Jesus, cf. L. G. Perdue, "The Wisdom Sayings of Jesus," 3–35.

[30] This is only one facet of the man's public persona (there are other sorts of similar authentic Jesus sayings besides aphorisms and parables), but it seems to be the most prominent one remembered by those who passed on the Jesus tradition.

least 70% of the Jesus tradition is in the form of some sort of Wisdom utterance such as an aphorism, riddle, or parable.[31] R. Riesner counts some 247 *meshalim* in the Synoptics.[32]

Several important studies have shown how fruitful it is to study Jesus' aphorisms and parables in the light of similar sorts of material not only in the Hebrew Scriptures, but in extra-canonical material of roughly the same era.[33] C. Westermann has shown how Jesus' parables are not free-standing entities but rather comparisons in the form of a story. As such, they are an extended form of another sort of figurative comparison, namely the simile. He is rightly critical of the attempts by Ricoeur and others to view such parables in the light of "a timeless and unhistorical linguistic phenomenon called 'metaphor'."[34] While it can be argued that the narrative *meshalim* are in a certain sense extended metaphors or perhaps similes, nevertheless because they are both created and used as a form of address or dialogue about specific historical matters, they take on a specific historical character. Jesus' parables were both timely and historical in character, meant to provide his audience with various sorts of comparisons between what God's Dominion and its inbreaking were like in analogy with their own more familar life experiences.[35] Westermann is also right that the parables should not be seen as mere illustrations, much less illustrations of Jesus' preaching. From all one can tell, they were one of the main vehicles of Jesus' proclamation in and of themselves.

The work of C. R. Fontaine on traditional sayings in non-Wisdom literature and their functions has led to several important conclusions that have a bearing on the study of Jesus' aphorisms in particular. First, normally traditional Wisdom sayings or proverbs are used to uphold the norms, rituals, beliefs, and institutions of the existing society, which stands in contrast by and large to the way Jesus uses his Wisdom sayings. But Jesus' sayings and traditional Wisdom sayings have this much in common – "their function is not

---

[31] While I am using the term parable in the more familiar narrow sense here to refer to the narrative *meshalim*, in fact the term *parabolos*, like the term *mashal*, could be used of a wide variety of forms of figurative speech. The term *parabolos* appears forty-eight times in the Gospels and nowhere else in the New Testament (except Heb. 9.9, 11.19). B. Gerhardsson, "The Narrative Meshalim in the Synoptic Gospels," 339–63, points to Mark 4 where the term *parabolos* includes more than just narrative *meshalim* (cf. Mark 4:2, 33–34).

[32] Cf. R. Riesner, *Jesus als Lehrer*, 392–94.

[33] I am thinking of the very helpful study by C. Westermann, *The Parables of Jesus in the Light of the Old Testament*; and B. Gerhardsson's two important articles, "The Narrative Meshalim," 339–63 and "If We Do not Cut the Parables out of their Frames," 321–335. One must also consult the important work now being done by W. F. Brosend on parable, allegory, and metaphor. Of some help, though these works are not without methodological flaws, are: B. H. Young, *Jesus and his Jewish Parables*; MacArthur and Johnston, *They Also Taught in Parables* and J. Drury, *The Parables in the Gospels*. On Jesus' aphorisms, cf. Williams, *Those who Ponder Proverbs*; J. D. Crossan, *In Fragments. The Aphorisms of Jesus*.

[34] Westermann, *Parables*, 182–83.

[35] This could include extreme crisis life situations, or even absurd or paradoxical though nonetheless real experiences.

so much to discover some pre-existent world order as to create and consolidate (cultural) order. "[36] This means that the so-called "observational nature" of Wisdom sayings is often overplayed, especially when the social context in which a saying is uttered conditions its meaning. Second, the key to proper proverb performance is not merely understanding the message one is conveying but knowing when and in what way to apply the saying. This may be of some relevance for the study of a saying like "the Sabbath was made for humankind, not humankind for the Sabbath."

Third, there are three elements that need to be attended to in the study of Wisdom sayings the form, content, *and* the context, although often the context of a proverb's performance is difficult if not impossible to recover. Fourth, the style of Wisdom sayings often violates regular syntactical patterns forcing the listener to carefully process and reflect on what s/he has heard.

Fifth, Wisdom sayings or proverbs are frequently used to bring about the final denouement in a pericope, or to conclude a discussion or speech. Sixth,

> The stimulus which elicts proverb performance is a situation in which conflict is felt on the part of the "Source" between the "true" state of affairs (as the Source understands the context) and the "perceived" state of affairs (as seen from the perspective of the "Receiver"). In other words, where the Source and Receiver disagree over the proper interpretation of the Context situation, the Source initiates proverb performance to highlight those differences in perspective and make a traditionally sanctioned case for his own side.[37]

All of the examples Fontaine presents are given in a context of cultural instability and conflict. It is noteworthy that a good deal of Jesus' teachings, both in content and in their present Gospel contexts, reflect an environment of instability and controversy, and like those traditional Wisdom sayings seek to give guidance about the problematic aspects of society.

Seventh, in *all* the examples Fontaine studies the person offering the Wisdom saying occupies the inferior position or is in some disadvantaged position in the current situation. Is it because he was not a recognized religious authority, a sage from below rather than from the well to do or the royal courts, that Jesus chose a sapiential form of expression, or is it because he operated at a disadvantage compared to other religious figures of his day? Eighth, the traditional Wisdom sayings studied present "a message 'coded' in traditional (hence 'authoritative') language. The receiver responds because of the famili-

---

[36] Fontaine, *Traditional Sayings*, 150–51. In all of what follows in this paragraph I am correlating Fontaine's conclusions about traditional sayings with my own observations of their implications for the study of the Jesus material.

[37] Fontaine, *Traditional Sayings*, 154–55.

arity with the culture's proverbial stock."[38] In this way even unconventional ideas can gain a hearing because they are presented in traditional, authoritative Wisdom garb. Ninth, because of the indirect and conventional form of the speech, the speaker is somewhat protected from immediate rejection, and his ideas, even if unconventional, are given time to gain a hearing.[39] Various of the above observations bear some close scrutiny when one considers Jesus' sapiential teaching and particularly his aphorisms.

The study of Jewish Wisdom literature earlier in this book led to the conclusion that *narrative meshalim* were *not* characteristic of the sages whose work made its way into the Hebrew Scriptures. Rather, they seem to have been a prophetic phenomenon, perhaps one may say a prophetic modification of a Wisdom form of utterance (cf. 2 Sam. 12:1–4; Ezek.17:3–10; and perhaps also Isa. 5:1–6).[40] In short, the narrative *meshalim* reflect the prophetic adaptation and expansion of a Wisdom and poetic form of speech, the simile, to serve prophetic narrative concerns. Basically they are comparisons that have been elongated into brief narratives.[41]

In the study of Ben Sira, important new developments were noted including: (1) a sage's claim to be inspired like the prophets and so offer some new revelation from God in sapiential form: "I will again pour out teaching like prophecy" (Sir. 24:33); and (2) the sage is said to study and draw on prophetic material (Sir. 39:1). In Wis. 7:27 one hears that when the spirit of Wisdom passes into someone's soul she makes them "friends of God, *and prophets*" (Wis. 7:27). Here the sage is seen as the one who delivers the prophetic word. Consider also the later saying from the Talmud (*B.T B.Batra* 12a) that God took prophecy from the prophets and gave it to the sages.

I submit that the vast majority of the Gospel sayings tradition can be explained on the hypothesis that Jesus presented himself as a Jewish prophetic sage, one who drew on all the riches of earlier Jewish sacred traditions, especially the prophetic, apocalyptic, and sapiential material though occasionally even the legal traditions. His teaching, like Ben Sira's and Pseudo-

---

[38] Fontaine, *Traditional Sayings*, 158.

[39] Fontaine, *Traditional Sayings*, 157. On all the above one should carefully read through 139–70.

[40] I leave out of account the fables found in Jug. 9.7–15 and 2 Kgs. 14.9. Fables are narrative fictions in which plants and/or animals discourse. These are not true parables though they are certainly a form of figurative speech. It is telling that Jesus does not offer any fables, and one would be hard pressed to find many in the prophetic corpus either. Narrative *meshalim* as we find them in the prophets, Jesus tradition, and in early Judaism have human actors; they do not involve the personification of animals or plants. Cf. Drury, *The Parables in the Gospels*, 7–20, 39ff. One could argue that a narrative *mashal* is a sapiential modification of a prophetic form of speech. In Jesus' case this may well be true, but originally it seems more likely that the Old Testament prophets were drawing on sapiential similes and expanding them into *meshalim*.

[41] Fontaine, *Traditional Sayings*, 165, also concludes that Wisdom sayings are not polyvalent but rather have a kernel of meaning that is "context-free".

Solomon's before him, bears witness to the cross-fertilization of the several streams of sacred Jewish traditions. However, what makes sage the most appropriate and comprehensive term for describing Jesus, is that he either casts his teaching in a recognizably sapiential form (e.g. an aphorism, or beatitude, or riddle), or uses the prophetic adaptation of sapiential speech – the narrative *mashal*. In either case, he speaks by various means of figurative language, thus choosing to address his audience using indirect speech. It is in part this which makes Jesus so enigmatic and hard to pin down, especially for many moderns. His chosen means of address required concentration and rumination to be understood. He did not come into Galilee spouting self-evident propositions, nor did he present his Wisdom in the form of syllogistic logic.[42]

To judge from the evidence, during and after the time of Jesus, narrative *meshalim* seem to have become an increasingly popular vehicle for all sorts of teachers to convey a message in early Judaism, as the works of B.H. Young, H.K. McArthur and R. M. Johnston show. Such surveys of the wider circle of Jewish parallels to the narrative *meshalim* in the Gospels lead to two important conclusions. First, parable and allegory, at least as used by early Jews, cannot be *radically* distinguished, despite the long standing dictum of A. Jülicher and those whom he influenced.[43] Parables, including Jesus', could and did include allegorical or symbolic elements at times. One must be able to distinguish between allegory, allegorical elements in what otherwise is not allegory, and allegorical interpretation.[44] What Jülicher basically was reacting against it seems is the *allegorical interpretation* of the narrative *meshalim* from the Middle Ages onward in the church. Whatever the merits or demerits of the medieval Christian hermeneutical approach to the parables, it does not have any bearing on the question of what the relationship of parable to allegory was in Jesus'

---

[42] As evidence that the meanings of the parables are not self–evident or crystal clear to moderns, note the proliferation of books on the parables that are thought to be must reading for their understanding and interpretation. There are, in the case of many *meshalim*, as many interpretations as interpreters! Cf. now Brosend, "The Recovery of Allegory," Chapter 6 on the definitions of parable and allegory. Both contain various elements that *require* interpretation and reference something outside the *mashal*.

[43] Cf. J. Z. Lauterbach, "Ancient Jewish Allegorists," 301–33. What Lauterbach's study shows is that some ancient Palestinian Jewish sages did interpret various texts from the Hebrew Scriptures figuratively as well as literally. We may call this a form of allegorical interpretation. This sort of approach was not confined to Diaspora Jews like Philo, or like Paul (cf. 1 Cor. 10:1–4; Gal. 5:22–31). What we do not find evidence of is what later in the West amounted to full–blown allegory where the author of the literary creation was deliberately trying to make most if not all elements in his narrative symbolic in character. S. L. Wailes, *Medieval Allegories of Jesus' Parables*, points out that allegory does not appear as a genre of Latin literature before about A.D. 400. There is nothing historically improbable with the idea that Jesus may have deliberately structured into his parables several symbolic elements.

[44] Brosend, "The Recovery of Allegory," has now analyzed Jülicher in detail and shown how his aversion to allegory led to his imposing a non–historical distinction on the early Jewish parables of the Jesus tradition. This being the case, allegorical elements in a parable cannot simply be assumed to be a sign of later Christian theologizing. The sliding scale between parable and allegory was already noted by, among others, R. E. Brown, *New Testament Essays*, 322ff.

day.[45] Second, parables often came with interpretations or explanations in early Judaism; they were not normally self-contained and self-explanatory literary units. J. Arthur Baird has pointed out that of the seventy-one or so possible parables in the Synoptics, forty-two of them have some sort of explanation with them.[46] In view of the fact that this is also very characteristic of other early Jewish parables, one should not automatically assume that an explanation of a parable in the Synoptics is necessarily a product of later Christian reflection on Jesus' parables, though in particular cases it may be.[47] One must probe further and ask the question, could or would this explanation have more likely arisen in a *Sitz im Leben Jesu* or from a later period?

It is also important to note ways that Jesus' *narrative meshalim* differed from other early Jewish parables. As B. Gerhardsson points out, Jesus never or almost never uses *meshalim* as a means of interpreting or illuminating Scripture. Nor does he use them to proclaim some sort of law or to clarify some regulation. Halachic questions do not arise at all in the narrative *meshalim*.[48] They also stand out in regard to their function. P. Perkins rightly remarks:

> What makes Jesus' use of proverbial traditions distinctive? Jesus is not simply teaching people truths of folk wisdom that they already had heard from others.... Jesus uses proverbs in defense of his vision of the Reign of God. Jesus wants people to see that it is time for a new experience of God's presence in human life. This new vision challenges old ways of thinking and acting. In order to show people how radical the challenge is, he often uses images that are extreme or even paradoxical. Unlike the commonplaces of much wisdom tradition, which says the world will always go on as a place in which the fools repeat the same mistakes, Jesus sees the coming of the Reign of God as an opportunity for radical change.[49]

Perhaps equally important is what J. G. Williams points to as a decisive difference between the sort of material we find in Proverbs and in the Jesus tradition. In the former work we find almost exclusively the products of the collective voice, speaking by way of generalizations. By contrast, in the Jesus tradition, we find by and large an individual voice.[50] Scott urges that "The construct of the voice of Jesus' aphorisms or parables embodies a distinctive, individual voice whose patterns, accents, styles, themes, and even ideology are recognizable. This is to be distinguished from other proverbs and parables whose voice, being 'anonymous' is the projection of common wisdom."[51]

---

[45] On medieval Christian use of Jesus' parables, cf. Wailes, *Medieval Allegories*, espec. 76ff.
[46] J. A. Baird, *Discovering the Power of the Gospel*, 9.
[47] Cf. Young, *Jesus and His Jewish Parables*, 164ff.
[48] Gerhardsson, "If We Do Not Cut the Parables," 329–32.
[49] Perkins, *Jesus as Teacher*, 44.
[50] Williams, *Those Who Ponder*, 40ff.
[51] Scott, "Jesus as Sage," 407.

Even in the case of Qoheleth, as his disciples' addendum tells us (Eccles. 12:9–10), one is largely dealing with a person who was a collector and arranger and refuter of some of the common Wisdom with its generalizations. Jesus by contrast was not merely commenting on common human experience, or even on his own private experience, but on experience, whether his or the experience of one who receives his message, as it may and ought to be now in the light of the inbreaking of the Dominion in his ministry. This required of him that for the most part he coin his own situation relevant *meshalim*.[52] This study will now examine in some detail a selection of arguably authentic aphorisms, riddles, and narrative *meshalim*.

APHORISMS OF COUNTER ORDER

Definitions and Distinctions. As has already been said in Chapter 1 there is a need to distinguish between proverbs, which are communications of "the generally accepted, the universal, the tried and true, not the striking or innovative"[53] and aphorisms. An excellent example of a proverb would be, "A slack hand brings poverty, but the hand of the diligent makes rich" (Prov. 10:4). This does not mean that proverbs intend to embody the whole truth, but rather they are generalizations that were very often found to be true. C. Carlston stresses that there is very little in the Jesus tradition that is purely proverbial in form.[54] To be sure, there are a few examples such as "no one can serve two masters" (Matt. 6:24 = Luke 6:43), or "life does not consist in the abundance of one's posessions" (Luke 12:15), or "a city set on a hill cannot be hid" (Matt. 5:14), but not many.

One may also be surprised to discover how many of the major themes of proverbial Wisdom are totally or almost totally *absent* from the Jesus tradition. For example there are no proverbs urging the seeking of Wisdom, or suggesting that the acquiring of it is difficult. Nor does Jesus urge that the fear of God is the beginning of Wisdom. There are, furthermore, no proverbs or sayings urging hard work or character building exercises *per se*. Jesus offers nothing like the conventional androcentric and patriarchal Wisdom about women found in Proverbs, much less what is found in Ben Sira. Even comments about strange or foreign women being morally dangerous or temptresses are notably lacking in the Jesus tradition. Indeed, as I have argued elsewhere, Jesus seems to locate the source of sexual danger for men in their own lust and desires.[55] Perhaps one of the reasons Jesus engages in none of the usual androcentric rhetoric about women that often peppered ancient proverbs of many cultures[56]

---

[52] I do not say that Jesus never drew on previous Wisdom. There are various places where it is likely he or at least the editors of the Jesus tradition did (cf. Luke 11:49, John 4:35).

[53] Cf. C. E. Carlston, "Proverbs, Maxims, and the Historical Jesus,", 87–105.

[54] Ibid., 93.

[55] Witherington, *Women in the Ministry of Jesus*, 18ff.

[56] Cf. Carlston, "Proverbs," 92ff., to whom I am indebted in this section at various points.

is because he, unlike Ben Sira, has no interest in inculcating or buttressing an androcentric honor–shame culture, in which women were at a distinct disadvantage. Further, he seems rarely if ever to comment about human nature in general, using stereotypes like "the sluggard".

When Jesus does on occasion appear to use a proverb, he often seems to use it in an aphoristic way, or place it in a context where it has an aphoristic thrust. He takes a general statement and retools it to say something specific about a situation in which he found himself. Consider the sayings found in Mark 2:27–28: "The sabbath was made for human beings, not human beings for the sabbath, so the Son of Man is lord even of the sabbath." It may well be, as J. D. Crossan avers, that Mark 2:27 was once a general saying which has been appropriated in the Jesus tradition.[57] It may have looked something like the rabbinic saying, "The sabbath was given to you, not you to the sabbath" (R. Simeon b. Menasya, *Mekilta* 109b on Exod. 31:14). The thrust of the combination now is to make a specific comment about Jesus, perhaps as the representative human being who felt free to act in accord with the real intention of the giving of the sabbath in the first place, namely to provide rest and restoration for human beings.

An aphorism, by contrast with a proverb, involves a personal and individual insight though like a proverb it is formulated in a non-narrative manner as an assertion. J. L. Bailey and L. D. Vander Broek put it this way: "In contrast to a proverb, the aphorism is attributed speech or, more precisely, 'a saying attributed to a specific person and perceived within the horizons of that person's wisdom and action.'"[58] Bultmann's taxonomy of the sayings material is still helpful in that it rightly encourages us to distinguish both proverbs and aphorisms from other types of sayings, such as purely prophetic, or apocalyptic, or legal sayings.[59] While this is in part a distinction based on content, it may also be said to be based on form, for aphorisms seldom involve imperatives. Out of 167 possible aphorisms carefully cataloged by D. Aune, only fifteen from the Gospel tradition now have an imperatival form, and it appears that several of these were originally in the indicative.[60] They normally involve observations or statements, a more indirect means of persuasion or changing behavior. There are also eight aphoristic beatitudes, which involve the melding together of two different sapiential literary forms.

Taking the 167 aphorisms together as a whole, the tradition suggests that Jesus usually spoke one line aphorisms, though there are also a considerable number of two line aphorisms as well. Aphorisms in a two line format

[57] The following section owes much to Crossan, *In Fragments*, 78–85.

[58] J. L. Bailey and L. D. Vander Broek, *Literary Forms in the New Testament*, 99.

[59] Cf. R. Bultmann, *Die Geschichte der synoptischen Tradition*, 8th edition, 73–113.

[60] D. Aune, "Oral Tradition and the Aphorisms of Jesus," *Jesus and the Oral Gospel*, ed. H. Wansborough, 242–58. Notice how the aphoristic beatitude in Mt. 5.7 is transformed into an imperative in *1 Clem.* 13:2a and Polycarp *Phil.* 2:3.

normally involve either synthetic or antithetical parallelism, which is not usually so with other types of sayings.[61] Some of the standard forms these aphorisms take are where/there (e.g. Luke 12:34/Matt. 16:21); as/so (e.g. Luke 11:30/Matt. 12:40); future reversal (e.g. Mark 8:35). In the latter category one could also include some sayings about reciprocity (e.g. "judge not that you be not judged," Matt. 7:1–2). This last saying is important, because if it goes back to Jesus, it suggests he affirmed the act–consequence schema in some form. As U. Luz says, because of its radicality this saying is almost universally assumed to be authentic.[62] Its meaning is, "Do not judge, in order that you not be condemned" (implied – by God at the final judgment).[63] That Jesus, like the earlier sages Ben Sira and Pseudo-Solomon, affirmed an eschatological resolution of things by a final judgment on the wicked which at the same time entailed a vindication of the righteous is not difficult to believe.[64] What is crucial to note about this is that it dramatically changes the character of one's Wisdom. Wisdom is shown to be right by divine intervention, not, or at least not primarily, by a general moral order in creation that rewards goodness here and now with health, wealth and the like.[65] This later Wisdom perspective on the act-consequence idea may explain why it is that Jesus combines traditional Wisdom forms and themes with themes from prophetical and apocalyptic traditions about reversal.

An aphorism has an air of authority, for it does not argue its point; it usually simply asserts *without* drawing on a generalization from nature or human nature that would be widely recognized as true. An aphorist is seeking to assert a counter order to the current *status quo*, or to urge a better and ideal set of affairs that, while not yet fully realized, can or will come to pass.[66] This ideal set of affairs, in the Jesus tradition, may be based on a creation order or

---

[61] I do not deny there are some admonitions, with verbs in the imperative, in the Jesus tradition which could be called aphorisms in the broad sense. It is suspicious to me that most of the examples that Aune can find are from Q (but cf. e.g. Mark 12:17 and par.). Even in the case of some of those within Q, however, they are not simple imperatives, for they have introductory clauses such as, "What I tell you in the dark," followed by, "utter in the light" (Matt. 10:27). But in the Lukan parallel to this saying we have no imperative at all but rather a simple sentence. This could lead to the conclusion that original aphorisms have been transformed into imperatives, if the Lukan form of the above saying (Luke 12:3), is regarded as closer to the original form. If the way Matthew and Luke use Mark is any guide, Luke when he takes over source material is slightly more likely than Matthew to preserve the source's exact words, while Matthew is much more likely to preserve more of the source's content. Cf. Aune, "Oral Tradition," 211–65.

[62] Cf. U. Luz, *Matthew 1–7*, 413.

[63] D. Allison and W. D. Davies, *The Gospel according to Saint Matthew*, Vol. I, 669.

[64] I have argued in *Women in the Ministry of Jesus*, 44–45 that the saying about the Queen of Sheba as a witness in the resurrection is very likely authentic.

[65] That Jesus argued for the latter as well can be urged on the basis of texts like Matt. 6:25ff/Luke 12:22ff. but it will be noted that there too it is not some ordering principle in creation but God's ongoing providential care (arguing from the lesser to the greater – if birds are cared for, then humans too).

[66] Cf. Williams, *Those Who Ponder Proverbs*, 80–88.

design that God originally intended for human beings, or on some new inbreaking work of God that changes the parameters of the possible, or will one day do so (cf. e.g. Mark 10:6). Thus, for example, one may think of an aphorism like, "But many that are first will be last, and the last first" (Mark 10:31 and par.), or "For whoever would save his life, will lose it; and whoever loses his life for my sake ...will save it" (Mark 8:35 and par.), or "You cannot serve both God and mammon" (Matt. 6:24/Luke 16:13), or "It is easier for a camel to go through the eye of a needle than for a rich person to enter the kingdom of God" (Mark 10:25).

In the case of aphorisms like these, it is not just that some of them are apparently paradoxical and counter-intuitive (is it always so that when a person tries to save their life they will in fact lose it?), but they often reflect an order that goes counter to traditional Wisdom. In proverbial Wisdom it is often assumed that riches are a blessing from God. How could it be that a person so blessed might always find it extremely difficult if not impossible to get into God's kingdom? These aphorisms of "counter-order" as Williams calls them[67] were often meant to challenge prevailing assumptions that Jewish Wisdom had traditionally inculcated. This could involve dramatic hyperbole (Mark 10:25), but it could also involve understatement.[68]

One of the things that must have been confusing about Jesus is that in some cases he affirmed traditional values and ideas, and in others he seems to have vehemently rejected them. Even when Jesus appealed to the Scriptures or traditional Wisdom he did so "in order to support his strong sense of personal destiny and authority as God's healer and messenger."[69] "In general his strategy is one of representing the divine reality (kingdom of God, life) while using paradoxes that disorient the listener..."[70] D. Aune is right to stress that "the tenacity with which aphorisms cling to their attribution to Jesus is an important theological and sociological feature of early Christianity, suggestive not only of the role played by the historical Jesus, but also of the role which later Christianity wished to have Jesus play."[71]

Since Qoheleth is not a personal name, it appears that Jesus is the first person mentioned *by name* in the literature that arose out of early Judaism, whose name is *explicitly* associated with a wide variety of aphorisms.[72] This in

---

[67] Williams, *Those Who Ponder Proverbs*, 82ff.

[68] Cf. Crossan, *In Fragments*, 27: "Overstatement and exaggeration, hyperbole and paradox, are often mentioned as facets of aphoristic truth. But understatement, the even more delicate art of letting everything hang on a single word, is also typical of aphorism."

[69] Williams, *Those Who Ponder Proverbs*, 85.

[70] Williams, 88.

[71] Aune, "Oral Tradition," 241.

[72] Ben Sira basically does not use the aphoristic form. He prefers the sort of poetry, mostly bicola in form, that is akin to what we find in Job, Psalms, and some parts of Proverbs (e.g., Proverbs 1–9). Often he uses the technique of composing 22–23 line units. Cf. Skehan and di Lella, *The Wisdom of Ben Sira*, 63, 74. Likewise in the case of the Wisdom of Solomon one will search for aphorisms in vain, though there are a few places where the sage seems to be reusing traditional proverbs. The very fact that this sage is anonymous, using an ancient persona, would not have led one to expect aphorisms, much less aphorisms of counter order from him (cf. e.g. Wis. 9.15).

itself leads one to think that Jesus represented himself to a significant degree in his public utterances as a sage. But what sort of sage?

It would seem, when one compares the writings of Ben Sira with the sayings of Jesus and the Synoptics in general, that while in Ben Sira's day there was a virtual equation of scribe with sage, the Torah scholar with the wise man (and with the king's counselor), in Jesus' day and case this equation no longer completely held. Jesus does not present himself as primarily a scribe or exegete of Torah, indeed he is repeatedly set over against such scribes in the Gospel tradition. The solution to this dilemma comes in recognizing that Jesus was a sage from below. That is, as was apparently the case in the time when the book of Proverbs and Ecclesiastes were being produced there were *some* sages who were not a part of, perhaps even in some cases alienated from, the religious and political hierarchy.[73] These sages were not employed as professional interpreters of the law for the temple hierarchy, nor as counselors or emissaries for rulers. Their provenance was the synagogue, the city gate, perhaps even an unofficial study house in their home. Their subject matter was wisdom from below, especially the wisdom of family and clan, and often they were highly critical of wisdom from above that supported the establishment and the wealthy landed class of society.

This may explain why Jesus often did not address some of the major concerns of earlier sages like Ben Sira whose writings were extant, and whose connections with the wealthy and the royal were obvious. Jesus was concerned with Wisdom that spoke to more than just the upper echelon of society for he was from a lower strata of society, and had chosen by and large a more plebian audience. This is not to say that he never addressed some of the reasonably well off in society, but when he did so it is notable how critical he was of many of their values, such as the accumulation of wealth (cf. Matt.6:24/Luke 16:13; Luke 12:16–21; Matt. 12:38–40). Jesus was highly critical of scribes who bilked widows.[74] Jesus' social position and orientation as a sage of the common people probably explains to a significant degree why he offered aphorisms of counter order. He identified with and believed that through his ministry God was doing something special to help the least, the last, and the lost as well as others. It is time for closer consideration of some of the aphorisms of counter order.

Cavils about Camels (Mark.10:25 and par.). One of the clearest indicators that Jesus not only coined a goodly number of aphorisms but also that aphorisms were a *characteristic* form of his teaching is that one finds aphorisms in all layers of the Synoptic tradition. Carlston has counted 102 Wisdom sayings with the following distribution: thirty-two in Mark, thirty-eight in Q, sixteen in Matthew, and sixteen in Luke.[75] The intent here is to examine a representative

[73] So Fontaine, *Traditional Sayings*, 166–68.

[74] Witherington, *Women in the Ministry of Jesus*, 16–17.

[75] Carlston, "Proverbs, Maxims," 91 and n. 24.

sample of these aphorisms, including some from each source. The first aphorism is the familiar one found in Mark 10:25 (and par.).

In its present Markan context it is connected to a discussion about the encumbrances of riches and brings the discussion to a climax, though there is a question and answer that follows by way of denouement. This aphorism may have originally been an independent saying for, as Aune points out, it is found as an isolated saying in *Gospel of the Nazarene* 16.[76] Furthermore, E. Best's careful study of the tradition history of Mark 10:23–27 also points in the direction that Mark 10:25 was not only pre-Markan but goes back to Jesus. As he says, "there is no reason to suggest Mark created [v. 25]; at no point does it bear any sign of his hand."[77]

As J. D. Crossan points out, this saying is striking in part because it is a "startling combination of comedy in form and tragedy in metaphorical meaning."[78] In form, this saying is much like the "better… than" aphorisms (cf. Prov. 15:16, 17; 16:8; Sirach 11:3; Mark 9:45). That Mark 10:25 is an aphorism of counter order is evident from the fact that while it addresses a familiar Wisdom topic, wealth, far from seeing riches as a good thing or a blessing from God as is the case so often in Proverbs and Job (cf. Job 1:10, 42:10), it sees them as that which blocks the door into God's dominion. This conclusion was obviously too much for some later Christian scribes, who changed the original *kamelon* to *kamilon*, which is a rope or ship's hawser.[79]

The image in the aphorism is deliberately absurd, for the camel was the largest animal normally found in Israel in Jesus' day, and the needle's eye certainly one of the smallest holes.[80] Thus one is talking about a real impossibility, unless the rich person does something about his wealth in advance of the time when he might enter the dominion. This teaching comports with what the Jesus tradition elsewhere suggests about the enslaving and encumbering power of wealth (cf. Matt. 6:24; Luke 12:13–21).

Elsewhere I have explored the dominion entrance sayings in the Gospel tradition, and came to the conclusion that such sayings, which envision the dominion as an actual realm that can be entered, turn out to be future oriented

---

[76] Aune, "Oral Tradition," 246.

[77] E. Best, "Uncomfortable Words: VII. The Camel and the Needle's Eye (Mk 10.25)," 85.

[78] Crossan, *In Fragments*, 222.

[79] Bruce Metzger, *Textual Commentary*, 50, 106, 169. It is possible that this change was facilitated because the sound of the Greek *i* and *e* became indistinct in later Greek (p. 169). There are also traces of this modification of the original saying in the Koran. Cf. R. Köbert, "Kamel und Schiffstau: zu Markus 10.25 (Par.) und Koran 7,40/38," 229–33.

[80] W. L. Lane, *The Gospel According to Mark*, 369. As Lane indicates, attempts to whittle off the hard edge of this saying should be resisted; for instance, the old dodge that Jesus was talking about some (non–existant) needle–gate in Jerusalem through which camels could only pass on their knees. The saying in the Talmud about an elephant passing through a needle (cf. *B. T. Berak.* 55b; *B. T. Baba* Metzia 38b) is late and probably has no relationship with our saying. When would Palestinian rabbis have had occasion to see elephants? Surely, the answer is rarely if ever. Cf. J. D. M. Derrett, "A Camel through the Eye of a Needle," 467.

sayings.[81] This aphorism then has a future eschatological thrust to it, as do many other aphorisms as well as various of the aphoristic beatitudes.

Sabbatical Plans (Mark.2:27-28 and par.). The pericope Mark 2:23–28 in its present form can be said to be a chreia, with v 27 seen as a maxim which leads in turn to the conclusion of the pericope in v 28.[82] Mark 2:27–28 may be an original unity or, less probably, a combination of two originally isolated sayings into an aphoristic compound.[83] In favor of there originally being two isolated sayings is that the general maxim in v 27 bears some resemblance to a later saying of Rabbi Simeon b. Menasya (*c* A.D. 180): "The sabbath was delivered to you, you were not delivered to the sabbath" (*Mekilta* on Exod. 31.13–14 cf. *B.T. Yoma* 85b). But the rabbinic saying was used only to justify action on the sabbath in life threatening situations. It was considered a specific saying, not a general maxim.[84] It is generally agreed that *kai elegen autois*, a typical Markan introduction (cf. Mark. 4:11, 13, 21, 24; 6:10; 7:9, 14; etc.), sets vv 27–28 apart from what precedes and since Mark 3:1 is clearly the beginning of a new pericope the question becomes whether v 27 and/or 28 could stand alone, or whether they belong together. Both Matthew and Luke very likely dropped v 27 because it diluted the force of a potentially christological statement in v 28. In fact they both made four changes: (1) dropping v 27; (2) dropping the *hoste*; (3) dropping the ascensive *kai*; and (4) changing the word order so that *kurios* comes first in the sentence followed by the verb and the clause "of the sabbath", leaving "Son of Man" until the end of the sentence.[85]

This bears witness to the potentially offensive character of vv 27–28 when taken together, and for that reason one should not be too hasty to deny an original connection.[86] As R. Guelich has pointed out, *hoste* introduces a result clause ('so that') in v 28, it is not simply the equivalent of the loose English connective "so".[87] Thus, at the very least Mark saw a significant connection between these two verses. The question is whether or not one can make sense of these two verses together.

---

[81] Witherington, *Jesus, Paul, and the End of the World*, 59ff.

[82] B. Mack, *Rhetoric and the New Testament* , 52.

[83] Crossan, *In Fragments*, 78ff.

[84] A. J. Hultgren, *Jesus and His Adversaries: The Form and Function of the Conflict Stories in the Synoptic Tradition*, 140 and n. 62.

[85] Crossan, *Fragments*, 79–80; R. Pesch, *Markusevangelium I*, 183ff. It is these sorts of minor agreements of Matthew and Luke which have fueled speculation that either Matthew knew Luke or vice versa, which is not impossible, but in this case the changes made are explicable on the grounds that both the First Evangelist and Luke found the connection of these two sayings awkward and potentially offensive. The changes in word order are simply stylistic improvements a good editor would make.

[86] In *Christology of Jesus*, I argued that v 28 may in fact be Markan editorial work (67). I now think this conclusion while still possible is less probable than that vv 27–28 originally went together.

[87] R. Guelich, *Mark 1 — 8.26* (Waco: Word, 1989), 125.

V. Taylor argues, "the thought is that, since the Sabbath was made for man, He who is man's Lord and Representative has authority to determine its laws and use."[88] This is perhaps saying too much, but probably he is on the right track. I have argued that Jesus did indeed use the phrase Son of Man of himself during the course of his ministry, alluding on various occasions to Daniel 7.[89] If this is so, then Jesus saw himself as the representative of God's people who would be given dominion over, among other things, kingdoms. C. M. Tuckett has detected in this present Son of Man saying the concept of the Son of Man's rejection, hence his need to assert his authority.[90]

That Jesus had controversies with other Jews over what was appropriate behavior on the sabbath seems highly likely since it is well attested in Mark here and in 3:1–6, in Luke's special material (cf. 13:10–17; 14:1–6); and also in John (cf. 5:1–18; 9:1–41).[91] In addition, other texts make clear that Jesus appealed to the creation order to establish some of his novel teaching (cf. Mark 10.:6 and par.).

This suggests that the meaning of these two verses is that human beings, not least because they were created before the sabbath and the sabbath was given for their rest and restoration, are more important than the observance of sabbath regulations. Giving them rest and restoration, which was the original purpose of the sabbath, takes precedence over the strict observance of Mosaic sabbath rules. The question then becomes, who has the authority to say when one is in a situation when the sabbath's purpose is better served and honored by not obeying its Mosaic strictures?[92]

Jesus argues that since the sabbath was made for (Jewish) humankind in the first place, and not the other way around, then surely the result of accepting the principle in v 27 is that the Son of Man, who is the representative of God's people given dominion over many things, has authority over the disposition of sabbath behavior. His authority is an extension of an authority given in principle to all God's people. Put another way, Jesus' authority over the sabbath is the logical outcome of the fact that: (1) the sabbath has been made for him and other Jews; and (2) as their representative he has both the right and authority to make rulings based on his understanding of the original purpose of the sabbath. This is a perfectly logical argument once one considers the larger context which involves Jesus' self-understanding as Son of Man and his sabbath controversies. The First Evangelist and Luke flinched at this argument because of the suggestion that Jesus' authority might be seen as an extension

[88] V. Taylor, *The Gospel According to St. Mark*, 219.

[89] Witherington, *Christology of Jesus*, pp 238ff.

[90] C. M. Tuckett, "The Present Son of Man,", 58–81; he is very likely right to argue for the overlap of present and suffering Son of Man sayings in Q and elsewhere.

[91] Allison and Davies, *Matthew*, Vol. 2 (1991), 304–05.

[92] Verse 27 should probably not be seen as a general maxim about humanity in general, since in Jesus' day the sabbath was seen as a provision of the Mosaic law given especially to Jews. This maxim is part of an internal Jewish debate.

or, better said, a result and representative expression of the authority given to Jews in general in regard to the sabbath. The one who was lord over disease and suffering had now been shown to be lord *even* over the sabbath.[93]

It is not impossible that we have here Jesus' answer to the kind of logic one finds in *Jubilees* 2:18ff. where it is argued that the sabbath was first kept in heaven, and afterward God created Israel in order to have a people to observe the sabbath on earth. This is the precise opposite of Jesus' argument here.

Whether or not Mark 2:27–28 is in its original setting, as a likely authentic utterance of Jesus[94] it reveals several points of importance for our study. First, the theology Jesus the sage appeals to in order to justify his novel behavior or that of his disciples is a creation theology, which is characteristic of Jewish Wisdom thought. Second, Jesus may be drawing on a traditional Wisdom maxim (v 27 in some earlier form), but he turns it into an aphorism of counter order standing over against a certain approach to the Mosaic sabbath strictures, and for good measure makes clear that he himself as the people's representative has authority to make such pronouncements, precisely because God gave such authority to his creatures at the outset.[95] Third, the way Jesus exercises his authority is much like the manner in which ancient sages operated. He does not try to justify his pronouncements on the basis of a "thus saith Yahweh" or a chain of citations from previous Jewish teachers, but assumes an authority based on his own personal observation or understanding of things (like Qoheleth), or perhaps on the basis of new revelation (like Ben Sira), although the latter is not alluded to in this text.[96] Fourth, here, as in Ben Sira, one sees a mixture of things. One or possibly two aphorisms are coined and used to make a statement about a legal matter, and v. 28 even draws on a phrase from the apocalyptic material in Daniel. The form of address is sapiential but legal and apocalyptic matters have been sapientialized and used in the service of Wisdom theology – namely creation theology.[97]

---

[93] The *kai* suggests that this is seen as exceptional authority, not, as Crossan suggests, that this power over the sabbath is "just barely achieved" (*Fragments*, 80).

[94] Would Mark or the early church before him really have made up or combined two sayings which could be understood to suggest (and were so understood by Luke and the First Evangelist) that Jesus' authority derived from the general authority given to God's people?

[95] E. Schweizer, *The Goods News according to Mark*, 73: "It is the presence of the Son of Man which makes such freedom possible, because in him God's will for man has been realized, namely, God's full and complete giving. Therefore, as Lord of the Sabbath Jesus gives the Sabbath back to man to be a help; he does not lay it on man as a burden."

[96] It will be noted that there is no evidence that v 27 originally had the phrase 'son of man' in it. Cf. Schweizer, *Mark*, 71. Schweizer notes that this saying does not easily comport with Mark's messianic secret theme which strongly suggests Mark did not invent it. Furthermore, the suggestion that in v 28 an original a–titular use of Son of Man was changed into a titular one comports neither with the tendency of Jesus to make personal and situation specific observations, not coin general proverbs, nor with the evidence of the Gospel tradition itself where it is always *the* Son of Man, whatever layer of tradition, or source of tradition (Mark, Q, Special L, M, or John) one may consult.

[97] The interesting *agraphon* where Jesus says to someone working on the sabbath, "Man if you know what you are doing you are blessed; but if you do not know you are cursed and a transgressor of the law" which is found at the location of Luke 6.5 in manuscript D (cf.

Right beverage, Wrong Container (Mark 2:22 and par. Gospel of Thomas 47b). Though one could focus on the saying about the unshrunk cloth sewn onto the old garment (Mark. 2:21 par.), because its significance is much the same as the saying in Mark 2:22 (and par.)[98] and because the two sayings are very likely an example of an aphoristic compound made out of originally independent sayings, the focus here will be on the second saying.[99] Wine was one of the standing topics discussed by sages and is the subject of both proverbs and more discursive kinds of Wisdom speech (cf. Prov. 20:1; 23:30; Sir. 31:25ff.). Here, however, is another example of metaphorical speech; Jesus is not really concerned to reflect on the problem of wine placed in the wrong sort of containers. More germane is the earlier Wisdom saying of Ben Sira: "Do not abandon old friends, for new ones cannot equal them. A new friend is like new wine; when it has aged you can drink it with pleasure" (9:10). Here as there one finds a metaphorical use of the subject, playing on the difference between new and old wine. There may be a certain fitness to the fact that our saying is grouped together with the discussion about fasting/feasting and proper garments – all three subjects could arise in a discussion of proper decorum at a wedding.[100] It is believable that this saying arose either in the context of Jesus contrasting his ministry and what was appropriate thereto with John the Baptist's, or perhaps in a more polemical discussion with opponents who wanted to know why Jesus was so unconventional.[101] There is little or no debate over the authenticity of this saying.[102]

The saying itself has a complicated tradition history, as has been shown by Crossan.[103] The original form of the saying seems to have read essentially the way one finds it in Mark. Luke seems to have assimilated the garment saying to the wine saying by changing Mark's shrunk/unshrunk to the old/new contrast in the wine saying (cf. Luke 5:36). The version in the *Gospel of Thomas*

Metzger, *Textual Commentary*, 140), may go back to Jesus. Cf. J. Jeremias, *Unknown Sayings of Jesus*, 49–54. On the other hand, as J. Fitzmyer, *The Gospel According to Luke I–IX*, 610 points out, the saying is similar to Copt. Gos Thomas saying 3 and 14 and probably belongs to the apocryphal Gospel traditions.

[98] Despite the protest of Crossan, *In Fragments*, 122ff. against assimilating the two sayings, in the end he admits that both are about "combinational impossibility" (127).

[99] Crossan, *In Fragments*, 122–24.

[100] But cf. I. H. Marshall, *The Gospel of Luke* , 223; Crossan, *In Fragments*, 121.

[101] There is no evidence he is contrasting a new and old covenant, or a new people of God versus an old one in some sort of replacement schema. On the opponents here being Pharisees, cf. J. A. Ziesler, "The Removal of the Bridegroom: A Note on Mark II.18–22 and Parallels," 190–94, here 192.

[102] Cf. Pesch, *Markusevangelium* I, 177–78. Throughout this chapter with rare exceptions, I am basically choosing to deal, with sayings and parables about which there is little or no debate in regard to their authenticity, at least in regard to their *ipsissima structura* if not their *ipsissima verba*. To be sure R. Bultmann, *The History of the Synoptic Tradition*, 102, thought these are secular *meshalim* here which have been taken up into the Jesus tradition and turned into dominical sayings. He does not substantiate this claim, however. Cf. A. Kee, "The Old Coat and the New Wine," 17.

[103] Crossan, *In Fragments*, 121–27

47b seems to be later than that of Mark, speaking of spoiled not lost wine, which may reflect a knowledge of the first evangelist's added comment "and so both are *preserved*'" (cf. Matt. 9:17). An even stronger case can be made for the dependency of the saying in Thomas on the Lukan version of the text, because both add a saying about drinking old wine, and the Lukan form of that saying seems more primitive.[104] In any case, the First Evangelist has muted the force of the contrast in the saying by his addition which suggests that both new and old are good things worth preserving. But was he right to read the saying as being about a new/old contrast?

Crossan has suggested that, "The point of the double aphorism is not the victory of the new over the old, but the impossibility of bringing together certain objects. The stress is on combinational impossibility, not on novel superiority."[105] In terms of the *stress*, this conclusion seems to be correct, especially if this saying is part of an original pair with the cloth saying, for its original form seems to have been about shrunk/unshrunk and incompatibility, not primarily about new/old.[106] But the element of new/old should not be neglected as a secondary point. After all, unshrunk cloth will be new cloth, and old wineskins, made of goatskin,[107] burst precisely because it is new wine, still involved in the early stages of fermentation, that is put in them.[108] G. Brooke has attempted to see this aphorism in the light of the reference to the new wine feast at Qumran (cf. 11QTemple 21.4–7). He stresses the contrast is not between old and new, as bad and good, but is about the incompatibility of acting in old ways when a new situation has arisen which calls for different behavior appropriate to the occasion.[109]

What then is the point of this aphorism? Is it that "new occasions teach new duties?" If one stresses the matter of incongruity and imagines this saying as arising out of the controversy caused by the difference in behavior between Jesus' and John's disciples, the point will be that certain kinds of traditional behavior (such as fasting or abstinence from wine), which are fine for John's

---

[104] Allison and Davies, *Matthew*, Vol. 2, 116; and especially Fitzmyer, *Luke 1–9*, 596. The reversal of the order of the aphorisms in both Luke and Thomas surely also points to some sort of relationship. Cf. also Schweizer, *Mark*, 67 on Thomas' saying being a later development in comparison to Mark's or Luke's. On the Lukan form of the saying, cf. J. Dupont, "Vin Vieux, Vin Nouveau (Luc 5,39)," 286–304. He sees the point of the aphorism as driving the listener to choose between two incompatible things.

[105] Crossan, *In Fragments*, 127.

[106] The question must be raised as to whether Jesus' penchant for pairing parables (cf. Witherington, *Women in the Ministry of Jesus*, 40ff.) carried over into the way he handled aphorisms. This is certain possible; cf. Marshall, *Luke*, 224.

[107] Cf. Allison and Davies, *Matthew*, Vol. 2, 115.

[108] The attempt by D. Flusser to argue for Lukan priority over Mark in general, and on that basis for the authenticity of Luke 5:39 is clearly a case of special pleading. He fails to come to grips with the counter order quality in many of the likely authentic sayings of Jesus. Cf. D. Flusser, "Do You Prefer New Wine?" 26–31.

[109] G. Brooke, "The Feast of New Wine and the Question of Fasting," *ET* 95 (1983–84), 175–76.

disciples since he is the last of the old line of prophets, are inappropriate for Jesus' followers because Jesus is doing a new thing. This saying would be fending off criticism of Jesus' disciples and by implication himself. A. Kee is surely missing the point in suggesting that the saying is about securing oneself against the danger of loss by avoiding ill-considered actions.[110] The issue is either inappropriate combinations or the old/new contrast or more likely both.

J. Jeremias has suggested that Jesus is here using traditional metaphors for the new or eschatological age.[111] This sort of idea does seem to be present in John 2:1–11, but in the one really appropriate text that might provide a backdrop to our saying, Gen. 49:11–12, the discussion is about about Judah's kingship and his conquering his enemies (cf. 49:8).[112] This latter point hardly seems to stand in the background here.

Thus, this saying very likely represents an aphorism of counter order used to fend off criticism of Jesus' disciples or Jesus or both. It was not unprecedented for a sage to say new things and coin new sayings as has been seen both in Qoheleth's aphorisms, and also to a lesser extent in Ben Sira who said, "If the great Lord is willing he [the sage/scribe] will be filled with the spirit of understanding; he will pour forth words of wisdom of his own" (Sir. 39:6). To a certain extent, Jesus was a sage who practiced reorientation by disorientation.[113] The new things he said and did, coupled with the new behavior of his disciples caught people off guard and raised questions as to how such things were compatible with previous Jewish traditions, Torah, Wisdom. Jesus' response was that it was time to do something new, something which was in some ways incompatible with previous ways of doing things. This response was very likely grounded in Jesus' conviction that God's eschatological reign was breaking into the midst of Israel through his ministry.[114]

Lost and Found (Mark 8:35 and par). If one really wants to talk about reorientation by disorientation, or in this case by paradox, in the aphorisms of Jesus, one must discuss a saying like Mark 8:35 (and par). By the criterion of multiple attestation this saying has a good chance of going back to Jesus in some form, for it is found not only in Mark but also in Q (cf. Matt.10:39/Luke 17:33), and in John 12:25.[115] Its original form seems to have read, "Whoever would save his

---

[110] A. Kee, "The Old Coat and the New Wine," 13–21.

[111] Cf. J. Jeremias, *The Parables of Jesus*, 115.

[112] The image, "he shall wash his garment in wine and his robes in the blood of new wine," seems to be understood as one of conquest (cf. Rev. 19.13, cf. 14.18–20) in the last book in the Bible, not one of celebration of new life. The other texts Jeremias cites (Gen. 9.20, Num. 13.23–24) seem quite irrelevant.

[113] Borrowing a phrase from Ricouer, "Biblical Hermeneutics," 71 and 122–28, though I am using it in a somewhat different fashion.

[114] Witherington, *Christology of Jesus*, 191ff. and Pesch, *Markusevangelium*, I, 177.

[115] For an extended argument for the authenticity of the Markan form of the saying, without "for my sake and the sake of the Gospel," cf. W. Rebell, "'Sein Leben verlieren' (Mark 8.35

life will lose it; and whoever loses his life will save it."[116] This saying is in antithetical format, and may be called an aphorism of reversal.[117] C. F. Burney has argued that of all the various sorts of Semitic parallelism, antithetical parallelism is the form most often found in the Jesus tradition, and in fact he takes it to be a pointer to when one has found an authentic word of Jesus.[118] Of equal importance is Jeremias' observation that while in an Old Testament saying in antithetical parallelism the dominant member of the saying is usually the first member, with the second illuminating and/or deepening the first, in Jesus' antithetical aphorisms one normally has end stress (emphasis is placed on the second half).[119] A careful examination of Proverbs 10ff. shows that this is often, though not always so (cf. e.g. Prov. 10:2). If Jeremias' observation provides the clue to understanding Mark 8:35, then the emphasis will be on the rewards of self-giving, presumably self-giving in the course of being a faithful disciple of Jesus. The form of this saying entails a conditional remark with *hos ean* introducing the protasis, and a future verb in the apodosis. As such it explains what will happen under certain conditions. Whether one "saves one's life" in the end or loses it is determined by the course of life now.

R. Pesch has rightly observed that here one has Jesus' own formulation of the act–consequence idea.[120] He stresses that in the light of other sayings like Mark 9:41 or Mark 11:23 which contain the act–consequence idea that this saying is about eschatological reversal of fortunes. The saying is trying to counter a self-seeking approach to things, and offers the advice that one who lives a self-giving and sacrificial life now will in the end be recompensed by God. The person who does not do this has not lived by placing his life in God's hands and acting accordingly. Rather the self-centered person lives as though life is not a gift, and one may do as one pleases with it ("it's my life!").

But by the principle of end stress it may be that Jesus is mainly interested in affirming that discipleship can prove very costly, one may even lose one's life.[121] Even if that should happen, one should not worry for God will right things in the end. There is certainly nothing here about wrongs being righted by means of the compensation of heaven and, in the light of sayings like Mark

parr.) also Strukturmoment vorund nachosterlichen Glaubens," 202–18, especially 203–09. Rebell argues that in this saying we find a key link between the pre– and post–Easter followers of Jesus, namely the call to radical self–giving as a mark of being a follower of Jesus.

[116] Schweizer, *Mark*, 176–77; Crossan, *In Fragments*, 88–95; Rebell, "Sein Leben," 209–10.

[117] R. C. Tannehill, "Reading it Whole: The Function of Mark 8.34–35 in Mark's Story," 67–78 calls it an antithetical aphorism.

[118] C. F. Burney, *The Poetry of Our Lord*, 73ff.

[119] Jeremias, *Parables of Jesus* (1971), 18.

[120] Pesch, *Markusevangelium* II, 58.

[121] W. A. Beardslee, "Saving One's Life by Losing It," 57–72, here 60. Beardslee has amassed numerous parallels to this saying which may suggest Jesus is appropriating a common saying for his own purposes.

8:38, 9:41, 10:25 (and other entrance sayings) and 14:25, it seems certain that Jesus is thinking of eschatological reversal, presumably in the kingdom.[122] This is significant because in this Jesus is not departing from a Wisdom perspective but rather further developing the one we have already found in Sirach and to a lesser degree in the Wisdom of Solomon.

It is possible that one should see this paradoxical saying as a kind of riddle. J. Crenshaw, in commenting on riddles as a form of Wisdom speech, says that a riddle,

> both puzzles the hearers and communicates to them. Riddles can only arise where language is ambiguous, for they employ the common vocabulary to dispense privileged information to those worthy of receiving it. In antiquity riddles tread on perimeters of myth and divination, particularly in rites of passage. Often constituting a judgment situation, they generate anxiety on the part of riddler and opponent. [They are] tests of worthiness more than intelligence.... In Israel *hidha*, riddle... serves as an umbrella term referring to enigmatic proverbs and allegories....[123]

This saying certainly seems to function in the way described above; it would create anxiety, but its paradoxical character would mean that its significance would not be immediately apparently. Surely it would only be penetrable by Jesus' disciples, those who had the context of his ministry and other teachings to interpret it by, if it could be understood at all. As such it can be taken as a comment indicating the cost and rewards of being Jesus' disciple. "What the saying demands is a readiness to give up even one's life for Jesus or the kingdom."[124] Thus, this saying, as W. A. Beardslee notes, is about self-transcendence through becoming and being a disciple of Jesus.[125] A human being "is caught up in self-defeating care to maintain himself in the world, but his great hope lies in the word that he is already valued by God.... One must give up the maintenance of a little self-order as the primary concern and give oneself over to the new divine order, in which the meaning of individual-in-community has everlasting significance."[126] By this sort of aphorism of a counter order fundamental human motivations such as the desire for safety and security in life are shown to be less important or of no importance in comparison to

---

[122] Witherington, *Jesus, Paul, and the End of the World*, 57ff.

[123] J. Crenshaw, "Riddle," 749–50, here 749. He adds that riddles deal in paradoxes.

[124] Fitzmyer, *Luke 1–9*, 788. The term *psuche* here means life or even self, not the Greek idea of soul. The parallel saying in *B. T. Tamid* 66a should be consulted, but both the form of the rabbinic saying and its probable lateness do not suggest a necessary relationship with our saying. Furthermore, the rabbinic saying suggests death comes by a life of pleasure, but there is nothing to that effect in Mark 8:35. Cf. Rebell, "Sein Leben," 204.

[125] Beardslee, "Saving One's Life," 67.

[126] Williams, *Those who Ponder Proverbs*, 52.

following the example of Jesus who did indeed save his life (and others) by losing it.[127]

Slaving to Gain Mastery (Mt. 10:24–25a/Luke 6:40). In another context I have shown that it is highly likely that Jesus was not only a teacher of godly Wisdom, but one who gathered disciples around him.[128] It would appear that this was the perspective of even Josephus, who is reported in *Ant.* 18.63 to have said, "Now at this time there lived... a wise man... He was one who performed surprising feats and was a teacher of the sort of people who accept the truth gladly. He won over many Jews..." While the so-called *Testimonium Flavianum* very likely has Christian interpolations, various scholars, both Christian and Jewish, have been inclined to take at least the portion quoted above as representing Josephus' actual evaluation of Jesus.[129]

This chapter has already begun to show considerable evidence that Jesus may be characterized as a sage or, as Josephus puts it, a *sophos aner*. Having already noted some of the ways Jesus seems to have differed from earlier sages, this aphorism suggests at least one important way in which Jesus may have been very much like a Ben Sira.

Did Jesus, like earlier sages before him, engage in a programatic transmission of his teachings to a group of disciples? We should recall the appendix to Qoheleth's book (Eccles. 12:9–12) and Ben Sira's words in various places throughout his book (e.g. Sir. 33:18; 39:1–3; 51:23–26). The appendix to Qoheleth indicates that the sage taught, and that in addition to creating *meshalim* of various sorts he studied and arranged and weighed them as well. The "Assembler" or "Collector" was one who deliberately sought to find pleasing words, words that could be learned and remembered. The collected sayings of such a sage are said to be like goads on the one hand, and like firmly fixed nails on the other. Here already there are clues about the programatic transmission of a collection of a sage's sayings. It was recognized that a sage was one who would reflect on previous godly Wisdom and carefully arrange and express it, as well as doing the same with his own contribution to the ongoing stream of Wisdom tradition.

---

[127] I think Tannehill, "Seeing it Whole," 70ff. is quite right that such sayings are meant to show how Jesus' teaching comes into conflict with basic human motivations and also, in the Markan outline to prepare the hearer for the passion story where Jesus himself proves the truth of this aphorism. The pattern pointed out by Tannehill of a three-fold announcement of coming passion (Mark 8:31, 9:31, 10:32) followed by a three–fold rejection of or resistance to this by disciples, which in turn is followed by the three–fold correction of that resistance by an aphorism of counter order or another similar corrective teaching (cf. 8:34 — 9.1; 9:35–37; 10:42–45) is intriguing. This suggests that such a climactic aphorism is meant to settle the issue, a function an aphorism at the end of a story seems to have elsewhere. On the call to risky and outrageous behavior in some of Jesus' aphorisms, cf. Crossan, *Historical Jesus*, 353.

[128] Witherington, *Christology of Jesus*, 179ff.

[129] G. Vermes, "The Jesus Notice of Josephus Re–Examined," 2–10; R. Riesner, "Jesus as Preacher and Teacher," 185–210, here 185–86.

Turning for a moment to Ben Sira, in Sir. 33:16ff the sage drew an analogy between himself and a gleaner who to his surprise turned into a grape picker, and indeed a cultivator of his own grapes. Ben Sira stresses that he did this for all who sought instruction. Jewish sages did not teach in a vacuum; they instructed disciples. The closing invitation, very likely from Ben Sira himself, is to come and study with him, even to lodge in a house of instruction. The point is that to gain Wisdom requires ongoing disciplined study, not just occasional listening. The sages gave their teachings in forms that would be both memorable and memorizable by those who were diligent to learn such things.

In view of the many similarities both in form and content of Jesus' teaching with the teachings of previous sages, coupled with the evidence that Jesus had ongoing listeners, even apparently going beyond previous sages by *gathering* disciples who had time to reflect on and hear again and again many of Jesus' teachings, it seems to me that we have a very plausible *Sitz im Leben* out of which to explain the rise of the Jesus tradition.

Without making too much of this, it is striking that the earliest Gospel suggests that Jesus instructs many *in house* and in depth, including especially his inner circle of disciples. This is said to have included the explanation of the meaning of various of his *meshalim* (cf. e.g. Mark 2:1–2; 2:13–14; 4:10–12; 4:33, 9:30). While doubtless some of this may reflect Mark's own special interests, the material cited above does not easily fall into the "messianic secret" category,[130] and the evidence elsewhere, including the Q saying about to be examined, is strong that Jesus did have an ongoing inner circle of disciples whom he deliberately instructed.[131] The pattern of public discourse of a Jewish teacher followed by private explanation for the initiates is found in early Jewish traditions outside the Gospels as well, involving another important first century Jewish teacher, Johanan ben Zacchai.[132] It may be that Jesus was following a common practice in this regard. [133]

It was always a problem for the Gerhardsson theory that it had to argue that Jesus' words were treated like Holy Writ, and to some extent this entailed envisioning the disciples as a group of *talmidim*.[134] Besides the obvious problem of anachronism when one projects later rabbinic practices back into pre A.D. 70 Judaism, there is also the further problem that the evidence is slim that the focus of both Jesus' teaching and the learning of Jesus' disciples was *Torah*. Jesus' teaching, while often drawing on Torah, does not, by and large,

---

[130] Witherington, *Christology of Jesus*, 263ff. argues that there are several motifs, and the teaching in privacy is something distinct from the so–called Messianic secret motif.

[131] Witherington, *Christology of Jesus*, 118–42.

[132] D. Daube, "Public Pronouncement and Private Explanation in the Gospels," 175–77.

[133] For examples from a somewhat later period (though some are from the later part of the first century A.D.) of rabbis teaching in the gate of the city (in Sepphoris, Jamnia, and Tiberias, *et al.*) or in the door of their house, and then having questions from their disciples, cf. A. Buchler, "Learning and Teaching in the Open Air in Palestine," 485–91.

[134] Cf. my critique of Gerhardsson in Witherington, *Christology of Jesus*, 180–81.

have the character of *halakah* or even *haggadah*. Rather, it is sapiential in character.

But there is nothing preventing the conclusion that Jesus systematically taught like previous sages, and his disciples both learned and even memorized various of his aphorisms and narrative *meshalim*. Anyone who has closely examined Wisdom teaching knows that much of it involves something that appears to be carefully and consciously pre-formulated, crafted so that it will be memorable, not usually something thought up on the spur of the moment in response to the immediate circumstances. Both the character of Jesus' teaching (normally given in poetic and/or some sort of memorizable form), and the evidence of the approach to learning by the disciples of earlier sages encourage one to think of rote learning as not merely possible but likely among Jesus' inner circle.[135]

Not only does the content of the Jesus tradition not encourage us to think that Jesus' teaching amounted to either *halakah* or *haggadah*, but it also does not seem to have been seen by the earliest Christian tradents primarily as prophecy, much less prophecy of the ascended Lord.[136] The vast preponderance of parables and aphorisms in the Synoptic tradition makes such a conjecture highly unlikely. J. Kloppenborg is right to point out that especially in Q,

> the dominant mode of address is sapiential, not prophetic. There is no indication that the *lego humin* is that of the Exalted Lord speaking through the mouth of his prophets; it is rather the *lego humin* of a teacher of wisdom speaking to followers. Q lacks the repetitive forms characteristic of prophetic genres: "The word of the Lord came to..." "Thus says the Lord," "As I live." The mode of persuasion is not prophetic – by appeal to the authority of God – but sapiential, by rhetorical question and appeal to observation of nature and ordinary human relations.[137]

---

[135] On education in Jewish antiquity, the raw data assembled by Riesner in *Jesus al Lehrer* is indispensable even though his methodology and conclusions are not always without flaws. Cf. also Crenshaw, "Education in Ancient Israel," 601–15, on the possibility of schools in the period before Ben Sira.

[136] It is for this reason that I continue to be skeptical of the theory of M. E. Boring, *The Continuing Voice of Jesus. Christian Prophecy and the Gospel Tradition* (especially 155ff.) and others, that there is any significant amount of teachings of the ascended Lord spoken through the mouths of later Christian prophets in the Synoptic tradition. Even when there are revelatory sayings in the Synoptics, it is not "thus saith the Lord" but rather the sort of revelation a godly sage like a Ben Sira or Jesus might claim to give. We have alluded to the tradition that tells us that the sages (during and after the time of Jesus) were gradually taking the place of prophets. This would presumably involve them offering new relevation, though in sapiential form. There is no reason why Jesus, like Ben Sira before him, could not have claimed to do this, believing *as Ben Sira believed* that he stood at the end of one era and thus also the beginning of another (cf. Sir. 33.16). Perhaps this may explain the cryptic comments in the Jesus tradition suggesting that John the Baptist was seen as the last great prophet before the eschatological age (cf. the Q material in Matt. 11:9–15; Luke 7:26–28).

[137] Kloppenborg, *The Formation of Q*, 321.

Jesus' words were seen to be examples of godly Wisdom, and were learned and transmitted accordingly. This very likely continued to be true at least during the era when Jewish Christianity, in particular Palestinian Jewish Christianity, was the primary if not sole matrix through which the Jesus tradition was transmitted. That is, the Jesus tradition was treated and transmitted in a sapiential fashion at least until the time when the Q material was first put into writing, probably in Palestine, and possibly as various Q scholars aver in Galilee.[138]

This is not to say that there was not redaction of the Jesus tradition, even from the earliest period of transmission. The very character of the sayings of Jesus in the Synoptics (and elsewhere) require such a conclusion. One's theory must account for the hard data of the various permutations and combinations of aphorisms and parables that have already been noticed in this chapter, and this requires careful work in tradition history. Nevertheless, the analogy with other sapiential material, coupled with what can be known about the process of learning amongst the Jewish disciples of sages, encourages one to think that the techniques used in the early transmission of Jesus' sayings would have placed more stress on *conservation* than on innovation. Recent studies of the Teacher of Righteousness sayings which demonstrate the fundamentally conservative way they were handled and redacted by his community of followers encourage one to draw this conclusion as well.[139] Conservation rather than innovation was the order of the day in the Wisdom tradition of teaching and learning especially since "a disciple is not above his teacher," which leads us to discuss the aphorism at hand.

The aphorism found in Matt. 10:24–25a/Luke 6:40 and in John 13:16/John15:20 has good claims to go back to Jesus in some form on the criterion of multiple attestation, for most scholars would accept that the Johannine forms of the saying represent an independent attestation to it.[140] It also seems likely that the Q form of the saying originally included both Matt. 10:24 and 10:25a, which Luke has then truncated in Luke. 6:40.[141] It appears that neither Matthew

---

[138] On the possible link of Q with Greek speaking Jewish Christians from Jerusalem and their mission, cf. R. Piper, *Wisdom in the Q Tradition: The Aphoristic Teaching of Jesus*, 184–92.

[139] Cf. S. Talmon, "Oral Transmission and Written Transmission, or the Heard and Seen Word in Judaism of the Second Temple Period," in *Jesus and the Oral Gospel*, 121–58. "It seems that in the transfer of the Teacher's message from one medium to the other, the one–time oral tradition became written transmission without undergoing any spectacular changes. Nothing gives grounds for thinking a dramatic hermeneutic shift occured when his spoken words became written text.... No other corpus of sacred traditions in the entire spread of Judaism at the end of the Second Temple period can as fruitfully serve as a model by which to gauge the behavior of sacred traditions in the Gospels" (158).

[140] Cf. the careful work of C. H. Dodd, *Historical Tradition in the Fourth Gospel*, 335–38.

[141] Cf. Crossan, *In Fragments*, 86; Fitzmyer, *Luke 1–9*, 642; J. S. Kloppenborg, *Q Parallels*, 38. It is not impossible that the first half of this saying is Jesus' use of a traditional proverb, and the servant analogy certainly seems to be quoting a traditional aphorism; cf. Allison and Davies, *Matthew*, Vol. 2, 193–94. On Matt. 10:25 (and par.), cf. the Sipra on Lev. 25:23 – "*dayyo le'ebed seyyihyeh kerabbo*."

nor Luke have placed this aphorism in its original context. Luke 6.39 is about leading and misleading, but Luke 6:40 is about following and being like one's teacher. Matthew has placed the saying in a persecution context in relation to the Beelzebul controversy. However, taken on face value this saying is about the proper relationship of a teacher and his disciples. It is implied that it is like the relationship of a master and a slave. The disciple has no authority over his teacher, any more than a slave has over his master. Since one is talking about a pedagogical relationship, this implies that the disciple's task is to learn, to receive whatever authoritative teaching the teacher may give, probably involving committing it to memory at least in some cases. There is also the further thought in both the Matthean and Lukan form of the saying about the disciple being like the teacher.

Luke specifies that this likeness comes about when the disciple is fully taught. The key verb here is *katartidzo* which literally means "made complete". It should be noted that this verb is used elsewhere in the New Testament of mutual edification and upbuilding which involves among other things instruction (cf. Gal. 6:1; 1 Cor. 1:10; 1 Pet. 5:10).[142] The disciple is like the master when s/he is built up, fully edified, or as Crossan rightly translates it, "fully taught".[143] This implies that an essential element in following Jesus and being like him is learning his teaching.

Several critical insights come to light from this aphorism. The first is that Jesus not only had disciples but that he very likely called them disciples, which is to say learners.[144] Second, Jesus assumed the authority of a sage, one who taught his pupils godly Wisdom. It was the job of the disciple to learn and conserve the teaching of the master. The disciple could not assume authority over his teacher or his teaching. Third, the disciple could only be equal to the teacher when s/he was fully instructed – then only was s/he complete. Here then in this aphorism we have a brief glimpse of and a window into the *Sitz im Leben* out of which the Jesus tradition very likely originally came.

Return to Sender (Matt. 10:40/Luke 10:16/John 13:20 and par.) This saying appears to have had a complicated tradition history. It would appear that the saying was known to Mark, the editors of Q and John, and so very likely in some form goes back to Jesus.[145] Mark, who is the only one who mentions children in this context (Mark 9:37), has introduced that idea from his other material on that

---

142 Marshall, *Luke*, 269.

143 Crossan, *In Fragments*, 86; Kloppenborg, *Q Parallels*, 39; J. Nolland, *Luke 1–9.20*, 305–07.

144 Cf. Riesner, "Jesus as Preacher and Teacher," who points out about both the Hebrew equivalents and *mathetes*: "All these expressions mean someone who learns. Interestingly, the word *mathetes* in the New Testament is restricted to pupils of Jewish teachers, pre–Easter disciples of Jesus, some post–Easter believers in close contact with the pre–Easter community and in one case to pupils of Paul (Acts 9:25)" (197).

145 E. Schweizer, *Mark*, 253.

subject (cf. Mark 9:36–37; 10:13–16).[146] Some consideration should be given to the fact that in the Jewish Wisdom tradition a learner is regularly addressed as the teacher's child or more particularly son (cf. Prov. 1:8; 2:1; 3:1; Sir. 2:1; 3:1; 3:17; 4.1). In the light of such usage in the Wisdom tradition, it is not out of the question that Jesus could have used the term child to refer to a disciple, but Mark 9:36 makes clear that the Evangelist understands Jesus to be talking about a literal child. It is better then to assume that Q and John reflect an earlier stage in the tradition.

This saying should be understood as reflecting the Jewish concept of agency – "a person's *shaliach* is like unto himself" (*Mish. Ber.* 5.5).[147] Agency could involve acting legally for a person or conveying a message for the sender. Whatever may have been the task, the one sent and his word were to be received as if the sender had personally delivered it. Coming as it does at the end of the Q missionary discourse, one is encouraged to see this as a saying indicating that Jesus did indeed send out his disciples, or at least the inner circle, as his agents to carry forth and carry farther his message and ministry. But it is also a saying that suggests that Jesus saw himself as a person under authority of the one who sent him, and sent for a specific purpose and duration.

The Matthean form of the saying seems to focus more specifically on the matter of hospitality ("who welcomes/receives you"), while the Lukan form focuses on being heard, though this may be a false dichotomy since the Aramaic word *qabbel* can mean either "receive" or "hear and accept".[148] In view of the parallel in John 13:20 it may be that Luke has altered the saying, but probably he has not altered its primary sense for if the disciples were sent out as Jesus' agents, then they were not sent simply to take advantage of the system of standing hospitality. They were sent to deliver a message which might or might not be received. Bultmann argues that the original form of the saying is found in Luke 10:16 and that the First Evangelist substituted a separate tradition (Matt. 10:40–42), but this seems less likely than that the First Evangelist and Luke are citing two forms of the *same* tradition.[149]

The import of this saying for this discussion is as follows. First, *if* as has been seen in the discussion of Matt. 10:24–25a (and par.), Jesus did indeed teach and fully train his disciples in godly Wisdom and then sent them forth during his ministry at least on a trial basis for a specific period of time, *then* there already is in the pre-Easter period an occasion for the transmission of Jesus' teaching by his disciples. Second, disciples endowed as *shalihim* with the authority of him who sent them have a limited commission, not to create a message but rather to convey one. I would suggest that at least to a large extent this message involved telling of the Good News of the inbreaking Dominion of

[146] Crossan, *In Fragments*, 109.
[147] Witherington, *Christology of Jesus*, 132ff.
[148] Marshall, *Luke*, 426.
[149] Bultmann, *Die Geschichte*, 152–53.

God, using various forms of Wisdom speech specifically and especially aphorisms and narrative *meshalim*. They were to be like goads or fixed nails giving people some substantive way to grapple with and hopefully grasp the meaning of Jesus' message and ministry. Third, if this did in fact happen, then it was all the more crucial that Jesus should explain various of these sayings to his disciples in full, especially the narrative *meshalim*.

Mourning and Evening; Hunger and Thirst (Matt. 5:4, 6/Luke 6:21). This section concludes by looking at two examples of what have been called aphoristic beatitudes. There are fifteen of these in the canonical Gospels and another thirteen in the *Gospel of Thomas*.[150] In view of the fact that one finds beatitudes in international Wisdom literature, in particular in Egyptian and Old Testament Wisdom literature,[151] or in contexts which have been influenced by sapiential concerns (cf. Job 5:17; Gen. 30:13; Ps. 1:1–2; Sir. 25:8–10; 28:19; 14:1–2), it is probable that one should call a beatitude a sapiential form of expression. It is also an example of yet another Wisdom form that is appropriated in prophetic or apocalyptic contexts to express some eschatological matters (cf. Dan. 12:12; Tob. 13:14; *Psalms of Solomon* 17:44; *1 Enoch* 58:2–3). This is especially relevant to the discussion of Matt. 5:4, 6 (and par.) for they too are eschatological beatitudes.

The two beatitudes now under scrutiny are Q beatitudes.[152] Though there are significant differences between the Matthean and Lukan forms, nevertheless they both retain the basic structure of *makarios* plus the subject plus a *hoti* clause. In making determinations about the original form of these beatitudes one must also take into consideration *Gospel of Thomas* 69b: "Blessed are the hungry, so that the belly of the one who desires will be filled." This is closer to the Lukan form of this macarism except it is *not in the second person*. On balance it seems likely that Luke has changed beatitudes originally in the third person to a second person form, perhaps so they would match up with the woes he includes in Luke 6:24–26.[153] Furthermore, the form of most of the earlier Jewish beatitudes favors the view that the third person address is original here.

Probably the original form of these two beatitudes was as follows: "Blessed are those who mourn, for they shall be consoled.... Blessed are those

---

150 Cf. the list in Aune, "Oral Tradition," 227ff.

151 J. Dupont, "Béatitudes egyptiennes,", 185–222.

152 Kloppenborg, *Q Parallels*, 26–27.

153 Allison and Davies, *Matthew*, Vol. 1, 435ff.; Fitzmyer, *Luke 1 — 9*, 632; Nolland, *Luke 1 — 9:20*, 280–01. For a detailed study of the beatitudes, cf. J. Dupont, *Les béatitudes*, though I would demur from his attempts to suggest that Luke has made major alterations from the meaning Jesus originally intended in these beatitudes. That Jesus saw the dominion and the eschatological reversal in it as especially good news for the poor, hungry, and disenfranchised is very likely indeed. Quite apart from the beatitudes there is clear evidence for this elsewhere in the Gospel tradition (Witherington, *Christology of Jesus*, 73ff.).

who are hungry, for they shall eat their fill.[154] "The passive form and the future tense... express the divine comfort integral to the promise for Israel's future (Isa. 49:13; 51:12; 66:13; Jer. 31:13)."[155] W. D. Davies is perhaps right that these arguably authentic beatitudes betoken the fact that "Jesus first appeared, not making a demand, but offering succour, his first concern, not the exaction of obedience, but the proclamation of blessing (4:23ff.; 5:3–11)."[156]

In the early Wisdom tradition, beatitudes expressed some sort of practical wisdom about the current condition or situation of some person or persons (cf. Sir. 14.20ff. – a person will be blessed or happy when they pursue a wise course of action). But in Matthew and Luke "the beatitudes only rarely express practical wisdom, since they usually stress a reversal of values that people put on earthly things in view of the kingdom now being preached by Jesus."[157] There is a strong element of paradox in the beatitudes that very likely goes back to Jesus, which makes them unique. What other sage was suggesting that the hungry or those in mourning were blessed by God?

In regard to the question of whether or not one should see these beatitudes as having an ethical thrust, it seems that in their original form as Jesus uttered them that was not their intended function.[158] He is not commending hunger or mourning to his disciples. These macarisms are intended as words of comfort and hope for those currently under duress, a hope based in an eschatological reversal of their current situation.[159]

---

[154] In view of the alliteration of the beatitudes in Matt. 5:3–6, it seems more likely that Luke has altered Q's "mourn" to "weep", than that Matthew has done the converse, though Luke's alteration does not really affect the meaning of the first half of his form of the beatitude. Cf. C. Michaelis, "Die 'p'–Alliteration der Subjektsworte der ersten 4 Seligpreisungen in Mt. V.3–6 und ihre Bedeutung für den Aufbau der Seligpreisungen bei Matt., Luke und in Q," 148–61. The second half of the beatitude in Luke is more positive – the weeping person will actually turn around and laugh one day. If "mourn" is original, then it is probable that console/comfort is as well. This is all the more likely if these beatitudes were originally framed with Is. 61:1–2 in mind. If Jesus is responsible for this (cf. and contrast Allison and Davies, *Matthew*, Vol. 1, 436–37 with Luz, *Matthew*, 235ff.), then there may be an implicit christological message in these beatitudes, namely that Jesus is the servant of God who will ultimately bring this reversal to pass. Luke has very likely added the 'now' to his beatitudes, but the more significant addition is Matthew's 'and thirst for righteousness.' In view of Luke's interest in the poor and hungry, it is not completely out of the question that the Matthean form could be earlier, but probably the parallel in the *Gospel of Thomas* tips the scales in favor of the Lukan form. Matthew in any case has a clear interest in righteousnes (cf. e.g. Matt. 3:15 and par). On *klaio* as a characteristically Lukan verb, cf. N. McEleney, "The Beatitudes of the Sermon on the Mount/Plain," 1–13.

[155] R. Guelich, *The Sermon on the Mount. A Foundation for Understanding*, 81. Guelich is perhaps right that Matthew has shaped his beatitudes and ordered them in the light of Isa.61:1–2, but there is no reason in the case of Matt. 5:4 that Jesus himself could not have drawn on the Isaianic material at this point. The redactional work of the First Evangelist is probably more in evidence in Matt. 5:6.

[156] W. D. Davies, *The Setting of the Sermon on the Mount*, 96.

[157] Fitzmyer, *Luke 1–9*, 633.

[158] For the argument that the two beatitudes we are examining go back in some form to Jesus, cf. Allison and Davies, *Matthew*, Vol. 2, 435.

[159] This comports with the promise of the meek inheriting the land which likely goes back to Jesus; cf. Witherington, *Jesus, Paul and the End of the World*, 134ff.

It will be seen that these beatitudes do not reflect some sort of realized eschatology but are more like what one finds in *Psalms of Solomon* 17:44, or *1 En.* 58:2–3: "Blessed are you righteous and elect ones, for glorious is your portion. The righteous ones shall be in the light..." Jesus then was promising that whatever forms of deprivation (of family or of food) one was experiencing now, in the Dominion of God these lacks would be made good. It is not impossible that there is an allusion to the messianic banquet in Luke 6:21. What the arguably authentic beatitudes suggest is that Jesus, like other early Jews and Jewish sages who believed in a eschatological reversal of things, had a rather materialistic view of what reversal must amount to. Not pie in the sky by and by, but a reversal and vindication that is seen to happen in this world seems to be what Jesus had in mind. In this he is a sage like unto both Ben Sira and Pseudo-Solomon before him (cf. Sirach 35; Wis. 5:1–20).

The importance of these beatitudes for this study is primarily that they show further corroborating evidence not only that Jesus was a sage, but that he was a sage who expressed his eschatological convictions in Wisdom forms. This is even more in evidence in the narrative *meshalim*, the next topic for discussion.

NARRATIVE MESHALIM:*THE ENIGMA VARIATIONS*

The discussion of the narrative *meshalim* in the teachings of Jesus, ever popular, has become a virtual cottage industry in the last quarter of a century. Further, there are almost as many approaches to the parables as there are books on the subject. It has been suggested that this subject ought not to be approached not first and foremost on the basis of modern theories about metaphor and the like, *if the intent is to get at the historical function and meanings of Jesus' narrative meshalim*. Rather, one should first do comparative research in early Jewish parables and discern how they work. It is surprising how few recent interpreters of the narrative *meshalim* have bothered to spend any concerted time doing this. At this juncture, we should consider a few examples of early Jewish parables from outside the Jesus tradition, bearing in mind that parables seem to have been a modification or extension of Wisdom speech first offered by Jewish prophets. Indeed Hos. 12:10 very likely reads: "I spoke to the prophets; it was I who multiplied visions, and through the prophets gave parables."[160]

[160] One more recent translation has at Hos 12.10: 'and through the prophets I will bring destruction' (NRSV, contrast RSV and NIV), but in one of the earliest extra-biblical references to this text in *Mekilta Shirata* 3.28–29, R. Eliezer ben Hyrcanus (*c* A.D. 90) is said to have understood this verse to mean 'and by the ministry of prophets have I used similitudes.' The debate is over the meaning of the radical *DMY* and whether it should read as likeness/figure of speech/parable or as ruin. F. I. Andersen and D. N. Freedman are very likely right that the former is much more probable in view of the chiasmus in vv 10a and b (11a and b in the Hebrew). Cf. Andersen and Freedman, *Hosea* (New York: Doubleday, 1980), 618.

"They also spoke in parables": Other Jewish Parables.[161] Jesus' near contemporary Johanna Ben Zacchai (*c* A.D. 70) offers us several narrative *meshalim* of which two may be cited.

> In the case of the first tablets: "And the tables were the work of God" (Exod. 32:16). In the case of the second set of tablets, the tables were the work of Moses, as it is written: "And he wrote on the tablets the words of the covenant, the Decalogue" (Exod. 34:28)
>
> They parable a parable [probably to be vocalized *mashlu mashal*] – unto what is the matter like? It is like a king of flesh and blood who became engaged to a woman. He brought the scribe and ink and pen and the document and the witnesses. But if the woman had been divorcing him, she would bring all the necessary items. It would be enough for it that the king provided his own signature for the document. (*Tosephta B. Kamma* 7:4 cf. Deut. R. 3:17; Exod. R. 47:2 both of which are later than the Tosephta version).[162]

Reflecting on the subject of repentance being needful now, since one does not know when one may die, and on "And Solomon said in his wisdom: 'Let your garments be always white; and let not your head lack ointment'" (Eccles. 9.8), Ben Zacchai says:

> A parable. It is like a king who summoned his servants to a banquet without appointing a time. The wise ones dressed themselves and sat at the door of the palace; they said "Is anything lacking in a royal palace?" The fools went about their work, saying: "Can there be a banquet without preparations?" Suddenly the king desired the presence of his servants. The wise entered properly dressed, while the fools entered soiled. The king rejoiced at the wise but was angry with the fools. He said. "Those who properly dressed themselves for the banquet, let them sit, eat, and drink. But those who did not adorn themselves for the banquet, let them stand and watch" (*B.T. Shab.* 153a).

This second parable is remarkably similar in some respects to what one finds in the Jesus tradition at Matt. 22:1–14 and par. and in other respects like Matt. 25:1–13. One of the features of the Jewish parables outside the Jesus tradition

---

[161] Here I have borrowed and modified the title of McArthur and Johnston's, *They Also Taught in Parables*. I am indebted to them and will be basically following their translations with some modifications. I am also appreciative of some of the work of B. H. Young, *Jesus and his Jewish Parables*, though I differ with both of these books in terms of critical methodology at various points. I am no advocate of the Jerusalem school of approach (D. Flusser, *et al.*) to the Jesus tradition. The older work by A. Feldman, *The Parables and Similes of the Rabbis. Agricultural and Pastoral*, is still of some general use.

[162] MacArthur and Johnson, *They Also Taught in Parables*, 23–24.

is that they often deal with the stock figure of the king and his dealings and this is much less true of the Jesus tradition. Mostly Jesus' parables draw on the everyday life of ordinary people. Nevertheless, the similarity in character between Ben Zacchai's parables, which seek to make points by a story about something or somethings *outside* the story, and some of Jesus' parables should be evident. They are of the same genre and ilk.

From a slightly later period, but still within the New Testament era, there is the parable of R. Jose the Priest (*c A.D.* 90), trying to explain an apparent contradiction between Deut. 10:17 and Num. 6:26.

> I will parable you a parable. Unto what is the matter like? It is like one who lent his neighbor 100 denarii and fixed a time for payment in the presence of the king, while the other swore to pay him by the life of the king. When the time arrived, he did not pay him, and he went to excuse himself to the king. But the king said to him: The wrong done to me, I excuse you, but go and obtain forgiveness from your neighbor. Even so one text speaks of offenses commited by a man against the Place [i.e a circumlocution for God], the other of offenses committed by a man against his fellow human being (*B.T. Rosh Hashanah* 17b–18a).

This parable is similar enough to the parable of the unrighteous steward found in Luke 16:1–13 that it may suggest that Jesus, like other of his Jewish contemporaries, was drawing on some well known stories and modifying them to make his own point. Again, the crucial point is that Jesus' parables must not be studied in isolation. They are drawn from the same well as some of these other early Jewish parables. One final parable will be mentioned which is found in *Mish. Aboth* 3:18 and is attributed to R. Eliezar b. Azariah (*c* A.D. 90).

> He whose wisdom is more abundant than his works unto what is he like? He is like a tree whose branches are abundant but whose roots are few. And the wind comes and uproots it and overturns it. As it is written 'He shall be like a tamarisk in the desert and shall not see when good comes: but shall inhabit the parched places in the wilderness' (Jer. 17:6). But he whose works are more abundant than his wisdom, unto what is he like? He is like a tree whose branches are few but whoose roots are many; so that even if all the winds in the world come and blow against it, it cannot be stirred from its place. As it is written: He shall be as a tree planted by the waters... (Jer. 17.8).

This is not a complete narrative but evidences that the roots of Jewish parables lie in simple comparisons. The comparison then may spawn an expansion into a full story, or at least encourage the fresh creation of comparative stories. If one keeps in mind that a narrative *mashal* is but one form of the larger category of *mashal* or comparison, which includes brief comparisons and riddles on one end of the spectrum all the way to what *today are called* allegories on the other end of the spectrum (e.g., Ezekiel 17), one will understand the larger context in which early Jewish parables were and should be understood. The comparison above is similar to what one finds in Matt. 7:16–20 (and par.) and 7:24–27. In both the Jesus tradition and in other early Jewish traditions involving parables, it was not uncommon to draw not only from the realm of human interaction and affairs but also from natural phenomena in order to construct a *mashal*.

There are many more such Jewish parables, some of which have striking similarities to various Gospel parables, e.g., R. Meir's parable of the wayward son in Deut. R. 2.24 to the prodigal son parable (*c*. A.D. 150). Care has been taken to limit the discussion to a few examples of some of the earliest of these parables which are unlikely to reflect any direct influence of the Gospel traditions.[163] Three examples of narrative *meshalim* and one example which may be called a briefer comparison that does not amount to a complete story but is closer to a simile have been chosen. In fact various of the earliest Jewish parables are very brief comparisons that have not been developed into anything like a narrative. For example, in *Tos. Kid.* 1.11 R. Gamaliel (*c*. 80) is said to have opined: "Everyone who has a handicraft, unto what is he like? He is like a vineyard that is surrounded by a fence, and like a vine tendril surrounded by enclosure." In such sayings one may be seeing how a parable began as a simple comparison, which would support Westermann's theory about the development of this form of Wisdom speech.

If one carefully studies the early Jewish parables several important conclusions come to light. Firstly, they are always comparisons, which have referents external to the story or similitude. This in itself should warn against too quickly assuming that Jesus' parables did not have external referents. One will need to provide evidence for such a conclusion, since elsewhere it is the character of Jewish parables to have such referents. Furthermore, Jewish parables outside the Jesus tradition often had more than just one point of comparison. Is one compelled to assume that Jesus' parables were fundamentally different in this regard? If so, one must argue for this conclusion not assume it, for it doesn't comport with the evidence of the wider body of contemporary Jewish *meshalim*. Secondly, the early Jewish parables frequently required and had explanations and applications with them. "The great majority of rabbinic parables (nearly 80 percent) have as one of their features an explicit interpretation of the story, usually following it."[164] Unless one wants to maintain that Jesus' parables were completely anomalous, one should not rule out that he may also have offered explanations to the disciples with at least some of his narrative *meshalim*. Thirdly, the rabbinic parables were illustrations, almost always illustrations of some Scriptural text or texts. That is,

[163] I am well aware that in various of the Jewish parables there is a problem of attribution, and then too many are anonymous. But about the ones cited there is little reason to doubt their accuracy. The attributions in the cited cases do not begin with a phrase like "said in the name of" but simply "said".

[164] MacArthur and Johnson, *They Also Taught in Parables*, 139.

parables *were* interpretations or illustrations, though sometimes they also needed explanations and applications.[165] While it is true that Jesus' parables were not, or were usually not, illustrations of some Scriptural text or principle, it does not follow from this that they were not illustrations of something. I would suggest they were illustrations and illuminations of the things that were happening in and through Jesus' ministry. In particular, they were illustrations of what was happening or would happen as a result of God's dominion breaking into Israel's midst in the person and ministry of Jesus the sage. In this regard, Jesus' *meshalim* are not Torah-centric like other early Jewish parables but are more prophetic in character, telling the truth about some present or future situation.[166]

Jesus' parables are more like those one finds in the Old Testament (e.g., 2 Samuel 12 – parable with application; Isa. 5:1–6 with explanation in 5:7; cf. Ezek. 17:1–10 with explanation in vv 11ff.). In fact, I would argue that Jesus' parables stand at the interface between revealed Wisdom and prophecy on the one hand, and Wisdom discovered from observing the world on the other. On the one hand Jesus seems to be operating with a disclosure or analogical model of reality. He is telling his audience something they could not simply deduce from wise observation of human life or the world of nature. Disclosure models of reality are *aspective* not pictorial of the reality they disclose. They reveal an aspect or some aspects of the truth about something. This means the images cannot be overpressed into some sort of elaborate allegory. Jesus is revealing some aspect of the character of God, God's inbreaking dominion, or God's saving plan. He is not *depicting* these things in detail. This explains how Jesus can even use an example of someone being unscrupulous to make his point (cf. Luke 16:1–8a).

Jesus in his parables draws on everyday occurrences which many had seen or experienced or heard about, into which he injects the unusual aspects of a counter order of things that causes a person to re-envision reality. The jarring is juxtaposed with the commonplace. The disclosure comes in the paradoxical or unusual elements, or in the way in which such elements interface with the picture of everyday life on which any wise sage could have discoursed. Neither the revelatory/prophetic character nor the Wisdom character and form of these sayings should be minimized. Sometimes it is the larger impression or overall surprising effect of the parable that Jesus is striving for, and thus the details are less crucial, sometimes even incidental.

While the narrative Jewish *meshalim* were not or not usually full dress allegories like a Bunyan's *Pilgrim's Progress*, it is not inappropriate to speak of some symbolic elements in these parables, if one wants to put it that way. This is a very different matter from an allegorizing interpretation especially one that ignores the original historical frame of reference of the parable, as has already

---

[165] MacArthur Johnson, *They Also*, 137.

been said.[167] It must always be kept in mind that what is primary in the relationship between parable and what it illustrates is the latter not the former. That is, the parable is told and shaped in such a way that it will aptly illuminate some reality that is already a given. As MacArthur and Johnson put it: "Clearly the story is subordinant to the illustrand."[168] It follows from this that where the parable seems to depart from what seems normal or natural, the parable has very likely been modified because of some aspect of the situation or subject it is meant to illustrate. The goal was not realism so much as apt commentary on the situation.

As time went on Jewish parables took on very stereotyped forms often repeatedly using the same stock characters, such as a king over and over, which is certainly less true of Jesus' parables. It is important to note that Jesus' parables do on occasion manifest some of the typical introductory formulae and also the formulae that provide transition to the interpretation or explanation. For example, there is sometimes a reference to the fact that what Jesus is about to say is in the form of a *mashal* (cf. Mark 4:2; 12:1) or that a comparison is about to be offered ("To what shall I compare," cf. Matt. 11:16; Luke 7:31–32), or he begins with a question (cf. Luke 11:5; 14:28; 17:7).

The transition to the interpretation in Jewish parables is usually made with the term *kak* meaning "thus," "similarly," "even so." To this one may compare the transitions in Matt. 13:49; 18:14; Mark 13:29; Luke 12:21; 17:10; (and par.); and Matt. 20:16. Doubtless some of these transitions and what follows them are the contributions of the evangelist or earlier Christian tradents (e.g., Matt. 20:16), but this is probably not always the case. What one must ask about an interpretation is, Could it or would it have more likely arisen in a *Sitz im Leben Jesu*, or in the early church? This matter must be decided on a case by case basis with careful historical scrutiny. Some of the features discussed above are readily apparent in the four examples cited; readers are urged to study the early Jewish parables for themselves.[169]

A judicious assessment of the similarities and differences between Jesus' and other early Jewish parables has been offered by C. Blomberg. He points to the following five shared features: similar introductory formulae, similar structure, similar length, similar topics, varied interpretations. He then singles out the following differences: rabbinic parables support conventional wisdom; the very frequent use of added interpretation in the rabbinic material; and the eschatological elements in Jesus' parables.[170]

---

[166] Jesus differs from Ben Sira in his apparent lack of intent to inculcate a Torah–centric or temple–centric approach to life. Instead he binds his disciples to himself and his own teaching.

[167] It is the merit of C. L. Blomberg, *Interpreting the Parables*, that he has seen this point, but his mechanistic one point per character in a parable does not do justice to their flexibility. Sometimes it is the action in the parable not the characters, or sometimes both, that allude to something outside the story.

[168] MacArthur and Johnson, *They Also Taught in Parables*, 168.

[169] One may wish to begin with Young's careful translations of the Hebrew originals, i.e., if one does not know Hebrew or has no access to the original Jewish sources.

[170] Blomberg, *Interpreting the Parables*, 58–68.

Jülicher's Eulogy, Jülicher's Legacy. Parable interpretation of late has been notable for its lack of clarity in regard to methodology. What is the relationship of simile and metaphor to parable and allegory? Though it is not often noted, A. Jülicher correlated simile with parable, and metaphor with allegory, and would not be best pleased to see scholars of today saluting him and then proceeding to treat parable as some sort of metaphor.[171] Nor is one helped much by those who try to use Aristotle as a basis for making major distinctions between parable and allegory, on the assumption of a supposed major distinction betweeen simile and metaphor. What Aristotle in fact says is that the difference between simile and metaphor is slight (*mikron* – *The Art of Rhetoric* 3.4, 1406b)! Jülicher in effect chose to ignore this statement in order to drive a firm wedge between parable and allegory. While I agree with Jülicher that a parable seems to be an extended form of simile, his further conclusion, that since Jesus spoke in parables he intended to convey a single universal truth in each one, is doubtful at best.[172] This does not seem to be always or even often the case with early Jewish parables.[173] In order for Jülicher to be right, all the evangelists must be wrong in how they handled Jesus' narrative *meshalim.*

B. B. Scott is much more helpful when he frankly admits that modern scholars have an unjustified bias against allegory and in favor of parable.[174] In fact, the Jewish use of the term *mashal*, translated *parabolos* in the Gospels, or even the more specific narrative *mashal* can include both what today is called parable and allegory (cf. Ezek. 17:2). If one denies the basis of Jülicher's distinction between parable and allegory (namely a radical distinction between simile and metaphor), the former distinction must also be reassessed. M. A. Tolbert is bold enough to say, "The whole foundation upon which Jülicher built his distinction has crumbled, but his distinction itself still reigns."[175]

A much more sane way to approach Jesus' parables is to recognize that sometimes they have several elements / figures / actions that represent or comment on several things / persons / events outside the narrative itself. One may then wish to say that a parable of Jesus may have one or more symbolic elements. I eschew the use of the term allegory at this point firstly because that has become a term for a particular *genre* of literature distinct from parables, but secondly also because I do not think that *all* or almost all the elements in a parable of Jesus correspond to something outside of the parable, in a way that

[171] I am indebted to Brosend for allowing me to read his dissertation on Jülicher and parables in typescript. In what follows in the next two paragraphs I am drawing on some of his insights. Cf. A. Jülicher, *Die Gleichnisreden Jesu*, Vol. I, 52.

[172] Jülicher, *Die Gleichnisreden Jesu*, I, 106–07.

[173] As Brosend shows, C. H. Dodd, while admitting his debt to Jülicher in the distinction between parable and allegory and the stressing of one point per parable, simply collapses simile and metaphor, seemingly ignorant of the fact that this would have caused Jülicher to turn over in his grave. Cf. C. H. Dodd, *The Parables of the Kingdom*, 5.

[174] B. B. Scott, *Hear Then the Parable*, 45ff.

[175] M. A. Tolbert, *Perspectives on the Parables*, 27.

a work like Bunyan's *Pilgrim's Progress* does. Rather, Jesus told narrative *meshalim* that had striking correspondences between *some* elements or aspects of the story and some elements or aspects of the world or events on which he was commenting. This allowed Jesus to draw on conventional customs, everyday occurrences, or events and alter them only minimally here and there to make the point or points he wished to get across. This is significantly different from a story that is entirely contrived on the basis of some set of abstract ideas or propositions about life that one wishes to get across, so that every element in the story is artificial and symbolic. Bearing these things in mind, it is time to examine a few of Jesus' narrative *meshalim*.[176]

Leaven Well Enough Alone (Matt. 13:33b/Luke 13:20–21) Since I have already commented on some aspects of this saying,[177] the intent here is to concentrate on some of the more recent discussions of this saying and what it indicates about Jesus the sage. In its Lukan form it receives the highest rating of the Jesus seminar, and in its Matthean form the second highest, among all of Jesus' parables in regard to the question of authenticity.[178]

Both in its Matthean and Lukan forms, and thus surely also in Q, this parable has an introductory formulae like those used in other Jewish *meshalim*. The standard formula "to what is the matter like?" (cf. *Mish. Aboth* 4:20; *Tos.Suk.* 2:6; *B.T. Pes.* 87b) has been modified slightly, probably by Jesus, to "to what shall I liken the Kingdom of God?" This is very important, since it makes quite clear that the parable is intended to be some kind of comparison, like other early Jewish *meshalim*. This means that one must ask about the point or points of comparison. This parable is one of only three in the Synoptic tradition where one is told that the subject being compared to something else is a thing, not a person. In this case it is leaven.[179]

---

[176] Brosend, in his chapter "Parable and Allegory Defined," argues that parable is comprised of one comparison or a cluster of comparisons with a single referent or referential cluster, while allegory is composed of a series of comparisons with a series of referents. This is rather like saying a parable has one main idea while an allegory has several controlling ideas. I am not sure this distinction is adequate. It appears that parables that have only one comparison or one main idea are usually very short ones (such as the leaven parable). Rather, there is a sliding scale between parable and allegory, the latter does have more points of comparison and tends to be more artificial because these external referents are affecting the presentation of the *mashal*'s plot line and presentation of characters, *but* a parable can have several points of comparison or symbolic elements, and not necessarily focus on just *one central idea*. A good example is indeed the Laborers in the Vineyard (Matt. 20:1–16). Here several different points are made (cf. below), but by no means are all or nearly all the elements in the story symbolic. For instance those hired at noon and 3 pm seem to have no such symbolic significance.

[177] Witherington, *Women in the Ministry of Jesus*, 40–41.

[178] R. W. Funk, *et al.*, *The Parables of Jesus*, 104.

[179] The argument of E. Waller, "The Parable of the Leaven: Sectarian Teaching and the Inclusion of Women,", 99–109, that the Thomas form has a woman, rather than leaven, as the subject of the parable is unconvincing. Precisely because of the offensive associations of leaven it is hardly likely that either Matthew or Luke would have replaced a woman as the subject with leaven if that had been the form of the parable when they received it.

In recent discussion of this parable, a good deal has rightly been made of the fact that leaven is almost universally seen in early Judaism and early Christianity (cf. 1 Cor. 5:6) as something unclean or even as a symbol of something evil (but cf. Philo, *Spec. Leg.* 2:184–85).[180] Is it possible that it has such an allusion here? If one associates this parable with Jesus' ministry to the outcasts, including the ceremonially unclean, such an interpretation is not beyond the bounds of possibility. The dominion of God, if indeed it is to be found in this world, is found amongst the unclean who are a small minority within the larger whole of Israel. The problem with this interpretation is that the leaven is the active agent in this story, not the result of that agent's work.

Perhaps a more promising avenue is to explore further why the leaven is hidden in (*enegkrupsen*) the dough. The verb in question usually means something stronger than "put into." As Scott says, "The figurative use of hiding to describe the mixing of the leaven and the flour is otherwise unattested in Greek or Hebrew." It is right to compare the use of the verb here to the use of *krupto* in Matt. 13:14, 44. The idea conveyed is that of concealment. Jesus is reversing normal expectations – how can God's dominion be like something unclean such as leaven, or be hidden, even concealed?

Again, when one finds something incongruous, something not true to life in a parable, it is fair to assume that an alteration has been made in order to make a point about the subject outside the story. Could this story be about how Jesus has hidden the Kingdom or Kingdom message in the midst of his audience through offering a mass of *meshalim*? In spite of its inconspicuous character, this dominion is still working as an agent of change in and through these *meshalim*. Jesus' dominion message could indeed have been seen as something unclean, since it apparently did not affirm traditional ritual barriers of clean and unclean.[182] But Jesus believed that this message would have an effect out of all proportion to what one might expect. If there is also a stress on the amount of flour used, one must see this as a message about remarkable results once the permeating process is finished. That is, this parable reflects an eschatological optimism about how things will finally turn out.

If this is a parable about proclaiming the dominion through parabling, and the foreseen results of that activity, one must ask whether there is any further significance in the fact that it is a woman who is the one kneading the dough until it is permeated with yeast. Some medieval exegetes considered the possibility that the woman might be an allusion to Wisdom.[183] Since it seems likely that Jesus deliberately portrayed himself as a sage, one must then ask, is Jesus identifying himself with or even as personified Wisdom in this parable?

---

[180] Scott, *Hear Then the Parable*, 321–29; Blomberg, *Interpreting*, 286; Allison and Davies, *Matthew*, 422.

[181] Scott, *Hear Then the Parable*, 326.

[182] Witherington, *Christology of Jesus*, 73ff.

[183] Wailes, *Medieval Allegories*, 113–17.

This is not beyond the realm of possibility in the light of other evidence that Jesus presented himself as Wisdom (cf. below). Whatever else one may say about this parable, it is certainly a parable about a counter order, an order where leaven is seen as something good, where hiding something important can have a good effect, where extravagance is seen as salutary.[184] E. Schweizer may be near the mark when he asks, "Is this meant to alert the listener through its alienating effect, using unheard-of, iconoclastic images for the Kingdom of God?"[185] This seems quite likely.

Beyond all Bounds (Luke 10:30b–35). The parable of the Good Samaritan has been so often used and abused that very few recent treatments of this *mashal* have shed much new light on its meaning. Its importance, coupled with the high degree of likelihood that at least Luke 10:30b–35 goes back in some form to Jesus,[186] means that we must step into the shoes of the Samaritan once more, even though the road he walked has been heavily traveled since his time and one sometimes despairs of finding evidence of his original footprints.

Luke shows a particular interest in Samaritans in his two volume work (cf. Luke 9:52; 17:11, 16; Acts 1:8; 8:1, 5, 9, 14, 25; 9:31; 15:3). For this reason among others, some scholars, such as G. Sellin, have argued that this parable, "ist ganze eine lukanische Komposition."[187] This conclusion is both unnecessary and unlikely. It is unnecessary because the Lukan style that the parable reflects simply shows he has made his source his own, as Luke is apt to do. It is unlikely because, so far as one can tell, offering up a counter order of things is hardly one of Luke's agendas.

More attention needs to be given to the tradition history of this parable, and to the question of whether in fact it is an 'example story' rather than a comparative *mashal*. In an example story there is no symbolic or metaphorical meaning latent in this or that feature of the story that refers to something outside itself; rather, an example is being offered by something *in* the story itself. It has always been suspicious that the only example stories in the Synoptic tradition are found in Luke (cf. Luke 10:30–37; 12:16–21; 16:19–31;

[184] Scott, *Hear Then the Parable*, 326ff. The argument that Jesus or the evangelist is warning against the leaven of the Pharisees here is quite unconvincing. The subject is God's Dominion and how it is working. On the suggestion that Jesus is parodying the way the Pharisees had characterized his followers (i.e., as unclean); cf. Beare, *Matthew*, 307–09.

[185] Schweizer, *Matthew*, adds: "Was Jesus perhaps even thinking of his own band of disciples, the tax collectors and ignorant fishermen who were worldly and unclean by Pharisaic standards?" (307). This suggestion seems less apt because Jesus apparently was notorious for hanging around with this sort of people. In short his companions could hardly be called hidden.

[186] It was ranked only behind the leaven parable by the Jesus seminar in regard to the question of authenticity, and no scholar gave it a black mark, meaning no one was willing to say it was certainly inauthentic. Funk, *Parables of Jesus*, 98.

[187] G. Sellin, "Lukas als Gleichniserzähler: Die Erzählung vom barmherzigen Samariter (Lk. 10, 25–37)," 31.

18:10–14). Accordingly, Crossan has argued that Luke or his source has transformed what were originally parables into example stories.[188] Each case must be weighed on its own merits, and the concern here is with the Good Samaritan parable in particular. Are there signs of such a transformation?

The giving of a parable as a means of clarifying a portion of Torah has abundant parallels in Jewish literature outside the New Testament, but not in the Jesus tradition. That Jesus might occasionally have done such a thing is not implausible. This parable then might be seen as a form of exegesis of the commandment to love thy neighbor as thyself. There are problems with this conclusion; for example, there is the oft-noted apparent incongruity between the question of the lawyer ("Who is my neighbor?") and the subject of the parable, which is about *how* to be a neighbor to someone. One might respond that it was characteristic of Jesus that he seldom answered a question directly (e.g., Mark. 12:18–27). After all, if one settles the issue about how to be a neighbor to anyone and everyone, one has by implication answered the "who" question. Nevertheless, two important considerations suggest that the framework of this parable may be of Luke's own devising. First, there is evidence elsewhere that Luke tends to *generalize* the or a major point of a parable in his introduction. For instance, in Luke 18:1 Luke introduces a parable about prayer of a specific sort, prayer for eschatological vindication, with the words, "Then Jesus told them a parable about their need to pray always and never to lose heart." There is no reason Luke could not have introduced the Samaritan parable using a similar technique. Secondly, as Crossan has shown, the question about eternal life in Luke, coupled with the answer about love, bears a considerable resemblance to Mark 12:28–31/ Matt. 22:34–40.[189] This probably means that one should see the framework as Luke's use of another source combining it with the parable proper. This does not mean that Luke has thereby profoundly misunderstood or distorted the parable; it is in part about neighborly love, and exceeding all bounds in regard to the usual limits of who would be treated as neighbor. But Luke has generalized or universalized in his framework what was considerably more specific on the lips of Jesus – a comment on the relationship between Samaritans and Jews, in order to offer a vision of a counter-order exceeding the bounds of usual Jewish thinking on this subject. In short, it seems likely that this parable is not merely an example story but another telling parabolic portrayal of how the inbreaking of the Dominion of God with its power to transform persons and lives, subverts and reorders normal thinking.

One must look for the unusual element in the parable in order to see what it is driving at. Clearly what is out of the ordinary in this parable, which may owe some significant debt to the material in 2 Chron. 28:8–15,[190] is the loving

---

[188] J. D. Crossan, "Parable and Example in the Teaching of Jesus," 63–104.

[189] Crossan, "Parable and Example," 5–6.

[190] J. D. M. Derrett, "Law in the New Testament: Fresh Light on the Parable of the Good Samaritan," 23ff.

acts of the Samaritan on behalf of a Jew. The antipathy between Jew and Samaritan before, during, and after Jesus' day is well chronicled and is apparent in earlier Wisdom literature (cf. Sir. 50:25–26; Josephus *Ant.* 18:2.2; John 8:48; *B.T. San.* 57a, where a Samaritan is not worthy of receiving aid from a Jew).[191] Samaritans were considered half-breeds and heretics, since their views on Torah and its limits differed from Jewish views. [192]

If it is true, as R. W. Funk avers, that the original hearer of this parable would very likely have identified with the victim (it is much less likely they would identify with the priest and levite, since the religious leaders were in most ways distinguished from ordinary Jews and had special restrictions about ritual uncleanness to follow),[193] then "the Samaritan is he whom the victim... could not expect to help, indeed does not want to help. The literal, i.e. historical significance of the Samaritan is what gives the parable its edge."[194]

It is not accidental that one is told that the victim, who in the *Sitz im Leben Jesu* would certainly have been presumed to be a Jew, has been stripped of all material evidence of his social status or ethnic identity. He is simply 'a certain man' once he has been mugged and robbed. The Samaritan's act must be seen then as one done *regardless* of the ethnic identity of the victim. His actions were not decided by a pre-determined set of categories that dictated who was in and who was out of bounds as an object of such mercy or compassion.[195]

From the victim's point of view, one of the last things a wounded Jew would have expected was help from a Samaritan. The idea of a good Samaritan was a contradiction in terms for such a person. But this is characteristic of Jesus the sage who seems to specialize in oxymorons like good leaven, light burdens and here a good Samaritan. As Crossan says, "[t]he focal point must remain, not on the good deed itself, but on the *goodness* of the *Samaritan*."[196]

The structure of this parable reinforces this point. By the rule of end stress, one would expect the last major character introduced to be the focal point of this story, and he is. There is also apparently some degree of contrast between the Samaritan and the priest and levite. This is evident first because the normal development of this parable which a Jew would have expected would have been that first a priest, then a levite, then an ordinary Israelite

---

[191] J. R. Donahue, *The Gospel in Parables*, 130.

[192] M. I. Boucher, *The Parables*, 127.

[193] As Derrett points out, when a priest or a levite became unclean it very likely meant disqualification from his priestly service and also inability to feed his family, since he could not then handle or eat the tithe. Cf. Derrett, "Law in the NT," 26–27. *Mish. Berak.* 7.7: "he that suffers uncleanness because of the dead is unqualified until he pledges himself to suffer uncleanness no more for the dead." In short, if the priest or levite did help this man, would they be able to attend to their own family members later after such a pledge? But the real question is, are we meant to assume that the priest and levite thought the man dead?

[194] R. W. Funk, "The Old Testament in Parable: A Study of Luke 10.25–37," 261.

[195] L. Ramaroson, "Comme 'Le Bon Samaritain', ne chercher qu'a aimer (Lc. 10,29–37),", 533–36.

[196] Crossan, "Parable and Example," 75.

would have been given a chance to help his fellow Jew (cf. *Mish. Hor.* 3:8).[197] Secondly, as Scott has shown, the very way the story proceeds with parallel language except when there is a crucial disjuncture suggests a contrast (cf. "a certain priest... and seeing he went by on the opposite side,... a levite... and seeing went by on the opposite side,... a certain Samaritan... *went up to him and seeing had pity/ mercy,'*).[198]

Anticlericalism in itself would not necessarily be surprising, but holding up the example of a Samaritan as opposed to those who were at least *supposed* to be paragons of holiness and virtue in Jesus' society is striking. This is especially so if one is meant to think that the priest and levite know the man to be still alive. "Given the upperclass status of the priest and Levite, the anticlericalism of the audience, and the importance of tradition as an interpreter of the Torah, an audience would look askance at the scandalous, merciless act of the priest and Levite."[199] Jesus was deliberately heightening the tension in the story, and playing on its shock value for his audience.

The Samaritan not only helps the victim but also makes sure he will be able to recover fully and return to normal life. He does this by a series of compassionate acts: (1) ministering to and binding his wounds; (2) carrying him to the inn; (3) paying the innkeeper; (4) making promise of future payment if needed. As has been pointed out, the man could have been taken as a slave by the innkeeper for failure to pay a debt, had the Samaritan not secured the man's debts, making sure he would be a free man at the end of his time of healing.[200] This Samaritan went well beyond a simple act of kindness or compassion. Indeed he went beyond all bounds, not merely ethnic bounds, but even the suggested bounds in the Old Testament of what compassion would look like. Herein one finds a clue to what this parable is about.

When the dominion of God breaks into human lives and situations, old prejudices pass away and a new and shocking pattern of behavior comes to pass. Jesus is commending such a pattern of behavior here, perhaps in part as an *apologia* for his own scandalous behavior but also for the behavior of those who followed him and took his message to heart.

One of the essential characteristics of Jesus' ministry was controversy over holiness issues.[201] Both Jesus and the Pharisees wished to spread holiness throughout the land, but they disagreed as to how to bring about such a reform. The Pharisaic program involved in part applying levitical laws to the everyday lives of ordinary Jews, though it also involved moral reform as well. The net effect of the ritual part of the Pharisaic program was to further divide and

---

[197] Scott, *Hear Then the Parable*, 198.

[198] Scott, *Hear Then the Parable*, 193.

[199] Scott, *Hear Then the Parable*, 197.

[200] Derrett, "Law in the NT," 29–30.

[201] Witherington, *Christology of Jesus*, 60ff. Rightly also stressed by M. Borg, *Conflict, Holiness, and Politics in the Teaching of Jesus*.

separate Jews from Samaritans, Gentiles, and others. It was a move that strengthened the ethnic purity of the religious group.

Jesus by contrast stressed an intensification only of the basic moral demands of the Old Testament such as fidelity in marriage, honoring parents, loving neighbor and a benign neglect or even possibly the dismissal of the more divisive of the ritual requirements of Torah in favor of the more important moral demands. The net result was a conflict between Jesus and the Pharisees over what holiness did and did not entail. This parable, since it was given in a context where ritual purity was an issue, should be read in the light of these considerations.

I suspect that the reason why there is a contrast between priests and levites (the ritually clean) on the one hand and a Samaritan (the ritually unclean) on the other coupled with a victim who may or may not have been viewed as unclean, is because Jesus is offering a defense of his approach to matters of clean and unclean. It is precisely because compassion is a weightier matter of the law, that all such ritually based distinctions are set aside when the dominion breaks into Israel's midst. Jesus is driving his people back to first principles in the light of the new thing God is doing through his ministry. This may be seen as another manifestation of the sage's creation theology, for the first humans in the garden had no such ritual requirements to meet, only a moral one.

Jesus as a prophetic or eschatological sage does seem to have operated with an *Urzeit–Endzeit* schema. God's dominion breaking in meant a remarkable outpouring of grace which called forth remarkable acts of compassion.[202] This is also evident in the next and last narrative *mashal* to which this study will turn after a final observation from A. N. Wilder:

> The focal image of Jesus' message was that of the Kingdom of God, viewed as imminent and constituting both grace and total demand. It is not enough to say that Jesus goes back to the prophets. The ultimate reference of his message and vision is that of creation itself. This is suggested by the cosmic–eschatological character of the Kingdom which he announced, in this respect different from the eschatology of the Pharisees associated with the age to come and the national hope.... It is as though for Jesus many of the intervening cultural strata in Judaism, with their long sedimentation of social and psychic habit, had collapsed like so many floors. We may take as illustrative his appeal back of Moses to the "beginning of creation"... This depth in the sanctions of Jesus explains the implicit universalism in his position, as in his attitude to the Samaritans... I am not saying that Jesus reverted to the creation motif alone, but that his imagery met the current dilemma by reordering all its symbolics in depth. One aspect of this is the

[202] In the end, I doubt that Jesus is comparing himself to the Samaritan, or vice versa, though it is not impossible, since some may have seen Jesus as an unclean northerner as well. The focus is rather on the deeds done by one who breaks down or goes beyond ethnic boundaries or even Torah's expectations.

convergence in him of the various roles and styles of the three main types of Israel's spokesmen – prophet, sage, and scribe.[203]

Equal Pay for Unequal Work (Matt. 20:1–15). Scholars are almost universally agreed that Matt. 20:16 should be seen as the First Evangelist's addition to a very likely authentic parable, so that he might use the parable to highlight the theme of reversal in which he has elsewhere shown evidence of being interested (cf. Matt. 19:30). This conclusion is very likely correct, but the verse is not entirely at odds with the parable in view of Matt. 20:8–9. It is not convincing to argue that vv 8–9 are redactional since they are integral to the story – the workers who worked all day must be present to see what happens when the last are paid, otherwise the story would conclude differently.[204] Nevertheless, reversal is not the main subject of the parable.

F. W. Beare has rightly labeled this parable the *mashal* of the eccentric employer.[205] On the one hand, he has not defrauded anyone by paying them less than promised. On the other hand, the impression that he has been unfair is strong, for those who worked all day got the same denarius as those who only worked an hour. Here is a feature of the parable that seems to reflect something out of the norm, and may point one to the meaning of this *mashal*.[206] The first workers are irate not because the employer has given the last hired a denarius, but because he has made the first *equal* with those last hired by paying all the same.[207]

It is very often argued that this parable is about divine generosity — but is this so? A denarius was the regular wage of a day laborer, and it was not worth a great deal. As Scott rightly says, while "a denarius for an hour's work is generous in comparison with a denarius for a full day's labor... in and of itself it is not generous... A peasant earning a denarius a day will live in the shadow of poverty".[209] The vineyard owner has doubtless done what is fair and in this

---

[203] Wilder, *Jesus' Parables*, 117–18.

[204] This parable is not about an exchange of lots or places since all the workers are paid the same amount. On the importance of vv 8–9 to the parable, cf. Beare, *Matthew*, 403.

[205] Beare, *Matthew*, 401.

[206] I say this despite J. D. M. Derrett's, *Studies in the New Testament*, Vol. 1, 48–75, learned argument that this parable does not present abnormal behavior on the part of the employer in view of the concept of *po'el batel* (i.e., that a person's leisure, if taken away, was worth something and should be compensated with at least a minimum honorarium). The parable shows no interest in this idea, and indeed if this concept did stand behind this parable it is hard to understand why the employer did not remind those first hired of the idea when they grumbled.

[207] This parable is a good example of the weakness of Blomberg's rather wooden one point per (*major*) character in the parable view. Were this the case one would expect this parable to have more than three points, since those hired between the first and last provide yet a fourth group in the parable. Cf. his *Interpreting the Parables*, 221–25. To make this a three–point parable Blomberg lumps together all the workers except those last hired, something the parable does not do. That destroys the first/last tandem in the parable.

[208] F. Gryglewicz, "The Gospel of the Overworked Workers," 190–98.

sense has been good, but this should not be seen as a parable about the abundance of divine generosity.[210]

Three things in the parable suggest that the vineyard owner has an urgent need to get some work done. First of all, he and not his steward goes to the marketplace to hire the workers. Secondly, he goes repeatedly to the marketplace even at the close of the day, the eleventh hour. Thirdly, though his steward pays the workers, he is present at the time, which suggests a special interest in the completion of the work and the rendering of accounts at the end of the day. Thus, the need of the employer was great and the value of all the labor was apparently considerable. Furthermore, it is this same urgency which leads J. D. M. Derrett to say that a "Jewish hearer of our parable would recognize from repeated trips to the marketplace that the crop is expected to produce a high superior vintage, of great value,"[211] hence the parable is very likely about harvest time. In view of all the facets of this story, it is unlikely that the message of the parable is about generosity.

In fact, the vineyard owner does things *de rigueur*. The law was clear about the need to pay the day laborer at the end of the day (cf. Deut. 24:14–15; Lev. 19:13), otherwise he and his family might go hungry the next day. Thus the vineyard owner follows Torah on this point. He had bargained with the first hired, and promised to pay what is right to the second, third, and fourth groups (vv 3–5). It is only to the last group that he made no promise but simply told them to go into the vineyard. With all of them he had been just, and paid them what was right, even a bit above what might have been ordinarily expected, but again a denarius was no great sum. He has done no one any wrong strictly speaking (cf. v 13), but he has created the appearance of unfairness and so he must answer the grumbling of the first hired workers.[212] Notice how the parable closes on the issue of envy – "is your eye evil because I am good." There is no justification for translating *agathos* as "generous".[213] It is at this juncture that one must ask about the *Sitz im Leben Jesu* of such a parable.

I would suggest the key clues are: (1) equal pay to all; and (2) the issue of envy broached at the end. 'The evil eye' was a concept frequently found in

---

[209] Scott, *Hear Then the Parable*, 283.

[210] If one is to think that the need of the employer was great, perhaps because this is a story about the crucial day when one must harvest the grapes, then it may be that the value of the work done at the end was as great to him as that which had been done throughout the day.

[211] Derrett, *Studies in the NT*, p.56.

[212] As Gryglewicz, "Gospel of the Overworked Laborers," 195 says, "Everything was left entirely to the discretion of the employer," except that he was obliged to keep the rules of Torah. In view of the scarcity of work and high unemployment of day laborers in Jesus' time workers were desperate and would take even a fraction of a day's work in hopes of earning something. This left them at the mercy of the employer. The picture this parable paints is of a society with some considerable economic problems. In such a setting this parable would be all the more volatile.

[213] One is not helped by translations that render *agathos*, by "generous" (cf. NRSV, NIV). "Good" and "generous" are not synonymous. The employer does what is honest, right, and therefore good, but he is hardly very generous.

earlier Wisdom literature (cf. Proverbs and Sirach). One must also take into account the fact that the vineyard is a stock symbol for Israel not only in the Old Testament (cf. Isa. 5) but also in the arguably authentic parables of Jesus (cf. Mark 12.1–9 and par.).[214] Furthermore, this parable is primarily about *employment*, not gifts or grace. We are told explicitly that all but the last hired were paid what was owed them or what was right (*dikaios*).[215] This leads to the conclusion that this parable is about service in God's vineyard. It has definite similarities to the parable of the Prodigal Son (cf. Luke 15:11–32) particularly when one compares the reaction of the first hired here with the reaction of the elder brother there.[216]

One can envision that this parable was told as an answer to those who objected to Jesus' approach to ministry. More particularly, Jesus was suggesting that his disciples, in part culled from the least, last and lost of Jewish society[217] and brought into service in the vineyard at the eleventh hour, would be 'made equal' or at least would receive equal treatment from the divine vineyard owner for the services they rendered. Some of Jesus' audience objected to this as unfair, for they had labored long and hard in the vineyard. I submit that this interpretation makes better sense of the parable in Jesus' life situation than the proposed alternatives, as Jesus on various occasions seems to have had to justify his ministry and the sort of people he called and used in his ministry.[218]

There is a sense in which all those who labor in the service of the Dominion of God are made equal in the end. "The parable relativizes justice to show that it is incapable of organizing the world of the kingdom... [for] the function of justice is not to make all equal but to ensure all their appropriate places."[219] The vineyard owner is anxious precisely because the time of harvest has come and the workers are insufficient in number to accomplish the task, unless he goes back out over and over and hires whomever he can find. "The harvest is plentiful but the laborers are few" (Matt. 9:37). This is a parable about eschatology and the benefits of working for the vineyard owner. It suggests again that Jesus saw the eschatological reign of God breaking into Israel's midst

---

[214] On the authenticity of this parable, cf. Witherington, *Christology of Jesus*, 213ff.

[215] Cf. G. de Ru, "Reward in the Teaching of Jesus," 202–222, who says "...the first are not condemned at all, but receive the wages that were agreed with them beforehand" (204). The address to them by the vineyard owner—*hetaire*, 'friend' or "companion" – is a term used in friendly rebuke (cf. Matt. 22:12; 26:50) and may suggest that the vineyard owner is not being pictured as a tyrant, though there is the appearance of unfairness.

[216] Rightly noted by R. T. France, *Matthew*, 289–90. Cf. R. H. Stein, *An Introduction to the Parables of Jesus*, 127. Stein is right that the rule of end stress places a premium on the dialogue between the grumbling workers and the employer at the end, revealing the essential thrust of the story.

[217] The "idle" are those who seemed not to be doing anything of any importance.

[218] Witherington, *Christology of Jesus*, 124ff.

[219] Scott, *Hear Then the Parable*, 297. I would demur from his conclusion that this parable is basically about invitation. To the contrary there is no stress on all being equally invited but rather on all being equally paid!

through his ministry, precipitating the time of harvesting and thus the need for workers, though the pay off would not come until the work was completed.[220]

Thus one must conclude that this is definitely not a reversal parable, unless one means by that a parable that reverses or dashes the expectations of the first hired.[221] The first do not exchange places or rewards with the last in this parable, however. G. de Ru rightly says, "the parable is not intended to preach a reversal of all earthly rank on the last day, for in respect of the amount of wages (and that is the whole point) there is no mention of anything of the kind, all receive exactly the same amount."[222] J. R. Donahue is also right that this parable seems to turn upside down the orderly structure of society with its pecking order established by things like seniority and years of service.[223] A disturbing conclusion that reorients one's thinking by disorienting is typical of Jesus' parables.[224]

The dominion of God has its own economy. All work in the vineyard is apparently equally valuable to the vineyard owner, regardless of the length of time one worker or another contributes to the overall task. The point may be that it requires a group effort, and just as a team's members all equally share in a victory, regardless of how many minutes one or another player has played, so too every worker equally shares in the remuneration in the dominion of God. About the divine vineyard owner it can be said, "He knows, he understands, he cares, he sympathizes, he is righteous, but his righteousness holds more in the balance of just judgment than time served and work accomplished. His call came to different [people] at different hours."[225] Jesus' Wisdom as expressed in his narrative *meshalim* was a Wisdom tempered, indeed molded, by his eschatological convictions. This can be seen to be true in all three of the

---

[220] Boucher, *The Parables*, 95 is quite right that 'reckoning' was a traditional Jewish metaphor for the coming of God's reign. The difference is that Jesus' teaching has an already – not yet quality to it – already it is the time for harvest, but the reckoning will not come until the labor in the vineyard is done.

[221] J. D. Crossan, "The Servant Parables of Jesus,", 17–55, is probably wrong to treat this with master–servant parables, for the social relationships of employer and day laborer differed from those between master and slave.

[222] De Ru, "Reward in the Teaching of Jesus," 205. He is quite right that the parable is not about a sudden burst of generosity in view of the amount given, a subsistence wage.

[223] J. R. Donahue, *The Gospel in Parable*, 81.

[224] Rabbi E. Friedman of Washington, D.C. suggested that Jesus was crucified because he told parables which spoke so revealingly of the human heart and condition. No one likes to look in the mirror when one knows deep down the image will not be beautiful.

[225] W. A. Curtis, "The Parable of the Laborers, (Matt. xx.1–16),", 5–10, here 9. This parable, though bearing some similarity to the Jewish parable (*Midrash Rabba* on Deut. 6:2 about R. Abba bar Kahana from about A.D. 325 at the earliest), is in fact about a king who concealed his pay scale and gave different pay for different work. This is the opposite of our tale. The parable told by R. bar Hiya (*J. T. Berak.* 2.8; Song of Songs R. 6.2) discussed by Donahue, *Gospel in Parable*, 81–82 is indeed apparently about equal pay for unequal work; *however*, one is told explicitly that the one worker called aside by the king to walk with him was more industrious and is said to have accomplished more in two hours than the rest did in a whole day. No such thing is stated in Jesus' parable.

parables studied here. It is a Wisdom unlike that of a Ben Sira because it tends to challenge or reverse conventional values rather than strengthen or reinforce them.

Throughout this discussion good reasons have been noted to say that Jesus taught a Wisdom that entailed a counter order, and often it was a Wisdom from below, not one that propped up the *status quo* or supported the values of the wealthy few. Paradoxically enough, the source of the counter order was indeed from above – the inbreaking eschatological dominion of God.

JESUS—THE WISDOM OF GOD

By reading the previous sections of this chapter, one might get the impression that Jesus only expressed himself by means of the various forms of Wisdom speech. This is not true, as on some occasions he draws on prophetic and apocalyptic modes of speech, as I have shown in the *Christology of Jesus*. One must also reckon with cross fertilization of these various modes of speaking as well. What seems to be the case is that Jesus usually sapientialized whatever he said, often expressing prophetic or apocalyptic ideas in some sort of Wisdom form of speech. It is for this reason that calling Jesus a sage is heuristically the most all-encompassing and satisfying term. It explains not only the form of the vast majority of his sayings, but also the content of some of these sayings. Wilder is right in urging that one must see Jesus as the sort of sage one would expect at the turn of the era, one influenced by the cross-currents of various traditions. He puts it this way:

> Now if the parables came out of the wisdom tradition to Israel, we also know that apocalyptic was closely related to wisdom. If Solomon was seen as the founder of proverbial wisdom, Enoch, for example, was a chief representative of wisdom of another kind. Jesus' eschatological outlook and imagery were related to the latter, as his parables were to the former. He united both styles and brought both into direct relation with the realities of his time... In the Book of Enoch the term *mashal* is prominent in the sense of a "revelation of secrets of God concerning the economy of salvation"... Thus in Enoch... a parable or *mashal* means a prophetic unveiling of the secrets of the future. In intertestamental Judaism there was a tendency for the old categories to be merged – law and wisdom, but also wisdom and prophecy or apocalyptic vision.[226]

This observation is essentially correct, though probably the narrative *mashal* is a prophetic adaptation of a Wisdom form. The reference to Enoch is intriguing for elsewhere we have shown evidence that Jesus in his use of the Son of Man

[226] Wilder, *Jesus' Parables and the War of Myths. Essays on Imagination in the Scriptures*, 79.

language reflects an indebtedness to Enoch's parables.[227] Did Jesus believe that he too was one to whom secrets about the Dominion had been revealed and who was called upon to reveal them to others, perhaps chiefly through the indirect method of the narrative *mashal*? Possibly Matt. 11:25–27 and par. points in the direction of Jesus seeing himself as a revealer of things hidden, and it appears that this tradition goes in some form back to Jesus.[228]

As noted earlier, at various points in the development of the Wisdom tradition there was some stress on the hiddenness of Wisdom (e.g. Job 28), and therefore the need for it to be revealed. It was, as Jesus says, for ears who were prepared to hear. As Ben Sira indicates, there are subtleties and obscurities to parables and hidden meanings to proverbs; it requires being filled with God's Spirit to understand these mysteries and to be able to reveal them (cf. Sir. 39:1–9). The Wisdom of Solomon pursues some of these ideas even farther by so closely identifying Wisdom and spirit that to have or be filled with the latter is to have or be filled with the former.

It may well be that in early Judaism the personification of Wisdom arose, at least in part, to cope with and make clear not only that some of life's Wisdom is hidden, but also that God intends to reveal it. Could Jesus then, as both sage and revealer of God's inbreaking dominion, have gone a step further and identified himself as the very embodiment of Wisdom on earth? I already made a start towards demonstrating this possibility when I investigated Matt. 11:25–27 and par., but there were also other hints along the way such as the earliest form of a sapiential saying that Wisdom will be vindicated by her deeds (Matt. 11:19b).[229] There is also the Q saying about one greater than Solomon being present (Luke 11:31 / Matt. 12:42).[230] One must ask, for a person like Jesus who spoke in the Wisdom tradition, a tradition which continued to attribute a wide variety of works to Solomon right up to the turn of the era, who or what could be greater than Solomon? Surely the implication is the presence of Wisdom herself.

More also needs to be made of the Q saying in Luke 9:58 / Matt. 8:20. This very likely authentic saying is not just about rejection or homelessness but also about rest.[231] If one allows the supposition for a moment that Jesus saw himself as Wisdom and interpreted his mission in the light of the earlier Wisdom poems/hymns, then Sir 24:7ff. becomes very revealing. In that text Wisdom is *seeking*, but not finding, a resting place *until* she comes to rest in Jerusalem having been commanded by God to go there (vv 8–11). In the hymn in Sirach

---

[227] Witherington, *Christology of Jesus*, 234ff.

[228] As argued in Witherington, *Christology of Jesus*, 221ff.

[229] Witherington, *Christology of Jesus*, 51–53.

[230] The essential authenticity was urged in Witherington, *Women in the Ministry of Jesus*, 44–45 and notes.

[231] L. E. Vaage, "Q and the Historical Jesus," 166–67 suggests that the very peculiarity of this saying assures its essential authenticity. Nowhere else in the Gospel tradition do we hear Jesus discourse about his sleeping patterns. Here alone is there the suggestion that Jesus lived a less civilized life than even common animals.

this amounts to cosmic and international Wisdom taking up residence amongst a particular people in their chief religious center. Is it not possible that Jesus heard the call of God for him to go up to Jerusalem through a careful meditation on Sirach 24 and a realization that he was experiencing rejection and no *shalom* elsewhere? Could this life orientation of Jesus not be behind the journeying up to Jerusalem motif so important to all the Gospels? But one must go back and ask if there is anything in earlier Jewish traditions which might have encouraged Jesus to see himself in this light, making the considerable step from presenting himself as a sage to presenting himself as the embodiment of Wisdom in the flesh.

Bearing in mind that the narrative *mashal* seems to have Jesus' dominant tool for public discourse, a tool that was a prophetic adaptation of the modes of Wisdom utterance, there seems to have been a way in which Jesus may have been encouraged by the prophetic tradition to be daring in the way he adopted and adapted Wisdom speech. I am referring to the fact that in the prophetic corpus on occasion a person presented himself or was viewed as *being* a *mashal*, a living symbol or figure of God's message to and for God's people.

There was ample precedent for this in traditions one finds in a variety of places in the Old Testament. For example, at Deut. 28:37 the nation is said to be a *mashal*, a figure or symbol of God's judgment. The same sort of use is found in Ps. 44:14, 2 Chron. 8:20, and Tobit 3:4. At Ps. 69:11, however, *mashal* is used of a particular individual and in this case apparently a royal individual who has become a "byword" – as *mashal* is so often translated in such cases. The idea here is of a person being a living symbol and often an object of derision and ridicule. Even more to the point are the places, especially in the late prophetic book of Ezekiel, where the one who relates *meshalim* himself becomes a *mashal*, perhaps by some sort of symbolic prophetic action such as one finds at Ezek. 24:3. In fact, at 24:24 one hears the Word of God say about him, "Thus shall Ezekiel be to you a sign; according to all that he has done you shall do." One may also think of the example of Hosea and his marriage to Gomer, so that the prophet and his very life becomes a *mashal* to God's people. The point of mentioning all of this is not to suggest that the case of Jesus was exactly the same as the case of Ezekiel or Hosea, but that there is at least one crucial point at which they are analagous, namely, that the spokesman for God might not just convey a message but be the embodiment of that message in who he was, in what he did, in how he lived.[232]

Realizing this, it would not be an improbable progression in early Judaism for Jesus not to be merely an utterer of Wisdom speech, but also to represent himself as the embodiment of Wisdom, Wisdom in person. The relationship of Jesus the sage and Jesus as Wisdom lies in part in one being the

---

[232] I am well aware that being a prophetic sign is not identical to claiming to be God's Wisdom in person. Nevertheless, the idea of being the embodiment of one's message provides a precedent for Jesus to take such a daring step.

personal embodiment of one's message, but also in the fact that for Jesus, *who* told the parable, and what his authority was, was as important as the *mashal* he told.[233] Jesus did not merely announce the inbreaking of God's dominion on earth, he believed that he brought it, and thus in some sense even embodied it. It is also not unimportant that it was because *Jesus* told these parables, aphorisms, and riddles that they were collected and passed down by his early followers. It was at least in part because it was believed that these sayings said something about *him*, that such collections were made. L. E. Keck makes the following apt observations:

> Jesus preferred parables not merely because he found them useful but primarily because there is an inner connection between the parabolic mode of speech and the mode and motive of his work. Jesus concentrated on parabolic speech because he himself was a parabolic event of the kingdom of God.... Jesus is himself a parable.... He not only tells shocking stories but leads a shocking life toward a shocking end. Just as the parables have familiar elements in unfamiliar plots, so Jesus' life has familiar features of Palestinian life in startling juxtaposition: he preaches in synagogues but at the beach as well, he consorts with scrupulous Pharisees but ignores ritual washing when he is their guest.... Precisely the offensiveness of the historical Jesus is congruent with his parabolic function, for he arrests the flow of trusts and thoughts and thereby invites us to reorder them, that is, to reorder ourselves (i.e. repent). It is not just the words of Jesus that call [us] to repent, but the man as a whole; for as in the case of the parable, one cannot attend to Jesus and still assume that one's knowing and trusting are unchallenged.[234]

What is especially daring about the idea of Jesus taking the personification of Wisdom and suggesting that he was the living embodiment of it, is that while a prophet might be seen as a *mashal* or prophetic sign, no one, so far as one can tell, up to that point in early Judaism had dared to suggested that he was a human embodiment of an attribute of God – God's Wisdom. Indeed, as M. Hengel has remarked to me, no known person in early Judaism other than Jesus between the time of Alexander and Bar Kochba was identified with the personification of Wisdom.[235] Some explanation for this remarkable and anomalous development must be given, and the best, though by no means the only, explanation of this fact is that Jesus presented himself as both sage and the message of the sage – God's Wisdom.

---

[233] This was also in part true of any authoritative word spoken in early Judaism. One needed to consider the source as much as the sort of utterance given by that source, hence the concern about false prophets, deceptive sages, unfaithful priests and the like. Early Judaism expected the messenger to comport with the message. The ultimate degree of such integrity would be found if the messenger could be seen to be the very embodiment of the message s/he offered.

[234] L. E. Keck, *A Future for the Historical Jesus*, 244, 246, 247.

[235] In a personal letter to me dated July 18, 1991.

Personified Wisdom is after all the highest form of *mashal*, of metaphorical and figurative Wisdom speech, and thus the development from being a *mashal* in the Old Testament prophetic sense to being Wisdom is not unnatural. Furthermore, the portrayal of the role of Jesus in the earliest authentic Gospel material is much like the role of Wisdom as described by one of Jesus' Jewish near contemporaries: "Wisdom rescued from troubles those who served her... she guided him on straight paths; she showed him the Kingdom of God, and gave him knowledge of holy things..." (Wis. 10:9–10).

This leads to the scrutiny of one text which is crucial to this discussion, i.e., Matt. 11:28–30 which has both a precedent and a close parallel in Sir. 6:23–31 (cf. 51:23–28), as already mentioned.[236] In Sirach it is clearly Wisdom's yoke[237] the disciple is to put on, and in Matthew it is Jesus'/Wisdom's yoke. The possibility of the authenticity of this saying must be seriously entertained in view of the fact that the idea of Jesus as Wisdom can be found in a variety of Synoptic sources: (1) Q: Matt. 12.42/Luke. 11:31; Matt. 11:27; Luke 10:22;[238] (2) L: Luke 21:15 and cf. 11:49; and (3) M: Matt. 11:19, 28–30. It is not simply an idea found in one Gospel source[239] and its absence from Mark can perhaps be attributed to two considerations: (1) Mark does not contain a great deal of Jesus' sayings and may not know Q at all;[240] and (2) what sayings he does include are basically either parables or the material found in the eschatological discourse in Mark 13. Mark offers little of the other forms of Wisdom material such as riddles or aphorisms and certainly no Wisdom discourses. Thus, he has little need or occasion to reflect on or develop the theme of Jesus as Wisdom (but cf. Mark 4:11 to Wis. 10:10; Sir. 39:1–9).

The following arguments also favor the essential authenticity of this saying. First, if Ben Sira could say words very close to what is found in this text, surely there is no reason Jesus could not as well. In view of how popular and apparently widely circulated Ben Sira's book was in early Judaism, there is no reason why Jesus could not have known it.[241] It is not so much the words themselves but the implication that Jesus is speaking as Wisdom and asking followers to learn of him, that some scholars have balked at. But it has already

[236] Cf. pp. 143–144 above, on the comparison of the teachings of Jesus and of Ben Sira.

[237] Which is not to be simply identified with the yoke of Torah, for as we have seen Ben Sira meant more than Torah when he spoke of Wisdom. The two are not simply synonymous.

[238] On the latter saying cf. Witherington, *Christology of Jesus*, 223–24.

[239] It is also present in the *Gospel of Thomas*.

[240] The one really strong argument for believing that Mark did know Q is the correspondence of the conglomerate Old Testament quote (Exod. 23:20 + Mal. 3;1) in Mark 1:2b and Q 7:27 (= Luke 7:27 and par.) in a form not otherwise known elsewhere. Since both Luke and Matthew have the phrase *emprosthen sou* which is not found in Mark, it is suggested that these two evangelists are drawing on Q material, not Mark. Cf. D. Catchpole, "The Beginning of Q," 205–221, here 214–15. This may be so *but* it is also possible that both Luke and the first evangelist have added the phrase *emprosthen sou* at the end of the second part of the sentence as a natural stylistic improvement to parallel the phrase *pro prosopou sou* at the end of the first half of the verse.

[241] On Ben Sira's widespread popularity, see pp. 76–77.

been shown that Jesus had a sage-disciple relationship with various people,[242] *and* there are other likely authentic texts where Jesus presented himself as Wisdom in the flesh.[243] That Jesus could have made an invitation to discipleship like Matt. 11:28–30 is not beyond the realm of plausibility. Second, if the saying owes anything to Hellenistic thinking,[244] then it does so no more than the material in Sirach, and early Judaism was to some degree Hellenized. In short this is no argument against the authenticity of this saying. Third, Paul seems to have known this saying, at least in part, for 2 Cor. 10.1 seems to be an echo of Matt. 11:29b. Fourth, there is a possible echo of Jer. 6:16 in its Hebrew, not LXX, form which favors its authenticity. Fifth, this saying reflects a characteristic trait of Jesus' teachings – the presentation of a counter order, offered in paradoxical terms. This saying is *not* about taking on the yoke of Torah, but rather Jesus' yoke which is said in oxymoronic fashion to be an easy yoke, involving a light burden! Sixth, many critical scholars have accepted the substantial authenticity of this saying including J. Dupont, J. Jeremias, C. H. Dodd, O. Cullmann, T. W. Manson, W. Grundmann, E. Stauffer, A. M. Hunter, D. Hill, R. Otto, and A. Schlatter, to mention a few.[245] This is an impressive and diverse list, and the judgment of these scholars should not be taken lightly.

In all likelihood Matt. 11:28–30 is independent of Matt. 11:25–27 and whether it stood in Q or not will be considered in Chapter 6. A variant of this tradition is found in *Gos. Thom.* 90 where Jesus says, "Come to me, for my yoke is easy and my lordship is gentle (*rmras*) and you shall find rest for yourselves." In view of the use of the term *rmras*, which may reflect knowledge of the First Evangelist's saying,[246] it looks like the Thomas version is secondary. Yet a case can be made for this saying being independently attested in Thomas, since the clauses of the saying are in a different order in Thomas than they are in Matthew.

While v 29bc may be redactional, A. R. Motte has argued that this saying mirrors the form of other Wisdom sayings in Sirach as follows: (1) there are two imperative clauses (vv 28a and 29a); (2) each of these is followed by a saying in the future introduced by *kai* (vv 28b and 29c); 3) there are also two subordinate clauses, a *hoti* clause in v 29b and a *gar* clause in v 30. This would make the

[242] Cf. pp. 175ff. above.

[243] Witherington, *Christology of Jesus*, 52–53.

[244] For a review of possible Hellenistic elements and of German scholarship's treatment of this passage in the twentieth century, cf. H. D. Betz, "The Logion of the Easy Yoke and of Rest (Matt. 11.28–30)," 10–24. He is likely right that Matt. 11:28–30 is taken up again in the promise and commission found in Matt. 28:18–20.

[245] On the authenticity of this saying, cf. A. M. Hunter, "Crux Criticorum–Matt. XI.25–30 – A Re-Appraisal," 241–49; S. Bacchiocchi, "Matthew 11.28–30: Jesus' Rest and the Sabbath," 289–316, especially 311–16, citing various scholars' views.

[246] Cf. Allison and Davies, *Matthew*, Vol. 2, 292, who argue that at least v 29bc is redactional, destroying the parallelism of 28 ab and 29 ad. This may be so, though I am not fully convinced that at least v 29b is redactional, especially since Paul seems to know precisely this part of the saying. For another view of the structure of this saying, cf. below on A. R. Motte.

structure of the logion A, B, A', C, B', C' which is rather peculiar and may suggest a redactional insertion, namely C, "because I am meek and humble of heart." If this is omitted, then one has an orderly progression with a final explanatory *gar* clause. A very similar structure is found in Sirach – imperative, indicative clause, causal or explanatory clause (Sir. 1.30, cf. 1.26; 3:1-2; 6:27-28).[247] This last parallel is important.

Sir. 6.27 is in synonymous parallelism with 6.26 and various parts of the larger context which beckons the disciple to heed Wisdom deserve citation: "Come to her with all your soul" (v 26); "For at last you will find the rest she gives" (v 28), "Her yoke is a golden ornament, and her bonds a purple cord" (v 30). This is much closer to our logion than Sirach 51. Only Sirach 51:26, "Put your neck under her yoke," from that chapter is closer to the language of Matt. 11:28–30, than what one finds in Sirach 6, and in any case Sir. 6:24 also says, "put your neck into her collar." If Jesus' audience had any memory of Sirach 6 they could have drawn the conclusion that when Jesus spoke the substance of what one find in Matt. 11:28–30, he was speaking as Wisdom.

The suggestion that in doing this Jesus should be seen as a new Moses fails to come to grips with the close parallels from Sirach and the development of the personification of Wisdom in early Judaism which is not completely identified with Torah even in Sirach.[248] The suggestion that Jesus is speaking *in persona sapientiae* has been championed by various scholars in this century, perhaps most strikingly by R. Otto.[249] While it is probably saying too much to claim that "[t]hese are perhaps the most important verses in the Synoptic Gospels,"[250] they are quite important for they reveal that Jesus the sage did not see himself as just another sage, or even just the last great Jewish sage. These verses point to a transcendent self-understanding.[251]

There are still some enigmatic aspects to this saying. What sort of burdens did Jesus have in mind to alleviate his followers from, and what sort of rest did he offer? On the former score perhaps Matt. 23:4/Luke 11:46 suggests the Pharisaic and scribal *halakah* was the burden in view.[252] On the latter score, eschatological rest is probably intended, especially in view of a

---

[247] A. R. Motte, "La Structure du Logion de Matthieu," 226–233, especially 227–28.

[248] For example, M. Maher, "'Take my Yoke upon You' (Matt. XI.29)," 97–103.

[249] R. Otto, *The Kingdom of God and Son of Man* (1938), 137; 171ff. I would disagree with Otto on the matter of whether or not there is a straight quote from Sirach 51. Hunter, "Crux Criticorum," 247–48 is correct in saying that elements have been taken up from several passages and Jesus has made his own new whole out of them.

[250] Hunter, "Crux Criticorum," 241.

[251] On a variety of other grounds this conclusion seems likely as well; cf. Witherington, *Christology of Jesus*, 263–75.

[252] Cf. Motte, "Structure du Logion," 231: "Le repos est présente d'un côté comme donné par le maître, de l'autre comme trouvé par les disciples. On passe d'une manière très suggestive du maître qui tient école a l'enseignement qu'il faut mettre en pratique. Ainsi est–il signifié que Jesus n'est pas un rabbi quelconque: plus qu'à son enseignement c'est a lui–même qui doit aller l'attachement du disciple."

likely authentic beatitude like Matt.5:4/Luke 6:21b.[253] Jesus does not suggest that in the interim his followers will not have a yoke or a burden to bear. Indeed, since Jesus seems to have upped the cost of discipleship and intensified Old Testament demands in various regards it would be as unwise to ignore the noun "yoke" as it would be to ignore the adjective "easy". This was yet another paradoxical teaching from the sage.

No one before or after Jesus during the biblical era identified themselves with personified Wisdom. While Ben Sira could invite disciples to come and study with him, in the end he would point them away from himself to the yoke of Wisdom. He was a much more traditional and conservative sage. Jesus spoke as Wisdom, and his yoke amounted to binding his disciples personally to himself and his teaching, a teaching about a counter order of reality that he believed was being brought about through his ministry. This would explain the concern by the later handlers of the Jesus tradition not only to preserve some of his teaching but to specifically identify that teaching as coming from a particular sage, Jesus. It would also explain at least to a significant degree how it came to be that christological reflection by the church became bound up with what was essentially sapiential material.[254]

If the validity of an interpretation is shown by its ability to explain a wide variety of data, then the thesis that Jesus presented himself as the embodiment of Wisdom has definite validity. As shall soon be discussed, sparked by the catalyst of this remarkable and so far as one knows unprecedented (in early Judaism) association by Jesus of a historical individual with God's personified Wisdom, the early church took this seed, planted it and raised a vast harvest of Wisdom Christologies, found in such varied contexts as Q, christological hymns, Paul, and the narrative framework of Gospels. How better to explain the appearance of the idea of the historical person Jesus being identified or portrayed as Wisdom in so many different sources, many of which have no likely interconnections, than to assume that Jesus in some way presented himself as Wisdom? It is to the further pilgrimage of Jesus as Wisdom in the church to which this study now turns.

---

[253] Betz, "Logion," 24: "The logion 11.28–30 is therefore theologically identical with the macarisms of the Sermon on the Mount (5.3–12)."

[254] Schweizer, *Matthew*, 447.

PART TWO
FROM JESUS TO THE CHURCH

5

Wisdom's Legacy: From Q to James

FOR at least significant portions of the early Christian movement, Wisdom in the person of Jesus was believed to have returned to heaven, exalted to the right hand of God, and to be reigning from there.[1] But Jesus as Wisdom had left both his legacy and his influence behind. This chapter will examine some of both in two different sorts of collections of sayings – one a collection of Jesus' own sayings (his legacy),[2] the other a collection of Wisdom sayings thought to have come from Jesus' brother James and reflecting the influence of Jesus.

RIGHT ON Q: DOUBTING THOMAS

GENERAL CONSIDERATIONS

I have elsewhere expressed my skepticism about the existence of a Q community, by which I mean a community for which the Q material *was* their Gospel or their only formative source of religious thought.[3] More recent studies by J. Kloppenborg, H. Koester, and J. D. Crossan have not persuaded me to change my mind on this issue.[4] Arguing there was a Q community is rather like arguing there was a Proverbs community, or an Aboth community. Besides the fact that it is wholly an argument from silence, with no data outside of Q by

---

[1] See Chapter 6 on the christological hymns found in Pauline and Johannine material as well as in Hebrews. One may also wish to point to the concept of the ascension of Jesus in Luke–Acts.

[2] For a helpful survey of research on Q up to 1981, cf. F. Neirynck, "Recent Developments in the Study of Q," 29–75.

[3] Witherington, *Christology of Jesus*, 222–24.

[4] J. Kloppenborg, *The Formation of Q*; H. Koester, *Ancient Christian Gospels, Crossan, Historical Jesus.*

which to check such a view, where is there any precedent in early Judaism for such a community? If Ben Sira is any clue as to how Wisdom material was being handled, the sages, well before Jesus' time, were pointing their disciples to a variety of sources for Wisdom *including Torah*. That is, the sages were not only drawing on and sapientializing a variety of types of sayings material, but Ben Sira at least was urging them to study not only the sayings of the sages but this other teaching material as well. One cannot *presume* that Q represents the entire theology of any Christian community.[5]

The analogy with the *Gospel of Thomas* is also made too much of in some quarters and too little of in others. In the first place, the Gnosticizing and ascetical tendencies of that book encourage one to see it as arising out of a provenance different from and probably later than Q.[6] Indeed it is the *only* early sayings collection arising out of Judaism or Christianity that really manifests a Gnostic tendency. In some respects it has more kinship with second-century Gnostic documents such as the *Pistis Sophia* than with Q. In the second place not only in its Gnostic agenda but also in form it differs significantly from Q in the following respects: (1) in Thomas there is some interest in dialogue, as in later Gnostic documents, which is not characteristic of Q; (2) in Q there is not only some interest in narrative (e.g. about Jesus" temptations) but also in miracle stories (cf. Luke 7:1–10/Matt. 8:5–13) which is not characteristic of Thomas. It also more than doubtful that one can argue that because Thomas does not really manifest future eschatological sayings of Jesus, therefore the earliest strata of Q did not do so either.[7] The editorial tendencies of the redactors of these respective sayings collections cannot be presumed to be the same. In view of its Gnosticizing agenda, it is more than likely that Thomas edited future eschatological material out of his source. Q gives prominent space to *future* eschatological sayings by placing them in a collection at the end of the document, though there is eschatological material throughout Q (cf. Q 3:17; 6:20–33; 6:36; 6:46; 6:47–49; 10:12–15; 11:2–13; 11:14–23; 11:31–32; 12:8–9; 12:31; 13:34–35; 17:22–37).[8]

Furthermore, the attempt to see Q as a collection of "*secret* Wisdom sayings" (cf. the incipit of Thomas) overlooks the fact that the Wisdom

[5] Cf. the important warning of A. D. Jacobson, *Wisdom Christology in Q*, 22, n. 39: "It is true that Q is striking as much for what it lacks as what it contains... However, the absence of certain material in Q (e.g., passion and resurrection narratives, miracle stories, Sabbath controversies, etc.) cannot be used as primary evidence for the theological character of Q."

[6] If one may judge by the company this document was found with at Nag Hammadi it arose from a very eclectic community with Gnostic tendencies. Cf. the Nag Hammadi book list in J. Kloppenborg, *et al., Q, Thomas Reader*, 80. The authors of this volume may be right that this is a first century document, perhaps from the last thirty years of the century, but its theological tendencies make a second century date more probable. On Thomas as later than Q, cf. P. J. Hartin, *James and the Q Sayings of Jesus*, 57ff.

[7] *Pace* Koester, *Ancient Gospels*, 150.

[8] C. M. Tuckett, "A Cynic Q?" 371–72.

pericopes in Q occur primarily in the first two–thirds of Q[9] and so Q as a whole cannot be categorized *simply* as *logoi sophon*, much less as *secret* Wisdom sayings. This is a Wisdom collection but it is more than just logia; it also involves narratives, and it certainly has only a distinct minority of material that could be characterized as esoteric or secret Wisdom. It stands in the tradition of earlier Jewish Wisdom collections such as one finds in Proverbs, Ecclesiastes and Sirach.[10]

This is not to deny the existence of sayings collections that primarily focused on Jesus' logia, or that there is a very sizable amount of Wisdom material in Q, or that sometimes here and there Thomas may provide a non–canonical saying of Jesus or an earlier form of a canonical saying.[11] One must agree with Kloppenborg that the genre of the Q material should be determined by examining the Q material itself, not simply by analogy, and certainly not simply by analogy with Thomas.[12] The great value of Thomas is that it makes plausible the argument that there *were* early collections primarily made up of Jesus' words in communities influenced by early Christianity.[13]

Q is *basically* a sayings collection, and the majority of the sayings are Wisdom sayings but it draws on diverse genres, including sapiential, prophetic and also other kinds of material, which are then redacted to serve certain agendas. It is helpful to ask whether or not a sapiential sort of editing has gone

---

[9] Jacobson, *Wisdom Christology in Q*, 3ff.

[10] Scholars owe a considerable debt to J. M. Robinson in his seminal essay, "*Logoi Sophon*: On the Gattung of Q," in *Trajectories through Early Christianity*, 71–113, for helping us to place Q in the trajectory of Jewish and Jewish Christian Wisdom collections. I would disagree that these types of collections necessarily had a gnosticizing tendency simply by being a sayings collection. Robinson's subsequent essay, "Early Collections of Jesus's Sayings," 389–94 is equally helpful in that it shows that in places like Mark 4 we find hints of early collections of parables (in this case parables grouped together because of the similarity of key words or themes – sower/seed).

[11] The judicious surveys of K. Snodgrass, "The Gospel of Thomas; a Secondary Gospel," 19–38; and C. M. Tuckett, "Thomas and the Synoptics," 132–57, must be given their due. Thomas manifests not only a knowledge of material found in all four Gospels, but more importantly the *redactional* work of all the Synoptic evangelists and perhaps John as well. Snodgrass' conclusion is fully warranted: "Thomas represents a late stage in transmission process and... its material is determined by oral tradition that is partly dependent on the canonical Gospels, but also on other material..." From this *other* material Thomas on occasion provides an earlier and independent form of a tradition also found in the canonical Gospels, or an authentic non–canonical saying. All these matters are further complicated by the fact that most of Thomas is available only in Coptic which appears to be a translation *and redaction* of an earlier Greek text (cf. POXY 654, 1, 655). In such circumstances sweeping claims about Thomas representing the earliest form of many sayings are dubious at best, and in any case not demonstrable.

[12] Kloppenborg, *Formation of Q*, 38ff.

[13] It is not completely clear, but at least eight places in Thomas suggest that Thomas knew and drew on material now found in the Synoptic Gospels, among a variety of other sources. Cf. *Thomas* 32 (Matt. 5:14b); *Thomas* 39 (Matt. 23.13); *Thomas* 45b (Luke 6:45); *Thomas* 104a (Luke 5:33); and *Thomas* 104b (Luke 5:33–35). Three further examples are less certain but cf. *Thomas* 32, 33b (Matt. 5:14b–15); *Thomas* 65, 66 (Mark 12:31–35, pars.); *Thomas* 92a, 93–94 (Matt. 7:6–7). On the Syrian and second century provenance of Thomas, cf. Snodgrass, "Gospel of Thomas," 22ff.

on in the arranging and use of the diverse sorts of Q sayings materials, similar to that found in Sirach. This will reveal as much about the intentions of the final redactor of Q as an examination of the sayings themselves.

Another problem that plagues research in the Q material, besides arguments from silence, inadequate analogies with Thomas, and conclusions about *logoi sophon* that outstrip the actual evidence in Q, is the persistent tendency by specialists in Q to favor the Lukan form of this or that saying sometimes without even an argument. I have always found this puzzling in view of the fact that there is a standard which can help one to judge such matters. A person who wants to figure out how the First Evangelist or Luke has edited the sayings material should first consider how Matthew and Luke edit Mark. One learns several very revealing things from such an investigation.

For instance, Matthew takes over more than 90% of his Markan source (606 out of 661 Markan verses), while Luke takes over only a little over 50%. The difference in degree of word for word appropriation of Mark in the pericopes and sayings that Matthew and Luke take over is minimal. Luke uses about 53% of Mark's exact words in the material culled from that source, while the First Evangelist uses about 51% of Mark's exact words of the 606 verses he appropriates. This means that Luke and the First Evangelist are about equally likely to preserve the exact wording of their source, and they do so about half the time. Luke, however, seems to make more of a consistent effort than Matthew to rewrite all his sources using his own style and syntax.

Unless one wants to argue that the First Evangelist and Luke used very *different* editorial techniques in handling the Q material than they did in handling Mark, for which view one would have to give evidence, then two things need to be kept in mind. The First Evangelist seems to reproduce much more of the *content* of his sources than Luke does. There are various pericopes, found only in Matthew, that certainly may have been in Q though Luke does not include them. One such example would be the saying already examined in the previous chapter, Matt. 11:28–30.[14] C. E. Carlston has argued that the balance of probability lies with its inclusion in Q.[15] There are several places where it might have been included, for example at the very end of the document, if Sirach 51 is any analogy. It seems more likely to have come at the end of the very first major section of Q, which then in turn is followed by the first section on discipleship. Another possibility would be that it came after the parable of the lost coin (Luke 15:1–10) at the end of Part 5 of Q and prior to the second major section on discipleship. Secondly, there is no good reason to suspect that Matthew had a much stronger tendency than Luke to add to or

[14] For the typical judgment that Matt. 11:28–30 was not in Q, based on a predeliction for following Luke's form of Q material, cf. R. A. Edwards, "Matthew's Use of Q in Chapter Eleven," 257–75.

[15] C. E. Carlston, "Wisdom and Eschatology," 104.

change the language of his source. In fact J. A. Fitzmyer has argued that Matthew is often more apt to preserve the original wording of a saying than Luke.[16]

In regard to the question of the order of pericopes in one's source, it does look like Luke was more apt to follow the order of his source material (basically alternating blocks of Markan and non–Markan material) than the First Evangelist was (who often groups material topically or by genre – e.g., parables grouped together). Thus, it is more probable that Luke follows the original order of the Q material than Matthew. The above discussion leads to the following plea – in regard to the earliest form of a Q saying or pericope, each example should be weighed on its own merits. No predilection for the Lukan form of the tradition should be allowed to determine the issue. One sometimes suspects that the Lukan form of a saying is preferred not on the grounds of the probable tradition history of the material, but because the Lukan form of the logion tends to be less explicitly Jewish in form and less eschatological or apocalyptic in content. A dislike for the idea of Jesus as an apocalyptic seer, or even as a Jewish prophetic sage, should not be allowed to skew one's judgments as to the original Q form of a saying.[17]

Recently, R. A. Horsley subjected J. A. Kloppenborg's conclusions about the formation and strata of Q to a searching analysis.[18] Perhaps the most important conclusion he arrives at is that

> [recent] attempts to distinguish major redactional strata in Q do not seem convincing. It is clear from Kloppenborg's and other's work that the material in Q underwent some development and shaping and... some passages are likely insertions into already shaped complexes of sayings. But the actual material in the various complexes gives little evidence for the existence of later "apocalyptic" or judgmental stratum significantly different from a formative "sapiential" stratum. Hence there does not seem to be an adequate evidentiary basis for tracing a "social history" of the Q tradents or community.[19]

Horsley arrives at this conclusion in part because:

---

[16] J. A. Fitzmyer, "The Priority of Mark and the 'Q' source in Luke," 154.

[17] On all the above, see Witherington, "Principles for Interpreting the Gospels and Acts," 35–70.

[18] R. A. Horsley, "Questions about Redactional Strata and Social Relations Reflected in Q," 186–203. Kloppenborg's response, "The Formation of Q Revisited: A Response to Richard Horsley," is found on 204–15.

[19] Horsley, "Redactional Strata," 195. R. A. Edwards, *A Theology of Q*, 146ff. warned against taking the two strata approach already found in one form in S.Schulz, *Q, Die Spruchquelle der Evangelisten*, if it meant drawing strata lines based on formal considerations about eschatological, prophetic, and wisdom materials. On some points (e.g. about the role of Christian prophets) I would disagree with Edwards, but on the point of Wisdom and eschatological traditions being interwoven in the earliest strata of Q I think he is right. Those who doubt this should read carefully his demonstration of this on 80–145.

> It seems abundantly clear, sociologically speaking, that the people who produced apocalyptic literature such as the various sections of 1 Enoch or the book of Daniel were some of the same people who taught wisdom and Torah. The mixture of "apocalyptic" and "sapiential" materials in the same text can be observed quite clearly in 1 Enoch. What was produced depended on the times and circumstances, but both apocalyptic and wisdom literature stemmed from the same numerically small social stratum.[20]

Kloppenborg has little answer to these criticisms. In fact he makes an important qualification: "It should be stressed that the assignment of a set of sayings to the framing redaction [of Q] implies nothing about their ultimate tradition–historical provenance or their authenticity; it is a literary observation."[21]

Yet this is precisely *not* how scholars such as Crossan and Koester have seen the matter. They seem to have assumed that redactional framing involving apocalytic material is later, and therefore inauthentic while sapiential material is at the earlier level of Q and therefore authentic. Furthermore, while Kloppenborg is right that there is an interest shown in the Son of Man and judgment ideas at the beginning and end of Q,[22] this is not the only redactional agenda in this document. In fact, if anything, the final editor has for the most part a sapiential editorial agenda. Even the eschatological material at the beginning and end of Q serves the purpose of announcing the coming of Jesus the sage, or the consequences of rejecting him.

Kloppenborg attempts to continue to support his general views with a somewhat more nuanced approach than is found in his *The Formation of Q*. For instance, he continues to argue that the "sapiential portions of Q are antecedent to the prophetic–polemical sections because... the prophetic–polemical blocks cohere most closely with the framing redaction of Q, and therefore... represent an ultimate or at least penultimate stage in redaction."[23] This is to overlook the fact that in Q there is a deliberate intention on the part of the final editor to bring together or highlight the *overlap* of the sapiential and prophetic traditions in Jesus (e.g. the rejection and suffering of Jesus is likened to *both* the rejection of Wisdom and the rejection and suffering of the earlier prophets).[24] G. Theissen's recent discussion of these matters deserves to be quoted at this juncture:

---

[20] Horsley., 191.

[21] Kloppenborg, "Formation of Q Revisited," 206.

[22] Kloppenborg, *Formation of Q*, 102ff.

[23] Kloppenborg, "Formation of Q Revisited," 209. It should be seen that this is a complete reversal of the view of earlier Q scholars such as D. Lührmann, *Die redaktion der Logienquelle*, 97ff who argues that the main Wisdom pericopes belong to the *later* layers of Q. Cf. also the older views of J. M. Robinson, "Jesus as Sophos and Sophia: Wisdom Tradition and the Gospels," *Aspects of Wisdom in Judaism and Early Christianity*, 1–16.

[24] C. M. Tuckett, "The Present Son of Man," 58–81, here 69. This had already been pointed out by O. H. Steck, *Israel und das gewaltsame Geschick der Propheten*, 107, 224–26.

> Form–critical criteria for the distinction of layers are also, in my opinion, unpersuasive. That the Sayings Source was first a book with a "wisdom" character, at a second stage incorporated prophetic sayings, and then finally developed into a "bios" of Jesus by integrating narrative traditions, cannot, I think be verified. Thus, in the double saying in Matt. 12.41–42Q, Jesus is compared with both Jonah and Solomon. He is both a prophet and a wisdom teacher. It is precisely this coupling of both aspects that is typical of Q (and probably of the historical Jesus).[25]

I quite agree with this judgment.

The recent detailed study by R. A. Piper has shown that the final redactor(s) of Q had a definite *sapiential* agenda, in addition to whatever other agendas he may have had.[26] In short, there is evidence for both sapiential and prophetic agendas operating at the redactional level of Q, and I would add in the earliest strata of Q as well. A. D. Jacobson had already argued at length that there was a Deuteronomistic–Wisdom agenda in the editing of Q.[27] I shall argue in this chapter[28] that *one* of the agendas of the final redactor(s) of Q was to portray Jesus both as prophetic sage and even at times as the embodiment of Wisdom.[29]

Q scholars need to take into account that there is evidence from Mark (e.g. 14:62), L (e.g. 18:8), and M (e.g 13:41) that future Son of Man sayings involving coming judgment circulated widely and early in the Christian community. In view of this other evidence, those who would argue that the prophetic Son of Man sayings in Q are later, redactional, or even inauthentic must prove their case on all three scores. There is no basis for assuming that such sayings in Q were created by the collectors of the Q material. This is all the more the case since Kloppenborg concedes that "there is no good reason to think that son of man language was formative for Q... or that it represents the heart of Q's christology."[30] The dispersal of such sayings in a variety of Gospel sources, even leaving Q out of consideration, suggests that at least some of the

---

[25] G. Theissen, *The Gospels in Context. Social and Political History in the Synoptic Tradition*, 205.

[26] Cf. R. A. Piper, *Wisdom in the Q–Tradition*, especially 161ff.

[27] Jacobson, *Wisdom Christology in Q*, but also his helpful summary "The Literary Unity of Q,", 365–89. He concludes: "The deuteronomistic–Wisdom perspective represents a shift away from the earlier view focused on the imminent expectation of the Son of Man" (389, cf. especially Luke 6:22–23 and par. and 11:29–32). The fact that equally adept scholars like Kloppenborg and Jacobson who are specialists in the Q material can argue completely opposite cases about the layers of Q and what appears to be earlier and what later simply reveals the high degree of subjectivity in such arguments since no Q document or documents have actually been found to which one may compare such hypotheses.

[28] Jacobson, *Wisdom Christology in Q*.

[29] It is instructive to compare the "mixed" portrait of Jesus that emerges from 1 Corinthians 1–4 where Jesus is seen as Wisdom, crucified Messiah, and reigning Lord among other things. The mixing of prophetic, apocalyptic and sapiential categories would hardly be surprising in Q in light of such evidence from the A.D. 50s from the Pauline corpus.

[30] Kloppenborg, "Formation of Q Revisited" 208.

prophetic material about a coming and judging Son of Man very likely goes back to Jesus in some form.

Furthermore, the attempt to use Q, at the expense of other Gospel sources, to conjure up a non–apocalyptic sapiential and even Cynic Jesus will not work. Nor should Q itself be seen as a Cynic tract, closely parallel to the lives of the Cynic philosophers. This has recently been demonstrated by C. M. Tuckett.[31] The following of Tuckett's arguments are especially telling. First, too often such arguments are based on a fusing or confusing of Cynic material and Stoic material. It is not justified to cite Epictetus, Dio, the Cynic Epistles, Demonax, and Diogenes indiscriminately in order to bolster an argument for a Cynic Q or even a Cynic Jesus. Second, too many times it is simply assumed without proof that Cynicism permeated the Roman Empire and in particular the environment out of which Q arose. *Dio* 32:9 does not say that there were Cynics on *every* street corner, he is speaking only of Alexandria. Extrapolating from what Dio says about Alexandria to Palestine is unwarranted. Furthermore, the Cynics from Gadara (Menippus, Meleager, Oenomaeus) while they "span the first century in time,...none of them actually dates from the first century itself; there is thus still the problem of dating..."[32] Third, Cynicism was primarily an urban phenomenon, but Jesus in Q is portrayed as avoiding the major Hellenistic centers, sticking to relatively small towns like Chorazin, Bethsaida, and Capernaum. Fourth, Q is not simply a collection of random sayings or chreia. It has both narrative and structure (cf. below) and must be distinguished from a work like *Demonax*.[33] Fifth, the Q missionaries are distinguished from the Cynic ones in that the strictures placed on them are more severe. This suggests "that there was a conscious differentiation between the Christian charismatics and the Cynics..."[34] In summary he says:

> There is doubt about whether some of the "Cynic" texts cited should be regarded as Cynic. The eschatology which underlies so much of Q is absent from the Cynic tradition and hence many of the parallels turn out to be at best superficial....The garb of the Q missionaries seems designed deliberately to avoid any possible confusion between the Q Christians and Cynic preachers; and the method underlying their...common appearance of itinerancy is widely different from the Cynic ethos. The stress on Q miracles bears no relation at all to Cynic views on health. Finally, no appeal is ever made in Q to Cynic traditions as providing precedents for the activity or experience of Christians. By contrast, Q does appeal frequently to the Jewish prophetic tradition as providing such precedents.[35]

---

[31] Tuckett, "A Cynic Q?" 349–76.

[32] Tuckett, "A Cynic Q?" 356–57.

[33] Kloppenborg, *Formation of Q*, 323–24 is basically forced to this conclusion.

[34] H. C. Kee, *Christian Origins in Sociological Perspective:*, 58. Tuckett also quotes Kee approvingly at this point.

[35] Tuckett, "A Cynic Q?" 375–76.:

Several of Kloppenborg's conclusion on the Q Jesus must also be heeded:

> The Jesus of Q is not a paradigm of Cynic *parresia*, or still less, *anaideia*, as an expression of the self–sufficiency of the sage. The idiom of Q is controlled not by a philosophic notion of freedom but a historical and soteriological schema of God's constant invitation to Israel to repent, and by the expectation of the imminent manifestation of the kingdom... [36]

It is time to provide evidence for the sapiential agenda of the redactor(s) of Q.

TABLE 2

A. The Story of Jesus the Sage/Wisdom

1. The Forerunner and the Announcement of the Sage's Coming (by John) – Luke 3:2–9/Matt.3:1–10; Luke 3:15–17/Matt. 3:11–12
2. The Anointment of the Sage with the Spirit – Luke 3.:21–22/ Matt.3:13–16[37]
3. The Testing of the Sage – Luke 4:1–13/Matt. 4:1–11
4. The Sermon of the Sage – Luke 6:20–49/Matt. 5–7
5. The Wonder Working of the Sage – Luke 7:1–10/Matt. 8:5–10
6. The Questioning of the Sage (by John) – Luke 7:18–23/Matt. 11:2–6
7. The Response of the Sage – Luke 7:24–28/Matt. 11:7–11[38]
8. The Rejection of the Sage by "this generation" – Luke 7:31–35/ Matt.11:16–19 "YET WISDOM IS VINDICATED BY HER DEEDS"

PART A ENDS WITH THE FIRST REVELATION OF JESUS AS WISDOM

B. Discipleship to Jesus the Sage–its Character and Mission

9. Discipleship's Cost – Luke 9:57–62/Matt. 8:19–22
10. Discipleship's Mission – Luke 10:1–24/Matt. 9:37–38; 10:5–16; 11:20–24; 11:25–27; 13:16–17
    a. The Mission speech – Luke 10:1–12/Matt. 9:37–38; 10:5–16
    b. Woes on Galilean villages – Luke 10:13–15/Matt. 11:20–24
    c. Authority of Missionaries – Luke 10:16–20/Matt. 10:40
    d. Thanksgiving and Blessing – Luke 10:21–24/Matt. 11:25–27; 13:16–17

---

[36] Kloppenborg, *Formation of Q*, 324.

[37] The arguments against there being a baptismal story in Q, at least in the brief form one finds it in Luke 3:21–22 are not convincing. If Q is attempting to present Jesus as a sage like unto but greater than Solomon, then this pericope about his being anointed by the Spirit is important, especially in the light of the parallels in the Wisdom of Solomon. The so–called minor agreements in Matthew and Luke's account over against Mark are at least in two cases not so minor: (1) the use of the verb *anoigo* in both Matt. and Luke; (2) the placement of *katabaino* before the qualifying comparative clause. However, cf. J. S. Kloppenborg, *Q Parallels*, 16.

[38] It is possible, but debatable, whether either Luke 16:16 and par. or Luke 7:29–30 (and par.) should be included in Q at this point. Cf. Kloppenborg, *Q Parallels*, 56–59 and A. Polag, "The Text of Q," in I. Havener, *The Sayings of Jesus*, 118.

11. The Disciple's Prayer and Praying – Luke 11:2–4; 11:5–13/ Matt.6:7–13; 7:7–11

PART B ENDS WITH THE DISCIPLES URGED TO SEEK HELP FROM ABOVE

C. The Wars and Woes of the Sage/Wisdom

12. Struggling with Satan – Luke 11:14–26; Matt. 12:22–30; 43–45[39]
13. Signs of Trouble – Luke 11:29–32 (cf. v 16); Matt. 12:38–42
14. The Light of One's Life – Luke 11:33–36/Matt. 5:15; 6:22–23
15. The Woes of Wisdom – Luke 11:42–52/Matt. 23:4, 6, 7, 13, 22–23, 25–31, 34–36[40]

THE WISDOM OF GOD SAID – SEVENTH WOE ON THOSE WHO WOULD BE SAGES (cf. Luke 11:52; Matt. 23:13 – scribes)

END OF PART C OF Q

D. The Revelations of Wisdom

16. Hidden and Revealed – Luke 12:2–3/Matt. 10:26–27
17. Wisdom's persecuted followers – Luke 12:4–7/Matt. 10:28–31
18. Acknowledging the Sage and the Spirit – Luke 12:8–12/Matt. 10:19, 32–33[41]
19. Wisdom in Nature – Luke 12:22–31/Matt. 6:25–33
20. The Treasures of Wisdom – Luke 12:32–34/Matt. 6:19–21
21. Preparation for Wisdom's Feast – Luke 12:35–40/Matt. 24:43–44[42]
22. Preparation for Wisdom's Return – Luke 12:42–48/Matt. 24:45–51
23. Wisdom's Second Baptism – Luke 12:49–50
24. Divisions over Wisdom and her Demise – Luke 12:51–53/Matt.10:34–36
25. Signs of Trouble II – Luke 12:54–56/Matt. 16:2–3
26. Time to Settle Accounts – Luke 12:57–59/Matt. 5:25–26
27. The Lament of Wisdom for Jerusalem – Luke 13:34–35/Matt. 23:37–39[43]

WISDOM IS REJECTED AT THE HEART OF THE NATION – JERUSALEM'S HOUSE FORSAKEN BY GOD'S PRESENCE; WISDOM NOT TO BE SEEN IN JERUSALEM AGAIN UNTIL THE BEATITUDE ON WISDOM IS PRONOUNCED

END OF PART D OF Q

E. The Narrative *Meshalim* and Aphorisms of the Sage/Wisdom

28. Seed and Leaven – Luke 13:18–21/Matt. 13:31–33
29. Gate and Door – Luke 13:23–27/Matt. 7:13–14; 22–23

---

[39] It is uncertain whether Luke 11:27–28 belongs in Q at this point.

[40] Some would include Luke 13:34–35 and par. at this point, but probably it belongs at the end of the next major section of Q, but cf. Kloppenborg, *Q Parallels*, 158–59.

[41] It is uncertain whether or not Luke 12:35–38, found only in Luke, belongs here.

[42] Luke 12:35–38 has no exact parallel in Matthew, but probably was in Q.

[43] For this placement of the lament, cf. Polag, "Text," in Havener, *Q. The Sayings*, 120.

30. East and West/Last and First – Luke 13:28–30/Matt. 8:11–12; 20:16[44]
31. Wisdom's banquet – Luke 14:15–24/Matt. 22:1–10
32. The Cost of Discipleship (Cross Talk) – Luke 14:5–27/ Matt.10:37–38
33. Old Salt – Luke 14:34–35/Matt. 5:13
34. Lost Sheep – Luke 15:3–7/Matt. 18:12–14
35. Lost Coin – Luke 15:8–10

PART E ENDS WITH WISDOM'S SEARCH FOR THE LOST

F. Discipleship at the Turn of the Era

36. Choose whom to Serve – God or Mammon – Luke 16:13/Matt.6:24
37. The End of Torah's era? – Luke 16:16–17/Matt. 11:12–13; 5:18
38. The End of a Marriage – Luke 16:18/Matt. 5:32
39. Sins and Forgiveness – Luke 17:1–4/Matt. 18:7, 21–22
40. Mustard Seed Faith – Luke 17:5–6/Matt. 17:20

PART F ENDS WITH THE ASSURANCE TO DISCIPLES THAT EVEN SMALL FAITH CAN WORK GREAT MIRACLES

G. The End of the Age

41. Vs. False Hopes – Luke 17:22–23/Matt. 24:26[45]
42. Like Lightning – Luke17:24/Matt. 24:27
43. Like Vultures – Luke 17:37/Matt. 24:28
44. Like Noah's and Lot's time – Luke 17:26–30/Matt. 24:37–39
45. No Turning Back – Luke 17:31–32/Matt. 24:17–18
46. Find Life by Losing it – Luke 17:33/Matt. 10:29
47. Division of Laborers – Luke 17:34–35/Matt. 24:40–41
48. Parable of the Talents – Luke 19:11–27/Matt. 25:14–30
49. At Table and on Thrones in the Dominion – Luke 22:28–30/Matt. 19:28

PART G ENTAILS AN ESCHATOLOGICAL DISCOURSE, ENDING WITH THE PROMISE OF ESCHATOLOGICAL REUNION AND ROLES WITH JESUS

JESUS THE PROPHETIC SAGE AND HIS WISDOM IN Q

We will first examine the order and arrangement of the Q material, the beginning and end of the Q material, the clustering of aphorisms in the Q material, and some key Wisdom sayings in the first half of Q. The table of contents and arrangement of the Q material is based on the view that Luke best preserves the order of Q.[46] It will be seen from this division of Q into seven parts

[44] It is possible Luke 13:34–35 belongs here.

[45] Luke 17:20b–21 may belong here, but it has no Matthean parallel.

[46] The seminal essays by V. Taylor establishing that it is basically Luke that preserves the original order of Q are still valid and useful; cf. their reprinted editions in V. Taylor, *New Testament Essays*, 90–118.

that Q oscillates between a focus on Jesus the sage or even Jesus as Wisdom on the one hand, and discipleship on the other until the seventh section of Q which functions as an eschatological discourse. This arrangement with the eschatological discourse last is appropriate not least because it comes after the several fold rejection of Jesus as Wisdom in the earlier material and so reveals the moral consequences of either discipleship to or rejection of Jesus. More particularly, Parts B and F focus especially on discipleship, while Parts A, C, D, E seek to present Jesus either as sage or as Wisdom or as both by a variety of means (e.g. presenting his nature wisdom, presenting his *meshalim*). The organizing principles here are clearly sapiential, as is also seen from several further facts.

First, sections A, C, D, E all end with the personification of Wisdom or Jesus speaking as Wisdom. This comports with how the two discipleship sections end, namely with the urging to seek help from above (i.e. from the now exalted Wisdom who can send good things/Spirit), or with an exhortation to keep the faith, in particular while Wisdom is gone.[47] Second, this document asserts the sort of view of act–consequence which was seen in the Wisdom of Solomon, but also in Sirach, namely that vindication of what is right and who is righteous will come finally by divine intervention at the end of the age. This is surely the function of the last section of Q.

Third, as Kloppenborg has rightly pointed out,[48] both Sirach and the Wisdom of Solomon begin, after preliminary remarks, with the trials and temptations of the sage. Sirach, after a preliminary hymn to Wisdom, begins his instruction with "My son if you come forward to serve the Lord prepare yourself for temptation. Accept whatever befalls you and in times of humiliation be patient. For gold is tested in the fire, and those he found acceptable in the furnace of humiliation" (Sir. 2.1, 4–5). The trials of the sage or wise man are also how the Wisdom of Solomon begins (cf. 1.16–2.20). One might also compare Ecclesiastes which after an initial poem about futility and life's meaningless cycle, then has the sage present himself with a number of tests or trials (cf. 2.1ff.). Perhaps even more telling is the fact that the instructional material in Proverbs 1–9 begins after the announcement of the leitmotif (Prov. 1.7) with an extended warning against temptations (Prov. 1.8–19). A. D. Jacobson has rightly pointed out that Jesus' second temptation especially has a striking parallel in Wis. 2.17–20:[49]

---

[47] The attempt to determine whether there is a Wisdom Christology in Q on the basis of a detailed analysis of Matt. 11:25–27 alone is doomed to failure because it narrows the proper subject matter for close scrutiny far to much. This is the major flaw in J. Kloppenborg, "Wisdom Christology in Q,", 129–47.

[48] Kloppenborg, *Formation of Q*, 278–79.

[49] Jacobson, *Wisdom Christology in Q*, 43–44.

> Let us see if his words are true, and let us test what will happen at the end of his life; for if the righteous man is God's son, he will help him, and will deliver him from the hands of his adversaries....Let us condemn him to a shameful death, for, according to what he says, he will be protected.

In the light of all this, the beginning of Q is not anomalous.[50] In fact, the discussion in the Temptation story takes on the character of a sapiential disputation, not unlike what one finds in Job 1–2 between Ha Satan and Yahweh. Jesus as sage passes the test by quoting Deuteronomy thrice. Thus Jesus is depicted at the very outset of Q as one who draws on the riches of God's Wisdom in Torah, as well as creating his own sayings.[51] That is, Jesus is depicted as doing what Ben Sira urged on his disciples, finding Wisdom in Torah as well as elsewhere.[52] Furthermore, the end of Q conveys a similar sort of message as the end of Sirach – the disciples have persevered through trials with Jesus and are promised reward in the life to come (Luke 22:28–30 and par.). H. Fledderman has shown that in the last Q pericope three key Q themes come together: (1) the judgment theme; (2) the coming together of Jesus with his disciples at the eschaton; and (3) eschatological reversal and vindication.[53] Ben Sira puts it this way: "Do your work in good time, and in his own time God will give you your reward" (51:30). The theme of rewarding the disciples is found at the end of both books, and Ben Sira has made clear his belief in the day of reckoning and the reversal and vindication of God's faithful then and there (cf. Sir. 16, 28:1, 35:21ff.).

Particular attention needs to be paid to the pericopes in the first section of Q for they reveal as much about the Wisdom agendas of the final redactor as any portion of the book.[54] Besides the obvious sapiential character of the

---

[50] The material about the Baptist is clearly preparatory, and meant to provide a means of introducing Jesus the sage as a contemporary of the Baptist, and one with a somewhat similar agenda. If Q was put together before all of the Gospels, it may have provided the pattern for the beginning of the Gospel story.Though I am not yet convinced, if D. Catchpole, "The Beginning of Q: a Proposal,", 205–21, is right that Mark draws on Q in the early pericopes of his Gospel, this would provide an additional piece of evidence that Q begins with the Baptist material including the Baptism story.

[51] Jacobson, *Wisdom Christology in Q*, 41 says he is depicted as a super scribe. The quotation of the LXX form of Deuteronomy in Jesus' responses is one more clue that this document, whatever its sources, was first assembled in Greek.

[52] L. G. Perdue, "The Wisdom Sayings of Jesus," 3–35, here 25–26. The setting and the actual disputation is not unlike other such disputations (besides Job, one may wish to compare the 'Babylonian Theodicy'). The various attempts to point the listener to resources for Wisdom beyond just the Q collection itself should not be ignored, and must count against the view that Q was a sort of Bible for some Christian community to the exclusion of other Jewish and Jewish Christian traditions. It may be that this narrative has been compiled by an early Jewish Christian sage/scribe concerned about scribal debates. Cf. E. Haenchen, *Der Weg Jesu*, 64–72.

[53] H. Fleddermann, "The End of Q," 10.

[54] Jacobson, *Wisdom Christology in Q*, 15 rightly warns: "The assumption that the introductory pericopes in Q were added later becaused they were not... sayings of Jesus is not a sound assumption." In part, it arises out of trying to draw too close an analogy with the *Gospel of Thomas*, but the final redactors of Q and of Thomas had different agendas (Thomas is more nearly a pure logia collection).

temptation narrative, the story about the anointing of Jesus by the Spirit coupled with a revelation of Jesus' identity in Luke 3.21–22 and par. should be compared to the story of the anointing of Solomon with "the Spirit of Wisdom" in Wisdom 7–9. In the course of those chapters one is told not only that Solomon called on God and received the Spirit of Wisdom (7:7) praying "send her forth from the holy heavens" (9:10), but also he calls himself the Son of your serving girl (9:5) and stresses, "Who has learned your counsel unless you have given Wisdom and sent your Spirit from on high?"(9:17). Only by this means are the paths of humans set straight "and people taught… what pleases you and… saved by wisdom." If one compares this material to Luke 3:21–22, which is the earlier form of this Q material, one will see that Jesus is portrayed as a Solomon or, as we learn later in Q, one greater than Solomon, since he is the very embodiment of Wisdom. Having been anointed with the Spirit of God, he is now prepared to embark on the career of a sage dispensing Wisdom, but also one making it possible for people to be saved by Wisdom. In this way, what follows in Q, beginning immediately with the first teaching pericope (Luke 6:20ff. and par.) is seen to be the teachings of a sage – one like Solomon endowed with all that the Spirit of Wisdom can convey.[55]

The so–called Sermon on the Mount, which in both Matthew and Luke is presented as a paradigmatic homily revealing the essence of the teaching of the sage, not only contains sapiential material but as Bultmann pointed out almost nothing else.[56] The ending of the sermon is particularly of interest to us as it shows the redactional tendencies of the final editor. The parable of the two houses (Luke 6:47–49 and par.) "conforms to the practice typical of the Wisdom tradition for ending collections of material."[57] Especially important is the parallel at the end of Eccles. 12:1–8, but one may also think of the end of the third cycle of speeches in Job 27 or the material in Prov. 9:1–6. Notice also that Luke 13:34–35 (and par.), the end of Part D of Q, reflects this selfsame motif. In this

[55] Additional factors to those mentioned above for seeing the baptismal story primarily in the form found in Luke 3:21–22 as in Q originally are: (1) the mention of Jesus' name; (2) probably the unusual *pneuma theou* in the Matthean form of the tradition; (3) the use of the aorist passive participle of *baptizo*; (4) the fact that Jesus is introduced as Son of God in the baptismal story or at least earlier in Q seems to be presupposed in the temptation narrative. On all this, cf. Jacobson, *Wisdom Christology in Q*, 35–36. It is difficult to know what to call this sapiential approach to the Jesus story. On the one hand, the mythological story of personified Wisdom who came to Israel and was rejected pre–existed the Jesus story, but was never identified specifically with a particular historical figure. Not even Solomon is said to be Wisdom incarnate in a book like the Wisdom of Solomon. Perhaps one could speak of the historicizing of the Wisdom myth by its use to interpret the significance of the historical Jesus. But cf. B. Mack, "Wisdom, Myth and Mythology," 46–60. In Old Testament interpretation this sort of use of myth to describe real people, events or creatures has in fact been called *demythologizing*. The point is, what is myth in Proverbs 8 or Sirach 24 is seen as coming on the historical stage in the person of Jesus.

[56] Bultmann, *History of the Synoptic Tradition*, 77ff.

[57] Jacobson, *Wisdom Christology in Q*, 49.

case it is God's house left abandoned, a very appropriate ending for a section of Q.[58]

It seems to have been common to end a Wisdom discourse with a warning about the consequences of disobeying the teaching. If one looks at the last section of Q carefully, this seems to be the function of the eschatological discourse. That is, the closing section of Q functions in such a way that the whole document concludes in a traditional sapiential way, though the author has appropriated eschatological material to accomplish that aim (cf. Sirach and Wisdom of Solomon)[59] One may also note that the very end of Q conforms to the general sapiential pattern of concluding a section not only with the curse sanctions for those who disobey, but also with the blessings or rewards for those who obey.[60]

Kloppenborg's thesis that the Sermon on the Mount was part of a collection of six sapiential speeches which formed the foundation of Q and to which were added prophetic speeches and material, must be considered for a moment. Kloppenborg makes this distinction not just on form critical grounds but also because, "in the case of the judgment speeches... the ostensible audience was 'this generation' i.e. impenitent Israel."[61] This is to be contrasted with the sapiential speeches which are addressed to the community. Frankly, however, this distinction is overdrawn. As Kloppenborg himself admits, impenitent Israel is also addressed in the sapiential speeches (he cites Q 10:12–15, 12:8–10; 13:26–30, 34–35; and 14:16–24)[62]. That is, the difference between the sapiential speeches and the prophetic ones is a matter of degree. There is the further problem that one must be able to distinguish between the audience *in* various parts of Q and the audience of Q. *All* of Q is addressed to the community of Jesus' followers, and some of it no doubt was intended for that community's use in its dialogue with non–Christian Jews, while other parts *of* Q were primarily meant to deal with matters internal to the community for whom Q was compiled. That we find Israel addressed *in* some parts of Q is no basis for drawing conclusions about stages in the literary composition of Q.

Kloppenborg also points out rightly that there are Wisdom elements in some of the prophetic speeches (cf. Q 7:35; 11:17b–18; 11:33–34; 12:54–55; 17:37).[63] One could also point out prophetic elements in sapiential speeches. Kloppenborg wishes to argue that in the latter case these are later insertions

---

[58] The motif of the house is one of the things which leads to the conclusion that this pericope was very likely found at the end, and not in the middle of a major section of Q.

[59] Jacobson, *Wisdom Christology in Q*, 110–11, n. 84.

[60] Ibid.; cf. the ending of each collection in M. Aboth and Sir. 50.28–29 with Q's end, but also compare the end of several small collections – Luke 6:20–23 (and par.), Luke 6:36–38 (and par.), Luke12:22–34, and Luke 17:22–33.

[61] Kloppenborg, *Formation of Q*, 238.

[62] Ibid.

[63] Kloppenborg., 239.

into sapiential speeches originally devoid of such material. If one considers two of his prime examples, Q 6:23c and Q 10:13–15, problems immediately arise. Q 6:23c will not stand alone; it belongs at least with 6.22. But 6.22 and at least 6.23b are part of an eschatological beatitude, a saying which is a mixture of eschatological and sapiential motifs. In such a context, it would hardly be surprising if 6.23c was joined to the saying when Q was first formed, not later. Ancient speeches and documents were not always composed on the basis of nice literary or genre distinctions. The mixture of material in other early Jewish Wisdom collections like Sirach and the Wisdom of Solomon does not encourage one to expect those sort of distinctions in Q. In practice, form is usually made flexible because content is normally of more paramount importance.

In regard to Q 10:13–15, a note of judgment on Sodom is already present in this speech at 10:12. If 10:12 could be part of the original sapiential speech, then both on form and content grounds so could 10:13–15. The argument that 10:12 is a redactional clasp to bind 10:13–15 to what precedes is weak. As Kloppenborg admits, *lego humin* is a sapiential not (or at least not usually) a prophetic locution (cf. Prov. 24.23; *1 En.* 91.3; 94.1, 3, 10).[64] More to the point, it is a locution that often provides a conclusion based on something said immediately before it (cf.Q 11.9, 12.5). Q was from the first primarily a Wisdom collection, but it was a Wisdom collection like Sirach and Wisdom of Solomon and thus it included prophetic and eschatological elements probably from the very beginning of its compilation. I would suggest this is because this was also true of the teaching of Jesus. In the arguably authentic material there is an irreducible amount of both sapiential, prophetic, and eschatological material. Q has faithfully reflected this fact. A bit more will be said shortly about the sapiential tendencies of the final editor of Q.

Further along in the first section of Q one find a story about Jesus performing a miracle. One must bear in mind that in the intertestamental and New Testament periods Solomon was seen as a wonder worker, one whose name could aid exorcisms (cf. Josephus *Ant.* 8.45 and evidence from Qumran cave 11).[65] Thus even the healing story in Luke 7.1 – 10 (and par.) should not be seen as out of character in a Wisdom collection, especially one which has set out to portray Jesus as a Solomon or even greater than Solomon.

As is suggested by the outline of Q above, the attempt to portray Jesus as Wisdom is evident not just in the first section of Q, but especially at the end of those sections which focus on Jesus and his words and deeds. At the end of the first section we hear in the earliest Q form of the tradition that Wisdom is vindicated by her deeds.[66] The saying in itself arises out of an environment of

---

[64] Kloppenborg., 239.

[65] Witherington, *Christology of Jesus*, 156, 189.

[66] Various scholars fail to see the awkwardness of the "Wisdom is vindicated by all her children" form of this saying that Luke offers. The reference in Luke 7:32 to "children" is to the audience of Jesus and John who did not respond to these two messengers. This makes the idea of a reference to Jesus and John in the "children" phrase in v 35 very suspect. What makes

controversy as to who Jesus truly was, and what could count as evidence of his character and identity. Probably it arises out of a setting in which Jesus as sage and as Wisdom have been rejected by some, and thus this identification requires vindication. It will be seen that this is precisely the theme that comes to the fore at the end of all the sections of Q where the focus is on Jesus rather than discipleship, with the possible exception of the end of Part F. There is then a connection between the theme of rejection and the revelation of the full identity of Jesus as Wisdom in the flesh. The connection seems to be that Israel is made to see the magnitude of this rejection–they are not just rejecting another sage, but Wisdom in the flesh.[67]

The pre–eminence of Jesus in the Q tradition is established in two primary ways: (1) as Robinson recognized, by the identification of Jesus with the Son of Man and in particular the future Son of Man who will yet come;[68] and (2) by the identification of Jesus with Wisdom who has already come and been rejected. One possible reason why, in the present Son of Man sayings, the phrase "Son of Man" seems virtually a synonym for I, and has little content borrowed from Daniel 7 is because essentially in those sayings Jesus is being portrayed as Wisdom and the *content* of those sayings comes from the Wisdom tradition.[69] This is particularly evident in a saying like Matt. 8:20/Luke 9:58.[70] This blending of Wisdom ideas and future eschatological or apocalyptic ideas can also be seen especially well in the way the lament over Jerusalem and the picture of dejection and rejection is followed immediately by Luke 13:35/Matt. 23:38–39. As Robinson puts it here, "the withdrawal of Sophia is put into the apocalyptic context of the future judgment by Jesus the son of man at his parousia."[71]

---

it all the more unlikely is that Luke seems to also have added to the phrase the word *all*. Were Jesus and John *all* of Wisdom's children? Jacobson and Robinson have seen the force of this point unlike Hartin, *James and the Q Sayings of Jesus*, 123. In Luke, all the children are surely those who do respond positively to Wisdom, but this fits quite awkwardly with 7:32, which suggests only rejection of Jesus and John and suggests a Lukan modification of the source.

[67] The care in the editing of this document is remarkable. The ending of Part A of Q is picked up in passing in the first pericope of Part B, even though it is a discipleship section. That is, the theme of the rejection of Wisdom is reiterated in Luke 9:58/Matt. 8:20 though now it has been placed in a framework where the subject matter is discipleship. Cf. Jacobson, *Wisdom Christology in Q*, 132–33. Since this document was put together after the time of Jesus, the theme has now become that the rejection of Wisdom betokens the rejection of those who would be followers as well. The theme of Jesus speaking as Wisdom, in response to the rejection of many, can also be seen at the beginning of Part D of Q, which in some ways is the most explicit section in revealing Jesus as Wisdom.

[68] Robinson, "Jesus as Sophos and Sophia," 6.

[69] For the argument that "Son of Man" at least in the present sayings is used in service of the Wisdom Christology of Q, cf. F. Christ, *Jesus Sophia. Die Sophia Christologie bei den Synoptiken*, 69–70; M. J. Suggs, *Wisdom, Christology, and Law in Matthew's Gospel*, 48–55.

[70] At this juncture, I am offering a further development of what I tentatively suggested about some of these present Son of Man sayings in *Christology of Jesus*, 248–49.

[71] Robinson, "Jesus as Sophos and Sophia," 13.

At the end of Parts A, C, and D of Q, especially in a saying like Luke 7:31–35/Matt. 11:16–19 the listener is meant to hear the allusion to a text like Prov. 1:24–28 where Wisdom says:

> Because I have called and you refused to listen, have stretched out my hand and no one has heeded, and you have ignored all my counsel and would have none of my reproof, I also will laugh at your calamity...Then they will call upon me, but I will not answer, they will seek me diligently but will not find me.[72]

The end of Part C of Q focuses on the matter of the *heilesgeschichte* of how Wisdom has sent her various messengers to the people, including prophets. This saying plus the lament in Luke 13.34–35 (and par.) are very important because they show that it is Wisdom who sends prophets. The final redactor of Q is emphasizing the confluence of the two traditions – prophetic and sapiential – not their distinction. Probably the Lukan form of the tradition (Luke 11:49, cf. Matt. 23:34) is earlier here than the Matthean one, and there seems to be an echo of Wisdom 7:27: "Though she is but one, she can do all things;... in every generation she passes into holy souls and makes them friends of God and prophets." The confluence of the two traditions has a precedent in Wisdom literature earlier than Q.[73] Matthew makes explicit what at most is implicit in Q, namely that it was the Christ who sent these messengers. In view, however, of the end of other sections of Q, it appears that the identification of Jesus with Wisdom, is at least implicit in Luke 11:49. It must be remembered that Luke 11:49 is found in the midst of a group of woe sayings by Jesus, and there is an especially close connection between Luke 11:47–48 and Luke 11:49, the former verses also discussing the former prophets. In these verses the present audience of Jesus is seen as in continuity with the previous generations of Israel who rejected the prophets, just as Jesus as seen as connected or identified with pre–existent Wisdom who sent the prophets in the first place.[74] Thus, the First Evangelist has not gone far beyond Q in simply restating things so that it is

---

[72] I owe this observation to Perdue, "Wisdom Sayings of Jesus," 27–28.

[73] Hartin, *James and the Q Sayings of Jesus*, 118.

[74] Jacobson, *Wisdom Christology in Q*, 190ff. has suggested a different interpretation of the Lukan form of this saying. He suggests that Wisdom is not speaking from the dawn of time, but is speaking in the present to this generation and is speaking about present and future prophets and their treatment. In favor of this view he argues that the verb speaks of how the blood of the prophets "has been shed". If pre–existent Wisdom is being quoted here then this reference to blood already shed makes no sense. The reference to "this generation" also makes no sense if these are the words of pre–existent Wisdom. But Jacobson's interpretation fails to come to grips with the fact that we are told that this is something Wisdom *said*. The dilemma is solved if Jesus is being identified with pre–existent Wisdom here. It would then both be possible for Wisdom to send the prophets in the past, and also in the person of Jesus to address this generation now, looking back on blood already shed.

made clear that Christ is the one sending the prophets.[75] Robinson is right to point out that this pericope is akin to what one finds in Wisdom 10–11 where one hears of Wisdom guiding and guarding God's special ones at the end of which it is said: "She entered the soul of a servant of the Lord, and withstood dread kings with wonders and signs (10:16)... [Wisdom] prospered their works by the hand of a holy prophet" (11:1).[76] Not only is the idea of Wisdom speaking through a series of messengers found in both texts, but also the idea of Wisdom dwelling within a particular servant of the Lord.

Since the lament of Wisdom that ends part D of Q has already been mentioned above and discussed elsewhere,[77] consider now the end of Part E. If the yoke saying is not the end of this section, then this section seems to have ended with the parable of the search for the Lost Coin (Luke 15.8–10 and par.). This parable has some striking affinities with earlier Jewish Wisdom material about personified Wisdom. Besides a woman being the subject of the search, the search for something precious (in this case a coin) has resonances with various Wisdom injunctions: "Happy is the one who finds Wisdom... its profit is better than gold. She is more precious than jewels, and nothing you can desire can compare with her... She is a tree of life to those who lay hold of her" (Prov.3:13–18). In Proverbs 8 Wisdom seeks out human beings both the simple and the foolish. Thus, when this parable is told, the listener is very likely meant to hear the allusions to the material in Proverbs. In a section of Q which involves among other things a collection of parables, what better way to round out the collection than with a parable that portrays the work of Wisdom seeking and saving the lost (cf. Wis. 9:18)? It seems likely that the listener was meant to hear this parable as a description of Jesus' ministry and thus, at least by implication, Jesus is portrayed as Wisdom seeking the lost.

But it is not just at the end of certain sections of Q that one can see the redactor's wisdom agenda. It may also be seen especially in the revelatory saying at the beginning of Part D. This important saying, which I have argued elsewhere goes back to Jesus in some form, at least in the case of Matt. 11:27 (and par.),[78] has clear echoes of Wis. Sol. 2:13–18. There one hears of a person who "professes to have the knowledge of God, and calls himself a child of the Lord... and boasts that God is his father. Let us see if his words are true... for if the righteous man is God's son, he will help him."[79]

One may also note how a sapiential theme appears in the midst of a prophetic setting as in the case of Luke 11:31/Matt. 12:42. Notice how it seems to imply that the prophets and Solomon or one greater than Solomon are not unnatural bedfellows. The final editor of Q sees Jesus as a prophetic sage, one

---

[75] On the way Matthew expands and expounds upon the Wisdom Christology of his sources, cf. Chapter 9.

[76] Robinson, "Jesus and Sophos and Sophia," 3.

[77] Witherington, *Women in the Ministry of Jesus*, 46–47, and *Christology of Jesus*, 222–23.

[78] Witherington, *Christology of Jesus*, 221–27.

[79] Hartin, *James and the Q Sayings of Jesus*, 128–29.

in whom the sapiential and prophetic/eschatological traditions come to full expression.[80] But this saying also implies that the phenomena that is happening through Jesus warrants seeing him in even higher categories than merely another sage like Solomon.

It is also interesting how certain Wisdom themes crop up in more than one section of Q, for instance, the banquet theme, or the baptism theme, or the signs theme. At least the first of these themes very likely owes something to Wisdom's banquet in Prov. 9.1–6, especially in the case of Luke 14.15–24 (and par.). It must also be kept in mind that the throne saying that closes Q is also a banquet saying as well, and there it is made very clear that the disciples will be sitting at Jesus' table when the Dominion comes on earth. The more one studies the Q material the more the echoes of earlier Jewish Wisdom material become clearer, which strongly suggests that the collection was compiled by Jewish Christians for Jewish Christians, very likely before the time when there was a significant number of Gentile converts on whom such allusions would likely be lost.

The sapiential shaping of Q can be seen not only on the macro–structure level but also within individual collections of aphoristic material and in the handling of specific sayings. For example, R. A. Piper has demonstrated that Luke 11:9–13/Matt. 7:7–11; Luke 12:22–31/Matt. 6:25–33; Luke 6:37–42/Matt. 7:1–5; Luke 6:43–45/Matt. 7:16–20, 12:33–35; Luke 12:2–9/Matt. 10:26–33 all reveal a similar structure.[81] Each collection begins with a rather general aphoristic saying (either a maxim or Wisdom admonition). This is normally followed by a general statement which supports the original maxim. The third part of the collection is marked by the presentation of two sayings similar in theme but differing in imagery; usually at this point we have two rhetorical questions drawing on some specific or concrete human situation (cf. Luke 6:39; 6.44b; 11:11–12). "The use of rhetorical questions here is significant, for it emphasizes the attempt to persuade by argument."[82] Lastly, the final saying or unit of the collection is crucial as it provides the key for interpreting the meaning of the whole collection (cf. e.g. Matt. 7.11). The collection as a whole moves from the more general saying to the more concrete and seeks to move the listener by persuasion. Piper's conclusion is worth quoting at some length:

> This pattern suggests that these small collections of aphoristic sayings did not grow at random from wide–ranging oral or written traditions into the form in which they now appear. *These are not haphazard collections of aphoristic sayings; they display a design and argument unique in the synoptic tradition.* This rather suggests

---

[80] Hartin, *James and the Q Sayings of Jesus*, 129–30; cf. Kloppenborg, "Wisdom Christology in Q," 129–47.

[81] Piper, *Wisdom in the Q Tradition*, 14ff.

[82] Piper., 63.

> that the material has been formulated into units so as to conform consciously to a general pattern of argument. This in turn argues strongly in favor of a unique "compositional activity" responsible for the formulation of these collections.[83]

If one asks the question whether there are any parallels to this form of argumentation then the answer is yes, in Jewish Wisdom collections. One may compare Prov. 6:25–29; or even more strikingly close is Sirach 13:15–20. It seems clear that this is a sapiential form of editing.

At this juncture it will be helpful to point out the way prophetic and legal traditions are sapientialized in Q. There is first of all the important saying in Luke 11:49–51 (and par.) which in its earliest form says the prophets have been sent to Israel by Wisdom. Secondly, one may consider the woe oracle against Chorazin and Bethsaida (Luke 10.13–15 and par.). This saying in content and form is much like the woe oracles against Zion and other places in Amos 6.1 or like various of the woe oracles in Isa. 28:1 — 33:24 (cf. 28:1, 30:1, 31:1, 33:1). But it will be noted that this woe oracle is now placed in the mission discourse in which Jesus sends out his disciples to share in the ministry and mission of the prophetic sage. More importantly this woe oracle is followed by the important Wisdom saying in Luke 10:21–22 and par. which makes clear that this mission and the words of both Jesus and his followers derive from the revelation of God to the "babes" and the special relationship and knowledge which the Son and Father share.

The use of the historical review for a variety of purposes (including a warning against possible judgment) is found in Luke 11:29–32 (and par.) and in Luke 17:26–30 and par. One also finds a historical review used for sapiential purposes in Sirach 44–50. Ben Sira's review ends with a benediction calling for peace in our time "as in the days of old" and deliverance in our days (50.23–24). The same sort of comparison – as it was then, so also it will be now – is found in the Q examples cited above. Furthermore, part of the function of the reviews in Q is to give the disciples hope of eschatological deliverance, which is precisely what Ben Sira prayed for in his benediction.

Yet another example of the way prophetic traditions are sapientialized in Q is seen in Matt. 11:19 (cf. Luke 15:2). Matthew in this case very likely preserves an earlier form of this saying than Luke does.[84] Thus note that while Jesus is said to fulfill the prophecy of Isa. 35:4–6 (in Matt. 11:4–5 and par.), the end of this part of Q makes clear that it is Jesus as Wisdom who has performed these deeds. Sometimes then it is not so much a case of modifying the actual saying in question as placing it in a larger sapiential context which gives it a different orientation.

The same sort of sapientializing of heterogeneous traditions can be seen in the handling of legal material in Q. Luke 16:18, for example, is placed in a

[83] Piper, *Wisdom in the Q Tradition*, 64, the emphasis is his.
[84] Witherington, *Christology of Jesus*, 52, 222–24.

context where it has just been said that the Law and prophets were *in effect until* John (Luke 16:16). In short, it becomes evident that the teaching of Jesus is not just an affirmation of the old Law which was in effect until John but something new and more demanding. By the context in which a saying is placed the listener is alerted that something new is happening.

This all too cursory review attempts to show that in many respects Q may be called a Wisdom collection but, even better, one might call it a Wisdom book with a design. It is not a mere random collection of sayings, and this is not just because of the sapiential content found especially in the first two thirds of Q. Kloppenborg has sought to argue that Q began as a collection of six Wisdom speeches or sermons to which has been added eschatological and apocalyptic material especially at the end of the collection and narrative elements especially at the beginning of Q.[85] I would want to suggest that the stages of composition are much less certain or discernible than Kloppenborg argues, particularly in view of the fact that when one considers a document like Sirach or the Wisdom of Solomon, one finds not only eschatology, but in fact future eschatology dealing with a coming or final day of judgment in ways that are quite similar to what one finds in Q (cf. Sirach 12, 16; Wisdom 5, especially cf. 5.15–16 to the end of Q). C. E. Carlston has rightly argued that the combination of sententious Wisdom with the wisdom persona and eschatological elements in Q is not without analogy:

> Yet we do have a few documents from the beginning of our era in which eschatology (or apocalyptic) and wisdom are closely associated: the Wisdom of Solomon, the Testament of the 12 Patriarches, 4 Ezra, Matthew, the Didache, and Hermas – to give but a few examples. So Q is not really without parallel in this regard.... Wisdom and eschatology must both be included in any summary of the teaching of Jesus as it is handed down to and by the Q community.... a critical winnowing of the eschatology still leaves us with material suggesting Jesus saw the eschatological crisis in terms of both present and future and understood that crisis as coming to a head, not simply in his own time, but in his own ministry.[86]

Besides the formal precedents for the combination of future eschatology and Wisdom, I would suggest there is also a material one. In an upside down world, where God's people were oppressed and under foreign rule, the act–consequence idea is sorely put to the test.[87] The way the later sages dealt with this dilemma was by introducing into their teachings future eschatological material. This was necessary not only because their own Wisdom upheld the idea of a moral universe where justice was ultimately done, but also because the character of the all wise God was at stake. Future eschatology is required in an upside down world if the concepts of act–consequence, a moral structure to

---

[85] Kloppenborg, *Formation of Q*, 37ff., 263ff., 317ff.
[86] Carlston, "Wisdom and Eschatology," 114, 116.
[87] See pp. 57ff., especially on Ecclesiastes, but also on the Wisdom of Solomon, pp.105ff.

human reality, and a just God are to be maintained. Especially on the basis of the precedents in the Wisdom of Solomon and Sirach, I maintain that Wisdom and future eschatological elements were very likely present in Q from the beginning, and that the overall collection has been edited to make clear Jesus was a sage, but not just any sort of sage.[88] He is a sage of counter order (like Qoheleth), but also a prophetic sage, like Ben Sira or Pseudo–Solomon in some ways (e.g. in his use of eschatology). In his use of revelatory Wisdom and the Son of Man concept he is like the sage who composed the parables of *Enoch*.[89] What the final redactor is most concerned to show, however, is that Jesus is one like Solomon, or even greater than Solomon, because in him Wisdom has taken on flesh.

CONCLUSIONS AND IMPLICATIONS

In Q one finds a variety of sayings and narratives which have been tailored or contexted in order to serve sapiential agendas, and thus in the end the only truly appropriate term for this collection is a Wisdom collection. It reveals Jesus' wisdom, but also sets out, from the very first section with its narrative components, to set those sayings and parables in the context of seeing Jesus not merely as just another sage, but as the prophetic sage, the one like, yet greater than, Solomon. He is anointed with the plenitude of the Spirit, resists every temptation (unlike Solomon) and performs wonders that surpass what even Jewish folklore had predicated of Solomon. Even more strikingly, at the climax or end of several of the sections of Q, the reader is left with the suggestion that Jesus is the very embodiment of Wisdom, one who is vindicated as Wisdom by his deeds, one who seeks the lost, one who laments over Jerusalem, as a mother over her children.[90] The sapiential agenda is evident throughout in many

[88] That is, while I would not agree totally with either Kloppenborg or Jacobson, the latter is more nearly right in suggesting sapiential editing on a corpus that included among other things future Son of Man sayings (but even more Wisdom logia) even in its earliest stages. If the development of the rest of early Christianity is any analogy one should expect more future eschatology at the earlier levels of the Q tradition. For example, the earlier Gospels (Mark, Matthew) certainly manifest more of this than do the later Gospels (Luke, and especially John). In the Pauline corpus as well, the earlier Paulines have more future eschatological content than the later ones, indeed future eschatology has all but disappeared in the Pastoral Epistles, and it is less evident in an Ephesians for example than in a 1 Thessalonians or a 1 Corinthians. Furthermore, one has evidence from 1 Corinthians 16:22 that the Aramaic-speaking Jewish Christians expressed a fervent hope for a return of their Lord from heaven. Is it really plausible to argue that those who first made the Q collection did not partake of this eschatological fervor as well? One would have to argue for a very isolated Q community indeed to make this plausible.

[89] Cf. on p. 201 above the quote by A. N. Wilder.

[90] I quite agree with Kloppenborg that one should not ignore the international character of even Israel's Wisdom collections, and so the argument that there are some chreia in Q and that in some minor respects Q resembles a Greek gnomologia is not without some plausibility. One should not be surprised at this in view of the fact that it appears that Q was in Greek from its inception and Greek models were ready to hand. Nevertheless, the dominating influence on Q, as this I have attempted to show in this half of the chapter is the Jewish Wisdom tradition. On the Greek influence, cf. Kloppenborg, *Formation of Q*, 289ff.

different ways, as this discussion has sought to show briefly. On the basis of these conclusions about the character of Q, a few hypotheses about its origins and authorship are in order.

In regard to the authorship, provenance, and date of Q several considerations arise as a result of the above discussion. If Q was a document intentionally formed and shaped for some specific purposes, and in light of the discussion in this chapter this seems likely, then one need to look for someone as author who was not merely literate but had considerable literary skills and was steeped in Jewish Wisdom material, and who sought to highlight that Jesus was likewise steeped in such material. One may wonder whether there might have been not only Jewish Christian scribes who transmitted the Jesus tradition but also, at least in this case, one Jewish Christian scribe who was enough of a sage himself to produce this remarkable document called Q.

There were after all scribes like Ben Sira who were also sages in their own right. But it may be objected that Ben Sira, like many earlier scribes, was a retainer of the court or at least the temple, and such scribes were supporters of traditional Wisdom as a prop to the *status quo*, which was true neither of Jesus, nor, so far as one can tell, of his earliest followers. But this is to overlook the fact that scribes,

> do not seem to have been a coherent social group with a set membership, but rather a class of literate individuals drawn from many parts of society who filled many social roles and were attached to all parts of society from the village to the palace and Temple.... Scribes were varied in background and allegiance and were individuals filling a social role in different contexts rather than a unified political and religious force.[91]

In short, the priests had scribes among them, as did the Pharisees, and there is no reason why Jesus or at least the post–Easter Jesus movement as it gained momentum, might not have had one or more Galilean scribes among his followers. They would have been retainers of local officials who copied documents or helped administer justice.

The lack of a Torah–centric orientation to Q does not discredit this hypothesis, for there were many different sorts of scribes and not all of them were Torah scholars, though in the late post–exilic period this seems often to have been the case especially in Judea and Jerusalem. No, the person who put together Q appears to have been a scribe, and one may say a sage in his own right, one steeped in Jewish Wisdom material but also most profoundly impacted by the Jesus who offered aphorisms, riddles, and parables of a counter order. This sage believed not only in Jesus' teachings but in Jesus

---

[91] A. J. Saldarini, *Pharisees, Scribes, and Sadducees*, 275–76.

himself, hence the central focus on Jesus in Q. He believed Jesus to be right about that counter order and sought to show it throughout Q. In order to make clear how Jesus stood apart from previous sages, he drew on both the idea of Jesus as Son of Man and to some extent the idea of Jesus as the embodiment of Wisdom.

It appears reasonably clear that Q and its author were rather close to the fount. Not only in the variety of Wisdom forms found in Q but also in its content it seems very much like Jesus' Wisdom teaching as examined in the previous chapter, provided one supplements this with some of the likely authentic Jesus material I have discussed in the *Christology of Jesus*. But even when this author or editor uses eschatological material, he seems to use it for sapiential purposes. At both the level of the *Sitz im Leben Jesu* and the stage at which Q was put together, Jesus is presented as both a prophetic sage and also something more. At least by implication Jesus is also presented as the embodiment of Wisdom. If Matt. 11:28–30 was part of Q originally, what is implicit in a text like Luke 19:41–44 and par. becomes explicit in Q as well. Perhaps W. A. Beardslee got the balance right when he said,

> Q, already at a very early date, interpreted Christ by means of the analogy with transcendent Wisdom, or possibly even identified Christ as the Wisdom of God. Something greater than the wisdom of Solomon is here with Jesus (Luke 11.31).... Almost no mythology of *sophia* is expressed in Q. Christ is Wisdom because he brings what the world cannot bring. The identification of Christ and Wisdom is not elaborated to give a picture of the transcendent Christ, but it is applied unspeculatively to give precisely to the concrete, present commands of Christ the numinous attribute of transcendence.[92]

In the light of C. C. Hill's recent study, it no longer seems possible to posit a radical dichotomy between the Hebrews and the Hellenists in Jerusalem and in the early Judean Christian community.[93] This being the case, certain old clues no longer seem helpful in determing the provenance of Q. Since it appears that the first composition of Q was in Greek (and not bad Greek either) rather than in Aramaic, all other things being equal it may be that the first compilation was made as the first generation of disciples was dying off, possibly in Galilee where there was very likely more contact with Greek speaking people on a regular basis, though this is not certain. There are some hints in Q of a wider and perhaps Gentile presence that is being held up as an example to a probably predominantly Jewish audience of Q (cf. Luke 7:1–10 and par.; 10:13–15 and par.; 11:32–33 and par.; 13:28–29 and par.).[94] It seems clear that the impetus for

---

[92] W. A. Beardslee, "The Wisdom Tradition and the Synoptic Gospels," 236–37.

[93] C. C. Hill, *Hebrew and Hellenists. Reappraising Division in the Early Church.*

[94] Jacobson, "Literary Unity of Q," 389.

such a collection would have been greatest before the composition of the Gospels, and certainly after Matthew and Luke were composed there would be less need. This suggests that this collection was very likely made sometime in the 50s or 60s A.D. but it could have been earlier. If there was actually more than one redaction of Q, which in my opinion is not yet clear at all, this might favor an earlier date than the 50s for the first compilation. What is clear is that Q was a fruit that had not fallen far from the tree of life from which it had come. Furthermore, "it is no longer possible to think of Q simply as a *collection*: one must reckon with a redactor,"[95] and in particular a redactor with definite sapiential agendas. The case being argued in the last chapter and a half has in part also been made by F. Christ. He was probably right in concluding that,

> Matt. und Luke empfingen die Sophia–Christologie hauptsächlich durch Q.... Auch Q hat aber die Sophia–Christologie nicht selbst gebildet, sondern ebenfalls höchstens ausgebildet und weitergebildet.... Der Entstehungsort der Sophia–Christologie ist aber schon vor Q zu suchen.... Möglich bleibt schliesslich, wenn auch nicht beweisbar, dass schon Jesus selbst sich als Sophia verstand.[96]

JAMES AND TRADITIONAL WISDOM

One of the mysteries of the scholarly study of Q is why, with few exceptions, James has been ignored as a possible parallel to Q. A start has now been made by P. J. Hartin in exploring the correlations between Q and James but much more work needs to be done.[97] It is the purpose of the brief discussion that follows to point out some facts pertinent to the further exploration of this subject.

Nothing in what follows is meant to deny that the author of this document had a good command of Greek. He is adept enough to engage in word play (e.g. *chairein/charan*, James 1:1–2; *apeirastosa/peirazei*, 1:13; *adiakritos/anupokritos*, 3:17), and to use alliteration (e.g. *"mikros melos megala,"* 3:5). He uses about 560 words of which sixty are found nowhere else in the New Testament.[98] His style is direct and pithy containing some fifty-four imperatives in the span of 108 verses (ten in 4:7–10 alone). It will be seen from this that

[95] Jacobson, *Wisdom Christology in Q*, 12.

[96] Christ, *Jesus Sophia*, 154. Christ approaches the matter rather differently, and focuses more on the issue of the development of the tradition up to and including its use in the Synoptics.

[97] Hartin, *James and the Q Sayings of Jesus*, especially 140ff.

[98] J. W. MacGorman, "Introducing the Book of James," 9–22. Some of these characteristics may suggest that this document was originally meant for oral performance in Greek, or at least some of the material in James was.

a particular kind of parenetic use of Wisdom material is being made – here one finds not just persuasion but command.[99] When one adds to these considerations the fact that some of this material seems to be linked by catchwords in Greek (cf. *"leipomenoi/leipetai,"* 1:4–5; *peirasmon/peirazomenos*, 1:12–13; *proseuchesthe/deēsis*, 5:16),[100] it becomes difficult to argue for this document being a Greek translation from some Semitic source.

L. G. Perdue has demonstrated that James has the four major features of Hellenistic parenesis: (1) it tends primarily though not exclusively to rely on traditional rather than original material; (2) it basically focuses on material of general applicability; (3) it is often addressed to those who have heard it before, thus one of its major functions is to stimulate memory, not offer new teaching; and (4) it uses human examples of virtue.[101] Yet these very features are also characteristic of traditional Jewish Wisdom material, as can be seen in Proverbs, Job, or Sirach.

In view of what has already been said about Hellenization in Palestine and its environs in the first century A.D., the evidence considered above may mean no more than that the author of James is a somewhat Hellenized Jewish Christian who nonetheless has a commitment to a conventional Wisdom agenda. The cast of the material may also be significantly conditioned by the character of the majority of the audience.[102] The likely function of this document is to reinforce the socializing process for those Jews who have recently become Christians, and due to pressure and/or persecution are now wavering in their faith. "In order for any group to exist, definite boundaries must be constructed which demarcate the group and its distinctive social world from other groups with differing social worlds. Thus paraenesis presents a group ethic designed to maintain a clear differentiation between in–group and out–group."[103]

It has been widely recognized, at least since J. B. Mayor's landmark study of James, that the author of James is heavily indebted not only to the Wisdom material found in the Hebrew Scriptures, particularly Proverbs (cf. e.g. Prov. 3:34 and James 4:6; Prov. 9:30 and James 3:18; Prov. 10:12 (LXX) and James 5:20),[104] but is even more heavily indebted to the writings of Ben Sira and

---

[99] J. B. Polhill, "The Life–Situation of the Book of James," 371.

[100] MacGorman, "Introducing the Book of James," 19.

[101] L. G. Perdue, "Parenesis and the Epistle of James," 241–56.

[102] Whatever else one may wish to say about James 1.1, it suggests an audience *outside* of Palestine, which may in part explain the cast of the material and its apparent use of the LXX not the MT. I would suggest it is probably addressing Jewish Christians, perhaps in Syria (Antioch?) in particular or Asia Minor in general. James may be intended as some sort of circular letter which may also partially explain its generalizing tendencies.

[103] Perdue, "Parenesis," 255.

[104] Cf. the entire detailed list in J. B. Mayor, *The Epistle of St. James*, cxiii. There are a few notable parallels with Job as well; e.g., Job 42:12 to James 5:11. What is notable for its absence are any significant parallels with Ecclesiastes. The only one cited by Mayor (Eccles. 7:9/James 1:19) is too weak and of too general a character to be sure if the author even knew Ecclesiastes. My own view is that he knew it, but chose not to draw on Qoheleth's works because it intended to correct some aspects of traditional Wisdom.

Pseudo–Solomon.[105] Mayor is able to cite over two pages of detailed parallels between James and these intertestamental sapiential writings.[106] In addition, major themes like the discussion of the tongue in James 3 owe a great deal to Sir. 19:6–12; 20:4–7, 17–19; 35:5–10; 38:13–26. James 1:12–18 seems also to echo Sir. 15:11–20. The importance of this for discerning the provenance of James should not be underestimated. This author stands in the same stream of thought as a Ben Sira. His is basically *not* a Wisdom of a counter order, as was true with Jesus and Qoheleth, but rather a more traditional and conventional form of Wisdom like that found in Proverbs and Sirach. The author also seems clearly to be operating with a Wisdom hermeneutic which tends to focus on or even create generalizations like the earlier traditions of Proverbial Wisdom discussed in the first chapter of this study.[107] James is an example not of "early Catholicism" but rather of a form of early Jewish–Christianity heavily indebted to early Jewish sapiential traditions, including the Jesus tradition, but the writer is also conversant with the larger world of Hellenistic discourse.[108]

The author of James returns to traditional topics, not only like guarding one's speech and passions but also enduring suffering (like Job) and temptations, looking into the "perfect law," seeking Wisdom (1:5) and the like.[109] By and large, such topics were notable for their absence in the Jesus material. Missing in James is any real sense of God's new eschatological activity or inbreaking reign in the present which changes the social order of things even now. Instead, the audience is only exhorted to be patient until the Lord comes (5:7). Even the beatitude about endurance through trials which results in receiving the crown of life (1:12) does not connect such blessedness with any future Dominion of God coming on earth (but cf. 2:5).[110] This in itself may explain why on the surface this book seems so foreign to much of the rest of the New Testament and has so often been maligned or neglected. R. Obermüller argues that in James, "die Verwandlung des Prophetischen ins weisheitlich Vernünftige, des Christlichen ins allgemein Menschliche, des Religiösen in ein auch weltliches Verhalten..." and that this constitutes the whole

---

[105] Davids, "The Epistle of James," 3636 reminds us that both of these Wisdom books were included in the early uncials of the New Testament: "and so the literate author of James would have read them even if his Judaism was tangential." This conclusion depends on when one dates James. More crucial is D. Bertrand's demonstration in "Le fond de l'épreuve. Épître de Jacques 1,12–18," 212–218 that James 1:12–18 seems to be drawing on Sir. 15.11–20.

[106] Mayor., cxvi–cxviii.

[107] R. Obermüller, "Hermeneutische Themen im Jakobusbrief," 234–44.

[108] E. Baasland, "Der Jacobusbrief als Neutestamentliche Weisheitsschrift," 119–39 for arguments that James arose out of a 'Wisdom milieu'. W. D. Davies in his classic study *The Setting of the Sermon on the Mount*, 403–05 says: "in the milieu from which James drew its materials, the words of Jesus were in the air, so that, as a living and formative tradition they moulded the life of the Christian community...."

[109] T. B. Maston, "Ethical Dimensions of James," 23–39, 31ff.

[110] James 1:12 may suggest the reward of a positive afterlife for the martyr, or at least one who remains faithful until he dies, regardless of the circumstances surrounding his death. Cf. especially Rev. 2:10, 3:11, 4:4, 10 on this. M. Dibelius, *James*, 88–89.

problematic of James' hermeneutics.[111] In part this will depend on how one views the date of this letter. If it is early, it may in fact reflect that the author, being one of the first Jewish Christians, brought with him into Christianity – a heavy indebtedness to Hebrew sapiential thinking and literature. Into this more conventional mold of Jewish Wisdom thinking he has tried to incorporate both some of the insights of the Q Sermon on the Mount material, and also some dialogue with Pauline ideas. Nevertheless, he is still basically operating from a perspective of conventional Wisdom. Obermüller may be right that James, being a Wisdom teacher like a Ben Sira, believes the way forward is in large measure to go back to a more traditional orientation. This makes it all the more urgent that one looks carefully at some of the parallels between this book and the Q material, as well as some of its apparent parallels with other Synoptic traditions.

As Hartin has shown, primarily the parallels between James and Q lie in the material now called the Sermon on the Mount, and in particular between James and the *Matthean* version of the Sermon on the Mount or perhaps QMt before it was redacted by the First Evangelist.[112] Whether this leads to the conclusion that the author of James knew Q and not just QMt or Matthew depends on one's views as to whether in general Matthew or Luke preserves the earliest form of Q in the texts in question. Probably the question should be pushed one step further back, for several scholars have presented significant evidence that James reflects a knowledge of a pre–literary form of Jesus" sayings.[113] The fact that the author has a good command of Greek and appears to use the LXX, in view of what we know now about Hellenization in first century Palestine, is no obstacle to seeing James as a document from the earliest period of the Christian movement, originating prior to the writing of any of the Gospels.[114] The discussion must now focus on the parallels between James and the Q material.

---

[111] Obermüller, *Hermeneutische Themen*, 244.

[112] Hartin, *James and the Q sayings*, 144ff. Cf. M. H. Shepherd, "The Epistle of James and the Gospel of Matthew," 40–51.

[113] Cf. J. B. Adamson, *The Epistle of James*, 21ff. drawing on his unpublished Ph.D. thesis "An Inductive Approach to the Epistle of James," 291–310; cf. also F. Hahn, "Die christologische Begründung urchristlicher Paränese," 90–99; B. S. Childs, *The New Testament as Canon. An Introduction*, 437; contra Shepherd, "James and Matthew," 47 who thinks the author heard the Gospel of Matthew in worship.

[114] It seems rather certain that the author or at least the original source of many of the traditions in James knew and perhaps also spoke Aramaic. Cf. F. Mussner, *Der Jakobusbrief* 30–32; Davids, "Epistle of James," 3640. The only really difficult obstacle to seeing one of the very first Christians, perhaps even James the brother of the Lord, as the author or ultimate source of this document is the discussion of law, works, and faith (James 2:14–26, especially 2:24) which seems to reflect a knowledge of the Pauline discussion of these matters. But this issue was already apparently being broached once Paul began his missionary work, some time in the late A.D. 40s, and perhaps even before if there really was a significant Gentile presence in the Church in Syrian Antioch. Perhaps then an early collection of James' teaching was redacted and edited sometime in the A.D. 50s in response to a misunderstanding of the Pauline gospel. Cf. R. P. Martin, *James*, lxxvi–lxxvii. On the question of Hellenization in Palestine, cf. pp. 119ff. above. On the issue of the authenticity of James, cf. R. Bauckham, "Pseudo–Apostolic Letters," 469–494. On the style of this document, cf. below.

The parallels may be listed as follows:

MATTHEAN PARALLELS		LUKAN PARALLELS
James 1:2	=	Matt. 5:11–12/Luke 6:22–23
James 1:4	=	Matt. 5:48
James 1:5	=	Matt. 7:7
James 1:17	=	Matt. 7:11
James 1:22	=	Matt. 7:24/Luke 6:46–47
James 1:23	=	Matt. 7:26/Luke 6:49
James 2:5	=	Matt. 5:3,5/Luke 6:20
James 2:10	=	Matt. 5:18–19 (cf. Luke 3:9)
James 2:11	=	Matt. 5:21–22
James 2:13	=	Matt. 5:7/Luke 6:36
James 3:12	=	Matt. 7:16–18/Luke 6:43–44
James 3:18	=	Matt. 5:9
James 4:2–3	=	Matt. 7:7–8
James 4:4	=	Matt. 6:24/Luke 16:13
James 4:8	=	Matt. 5:8
James 4:9	=	Matt. 5:4/Luke 6:25
James 4:11	=	Matt. 7:1–2/Luke 6:37–38
James 5:2–3	=	Matt. 6:19–21/Luke 12:33
James 5:6	=	Matt. 7:1/Luke 6:37
James 5:10	=	Matt. 5:11–12/Luke 6:23
James 5:12	=	Matt. 5:34–37[115]

These parallels, some of which will be examined in detail in a moment, are sufficient to show that the author of James either knew some of Jesus' sayings in a pre–literary form or a collection of Jesus' sayings.[116] Both the character and the distribution of the parallels throughout James make unlikely the argument that James was originally a Jewish document to which was added a few Christianizing phrases (e.g. 1:1, 2:1). As P. H. Davids has argued, "While James ultimately has wisdom material as his background, this is refracted... through the pregospel Jesus tradition."[117] That the book of James is not just indebted to earlier Jewish Wisdom material, but more specifically to the Jesus tradition may also be suggested by the author's use of the narrative *mashal* form (cf. James 1:23–24; 2:2; 2:15–17), which was not characteristic of Wisdom books that antedate the time of Jesus.[118]

---

[115] I have adopted with some changes the lists found in Hartin, *James and the Q Sayings*, 144, n. 3; 145, n. 1.

[116] The attempt to date James very late possibly even in the second century and see it as drawing on one or more Gospels has been made very unlikely by various recent studies. Cf. Hartin, *James and the Q Sayings*, 171–72; R. P. Martin, *James* lxix–lxxvii; Davids, *Commentary on James*, 33–34. It appears likely that the author of the Shepherd of Hermas knew James; cf. Herm. *Mandates*, 11.8 to James 3.17, and *Mandates* 9.4 to James 1.6.

[117] Davids, "The Epistle of James in Modern Debate," 3638.

[118] Hartin, *James and the Q Sayings*, 75. All of the James narrative *meshalim* are of the most elementary and brief sort, being very close to the basic comparison form. The fact that one

One immediately notices that the author of James does not cite the Jesus tradition directly, but rather weaves various ideas, themes, and phrases from that tradition into his *own* argument. Unlike Q, the material in James is not presented as sayings of Jesus, but rather as the teaching of James, which in turn has evidently been influenced by the Jesus tradition. Childs observes that, "the sayings of Jesus... function as a prism through which the Old Testament is now understood..."[119] This is only partly accurate. It seems more often to be the case that the controlling orientation goes in the other direction. For example, when one examines the way James uses some of Jesus' aphorisms and aphoristic beatitudes he seems to be turning them back into proverbs of a conventional sort (cf. e.g. James 4:9, 5:1 to Matt. 5:4). It might be better to say that James mainly sees the Jesus tradition as a development of the earlier Jewish sapiential traditions, and uses Jesus' sayings to reinforce some traditional Wisdom agendas. Davids asks, "Is the tradition so common that he expects the reader to have memorized it?"[120] Though this question is impossible to answer, the author certainly seems to assume some degree of familiarity with the Jesus tradition as one finds it in Q. Does he also reflect and assume a knowledge of material beyond Q? A glance at the chart above might lead one to answer that a knowledge of special M material is also in evidence. This view does not stand up under closer scrutiny.

Perhaps the best example that might suggest that the author of James knows special M material is found in Matt. 5:33–37 and James 5:12. In both texts one has a direct prohibition of all oaths followed by examples (e.g. swearing by heaven or earth), followed by a call to absolute truthfulness, letting one's yes or no be a sufficient answer, which is finally followed by a reason given. Hartin shows how the Matthean form of this tradition is further developed in Matthew than in James (e.g. the additions about swearing by Jerusalem or by your head).[121] Hartin then concludes that James must have known this material in its special M form before the first evangelist redacted it. There is, however, another strong possibility, namely that this tradition was originally present in Q and Luke has omitted it.[122] This material is found in the Sermon on the Mount, and there is no good reason why it could not have been part of that collection from the beginning. In that case, James bears witness to an earlier form of this tradition than is found in Q.[123] The other alleged parallels with special M material are so slight as to be inconsequential. For instance, the discussion

---

does not find parables in the earlier Wisdom material, except in the Jesus traditions, points to the interlinking of James with the Jesus material.

[119] Childs, *New Testament Canon*, 437.

[120] Davids, "The Epistle of James", 3638f.

[121] Hartin, *James and the Q Sayings*, 188–89.

[122] Bearing in mind the tendency (noted above pp. 214ff.) that Luke has to use less of a source than the First Evangelist does. Luke may well have omitted this material because Jewish oath taking and its various forms was of no direct relevance for Luke's Gentile audience.

[123] In view of the unprecedented nature of this teaching on oaths in a Jewish setting it is very likely it goes back to Jesus. Cf. S. Laws, *A Commentary on the Epistle of James*, 224.

about the care of the needy in James 2:15–16/Matt. 25:34–35 reveals no striking parallel phrases, and may be Q material anyway (cf. Luke 3:11). Even the order of discussion of care for the hungry and care for those needing clothes is different in Matthew and James. In fact the order of Luke 3:11 is closer to the saying of James than the Matthean form, but the vocabulary is completely different (Luke has *chiton, Bromata* while James has *gumnoi* and *ta epitedeia tou somatos, trophes*). The obligation to help needy members of the faith community is already made clear in the Hebrew Scriptures (cf. Lev. 19:10, Job 31:16), and thus the author of James need not have derived such a concern from the Jesus tradition. Another possible parallel is found in James 1:12 and Matt. 24:13 /Luke 10:22b, a text to which Hartin gives insufficient attention. The James version speaks of a crown of life, not unlike those texts in early Jewish literature that speak of a crown of glory or of righteousness (cf. *Test. Lev.* 8:2,9; *Test. Ben.* 4:1; of. 2 Tim. 4:8), while the First Evangelist speaks of being saved. It will be noted, however, that the James form of the saying seems in various ways close to the saying in Wis. 5:16–17: "But the righteous will live forever, and their reward is with the Lord;... Therefore they will receive a glorious crown and a beautiful diadem from the hand of the Lord." This is said in a context where the listener has already been exhorted to endure trials and temptations and be of good character (cf. Wis. 2–3). Thus, while it is possible that James 1.12 reflects a knowledge of special M material, it may simply be a parallel development of earlier sapiential ideas.[124]

Next, questions must be asked about some of the parallels between James and Q, beginning with James 2:10–11 and Matt. 5:18–19/Luke16:17. The attitude that when one has violated one commandment one has violated the Law as a body of legislation is not an idea unique to Matthew. In fact the closest parallel to James 2:10 is *B.T. Hor.* 8b which says that "whoever is liable for one [Mosaic commandment] is liable for all." The idea of the law being observed or being violated as a whole is also found in Gal. 5:3 where Paul warns, "I testify to everyone who receives circumcision that he is bound to keep the whole law." The discussion about killing followed by the discussion about adultery is found in a different order in Matt. 5:21–22 than it is in James and in any case both passages are expositions of some of the Ten Commandments, and do not reflect a relationship of dependence. This parallel, which was weak to begin with, seems to be non–existent on closer scrutiny. There is nothing in James 2:10–11 that requires one to assume that James knew Q material.[125] It must be admitted that some of the other parallels on Hartin's list seem to be equally insubstantial (e.g. James 3:12 and Matt. 7:16–18/Luke 6:33–34), but many of them cannot be lightly dismissed. Hartin has made a strong enough case to

[124] Shepherd, "James and Matthew," 43ff is quite right that James is closer to the Matthean form of Q with perhaps only a rare exception, but his evidence that James knew Matthew in general is no stronger or different than Hartin's.

[125] On the parallel with Paul, cf. Dibelius, *James*, 146.

show a knowledge of at least the material in the Sermon on the Mount on the part of the author of James, whether in its Q form or in some pre–literary form.[126] The contention that he knew QMt, however, needs closer scrutiny.

For example, when one examines James 1.5, 17 / Matt.7:7–11 / Luke 11:9–13, Hartin argues that Matt. 7:11, which speaks of good things being given by God, is very likely later than the Lukan form of the saying which speaks of the gift of the Holy Spirit. In view of Luke's great interest in the Holy Spirit in both Luke and Acts[127] this conclusion is doubtful at best. On the other hand, the rather striking parallels between James 1:4 and Matt. 5:48 on perfection, or James 3:17–18 and Matt. 5:5, 9 on peacemaking (the only two references to peacemakers in the New Testament), both of which sayings are usually seen as part of QMt gives some credence to Hartin's argument. But it must be stressed that the First Evangelist, if his use of Mark is any indication, is much more apt to include the substance of his source in his own work than Luke is. There is no good reason why this QMt material cannot simply represent the substance of what was originally in Q. It has already been pointed out that Luke may have omitted a beatitude or two in order to make room for some woes, and there is no evidence elsewhere in Luke–Acts that Luke shows any interest in the theme of perfection. Luke may well have changed Q's *teleios* to *oiktirmones* in Luke 6:36, for the theme of mercy is definitely important to Luke (cf. Luke 1:50, 72; 10:37; 16:24; 18:38). The tendency to favor the Lukan form of Q sayings most of the time has skewed some of Hartin's otherwise apt and important conclusions. All of the evidence that he presents for James knowing QMt may turn out in the end to be simply evidence that James knew Q or at least the material that came to be incorporated in Q.[128] Putting the matter the other way around, if James represents a very early appropriation of Q material, at least as early as the 50s A.D., and I think Hartin has made his case on this point, it must be said that the evidence of James seems to suggest that Matthew's Gospel, not Luke's for the most part, represents the original Q form of the material, especially if the question is about the *substance* of Q rather than the specific wording of a saying. Even on the latter score, however, the material in James should cause one to abandon any predispositions to favor the Lukan wording of a Q saying.

Another critical question to be raised is whether James reflects knowledge of the wider Gospel tradition as it is represented in Matthew, Mark and Luke. Here the evidence, as Hartin recognizes, is weak. The only real parallel in Luke from the wider Gospel material is the example of Elijah used in both

---

[126] Martin, *James*, lxxvff. on parallels with Matthew.

[127] Cf. Luke 1:15, 41, 67, 80; 2:25, 27; 3:22; 4:1, 11, 14; 11:13. In Luke 3:22; 4:11 and 11:13 it appears to be a redactional addition. Holy Spirit also appears 42 times in Acts; cf. H. Conzelman, *The Theology of Saint Luke*, 180 and n. 1.; Fitzmyer, *Luke 1–9*, 227ff.

[128] This in turn would argue for an earlier date for James, than is often the case. Cf. R. Bauckham, *Jude and the Relatives of Jesus in the Early Church*, 128, n. 225; 133, n. 233, who believes at least many of the traditions in James go back to James the brother of the Lord.

Luke 4:25–26 and James 5:17. In Luke the focus is on aid to a widow, in James on rain being withheld or sent, and the notable parallel about three years and six months may simply reflect a widely used round number for a period of judgment (cf. Dan. 7:25; 12:7; Rev. 11:22; 12:14, making more specific the reference in 1 Kgs. 18:1).[129] The use of Elijah as an example in sapiential material is found in the earlier material in Sir. 48:1–11. There are really no other examples of any force whatsoever from the Lukan material. From Mark one may cite perhaps Mark 11:2 (cf. James 1:6), but this is also found in Matt. 21:21. But the theme of praying in faith without doubting is surely of too general and widespread a character in early Judaism to warrant any firm conclusions about borrowing from Mark or Matthew (cf. Sir. 7:10). The more substantive of the parallels in uniquely Matthean material has already been considered. There are, however, places where the discussion of important topics like warnings against the rich (Matt. 19:23–24/James 2:6–7), help to the poor (Matt. 25:35/James 2:16), and eschatological imminence (Matt. 24:33/James 5:9) seem to point to a knowledge of some traditions that have come to be called special M material. In each case, one would need to ask whether this material is redactional, or whether it might in some form go back to Jesus. The most one can say without a detailed study of the tradition history is that it is possible that the author of James also knew some of the special M material.

The general impression left from examining the parallels between James and Q and, in particular, the Q Sermon on the Mount is that the only area where firm conclusions are warranted is in regard to a common knowledge of the Q Sermon on the Mount material. It may also be true that James knew QMt and the special M material but this is less certain. In general, James' use of the Q material does not amount to direct quoting but is allusive in character, and clearly the author of James uses the material to his own ends. Only rarely would it seem warranted to suggest that James preserves an earlier form of a Q saying than either Luke or Matthew because of the freer way he handles the material. This may be because James reflects a pre–literary use of the Jesus material.

The far more important questions for our purposes are *how* and *to what ends* is James appropriating the Q material. Here tell–tale signs show how the material has been made to serve a more conventional Wisdom approach to life than is generally characteristic of the Jesus tradition.

First, from the very outset of James, the author makes clear that it is Wisdom, conventional Wisdom of a practical sort, that one is to seek to cope with the trials and temptations of life (cf. James 1.2–6). The listener is not exhorted to seek first the Dominion of God in the here and now, or to learn the teachings of Jesus, but rather to pray to God for Wisdom from above. The beginning of the book of James resonates with the exhortation in Wis 7:7–8: "Therefore I prayed and understanding was given me; I called on God, and the

[129] Dibelius, *James*, 256–57, and n. 91.

spirit of wisdom came to me."[130] In James the suggestion is that Wisdom should be sought from God since it comes from above. James does not really exhort his audience to observe life or nature to gain Wisdom. It is something passed down to one from one's teachers or directly from God.[131]

Yet one might ask, what about the way James deals with the rich? Do not James 2.6 and 5.1–5 sound like the teaching of Jesus, and unlike the old Wisdom view that riches are a blessing of God? The answer to this query is yes, but only in part. James does reflect a sort of Wisdom from below, a Wisdom of the oppressed and disenfranchised, but the advice he gives the poor and oppressed is basically endurance until the Lord returns at which point the rich oppressors will be dealt with (cf. James 5:1–7). Missing is the note of joy about the present inbreaking of the Dominion of God and how that should cause a transvaluation of values. In James one has parenesis juxtaposed with some future eschatology. This at best reflects only one side of the Jesus tradition. The dialectic of already and not yet is largely lost.

There is also no evidence of any thrust amounting to a proclaiming of Good News about the present, or to those outside the community, unless a bare passing hint like James 1:18 suggests it. Indeed, the basic exhortation is not that all should go and make disciples but rather, "Let not many of you become teachers... " (James 3:1)! James is focused specifically on inculcating a certain kind of community ethic, concentrating almost exclusively on behavior within the community (cf. James 4:11; 5:9). It is to good works and the good life that James is exhorting his charges (James 2:14ff; 3:13–18), not to a proclaiming of Good News to the world. And the works to which James is exhorting his audience are the following: (1) to care for widows and orphans in the community (1:27); (2) to keep oneself unstained from the world (1:27b); (3) to fulfill the royal law, according to Scripture (which entails the Ten Commandments among other things (cf. 2:8–13); (4) bridling one's tongue and one's passions (3:1–12; 4:1–10); (5) persevering in faith through suffering and trials (1:2–15; 5:10–11); (6) prayer for the sick and suffering (5:13–15, 16b–17); (7) confession of sins to one another in the community (5:16); and (8) retrieving the erring community member (5:19).

There is very little here that Ben Sira could not have said except the unreserved condemnation of the rich in James (cf. Sir. 31:1–8), and there are various places where the echoes are clear. For example in Sir. 35:15–16 one hears, "for the Lord is the judge, and with him there is no partiality. He will not show partiality to the poor, *but* he will listen to the prayer of one who is wronged. He will not ignore the supplication of the orphan, or the widow when she pours out her complaint" (cf. James 1:27–2.9). Or again the concern

---

[130] On the association of Spirit and Wisdom in both James and earlier Jewish sapiential material, cf. J. A. Kirk, "The Meaning of Wisdom in James: Examination of a Hypothesis," 24–38.

[131] This book then reflects a knowledge of the "hidden" quality of divine Wisdom, but does not develop the idea of personified Wisdom.

for carefully controlled speech is expressed in Sir. 23:7–15, 27:4–5 in similar ways to James 3:1–12 especially in regard to the avoiding of cursing and abusive speech. Even the connection of Wisdom and the Law is at least implied in James, which may be yet another echo of Sirach (cf. James 1:5, 2:8ff. with Sir. 24:23).

As the cultural anthropologists inform us, the sort of advice the author of James gives suggests that he is trying to inculcate a community with carefully controlled boundaries, as is shown by the attempts to carefully limit behaviour, relationships, and speech.[132] He is deeply concerned with matters of moral purity both in regard to behaviour and in one's emotions and attitudes. The sacred space is the community itself, the world is the zone of defilement (cf. James 1:27b). This is the sort of ethic one finds in part in Ben Sira and more fully in Pseudo–Solomon set forth in order to help Judaism survive in a hostile environment. James, in view of various trials and possible persecutions, is also suggesting battening down the hatches in a manner somewhat similar to the Johannine epistles. His aim is to have his listeners control all three zones of the human being – the zone of emotion infused thought (cf. 1:14–16; 3:16–18), the zone of self–expressive speech (cf. 3:1–12), and the zone of purposeful action (cf. 2:1–26).[133] How very different a note this sounds to the Jesus tradition which speaks of Jesus' free association with sinners, his reaching out to the least, last and the lost, his sending out of his own followers to be extensions of his ministry and the like. I would suggest the reason for this difference is the absence in James' teaching of a sense of the inbreaking Dominion of God and the way it reorders both community and world.

Then too, despite the pervasive sapiential content of the book there is no reflection in James whatsoever on the concept of Jesus as Wisdom. Also notable for its absence is any of the more radical teachings of Jesus about, for example, loving enemies or leaving the dead to bury the dead. James has chosen either to draw on the more conventional parts of the Jesus tradition, or to use the often unconventional teaching of Jesus for some very conventional and traditional purposes, or to remain silent about certain aspects of Jesus' teaching that inculcated a counter order of things.

Qoheleth offered aphorisms and meditations of a counter order because of the limits and in some case the bankruptcy he saw in conventional Wisdom. Jesus offered aphorisms and parables of a counter order not merely as a critique of the *status quo* but as a positive alternative made possible by the inbreaking of God's eschatological reign even in the present. James basically offers neither, in the main returning to the sort of things which by now are quite familiar to the reader of this study from Proverbs or Ben Sira.

In many ways the Letter of James comports with what other sources suggest was the attitude, lifestyle, and teaching of Jesus' brother James (cf. Acts

---

[132] Malina, *New Testament World*, 122ff.
[133] Malina, *New Testament World*, 61.

15:12–21; 21:17–26; Gal. 1:18–2:10; 1 Cor. 9:5; Eusebius, *Historia Ecclesiae* 2.23, quoting Hegisippus, and Josephus, *Ant.* 20.9.1).[134] It does appear also, as N. Turner has shown, that in style James is most like Jewish sapiential synagogue homilies, not Cynic diatribes.[135] As such, it is not difficult to accept that in some form most if not all of the document went back to a somewhat Hellenized early Jew like James, Jesus' brother. If J. B. Adamson is correct that the "Epistle of James comes from the center and head of the Christianity of its day, and speaks with all the pastoral authority of its source," then certainly it deserves closer scrutiny than it has usually received in the past two centuries.[136] It suggests that at least one form of early Jewish Christianity could be very traditional indeed, *even though it drew on the Jesus tradition in numerous ways and places.* This author was capable of using aphorisms and aphoristic beatitudes of Jesus in a proverbial way, and I would suggest that it is because of this author's intention to do precisely this that he does not attribute any of his material to Jesus. Proverbial wisdom was normally anonymous or the collective and accumulated wisdom of many generations of sages. James is handling the Jesus tradition as though it were proverbial Wisdom.

Whether or not Jesus' brother James was actually responsible for the book of James either as a source or as its author, clearly this book is a piece of Jewish–Christian sapiential material, probably a very early one, and in any event one that uses the Jesus tradition in a way that differs in significant ways from the use of it made in Q. Early Christian use of Jewish Wisdom or even Jesus Wisdom material was in other words not a uniform matter. Different authors used the sapiential material in differing ways.

The Wisdom that is from above in James produces or at least leads to good and godly character and behavior (James 3:13–18).[137] This is very different from the Wisdom that is said to be from above and now has returned to that same location in the early Christological hymns. It is to these early expressions of Wisdom Christology in the hymns that we must now turn.

---

[134] These sources must be critically sifted, but the overall impression they leave is of a Jewish follower of Jesus who continued to keep the Mosaic law. This also comports with the impression left by the Epistle of James, with the added dimension that in James, we see a person who relied heavily on Wisdom material and seems to have taken a sapiential approach to Torah not unlike that of Ben Sira. On how the life of James the Just comports for the most part with the impression left by this epistle, cf. F. F. Bruce, *Peter, Stephen, James, and John,* 113ff. On whether its style is possible by a Jerusalem Jewish Christian, cf. N. Turner, *Grammatical Insights,* 116ff.

[135] N. Turner, "The Style of the Epistle of James," in *MHT, A Grammar of New Testament Greek,* 114–20.

[136] Adamson, *James,* 21.

[137] The character formation elsewhere predicated of the Spirit is in James predicated of Wisdom (cf. and contrast Gal. 5:22–23 with James 2:17). This move is not unexpected in view of the close connection of the Spirit and Wisdom in earlier Wisdom books such as the Wisdom of Solomon.

6

Singing Wisdom's Praise

ONCE Wisdom became identified with Jesus of Nazareth in the Q tradition (perhaps drawing on Jesus' own ideas), and Jesus became an object of worship for early Jewish Christians, it is not entirely surprising to discover that some of these same people, steeped in Jewish Wisdom traditions, soon appropriated the hymn–like praise of personified Wisdom in order to express their devotion to Jesus Christ. It is the major thesis of this chapter that the christological hymn fragments found in the Pauline corpus, the Fourth Gospel, and Hebrews are fundamentally expressions of a Wisdom Christology that goes back to early Jewish Christianity and reflects the fact that some of the earliest christological thinking about Jesus amounted to what today would be called a very "high" Christology indeed. Indeed, it was a Christology which ultimately led to a full–blown doctrine of the pre–existence of the Son and in due course when the logical implications of that idea sank in, to a doctrine of the incarnation. It is the plan of this chapter to examine each of the christological hymn fragments in chronological order in the light of the earlier sapiential material, starting with Phil. 2:6–11, then Col. 1:15–20, 1 Tim. 3:16, Heb. 1:2–4, and finally probably the latest of these hymn fragments John 1:1–5, 9–14.

TUNING UP

Though it is perhaps an exaggeration to say that early Christology was born in song, one may certainly say that early Christology grew out of the worship of Christ and was accordingly expressed in various liturgical forms – hymns, prayers, credal statements, testimonia, and doxologies. Some of these forms no doubt came initially from a spontaneous response in worship to what was felt to be the leading of the Holy Spirit, but some also seem to reflect a careful and calculated composition prepared in advance for use in worship. Various sources suggest that psalms, hymns, and spiritual songs were perhaps the most crucial forms not only in the earliest period (c. A.D. 35–55) but at least well into the second century. It is not just Pliny the Younger (*Ep.* 10.96.7) who bears witness to the fact that what distinguished early Christians was "carmenque Christo quasi deo dicere secum invicem."[1] Indeed there is telltale evidence of such practices well before the time of Pliny.[2]

One may begin, for instance, by noting the reference in 1 Cor. 14:26 to each one having a *psalmos* to share in worship. Paul wrote this in the early 50s. Somewhat later we hear of a threefold characterization of the singing as involving *psalmois, humnois,* and *odais pneumatikais* (Col. 3:16) a passage that seems to be further expanded upon in Ephes. 5:19.[3] It may be possible to make a distinction between these three types of songs. The first may reflect the deliberate early Christian use of the psalms in a messianic way; the second would refer to newly composed Christian hymns; and the third to spontaneous songs offered in worship at the prompting of the Holy Spirit. There probably was some overlap, especially between the psalms and the composed hymns (cf. below), and it is not possible to make hard and fast form critical distinctions on the basis of the slender evidence available. It is also probable that these songs included hymns to God as well as to the Lord Jesus, but it would be the latter that made Christians stand out and be recognizable to even the outside observer such as Pliny. Moreover, in the pagan world there was already a close connection between hymn writing and singing in temples coupled with significant theological content. In fact, the *hymnodes* could also be called *theologoi* (cf. *OGIS* 513 – in Smyrna and Rome).[4] Menander of Laodicea at a somewhat later period instructs pagan hymn writers to dwell on "the naming of the god, or a valedictory, or on the god's nature or story or birth or form..." (*De Hymn.* 1ff.).[5] Christianity needed hymns to match or outstrip its competitors in the Greek speaking world.

W. Wink points to evidence from the Nag Hammadi *Tripartite Tractate* that makes quite clear that the material found in a somewhat different form in Col. 1:15–20 was viewed and used as a hymn. He also refers to evidence from the *Odes of Solomon* (cf. e.g. 16:1–2) as well as the *Acts of John* (94:1–96:51) that both groups on the fringe of Christianity as well as orthodox groups were

[1] That Pliny is refering to hymn singing seems clear in light of the way Tertullian interprets the text in *Apol.* 2.6.

[2] In what follows I am indebted to M. Hengel's seminal essay, "Hymns and Christology," in *Between Jesus and Paul. Studies in the Earliest History of Christianity,* 78–96.

[3] It still seems more probable to me that Paul wrote Colossians and possibly even Ephesians toward the close of his ministry and life (perhaps in the early 60s), than that they are the creations of a later Paulinist.

[4] Cf. also the evidence of an inscription from Nysa mentioning a "poet, rhapsode, and theologue" in R. MacMullen, *Paganism in the Roman Empire,* 150, n. 89.

[5] Cited in MacMullen, *Paganism,* 17 from a source unavailable to me.

regularly in the practice of composing and singing hymns to and about Christ.[6] Also important for our purposes are the words of Philo (*Vit. Cont.* 28–29,68–80) about the Jewish Therapeutae in the first century A.D. who were "yearning for Wisdom" (68) and so they studied Scripture.

> Then the President rises and sings a hymn composed as an address to God, either a new one of his own composition or an old one by poets of an earlier day who have left behind them hymns in many measures and melodies.... They all lift up their voices, men and women alike (80).... [in] two choirs one of men and one of women (83)... After choric dancing they form a single choir and sing until dawn (89).[7]

Especially telling is the fact that Eusebius interprets this discussion in Philo as referring to early Christian worship (cf. *Hist.Ecc.* 2, 17, 21ff.).

If one considers the possible analogies with Qumran, one will not be surprised that Christians were in the business of composing hymns. Certainly this was a regular practice in the Qumran community (cf. especially the 1QH material), and there is evidence that the psalms and perhaps also the hymns were the outcome of being filled with God's wisdom and Spirit which resulted in a prophetic utterance. This is, in fact, what is claimed for David in 11QPs.[8] which reads in part, "And Yahweh gave him a wise and enlightened spirit... the sum (of his songs) was 4050. These he uttered through prophecy (*bnbw'h*) which had been given him by the most high." This should be compared with the previous discussion in this study about Solomon and his songs[9] but also with what is said about Solomon in Wis. 7:7 – "Therefore I prayed, and understanding was given me; I called on God and the spirit of wisdom came to me." This is followed by the Wisdom hymn in 7:22ff which near its conclusion says, "in every generation she passes into holy souls and makes them friends of God and prophets; for God loves nothing so much as the person who lives with Wisdom." The point of the previous discussion was to show that there is a precedent and also parallels both in early Judaism and elsewhere for the earliest Christians composing hymns and, in particular, hymns influenced by sapiential material.

In large measure the earliest Christian worship practices seem to have reflected and grown out of early Jewish worship and so the quote from Philo is important especially in view of the Pauline texts mentioned above. The connection between Wisdom and the singing of hymns in the Philo quote, and also in the quote from the Qumran material should not be missed, for there is

---

[6] W. Wink, "The Hymn of the Cosmic Christ," in *The Conversation Continues. Studies in Paul and John in Honor of J. L. Martyn*, 235–39.

[7] Cf. above what Pliny says about Christians singing at dawn.

[8] J. A. Sanders, "The Psalms Scroll of Qumran Cave 11," 91–92.

[9] cf.pp.16ff. above.

also such a connection in the christological hymn fragments in the New Testament as shall be shown shortly.[10] It was the focus on Christ, not the composition of hymns, even sapiential ones, that made early Christian worship and hymns stand out.[11]

It is not historically improbable that the theological thinking which eventually led to the christological hymns originated very early and on Palestinian soil. It must be borne in mind that "after a more than three–hundred–year history under the influence of Greek culture Palestinian Judaism can also be described as 'Hellenistic Judaism.'"[12] Thus, when one is dealing with first century A.D. Palestine, it is no longer possible with any certainty to make *sharp* distinctions between Jewish ideas and thought forms which might go back to Jesus or the early Jewish Christians, and Hellenistic ideas and thought forms that could *not* have arisen in such a *Sitz im Leben*.[13]

This conclusion cuts several ways. For instance, the use of the old Judaism/Hellenism dichotomy as a tool to trace the development of New Testament thought, and most especially christological thought, is questionable at best.[14] This is also true in the case of attempts to trace the path of Wisdom thought, which more than other forms of Jewish thought and literature seems to have been open to cross–cultural and even Hellenistic influences. It has already been seen in the case of the Wisdom of Solomon that significantly Hellenized Jewish Wisdom traditions were possible, albeit on foreign soil.[15]

---

[10] I agree with E. Schweizer, "Paul's Christology and Gnosticism," in *Paul and Paulinism. Essays in Honour of C. K. Barrett*, 115–23, that the parallels between the Gnostic use of hymns and Wisdom and Paul's use diverge in important ways. The hymns in Paul and elsewhere in the New Testament do not devalue creation nor do they stress the idea of a redeemer figure who in essence passes through the intervening layers of creation separating God and humanity escaping the taint of the material universe. Indeed in the christological hymn fragments in the New Testament not only is creation seen as good but the Redeemer has a hand in making it. "While Gnosticism took up and radicalized a notion which had, perhaps, been at the root of Jewish Wisdom literature, the idea of a divine order inherent in all things and particularly in man's mind, Christianity, on the contrary, did so with the typically Jewish idea of Wisdom as a gift of God to his elect people, manifest… definitively, 'eschatologically' (Heb. 1:2) in Jesus Christ" (120).

[11] Another text pointing to early evidence of christological hymn singing is Ignatius, *Ephes*. 4. 1–2, which speaks not only of singing through Christ to God but also of Jesus Christ being sung.

[12] Hengel, *Hellenization*, 53.

[13] Such distinctions are still possible to some degree in the case of earlier Jewish Wisdom literature, but demonstrating that a particular "Hellenistic" idea or literary form *could not* or *would not* have been used by Jesus or those who first gathered his traditions in Palestine is now virtually impossible.

[14] Hengel, *Hellenization*, is bold enough to claim "the whole development of christological doctrine *could* have taken place completely within Palestinian Judaism. There it was possible to find several pre–existent heavenly mediators closely bound up with God" (55). He also points out that, "The roots of the 'Jewish–Christian/Hellenistic' or more precisely the Greek–speaking Jewish Christian community in which the message of Jesus was formulated in Greek for the first time clearly extend back to the very earliest community in Jerusalem, and accordingly the first linguistic development of its kerygma and its Christology must have already taken place" (18).

[15] Cf. above on the Prologue to Ben Sira pp. 80ff. and the notes there.

The earliest use of christological hymn fragments is found in the Pauline corpus, and it is appropriate at this juncture to ask where Paul may have heard such hymns.[16] Perhaps the most likely answer is in contexts where Greek was the primary language of worship amongst Christians and thus such hymns would have been composed in Greek so that everyone might participate in the singing.[17] Some of the hymns, such as the one in Philippians 2, but especially the ones in Hebrews 1 and Colossians 1 which so clearly draw on the *Greek* text of the Wisdom of Solomon, were surely first composed in Greek.[18] This may mean that Paul could have first heard such hymns in Syrian Antioch, or possibly even in Damascus in the early years of his Christian life. Since, however, the fragments appear in some of Paul's *later* letters, the apostle could have drawn on traditions familiar in Philippi or Colossae. To judge from the fact that one finds hymn fragments in a variety of places including in Hebrews, the Fourth Gospel, *and* the Pauline corpus it appears that such hymns and their composition must have been a widespread phenomena. Paul was very likely not the originator of the christological hymns, nor of the use of Wisdom traditions to construct them. These hymns suggest a rather widely held common form of Wisdom Christology in early Christianity.

There seem to have been three primary sources which are drawn on to compose the christological hymns: (1) earlier Jewish discussions about personified or even hypostasized Wisdom; (2) the earliest Christian preaching about the life of Jesus, in particular, about his death and vindication beyond death; and (3) the Christological use of the psalms, especially Psalms 110 but also Psalm 8 among others.[19] Though this study intends to focus on the degree

---

[16] One must distinguish between where Paul very likely first heard such hymns and where they originated. I would not rule out a Palestinian origin at least for the primitive V pattern that stands behind all these hymns. In view of what was said about personified Wisdom in earlier Wisdom literature (cf. the summary on pp. 114–15 above) it is neither necessary nor plausible to insist on a Gnostic redeemer myth as the basis of the Christological hymns. Cf. Schweizer, "Paul's Christology and Gnosticism," in 115ff., but also L. W. Hurtado, "Jesus as Lordly Example in Philippians 2:5–11," in *From Jesus to Paul: Studies in Honour of F. W. Beare*, 113–26, 117. "In general, and for reasons sufficiently well known to require no explanation here, the appeal to a pre–Christian Gnostic redeemer–myth has fallen on hard times in recent years..." cf. E. Yamauchi, *Pre–Christian Gnosticism: A Survey of Proposed Evidences*, (Grand Rapids: Eerdmans, 1973).

[17] It is possible that some of the hymns were originally composed in Aramaic or even Hebrew (though this seems less likely than Aramaic); cf. e.g., H. Gese, *Essays on Biblical Theology*, 174–75 on the Logos Hymn in John 1.

[18] Even in regard to the earliest of these hymn fragments in Phil. 2, N. T. Wright, *The Climax of the Covenant. Christ and the Law in Pauline Theology*, 98 is quite right to point out that Phil. 2:6 with its "nuanced idiom [used] in a characteristically Hellenistic way... does not *prove* that the passage was originally composed in Greek, but it makes it very easy to imagine it was" (98). I would say it makes it quite likely.

[19] Cf. the important article by M. Hengel, "Psalm 110 und die Erhöhung des Auferstandenen zur Rechten Gottes," in *Anfänge der Christologie*, 43–73. The attempt to argue that the hymns were originally thanksgiving hymns on the basis of what comes before Col. 1.15–20 seems strained at best. As E. Schüssler Fiorenza points out in "Wisdom Mythology and the Christological Hymns of the New Testament," in *Aspects of Wisdom in Judaism and Early*

of indebtedness to the first source, the importance of the other two is not being minimized. It appears that in general the protological and incarnational language draws on the sapiential material; the language about Jesus' death or sacrifice draws on the passion material and the early preaching; and the references to Jesus' exaltation and vindication draw on material from the psalms. The V narrative *pattern* of these hymns, discussing in turn the pre–temporal, temporal, and post–temporal nature, life, and activity of the Son, favors the suggestion that the dominant influence on these hymns is the earlier Jewish reflection on the career of Personified Wisdom. Even the return of Wisdom to a place in glory once she was rejected is found in the material from 1 Enoch. All of the hymn fragments include protological material at least by implication, which is hardly surprising if the Wisdom material is the dominant influence here. As has already been mentioned on various occasions, Wisdom thinking to the extent that it is theology is a form of creation theology and thus one should not be surprised that a considerable amount of space could be devoted to what was true of the Son before and during the event of creation in a Christian Wisdom hymn. Indeed, in some of the christological hymns at least as much time (and in some instances more time) is spent on protological matters than on anything else (cf. e.g. Colossians 1 and John 1). Christ's career is envisioned as having both heavenly and earthly scope and the attempt to express adequately the theological significance of this career led early Jewish Christians to draw on the most exalted language they could find – Jewish Wisdom speculation, coupled to some degree with messianic interpretation of the Psalms, and soteriological reflections on Christ's death. Since Wisdom thought is a form of creation theology it is also not surprising that it is in these sorts of Christian hymns (rather than, for instance, in hymns which were simply a form of messianic exegesis of a psalm) that we find the first reflections about what it might mean to say that the pre–existent redeemer took on human flesh or became a human being.

I would thus differ with Hengel about the sapiential influence reflecting a later stage of development of these hymns.[20] In view of the degree of development of the personification of Wisdom in early Judaism well before these christological hymns were composed, there is no good reason in principle why this material could not have been used by the earliest Jewish Christians when these hymns were first composed. Indeed, the use of *both* the sapiential material and the Christological use of the psalms to compose these hymns points to early Jewish Christians, still closely connected with Judaism and its living holy traditions and ways of contemporizing Scripture, as the composers of these hymns. If any elements seem to be added later by Paul and others, it

Christianity, 17–41, a standard psalmic thanksgiving formula is not used in connection with these hymns, and furthermore, the psalms of thanksgiving do not seem to have been the main quarry used to construct these hymns (25).

[20] M. Hengel, *Between Jesus and Paul*, 94.

is the making explicit that the rejection of Wisdom in the person of Christ entailed death on a cross, the making of peace thereby, the offering of purification for sins, and the like. In short, particulars are added later about the historical death of Jesus and its significance. It does not necessarily follow from this that atonement theology is a later invention of Paul, Mark, or others but it does mean that the passion and resurrection narrative material or the early preaching about the same is not *the* primary source for these hymns.[21] Indeed, in the later hymns or hymn fragments found in 1 Tim. 3.16 and John 1 references to Christ's death and its implications are notably absent, and in the hymns in general not resurrection *per se* but exaltation to heaven (in particular to the right hand of God) or vindication is spoken of (cf. Phil. 2:9; 1 Tim. 3:16; Heb. 1:3b).[22]

R. P. Martin argues that the descent/ascent model replaced an earlier "Judaic" contrast involving rejection/vindication seen in the Acts kerygma. This, however, is too simplistic; both descent/ascent and vindication are seen in Philippians 2, the earliest of these hymns, as well as vindication in one of the latest, 1 Tim. 3:16. One must keep steadily in mind that the V pattern *and* the theme of rejection are already found in the earlier Jewish material about personified Wisdom.[23]

The point of these remarks is just this – these hymns do not appear to be hymnic adaptations of the early Christian kerygma or basic teaching about Jesus' death and resurrection. One should look for their provenance elsewhere. Even where soteriology is suggested in these hymn fragments one must not forget that in the Wisdom of Solomon, written probably only a few decades before the Christological hymns, not only does one find various hymns

---

[21] One must be careful about judging such matters purely on the basis of Q, since it is unlikely that Q reflects any community's whole christological or soteriological thinking. On the other hand, the general lack of much developed atonement theology in Acts, *except* possibly on the lips of Paul in Acts (cf. e.g. Acts 20.28), makes one wonder if it did not take a while for the early Christians to fathom the full weight and significance of Jesus' death and draw out its positive implications. The early summaries in Acts suggest that the earliest Christians continued to go to the temple (cf. Acts 2:5ff, 2:46, 5:20), and one wonders if this did not include, among other activities, offering sacrifices. Even the speech of Stephen in Acts 7 does not critique the offering of sacrifices *per se*, but only Jewish corruption and sin in various forms, and the supposition that God dwells in houses made by human hands (7:47ff). Surely the Pauline letters, especially Galatians, bear clear witness to the fact that many early Jewish Christians continued to be observant Jews. Paul is castigated by some for living like a Gentile and breaking down the barriers of customs that separate Jew and Gentile (e.g. circumcision, table fellowship). Paul's letters are all written to people who lived in the Diaspora and thus it is not surprising that temple sacrifices are not a topic of any significant discussion in the apostle's writings. Perhaps Paul was the first to clearly articulate a theology of the atoning death of Christ.

[22] It is possible that the reference in John 1:14 about having seen his glory may allude to the resurrection, but Jesus in the Fourth Gospel is presented as full of grace and truth throughout his career, so even here it seems doubtful. The difficult phrase "vindicated in spirit" or "by the Spirit" in 1 Tim. 3.16 could possibly allude to resurrection. In any case this is not the language of the early kerygma about Jesus' death and resurrection.

[23] R. P. Martin, "Some Reflections on New Testament Hymns," in *Christ the Lord. Studies Presented to Donald Guthrie*, 37–49

praising Wisdom but also the words, "Who has learned your counsel, unless you have given Wisdom and sent your Holy Spirit from on high? And thus the paths of those on earth were set right, and people were taught what pleases you, and were saved by Wisdom" (Wis. 9:17–18). E. Schüssler Fiorenza is right to stress how astonishing the exalted language of the christological hymns is, for "they do not belong to a later stage of christological development but are among the earliest christological statements found in the New Testament."[24]

In one of the more helpful studies of the christological hymns, J. T. Sanders argues with some force that "the New Testament Christological hymns had their formal matrix within the Wisdom school, and this of course coincides with the thesis that they represent a stage of a developing myth which had its prior development in Wisdom speculation."[25] Fiorenza, among others, is right to critique Sanders on the latter point and urges that what one seems to find in the christological hymns is "reflective mythology"[26] and

> "Reflective mythology" is not a living myth but is rather a form of theology appropriating mythical language, material, and patterns from different myths and uses these patterns, motifs, and configurations for its own theological concerns. Such a theology is not interested in reproducing the myth itself or the mythic materials as they stand, but rather in taking up and adapting the various mythical elements to its own theological goal and theoretical concerns.[27]

But the essential question is, what happens when one takes ideas applied to a personification or at most a hypostasization of God's Wisdom and applies them to an historical person? Does this not amount to an historicizing of the supernatural story, or to put it another way, a demythologizing of the story? Is it really helpful simply to continue to call such an adaptation a myth or even reflective mythology under such circumstances? What happens when the abstract becomes historical, concrete and particular?[28] At least from the perspective of Paul, and possibly his predecessors who created the christological

---

[24] E. Schüssler Fiorenza, "Wisdom Mythology," 19. Cf. also the new preface to the revised edition of R. P. Martin, *Carmen Christi: Philippians 2.5–11,* xiff.

[25] J. T. Sanders, *The New Testament Christological Hymns,* 136.

[26] I use the term myth to mean a story about supernatural beings, events or places without prejudice to whether and in what sense such things may be true or not. What is clear is that extra-temporal events, times, or conditions of persons *cannot* by definition be ruled in or out of existence by historical inquiry using the historical critical method, which must limit itself to data from within the time–space continuum. This is why the resurrection of Jesus on the one hand – if it was an historical event – *is* subject to historical discussion while events in heaven, for example, are not.

[27] Schüssler Fiorenza, "Wisdom Mythology," 29. She is here developing some ideas of, among others, B. Mack. Cf. Mack, "Wisdom Myth and Mythology," 46–60.

[28] This same question may be raised in the case of Ben Sira's attempt to suggest that Wisdom came to full historical expression in Torah.

hymns, it appears likely that they really believed not only in the existence of Christ beyond death in heaven as a ruling Lord but also in the existence of God's divine Son before space and time as well.[29] The latter idea, despite Dunn's qualms, apparently put no more strains on Jewish monotheism in the mind of early Jewish Christians than did the former idea.[30] In both cases, some sort of divinity or deity seems to have been predicated of Jesus, for nearly all of these hymns reflect not only on Christ and his divine doing but also on his divine being.

The Christological hymns make it very difficult to argue for a straightforward evolutionary development of early Christology. If the earliest Jewish Christians adopted and adapted Wisdom ideas and applied them to the one they worshipped as a risen Lord, one may have to speak of devolution rather than evolution of christological thought in early Christianity.[31] Bearing these things in mind, it is time to turn to the Christological hymns themselves and offer a fresh translation and interpretation of each one in turn, and then draw some conclusions about these hymns and what they tell us about the Christology and Wisdom thinking of some of the earliest Christians.

THE SERVANT SONG: PHILIPPIANS 2:6–11

Part I — Who being in the form of God,
Did not consider the having of equality to God something to take advantage of
But stripped/emptied himself
Taking the form of a servant
Being born in the likeness of human beings
And being found in appearance like a human being
Humbled himself, being obedient to the point of death, even death on the cross

Part II — That is why God has highly exalted him
and gave him the name, the one above all names,
in order that at the name of Jesus
all knees will bend–heavenly, on earth, and under the earth
and all tongues confess publicly that Jesus Christ is LORD
unto the glory of God the Father.

---

[29] Cf. especially the excellent rebuttal to Dunn's view of the pre–existence and incarnation issue in Wright, *Climax of the Covenant*, 74ff.

[30] J. D. G. Dunn, "Was Christianity a Monotheistic Faith from the Beginning?" 303–36.

[31] I submit that while it is often possible, as this study argues, to trace the development of various ideas through time, one must bear in mind that the development need not always be of an evolutionary sort – from a lower to a higher order. Indeed, often when one compares some second century Christian documents with the New Testament just the opposite seems to be the case in the realm of Christology.

The literature on this hymn, as on the Logos hymn in John 1, is so voluminous that it is impossible to survey or summarize it all.[32] Instead, the goal of this chapter is to point out the indebtedness of these hymns to Wisdom material and provide an explanation of the form and meaning of these hymns in the light of that indebtedness. The thesis of this chapter is that Wisdom material applied to Christ provides the primary source for the ideas and trajectory of these hymns at least in so far as they discuss protological matters.

There have always been those who have been skeptical about the view that the fragments under scrutiny in this chapter were originally parts of christological hymns.[33] Almost all such skeptics share one notable trait in common – they have failed to evaluate these hymns adequately in the light of late Jewish sapiential material, and especially in light of the personified Wisdom material which itself in some cases appears to be hymnic material.[34] But the degree of similarity in grammatical form, key terms, overall pattern, and often in substance in these hymns surely points to more than a remarkably similar appropriation by various New Testament authors of some common early Christian ideas that were "in the air." The correspondences are too notable not to suggest the use of earlier Christian material.

Let it also be clear from the outset that I am not arguing that the New Testament writers are simply "quoting" hymn fragments. Rather they take material over, sometimes modifying it slightly to suit the purposes for which and the contexts in which they intend to use it. Furthermore, their uses of this material in the context of their own documents undoubtedly means they agree with the sources they are using, so naturally the hymn material can also be used to deduce something about the views of Paul or the author of Hebrews, for instance, on various matters.

Christological hymns or hymn fragments are normally introduced with *hos*, in particular when they are quoted in mid–sentence. J. C. O'Neill has pointed out that this sort of usage is characteristic of the style of the late sages such as Ben Sira (cf. Sir. 46:1; 48:1ff., 12).[35] This does not mean that they are not frequently well integrated into their present context. For example, Philippians 2 consists of an exhortation to unity by means of humble mutual service and the example of Christ is appealed to as a model.[36] As G. Strecker points out, there

---

[32] For a helpful summary of the literature on Phil. 2:6–11 cf. Martin, *Carmen Christi*, xi–xxxix, 63–95.

[33] Gordon Fee, unpublished IBR lecture on Phil. 2.5ff. given at the 1990 SBL meeting; J. F. Balchin, "Colossians 1:15–20: an Early Christological Hymn? The Arguments from Style,", 65–94; J. Frankowski, "Early Christian Hymns Recorded in the New Testament. A Reconsideration of the question in light of Heb 1.3," 183–94.

[34] For the suggestion that in the Wisdom of Solomon we have parallel and polemical use of a hymnic form used elsewhere to praise Isis, cf. pp. 108ff. above.

[35] J. C. O'Neill, "The Source of Christology in Colossians," 90ff.

[36] Despite the protests of some. Contrast Martin, *Carmen Christi*, xii, to Hurtado, "Jesus as Lordly Example," 113–26.

is a terminological and possibly compositional connection between the hymn and its context by means of the theme of *tapeinoun* and *hupakon* (cf. vv 3–8 and 12).[37] The parenetic function of this Christ hymn should be clear from its introduction. The chapter is rounded out by Paul speaking of two emissaries he is sending to Philippi, Timothy and Epaphroditus, both of whom serve as further examples of humble service that leads to unity and the building up of the body of Christ. Paul is calling Christians to be self–forgetful, as the following example of Christ suggests.

The word *tapeinophrosune* is an important one. Humility was not seen as a virtue in antiquity. This word means something like base–minded, shabby, of no account, and in its adjectival form it was no compliment at all; it meant having the mentality of a slave. It is true that in the Old Testament one already finds humility and lowliness exalted, for instance in the Psalms. Paul's contribution to this development is that he connects this idea with the founder of his faith; indeed, he sees Christ as Exhibit A of what humility ought to mean. Jesus was one who took the form of a slave, or perhaps better said, a servant.

This hymn is not an attempt to contrast Christ with Adam,[38] a view largely based on a very doubtful interpretation of *harpagmos*.[39] The language of the last Adam is missing entirely from this hymn. There is nothing here about Christ beginning a new race of people, or being the first fruits of the resurrection, or being a life–giving Spirit. When one comes to the climax of the hymn where Christ is given the name *Kurios* it is appropriate to ask whether a monotheistic Jewish Christian could ever have thought that a mere human being such as Adam, even an obedient and resurrected one, had the right to be called, treated, and worshipped as the God of the Old Testament was worshipped.[40] Nor is there anything here about Jesus making a choice while on

---

[37] G. Strecker, "Redaktion und Tradition im Christushymnus Phil. 2.6–11," 63–64. In its present form of course this hymn is Pauline, as he has adopted it and adapted it for his purposes. It is not really possible to decide whether the hymn originally had a parenetic function apart from the Pauline context, but cf. Hurtado, "Jesus as Lordly Example," 113–26.

[38] The best attempt to make a case for such a view is Wright's in *The Climax of the Covenant*, 56ff., but he is trying to have it both ways – both an Adamic Christology and a Christology of pre–existence and incarnation in this hymn. Here C. F. D. Moule's critique of Dunn applies also to Wright: "Phil. ii speaks not of man's glorious destiny as something to be achieved. It speaks of one for whom it was a humiliation to take man's likeness, and who only thereafter was exalted – and exalted not to the status of man but of *Kurios*. Can this be squeezed into a purely Adamic pattern?" (Review of Dunn's *Christology*, 260.) Not only is Paul not engaging in speculation about some Ur–Adam who pre–existed in heaven, he is also not identifying Christ as an Adam figure by saying he took on the form of a *doulos*.

[39] Very helpful is the philological study of R. W. Hoover, "The Harpagmos Enigma: a Philological Solution," 95–119. He is right in stressing that the word *harpagmos* here must be evaluated as part of an idiomatic phrase, not as an isolated term. His suggested translation "as something to take advantage of" or "as something to use for his own advantage" is on the right track. His suggestion of a parallel with Rom. 15.3 is helpful, and one must stress his final conclusion: "in *every instance* which I have examined this idiomatic expression refers to something already present and at one's disposal. The question in such instances is not whether one possesses something, but whether one chooses to exploit something" (118, emphasis mine).

[40] As the allusion to Isaiah 45 surely indicates; cf. Wright, *Climax of the Covenant*, 75, 93ff.

earth parallel to Adam's choice while in the garden.[41] C. A. Wanamaker is quite right that Dunn fails to give an account of what glory or status Christ could have had and given up that was not available to other human beings. "In effect Dunn mythologizes the humanity of Christ by making him qualitatively different from the rest of humanity without any explanation of the origin of the supposed difference."[42] Also, as T. F. Glasson points out, the Genesis story says nothing about Adam or Eve desiring absolute equality with God, but rather desiring to be *like* God in the knowledge of good and evil. *En morphe Theou* is not simply equivalent here to *kata eikona Theou*, for Christ is said to set aside the former *morphe* for a *morphe doulou*.[43] Rather, one must ask whether the servant language, which distinguishes this hymn fragment from others, draws primarily on material from the Servant Songs of Isaiah or on Wisdom material, or on the former by means of its use in the latter.

It was always awkward for L. Cerfaux, J. Jeremias, D. Stanley, and others who wished to interpret this text purely in light of Isaiah, that the text has *doulos* not *pais*,[44] and furthermore that the term *doulos* seems crucial to the contrast in the hymn.[45] The insights of these scholars are not to be lightly dismissed but the problem is, as Sanders rightly points out, that they fail to notice that the servant language here comes to Paul, or whoever composed this hymn, through the later reflection on such language in Sirach and especially the Wisdom of Solomon.[46] That it is not merely a recapitulation of earlier ideas, however, is shown by Phil. 2:5–7.

---

[41] Pace J. D. G. Dunn, *Christology in the Making*, 119.

[42] C. A. Wanamaker, "Phil. 2.6–11: Son of God or Adamic Christology?" 183. The alternative to Dunn's view offered, i.e., a sonship Christology which totally neglects the Wisdom overtones of this material, is not much more convincing. Jesus is never called Son in the hymn or in its immediate context. Nor is the relevance of the observation that children bear a likeness to their parents immediately apparent. This hymn is not about parent–child relationships, even divine ones.

[43] T. F. Glasson, "Two Notes on the Philippians Hymn (II:6–11)," 133–38.

[44] Cf. L. Cerfaux, "L'hymne au Christ – Serviteur de Dieu (Phil. 2:6–11 = Isa. 52:13–53:12)," *Miscellanea Historica in honorem A. de Meyer*, Vol. I., 117–30; J. Jeremias, *The Servant of God*, and "Zu Phil. 2:7," 182–88; D. Stanley, "The Theme of the Servant of Yahweh," 421ff. That *doulos* is sometimes used to translate *ebed* in the early Servant passages (Isa. 42:19; 48:20; 49:3, 5) may not be relevant since in each case the nation of Israel is in view, not an individual person, as seems to be the case in the later Servant passages particularly Isa. 53 (noting the dialectic between "he" and "our" in the suffering servant passage, where the our is God's people collectively).

[45] Hurtado, "Jesus as Lordly Example," 122, n. 36, points out that in Paul the distinction between *doulos* and *diakonos* is important, the latter characteristically being associated with evangelistic activities and service, the former with general Christian life and obedience. Sander's suggestion that *doulos* here be used as it is in Philo (cf. *De Virtu* 74 and Heb. 1:14) of angels who are noted for their divine service is not impossible but seems more remote than the suggestion argued for here. But cf. his "Dissenting Deities and Philippians 2:1–11," 279–90.

[46] Cf. Sanders, *New Testament Christological Hymns*, 73–74. I agree with him that it is unnecessary to posit as Georgi tried to do, a specific Jewish hymn behind Philippians 2. The background is more general than that.

It cannot be stressed strongly enough that vv 5–7 are talking about a being who has a particular mindset and makes particular choices – a mindset and choices which Paul wishes his audience to emulate. Furthermore, as I. H. Marshall points out, the recapitulatory phrase, "and being found in form as a human being," is all but inexplicable if it refers to a person who has never been anything else but a human being. "[A]gain the *contrast* clearly expressed between "being in the form of God" and "becoming in the form of [human beings]" is extremely odd if the contrast is between two stages in the career of a man."[47] Furthermore, all such language is very odd indeed if Paul is simply applying the suffering servant language to Jesus here. In the Isaianic material the suffering servant gave up no divine prerogatives or heavenly existence to become a servant. It is much more convincing to suggest that various sorts of Wisdom ideas are here being predicated of Christ, including the concept of servanthood, but the Wisdom material in Sirach and the Wisdom of Solomon to some degree draws on the Isaianic material.[48] That J. Murphy O'Connor's approach to this hymn as a Wisdom piece is significantly flawed has been demonstrated by both Wanamaker and earlier by G. Howard,[49] but their criticisms are rightly directed against Murphy O'Conner's attempt to apply a Wisdom *anthropology* to this hymn, and do not apply to the case being made in this chapter.

After talking about the Wisdom who has formed humankind, Solomon in Wis. 9:4 prays "give me the Wisdom that sits by your throne, and do not reject me from among your servants, for I am your *doulos*, the son of your serving girl" (i.e. Wisdom). As the interplay in Q between Jesus as Wisdom and Jesus as Solomon figure has already been noted, it should not surprise us to find the same sort of thing here. D. Georgi was in part on the right track in pointing to the Wisdom of Solomon as the background of this material.[50] In particular, the material in Wisdom 5–7 can illuminate the second half of this hymn as well as the first half. For example, in Wis. 5:16 one hears of the righteous ones (called servants of God's kingdom in 6:4) who will receive a glorious crown; or again in 6:3ff, "for your dominion was given you from the Lord" for being obedient servants while on earth. Earlier in 5.1 the righteous are promised that they will at the final judgment stand in the presence of their oppressors who will be amazed and forced to confess the truth about them (cf. 5:4). All of this is interspersed with the discussion of hypostasized Wisdom (cf. e.g. 7:22f). Seen in this light, Philippians 2 becomes a hymn on the one hand about a royal figure who, like Solomon, humbles himself by becoming God's servant, obeys God,

[47] I. H. Marshall, "Incarnational Christology in the New Testament," in *Christ the Lord. Studies in Christology Presented to Donald Guthrie*, 6.

[48] Sanders, *New Testament Christological Hymns*, 66ff.

[49] G. Howard, "Phil. 2:6–11 and the Human Christ," 369–72.

[50] He argues in particular for Wisdom 5 and 8 (!) being alluded to here, the latter of which is somewhat problematic. D. Georgi, "Der vorPaulinische Hymnus Phil 2, 6–11," in *Zeit und Geschichte Dankesgabe an R. Bultmann zum 80 Geburtstag*, 263–93.

and is rewarded in royal fashion in the end, and on the other hand it is a story about a king who *is* the very embodiment of Wisdom, both before, during, and after his earthly career, as is shown by his behavior during all three stages of his career.

One may also consider the words of Ben Sira: "The wisdom of the humble lifts their heads high, and seats them among the great. Do not praise individuals for their good looks, or loathe anyone because of their appearance alone [cf. e.g. Isaiah 53]... Many kings have had to sit on the ground, but one who was never thought of has worn a crown" (Sir. 11:1ff). One may also consider Sir. 3:17ff: "My child perform your tasks with humility . . . the greater you are the more you must humble yourself; so you will find favor in the sight of the Lord. For great is the might of the Lord; and by the humble he is glorified." Is Phil. 2 not a story about the exaltation of the obedient and humble one, one who had humbled himself willingly? The juxtaposition of: (1) pre–existence language; (2) servant language; (3) humility and exaltation language; and (4) the bestowal of kingship and kingdom is found in both the Christ hymn in Phil. 2 and also in the sapiential material in Sirach and the Wisdom of Solomon. I submit that the whole of this hymn, except the Pauline additions (e.g. "even death on the cross"), probably derived from early Jewish Christian attempts to paint an adequately laudatory portrait of Christ reflecting on and using sapiential material. A few comments on some exegetical particulars and implications of such an interpretation must now be made.

G. Hawthorne is right that v 5 really does parallel the frame of mind Christians ought to have, and the frame of mind Christ both as pre–existent one and as incarnate one did have. He deliberately took a lower place. He deliberately did not take advantage of the divine prerogatives which he had and were rightfully his. He deliberately submitted to death on a cross – a punishment reserved for the most notable and notorious criminals, slaves, and rebels.

Three words are used to describe Christ's "form", likeness, or appearance – *morphe, homoioimati, schemati*. Of these three the one that most obviously connotes outward recognizable appearance is *schemati*, not the other two. *Morphe* suggests the way in which a thing or person appears to one's senses. However, *morphe* always signifies an outward form which truly, accurately, and fully expresses the real being which underlies it. Thus, when applied to Christ it must mean that he manifested a form that truly represented the nature and very being of God. This is why there is the further phrase, "the having equality to God". The hymn makes clear that Christ really had this. Grammaticially *isa* could be a adverb which if translated as such would lead to an elliptical rendering such as, "the being *equally* (something) to God". Presumably the something is the phrase *en morphe theou* from v 6a. Thus the expanded phrase would mean, "the being equally in the form of God as God [is]". Wright points out that the use of the articular infinitive (*to einai*) normally refers to something previously mentioned, and this usage is known elsewhere in Paul (cf. Rom. 7:18; 2 Cor. 7:11).[51] It has been argued that this adverb has a neuter plural ending and is being used adjectivally.[52] If so, then one must ask why a masculine adjectival form was not chosen and why it is in the plural. This would lead to a rendering something like "the having equal (attributes) to God".[53] In either case the meaning is that Christ by right and by nature had what God had.[54] As for the third term, *homoiomati*, it does mean likeness, but again the sense is not an illusory outer appearance that belies the real nature, but rather what is being said is that Christ really took on human likeness. He was truly human.

Dunn's interpretation of the combination *morphe doulou* as becoming a slave (like Adam as a result of the fall) makes no sense of the text or its context. The function of this hymn as Paul uses it is to inculcate humble self–sacrificial service, not slavery. Furthermore, it is hardly likely that Paul is trying to argue here that Jesus, like Adam, became a slave to sin.[55] The great failure of Dunn's interpretation is that while admitting in general that Wisdom material affected early christological thinking, he fails to apply this insight to the hymn in Philippians 2. When Wisdom's attributes are transferred and predicated of Christ, it is only natural to assume that since it is said of Wisdom that she was present at the creation of the world, and in the later Wisdom hymns apparently a helper in the act of creation, this is also assumed or stated to be the case about the person Jesus Christ. This becomes especially clear in the christological hymns at least as early as the one in Colossians 1, but the idea is very likely not absent here in Philippians 2. The choice being described in Philippians 2 is the choice to take on human flesh, a choice only a pre–existent one could make.[56] Furthermore, as the parallel passage in 2 Cor. 8:9 suggests, not only was a conscious choice made by the pre–existent one but also an *exchange* of something was involved – some sort of riches for some sort of poverty. Note also both the contrastive *alla* in Philippians 2, and the verb *ekenosen* which must have some significant content to it.

---

[51] Wright, *Climax of the Covenant*, 83.

[52] BDF 434.1.

[53] J. B. Lightfoot, *St. Paul's Epistle to the Philippians*, 110 is right to say that if the reference was to the person one would have expected *ison*, not *isa*.

[54] It makes no sense, if this is a *plural* predicate adjective, to render it "having equal office, equal status, equal position." It must refer to something Christ could have had that amounted to more than just an abstract singular concept like status. Nor does the rendering "equality" as in "the having equality to God" much improve things. It would be better either to render it as an adverb modifying *einai* or as a plural neuter adjective.

[55] *Pace* Dunn, *Christology in the Making*, 115ff. and cf. the telling critique by C. E. B. Cranfield, "Some Comments on Professor J. D. G. Dunn's *Christology in the Making* with Special Reference to the Evidence of the Epistle to the Romans," in *The Glory of Christ in the New Testament*, 271.

[56] The arguments of J. Murphy O' Connor, "Christological Anthropology in Phil. 2.6–11," 25–50, are no more convincing than Dunn's. The pre–existence issue is raised immediately by the use of the Wisdom material in the hymns to say things about the career of Christ even before his earthly existence. Only by ignoring this background can one claim that one has to bring the pre–existence idea to the text to find it here.

The word *harmagmos* has caused endless debate and dispute. It has been assumed to mean either robbery (as the Western Church came by and large to interpret it), in which case the verse reads that Christ did not consider it robbery to be equal in attributes to God (i.e. he was no usurper or interloper grabbing for more than what was rightfully his)[57], or it may mean as J. B. Lighfoot suggested that Christ did not consider being equal to God consisted in clutching at something,[58] perhaps his rightful divine prerogatives, or most likely as R. W. Hoover has argued it means not taking advantage of something one rightfully has.[59] This latter sense makes the best sense of the text.

It is important that one should give full weight to the contrast between vv 6b and 7a; Christ did not see being equal with God something he had to take advantage of, rather he stripped himself or emptied himself. G. F. Hawthorne is frankly too anxious to deny that Christ stripped himself of anything when he became incarnate.[60] However, the verb stripped or emptied must have some content to it, and it is not adequate to say that Christ did not subtract anything because he actually added a human nature. The latter is true enough but the text says he *did* empty himself or strip himself. It does not tell us explicitly what he emptied himself of. However, the contrast between vv 6b and 7a is very suggestive. It suggests Christ set aside his rightful divine prerogatives, or perhaps his *doxa*.[61] This probably does not mean he set aside his divine nature, but it does surely indicate some sort of self–limitation, some sort of setting aside of divine rights or privileges or glory.[62] He lived among humans as one of them, drawing on the power of the Spirit and prayer through which God revealed much to him. He lived as a servant king among humankind, even outshining Solomon in this regard.

---

[57] C. F. D. Moule, "Further Reflexions on Phil. 2:5–11," in *Apostolic History and the Gospel*, 264–76. On 266 he argues for the translation 'as consisting in snatching.'

[58] Lightfoot, *Philippians*, 111, argued in the last century that *harpagmos hegesato* was an idiomatic phrase meaning to prize highly, to set store by, or to clutch greedily. The idea of robbery for *harpagmos* had largely dropped out of sight by New Testament times, and the Greek Fathers almost universally understood the phrase as Lightfoot suggests. Cf. Glasson, "Two Notes on the Philippians Hymn," 133–36. Clearly the weakest of the translations in terms of the philological evidence is the robbery/seizure translation.

[59] Hoover, "Harpagmos", 118–19, points out against a common view that the idiomatic expression with *harpagmos* does not mean 'to retain something' or 'to hold something fast'. The linguistic evidence is against such a translation; cf. also rightly Moule, "Further Reflexion," 267.

[60] G. F. Hawthorne, *Philippians* (Waco: Word, 1983), 78ff. So too Wright, *Climax of the Covenant*, 83ff. who seems at first to assume that *ekenosen* means no more than that Christ took a different *attitude* towards the attributes or rights he had and kept all along. But surely "emptying" in v 6 refers to an action that parallels the action in v 7 of "taking on". Later Wright (p. 92) says Christ renounced the rank and privileges which he had. This is right, but what does this entail? If he renounced certain rights and privileges, this means at the very least that during his human existence he did not draw on these things. In short he accepted certain limitations.

[61] Wanamaker, "Phil. 2.6–11," 184–86.

[62] Perhaps it means that Christ did not act or draw on his ability to be omnipotent, omnipresent, and omniscient (that is, he accepted human limitations of time, space, and knowledge).

But Christ not only stripped himself in this way but also shunned any rightful human accolades or dignity; he took on the very form of a servant or slave. He identified himself with the lowest of the low, and he died a slave's death. This hymn places an especial stress on the fact that the pre–existent Christ had a choice about these matters and he *chose* to act in the way he did. Thus it is stressed that Christ was *obedient* even to the point of dying on the cross. He could have done otherwise.

The reason for this stress is that Paul is engaging in an argument about what the *imitatio Christi* means. Paul does not think it is ridiculous idealism to appeal to the example of Christ as a moral pattern for believers; rather, he believes by God's Spirit and grace Christians can be obedient even unto death. Paul seems to stress the Gospel principle in this hymn that those who humble themselves (an action, not an inferiority complex) will be exalted. If this is so, then Paul is suggesting to his converts that there will be a crown of glory for them as there was for Christ whom God exalted to the highest place.

The name which is above all names is surely the name of God, and in this hymn the name that Jesus is given when he is raised and exalted beyond death is not Jesus – he had that name since human birth – but the name of God in the Old Testament, i.e., LORD, which is the LXX equivalent to Yahweh. This is especially clear because Paul is alluding here to Isa. 45:21ff. where it is says that only God is God and Savior of his people, and only to God should anyone bow. At the name of Jesus all will bow and recognize his new and rightful title of Lord when history ends. This is an example of what Wright calls "christological monotheism" which while asserting the divinity of Christ at the same time "never intends to assert that Christ is divine in a sense apart from or over against the one true God."[63] This is unquestionably a new formulation of Jewish monotheism which draws strongly on what was previously said of Wisdom, but transforms it and goes beyond it, not only applying Wisdom ideas to Christ, but transforming them so that the author could speak about a divine person, not simply a personification of a divine attribute.

The hymn then is divided into two parts between what Christ chooses to do (he is the actor in vv 6–8) and what God has done for him in vv 9–11. Notice that confessing Jesus is Lord (very likely the earliest Christian confession) does not detract from but in fact adds to the Father's glory, for he has made all this possible by raising and exalting Jesus. Verses 10–11 suggest that all sentient beings will make this confession including angels, humans, and demons. This does not necessarily mean all will in the end be converted. More likely as in Wisdom 5 it means all will be forced to recognize the truth.

As the discussion of these hymns proceeds, it is important to bear in mind that if they all came out of the same sort of early Jewish Christian environment, then interpretations of them that make clear their general

[63] Wright, *Climax of the Covenant*, 116.

similarities are more likely to be correct than interpretations that radically distinguish one hymn from another. That is, these hymns share a cluster of ideas in common, and all things being equal the interpretation of these ideas in one hymn ought, with some room for novelty, to comport generally with their interpretation in the other hymns. In regard to the hymn just investigated, one can say that already as early as the formulation of the hymn in Philippians 2 or at the very least as early as the Pauline use and modification of the hymn one finds a new view of monotheism emerging which involves Christ as God's Wisdom in person – someone who had and has equal attributes with God, and in the end is given the same throne name.[64]

ODE TO THE COSMIC CHRIST: COLOSSIANS 1:15–20

Part I — Who is the image of the invisible God,
firstborn of all creation,
because in Him were created all things
in the heavens and upon the earth,
the seen and the unseen,
whether thrones or dominions
or sovereignties or powers.
Everything [created] through Him was also created for Him.
And he is before everything and everything coheres in Him.
And he is the head of the body, the Church.

Part II — Who is the beginning (source), the firstborn from the dead in order that he may take precedence in all things,
because in Him is pleased to dwell all the "pleroma"
and through Him is reconciled everything for Him,
making peace through the blood of his cross
whether things on earth or in the heavens.[65]

The parallels between this hymn and the Wisdom of Solomon are so numerous that they must be listed at the outset of the discussion.[66] W. Wink rightly argues that most of those who have tried to parcel out the hymn to source and redaction have failed to take into account "the heavy dependence of the entire passage on the Wisdom of Solomon,"[67] with a few possible minor Pauline additions.

---

[64] I will argue in the next chapter that as 1 Cor. 8:6 shows Paul had already made this sort of mental leap at least by the early 50s.

[65] For another, though similar, view taken here of the structure, cf. Wright, *Climax of the Covenant*, 102–104. Wright argues for an ABBA pattern with vv 15a and 18c being parallel and vv 17 and 18a being parallel.

[66] E. Schweizer, "The Church as the Missionary Body of Christ," 7: "One could quote the parallels to the first stanza word by word in Wisdom literature."

[67] Wink, "Hymn of the Cosmic Christ," 235. The hymn in Colossians 1, however, is as far as it could be from a Gnostic hymn, in view of the very positive outlook it takes of both creation and redemption in Christ. Cf. Wright, *Climax of the Covenant*, 107.

(1) Wis. 7:26 – "For she is… a spotless mirror of the working of God, and an image of his goodness" (cf. Col. 1:15a).
(2) Wis. 6:22 – "I will tell you what Wisdom is and how she came to be… I will trace her course *from the beginning of creation*" (cf. Col. 1:15b).
(3) Wis. 1:14: "for he created all things so that they might exist" (cf. Col. 1:16a).
(4) Wis 5:23d; 6:21; 7:8 – on thrones, scepters (Col. 1:16d).
(5) Wis. 7:24b – "For Wisdom… because of her pureness pervades and pentrates all things" (cf. Col. 1:16–17, 19);
(6) Wis. 1:7 – "that which holds all things together knows what is said" (and) 8.1b – "She reaches mightily from one end of the earth to the other, and she orders all things well" (cf. Col. 1:17b).
(7) Wis. 7:29c – on priority and superiority (cf. Col. 1:17a, 18d).

One may also wish to compare the Wisdom hymns in Sirach, particularly 1:4: "Wisdom was created before all other things" and in the first person in 24:9: "Before the ages, in the beginning, he created me, and for all ages I shall not cease to be."[68]

It might be possible to conclude from the listing of these parallels that the Christ hymn very likely stopped at Col. 1:18 or 19 originally, but it is more likely that what this shows is that Wink's judgment must be somewhat tempered – some of the material in this hymn, though only a minority, is drawn from reflection on some other source, in this case probably the story of Jesus' death.[69] One cannot say of Sophia that she is the head of the body.[70] Even if Col. 1:20b proves to be a Pauline addition, it is possible that the original phrase is found in Col. 1:22 which speaks of reconciliation in his body through death. E. Schweizer argues that while the first stanza can be explained from the sapiential material in Sirach and the Wisdom of Solomon, stanza two is originally Christian.[71] But only parts of the second stanza, in particular the so–called Pauline additions plus the body = Church language seem to be specifically Christian – the Wisdom influence is not absent even in the second stanza.

When one studies these parallels closely, it also becomes evident that the composer of this hymn is not simply transferring what was once said of Wisdom to Christ, for there are various small emendations or additions along the way. Thus, for example, while it appears in the Wisdom hymns in both Sirach and the Wisdom of Solomon that the authors are speaking of something

---

[68] J. Jervell, *Imago Dei. Gen. 1.26f im Spätjudentum, in der Gnosis und in den paulinischen Briefen*, 200–13.

[69] It is a puzzle why Wink, having cited all these parallels, then proceeds to focus on parallels with a Gnostic source, the *Tripartite Tractate* (Trimorphic Protennoia), which is clearly later than the New Testament data. As J. Ashton, "The Transformation of Wisdom. A Study of the Prologue of John's Gospel," 182, n. 4, notes, this material is much too late to have been of direct influence on New Testament hymns, even the one in John 1.

[70] Sanders, *New Testament Christological Hymns*, 82.

[71] E. Schweizer, "Die Kirche als Leib Christi im dem paulinishcen Antilegomena," 243–44.

created by God, this is not so certain in the Colossian hymn (cf. below). Furthermore, the composer is not simply interested in form for form's sake. O'Neill says the hymn uses the language of public declaration, where clauses and phrases and participles are piled up as an act of praise without proper connectives or regard for proper grammar.[72]

E. Norden long ago pointed out that the absence of articles, piling up of participles, and the frequent use of relative clauses is a formal clue that one is dealing with a hymn as is a closing doxology of some sort (cf. Phil. 2.9ff).[73] To this can be added the absence of the name of the one praised and frequent use of third person singular aorist verbs.[74] What this suggests is that the praise and the greatness of the theme to some extent engendered and explains the form. The composer cannot pile up enough superlatives.

The similarities between the hymn in Philippians 2 and that in Colossians 1 have often been noted, yet there is no servant language in Colossians 1, a fact which in itself suggests that Philippians 2 can not be explained by means of Isaiah alone.[75] Philippians 2 and Colossians 1 being the most similar of the hymns may suggest that they are the earliest and least revised of the lot. But this should not cause one to overlook the differences – Colossians 1 is about a cosmic victory while Philippians 2 is primarily about a personal vindication.[76]

The majority of scholars are very likely right that this is a pre–Pauline hymn for at least two important reasons. First, there is the distinctive non–Pauline vocabulary and content (e.g. Paul calls Christ the first fruits from the dead in 1 Cor. 15 not the firstborn). Secondly, this hymn manifests the basic V pattern so characteristic of early sapiential christological hymns, chronicling the drama of creation, salvation, and glorification in its three christological stages. Christ is seen as creator, sustainer, and redeemer all wrapped up into one in Col. 1:15ff. These hymns reveal that early Christians were not at all bashful about not only giving Christ divine names but also ascribing the deeds that only deity can do to him. Here we are told that in him the "pleroma," i.e., the fullness [of God], not just a part, was pleased to dwell – a point Paul amplifies in 2:9.

It is quite possible that Paul has added several elements to this hymn. The phrase "the church" may be a Pauline explanatory addition in v 18. What is interesting and unique about this particular hymn is that the nadir of the V is not the incarnation, but rather the body. Though this might originally have referred to the cosmos, it does not in Paul's use – it refers to the church which

---

[72] O'Neill, "Source of Christology in Colossians," 87–100. He does not think there is a hymn here, but apparently some sort of hymnic prose.

[73] E. Norden, *Agnostos Theos*, 168ff., 201ff.

[74] Martin, *Carmen Christi*, xxxiv.

[75] Rightly, Sanders, *Christological Hymns*, 75.

[76] Sanders, *Christological Hymns*, 86, n. 1. The theme of cosmic victory seems also to be found in the so–called "Song of the Star" in Ignatius, *Ephes*. 19:2–3.

is the locus where Christ is even now present on earth. Paul does go on to refer to "making peace through the blood of his cross" which was perhaps the original nadir of the song which the apostle then transposed to later in the hymn.

Those scholars who see only two strophes in this hymn – vv 15–18a and vv 18b–20 – are likely right. It is possible that 18a should be seen as a sort of transitional part of the hymn. That there are only two strophes is shown by the following parallels in the two parts: (1) *hos* and *hos* begins each strophe in 15a and 18b; (2) "he is the image" corresponds to "he is the beginning or source"; (3) *prototokos* in v 15 and v 18; (4) each of the relative clauses is in turn followed by a causal clause *hoti* in v 16, "because in him all things were created" and v 19, "because in him the fullness"; (5) the cosmic dimension rounds out each strophe: first the cosmic dimension of his creation role, v 16 – "whether thrones" – and then the cosmic dimension of his redemption role—"whether things on earth." The term *pas* recurs frequently and we have the emphatic use of *autos* in vv 17–18. The hymn keeps ringing the changes on in *him*, through *him*, for *him*, *he himself*, stressing the christological focus.

In regard to the meaning of the hymn, several key points need to be mentioned. Christ is said to be the image of the invisible God, but this does not mean he is merely a likeness of him, but rather that he is the exact representation of him, in character and otherwise. When the hymn says he is the firstborn of all creation this probably does not refer to his being created, for it is about to go on to say he is the author of all creation. Clearly he is depicted here as on the side of the creator in the creator–creature distinction. *Prototokos* then emphasizes Christ's relationship to that creation, just as *eikon* emphasizes the relationship to the creator.[77] Schweizer points out that in Philo "image" and "beginning" are two interchangeable predications of heavenly Wisdom.[78] Possibly the term *prototokos* reflects the Old Testament idea found for instance in Ps. 89:27 where God promises to make the King his firstborn – the meaning is preeminent, supreme in rank, not necessarily created. In this usage there is also some sense of temporal priority. Thus the point is that he is prior to and supreme over all creation. When the term is used again in v 18 the meaning is also of temporal priority but again the idea of being created is not present – Christ was not literally born or created by the resurrection – he was transformed by it. Thus in both cases the term connotes temporal priority and supremacy, not createdness.[79]

---

[77] It is interesting, however, that T. F. Glasson, "Col. 1.18, 15 and Sirach 24," 154–56 notes that the Old Latin of Sir. 24:3 reads, "I went forth out of the mouth of the Most High, firstborn before every creature… and in every people and in every nation I had the preeminence." Cf. Ps. Cyprian, *Testimonies* 2:1. Philo, *Quest. in Gen.* 4:97, calls Wisdom "first born mother of all things." Cf. *De Fug.* 109; *De Virtu.* 62. In some cases it is as important to note how the biblical writers alter their Wisdom source as how they re–present it.

[78] Schweizer, "The Church as the Missionary Body of Christ," 1–11; cf. Philo, *Leg. All.*, 1.43.

[79] In view of the parallels with the Wisdom material, it is possible that this hymn originally did speak of some sort of pre–temporal creation of the redeemer, but Paul does not understand the hymn in that sense, and it is impossible to reconstruct in any full sense the hymn's earlier form.

Verse 16 stresses that Christ even created the supernatural powers. The names – thrones, dominions, sovereignties, powers – were apparently rather common terms for such beings.[80] What is not clear is whether or not Paul envisions all of these as good angels/supernatural forces. Apparently he does. What this hymn seems to presuppose but does not speak of is the fall of some of the angelic host as well as humans for otherwise they would not need reconciling and clearly v 20 speaks of reconciling things in heaven.

I. H. Marshall is right to say that the language of Col. 1:15–20 surely refers to the personal activity of one who is the image of God and participates in the acts of creation. This is the only logical conclusion when one sees that the author is applying the language about the role of Wisdom in creation to a person whom the author worships. The first stanza of this hymn is not merely about the *power* that God exercised in creation being fully revealed or embodied in Christ.[81] The concept of incarnation is present, however inchoate or unexplained, in *all* these christological hymns, probably even including 1 Tim. 3:16. This is hardly unthinkable for early Jewish Christians. It is in fact simply a further development of the idea found in Sir. 24 which suggests that Wisdom expressed herself in concrete historical form in the Torah. To be sure this does not amount to a discussion of a *personal* incarnation, but once early Christians began to transfer what had previously been said about Wisdom and in particular Wisdom as manifested in Torah to Jesus, such a development is not totally surprising or unexpected. C. R. Holladay is right to criticize Dunn for giving too little attention to the partial antecedents for the idea of the incarnation.[82]

While there is an element of uniqueness involved in talking about the pre–existence and incarnation of a personal being who took on flesh and became Jesus the Messiah, the sapiential material with its exalted praise of Wisdom helped prepare the way for such an idea. It is not accidental that the most clearly Incarnational hymn, the Johannine Prologue, is also the most clearly sapiential one, as shall be made clear shortly. It is equally clear that some of the earliest interpreters and users of the Christological hymns and hymn patterns understood these hymns in such a sense. Consider for example the quotation of the so–called Naasene hymn found in Hippolytus *Refutatio* 5.10.1 where the redeemer is clearly presented as a heavenly being distinct from the

[80] In addition to the already listed references from the sapiential material, cf. *Test. Levi* 3:7–8 – "in heaven below them are…thrones and dominions"; *1* Enoch 61:10 – "all the angels of power"; 2 Enoch 20:1 – "I saw there [i.e. in the seventh heaven] dominions,… and the authorities, cherubim… thrones".

[81] Contrast Marshall, "Incarnational Christology," 9 to Dunn, *Christology in the Making*, 187–94. Marshall is also right that the mention of the body of his flesh in 1:22 would be quite gratuitous if the redeemer was here envisioned as simply a human being. "[T]he phrase is meaningful only as a way of emphasizing the fact that the One described in the preceding 'hymn' became incarnate in order to die on the cross" (8).

[82] C. R. Holladay, "New Testament Christology: Some Considerations of Method," 264.

Father who pleads: "Therefore, send me Father; Bearing the seals I will descend, I will pass through all the Aeons, I will disclose all mysteries...."[83]

Verse 17 indicates not only the priority of Christ to all things, but also that he is the glue, the one in whom all things cohere or are established. He is the sustainer of all things, which is a present ongoing role. These same sorts of things in regard to a role in creation and sustaining the universe are said about Wisdom in Wis. 1:7ff (cf. Sir. 43:26).

Despite P. T. O'Brien's special pleading, the term *ekklesia* surely does refer to the universal church which is Christ's body, for the emphasis in this hymn is on "all", on the universal, both in the human and in the natural realm.[84] The point is, the term *ekklesia* refers to the people of God, and does not always carry the sense of the assembled people of God. This is made clear with the body metaphor here, for that metaphor in a cosmic context like this has universal implications, and does not just refer to the body of believers in one place. Here one finds the first development of the idea of Christ as head of the body. That is, Christ is identified with a particular part of the body, whereas in 1 Corinthians and Romans "body" is simply a metaphor about the interrelationships between believers in the church. It is used here to speak of the relationship of Christ to church and this is a further step christologically speaking.

The second strophe begins by saying that Christ is the beginning or source (probably the former) of the resurrection from the dead (note it does not say from death, but from the realm of dead persons). Verse 18c makes clear the sense of *prototokos* in both cases – it is a matter of Christ taking precedence both in the realm of creation and in the realm of redemption. Glasson points out that the Old Latin version of Sir. 24:10, which may preserve the original reading, has *primatum habui*, in which case Col. 1:18c may be another example of the use of Wisdom material to construct the hymn.[85]

The term "pleroma" in later Gnostic thought came to mean all the intermediaries, the aeons, and things that existed between God and the material realm as a sort of buffer zone so that God would not be tainted by the material which was thought to be inherently evil. The term does not have that meaning here. Colossians 2:9 is the proper commentary on what it means here. In Christ the fullness of deity was pleased to dwell. This is very likely a polemical statement against the idea that there were other divine beings that

---

[83] This is the translation of R. McL. Wilson found in W. Forester, *Gnosis. A Selection of Gnostic Texts*, Vol. 1, 282. Cf. D. M. Mackinnon, "Review of Dunn's *Christology in the Making*," 364. To be sure this is very likely a Gnostic hymn, but Gnostics probably did not invent the idea of the pre–existent Son of God.

[84] P. T. O'Brien, *Colossians, Philemon*, 48–50, 57–61.

[85] Glasson, "Col. 1.18, 15 and Sirach 24," 154–56. Glasson is also right to point out that in the same context in Sir. 24:3ff. there is reference to Wisdom covering the earth, dwelling in the highest heaven, compassing the vault of heaven and the like, which should be compared to Col. 1:16: "in the heavens and upon the earth."

had some divinity in them. This seems to have been part of the theology of the false teachers in Colossae (cf. Col. 2:18 on reverencing or placating angels).

It is often asked whether "all" really means all in v 20 in which case there is universalism here – Christ will in the end save all persons and creatures and the universe. No one will finally be lost. O'Brien, however, rightly suggests that some will bend the knee to Christ by being forced to do so in the end, not because of faith in and trust in Christ. The universe will indeed be at peace in the end, but some will have that peace in them, and some will simply be pacified – laid to rest.[86] The material already referred to in Wis. 5:1ff. supports such an interpretation, and in view of the other parallels between Wisdom of Solomon and the Colossian hymn, such an interpretation is likely correct. This verse does make clear the idea that redemption is not just for those on earth.

Some have seen a christological hymn fragment in Eph. 2:13 or 14–18, but for formal and content reasons this appears to be a soteriological reflection on the implications of the death of Jesus, perhaps in particular as it is expressed in the hymn in Col. 1:20. The Ephesians passage then seeks to make clear the implications of Jesus' death for the reconciliation of Jews and Gentiles. Now, through Christ's death, even Gentiles have been brought near to God. This has happened because Christ himself (noting the emphatic *autos*) is the believer's peace. It is interesting that the author of this material seems to be attempting to answer or rebut the arguments of a Ben Sira who maintains that Torah is the locus of Wisdom on earth and that which brings God's people together. In Ephesians the abolition of Torah is necessary in order that one new person could be created out of the two peoples, Jew and Gentile. In this way both groups could be reconciled to God in one body, rather than having separate plans of reconciliation for Jews and Gentiles. As Eph. 2:13–18 is likely not a hymn but rather a theological reflection on the Colossians hymn, it is time to turn to another hymn fragment.

THE VINDICATION VERSE: 1 TIMOTHY 3:16

Who was revealed in flesh,
vindicated by the Spirit,
seen by angels,
proclaimed among the nations,
believed in throughout the world
taken up in glory.

This hymn fragment is not merely another variant of the the sort of hymn found in Philippians 2 or Colossians 1 but a separate hymn altogether. Evidence that

[86] O'Brien, *Colossians*, 53ff.

it was not simply created by the author of the Pastorals comes from the observation that it seems to be discernible in 1 Pet. 3:18–22 which says in part:

> For Christ also suffered for sins
> Once for all, the righteous for the unrighteous...
> He was put to death in the flesh,
> but brought to life in the spirit,
> in which also he went and made a proclamation
> to the spirits in prison...
> through the resurrection of Jesus Christ,
> who has gone into heaven
> and is at the right hand of God,
> with angels, authorities, and powers
> made subject to him.

Some have questioned whether it might be better to speak of a confessional fragment here, as it is missing many of the formal features of early christological hymns such as the use of participles and *parallelismus membrorum*. It is also far too brief for stanzas, and in this fragment the redeemer is not an actor, but is rather acted on – the verbs are all passives.[87] It must be remembered that in the second stanza of the christological hymns Christ is basically acted on, not an actor, and I would suggest that the lack of some of the other formal features is a sign of the *lateness* of this hymn fragment, but it does begin like other christological hymns with *hos*.[88]

Though 1 Tim. 3:16 is very likely a quotation from a popular early Christian hymn, it is not perfectly clear how one should divide it up into verses (three sets of two, six different lines). It has assonance as well as a certain rhythm and as already mentioned is introduced by *hos*.[89] The subject matter is again the career of Christ, but in 1 Tim. 3:16 there is only the barest hint of protology (*ephanerothe* presumably implies pre–existence), and none at all in 1 Pet. 3. Jeremias has even suggested that all of 1 Tim. 3:16 refers to an ascent to a heavenly throne, followed by the presentation and enthronement of the king, but in the light of 1 Pet. 3:18 *ephanerothe en sarki* surely refers to earthly existence, or possibly even death.[90] The vast majority of scholars would accept the view that the material in the Pastorals represents a later development than that in Philippians or Colossians. This being the case, this may suggest that an increased focus on the post–existence part of Christ's career to the general

[87] Sanders, *NT Christological Hymns*, 16.

[88] The thorough study of this hymn by R. H. Gundry, "The Form, Meaning and Background of the Hymn quoted in 1 Timothy 3.16," in *Apostolic History and the Gospel*, 203–22 should be consulted.

[89] "Who", not *ho* or *theos*, both later modifications due to copyist error or misunderstanding the reference to be to the mystery of the faith.

[90] J. Jeremias, *Die Briefe an Timotheus und Titus. Der Brief an der Hebräer*, 23ff., and the proper critique of this view in Sanders, *New Testament Christological Hymns*, 94.

neglect of protology may be a *later* development in these hymns. In view of the fact that 1 Pet. 3 reflects *no* protology and instead involves among other things an application of Ps. 110.1 to Christ,[91] one may properly ask whether in the later stages of the development of the christological hymns there was a move *away* from sapiential interests and towards the use, or at least a greater use, of the messianic reading of the Psalms.

There is also no agreement as to whether one should see a strict V pattern or chronological progression in the hymn in 1 Tim. 3:16, as one finds in Philippians 2, John 1 and elsewhere. There may be an earth, heaven, heaven earth, earth heaven pattern to the phrases, i.e., a, b, b, a, a, b.[92] This, however, would make a strict chronological progression impossible, it would seem, but consider the following: (1) incarnation comes first – "he appeared in flesh;"[93] (2) he was vindicated in Spirit (or by the Spirit, cf. below) which may be a reference to resurrection; and (3) he appeared before angels.[94] Either this refers to Christ's appearance before angels in glory,[95] *or* here is a reference to what is also mentioned in 1 Pet. 3:19 and Jude 6,[96] i.e., Christ's appearing to the imprisoned spirits. This has traditionally been referred to as the descent to Hades, but in fact there is no reason why this could not be happening on the way to heaven. This would be not in hell but in some form of limbo. (4) The phrase, "preached on *en ethnesin*", may mean amongst the Gentiles, though it can also be translated among the nations. Since the author is quoting here it is probably the latter. "Believed on in the world" is next mentioned, which alludes to the general spread of the Gospel and faith in Christ, (5) "Taken up in glory" then would refer to Christ's enthronement at the right hand of the Father, or his resuming of his glorious cosmic position having finished the work of salvation. On this showing this is a hymn about salvation history (*heilsgeschichte*) to a greater degree than either of the previous hymns thus far examined.

Many stress the antithesis between flesh and spirit, angels and nations, world and glory, and point out the universal scope of Christ's work and reign. It is not at all certain whether spirit in v 16a is a reference to Christ's spirit or the Holy Spirit who raises Jesus up and thus vindicates him. Probably the latter is what is meant especially if one compares Rom 1.3–4 where there is a similar contrast between the flesh of Christ and Holy Spirit.[97] There is some possibility that enthronement imagery of a king is being applied to Christ here perhaps

---

[91] But cf. Hengel, "Psalm 110," 68ff.

[92] Gundry, "Form, Meaning, and Background," 206–07.

[93] Not "in the flesh" – the point is he became fully human.

[94] Probably *angelos* does not mean messengers or witnesses here, in view of the parallel in 1 Peter 3. If it did mean messengers or witnesses then it could refer to the resurrection appearances.

[95] But if so what is the point of the last phrase, "taken up in glory"?

[96] The definitive study on the material in 1 Peter and Jude about the spirits in prison is W. J. Dalton's *Christ's Proclamation to the Spirits. A Study of 1 Peter 3:18–4:6.*

[97] But cf. Gundry, "Form, Meaning, and Background," 211–12.

from Ps. 110:1 but this probably should not be overpressed at least in the case of 1 Tim. 3:16.[98]

Several points stand out that are of importance for our discussion. If the hymn fragment quoted in 1 Tim. 3:16, and in a somewhat different form in 1 Pet. 3:18–22 does represent a later development in the creation of Christological hymns, it may reveal that there was a development *away* from a sapiential treatment of Christ's career as time went on. Since, however, the author is likely paraphrasing a source here, one cannot be sure about the relative age of this hymn fragment compared to others. Secondly, though protology is certainly not the focus of 1 Tim. 3:16, nevertheless to say that someone was "revealed in flesh" surely implies some sort of existence prior to becoming human, otherwise *ephanerothe* is a very strange verb to use. Thirdly, it is not impossible that "seen by angels" is an allusion to the sapiential material found in *1* Enoch 42 which speaks of Wisdom seeking a dwelling amongst human beings and when she does not find one returning to heaven and taking her place among the heavenly beings. This explanation seems less likely than the one suggested above, especially in view of the parallels in 1 Peter 3. This hymn also, like the one in Philippians 2, is in part about the vindication of an individual who was apparently rejected.[99] The implied context for understanding this could be the story of the rejection of Wisdom and her return to heaven, but one cannot be sure about this. Finally, this hymn is the *only one* amongst the generally recognized Christ hymns that does not strongly manifest a sapiential character, drawing on material especially from Sirach and the Wisdom of Solomon. It is very likely not accidental that the hymn fragment in 1 Tim. 3:16 begins with the incarnation, for it was the Wisdom material which provided the protological concepts and terminology and also the V pattern and this hymn eschews such Wisdom material. In 1 Tim. 3:16 the V pattern is reduced to a check mark.

THE RADIANCE REPRISE: HEBREWS 1:2b–4

Whom he appointed inheritor/heir of all things,
through whom also he made the aeons (i.e. created
worlds = universe);
who being the radiance of glory and the exact impress/stamp/
representation of his being/substance/reality,
upholding all things by his powerful word;
having made purification for sins,
he sat down on the right hand of the majesty on high,

[98] But cf. J. N. D. Kelly, *A Commentary on the Pastoral Epistles*, 91–93.
[99] Sanders, *New Testament Christological Hymns*, 97.

having become as much better than the angels as he has
inherited a more excellent name in comparison to them.[100]

Hebrews 1:1–2:4 is part of the first great segment of the letter 1:1–4:13 which in the main deals with the speaking of God in the Son, and particularly the superiority of the revelation in the Son to all previous revelations. The section begins with a prologue and integral to that prologue is the hymn fragment. Part of the point of this prologue and what follows is, as D. Guthrie says, that the revelation in the Son is not only superior to all previous ones, being a fuller representation of God's truth, but also the final, definitive revelation, and what happens at the end of the story is decisive for interpreting all that has come before.[101] It is not just a case of fulfilling earlier promises, but a case of going beyond any previous revelations. What follows tries to establish not only that Jesus fulfills previous hopes and promises, but also that he surpasses previous forms of revelation. Only the Son is the exact representation of the being of God. It may be worth noting as well that our author rounds off the first major section of the letter with another hymnic piece at 4:13.

In the first major subsection, 1:1–2:4, there is a prologue (vv 1–4), then a catena of Old Testament citations with linking commentary (1:5–14). Notice that the quotes function as a direct part of the author's argument, not merely as a proof text quoted to back up the argument. Finally he offers an exhortation in 2:1–4 based on what has come before. A. T. Lincoln sees the following structure in chapter 1:[102]

(1) 1:1–2a is commented on in v 5 where Ps. 2:7/2 Sam. 7:14 are cited as commentary on Christ's role as creator and divinity;

(2) 1:2b–3a is commented on in vv 6–12, where Deut. 32:43/Ps. 104:4, Ps. 45:6–7/ Ps. 102:25–27 are cited as illustrating the attributes mentioned in 2b–3a;

(3) 1:3b–4 which speaks of Christ's exaltation and enthronement is commented on in v 13 where Ps. 110:1 is cited for the first of several times. In fact the only part not directly commented on is the part in v 3 about making purification for sins; however, that will be taken up in detail later in the homily.[103]

Section 1:1–4 is basically one long sentence in the Greek with alliteration and rhythm. This is not surprising if it is in part a hymn fragment – it makes it easier

---

[100] There is one textual variant of some possible significance. In v 3 some MSS (p. [46] and 1739) have added *di eautou* "through himself", which must be construed with what follows power, and they omit "his" before power. D* K and L and most later MSS have both readings: "his power, when he through or by himself..." It is perhaps best to accept the simplest reading (*autou*) in many cases but how then to explain the *di eautou*? Thus some accept only *di eautou* as the original. On the basis of more support *autou* is probably to be preferred.

[101] D. Guthrie, *The Letter to the Hebrews*, 61–71; cf. H. W. Attridge, *Hebrews*, 38.

[102] Here I am drawing on a lecture which Dr. Andrew Lincoln gave in 1976 in S. Hamilton, Mass. which has not been published.

[103] A similar sort of paralleling of the prologue and the catena of quotes can be found in J. P. Meier, "Structure and Theology in Heb. 1.1–4," 168–89.

to sing or learn. It will be seen from the quoted fragment above that while in the fragment itself Christ is not called the Son, the author uses the fragment to speak about the Son, which is a major christological concept for this author. In fact, it is very striking that in *none* of the christological hymns under present scrutiny is Jesus called the Son. Sonship Christology seems to have arisen from another quarter. Here, then, several sorts of christological reflection are skillfully combined. D. W. B. Robinson has shown that the core affirmations about the Son begin with a predication drawing upon Psalm 2 and another drawing on Psalm 110, with familiar affirmations about Wisdom being used in between. This structure seems intended to establish two premises: (1) the royal Son of Psalm 2 can be identified as divine Wisdom, the agent of creation (cf. v 2b, c); and (2) divine Wisdom who is God's agent in the world and the world's sustainer is also identified as the royal priest of Psalm 110.[104]

Our author starts by saying that God had previously spoken through prophets, which here probably means all God's previous messengers including Moses and not just the later well known prophets, for the contrast is between all that went before and the revelation in the Son. Of this previous revelation he says it was partial or fragmentary and came in a variety of ways (dreams, visions, theophany). Very clearly this author operates with a concept of progressive revelation, but it is important that one understand what this means. The writer is not suggesting that what came before was bad. His comparison is between a good which was partial and piecemeal, which came little by little, and something better that came all at once in the Son. The comparison is between good and better, partial and definitive, ongoing and final.[105] The author in borrowing the phrase used in the LXX to refer to the end times (cf. Mic. 4:1, Num 24:14), suggests that God has now offered his *last word*, the final revelation. The point he will be driving towards is that one dare not refuse God's final and definitive offer, or neglect it now that one has received it. There can be no turning back.

Having considered the context in which the hymn is used, it is time to turn to the content of the hymn itself. In v 2b one is told that God set or appointed the redeemer to be the inheritor of all things and that through him he also made all created worlds. In short, the universe was made through him, but he is the one to whom it will belong and does belong. Here the pre-existent One is involved in creation, while also being the one who at the end of all things inherits it all.[106] In v 3b one learns that the Redeemer is involved not only at the

[104] Cf. D. W. B. Robinson, "The Literary Structure of Hebrews 1:1–4," 182–84, and also W. L. Lane, *Hebrews 1–8*, 6.

[105] Cf. G. Hughes, *Hebrews and Hermeneutics*, 5ff.

[106] Meier, "Structure and Theology," 175ff., makes too much of the fact that the hymn begins with an eschatological word about the Son. He tries to argue that the hymn is in the form of a ring. But the author of Hebrews views both the person and work of Christ from the end of things throughout this book – even protology is seen in the light of eschatology. This is not unlike Paul's procedure as well. Cf. Witherington, *Jesus, Paul, and the End of the World.*

beginning and end of things but that all along he is upholding the universe by his power on a continual basis (*pheron* is present continual tense – this is his ongoing task).[107] The world is held in being by him, not by some watchmaker–God who has wound it up and let it run on its own.

For christological purposes v 3a is one of the most crucial in the letter and much depends on how one understands two key words – *apaugasma* and *charakter*. While the former word is found several times in the New Testament (cf. 2 Cor. 4:4, 2 Pet. 1:19, Acts 20:11), the latter is a hapax legomena. The former word can be taken in an active or a passive sense. Actively it means radiance or effulgence; in the passive sense it means reflection. In view of the fact that this is a passage attempting to praise the redeemer as highly as possible, exalting him over other possible forms of God's revelation; and in view of Wis. 7:25f where the active sense is required (for Wisdom is called "a clear effulgence of the glory of the Almighty, an effulgence from everlasting light… and an image of his goodness"), it is likely that the active sense is to be preferred here as well. The difference is that a reflection, like an image of oneself in the water, is like a shadow cast but not directly connected to the light source, whereas if one translates it radiance or effulgence the idea is of a light beam coming forth from the light source as an integral expression of it.[108] This is not merely a matter of a person being a bearer of divine Wisdom or light that comes from some other source.[109] Rather, here the redeemer is said to be the beacon of divine light, Wisdom herself. Philo *Special Laws* 4:123 speaks of what God breathed into Adam as the effulgence of his nature, i.e., a life force or expression that came from the depths of his being. In short the redeemer does not merely reflect the light of God, he radiates it, as Wisdom is said to do in Wisdom 7.

In regard to the second word, its normal secular meaning is the stamp or impression that a signet ring would make on wax or a stamp would make on a piece of metal turning it into a coin.[110] Thus here it very likely means that the

---

But apart from the preliminary clause about Christ the inheritor, which could be the author's addition in any case, the hymn maintains the V pattern, like the other hymns. It may be that one should make a distinction between the Son being appointed the heir (from the beginning of things?), and his obtaining his name and inheritance after his exaltation. If this is so, the beginning and end clauses do not both refer to eschatology.

[107] The sudden change of subject in v 3 from God to Christ is also very likely a tip off that the author is using a source here. Cf. Frankowski, "Early Christian Hymns," 184.

[108] In view of this verse, L. D. Hurst's arguments, following his mentor G. B. Caird, which try to minimize or eliminate the idea of a pre–existent divine One here are hardly persuasive. Cf. his "The Christology of Hebrews 1 and 2," in *The Glory of Christ in the New Testament. Studies in Christology*, 155. Verse 3 is not refering to a mere human being, but rather to the Redeemer in his pre–human condition. Cf. rightly, R. G. Hammerton–Kelly, *Pre–existence, Wisdom, and the Son of Man*, 243–44. Hurst neglects the fact that the Christological hymns speak about pre–existence, earthly existence, *and* post–existence, not just the latter two of these. Even 1 Tim. 3:16 seems to hint at protology.

[109] Pace Hurst, "Christology," 156.

[110] Cf. Attridge, *Hebrews*, 43–44.

redeemer bears the exact likeness or representation of God's nature. One is immediately struck by how close this is to Col. 1:15–17 though the clauses are a bit rearranged.[111] The Wisdom parallel is important here as well. This author knows he is not merely talking about a personification or a hypostasization but about a person when he refers to the Son. This Wisdom figure he identifies with and as Jesus. Yet he chooses the Wisdom language probably because he wants to indicate that Jesus is not merely a good likeness of God, or a copy of him, or a reflection of him, but in fact God in God's final self–expression, beaming forth to humankind. The point is that the Son is the exact likeness of God, and therefore in a true sense may be called God, or God's Son, or divine, for what other term is left if he is above the angels and the exact representation of God? The author views the Son as not merely an act or power or an attribute of God but as a person who exactly represents or bears the impress of God, and as such is to be worshipped as no mere angelic being should be.

Though it is a bit less explicit than the prologue in John 1, it is striking that the author holds the human name of the redeemer in abeyance until 2:9, perhaps because the redeemer was not properly speaking Jesus (the human being with a human nature) until after the incarnation. In Heb. 1:1–4 he is at least in part talking about the pre–existent condition of the redeemer at creation, as well as his earthly act of purification and also his post existence. W. L. Lane is very likely right in his conjecture that

> The writer's decision to present Jesus as God's Son who performs the functions assigned to Wisdom may have been motivated by a pastoral concern to achieve a hearing for what he had to say.... The concentration of unusual and distinctive vocabulary in v 3 suggests a congregation for whom the tradition preserved in Wis. 7:24–27 was normative. This Christian assembly has been significantly influenced by the hellenistic synagogue in terms of theological concept and vocabulary.[112]

One notes again the full familiar V pattern of this christological hymn, the one who comes down then is said to go back up, without in this case any mention of resurrection.[113] Various of the important formal features pointing to a hymn are also in evidence: (1) the opening *hos*; (2) participial predications; (3) using substantive participles without the article; (4) the aforementioned alliteration and rhythm; (5) the parallelism of key phrases (e.g. cf. *charakter tes hupotaseos autou* to *remati tes dunameos autou*, v. 3 seems to be in meter).[114]

---

[111] Cf. Frankowski, "Early Christian Hymns," 188.

[112] Lane, *Hebrews 1–8*, 18.

[113] It would appear that 1 Tim. 3:16 is the only text which alludes to the resurrection amongst these christological hymns, unless the Johannine Prologue's reference to "we have seen his glory" is such a reference. In any event, it appears not to have been a regular feature of these hymns.

[114] Sanders, *New Testament Christological Hymns*, 19.

E. Käsemann has shown how closely related Heb. 1:3 is to Phil. 2:6–11. He argues that they are chiefly distinguished by the fact that obedience is cosmically related in Philippians while it is community related in the Hebrew hymn. In the latter, Jesus' death is seen to have community benefits – purification is made for the community, while in Philippians it has a cosmic effect.[115]

Saying that the redeemer, after making purification (*katharismos* usually refers to the objective cultic cleansing, not the internal cleansing of conscience) then sat down at the right hand of God has a twofold point. First, in Wis. 9:4 the same is said of Wisdom; she sits by the throne of God as God's consort (because Sophia is a female personification or hypostasization).[116] The implication is that the redeemer is in some sense divine and divinely favored by God. Secondly, the point may be that the purification that the Son made was definitive, once for all time, and so thereafter he sat down, in contrast to the levitical priests who could only stand and offer sacrifices in God's presence which had to be offered over and over as sinning went on. This idea is developed further in Heb. 10:11ff. Though it is sometimes thought that the reference to making purification for sins is an alien intrusion into this hymn, it should be borne in mind that such an act is the work of a priest ministering in the tabernacle of God. It is thus not irrelevant to point out that it is said of Wisdom in Sir. 24:10, "In the holy tabernacle I ministered before him, and so I was established in Zion" while immediately after it is said, "and for eternity I shall not cease to exist." It will be seen that here one has some precedent for two of the major tenets of the high priestly Christology of Hebrews – that Christ was a holy priest, and that his priesthood is forever because he is an eternal being. Thus, even in the apparently least sapiential portions in these christological hymns, a sapiential explanation seems possible and helpful.[117]

The right hand in Semitic thinking is the hand of honor or power. It is possible to envision an enthronement scene here where the royal one enters, having completed the prerequisite task to being royal, is presented, and then enthroned. Meier is very likely right in saying, "What the author is doing is bringing together in one periodic sentence a Christology of pre–existent Wisdom and a Christology of Jesus who is enthroned as Son or Lord at the time of his resurrection/ascension..."[118] In any case, one is meant to see this as God's endorsement of what the redeemer has accomplished, and his exaltation

---

[115] E. Käsemann, *The Wandering People of God. An Investigation of the Letter to the Hebrews*, 97ff.

[116] The mention of "at the right hand" suggests here the first real hint in the hymns of the influence of Ps. 110:1, along with the sapiential influence. If this is a later hymn fragment than that found in Philippians or Colossians, this may suggest that the use of the Psalm to fill out the picture represents a later development in the composition of these hymns. We cannot be certain of this, however.

[117] H. Gese, *Essays on Biblical Theology*, 200–02.

[118] Meier, "Structure and Theology," 185. On the other hand, even some of the enthronement language seems to owe something to sapiential material.

indicates he has successfully completed the work he was sent to earth to do and is recognized in heaven for it by this most honorable of seats. The point also is that he is now in a position of ultimate power and authority, and thus can be a great help to those in need.

It may be that v 4 refers to the redeemer receiving a throne name, having assumed the seat at the right hand, for one is told that he has not only a superior position to the angels but also a superior name. This seems to reflect the same sort of motif found in Philippians 2 where one is told that the throne name is Lord. This may be the case here as well, but it is at least implied by the author that he was the pre–existent Son (cf. v. 2a, "spoken by a Son," to vv 5–6). One must bear in mind the idea that in regard to a royal son he assumes the throne when he inherits his kingdom, and at that point takes up the throne name. When this sort of thinking was later applied to the messiah, it was sometimes said that when God's eschatological anointed one comes he can only be called or named Messiah when he has completed the work of the messiah, and can thus be recognized by all as such.[119] These ideas may come into play here, for here it is said that he *inherited* a more excellent name. It may be that the term Son is used in two different senses – one as the divine pre–existent Son, and then under the royal enthronement imagery, as the royal Son, i.e., Messiah who is proclaimed as such, inheriting the name after completing the work of purification. If this is correct, then this author envisions the Son already being a priestly messiah, though not of the line of Levi or Aaron.

One final point – why this stress on the Son being superior to the angels? Perhaps because angels were believed to be the mediators of the Mosaic covenant (cf. Gal. 3:19, Acts 7:53; Jub. 1:29). More conjectural is the suggestion that the audience, like that at Colossae, was involved in some sort of esoteric Jewish angel worship or adulation, or was considering Jesus as an angel, since they too were called sons of God in the Old Testament, though no one of them in isolation is ever called the or a son of God. If this last idea was floating around, then our author attempts to make clear that the Son he is talking about is no mere angel but in some sense is divine.

The evidence of the influence of Wisdom material is quite clear in this hymn and may be summed up as follows. First, v 2 with its idea of an agent through whom God created all worlds is found already in the Wisdom of Solomon where Wisdom is called the fashioner of all things (7:22), an associate in God's works (8:4–5), the "active cause of all things" (9:2), the means by which God formed humankind, but it may already be present as early as the praise of Wisdom in Proverbs 8. More certainly the pre–temporal existence of Wisdom is affirmed as early as Proverbs 8.[120] Second, v 3a seems to be a direct use of Wis. 7:25 to describe the redeemer, especially in the use of *apaugasma* in an active

[119] On the idea of being granted a name such as Son, or even a divine name *after* recognition by God, cf. *Test Levi* 4.2, *3 Enoch* 12:15.

[120] Cf. pp. 45ff. above.

sense. Third, Wisdom/Spirit is said to hold all things together in Wis. Sol. 1:7 (cf. Sir. 24:3) which may provide a partial background for Heb. 1:3b. Fourth, already in Wis. 9:4 one hears of Wisdom sitting beside God's throne, and there is the plea in 9:10: "from the throne of your glory send her." This, perhaps coupled with Ps. 110:1, seems to be the source for v 3d. Fifth, the reference to angels and superiority over them may in part owe something to what is said of Wisdom in *1 Enoch* 42, that Wisdom took her place among but as superior to the angels.

THE LOGOS HYMN: JOHN 1

First Strophe — In the beginning was the Word;
and the Word was with God,
and the Word was God.
He was with God in the beginnning.

Second Strophe — Through him all things were made.
Without him nothing came to be.
In him was life,
And this life was the light of humanity.
The light shines in the darkness,
and the darkness has not overcome/understood it.

Third Strophe — He was in the world,
and though the world was made by him,
it did not recognize/respond to him.
To his own he came.
Yet his own did not receive him.
But all those who did accept him,
he empowered to become children of God.

(Verses 12b–13 are an explanatory insertion by the author about how one becomes such a child).

Fourth Strophe — And the Word became flesh,
and dwelt among us.
And we beheld his glory.
The glory of the only begotten Son of the Father,
full of grace and truth.[121]

There is some question as to whether vv 16–18 should be seen as a fifth strophe, but probably it should not be included. Roughly speaking the hymn can be

[121] I have basically followed R. E. Brown's division of the hymn with minor modifications; cf. Brown, *The Gospel according to John I–XII* (Garden City: Doubleday, 1966), 3ff.

broken down into several major themes: (1) the pre–existent Word (*logos*); (2) the Word and creation; (3) the response of those created – rejection; (4) the incarnation and revelation; (5) the response of the faithful community (i.e. "we have seen his glory"). Without question, John 1:1–18 has had more impact on Christian thinking about the Son of God as pre–existent and a divine being than any other New Testament passage. Here is where the early church derived its *logos* (i.e., the Son of God as the "Word") Christology and its basic understanding of the incarnation. In its pattern it is not unlike the two hymns in Phil. 2:6–11 and Col. 1:15–20 (cf. also Hebrews 1:2–4). Like the hymn in Hebrew 1 this material serves both to establish the identity and reveal the scope of the deeds and career of the main character of the book. While in Hebrew 1 the hymn is part of the Prologue, in John 1 it has basically become the Prologue, along with the parenthetical remarks about the Baptist and the birth from above.

In John 1 there is only really an account of the first two of the normal three stages in the V pattern, perhaps because this author is interested in focusing on the incarnate Son of God in this Gospel and the human reaction to him, or perhaps because he wishes to develop the glorification theme later in the Gospel. He is trying to make clear that Jesus' ministry and person can only be understood if one recognizes where Jesus came from and where he is going. In short, the Son of God is only explicable if one understands that here is a divine being who came from and returns to heaven. Yet it is striking also in this Gospel that in order to make clear that the Son of God does not exhaust the Godhead we are constantly being told in John that Jesus is dependent on the Father – he cannot speak or act except as the Father grants him to do so.

The evidence that this is an independent hymn that has been incorporated into this Gospel is strong, for there are various key terms in this hymn that one finds nowhere else in the Gospel, including the word *logos*, the word for grace (*charis*), and the word for fullness (*pleros*).[122] Further, the idea found in v 14 of the Word coming and tabernacling or setting up his tent in our midst is found only in this passage of the Gospel.

The best way to describe this hymn is to call it poetry, with some lapses into prose, or poetic prose at the end.[123] In the Greek it has a certain rhythmic cadence which can even be picked up in a good English translation. The cadence is established by the repetition of certain key words (v 1 Word, Word, God, God; vv 4–5 life, life, light, light, darkness, darkness; vv 10–12 the world, the world, the world, his own, his own, receive, receive). Note also that the phrase "his own" has a different meaning in the hymn than elsewhere in John.

---

[122] More words could be added; cf. J. Painter, "Christology and the History of the Johannine Community in the Prologue of the Fourth Gospel," 462 citing among other words *photizei, eskenosin, exegesato*.

[123] Painter, "Christology," 463–64 notes that vv 1–5, 10–12b, 14a–c are markedly poetic, and adds that while the poetry is basically in vv 1–14, the peculiar or unique vocabulary is basically in vv 14d–18.

The only real difficulty is in deciding what originally belonged to the hymn. The simplest solution is to see the material on the Baptist in vv 6–9 as an addition by the evangelist. There is certainly a stylistic difference between vv 6–8 and the rest of the hymn up to v 11.[124] While this hymn lacks the *hos* and the *parallelismus membrorum* of some of the hymns, the former difficulty is very likely explained by the fact that here for the first time a hymn is used at the very outset of a book, and thus should not begin with *hos*. One must always bear in mind that the Christian authors who used these hymns or hymn fragments also edited them to some extent to suit their own purposes.

There is in this hymn an obvious drawing on material from Genesis 1. Both documents begin with the words, "In the beginning." Then too the Genesis story is about how God made a universe by means of his spoken words. Here too creation happens by *the* Word. But whatever debt the author of this hymns has to Genesis, Genesis 1 is not about either a personified attribute, much less a person assisting God in creation. It is the use of the Genesis material in the hymnic material about Wisdom both in the Old Testament and in later Jewish sapiential writings that provides the font of ideas and forms used in creating this hymn. Not only Prov. 3 but also Proverbs 8:1–9.6 should be considered.[125] There one learns that personified Wisdom was present at creation, but also that she called God's people back to the right paths and offered them life and favor from God (cf. 8:35).[126] These are the very things being said of the Word as well in this hymn. This sort of Wisdom speculation had gone a step further by the time of Ben Sira to include speculation about God's written word the Torah. Torah and Wisdom were seen as interrelated, the former being the consummate expression of the latter (cf. Sirach 24). At the end of the hymn in John 1 it is said that the Son eclipses this Torah, for Torah which came from Moses gave the law, but through the *logos* one gets grace and truth.

The Wisdom character and background of the Logos hymn has long been recognized. R. Bultmann, before he favored the Gnostic redeemer myth theory, argued at length for the sapiential character of this hymn.[127] In view of the general demise of the use of Gnostic redeemer myth theory to explain these hymns, especially due to the problem of anachronism,[128] Bultmann's earlier suggestion needs to be heeded. Dodd also has shown the extensive indebtedness of this hymn to Wisdom material.[129] Gese has now taken the argument a

---

[124] Sanders, *New Testament Christological Hymns*, 20–21.

[125] Cf above. pp. 41ff.

[126] On all of this cf. pp. 42ff. above and the discussion of this material there.

[127] R. Bultmann, "Der Religionsgeschitliche Hintergrund des Prologs zum Johannes–Evangelium," *in Eucharisterion Festschrift für H. Gunkel*, Vol. 2, 3–26.

[128] Hurtado, "Jesus as Lordly Example," 117: "the appeal to a pre–Christian Gnostic redeemer myth has fallen on hard times in recent years..." Cf. Sanders, *NT Christological Hymns*, 58ff. and especially Hengel, *The Son of God*, 33–35.

[129] C. H. Dodd, *The Interpretation of the Fourth Gospel*, 274–78.

step further, providing even more evidence of indebtedness than Dodd.[130] One can also point out the remarkable parallel in 1QS 11:11: "All things come to pass by his knowledge. He establishes all things by His design, and without Him nothing is done [or made]."[131]

It is not necessary to reiterate all the parallels cited in this chapter which deal with Wisdom present at or participating in the events of creation. On the idea of Wisdom providing life and light one thinks again of Wis. 7:27 where Wisdom is said to be the effulgence of eternal light, and very life breath of God in Wis. 7:25a.

In regard to the old problem of why *logos* and not *sophia* is used here, it seems doubtful that the reason is because Jesus was a male. Certainly that did not stop the other evangelists from using *sophia* of Jesus (cf. Matt. 1:19; Luke 11:49).[132] It has also been pointed out that in Wis. 9:1–2 word (*en logo*) and Wisdom are used in synonymous parallelism, an idea which Philo takes much further.[133] Furthermore, the *logos* is already personified in Wis. 18:15 where it is said that God's "all–powerful Word leaped from heaven, from the royal throne into the midst of the land..." Since it had already been said in 9:10 that Wisdom was present and sent forth from the throne, one can see how interchangeable the terms were in the Wisdom of Solomon. This is also the case in the earlier writing of Ben Sira for at Sir. 24:3 it is Wisdom which is said to come forth from the mouth of God. It may be that the evangelist simply used the term *logos* to better prepare for the replacement motif – Jesus superseding Torah as God's *logos*.[134] It may be, as Gese suggests, that it was thought that the *logos* concept better united creation and salvation history.[135] It is quite unnecessary to posit a Stoic background for the material in John 1.[136] Whatever Hellenized thought may be reflected in this hymn is probably due to the heavy dependence of the hymn on Sirach and especially on the Wisdom of Solomon, both of

[130] Gese, *Essays on Biblical Theology* , 167–22, especially 190ff.

[131] This supports the contention that we are dealing with hymn material in John 1 which draws water from Jewish wells to create it. The translation cited is that of G. Vermes, *The Dead Sea Scrolls in English*, 93.

[132] Sanders, *NT Christological Hymns*, 35, and n. 1.

[133] C. K. Barrett, *The Gospel according to John*, 154: "Philo's Logos, broadly speaking, takes the place Sophia had occupied in earlier Hellenistic Judaism, and in particular exercises a cosmological function."

[134] I would not rule out that the hymn may originally have spoken of *Sophia* rather than *Logos*, but this is simply an unsupportable conjecture.

[135] Gese, *Biblical Essays*, 198.

[136] Gese, *Biblical Essays*, 199 conjectures the term *Logos* is used here because the historical appearance of Jesus is the revelation of the original order of the universe. But is this hymn really so concerned with that matter? Is it not more concerned with the disorder of the universe that the *Logos* now comes to set right? It is interesting that in the Greek–speaking world there was among the Stoics some speculation about a *logos* as well, but they understood it to refer to a sort of divine rational principle or moral structure to all of the universe, not to a personal being. One can argue that the evangelist has chosen terminology familiar to both Jews and Greeks, but he does not use it in a Stoic way.

which manifest such an influence already. Finally, there is also the matter of the tabernacling of the *logos* with God's people.[137] This idea was already manifested in Sir. 24:8 where it speaks about the creator choosing a place for Wisdom to tent, namely in the earthly tabernacle in Zion (v 10), and in particular in the book of the covenant in that tabernacle (v 23). In the Logos Hymn one finds the idea of Wisdom in the person of the divine Logos tabernacling in the midst of God's people. As Dunn avers, it is the idea of the Word taking on human flesh (not historical form of just any sort) that makes the Logos Hymn stand out from its sapiential background.[138] I would add that the explicitly incarnational expression in John 1:14 is just a further clarification of the already incarnational thought present in the earlier christological hymns.

It may be that this hymn was added in part to combat heretical ideas that plagued the church even in the first century. For instance, the idea of docetism (that Jesus only appeared to be human and have a human body) and one of the ideas of proto–Gnosticism (that there were many intermediaries between God and human beings) may be in view here.[139] The evangelist makes clear that the Logos really took on human flesh, and that he is the only intermediary between human beings and God.

This hymn causes one to reflect upon many important theological ideas, but this study can only mention a few of the more important ones by looking at several verses in more depth. This *logos* or Word was present with God before the space–time continuum or universe was created. Not only so, this Word is said to be God. The key phrase *kai theos en ho logos* does not mean "the Word was a god", but rather "the Word was God". Notice it does not say "the Word was *the* God" for this would then mean that the Word was all there was to the Godhead, and the Evangelist does not want to convey that idea. It is also pertinent to note that there is mention of the *pleros* of grace and truth in the Logos, as in Col. 1:19 we are told that the *pleroma* (the fullness of God, cf. Col. 2:9) dwells in him. The various parallels and similarities between the hymns should not be overlooked as they suggest they all came out of the same sort of *Sitz im Leben*, prone to thinking in certain sapiential ways about Christ.[140] The interpretation of one hymn should accordingly be checked against and compared to that of the others, and surely the most satisfying interpretation is the one that makes best sense of them all, while allowing for certain particularities in each hymn.

---

[137] It is not really so puzzling that the *Logos* is nowhere specifically identified by name in the hymn with Christ and J. Ashton, "The Transformation of Wisdom," 172ff., tries to make more of this than he should. Had he studied all the christological hymns together he would have realized that the absence of a named subject is a characteristic of these hymns. J. Jeremias, "Zum Logos–Problem," 82–85 suggests that the absolute use of *ho logos* in John 1:1, 14 suggests the audience knew this title already before reading the Gospel. The author was referring to "the (well known) *logos*."

[138] Dunn, *Christology in the Making*, 239ff.

[139] R. Schnackenburg, *The Gospel According to St. John*, Vol. I, 165ff.

[140] On the concept of fullness applied to Wisdom, cf. Wis. 7:24, 27 and 8:1.

M. D. Hooker has argued that the whole of John's Gospel must be read in the light of this Prologue, and this is surely correct.[141] She maintains that the "messianic secret", if one should call it that, in the Fourth Gospel is that Jesus is the Logos, the one who has come from above and returns to the Father. But this is hidden to all but the reader who starts with John 1, just as in Mark 1 the story is incomprehensible without knowing the content of the very first verse. Thus the christological hymn is used as a christological basis for the argument in the rest of the Fourth Gospel. This argument is supported by the point that P. S. Minear makes that understanding Jesus in the Fourth Gospel depends on knowing where he has come from and where he is going.[142] As I will argue in Chapter 8, there is a sense in which the whole of the Fourth Gospel is dependent on the Wisdom hymn in its first chapter to set the stage for the story about the one who comes from and returns to the Father. This is why on the one hand the Johannine Jesus can say, "before Abraham was, I am" and on the other hand can convey the idea that he is not glorified until he is first lifted up on the cross and then returns into heaven. It should also be stressed that this is the only christological hymn that begins a *Gospel*, and it is likely because of this fact that the normal second half of the V pattern is basically missing here. Had it been fully included here it would have pre–empted the conclusion of the Gospel story. The hymn is meant to introduce the Gospel, not provide a synopsis of the whole plot.

I would go further than Hooker and suggest that the whole of this Gospel must be read in light of this very first verse for it means that the deeds and words of Jesus are the deeds and words of a divine being, and not a created supernatural being either, for he existed prior to all of creation. Later one hears that this Son of God is the *monogenes* Son but this may mean the unique (only one of its kind) Son, or it may mean the "only begotten Son" as distinct from a created Son. This latter understanding would suggest that in eternity the Son proceeded from the Father as like produces like kind, but he was not created by the Father as something that was inherently distinct from the Father's being.[143] Jesus is then the natural Son of God, while mere mortals may be the adopted sons and daughters of God through the new birth. Thus the Son is set apart from other human beings in his divine nature.

This Word was involved in the whole act of creation. Nothing was made without him. Also he is involved in the whole work of redemption. Nothing is saved without him. The words "light" and "life" are major theological terms in this Gospel and they begin to be used here in this hymn. It is helpful to remember that light is a metaphor for revelation or enlightenment that comes from God, and life or eternal life is Fourth Gospel language for salvation, or at least the benefit of salvation. The light and life offered through the Son are not

---

[141] M. D. Hooker, "The Johannine Prologue and the Messianic Secret," 40–58.

[142] P. S. Minear, "'We Don't Know Where...' John 20:2," 125–39.

[143] Schnackenburg, *John*, Vol. 1, 271–73.

temporal or temporary like the life and light referred to in Genesis 1 which are part of material creation. This hymn is saying that in the Logos lie the gifts of eternal life and eternal light. The darkness the author talks about is not just physical darkness like that referred to in Genesis 1 but a spiritual darkness which involves not only ignorance of the truth but also moral darkness and fallenness, which leads one to reject the light and life even when they are offered. Thus our author wishes to stress the ultimate irony of all this. The creatures reject their own creator when they reject the Son of God. At v 5b we probably have a double entendre – the darkness has not understood the light, but in addition the verb *katelaben* may also mean the darkness has not overcome that light, it has not snuffed it out.[144] This rejection motif is a part of what had already been said about Wisdom, in particular in *1 Enoch* 42, but it is not irrelevant to point out that this same theme of the rejection of Wisdom can be found in the Q material (e.g., Matt. 23:37–39/Luke 13:34–35).

At v 14 the *logos* finally reaches the human stage. The strophes before this were not in any direct way talking about the incarnation, but here the subject is directly treated. Here one finds "*ho logos sarx egeneto.*" This means "the Word became flesh". It certainly does not mean that the Word turned into flesh with no remainder, because he remains the Word who is beheld by the community at the end of the hymn. Thus it might be better to say that what is meant is either the Word took on flesh, or "the Word came on the human scene".[145] The Word became more than he was before, not less. To his divine nature he added a human one.[146] The word translated "tabernacled" or "set up tent" seems to allude more remotely to the Tabernacles period of Jewish history when God's presence was to be found in the Tent of Meeting. Just as the Israelites saw the Shekinah glory, so the believers now have seen an even greater glory, *the* glory, the bright and shining presence of the only begotten Son. As has already been said, however, its more proximate parallel is found in Sirach 24 which speaks of Wisdom in the tabernacle, and Wisdom as the book of the covenant, God's holy Word.

Glory is a familiar concept from the Old Testament which refers to the splendor or majesty or overwhelming weightiness of the divine presence here. It is in order to note that *doxa* or radiance is regularly associated with Wisdom as well (cf. Wis. 6:12; 7:10; 7:26; 9:10). From the tabernacling of the Word temporarily here on earth came not just the benefit that some believers saw his glory (possibly an allusion to Jesus' resurrection appearances) but also that all believers receive grace (God's unmerited favor) and truth (something the Spirit conveys to people who have been born anew by the Spirit). Truth in this Gospel refers to saving truth, not just any sort of accurate information. This

---

[144] Painter, "Christology and the History," 470.

[145] So rightly Barrett, *Gospel of John*, 164–65.

[146] In this case the subject is ontology, not primarily status or prerogatives as was true in the Philippian hymn. This fact as well may suggest this hymn is a later development than the one in Philippians 2.

grace and truth have led to one blessing after another. Thus while Moses/Torah provided a certain knowledge of God's will, Jesus gave the ability through dispensing grace to know the truth *and* to perform it. The great theme of this hymn is that God, in the person of the Word, did what was necessary not only to inform humankind about the gift of salvation but also to reach out and transform some with that gift so that they might be like the Logos who is the Son, children of God.

In this hymn there are two ways that the Logos is given historical location and presence: through the mention of the incarnation in v 14, and by associating the coming of this *Logos* with an historical person, John the Baptist. The story of Wisdom is thereby given further historical concreteness and specificity. It is probably wrong to suggest that the Logos hymn marks a significant new step or radical departure in early Christology. Closer to the mark, though underestimating things a bit, is the judgment of E. D. Freed that "It may not be going too far to say that the writer of the *logos* verses in John has scarcely done more than add the technical term *logos* to a Christology which had already been formulated by Paul and others...."[147]

CONCLUSIONS AND FURTHER IMPLICATIONS

It would appear that the composers of all these christological hymns were concerned that their respective audiences should not be allowed to assume that the subject was a mere personified attribute or activity or power of God. In each case whether through reference to flesh, or death on the cross, or making purification for sin, or by associating the person in question with the Baptist, the composers were trying to ensure that these hymns would not be treated as mere myths or discussions about abstract concepts or attributes of God or the world. In short, in one way or another there was a felt need always to say more of an historical nature than had been said in previous Wisdom hymns, all the while still appropriating a considerable amount of the form and content of those hymns. When the Jewish Christians, whether Palestinian Jews or, more likely, Diaspora Jews, composed these hymns they were looking for exalted language from their heritage that gave adequate expression to their new found faith in Jesus Christ. They found no language better suited for such praise than the paeans about personified or hypostasized Wisdom found in Proverbs 8, Job 28, Sirach 24, Wisdom 7, 9 and elsewhere. With the partial exception of 1 Tim. 3:16 (and par.) evidence has been presented or cited that the influence of the earlier praise of personified Wisdom was both extensive and intensive on all these christological hymns, effecting both form and content of the hymns. In particular, it was the latest of the Wisdom hymns in Wisdom of Solomon that seems to have had the greatest impact on the christological hymns. That is, Jewish Wisdom speculation probably outside of Palestine and certainly Hellenized to some degree provides the background for the New Testament

---

[147] E. D. Freed, "Theological Prelude and the Prologue of John's Gospel," 266.

christological hymns. It was admitted that there are other influences evident in the christological hymns, particularly evidence of messianic reflection on the royal psalms and also on the passion story about Jesus, but these influences are not nearly as strong, and in fact do not seem to affect the first half (the pre–creation and creation side) of the christological hymns to any real degree. If there is any basis at all for chronological speculation, it would appear that the Wisdom speculation *preceded* at least some of these other sorts of reflection. In any case, Wisdom thinking is certainly more dominant in these hymns than other sorts of ideas. The overlap in ideas and terminology in these hymns suggests that they all arose (with the possible exception of 1 Tim. 3:16) out of the same sort of early Jewish Christian *Sitz im Leben*. It seems unlikely that one can argue for either just one original Wisdom Christology hymn which spawned all these variants, or for some sort of chronological development in which the Colossian hymn grew out of the Philippian hymn, or the Johannine hymn grew out of any of the earlier hymns. There are enough distinctive features in each of these hymns to make such an argument implausible. Rather, it appears that these sorts of ideas were widely shared and expressed variously by a variety of early Jewish Christians.

Wisdom Christology, as it is expressed in these hymns, is a very high Christology indeed. When the sapiential hymn material was applied to the historical person Jesus, this led to the predicating of pre–existence, incarnation, and even divinity to this same historical person. The existence of these hymns in so many different sorts of sources – Pauline, Johannine, in Hebrews, and probably 1 Peter as well – strongly suggests that this Wisdom christology was both widespread and popular with a variety of Christian writers and their audiences. The fact that one finds such christology already in nearly full flower used by Paul in Philippians 2, suggests that this Christology had already developed within the first two or three decades of early Christianity. That is, this christology had developed *before* the writing of any of the canonical Gospels. To be sure, John 1 may be a further amplification especially of the ideas of incarnation and divinity but such ideas are already present, though not as fully expressed, in the earlier hymns. The Fourth Evangelist did not invent such ideas; he had very likely heard them sung about for many years.

These conclusions are made all the more probable if the conclusions of the previous two chapters are even partially correct. It is more likely than not that Jesus was identified as Wisdom in Q. This must have happened no later than the 60s in order for these traditions to be used by both the First Evangelist and Luke. If James is any clue about the date of Q, then possibly as early as the 40s the Q material (or at least the Sermon on the Mount), apparently in a rather Matthean form was already circulating. In any event, the final editor of Q had a pronounced Wisdom agenda. It was also argued in Chapter 4 that there even appears to be some credible evidence that Jesus spoke of or alluded to himself as Wisdom.

There is then a historically plausible path that can be traced from Jesus to the early church in christological matters:

Stage One: Jesus speaks of or at least alludes to himself as Wisdom to his followers.

Stage 2: This hint is picked up and amplified by the collectors of the Q material, in particular by the final redactor of this material who strives not only to present a Wisdom book, but to present Jesus as Wisdom in that book. This development was obviously not the only sort of development of thought in early Christianity, but it is striking that even when one finds something different (e.g., in James), it is simply a different sort of sapiential thinking – Wisdom of a more traditional and less daring order rather than Wisdom of a counter order. One is hard pressed to find much in earliest (pre–canonical Gospel) Christianity that *was not* some sort of development of sapiential thinking either about Jesus or the Jesus tradition.

Stage 3: Once Christianity, beginning in the late 40s if not somewhat earlier, began to have a significant following in the Diaspora both among Jews and Gentiles, the composition of sapiential christological hymns followed shortly thereafter, probably in Greek, as is suggested by the prevalent use of the Wisdom of Solomon material. It must be remembered that Jewish sapiential material was already the most international in character, and perhaps in some ways also the most Hellenized well before the New Testament period, and thus in various ways such material was the most *ideal* Jewish material for a missionary religion to use to branch out to non–Palestinians, both Jew and Gentile alike. It does not seem to be an accident that the Wisdom source most used or alluded to in these hymns is itself very likely a composition of a somewhat Hellenized Diaspora Jew – the Wisdom of Solomon. Sirach also seems to have had widespread influence first in a Diaspora setting. The christological hymns are a further development, with some novel elements thrown in, along these sorts of lines.

Stage 4: The Christological hymns, as well as other Wisdom material such as that found in Q, begin to be used by those who composed letters to various Christian communities, in particular Paul, whoever wrote Hebrews, and in the case of some of the (orally circulating?) Q material, James. This entails some modification, additions and subtractions from these hymns and other Jewish Christian Wisdom sources for they are not just quoted but used to serve the various writer's purposes.

Stage 5: The evangelists begin to take up the Wisdom material, and in the case of the Fourth Evangelist even the christological hymn form, and use it to tell the story of the historical Jesus in a sapiential way. This is especially evident in Matthew and John (cf. Chapter 8 below), but there is some evidence of a Wisdom agenda even in the earliest Gospel – Mark.[148] It is possible that Luke actually wrote the Pastoral Epistles, whether at the behest of Paul or not, and thus 1 Tim. 3:16 would be another example, certainly later than those found in

[148] H. M. Humphrey, "Jesus as Wisdom in Mark," 48–53.

Philippians or Colossians, of an evangelist appropriating the christological Wisdom hymn form.[149] This leads to a question – and it is only that. Is there a connection between the fact that the hymn in 1 Tim. 3:16 is the least sapiential of the lot and the possibility that it is also perhaps the latest hymn fragment? It seems to me that the answer is yes. Wisdom Christology is not late, it is early, and various other christologies, some of which are not as "high" as Wisdom Christology reflect what can only be called the devolution or at least non–development of christological thinking, which in some cases continues on into the second century of early Christianity.[150] If one combines the evidence discussed in Chapters 4 to 6 of this study, one cannot help but be impressed with the extent of the influence of Wisdom Christology in all sorts and forms of different traditions, all *before the writing of any of the canonical Gospels*, indeed apparently before the writing of any of the canonical books of the New Testament with the possible exception of Paul's earliest letters. The cumulative evidence is impressive even if one might wish to quibble about this or that piece of evidence along the way.

Wisdom Christology turns out to be a very high Christology indeed, ultimately entailing, at least in the christological hymns, the discussion of protological matters including the pre–existence, incarnation, and divinity of Christ. At the least one sees here already the roots of a sort of binitarian thinking, all the while without seeking to deny monotheism. Jesus is nowhere simply identified *as* Yahweh in these hymns, nor is he said to be "the God" without remainder. The prepositions in some of these hymns indicate that creation happens *in* or *through* or *for* him, which implies another actor than just Wisdom involved in these deeds. There is an interplay between God and Wisdom in these hymns just as there was in the earlier Jewish Wisdom hymns. The two are closely related and can be discussed in the same terms, but they are also distinguishable. What is new is that the composers of the christological hymns believe they are talking about a person when they talk about Wisdom or Logos – a person who can choose (Philippians 2), or be involved in the making of creation (John 1) during his pre–existence. Of course early Judaism was familiar with the idea of other supernatural beings, namely angels, being present with God in heaven, perhaps even before the creation of the world, or at least before the creation of human beings,[151] but the christological hymns are groping for words to say something more than this. Dunn is right that there is no evidence in the New Testament that deserves even a second glance of the development of an angel Christology – Christ as a preeminent angel.[152] Indeed, a text like Hebrews 1 very likely reveals a polemic against any such idea.

---

[149] S. G. Wilson, *Luke and the Pastoral Epistles*.

[150] I am thinking of documents like the Shepherd of Hermas, or the Epistle of Barnabas, or some of the material from Justin Martyr.

[151] L. W. Hurtado, *One God, One Lord. Early Christian Devotion and Ancient Jewish Monotheism*.

[152] Dunn, "Was Christianity," 320ff.

Something must be said about the fact that nowhere in these, hymns is Christ ever directly called Wisdom, but in many places Wisdom's actions, status or attributes are predicated of Christ. I do not think this is because the composers were trying to *avoid* portraying Christ with feminine imagery, though most of the specifically feminine attributes predicated of Wisdom in the earlier sapiential material seem to be omitted in these hymns. The hymn writers' interests were not with the gender issue at all; they were neither trying to exalt or belittle the feminine traits of Christ nor trying in a polemical way to replace the implications of femininity by using a masculine word such as *logos*. Philo, when he predicates both male and female traits and actions to *Sophia*, remarks: "Let us then pay no heed to the discrepancy in the gender of the words and say that the daughter of God, *Sophia*, is masculine and so even father sowing and begetting in souls aptness to learn..." (*De Fug*. 52).[153] Our anxieties about genderized God–talk are modern concerns with which the ancient hymn writers, like other ancients, do not seem to have been dealing.[154] Their interest was simply in transferring adequately exalted language to the one they worshipped. Whether the nouns or participles were male or female in gender was irrelevant – *logos* was probably not chosen because it was a masculine word, any more than *harpagmos* was. The issue was the content conveyed by the word, not its gender. The use of *logos* in John 1 probably owes little or nothing to Philo's androcentric predilections, but rather is drawing on the parallelism between Wisdom and Word in the Wisdom of Solomon, and/or has a special concern to show Jesus' greater character than the previous Word in Torah. There is no indication of a specific stress on maleness in the use of *logos* in the Wisdom of Solomon, and I doubt there is in John 1 either, even though the Logos hymn is about a person. Johnson is right to remind all that in early Christianity "there were no priests or temples of Sophia. They were not, in other words, introducing a second deity into the structure of their monotheism and so surrendering their faith."[155] Rather, the early Christians were groping for a way to predicate divinity of Christ and at the same time *not* relinquish a belief in only one God. Wisdom material made possible the adequate expression of this sort of monotheistic faith.[156]

---

153 I owe this reference to C. Deutsch, "Wisdom in Matthew: Transformation of a Symbol," 13–46 though she mistranslates the *te kai* as "*not*... but" (26) and cites the wrong reference on 27. One could render it "not only... but", or "and so even".

154 Indeed one suspects that in a language which has only gender inflected substantives (counting neuter as a gender), such a usage was just part of the structure of the language and seldom if ever became a real gender issue, unless there was a point in time when there was some real concern in Jewish monotheism about actual worship of goddesses among the faithful. Cf. pp. 41ff. above and Johnson, "Jesus the Wisdom of God," 269. It may not be accidental that such issues today are chiefly being raised in the English speaking world, where nouns and some other substantives are *not* gender specific.

155 Johnson, "Jesus the Wisdom of God," 271.

156 It is not adequate to say of Wisdom in the Wisdom hymns that Wisdom is simply Yahweh acting wisely for the two are not fully equated. They can be distinguished with both being spoken of at the same time. Nor is the Logos in John 1 fully equated with God *without*

On another front, it must be admitted at this juncture that chronology does not determine truth – either historical or theological truth. That is, arguing for the earliness of Wisdom Christology does not *in itself* demonstrate either the truth or falsity of such ideas. Truth can be latent for a long time before it is discovered. Then too first reflections can be false or misleading. Nevertheless, what the evidence in this chapter and the previous two chapters does tend to show is that the argument that "high" Christology is late and therefore *necessarily* a creation of the church *imposed* on an earlier non–christological Jesus or Jesus tradition is very doubtful.[157]

One must reckon with the earliest Diaspora Jewish Christians, as well as the Palestinian gatherers and editors of the Q tradition before any Gospel was written *already* thinking of Jesus in rather exalted sapiential terms. One may even have to reckon with Jesus speaking in such a way as to provide the catalyst for such thinking. This being the case, those who have a problem with "high" Christology in all likelihood have a disagreement with some of the earliest Christians about the matter, possibly even with Jesus himself. The "problem", if it should be called that, does not simply arise when one reaches the composition of what are now the canonical Gospels, sometime during the last third of the first century A.D. Earliest Christianity, even from the outset, seems already to have been groping for and starting to express its faith in Jesus in various sorts of exalted christological language, much of it sapiential.[158] It is time now to turn to the first and earliest evidence of material composed by a *canonical* writer, Paul, and examine its sapiential character.

---

remainder. The Logos is God, but the Logos does not exhaust the Godhead, in the hymn writer's mind. The mistake made by E. Schüssler Fiorenza, *In Memory of Her: A Feminist Theological Reconstruction of Christian Origins*, 133, is in simply equating Sophia with Yahweh without remainder. She says, "Divine Sophia is Israel's God in the language and *Gestalt* of the goddess" (emphasis mine). Rather, Sophia in Jewish speculation expresses an aspect of God's character or an attribute of God. It does not swallow up other attributes such as God's *Hesed*, for example. This is also the same mistake found in Johnson. "Jesus the Wisdom of God," 275–76 in her eagerness to polemicize against androcentric images or names for God.

[157] Holladay, "NT Christology," 268, is quite right that Dunn's *Christology in the Making* is vulnerable to just such an argument as this.

[158] Even in the non–sapiential invocation *maran tha* used by the early Palestinian Aramaic speaking Christians, there is already evidence of thinking of Jesus in transcendent terms, for one does not pray to a mere deceased rabbi or sage to come.

7

Paul the Apostle: Sage or Sophist?

In this chapter, for the first time, the point has been reached where discussion about actual canonical documents and their Wisdom tendencies can begin. In order to better track the pilgrimage of Wisdom up to and beyond this point, a simple diagram is in order to clarify matters.

Conventional Wisdom		**Wisdom of a Counter–Order**
Proverbs	Job	Ecclesiastes
Sirach		
	Wisdom of Solomon	
		Jesus' Teaching
		Q
James		Christological hymns
	Paul	
	John	
Matthew		

It will be seen in this diagram that Job, while showing the limitations of conventional Wisdom thinking, at least in the Epilogue resorts to a traditional Wisdom resolution of the dilemmas discussed. Thus, Job is of a mixed character. Jesus basically stands in the category of a proponent of a counter order sort of Wisdom, *but* there are some traditional elements in his teaching, as is also true with Qoheleth, and therefore while both mainly belong under the second heading neither can be wholly placed under the heading of Wisdom of a counter order. Q and the christological hymns continue to be outgrowths of this counter order or alternative Wisdom thinking, while James by and large amounts to a return to traditional sapiential agendas and approaches. In the next chapter it will be argued that this is also the case with Matthew, which deserves to be called a Wisdom Gospel, and to a lesser extent with John. Paul is an important bridge figure who appropriates a good deal of what lies above him on the chart. In some ways he seems as radical as Jesus, but apparently more often than Jesus he draws on traditional sapiential material, particularly in his parenesis.

WHEN THOUGHT WORLDS CONVERGE: ESCHATOLOGICAL WISDOM

Though the last chapter did not discuss this aspect of the matter, one thing that the study of the christological hymns reveals is how it was possible to weld together Wisdom ideas and forms (e.g. the V pattern) with eschatological ideas such as the the coming of the messiah, the vindication of Christ beyond death, and his present lordship. I use the term eschatological (rather than apocalyptic) deliberately, for Paul, in his discussions about God's climactic saving acts in history, basically does not use either the genre form "apocalyptic" such as one finds in the book of Revelation, or by and large, hyperbolic or bizarre apocalyptic symbols to convey his message about the end things.[1] This is not to say that some of his ideas or modes of expression are not apocalyptic but that it is better not to use this as the umbrella term describing Paul's thought world.

Evaluating Paul's propensities to use either sapiential or eschatological discourse or both at once cannot rest purely on an evaluation of his appropriation and modification of christological hymns such as one finds in Philippians 2 or in Colossians 1 if, as I think, Colossians is Pauline. This is too slender a foundation for the conclusion that Paul sought to present himself as a sage. Furthermore, I do not think that one can argue that "sage" is the *primary* way Paul viewed himself. Rather, God's or Christ's *apostolos* seems to be the chief category in which he placed himself.[2] Nevertheless, there is some important evidence that Paul not only self-consciously drew on Wisdom material in various ways, but also sometimes, when the occasion warranted it, presented himself as a prophetic sage. It is this evidence that this chapter seeks to present and carefully evaluate.

As E. E. Johnson has accurately shown, the scholarly discussion of Paul in the last 100 years has vacillated between an eschatological Paul *or* a sapiential Paul, with very few mediating voices being heard.[3] "For most, the differences between the Wisdom and apocalyptic traditions – and their respective influences on Paul – have appeared too drastic to permit anything but a

---

[1] Witherington, *Jesus, Paul, and the End of the World*, 15–20

[2] Cf. Pearson, "Hellenistic Jewish Wisdom", 59: "it is clear that Paul does not regard himself primarily as a 'sage' or a 'teacher' but especially as an *apostle*, as the special recipient of revelation which he is to mediate to the Gentiles..."

[3] E. E. Johnson, *The Function of Apocalyptic and Wisdom Traditions in Romans 9–11*, 23–54.

forced choice: Paul is *either* an apocalypticist *or* a Wisdom thinker."[4] H. C. Kee recently called those who think this way "abortive Hegelians" – positing dualisms with no further synthesis.[5] He has isolated at least five ways Greco–Roman Wisdom (and I would add late Jewish Wisdom such as Sirach or Wisdom of Solomon) shared certain features with eschatological and even apocalyptic thinking: (1) a concern for maintenance of cosmic order; (2) human beings held accountable for their actions; (3) oracles making clear the purpose of the universe; (4) a belief in divine choice of human agents to fulfill God's purposes; and (5) imagery used to express these expectations drawing on traditional mythical language.[6]

While von Rad was very likely wrong to think of Wisdom as being the mother of apocalyptic (prophecy being a more likely candidate), there is no doubt that by the time one gets to prophetic–apocalyptic literature in Daniel and its succesors there is evidence of the appropriation of Wisdom ideas and forms in such material.[7] This study has already had occasion to point out that not only did Ben Sira claim prophetic inspiration for his Wisdom, he also used the final eschatological intervention of God as a sanction (something also found in the Wisdom of Solomon). It has also been noted that it is unlikely that one can separate Wisdom and future eschatological material in the case of Jesus or Q into earlier and later strata of the material purely on the basis of its being Wisdom or eschatological material, for the very good reason that often eschatology may be expressed in a Wisdom form (e.g. a narrative *mashal*), or Wisdom may be expressed in a prophetic form. Then, too, as Kee and others have pointed out, there is sometimes an overlap not only of forms but also of Wisdom and eschatological *ideas* as well. This is also the conclusion of J. G. Williams, who argues that "[a]pocalyptic and other forms of eschatology are not unreceptive to Wisdom orientations and vice versa... [and] the Jewish tradition did not exclude the possibility of combining the sage and the prophet – that is, of *perceiving* a given figure as both a teacher and a prophet, or as a sage and a charismatic."[8] This is correct and it has already been argued in this study that "prophetic sage" is the proper category in which to view Jesus and to explain most of his utterances. If one has read carefully the late Jewish

---

[4] Johnson., 49. Johnson is following her mentor, J. C. Beker who supervised her dissertation, in the (mis)use of the term apocalyptic, when normally what is meant is eschatology which may or may not take an apocalyptic form.

[5] H. C. Kee in a not yet published lecture, "Wisdom and Apocalyptic," given at the SBL (Kansas City in Nov. 1991).

[6] Kee sees a certain influence of Stoicism on Ben Sira, and he may well be right; cf. above pp. 71ff.

[7] On von Rad's view, cf. *Wisdom in Israel*, 263ff. I use the term prophetic–apocalyptic to make clear the sort of apocalyptic literature to which I am referring. Apocalyptic literature can, in fact, involve little or no eschatology, concentrating, for instance, on a heavenly journey or other matters, and this sort of literature should probably not be called prophetic–apocalyptic.

[8] J. G. Williams, "Neither Here nor There, Between Wisdom and Apocalyptic in Jesus' Kingdom Sayings," 28.

sapiential material *and* the late prophetic–apocalyptic material it will not be surprising to find someone like Paul combining sapiential material with other sorts of material, including revelatory material.[9] In this regard he was not doing anything novel.[10]

There is also another factor that must not be neglected in evaluating Paul's synthesis of Wisdom and eschatological thought. There was, at least as early as the earliest Wisdom hymns found in Proverbs, a recognized complexity to the character of Wisdom. On the one hand some aspects of Wisdom could be discerned by observing nature, human behavior, and the logical consequences thereof. Wisdom in this sense was immanent in creation and discernible by careful human scrutiny. But there was recognized to be another face to Wisdom as well, i.e., a transcendent Wisdom which could not be found in creation no matter how long a human being looked (cf. Job 28), *unless* God revealed it. Probably one of the main functions of the personification of Wisdom was to reassure God's people that God intended to and did reveal this important hidden Wisdom. It may also be relevant to point out that the personification of Wisdom may have arisen precisely to deal with problems of theodicy.[11] It is Wisdom for a world gone wrong, where it may be hard to discern any Wisdom immanent in creation or in immediate historical circumstances. At least in such circumstances, the Wisdom that comes from human reflection or scrutiny of the world was seen to be inadequate. These considerations have some direct bearing on the study of Paul's use of Wisdom material.

In the study of the Jesus tradition evidence was presented that Jesus drew on both sorts of Wisdom traditions (immanent and transcendent), but when he wished to speak of *himself* as Wisdom, or of the inbreaking dominion of God, he was drawing on the revelatory side of the tradition. This must also be kept squarely in mind when one evaluates Paul's use of godly Wisdom because while Paul does on occasion offer a common sense aphorism (e.g. 2 Cor. 9:6), his primary form of discourse does not involve traditional Wisdom embodied in narrative *meshalim*, riddles or the like. Normally when he draws on sapiential material it is of the revelatory sort, and not surprisingly it is most often about the nature of Christ or of God's salvific plan in Christ. It is not only in his Christology that Paul draws on Wisdom material, but that is most often the case. Out of necessity this chapter will focus on two relevant critical examples: (1) material in the Corinthian correspondence, and (2) material in Romans, with a few words in conclusion about other Pauline texts.

---

[9] For example, A. Feuillet, *Le Christ Sagesse de Dieu. D'apres les Épîtres Pauliniennes*, 41: "le vocabulaire apocalyptique et le sapiential se melent souvent de façon inextricable dans le Nouveau Testament, et cela tout particulièrement dans les Épitres pauliniennes."

[10] On the development of the idea of revelation in Wisdom literature, cf. J. C. Rylaarsdam, *Revelation in Jewish Wisdom Literature*, especially 74ff.

[11] Cf. above pp. 38ff.

WISDOM ON THE CROSS AND THE WISE MASTER-BUILDER: 1 CORINTHIANS 1–4

The amount of discussion of the *sophia* content of 1 Corinthians 1–4 among scholars since Conzelmann's 1965 programmatic article, "Paulus und die Weisheit," has been nothing short of staggering.[12] There have been certain notable trends in the discussion. First, it is increasingly agreed that it is probably anachronistic to describe either the Corinthians' or Paul's views as Gnostic in the second century sense of the term, though clearly both are interested in some sort of *gnosis*.[13] Secondly, instead of such a background, probably the majority of scholars believe that the sapiential material in 1 Corinthians 1–4 should be read against the background of Hellenistic Jewish Wisdom material.[14] This being the case, it is not surprising that there has also been a rise in the speculation that either Apollos or an Apollos party was causing a good deal of the difficulties in Corinth that Paul attempts to answer in 1 Corinthians 1–4.[15] Since this matter affects how one

---

[12] Besides the commentaries and the Conzelmann article which appeared in *NTS* 12 (1965–66), 213–44, drawing on older suggestions of H. Windisch and others the following is a representative sampling of the most helpful studies on the relevant data: among monographs or doctoral theses one may cite U. Wilckens, *Weisheit und Torheit*, though it came a bit before Conzelmann, and Wilckens later changed his mind about the Gnostic background, and the lack of relationship between Paul and a Wisdom Christology (cf. his article, "Zu 1 Kor. 2.1–16," in *Theologia Crucis–Signum Crucis, Festschrift für E. Dinkler*, 501–37); A. Feuillet, *Le Christ Sagesse de Dieu D'après les Épîtres Pauliniennes;* J. A. Davies, *Wisdom and the Spirit. An Investigation of 1 Corinthians 1:18–3.20 against the Background of Jewish Sapiential Traditions in the Greco–Roman Period*; and Schnabel, *Law and Wisdom from Ben Sira to Paul*, 227ff. The following essays or articles also are quite helpful: R. M. Grant, "The Wisdom of the Corinthians," in *The Joy of Study*, 51–55; R. Scroggs, "Paul – *Sophos and Pneumatikos*," 33–55; A. van Roon, "The relationship between Christ and the Wisdom of God according to Paul," 207–39; K. E. Bailey, "Recovering the Poetic Structure of 1 Cor. 1:17–2.2," 265–96; B. A. Pearson, "Hellenistic–Jewish Wisdom Speculation and Paul," in *Aspects of Wisdom in Judaism and Early Christianity*, 43–66; R. A. Horsley, "Wisdom of Word and Words of Wisdom in Corinth," 224–39; E. E. Ellis, "Wisdom and Knowledge in 1 Cor.," in his *Prophecy and Hermeneutics in Early Christianity*, 46–62; J. M. Reese, "Paul Proclaims the Wisdom of the Cross: Scandal and Foolishness," 147–53; W. Bender, "Bemerkung zur Übersetzung von 1 Korinther 1.30," 263–68; G. Sellin, "Das 'Geheimnis' der Weisheit und das Rätsel der 'Christuspartei' (zu 1 Kor. 1–4)," 69–96; R. McL. Wilson, "Gnosis at Corinth," in *Paul and Paulinism. Essays in Honour of C.K. Barrett*, 112–14; and in the same Festschrift, E. Schweizer, "Paul's Christology and Gnosticism," 115–23; J. B. Polhill, "The Wisdom of God and Factionalism: 1 Cor. 1–4," 325–39; P. Richardson, "The Thunderbolt in Q and the Wise Man in Corinth," in *From Jesus to Paul. Studies in Honour of F. W. Beare*, 91–11; B. Fiore, "'Covert Allusion' in 1 Corinthians 1–4," 85–102; P. Stuhlmacher, "The Hermeneutical Significance of 1 Cor. 2.6–16," in *Tradition and Interpretation in the NT. Essays in Honor of E. E. Ellis for his 60th Birthday*, 328–43; T. H. Lim, "Not in Persuasive Words of Wisdom but in the Demonstration of the Spirit and Power," 137–49; E. E..Johnson, "The Wisdom of God as Apocalyptic Power," in *Faith and History. Essays in Honor of P. W. Meyer*, 137–48; P. Lampe, "Theological Wisdom and the 'Word about the Cross'. The Rhetorical Scheme in 1 Corinthians 1–4," 117–31; M. D. Goulder, "*Sophia* in 1 Corinthians," 516–34.

[13] Wilson, "Gnosis at Corinth," 109ff.

[14] One may wish to compare this growing consensus to the older suggestions of C. K. Barrett in "Christianity at Corinth," in *Essays on Paul*, 1–27.

[15] Sellin, "Das 'Geheimnis'," 71ff. who says it is natural if late Jewish Wisdom is the background against which Apollos stands in the foreground.

views Paul's use of Wisdom traditions it is necessary to point out several things at this juncture.

First, I have made a case for the essential historicity of the material in Acts 18:24–28.[16] If this assessment is correct, then it is in order to note the various parallels between what the material in 1 Corinthians 1–4 suggests about the Corinthians' Wisdom orientation and the assessment of Apollos in Acts 18:24–26. Apollos is said to be from Alexandria and an *aner logios* which can mean he was eloquent and possibly implies he was one who used Greco–Roman rhetoric in the presentation of the Gospel. He is also said to be powerful in the Scriptures. He had been instructed in the way of the Lord, taught accurately the things concerning Jesus, and he was "boiling over in the Spirit," an idiomatic phrase which seems to mean he was full of the Holy Spirit not merely that he was enthusiastic (but cf. Rom. 12:11). In any event, this spiritual capacity propelled his speaking and teaching the things concerning Jesus. There was, however, one deficiency that he had – he knew only John's baptism. It is also said that he did his teaching in the Ephesian synagogue and that when he was heard by Paul's co–workers he was instructed more accurately in the way of God (which presumably includes teaching on Christian baptism). Finally it is said that his desire was to go to Achaia and the Christians in Ephesus wrote him a letter of reference or introduction so that he would be received there. This episode is placed *after* Paul's first visit to Corinth (Acts 18).

When one reads this narrative and compares it to 1 Corinthians 1–4 it is difficult not to see various connections. First, the issue of baptism is raised in 1 Corinthians 1 precisely in the context where the issue of divisions amongst the Corinthians ("I am of Apollos", "I am of Paul") is also raised. Second, Paul goes to some length to say that he was eschewing the use of *sophia logou* in his preaching, lest the cross of Christ be emptied of its power. Third, it becomes quite clear that not only baptism or Wisdom seem to be at issue in Corinth but also who was a *pneumatikos* and what this entailed. These three things together seem to have something to do with the divisions in Corinth. Fourth, Paul takes some pains in 1 Corinthians 3 to stress that he and Apollos are working together in harmony on the same task for God, not as competitors. Notice also it is *only these two* who are mentioned when the slogans "*Ego eimi*" followed by an apostle's name appear again in 1 Corinthians 3:4. The Corinthians are warned against taking pride in mere human beings (3:21) whether it be Paul, Apollos, or even Cephas. The crucial thing is not that they belong to one or another of these apostles but rather that they belong to Christ. Fifth, 4:6b must be taken quite seriously, for whatever 4:6a means, the second half of the verse states the nub of the problem – the Corinthians were taking sides, being inflated with

---

[16] For the general discussion, cf. Witherington, *Women in the Earliest Churches*, 153–54; for the authenticity of this material, cf. Witherington, *Women and Their Roles in the Gospels and Acts* (1981), ad loc.

pride for one apostle over against the other,[17] and in the context of what was said earlier this must surely mean Paul and Apollos. Paul must counter these divisions and does so in a variety of ways including using himself and Apollos as exhibit A of the lesson the Corinthians must learn – unity and cooperation (cf. 3:5ff.; 4:6–7).[18] This leads to a reconstruction of the situation which Paul addresses in 1 Corinthians 1–4.

While it is probably too much to speak of clear cut factions or parties in Corinth because not only is Paul still able to address the converts in Corinth *as a whole* in this letter, but also the term *schismata* (1:10) means cracks or fissures in a rock or tears in a garment, not separate rocks or garments,[19] *nevertheless* there seem to be serious divisions amongst a still somewhat unified group.[20] If one reads behind remarks like 1 Cor. 2:15 it also appears that the divisions involved a personal attack or at least a very critical judgment on Paul himself.[21] How had this happened if, as Paul says, he and Apollos were working as a team?

Paul was first in Corinth and responsible for the initial preaching and setting up of the congregation there. He had apparently stayed a considerable period of time in order to accomplish this task (cf. Acts 18:11, a year and a half). This would have entailed not only preaching in the synagogue and elsewhere but also teaching which followed up on the preaching as well. Paul speaks in 1 Cor. 2:1–2 of a conscious decision *not* to use sublime words or *sophia* but rather to preach only Christ and him crucified. The focus here seems to be on avoiding purely ornamental rhetoric in the preaching lest the audience be carried away by the form of the message rather than by the plain unvarnished truth that Paul wished to convey. As 2:6ff. goes on to reveal, however, Paul himself does speak Wisdom of a sort, a Wisdom not of this age but rather a Wisdom of God in a mystery, a Wisdom that involved a revelation from God through the Holy Spirit (2:10). For Paul, receiving the Spirit seems to be the primary thing and Wisdom and knowledge comes through the Spirit.[22] While it is probably

---

[17] G. D. Fee, *The First Epistle to the Corinthians*, (Grand Rapids: Eerdmans, 1989), 169–70; C. K. Barrett, *The First Epistle to the Corinthians* (New York: Harper and Row, 1968), 107. Goulder, "*Sophia*", 519, in order to make his view of pitting Paul vs. Peter work, interprets 4.6b to mean that the 'one' is Paul and Apollos together, and the 'other' is Peter standing for a Torah–centric approach to things. This is nowhere suggested by the text and requires one to read more into the term 'one' (*eis*) than is warranted.

[18] Polhill, "Wisdom of God," 336.

[19] For example, BAGD; Fee, *First Corinthians*, 31. *Schismata* is not as strong a word as the word schism in English.

[20] One suspects in view of 4.6 that there were at most only two significant groups – those who tended to favor the teaching of Paul and those who favored Apollos. It is hard to conceive of a Christ party, for surely had there really been such Paul would simply have said that all Christians belong to it. Had there really been a Christ party is it likely that Paul would have worded 1 Cor. 3:21–23 as he does, where the phrase "you are of Christ" is used positively (cf. 2 Cor. 10:7)?; cf. Sellin, "'Geheimnis'," 92; Fee, *First Corinthians*, 54ff.

[21] Polhill, "Wisdom of God," 336.

[22] So Davies, *Wisdom and the Spirit*, 108.

overreaching to think of Paul establishing a Wisdom school *per se* at Corinth, on the order of what Conzelmann assumes was set up in Ephesus,[23] nevertheless it does appear that Paul made it a practice to engage in Wisdom teaching, at least *en tois teleiois*, and this Wisdom seems to have something to do with further explication of the initial preaching about God's salvation plan operating in and through the crucified Christ.

Paul was succeeded in Corinth by Apollos, a fact suggested by Apollos being called a "waterer" (3.6), following Paul's role as a planter. If the description of Apollos in Acts 18 is anything close to accurate one may suspect that watering entailed at least the following things. First, he used ornamental rhetoric in public proclamation and presumably also teaching (cf. Acts 18:26 – he spoke with *parresia* as well as eloquence)[24]. Second, he drew on the Alexandrian Hellenistic Jewish Wisdom speculation in the process, perhaps especially in the exegesis of Scripture (cf. 1 Cor. 4.6a[25]). It seems likely the Corinthians picked up the hints of such things in the teaching of Apollos and went well beyond them on their own. Paul is not happy with this development and insists they must stick with what is written in Scripture.[26] Third, the baptizing of certain people in Corinth whom Paul had not yet baptized. Fourth, the stress on the pneumatic character of both his Wisdom and the Christian life. Whatever the intent of Apollos, the effect of his eloquent sapiential and pneumatic teaching was that factionalism, individualism, and sapiential spiritualism resulted. It is probably not by chance that Paul mentions that Greek desire *sophia* (1:22). Clearly at least some in Corinth were looking for *sophia*, and they believed they had found it in the eloquent discourses of Apollos. There is

---

[23] But cf. H. Conzelmann, *1 Corinthians* (Philadelphia: Fortress, 1975), 14ff. I would not entirely rule out this possibility. On Sirach being used in Jewish Wisdom schools, cf. H. Stadelmann, *Ben Sira als Schriftgelehrter*, 27–30. On the Wisdom of Solomon as possibly being a school product, cf. D. Georgi, *Weisheit Salamos*, 393.

[24] Cf. Horsley, "Wisdom of Word," 231–32 who suggests that Apollos introduced a Philonic sort of Wisdom to Corinth. This might explain the individualistic approach to religion in the Christian community there. As Horsley, 236, says, "Philo's whole discussion of speech is rather single–mindedly oriented toward the relation of the individual soul and the divine Wisdom." To counter this Paul offers a more community oriented sort of Wisdom, drawing on a variety of other Wisdom sources.

[25] Possibly 1 Cor 4.6a refers to Scripture, in which case the Corinthians are being warned not to go beyond Scripture (into Jewish halakah or, perhaps more likely, esoteric Wisdom speculations like one finds in Philo). This might be supported by the reference in 1 Cor. 1.20 to the *grammateus*, the expert in the Law.

[26] M. D. Hooker's handling of 1 Cor. 4.6a may be correct; cf. *From Adam to Christ. Essays on Paul*, 109: "The 'Wisdom' which was paraded by these teachers was something additional to Paul's own message of Christ crucified, the message which he saw as the fulfillment of God's purposes and of the 'things which are written.' It was a Wisdom which was centred on ideas extraneous to the gospel, and which therefore was the Wisdom of men, and not the Wisdom of God. In following this worthless and harmful teaching the Corinthians were not simply adding to that of Paul, but were also going 'beyond the things which are written', and it was this search for additional 'Wisdom' which had led to their divisions, and to the situation where one was 'puffed up against the other'."

nothing in 1 Corinthians 1–4 that suggests, even remotely, that Peter is the real culprit here. It is not even clear that Peter had even been to Corinth, though certainly the Corinthians know about him and his work.[27]

1 Cor. 16:12 supports the above reconstruction. Apollos is apparently with or near Paul in Asia when Paul writes this letter, and though Paul urged him *many times* to go to Corinth "with the brothers" he was *"not at all willing to come at the present time."* Paul is confident he will come when he gets a good opportunity. 1 Cor. 16:12 suggests several things. First, whatever the divisions between those who looked to Apollos and those who looked to Paul as their chief prophetic sage, Paul and Apollos were still working together. Paul would not have urged him many times to go to Corinth (perhaps to straighten out the mess that had arisen there) if he did not think the problem ultimately lay with the Corinthians and not with Apollos and his teachings.[28] Secondly, Apollos' unwillingness to go in the midst of the problems arising in Corinth may suggest that he realized he was the unwitting catalyst of some of these difficulties and in order not to cause Paul any further trouble he was going to stick with the work in which he was currently involved in Asia.[29]

Paul, with sarcasm, says of the *pneumatikoi* in Corinth, "Already you are satiated, already you have become rich (*eploutesate*, in Wisdom), already you reign (*ebasileusate*). It is hard not to hear echoes from sources deeply indebted to Hellenistic Jewish Wisdom material. Philo says, "And thus they laid down the dogma for the students of philosophy, that the sage alone is a ruler (*archon*, cf. 1 Cor. 2:6), and king (*basileus*), and virtue a rule and a kingship (*basileia*) whose authority is final" (*De Somn*. 2:243–44). Wis. 10:10 speaks of Wisdom guiding Jacob on straight paths "and showed him the kingdom of God, and gave him knowledge of holy things... she stood by him and made him rich." In the *Sentences of Sextus* 309–11 one reads: "Next to God nothing is as free as a *sophos aner*. Whatever God possesses so also the sage. A *sophos aner* shares in the *basileias tou theou*."[30] It appears the Corinthians were steeped in Hellenistic Jewish Wisdom and were taking the promises made in that material quite seriously.[31] They had a kingdom mentality

---

[27] But cf. Barrett, "Cephas and Corinth," in *Essays on Paul*, 28–39; Polhill, "The Wisdom of God," 234. Polhill suggests that Paul mentions one he has a harmonious relationship with, namely Apollos, in order to critique indirectly those really responsible for the divisions (perhaps another apostle). This is oversubtle and neglects the clear implications of 4:6b.

[28] Cf. Sellin, "Das 'Geheimnis'," 74. As Stuhlmacher, "The Hermeneutical Significance," 335 points out, Paul only criticizes the Corinthians, not Apollos, for he is rejecting *their* false estimation of their leaders. In view of Galatians one can hardly argue that Paul would not have criticized another apostle in a public letter.

[29] The speculation of Sellin, "Das 'Geheimnis'," 79ff. that Apollos presented himself as a redeemer figure (!) while in Corinth has no basis in the text whatsoever.

[30] On these texts, cf. Williams, "Neither Here nor There," 11.

[31] I take it that the composition of the Corinthian congregation was as follows: (1) Diaspora Jews converted from the synagogue(s) in Corinth; (2) Gentiles who had been synagogue adherents before becoming Christians; and (3) some Gentiles who had been pagans before conversion. While I would certainly not wish to minimize the influence of Greek Wisdom and

believing that through the Spirit and the Wisdom it conveyed they had already arrived at and even obtained the state of perfection, for they themselves were *sophoi* and as *M. Berak.* 2:2 says it is the task of the wise person "to take on the [yoke of the] kingdom of heaven." Again the close connection made between Wisdom and the Spirit in Wis. 1:6; 7:7, 23–24 as in 1 Corinthians 1–4 must be stressed. Through the Spirit at least some of the Corinthians believed they were already *teleioi*, already having esoteric knowledge and Wisdom about God and the power that comes with it.

How then does Paul respond to the crisis over pneumatic Wisdom in Corinth? He does so by offering a counter–order Wisdom, one that goes against natural human predilections and even against common sense Wisdom.[32] It is a Wisdom that lifts up the humble and humbles the proud, a Wisdom that builds up the congregation rather than puffing up the individual. He will present the Gospel in a sapiential way so as to offer a different sort of Wisdom to his audience. Paul offers a revelatory Wisdom, a Wisdom that must be called a *musterion* for unless it is revealed it could never be known; it is not the sort of Wisdom one could deduce from close scrutiny of the world or human behavior. He offers a Wisdom that squashes individualism, elitism, and human pride and counters factionalism in the congregation. What is interesting about this is that while Paul in this letter does not engage in any sort of rhetoric that might be called eloquence or ornamentation for its own sake, he does engage in rhetoric, the content of which is counter–order Wisdom, particularly in 1 Corinthians 1–4.[33] I would argue further that Paul's approach to Wisdom in these chapters is significantly indebted to the closing sections of Job (28–42) in the following ways. First, his presentation of hidden Wisdom, only revealed by God or God's agent, owes something to the discussion which begins in Job 28ff. Secondly, his statements about the Spirit within a person (God's breath) giving illumination draws on the words of Elihu in Job 32:8: "But truly it is the spirit in a mortal, the breath of the Almighty, that makes for understanding" (cf. 1 Cor. 2:10ff). Thirdly, Paul, like Elihu, proclaims revelatory Wisdom and as such makes clear that God's mouthpiece can be even the most unlikely of people – a young, apparently foolish, and inexperienced man, or the weak and lowly, including an impoverished and outwardly unimpressive apostle. Fourthly,

---

pagan religion on the Corinthians (this is suggested by the issue of eating in pagan temples, and perhaps also by the Corinthians attitude toward baptism – they seem to have seen it as a rite of initiation perhaps rather like that in some of the Mysteries, in which the initiator becomes important as a guide into the esoteric mysteries), I would suggest that probably the more dominant influence came from Hellenistic Jewish Wisdom, not least because probably most of the Corinthian Christians had formerly been Jews or synagogue adherents.

[32] G. Theissen, *Psychological Aspects of Pauline Theology*, 368ff., calls it an anti–Wisdom sort of Wisdom.

[33] I plan to argue the case for this at length in my forthcoming socio–rhetorical commentary on 1 and 2 Corinthians to be entitled *Conflict and Community in Corinth* (Grand Rapids: Eerdmans, 1994); cf. now M. M. Mitchell's dissertation, *Paul and the Rhetoric of Reconciliation*.

in the case of both Paul and Elihu the message is conveyed in the way it is, in order to rebuke what is taken to be arrogance in regard to human Wisdom.

I would suggest then that Paul's missionary strategy in Corinth[34] was originally not to use sophistic rhetoric in his preaching[35] which involved significant ornamentation, lest in that environment it be seen as an exercise in eloquence much like that of other great orators of the day. Paul wanted to be sure that the message, not the medium, won converts. He did not want to do anything to detract from the power of the message about the crucified Christ. The problem with this strategy was that in the Jewish Wisdom tradition the one who has Wisdom is known to have it by the way he speaks – "For Wisdom is known through speech, and education through the words of the tongue" (Sir. 4:24). Lim puts it this way: "In 1 Cor. 2:4 Paul is not rejecting rhetoric altogether, but that specific emphasis and practice of the Corinthian preachers to employ Wisdom of words in preaching."[36]

It appears from 2 Cor. 10:10 that "some" were complaining that while Paul's letters were weighty and strong, his oral speech, his preaching rhetoric, was ineffective. This amounted to calling him an *idiotes* – a rank amateur in his rhetoric or oral proclamation (2 Cor. 11:6).[37] The point of this is that the Corinthians had rightly noticed, as Paul admits, a distinction between Paul's oral proclamation which involved both bodily weakness and apparently unvarnished proclamation and the character of his letters. Paul came across differently in oral and in written communication and, at least in the case of the Corinthian situation, this was in part by design as 1 Cor. 2:2 suggests.

It is well to remember, however, lest one too quickly conclude Paul was no rhetorician, that while sophistry in the first century A.D. was a movement of professional orators who *all* traveled to major cities like Corinth, exhibiting their eloquence and charging students fees for lectures (using rhetoric patterned on that of the fourth to fifth centuries B.C.),[38] these sophists may be divided into two different sorts. The so-called *pure* sophist focused on developing students in elocution and declamation, but there were also philosophical sophists like Dio Chrysostom who used rhetoric to expound on his views on

---

[34] It is not clear that this was Paul's preaching strategy everywhere for he says in 2.2, "*ekrina ti eidenai* ***en humin***."

[35] Lim, "Not in Persuasive Words," 146, is right that Paul appears to be rejecting persuasive speech as it was practiced by some rhetoricians, but sometimes this was a rhetorical strategy in itself (cf. Dio 12.15–16; 42.2–3). The term *peithois* is frequently used to describe the skill of rhetoricians (cf. 1 Cor. 2.4 Philostratus *Lives* 503). The term *apodexei* is used in rhetoric for a proof from commonly agreed premises (cf. 1 Cor. 2.4). Barrett, "Christianity at Corinth," 8 is very likely right that what Paul is rejecting is the sort of rhetoric that relies on human device and artifice, rather than on the power and message of God.

[36] Lim, "Not in Persuasive Words," 148.

[37] On *idiotes* as a term for one who is an amateur in rhetoric rather than a professional rhetor, cf. Dio 42.3, possibly 54.1; Plato, *Ion*, 532D.

[38] On the charging of fees by rhetoricians, cf. Philostratus *Lives* 494, 591.

morality, politics, and other subjects.[39] At least in his letters, Paul comes across as the second sort of rhetor. Like Philo, Paul believed that being truly sagacious meant a good deal more than being a mere sophist for the difference between *ho sophistes* and a *sophos* was like the difference between a mere babe (*paidion neanias*, cf. 1 Cor. 3.1) and a mature person.[40] Paul's claim is not that the Corinthians have no Wisdom, but that, as Philo's distinction implies, there is a difference between settling for ornamental sophistry and partaking of the real meat of the Gospel, that makes one a true *sophos*. To be a real lover of Wisdom (*philosophia*) one must not pursue "the philosophy which is pursued by the present day crowd of sophists (*ho nun anthropon sophistikos homilos*) who use the craft of words against the truth...." though they call it Wisdom (*Post*. 101, cf. also *Mig*. 171). Paul shares Philo's disdain for mere sophistry, rather than the art of persuasion used to some good purpose.

A good example of Paul's use of rhetoric in 1 Corinthians 1–4 can be seen in 1 Cor. 4:6a where he tells his converts that in regard to the metaphors he has been using (in 3:1ff.) he has *metaschematisa* them to himself and Apollos. This fits into the category of veiled allusion or disguised speech. As Philostratus, *Lives* 597, 561 makes clear this is a rather standard figure of speech in rhetoric,[41] and the term *metaschematidzo* means "to hint at something in a disguised speech without saying it *expressis verbis*." Thus, as P. Lampe puts it, Paul is saying, "For your sake I have clothed the thoughts of 3:5—4:2 in... disguised speech about planting and watering, about preparing a foundation, building on it, and about examining a steward's housekeeping. And I have applied these disguised metaphors to me and Apollos... that you may learn not to be puffed up in favor of one (apostle) against another."[42] B. Fiore points out how the use of the rhetorical device of "covert allusion" to speak of the example of apostolic cooperation is meant to deal with the issue of factionalism. The apostolic example is meant to depict the approach to community the Corinthians should take.[43]

---

[39] On all this, cf. Lim, "Not in Persuasive Words," 143 and n. 20.

[40] As Philo claims in *Sob*. 9.

[41] Though it was considered a difficult type of speech to use well and in sophistic rhetoric it often becomes mere ornamentation. The person who used it well was demonstrating he was a very good rhetorician. Paul's decision to use this form shows his intent to present himself as a good rhetor. Cf. W. C. Wright's comments in the Loeb edition of *Philostratus and Eunapius* (Cambridge: Harvard University Press, 1968), 570.

[42] Lampe, "Theological Wisdom," 129. Quintilian, *Inst. Or.* 9.2.66–79 stresses that the thought figure of a *schema* is employed and positively received when the orator is "hampered by the existence of influential persons whose feelings he or she does not want to hurt by messages directly conveyed". On the use of rhetoric in 1 Corinthians in general and 1 Corinthians 1–4 in particular, cf. W. Wuellner, "Greek Rhetoric and Pauline Argumentation," in *Early Christian Literature and the Classical Intellectual Tradition. In Honorem R. M. Grant*, 177–88, here 182ff. He sees 1:19–3:20 as a digression.

[43] Fiore, "Covert Allusions," 101–02. Hooker, *From Adam to Paul*, 111 takes the meaning to be simply 'a figure of speech' but the verbal form of *meteschematisma* is not used in this sense anywhere else in Greek literature.

It has often been argued that Paul's use of the term *sophia* (seventeen times in 1 Corinthians, sixteen times in 1 Corinthians 1–3, only eleven times elsewhere in Paul's letters; *gnosis* is used ten times in 1 Corinthians out of a total of twenty-three)[44] and of Wisdom material in 1 Corinthians 1–4, is "best explained by the assumption that Paul picked up on a key word of the Corinthians here",[45] in short he was taking up and redefining the favorite vocabulary and phrases of his opponents. Thus, according to this line of thinking one should not look for a positive expression of his own thought in 1 Corinthians 1–4. While I would agree that this in part may explain Paul's *concentration* on the subject here, it is definitely not the case that this is the only place Paul uses sapiential material (cf. e.g. 2 Corinthians 11, the so–called Fool's Discourse; Phil. 2:6–11ff.; Rom. 10:6–8; in the Wisdom hymn Rom. 11:33–36; Col. 1:15ff.).[46] Such an argument also overlooks the fact that of all the extra–canonical books Paul cites or alludes to, Sirach and the Wisdom of Solomon are used more than any other sources, and in fact more than many sources in the Old Testament itself.[47] It cannot be argued that only the Corinthians or only Apollos drew on Hellenistic Jewish Wisdom material to formulate their views.[48] Paul does so as well.

The judgments of F. Lang and P. Stuhlmacher bear repeating at this point. Both claim that what one finds in this section of 1 Corinthians is Jewish Hellenistic Wisdom material bound up with an apocalyptic understanding of revelation. Paul uses this combination to interpret these traditions in a new way, from the standpoint of the Wisdom and power of God in Christ crucified and risen. This results in a strong concentration of Wisdom and apocalyptic ideas given a christological and soteriological focus.[49]

---

[44] Ellis, "Wisdom and Knowledge," 49. Reese, "Paul Proclaims," 149 reminds us that in the Hellenistic world sophia = a teaching or doctrine which leads to salvation. This development is already evident in the Wisdom of Solomon.

[45] Lampe, "Theological Wisdom," 118–19.

[46] Ellis, "Wisdom and Knowledge," 46 rightly points out the danger of reading 1 Corinthians overly much in the light of the later situation expressed in 2 Corinthians.

[47] He alludes to Sirach twenty–six times according to Nestle–Aland, *Novum Testamentum Graece* (1979), 769–75, and these allusions are spread throughout the Pauline corpus including in Romans 1, Corinthians, Ephesians, Philippians, Colossians, and 1 Thessalonians. Cf. Schnabel, *Law and Wisdom*, 231 and n. 26. He cites or alludes to the Wisdom of Solomon some forty times, including notable examples in Romans and 2 Corinthians. Cf. C. Romaniuk, "Le Livre de la Sagesse dans le Nouveau Testament," 503–13.

[48] It is possible, as Grant, "Wisdom of the Corinthians," 55, suggests, that the Corinthians, having been encouraged to interpret their faith as a form of Wisdom philosophy by Apollos, drew on the Greek heritage to some degree where there were at least two sorts of *sophoi*: (1) one could follow the Cynic and stress the irrelevance of bodily behavior and thus the freedom to act with license; or (2) or one could follow the ideal of the later Stoics and stress absolute continence. Perhaps the Corinthians were advocating some sort of synthesis of Alexandrian Jewish *and* Greek Wisdom ideas.

[49] F. Lang, *Die Briefe an die Korinther*, 38–41, especially 41: "Das hat eine Reduktion und starke Konzentration der weisheitlich–apokalyptischen Vorstellungen auf Christus geschehen zur Folge." Stuhlmacher, "Hermeneutical Significance," 330–32; cf. also the conclusion of Davies, *Wisdom and the Spirit*, 124. His particular insight is that "the pattern of religion at

It is instructive to note how Paul handles Scripture. For example, in 1 Cor. 2:16 Paul quotes Isa. 40:13 but by way of its use in Wis. 9:13. Isaiah says, "Who has directed the spirit of the Lord, or as his counselor instructed him?" The Wisdom of Solomon modifies this to, "For who can learn the counsel of God? Or who can discern what the Lord wills?" Paul has, "For who has known the mind of the Lord so as to instruct him?" This seems to be a combination of the two previous renderings, suggesting that Paul knew and used both.[50]

But this is not all; it appears from a comparison of 1 Cor. 1:19–20, 2:9 and Matt. 11:25–27 that Paul knows and draws on the so–called thunderbolt saying in Q.[51] As P. Richardson suggests, since Jesus or at least the editors of Q were very likely influenced by the speculations about Wisdom in late Jewish sapiential traditions, it should not surprise us if Paul in composing a Wisdom discourse draws on previous traditions about God's revelation of true Wisdom.[52] It is necessary now to examine some particularly crucial points about what may be called Paul's Wisdom discourse in 1 Corinthians 1–4.

Paul makes several notable contrasts in 1 Cor. 1:18ff., in particular between human and divine Wisdom and between what is wise and what is foolish (a more traditional sapiential contrast), and between sapiential form and sapiential content.[53] There are persons who are *sophoi kata sarki* (1:26); that is, they speak *en sophia anthropon* (2:5) which in light of 2:4 is said to entail "persuasive words of Wisdom". This Wisdom is also said to be a *sophian...tou aionos toutou* (2:6). Now in view of the fact that in his rhetorical questions in 1:20 Paul mentions three categories: (1) the (Jewish?) sage; (2) the expert in the law (*grammateus* is not used in Greek literature of non–Jewish scholars or teachers)[54]; and (3) the skillful debater (presumably a reference to Greek philosophers or sophists), it will be seen that Paul seems to have several things in mind when he speaks of a human Wisdom or a Wisdom of this age.[55] The allusion to Isa. 19:11–12 where the wise counselors or sages of Pharoah claim "I am one of the sages, a descendent of ancient kings" suggests that Paul has in mind the

---

Corinth resembled the pattern of sapiential achievement... in late Jewish Wisdom circles.... [I]t seems to have approximated most closely to the general contours of Hellenistic–Jewish Wisdom as represented by Philo." If this is correct, then perhaps one could argue that Paul is countering this with a Wisdom more closely tied to Israel's historical traditions, and thus more closely linked to works such as Sirach and the Wisdom of Solomon as well as the Christian kerygma about the climax of Christ's earthly career.

[50] Stuhlmacher, "Hermeneutical Significance," 338.

[51] This may support a rather early date for Q, or at least this particular tradition which was likely in Q; cf. pp. 211ff. above H. Koester, *Ancient Christian Gospels*, 55–62, thinks Paul may be drawing from a sayings collection other than Q, but the parallels that he draws from Thomas and elsewhere to other parts of 1 Corinthians 1–4 seem too remote to warrant such a conclusion.

[52] Richardson, "The Thunderbolt in Q," 95.

[53] Scroggs, "Paul – *Sophos* and *Pneumatikos*," 34.

[54] Fee, *First Corinthians*, 71.

[55] Another view is that *sophos* refers to the Greek wise man and the term debater includes both the previous two terms; cf. Mitchell, *Paul and the Rhetoric*, 87–88.

purveyors of Wisdom on an international scale, not just Jewish sages. This also makes sense in view of the way he characterizes it – Wisdom that is of this age in general. In the Jewish tradition this would amount to a critique of the Wisdom that sages could deduce from examining the world and human behavior, in short, the sort of Wisdom enshrined in Proverbs 10ff. Paul contrasts a revelatory Wisdom to this. But Paul's critique also applies to those called upon to interpret and indeed on occasion embellish Torah to make it applicable to a current situation.[56] Finally, the critique extends to the debater and here the focus seems clearly to be on a spoken Wisdom as well as perhaps a way of speaking in a "Wisdom of [human] words", in short sophistry or sophistic rhetoric.[57] It may be of some relevance that Philostratus in his biography characterized Apollonius of Tyana as a *sophos*, a *dunatos*, and having prominent blood lines (*eugenes*), and Paul reminds his converts that not many of them were any of these things (1 Cor. 1:26).[58]

What Paul offers as an alternative is described as the mystery of God (2:1) or, more vividly, as the Wisdom of God in a mystery. As R. E. Brown has pointed out, it is not necessary to look elsewhere than in Jewish sources, both prophetic–apocalyptic and late sapiential, to explain Paul's use of the term *musterion*.[59] For example, in Sirach 4:18 Wisdom is the one who reveals the secrets of God and in 14:10 she is said to have secrets herself. In Wis. 6:22 the origin of Wisdom is called a *musterion*, and in 7:21 Wisdom teaches "mysteries." Mysteries or secrets are things one would not otherwise have known, and cannot know by mere human inquiry or effort.[60] The content of this particular mystery seems to be what Paul preached and is now amplifying on – Christ crucified as the Wisdom and power of God (1:24).[61] This is a Wisdom that

[56] That either Torah–centric Wisdom is the particular or sole target of Paul's critique (cf. Davies, *Wisdom and the Spirit*, 141ff) or that the *sophia* in 1 Corinthians 1–3 that is being critiqued is Torah as a way of life, a view held by a Peter party in Corinth (Goulder, "*Sophia*," 521ff.), entails much too narrow a focus. Paul is critiquing all human Wisdoms that are at odds with the Wisdom of God which is Christ crucified. Most peculiar is Goulder's insistence that Paul is not talking about non–Christians in 1 Corinthians 1 where he refers to those seeking Wisdom or signs.

[57] Polhill, "Wisdom of God," 325, who stresses how Paul lumps together all human Wisdoms here and chastises the lot.

[58] Cf. Philostratus, *Vita Ap*. 1.2; 1.4, 3.38–39 and the discussion in Polhill, "Wisdom of God," 329–30.

[59] Cf. R. E. Brown, *The Semitic Background of the Term "Mystery" in the New Testament*, 40–50. Ellis, "Wisdom and Knowledge," 53ff., tries to merge the two categories of sage and prophet under the heading of prophet which leads to odd translations, for instance of 1 Cor. 13:2 – "If I have prophecy, *that is* know all mysteries..." That one may speak of a prophetic sage like Ben Sira is quite right, but Paul does not simply merge these categories as is shown by 1 Cor. 1:20a.

[60] Cf. 1 QpH 7.5 where God revealed to the Teacher of Righteous the mysteries of final eschatological events; cf. 1 QS 4.18.

[61] It is inadequate to say, as Johnson, "Wisdom of God," 140–41, does, that Paul's debate focuses on the nature of Christian preaching and preachers and *not on* Christology. Clearly the debate involves both, and Paul wishes to inculcate a Christocentric approach to Wisdom that rules out human pride and the like. I agree with her (144), however, that Paul's advanced teaching is not something wholly distinct from the simple preaching of Christ, for both are able to be summed up under the term of the gospel (cf. 2:1–5).

shames the wise, powerful, and well born of the world because it is something they did not generate, nor could have deduced, nor could have bought, nor could have inherited. It is strictly from God and therefore when one obtains it one has no grounds whatsoever for human pride or boasting.[62] Such Wisdom is folly to the Greeks and a scandal to Jews for how could a crucified manual worker from Galilee possibly be the locus of God's Wisdom and power for humankind?

In 1:18ff. Paul says that the old ways of reckoning what amounts to wisdom and what amounts to folly must be abandoned to understand the Gospel. There is no way the sort of advice found in Proverbs about human Wisdom and folly can help at this point. The spirit of what Paul says and the assumptions behind it seem very close to what one finds when Wisdom and prophecy are spoken of together at Qumran: "As one of the wise, I have knowledge of you, my God, by the Spirit that you gave to me... By your Holy Spirit you opened to me knowledge in the mystery of your Wisdom" (1QH 12:11–12). At Qumran those who are given leadership are the wise, the understanding, and the mature in the way (1QSam. 1:27ff). According to CD 9:12, 18–19 the job of the wise person is to guide members of the community with knowledge and Wisdom in the mysteries so they can walk maturely (*tamim* = *teleioi*). Paul's appropriation of the Wisdom and prophetic traditions in a community–oriented way is much more like what one finds in Qumran, Sirach, or the Wisdom of Solomon than like what one finds in Philo.

One of the most important verses in this Wisdom discourse is 1 Cor. 1:30. W. Bender has made several important points on the structure of this sentence:[63] (1) *en Christo* seems likely to be used in an instrumental sense here as it often is elsewhere in Paul; (2) if one considers the parallel in 1 Cor. 1:23–24 one is encouraged to see Christ being identified there as God's power and God's Wisdom, but not as some of these other terms found in 1:30; (3) more pertinently in 2 Cor. 5:21 one not only finds the instrumental use of *en* with Christ as the object but even more to the point it is the believer, *not* Christ, who is said to become the *dikaiosune theou*. This happens through Christ and because of what happened to him. Finally, 1 Cor. 6:11b must not be overlooked where it is said that *believers* were washed, consecrated, and justified through the name of Christ and through the Holy Spirit. Putting these things together, they strongly suggest the following translation for 1:30: "But from God *you* are through Christ (who was made Wisdom for us by God), righteousness and sanctification and redemption." These are the benefits one gets through Christ as a result of what God has accomplished in him. Christ is not said to be these

---

[62] Johnson, "Wisdom of God," 145 is likely right to stress that the conflict between human and divine Wisdom is seen as more than a mere human struggle for it also involves an eschatological struggle between cosmic forces. How much stress one places on this depends on whether the *archontes* are viewed as more than just human rulers.

[63] W. Bender, "Bemerkung zur Übersetzung von 1 Korinther 1.30," 263–68.

latter three things for believers nor are these latter three things a further explanation of what Christ's being Wisdom amounts to.[64]

What then is meant by Christ being made *Sophia* for believers? In the first place one must note the qualifier, "for us." This is a Wisdom which only belongs to believers, not to the world. The phrase about being made Wisdom by God suggests the parallel in 2 Cor. 5:21 which speaks about Christ being made sin (by God) for us, which in turn suggests that Paul is continuing to think of what happened when Christ was crucified. It was at that point that all worldly forms of Wisdom were made of no effect in so far as the matter of salvation is concerned. The world in its Wisdom crucified God's Wisdom, but paradoxically by so doing put God's Wisdom into effect so that through Christ, believers might have right–standing and all other aspects of salvation. To sum up, that Paul says Christ was made our Wisdom (on the cross) suggests that he is not here discussing Christ as God's pre–existent Wisdom. The focus here is soteriological, and Paul wishes to explain how things have changed in regard to Wisdom as a result of Christ's death on the cross. Because of that paradoxical event, all human Wisdom can now be said to be of no use soteriologically speaking. The only wisdom that has any power, effect or benefit is God's Wisdom as both expressed and embodied in the crucified Christ. This does have *implications* here for a developing Wisdom Christology, for it is not merely the cross of Christ or the event which happened at Golgotha but the person of Christ crucified who is said to be this Wisdom.[65] Paul does not choose to draw out the implications of a Wisdom christology *vis-à-vis* protological matters at this juncture, but he will do so later in the letter (1 Cor. 10.4). E. Schweizer puts it this way:

> With Paul, the starting point is... the life and, especially, the death and resurrection of Jesus Christ which attracted Wisdom language. The Jewish description of Wisdom as rejected by all nations fitted Paul's interpretation of Jesus, the one crucified by the Romans [cf. 1 Cor. 2:6]. It had merely to be radicalized: Israel also rejected God's Wisdom. She became a folly for Gentiles and a stumbling block for Jews.[66]

[64] There have been numerous misreadings of this crucial verse. Cf. Fee, *First Corinthians*, 86. He is right to say, "Thus Paul is not suggesting, as the KJV implies, that Christ has been made these four things for believers." But then he adds, "True Wisdom is to be understood in terms of these three illustrative metaphors." Barrett, *First Corinthians*, 59 rearranges the sentence so that it will read, "who as God's gift became Wisdom for us, and righteousness and sanctification and redemption too." Conzelmann, *1 Corinthians*, 51–52 likewise skirts the natural sense of the grammmar. F. Lang, *Die Briefe an die Korinther*, 33–34, alludes to Col. 2:3, 9–10, but then does not follow up on this lead. The point is that God through Christ has provided for believers right–standing, santification, and redemption, not that Christ is these things for believers or that these things fully explicate Christ being Wisdom. Cf. also Feuillet, *Le Christ Sagesse*, 22.

[65] Here Johnson, *Function of Apocalyptic*, 43ff., 136ff. overreaches by trying to deny all christological implications of this text.

[66] Schweizer, "Paul's Christology and Gnosticism," 121.

Even this Wisdom is only of benefit to those who accept it by faith. In short, the only Wisdom that is salvific is that revealed by God, not that discovered by humanity. This puts human Wisdom properly in its place and makes clear there is no place for human boasting about Wisdom in the presence of God and in view of God's mighty Wisdom. Paul in this section of his argument which climaxes with a quote of Jer. 9:24 in 1.31, can be said to be developing an idea already expressed in part (though without reference to the cross) in Wis. 9:17–18: "Who has learned your counsel unless you have given Wisdom and sent your Holy Spirit from on high? And thus the paths of those on earth were set right, and people were taught what pleases you and were saved by Wisdom." Beginning in 2:6ff Paul will further expand his argument by making clear that the only way the Corinthians could have such Wisdom was through the Holy Spirit, as the quote from the Wisdom of Solomon also stresses.

R. Scroggs has raised the issue of whether Paul did or was prepared to impart what might be called advanced sapiential Wisdom to the *teleioi* as 1 Cor. 2:6 suggests.[67] The answer to this question seems to be yes on several grounds. Paul is willing to say that the Corinthians are in fact *nepioi* (3:2), who are not able yet to receive solid meat. Now this suggests that Paul recognizes that there are levels of spiritual maturity and levels of sapiential teaching appropriate to each, and the Corinthians might one day reach such a level. Though the Corinthians, or at least some Corinthians, may have thought of themselves as mature or even perfect (depending on how one reads the use of the term *teleioi* in 2:6 and elsewhere), Paul disputes this. It does not follow from this that he thinks no one should hear teaching that goes beyond the basic kerygma of Christ crucified.

If one examines other texts where the term *musterion* appears in Paul, in particular in 1 Cor. 15:51 or Rom. 11:25, it does appear that Paul has what might be called some advanced teaching about such matters as whether all believers will be involved in the resurrection or the temporary hardening of some Jews so that Gentiles may be saved. It would seem then that Paul has to argue very carefully at this point. On the one hand in regard to salvation all are equally indebted to Christ, the Wisdom of God. Furthermore, there is no place for boasting about whatever spiritual gifts or abilities God has given a person since they are just that – gifts. Nevertheless, it appears Scroggs conclusion stands: "Paul nowhere denies that valid *distinctions* in maturity, spiritual gifts, intellectual levels, or productivity exist. What he attacks is rather *divisions* based upon a prideful evaluation of such distinctions."[68] In short, he attacks the wrong sort of assessments of the distinctions and differences that do exist in Christ's body.

---

[67] Scroggs, "Paul – *Sophos* and *Pneumatikos*," 34ff. One need look no further than Sirach and the Wisdom of Solomon for the use of the term *teleios/tamim* in the way it is used here; cf. Sir. 34:8 with 31:10 and 44:17; and Wis 9:6 (cf. 6:15).

[68] Scroggs, "Paul – *Sophos* and *Pneumatikos*", 38., n. 4.

The later distinction that Paul himself uses between the weak and those who do not suffer from a particular kind of scruples in 1 Corinthians 8. surely implies that Paul was willing to admit there were such distinctions among believers.

I have argued that at various points one can detect the influence of Pauline thought and perhaps even Pauline letters on the writer of Hebrews.[69] If so, then it is perhaps relevant to note that Heb. 5:11 — 6:2 seems to reflect a knowledge of the discussion in 1 Corinthians 1–4. Not only is there the exhortation to go on to *teleioteta*, but a distinction is made between the laying of the foundational teaching and by implication the building on top of it, and between those who need milk who are called *nepios*, and those prepared for solid food who are called *teleion*. The writer of Hebrews laments in a fashion not unlike Paul that his audience is dull of understanding (Heb. 5:11) and not prepared for the harder teaching.[70] These parallels would be all the more revealing if Hebrews was written by Apollos expositing his sapiential teaching.

Sometimes the reference to the *archontes* in 1 Cor. 2:6 has been seen as puzzling, but if in fact Paul is offering a Wisdom discourse it is not puzzling at all. The rulers in the Ancient Near East were those most often assumed to be gatherers and purveyors of true *sophia*. Paul's point could be that his Wisdom is no conventional Wisdom, the sort associated with courts and generated by the ruler's retainers–sages, scribes, counselors and the like.[71] It was traditional in Wisdom literature to address and even admonish rulers to seek Wisdom (cf. Wis. 1; 6:1; Sir. 10:1–4). Christ was crucified in part because the rulers of this world relied on their traditional and conventional forms of Wisdom, not on the revelatory message about the Wisdom of God, and so crucified Christ in ignorance.[72] This echoes the idea of Wisdom being rejected by the nations (cf. Sir. 24:6–7). The reference to the rulers also supports the conclusions that Paul in his critique here is taking on all forms of human Wisdom, whether Greek or Jewish. When one believes, as Paul does, that the *schema* of the world is passing away (1 Cor. 7:31), then any sort of Wisdom based on deduction from analysis of that world has also been put into the shade by the Christ–event which relativizes all human Wisdom.[73]

Paul's stress on the revelatory character of true Wisdom, stands in the line of the late Jewish sapiential traditions which stressed that God's counsel or plan could only be known if God revealed it, which in turn meant that one could only know such Wisdom through God's Spirit coming down and revealing it or inspiring the receiver (cf. Wis.. 7:27; 9:17; Sir. 24:33). The connection then between godly Wisdom and the Holy Spirit then became an

---

[69] Witherington, "The Influence of Galatians on Hebrews," 146–52.

[70] Scroggs, "Paul – *Sophos* and *Pneumatikos*", 38.

[71] On all this cf. above pp. 4ff.

[72] Cf. *1 Enoch* 63:2 – rulers bemoan their own ignorance which led to their punishment, and now they know God is both Lord of glory and of Wisdom.

[73] Cf. Pearson, "Hellenistic Jewish Wisdom," 49.

important one, and the connection between being a *sophos* and being a *pneumatikos* was a natural further development. The word *hemin* is in an emphatic position in 1 Cor. 2:10: "But *to us* God revealed [Wisdom] through the Spirit, for the Spirit examines everything, even the depths of God."

The term *bathe* seems to occur with some regularity in sapiential contexts where the subject is God's secret plan (cf. below on Rom. 11:33 and Eccles. 7.24, *1 Enoch* 63:3). The claim to have the mind of Christ (2:16) is a claim to know God's secrets because one has access to the the mind of Christ through the Spirit and Christ is God's Wisdom. Christ revealed in his person and in his deeds what the mind of God is (cf. Wis. 1:4–7; 7:22–23). As Scroggs says, the whole section 1 Cor. 2:6–16 should be read in the light of Wis. 9:9–18.[74]

Paul, when he assesses his missionary work, says many things including that he, being an assistant of Christ, is a steward of the mysteries of God (1 Cor. 4:1), but he also indicates that he views himself as a wise master builder (*architecton*, 3:10). That is, he sees it as his primary task to lay the foundations of the Christian community wherever he goes. This being the case, it is not surprising that Paul chose to preach the basic Gospel message in Corinth, and very likely elsewhere as well since there was no other foundation that should be laid than Christ Jesus (3:11). Without the possession of the Spirit the audience would not be prepared for higher or deeper spiritual things in any case. All of this suggests that one should not underestimate the considerable difference between what one finds in Paul's letters written to those who are already Christians, and the content and form of his missionary preaching. The Pauline kerygma and the didache while overlapping somewhat were not identical. It is time to look further in Corinthians for more evidence of Paul's Wisdom teaching.

THE CHRISTIAN *SHEMA* AND THE CHRIST OF THE EXODUS: 1 COR. 8:10 AND 2 CORINTHIANS 3–4

1 Cor. 8:6 comes in the midst of an argument about food offered to idols and is part of Paul's polemic against polytheism in general and participating in feasts in the presence of idols in particular. For our purposes, it is crucial to note that the discussion begins in 8:1 with Paul quoting the Corinthians' claim to all possess *gnosis*. The connections between Wisdom and knowledge are plentiful in Hellenistic Jewish sapiential material, as R. Horsley has shown.[75] For example, in Wis. 7:15–17 Solomon claims that God is the corrector even of the wise and has given him "unerring knowledge of what exists". While this seems to fall into the traditional category of nature Wisdom, in 10:10 the further claim is made that Wisdom gave the righteous man knowledge of holy things, which is paralleled with a phrase about being shown the kingdom of God. In

[74] Scroggs, "Paul – *Sophos* and *Pneumatikos*," 54.
[75] Horsley, "Gnosis in Corinth: 1 Corinthians 8.1–6," 32–51.

Wis. 15:3 it is stressed that to know God "is complete righteousness, and to know your power is the root of immortality."

After examining the relevant data, Horsley concludes that one may read the Corinthians' views in light of such material and so "*gnosis* was not identical with *sophia* for the Corinthians, but apparently was an expression of the *sophia* they possessed. 'Knowledge' probably referred to the particular religious content of *sophia*, including such fundamental theological principles as 'there are no idols in the world' and 'there is no god but One.'"[76] It is apposite to point out that if in fact "there are no idols in the world" is a *Corinthian* slogan which Paul quotes, the use of the term *eidolon* points to the Jewish critique of polytheism and encourages one to think that Jewish polemic against idols (such as that found in Wis. 13:10–14, or in the Old Testament in Isa. 44:9–20 or Jer. 10:1–16, or in prophetic–apocalyptic literature such as in *1 Enoch* 19; 99:6–10) was being drawn on.[77]

The close association of God with *Sophia*, even to the point of *Sophia* being said to sit by or even on God's throne in Wis. 9:4,10 is significant. In this source *Sophia* is also said to reach mightily from one end of the earth to the other and to order all things well (8:1). "For she is an initiate in the knowledge of God, and an associate in his works... who more than she is fashioner of all that exists?" (8:4, 7). Philo in *Quod Det.* 54, 84 urges faithful Jews to "Accord a father's honor to Him who created the world, and a mother's honor to Sophia, through whom (*di' hes*) the universe was brought to completion." In addition, it was pointed out earlier in this study that the use of the term "Father" for God is rare in early Judaism before the turn of the era, but when it is used it almost always appears in sapiential literature (cf. e.g. Wis. 2:17; Sir. 23:1 – in prayer coupled with Lord).[78] It seems quite possible, as Horsley argues, that the Corinthians or at least those who had previously been involved in the synagogue in Corinth had already been exposed to this sort of Hellenistic Jewish Wisdom thinking about idols and proper monotheism even before Paul came to Corinth.[79] "What Paul responds to, therefore, is not a Gnostic libertinism... but a Hellenistic Jewish *gnosis* at home precisely in the mission context."[80]

The Corinthians, or at least those not called weak by Paul, seem to have drawn some wrong conclusions from the slogans about only one God and no idols. They had assumed, since idols were nothing, that there could be no harm in participating in feasts in pagan temples. Paul must correct this mistaken assumption and he does so by drawing on some of the same Hellenistic–Jewish sapiential material from which the Corinthians themselves had drawn their conclusions.[81]

---

[76] Horsley, "Gnosis in Corinth," 35.

[77] So Horsley, "Gnosis in Corinth," 37.

[78] Cf. above pp. 71ff.

[79] R. A. Horsley, "The Background of the Confessional Formula in 1 Kor. 8.6," 130–35.

[80] R. A. Horsley, "Gnosis in Corinth," 48–49.

[81] I agree with Wright, *Climax of the Covenant*, 124 in his critique of Horsley that Horsley, distinguishes too sharply between different sorts of polemic against idols, on the basis of a

Paul, in order to counter this, goes back to first principles, drawing on the Jewish Shema and putting Jesus right in the midst of the most fundamental assertion in early Judaism of its monotheistic faith.[82] I would suggest that, as was the case with his use of Isaiah spoken of in the previous section of this study, so here he is reading the Shema through the later sapiential reflections on monotheism, Wisdom, and idolatry. The quote from Philo (*Quod Det.* 54, 84) is especially relevant at this point. Paul is taking what was formerly said of God the Father and *Sophia*, and now saying the same of the Father and Jesus Christ. But there is even more to this because Paul is also willing to use the term Lord of Christ, which in the Shema refers to Yahweh.[83] Whatever the Corinthians may have been looking for in terms of divine knowledge or Wisdom, Paul's assertion is that they will find it in Christ.

> [I]f – as Paul clearly believes – Jesus is the one through whom his people are reconciled to the creator, through whom therefore is being brought about the dawn of the new creation, then it must follow that he is indeed the *sophia theou*, the one through whom the creator himself is operating to remake that which, already made, had been spoilt through sin and corruption.[84]

This formula has to do not just with redemption but even more with creation, as would be expected in the light of the immediate context which discusses matters of creation (are idols anything?) and also in the light of the sapiential background and the roles predicated of Wisdom in texts like Wisdom 9. Dunn's and Murphy–O'Connor's views will not stand up to close scrutiny in view of these contexts.[85] Christ is the one through whom God made the universe, just as the same was said in Wisdom of Solomon. Once one believes this, then a statement like 1 Cor. 10:4 hardly comes as a surprise. Furthermore, Paul makes clear that since the initiative for both these things stands with God, then religious knowledge must be conceived as primarily theocentric rather than anthropocentric. What really matters is loving God and *being known* by God (8:3).

Thus Wright is correct that this new Christian Shema is exactly what Paul needed at this juncture of his argument to reassert a proper Christian monotheism and also the primacy of love as well, and perhaps also counter any under–estimation of Jesus Christ that might have existed in Corinth at the time.[86]

---

false dichotomy between Palestinian and Hellenistic Jewish thinking about such matters. This does not negate the fact that he seems to have put his finger on the proper background for understanding the discussion here.

[82] Rightly, Wright, *Climax of the Covenant*, 129.

[83] Paul it appears also does not flinch from calling Christ God as well, for instance, in Rom. 9.5 on which, cf. Wright, *Climax of the Covenant*, 237–38.

[84] Wright, *Climax of the Covenant*, 131.

[85] Contrast Dunn, *Christology in the Making*, 181–82; J. Murphy O'Connor, "I Cor. VIII.6: Cosmology or Soteriology?" 253–67 with Wright, *Climax of the Covenant*, 131ff.

[86] Wright, *Climax of the Covenant*, 132.

When a crucified Christ who took on the form of a slave for the world's redemption becomes part of the definition of deity there is no more room for self–indulgent practices such as eating in pagan temples in religious feasts that violate the conscience of fellow believers. No *gnosis* but the *gnosis* of one God the Father and one Lord Jesus Christ will do as the heart of the Christian faith.

1 Cor. 10:4 has often been seen as an example of odd and abstruse Jewish eisegesis, typology, or even allegorizing of the Exodus–Sinai story which stands at the heart of Jewish faith. But it is in order to point out that Paul is not dealing with this text directly but through the use of it in late Jewish sapiential material, in particular the Wisdom of Solomon and perhaps also Philo. Wis. 11:4, in the course of recounting Wisdom's role in guarding and guiding the Israelites through their wilderness wandering period says, "When they were thirsty, they called upon you [i.e. Wisdom], and water was given them out of the flinty rock." Philo *Leg. All.* 2:86 goes further and says, "For the flinty rock is the Wisdom of God, which he marked off highest and chiefest from his powers, and from which he satisfies the thirsty souls that love God."[87] The differences between Paul's interpretation and that of Philo are important. Philo is engaging in pure allegory it would appear, while Paul would seem to be making an actual claim about a historical situation (cf. below). The combination of interesting parallels and notable divergences between Paul's interpretation and that of his predecessors shows that there is a common sapiential tradition that all three authors are drawing on and modifying to suit their own purposes.[88]

It is incorrect to argue that Paul is merely doing a typological allegory of *present* Christian spiritual realities.[89] The point is, as it usually is in biblical typology, that as the case *was* in the past in God's dealings with believers, so it is also now in the present. The durative imperfect verbs here must be taken seriously in the context (cf. *egenethesan* in v 8, *sunebeinen* in v 11) and in the text itself (*en*, v 4b). Paul is talking about what *was* the case as well as what is the case. The point is that just because the Old Testament people of God had, so to speak, comparable sacraments, and just because Christ was there providing sustenance for them this did not prevent the majority of them falling by the wayside and never making it to the promised land.

Lest the Corinthians should think they were somehow immune from such a spiritual disaster because they had Christ and the sacraments, Paul wished to disabuse them of such a delusion by citing an historical precedent that parallels the current situation in various ways. As Paul says in 10:6, these things really occurred, and with hindsight they can be said to have occurred as

---

[87] Fee, *First Corinthians*, 449 is hardly convincing when he tries to dismiss such parallels as remote at best.

[88] Rightly, Schnabel, *Law and Wisdom*, 247.

[89] Pace Dunn, *Christology in the Making*, 183–84.

examples or *tupoi* for the Corinthians. A *tupos* by definition in this sort of argument requires a historical precedent.[90] As Hengel concludes, "So it is the pre–existent Christ who must accompany Israel on its journey through the wilderness as the 'spiritual rock' (1 Cor. 10:4)."[91]

Here again one finds the same sort of phenomenon as earlier. Paul takes up his Jewish heritage and reinterprets it with the help of late sapiential traditions in the light of Christ. Since Christ can be said to be the Wisdom of God, what was formerly said of Wisdom can now be said of Christ. The implications of 1 Cor. 10:4 should be allowed to have their full force. Paul very likely believed in a pre–existent Christ, and one not just involved in heaven but one intimately involved in helping the people of God in their historical pilgrimage toward the promised land. There was a precedent for this sort of conclusion in Wisdom 10–11 where Wisdom there assumes tasks in history to help God's people along their way. What is especially striking about both 1 Cor. 8:6 and 10:4 is that Paul is willing to take not just marginal ideas or events, but the very heart of the Jewish faith, its Shema and the Exodus–Sinai events that made them into the unique people of God they became, and redefine these traditions in the light of what Paul now believed to be true about Christ. Paul does not fully draw out the implications of the pre–existence of Christ here, but this text shows he is already thinking along such lines.[92] Wright is correct to say that the hallmark of Paul's thought is that he takes what is central to Jewish faith, monotheism and election, and redefines both by means of his christology.[93] His faith is rightly called christological monotheism.[94]

Before turning to material in Romans, the difficult passage in 2 Corinthians 3–4 about the two covenants deserves mention.[95] As Van Roon has noted, there is a rather striking lexical affinity between Wis. 7.25–26 and various parts of 2 Cor. 3:18 — 4:6.[96] In particular, Wisdom is said to be a pure emanation of the glory of the Almighty, a reflection of eternal light, "a spotless mirror of the working of God, and an image of his goodness" (Wis. 7:25). Paul says in 2 Cor. 3:18 that believers with unveiled faces see the glory of the Lord as though reflected in a mirror, and "are being transformed into the same image from one degree of glory to another." To this he adds in 4:6 that God gives the light of the

---

[90] For a study of this material which simply ignores the connections with Wisdom material, cf. P. J. Tomson, *Paul and the Jewish Law*, 198–203.

[91] M. Hengel, *The Son of God*, 72. He goes on to argue that this type of exegesis is not typical of Paul and so he concludes it must have come from the non–Pauline Greek speaking Jewish Christianity. I suspect, in view of 1 Corinthians 1–4, that it was Paul himself who conjured this up, especially in the light of the way he is able to handle the promise to Abraham and the Sarah and Hagar stories in Galatians 3–4.

[92] But cf. D. B. Botte, "La Sagesse et les Origenes de la Christologie," 60–61.

[93] More of this can be seen below in Paul's handling of the fate of ethnic Israel in Romans 9–11; cf. below.

[94] Wright, *Climax of the Covenant*, 119.

[95] Witherington, *Jesus, Paul, and the End of the World*, 109–12.

[96] Van Roon, "Relation," 228.

knowledge of the glory of God in the face of Jesus Christ. Though the terms in Greek are not all identical here (e.g. the Wisdom of Solomon has *esoptron* for mirror, Paul the participial form *katoptrizomenoi*) nonetheless the parallels of thought and terms (cf. *apaugasma* to *augasai* in 2 Cor. 4:4) in general is striking. Feuillet stresses that what really sets these two texts apart from other statements about mirrors or images is the association of *doxa* and image.[97] In view of the parallels to the Wisdom of Solomon it appears that what 2 Cor. 3:18 means is that the believer sees the glory of God reflected in the face (i.e. character) of Christ, who is both the mirror and the image of God.[98]

The believer is in the process of being transformed into the image of the glorified Christ.[99] It may be that Paul is also thinking of the material found in 2 *Bar*. 51:3, 7, 10: "they shall be changed... from beauty into loveliness, and from light into the splendour of glory." If this exegesis is correct, then it is apposite to point out that Paul not only seems to be drawing on Wisdom 7 but is once again taking the attributes of Wisdom and predicating them of Christ, for in the Wisdom of Solomon it is *Sophia* who is said to be the glory, the mirror and image, and the reflection of eternal light.[100] There is more because one of the points of Wisdom 7, as with 2 Corinthians 3–4, is to talk about the transformation of believers. In Wis. 7:27 one finds "while remaining in herself, she renews all things; in every generation she passes into holy souls and makes them friends of God and prophets." One may also wonder if the enigmatic discussion about the Lord and the Spirit in 2 Cor. 3:17 owes anything to the fact that not only in Wis. 7:23 is *Sophia* said to have a spirit in her that is holy, but in Wis. 1:6 one hears "For Wisdom *is* a kindly spirit," which is followed in the next verse by "because the spirit of the Lord has filled the world." Might Paul's version of this be, "For the Lord (Christ/Wisdom?) is the Spirit?"[101] Whether this last conjecture has any merit or not, there is certainly enough here to provide one more example of the christological appropriation of the sapiential material about Wisdom to serve the apostle's own ends or, perhaps better said the reading of the key Old Testament traditions here about Moses and the giving of the covenant, through a sapiential filter and with a christological agenda.[102] In this text the apostle has stressed that one becomes like what one beholds and admires.

---

[97] Feuillet, *Le Christ Sagesse*, 151. He is also right to point out that in the material world in antiquity what one saw in a mirror and the actual image often did not comport with one another very well (cf. 1 Cor. 13:12). In both of these texts the author has in mind an absolutely accurate reflection or image.

[98] One may also wish to compare *Odes of Solomon*, 13.1: "Behold, the Lord is our mirror."

[99] Barrett, *Second Corinthians*, 125 is the only English speaking commentator of late who pays much attention to the parallels with the Wisdom of Solomon. He is right that the transformation of the believer does not involve deification but rather glorification as believers come to bear the image of Christ as he bears the image of God.

[100] V. P. Furnish, *2 Corinthians* (New York: Doubleday, 1984), 241.

[101] For an extended discussion of this passage along the same lines, cf. Feuillet, *Le Christ*, 113–61.

[102] Cf. on all this C. K. Barrett, *The Second Epistle to the Corinthians* (New York: Harper and Row, 1973), 133–34.

WITH FAITHFULNESS AND JUSTICE FOR ALL: ROMANS 1–2; 9–11

Certainly one of the more important concerns of Jewish sages was with the justice of God. The theme of God's impartiality coupled with the act–consequence idea led to the conclusion that sooner or later all wrongs would be righted and all rights rewarded by a fair and impartial Deity. But the Jewish sages, after witnessing various disasters at the hands of the likes of the Babylonians or the successors of Alexander, came in due course to incorporate into their thinking first the prophetic notion of the *Yom Yahweh* (cf. Sir. 35:14 — 36:22), and even some sort of belief in an afterlife (Wis. 3:1–8). These were significant changes from the early sapiential literature and in part they reflect the unwillingness on the part of the sage to give up on the ideas of God's impartial justice or his faithfulness to his promises to his people.

In a world gone wrong, impartial justice amounts not just to rewards for righteousness but also a reversal of the present evil circumstances. Thus it was that more and more in Wisdom literature when God's impartiality was mentioned there was usually added things like "and he will listen to the prayer of the one who is wronged" (Sir. 35:16) or "And the Lord will not delay, and like a warrior will not be patient until he crushes the loins of the unmerciful and repays vengeance on the nations; until he destroys the multitude of the insolent and breaks the scepters of the unrighteous" (Sir. 35:22–23).

Paul, like Ben Sira and other sages before him, is very much alive to the need to stress God's impartial justice and also God's faithfulness to divine promises in a world gone wrong. This theme had importance on a variety of levels, not the least of which is that Paul could hardly call for equality or balance or fairness amongst his converts (for instance, in their giving, cf. 2 Cor. 8:13ff. and the use of *isotes*) if God was not one who also exhibited such characteristics in the divine–human encounter.[103]

J. M. Bassler in a helpful study on divine impartiality has shown that Rom. 2.11 sets forth a major theme that concerns Paul in Romans.[104] If it is true that God shows no partiality, that all shall be rewarded or punished depending on whether they have done good or ill (Rom. 2.9–10), how can it also be said that God will be faithful to his promises to Israel? In short, how does fairness comport with faithfulness? These questions are all the more pressing since it apparently seemed to some Christians on the surface of things that God has forsaken the first chosen people (Jews) for a second one (Gentiles). How can the

[103] Georgi, *Die Geschichte der Kollekte des Paulus für Jerusalem*, 62–67 sees Wisdom traditions behind Paul's appeal to equality in 2 Cor. 8:13ff. He even goes so far as to maintain that the important theme of *dikaiosune* in Paul goes back to this same set of ideas for when one talks about the righteousness of God giving right standing to all on the equal basis of divine grace one is drawing on the traditional Wisdom concern for balance and equality.

[104] J. M. Bassler, *Divine Impartiality*, 121ff. in fact argues that the first major unit of Romans is 1:16 — 2.11, climaxing in the statement about divine impartiality.

Gospel of Christ be the power of God for salvation for both Jew and Gentile when at present most Jews have rejected this Gospel and many Gentiles have accepted it? If God's promises are being fulfilled in Christ, but Jews are rejecting Christ, how then is God being faithful to the promises made to Israel? Paul answers these questions with a variety of arguments intended to show both God's impartiality in grace but also his faithfulness to Jews. These include not only the initial argument that the Gospel is God's saving power *for the Jew first* (presumably because God chose them first, 1:16b) and so God has not forgotten his promises to them as well as the Gentiles, but also the elaborate argument about the temporary breaking off of Jews from God's people, grafting in of Gentiles, and then the salvation of "all Israel" at the eschaton in Romans 9–11.[105] Right from the beginning of the first main section of Romans where the theme of the revelation of God's wrath against all unrighteousness is given full exposure (cf. 1:18ff) there is a deep seated concern to show that history is worked out by God according to "a pattern which emphasizes the exact correspondence between deed and reward."[106] This heightened concern can be said to be an example of the expression of the sapiential theme of act–consequence played out not only in part in the present but in full at the eschaton.[107] Furthermore, in the argument in Rom. 1:18ff Paul stresses two other aspects of this concept of divine impartiality: (1) that some sort of knowledge of the divine nature and power is available to all for these qualities are evident from the creation and so all are without excuse if they do not respond to God and his will; and (2) God will fairly judge all according to the light they have received. As 2:12–15 says, if they had the law they will be judged by it, if not they will be judged apart from the law. Rom. 2:16 says that on judgment day God through Christ will judge the secret thoughts of all. This is much like what the sage says in Wis. 1:6–8: "God is a witness of their inmost feelings, and a true observer of their hearts... therefore those who utter unrighteous things will not escape notice, and justice when it punishes will not pass them by." The point here is *not* that such themes cannot also be found for instance in the prophetic corpus, but that Paul stresses and expresses them in ways that reveal he evaluates and uses such themes in line with previous Jewish sages. This is also true elsewhere in the Pauline corpus for example in 1 Cor. 3:13–15 and 4:5, where the same sort of sapiential argument about divine impartiality is found,[108] or in Rom. 9:20ff. where in surprising fashion Paul recasts statements about Israel's election in order to show God's impartiality

---

[105] I have dealt at length with this latter argument in *Jesus, Paul and the End of the World*, 111–25.

[106] Bassler, *Divine Impartiality*, 136.

[107] It is often overlooked that Paul says that God's wrath is already at work against all unrighteous and so, like earlier sages, he has not entirely discarded the notion of divine recompense in the present. Act–consequence is simply the expression of what God's justice and impartiality mean when they are worked out in human affairs and history.

[108] Cf. Bassler, *Divine Impartiality*, 174–76.

even mercifully calling and choosing Gentiles, creating a people out of nothing. The Wisdom tradition about the potter's vessels is surprisingly used to say something about impartiality rather than simply Israel's election.[109] It appears that Paul's own contribution to this sort of Wisdom thinking is to parallel God's impartiality in judgment with his impartiality in grace toward both Jew and Gentile.[110]

The question raised over and over again in regard to Rom. 1:19–20 about the possibility of a "natural" theology is too often raised without realizing that Paul says what he does on the basis of certain sapiential assumptions about the world. Wisdom thinking can be said to be a creation theology and one of its major tenets is that there is "a universal divine self–disclosure" in God's creation.[111] The point of this theology is not pantheism but rather that all of creation reflects the imprint of its Maker and so to some degree reveals something about the reality and character of God. Paul's theological assumptions do not entail the idea that as a result of the fallen quality of all creation since Adam there is now *no* positive revelation of God in creation. "On the contrary, Paul states that in spite of a *positive* revelation of God's presence, of God's invisible nature in things which have been made, humanity has nevertheless chosen to reject both the revelation and its giver. It is for this reason that they are without excuse 'for although they *knew* God they did not honor God as God or give thanks to God' (1:21)."[112]

Paul, like previous sages, still believed in an inherent reflection of God in creation, *but* he also believed in *human* fallenness that led humans to falsely evaluate or reject the evidence of God in creation, as did the author of the Wisdom of Solomon. (cf. Wis. 2:23–24). They claimed themselves to be *sophoi*, but they became fools because they exchanged the glory of God for human images of creation, they exchanged the truth of God for a lie. As a result, God gave them up to the consequences of their chosen fallenness. Now this argument, which uses so many sapiential concepts (creation theology, act–consequence, contrast of wise and foolish) comes to a crashing halt in Rom. 2:1ff. with the surprising assertion: "therefore you have no excuse, whoever you are, when you judge others, for in passing judgment on another you condemn yourself..." Judgment is reserved for God alone; only God knows all and thus only God can be totally fair and impartial in judgment.

Commentators have long suspected that Paul is here drawing on traditional Jewish polemics against pagan immorality, and they are right, but not often enough do they point out that Paul is following the same sort of sapiential logic about these things that one finds for instance in Wis. 13:5 — 14:30 where it is said:

---

[109] Rightly, Johnson, *The Function of Apocalyptic*, 149–50.
[110] Johnson, 185ff.
[111] W. C. Bouzard, "The Theology of Wisdom in Romans 1 and 2," 281.
[112] Bouzard, 283–84.

> For from the greatness and beauty of created things comes a corresponding perception of their Creator. Yet these people are little to be blamed, for perhaps... while they live among his works, they keep searching, and they trust in what they see, because the things that are seen are beautiful. Yet again, not even they are to be excused; for if they had the power to know so much that they could investigate the world, how did they fail to find sooner the Lord of these things? But miserable with their hopes set on dead things, are those who give the name "gods" to the works of human hands... For the idea of making idols was the beginning of fornication, and the invention of them was the corruption of life... But just penalties will overtake them.[113]

The telltale signs that Paul is following a sapiential way of viewing these matters are evident in a variety of places. For example, in Rom. 1:24 the use of the term "uncleanness" (*akatharsia*) has little or no cultic sense here, as is true also in Wis. 2:16, but rather in both texts it refers to moral uncleanness. Or again in that same verse the term *"epithumia"*, used in a negative sense to mean sinful (and often illicit sexual) desire, is used in the same sense in Wis. 4:12; Sir. 5:2; 18:30–31; 23:5. One may also wish to point to the incorruptible/corruptible contrast here which is already functioning in Wis. 2:23. Paul and Pseudo–Solomon both stress how fallen human beings become futile in their thinking (cf. Rom. 1:21 with Wis. 13:1). If they ignore God they are said to be foolish by nature and futile in thinking. The refusal to acknowledge God properly is stressed in both Rom. 1:21 and Wis. 16:16.[114]

It will be seen that Paul is sterner in some respects than the sage who wrote the Wisdom of Solomon, but the thought pattern is quite similar. In both texts Gentiles are being castigated and in much the same way. Even the idea of God giving up such people to their own folly and letting them have the consequences of their sin is found expressed shortly before the above cited passage: "Therefore those who lived unrighteously, in a life of folly, you tormented through their own abominations" (Wis. 12:23). It is not first in Christian literature but already is earlier Jewish Wisdom and prophetic–apocalytic literature that one finds the interesting juxtaposition of a world which reflects God, and yet also a human world gone wrong. It may be seen at least as early as Qoheleth who already saw the need for counter–order Wisdom, but it is expressed in a book like the Wisdom of Solomon in a way that already foreshadows what Paul will say. The sage argues in the Wisdom of Solomon that in such a world one needs God to be revealed through Wisdom, through God's Spirit. Paul argues that in such a world one needs God to be revealed through Christ, by means of God's Spirit. "Very relevant for the background of Paul's thought at this point, then, is the interplay in Jewish

---

[113] But cf. U. Wilckens, *Der Brief an die Römer (Röm. 1–5)* (Zurich: Benziger Verlag, 1978), 96ff.; J. D. G. Dunn, *Romans 1–8*, 58–62.

[114] On all this cf. Dunn, *Romans 1–8*, 56ff.

Wisdom between the hiddenness and revelation of divine Wisdom (see particularly Job 28; Bar. 3:15—4:4) which forms the warp and woof of a natural theology."[115]

Again it is the christological turn to the argument that sets Paul's argument apart from his predecessors in the Wisdom tradition. Both Paul, and writers like Pseudo–Solomon, reflect the concept of a human world gone wrong and hence the need for Wisdom to be revealed by God, for both reflect that convergence of sapiential and prophetic–apocalyptic thinking about God, history, Wisdom, and salvation. For Paul, it is Christ as proclaimed in the Gospel who is capable of setting things right, and thus Rom. 1.18ff. as bleak as it may sound is meant to be read in the light of 1.16–17.

After a careful study of the sapiential material E. E. Johnson comes to this conclusion about the sages:

> the more a writer relies on traditional apocalyptic traditions, the less traditional is his use of Wisdom material and *vice versa*.... the more he views God's Wisdom as transcendent, the more he anticipates eschatological order; the more immanent is God's Wisdom, the greater the possibility for meaningful life in the present.[116]

It will be seen that the sage who wrote the Wisdom of Solomon and Paul do stress the necessity of revelatory Wisdom, and the folly of humans trying to be wise on their own, but they have *not* entirely given up on the idea of God's imprint in creation, or immanent Wisdom. Hence in both one finds the interesting juxtaposition of good creation and fallen humankind, some meaning in life here and now, the real glory later. All of this prepares one for the further revelations of the apostle in Romans 9–11.

In some ways the material in Romans 9–11 is presented in the style of a diatribe where dialogue comes to the fore.[117] One does detect in at least three places the strong influence of sapiential material, thinking, or exegesis. The first of these occurs in Rom. 9:20–23. As has been pointed out before, Paul will use an Old Testament text (in this case Isa. 29:16 is used in 9:20a; cf. Jer. 18:1–11), but then he will combine it with material that clearly does not come from that same fount. Johnson rightly notes that in neither Isaiah 29 nor Jeremiah 18 are there two sorts of vessels created for two different purposes involved.[118] Wis. 15.7, however, says "a potter kneads the soft earth and laboriously molds each vessel for our service, fashioning out of the same clay both the vessels that serve clean uses and those for contrary uses, making all alike; but which shall be the use of each of them the worker in clay decides." In Wisdom this

---

[115] Dunn, *Romans 1–8*, 57.
[116] Johnson, *The Function of Apocalyptic*, 109.
[117] Cf. S. K. Stowers, *The Diatribe and Paul's Letter to the Romans*, 179ff.
[118] Johnson, *The Function of Apocalyptic*, 132.

discussion comes in the course of a polemic against the making of idols (cf. Wis. 15:8ff.), but in Sir. 33:12–13 Ben Sira is discussing the creation of human beings and says that God distinguished them, appointing them to different ways. Some he blessed and exalted, others he cursed and brought down. "Like clay in the hand of the potter, to be molded as he pleases, so are all in the hand of the Maker to be given whatever he decides." The conclusion is fully warranted that Paul draws on the material from Isaiah and perhaps also Jeremiah but the form of the tradition he uses is dependent on the later use of the material in the Wisdom of Solomon and Sirach.[119] In addition it appears that the question "Why have you made me like this?" in Rom. 9:20 seems indebted to the rhetorical questions in Wis. 12:12.[120]

In Rom. 10:6–8 Paul is doing an exegesis of Deut. 30:12–14 but again there seems to be a significant indebtedness to a later sapiential treatment of the Deuteronomistic material, this time in Bar. 3:29–30 where the author asks, not about the commandment as in Deuteronomy, but about Wisdom "Who has gone up into heaven, and taken her, and brought her down from the clouds? Who has gone over the sea, and found her, and will buy her for pure gold?"[121] It is important also to note the difference in context in the material in Deuteronomy 30 and the material in Baruch 3. In the latter text, there is a contrast between human inability to find or gain Wisdom and the granting of Wisdom in the form of Torah to Jacob. In the former text the point is to admonish Israel to hear and do the law, for it is near at hand. It is intriguing that while Paul does not cite Deut. 30:12b at all, as Baruch does, nevertheless his interpretation which involves the phrase *christon katagagein* seems to reflect the way Baruch markedly altered Deuteronomy by substituting *kai katebibasen auten* for *kai akousantes auten*. This sort of influence also seems apparent when both Baruch and Paul, drawing on Deut. 30:13b both substitute a form of the verb *baino* for *diaperadzo*. Yet it is clearly not just Baruch that Paul is following for he uses Deut. 30:14 and Baruch does not though, as M. J. Suggs has pointed out, the intention of Baruch is similar to Paul's – stressing the nearness or closeness to the audience of the word of faith.[122]

Several further sapiential texts deserve attention here. Prov. 30:3–4 says, "I have not learned Wisdom, nor have I knowledge of the holy ones. Who has ascended to heaven and come down?"[123] In Sir. 24:5 Wisdom says, "Alone I

---

[119] On the use of the Wisdom of Solomon, cf. C. E. B. Cranfield, *Romans, Vol. 2*, 491–92; on the use of Sirach, cf. E. Käsemann, *Commentary on Romans*, 272.

[120] R. B. Hays, *Echoes of Scripture in the Letters of Paul*, 65–66 and 206, n. 64, is right about the complexity of the intertextual matrix from which Paul's discussion emerges, but he fails to see Paul's dependency on the later sapiential handling of the material in Isaiah and Jeremiah.

[121] In the discussion which follows I am principally following Johnson, *The Function of Apocalyptic*, 134ff.

[122] Cf. M. J. Suggs, "'The Word is Near to You.' Rom. 10:6–10 within the Purpose of the Letter," in *Christian History and Interpretation: Studies Presented to John Knox*, 289–312. It appears Paul is following the LXX of Deut. 30.14 and is offering a citation as there is a citation formula here "but it says".

[123] Suggs, "'The Word is Near You'," 305.

have made the circuit of the vault of heaven and I have walked in the depths of the abyss."

Now what is most intriguing about the parallels between Baruch and Paul is that Baruch is affirming of Wisdom as it is embodied in Torah what Paul is affirming either about Christ, or Christ as he is conveyed through the word of faith. In Baruch, as in Sirach, one is already to the stage where Torah is seen as *the* locus where Wisdom has manifested herself. By way of parallel, Paul seems to be asserting that Christ as the true embodiment of Wisdom has manifested himself or made himself available in the word of faith "that we proclaim".

It is now necessary to go back and look at the context of Paul's argument to see what an astounding *tour de force* it is. Beginning in Rom. 10:1ff. Paul contrasts the attempt to establish human righteousness (cf. 10:3) by means of a righteousness that comes from the law (10:5), with the righteousness that comes from God, that is to say the righteousness that comes from faith. In this context appears the crux of Rom. 10:4, a verse about which more ink has been spilt especially since the Reformation than about almost any other Scripture verse.[124] Though previously I have argued that Rom. 10:4 seems primarily to mean that Christ is the end of the Torah insofar as it is a way of obtaining right standing with God,[125] in light of further study of the sapiential context of this entire discussion and in the light of the intertextual echo, I now think that probably the primary sense of what Paul means is that Christ is the goal or aim of Torah.[126] Several things lead to this conclusion.

Firstly, it will be remembered that in Sir. 24:5, Wisdom is speaking about herself, and in Baruch 3 the subject matter is Wisdom, while in Proverbs 30 the issue is the human search for Wisdom. Now if a non–Christian Jew of Paul's day had been asked where one can find Wisdom, or for that matter where one can find the reflection of God's righteousness, the answer surely would have been *in Torah*.[127] The aim of Torah is Wisdom, which entails God's righteousness and the expression of his righteous will for humankind as the late Jewish sages who wrote Sirach and Baruch clearly assert. Paul, however, wishes to argue something rather different.

Secondly, R. B. Hays is on target when he says, "[t]he conjunction *gar* (for) in 10:4 is the crucial logical connective. This sentence explains what was said in the foregoing sentence: the real aim of the Law, the righteousness of

---

[124] For the history of the interpretation of this verse, cf. R. Badenas, *Christ the End of the Law. Romans 10.4 in Pauline Perspective*, 7–34, on the history of interpretation.

[125] Witherington, *Jesus, Paul and the End of the World*, 118–19.

[126] The implication of this is still that Christ and his work put an end to seeking righteous by means of the law, but that is not the main point Paul is making.

[127] Suggs, "'The Word is Near to You'," 307 rightly notes that there is basically no Law free Wisdom writing later than Sirach. Once that association was made in Sirach it had a tremendous impact. On the widespread use of Sirach in early Judaism, cf. pp. 76ff. above

God, *is* Jesus Christ."[128] The point is then that one will find the crucial things one has been looking for in the Law (Wisdom, righteousness and the like) only in Christ, not least because Christ rather than personified Wisdom or even personified Righteousness (cf. 10:6) is what Torah has been pointing to all along. Here is simply another example of Paul's christocentric use of Scripture. What one does *not* have here is the equation Torah = Wisdom = Christ.[129] The Torah pointed forward to Christ, for *he* rather than Torah is the incarnation or full embodiment of Wisdom.[130] In short, Torah points to Christ who is God's Wisdom and righteousness. This interpretation explains both the contrast between the righteousness that comes from the law and the righteousness that comes from faith in Rom. 10:5, *and* the reason for the close association of Christ and Torah in Rom. 10:4.[131]

This brings one back once more to the argument that follows it. While it is not certain, it may be that the personification in Rom. 10:6 ("the righteousness that comes from faith says") in fact refers to Christ speaking as pre–existent Wisdom, remembering again the parallels from the late sapiential material in Sirach especially. In any case, in Rom. 10:6–7 Paul is talking about human efforts to obtain righteousness (i.e., Christ/Wisdom). This is also the case in Proverbs 30 and in Bar. 3:29–30. But Paul may have combined this idea with Wisdom herself speaking in Rom. 10:6.

Paul's running commentary in vv 6–8 makes clear that the object of the search is Christ who has already come down from heaven, come up from the dead, and is now available to all through the word of faith. Hays is right that Rom. 10:8b–10 is an expansion upon the quotation in v. 8.[132] Thus, in the end Paul concludes this part of his argument by contrasting the Gospel which is the word of faith that is near to you, with the Law. The Law only pointed forward to the real embodiment of righteousness and Wisdom/Christ; it did not make him available. The Gospel, however, if received by faith, brings near Christ who is now in heaven and all his benefits. Put the other way around, Christ is the embodiment of God's Wisdom and righteousness and he is made available through the preaching of the Gospel, as even the Law pointed to all along.[133]

---

[128] Hays, *Echoes of Scripture*, 75–76.

[129] *Pace* Suggs, "'The Word is Near'," 311–12

[130] Cf. the argument about the fading splendor of the Old Covenant in 2 Corinthians 3–4 and my *Jesus, Paul, and the End of the World*, 109–111.

[131] The association of Wisdom and righteousness is very close in sapiential material (cf. Prov. 10:31; Ps. 37:30). Note how in Wisdom of Solomon the rulers are urged to love righteousness: "because Wisdom will not enter a deceitful soul" (1:4). Since Wisdom material is often largely persuasion about how to live rightly by means of godly Wisdom, such an association is not surprising (cf. Wis. 9:2–3). Royal figures (and certainly Paul) saw the Christ as such a one who was especially expected to manifest Wisdom and righteousness.

[132] Hays, *Echoes of Scripture in Paul*, 81–82.

[133] Johnson, *Function of Apocalyptic*, 136ff. fails to grasp the subtlety of Paul's argument. Paul clearly says in his commentary in Rom. 10:6–8a that he is speaking about Christ in the same way Baruch and Ben Sira were speaking about Wisdom. The Wisdom that is near the believer is Christ who they must confess, not merely the preached word which is only the

Lastly, Paul is apparently drawing on the descending–ascending Wisdom pattern to speak of Christ (as he surely does in Philippians 2). The implication is that the Christ who is Wisdom is indeed a hidden (in heaven) Wisdom which must be revealed through the Good News preached. By this means he becomes accessible. This comports with the earlier discussion of Paul's views on revelatory Wisdom in 1 Corinthians 1–4.[134]

The study of Wisdom material in Romans would not be complete without an examination of the magnificent Wisdom hymn in Rom. 11:33–36. The study of late Jewish hymns and prayers in their own right is in its nascent stages, although a good deal has been done on some of the Qumran hymns.[135]

The apparent hymn in Rom. 11:33–36 has been shown by Norden to have a strophic arrangement involving a parallel construction of nine lines as follows:

O the depths of the riches and Wisdom and knowledge of God
how unsearchable are his judgments
and inscrutable are his ways.
For who has known the mind of the Lord?
Or who has been his counselor?
Or who has given a gift to him
and received one from him?
For from him and through him and to him are all things;
To him be the glory forever. Amen.[136]

The hymnic features are almost evident in English and they include the typical use of the pronoun *autos* (nine times!), the rhetorical questions, the exclamatory *hos*, and the final doxology (cf. Phil. 2:11b; 4 Macc. 18:23).[137]

Besides the obvious fact that God's Wisdom is being praised here, the following Wisdom features may be noted: (1) the use of *bathos* which has already been noted in 1 Cor.2:10 and is found in earlier Wisdom contexts to discuss the depth of God's Wisdom (cf. e.g. Eccles. 7:24; *1 Enoch* 63:3); (2) the use

---

vehicle for making Christ accesible. Only in a derivative sense is Paul suggesting that the Gospel is God's Wisdom here, and only because its content is Christ. Torah and Gospel are the instruments, but Wisdom and Christ are the key focal points of the discussion in Baruch and Romans respectively.

[134] Cf. Schnabel, *Law and Wisdom*, 247–48. It is doubtful, however, that Schnabel is right that Paul when he uses the phrase "the law of Christ" is referring to Torah as interpreted in light of Christ but cf. his discussion on 297ff.

[135] J. H. Charlesworth, "Jewish Hymns, Odes, and Prayers (ca. 167 B.C.E.–135 C.E.)," in *Early Judaism and its Modern Interpreters*, 411–36. Surprisingly, Charlesworth does not mention Rom. 11:33–36 as a possible case of the use of Jewish hymnic material (cf. 418–19).

[136] Norden, *Agnostos Theos*, 241. Norden rightly notes that v 36 has no direct Old Testament parallels, but rather is like what one finds in 1 Cor. 8:6 and Col. 1:16–17.

[137] R. Deichgräber, *Gotteshymnus und Christushymnus in der frühen Christenheit*, 61–64.

of the term unsearchable which is found also in LXX Wisdom contexts (cf. Job 5:9; 9:10; 34:24)[138]; (3) the combined citation of Isa. 40:13 and some form of Job 41:3. This sort of combined citation with sapiential intent we have seen to be characteristic of Paul, and so it is possible that Paul composed this paean. Fourthly, the three parallel rhetorical questions are reminiscent of *2 Bar.* 14:8–10 – "But who, O Lord my God, understands your judgment, or who searches out the depth of your way, or who considers the heavy burden of your path, or who can reflect on your incomprehensible decree, or who of those ever born has found the beginning and end of your Wisdom?"[139] One may also wish to compare 1QH 7:26–33 and 10:3–7 which make clear that Paul's words here would have been seen as some sort of hymn. Fifthly, the four *hapax legomena* very likely point to the use of a source (*anexepaunta*, v 33b; *anexichniastoi*, v 33c; *sumboulos*, v 34b; and *proedoken*, v 35a.[140]

There does not appear to have been very much editorial work done on this hymn. Johnson suggests only a possible change from *en* to *dia* in v 36, as may have been the case in 1 Cor. 8:6, as a sign of Paul's hand.[141] In view of the whole argument of Romans 9–11 it does not seem that Paul has Christ specifically in focus. Rather the mysterious secret of God's eschatological plan not only to include Gentiles but to reinclude at the eschaton Jews who were temporarily broken off from God's people in order to allow Gentiles in seems to be the cause for this exclamation.[142] In short, God's faithfulness, fairness, and impartiality are all upheld, as is revealed in this Pauline *musterion*.[143]

Before concluding this chapter it is in order to point out that a good deal more could be said about sapiential material in the Pauline Epistles. For example the relationship between Pauline parenesis and Wisdom traditions in regard to the matter of motivations could be studied at some length. P. Grech, for example, has pointed to Paul's appeal to common sense or nature (cf. 1 Cor. 5:6; 6:12; 11:15–16); the appeal to a sense of shame (1 Thess. 4:4; 1 Cor. 11:6; 2 Cor. 9:4), and the appeal to social reasons (1 Thess. 4:12; 1 Cor. 7:4; Rom. 13:1–6) as essentially sapiential in character.[144] To this one might add a discussion of things like Paul's appeal to the order of creation (cf. 1 Cor. 11:8ff); or the appeal to conscience (cf. Rom. 2:15) to mention but two possibilities. As Schnabel says,

---

138 Johnson, *The Function of Apocalyptic*, 167.

139 Käsemann, *Romans*, 319, rightly points out how differently Paul's passage and the one in Baruch function. The latter expresses despair of knowing God's ways; the former expresses gratitude for the revealing of this great eschatological *musterion* of redemption for both Jew and Gentile in Christ.

140 So Johnson, *The Function of Apocalyptic*, 171.

141 Johnson, *The Function of Apocalyptic*, 173.

142 Witherington, *Jesus, Paul and the End of the World*, 122–28.

143 Schnabel, *Law and Wisdom*, 250–51 is right that Paul sees God's Wisdom as "in Christ" but Christ is only indirectly in view here – the focus is on the larger eschatological plan in which Christ plays the crucial role.

144 P. Grech, "Christological Motivations in Pauline Ethics," in *Paul de Tarse*, 542–43.

"The issue of the place of Wisdom in Paul's ethics seems never to have been dealt with systematically even though scholars are aware of the formal and material links between Paul's parenesis and the Jewish Wisdom."[145]

On a different front, Scroggs long ago pointed out how Colossians and Ephesians are letters filled with Wisdom language, concerned with words like Wisdom, mystery, knowledge, creation theology, rulers of this age and the like.[146] Ellis too has pointed out how Col. 2:3 and Eph. 1:8–9 and 3:9–10 only restate conclusions already drawn by Paul in the sapiential material in 1 Corinthians 1–4 and Romans 11.[147] Apart from rather brief discussions of such matters in recent commentaries, a detailed study of Colossians and Ephesians as heavily indebted to sapiential thinking and forms of expressions remains to be done.[148]

CONCLUSIONS AND CONJECTURES

The chapter title raised the question of whether Paul should be seen as a sage or a sophist. Certainly, if 1 Corinthians 1–4 is any indication, Paul had no desire to be seen as a sophist, or one who offered purely sophistic rhetoric. This does not mean that he did not use rhetoric or the art of persuasion, but apparently especially in his preaching he was very cautious to let the message speak for itself, lest the medium draw the most attention. As a missionary strategy this may apply especially to Paul's dealings with the Corinthians. 1 Cor. 2:1–2 is speaking about the initial proclamation of the Gospel, not later teaching by way of letter.

In regard to whether or not Paul is a sage, certainly this is not the main or even a major way that he categorizes himself in his letters. Nevertheless, the evidence surveyed in this chapter provides ample evidence that Paul operated as a prophetic sage like unto a Ben Sira or the author of the Wisdom of Solomon in various ways. First, while it is true that one does not find an abundance of proverbs, aphorisms, riddles, or narrative *meshalim* in Paul, Paul does frequently adopt the various modes and techniques of discourse that one finds in the late Wisdom material where prophecy, eschatology, apocalyptic, and Wisdom material cross–fertilized.

Especially striking is the way Paul draws on late sapiential handling of the Hebrew Scriptures when he uses the Old Testament to make a point. He is

[145] Schnabel, *Law and Wisdom*, 300.

[146] Scroggs, "Paul – *Sophos* and *Pneumatikos*," 42–43.

[147] Ellis, "Wisdom and Knowledge," 60.

[148] Cf. e.g. E. Schweizer, *The Letter to the Colossians* (London: SPCK, 1976), 63ff. J. Gnilka, *Der Kolosserbrief* (Freiburg: Herder, 1980), 51ff.; A. T. Lincoln, *Ephesians* (Waco: Word, 1990), 17ff. Basically none of these commentators give consideration at length to the sapiential shaping of the Gospel material in general. Rather, they focus in particular just on the Wisdom connections in the hymnic material or the like.

also quite happy to adopt or adapt a Wisdom hymn to his own ends, but uses it in a fashion not unlike the use of such material in Baruch or elsewhere. There is also a strong stress on revelatory Wisdom in Romans and the Corinthian correspondence as there is in late sapiential sources like Sirach and the Wisdom of Solomon. One may also point to the way Paul draws on key sapiential themes like divine impartiality, the act-consequence schema, and creation theology to mention but three.

For Paul the revealed Wisdom that he claims to be privy to is Wisdom about God's eschatological plan of salvation in Christ for all the world. Sometimes this amounts to talking about that plan in a specific way, so the *musterion* he reveals is limited to just christological matters. Sometimes broader soteriological issues are in focus as is the case with the Wisdom that Paul praises God for at the end of the discourse in Romans 11.

The majority of the time, the issue is specifically christological and on these occasions one finds Paul engaging in various forms of transference which sets his work apart from non–Christian Jewish sapiential material. Sometimes Paul transfers what the sages have said about Wisdom to Christ (e.g. 1 Cor. 10:4). Sometimes what the sages were prepared to say one got from Torah, Paul now claims one gets from Christ (Rom. 10:4),[149] and sometimes what was said of God is now said of Christ (1 Cor. 8:6).[150] Beyond even this Paul seems prepared to call Christ Wisdom (1 Cor. 1:30). In the text in question he means that as a result of Christ's death (and resurrection) Christ was made Wisdom for believers, making all human forms of wisdom pale into insignificance and in fact become folly. In texts like 1 Cor. 10:4 or the hymn in Philippians 2 (and Colossians 1 if by Paul) Paul is willing to pushes matters further and talk about Christ's pre–existence drawing heavily on Wisdom ideas to do so. While there is not yet a fully developed Wisdom Christology in Paul there are the rudiments of one present. On the basis of this evidence and on the basis of the fact that Paul claims that the Wisdom he has to convey is a revealed Wisdom, a *musterion* he has been called upon to make public, one may say that Paul operates as a prophetic sage in various ways on various occasions and that the Wisdom he has to convey is eschatological in terms of its historical horizon, soteriological in terms of its general focus, and on more than a few occasions christological in terms of its intent and content. Paul reads the Hebrew Scriptures with Christ in mind, but he often allows earlier sapiential ways of handling the text to guide the way he will use it to point to Christ.

Paul does not equate Christ with Torah, but he does believe that Torah, rightly interpreted, points not to itself but to Christ as the locus of God's Wisdom. Paul parallels the Torah and the Gospel as instruments and is willing to say, unlike previous sages, that the Wisdom they were looking for and thought they had found in Torah is actually to be found in Christ.

---

[149] On the benefits one got from Wisdom; cf. above pp. 319ff. on 2 Corinthians 3–4.

[150] Though here the sapiential use of the Shema may be a more immediate partial source for this modification of monotheism.

Where did these remarkable sapiential and christological thoughts come from? Perhaps a hint is provided in 1 Corinthians 1 where it appears that Paul knows and uses the so-called "thunderbolt saying" very likely found in the Q material. If Jesus characterized himself as Wisdom, or the editors of Q did so, or both, Paul may have gathered the spark from these sources and fanned it into a somewhat more intense and sizable flame. If Paul did know some form of Q and drew some of his Wisdom ideas from it, then one would have to date Q no later than the late 40s since 1 Corinthians was written in the early 50s.

One gets the sense from 1 Corinthians 1–4 that Paul was by no means the only Christian to use somewhat Hellenized Jewish sapiential material in his preaching and teaching. Apollos appears to have done so, and in view of the earlier investigation of Q and the christological hymns perhaps many others did so as well. At this point it is possible to state that Hellenized early Jewish Christianity seems to be the matrix out of which an early and rather high Wisdom Christology arose, a development for which Jesus himself seems to have provided the catalyst.

It is interesting to compare and contrast Jesus and Paul as prophetic sages. The vast majority of the Jesus tradition would seem to fit into the category of prophetic sapiential material which often had an eschatological content, while only a minority, though a significant minority, of Paul's teaching seems to be specifically sapiential in character. Both Jesus and Paul seem to have offered a revelatory sort of Wisdom of a counter order character that spoke of an eschatological reversal and of God's choosing the least, the last, and the lost to convey the Good News (cf. 1 Cor. 1:26ff with Matt. 11:25). Paul does not seem to have used parables of the kingdom as his major vehicle for public proclamation but rather a form of the early Christian kerygma that focused on the death and resurrection of Christ and its effects on those who believe. But he does engage in sapiential teaching in his letters to Christians.

It will be noted that Paul, like Jesus, never bothers to introduce his own authoritative teaching, which each took to be binding on their believing audience, with "Thus saith the Lord." Though Paul speaks prophetic words he does so as a prophetic sage who has received revelation from God and speaks as a steward of God's mysteries without need for such formulae. It would appear that both Jesus and Paul had what might be called advanced sapiential teaching for the more mature among their believing audiences. Jesus gave some explanations for his parables to his disciples; Paul explicated further the content of the christological and soteriological mystery he was charged to unveil. Both were convinced they offered God's Wisdom and not mere human Wisdom on such occasions. Paul sees the Holy Spirit as the agent through whom one is taught such Wisdom (1 Cor. 2:12–13) and probably Jesus also saw himself as given revelation by the Spirit (cf. Mark 3:29/Matt. 12:32).

Paul's activity as a prophetic sage does not try to duplicate that of Christ, the editors of Q, or of the creators of the christological hymns but rather to reflect on the meaning of Christ and the Christ event in general in the light of his own Jewish heritage, particularly the prophetic and sapiential sources. In this comparison one sees what fertile soil sapiential thinking and traditions proved to be both for Jesus and his early Jewish Christian followers like Paul.

But was there anyone who had the imagination to conceive of the entire story of the earthly life of Jesus within a sapiential framework? Could Wisdom progress beyond being a sayings collection for Christians to being a whole telling of the Gospel? In the final chapter in this study on the biblical data, the First and Fourth Gospels will be examined to see if they might well be called Wisdom Gospels and Gospels about Wisdom.

8

The Gospels of Wisdom: Matthew and John

WISDOM, as we have shown in this study, was expressed in many ways in early Judaism and early Jewish Christianity. Narrative is one of the ways Wisdom was expressed even as early as the composition of some parts of Proverbs 1–9, when space was given to meditating on personified Wisdom and her roles in creation and in daily life. A different form of narrative Wisdom arose in the narrative *meshalim* which are found in early Judaism both within and outside of the teaching of Jesus and the Gospel traditions.[1] But what happens if there are hints in the Gospel material itself that Jesus, who had an earthly career, had intimated that his own story was the story of Wisdom in person? What happens if in both word and deed Jesus presented himself and his life as the great parable of God's Wisdom, like and yet even greater than Solomon? Here one is beyond mere myths about personified attributes, or fictitious stories about prodigal sons and the like, and is dealing with the intermingling of history and theology presented in narrative form. What would it have looked like to tell the story of Jesus in the light of Jewish sapiential thinking about wisdom in general and personified and even hypostasized Wisdom in particular. I submit that it would have looked rather like what one finds in the First Gospel, and to a lesser but nonetheless real extent what one finds in the Fourth Gospel. It is not the purpose of this chapter to do detailed exegesis of all the relevant passages in Matthew and John but to provide some evidence that these Gospels can and were intended to be read as, among other things, expressions of Wisdom thinking about Jesus. To this end, things like the plots, key motifs, and

[1] Cf. Carlston, "Wisdom and Eschatology in Q," 101–02 on Wisdom in narrative in Q.

redactional tendencies should be reflected on. I am producing here not an exhaustive study but an evocative sketch of Wisdom's Gospels, after a few necessary preliminary remarks.

MATTHEW AND JOHN: DIFFERENT SONS OF THE SAME MOTHER

On first sight the First and Fourth Gospels seem to be distinctly different. After all, there is no Logos Prologue, "I am" discourses, or signs narratives in Matthew, nor a genealogy, Sermon on the Mount, or any real parable collections in John. But on closer inspection there is quite a lot that these two Gospels have in common. Both Gospels begin with a statement about the origins of the central character Jesus; both have a heavy stress on Jesus as a teacher which in both cases takes the form of a series of discourses;[2] and both bring their Gospels to their respective climaxes with an extended presentation of the death and resurrection appearances of Jesus, but then conclude with one or more scenes involving the recommissioning of the re-gathered disciples.

In addition both Gospels seem to have been written by the same sort of person, out of the the same sort of milieu, and for the same sort of audience; that is, these two Gospels were written by Jewish Christians, writing in the last quarter of the first century to a community which had recently experienced the "parting of the ways" with non–Christian Judaism, and for a predominantly Jewish Christian audience.[3] Thus, the disciples of Jesus, even Jewish ones in these evangelists' days, can be distinguished from "the Jews" (cf. Matt. 28:15; John 10:19, 24; seventy-one times in John).[4] Both Gospels are significantly shaped not only by whom they are written for (a group of predominantly Jewish–Christians, though some Gentile Christians seem to be in the audience), but also by whom they are written against (in Matthew, the Pharisees in particular but also the Jewish religio–political leadership in general; in John, "the Jews", which seems in the main to refer to Jewish religio–political leaders). They both seem to have arisen out of a context of conflict and probably even persecution.[5]

The understanding of the story in both the First and Fourth Gospels turns to a large degree on understanding the relationship among the protagonists (Jesus and his followers) *and* between the protagonists and antagonists.

---

[2] The term sermon is a misnomer for the Matthean discourses, including Matthew 5–7; Matt. 5:2 is quite explicit that what follows is teaching, not preaching.

[3] G. N. Stanton, *A Gospel for a New People. Studies in Matthew*, 111ff. I borrowed the phrase "parting of the ways" from him.

[4] O. L. Colpe, *Matthew: A Scribe Trained for the Kingdom of Heaven*, 129.

[5] D. R. A. Hare, *Jewish Persecution of Christians*, 80ff; R. T. France, *Matthew – Evangelist and Teacher*, 216ff; J. Painter, *The Quest for the Messiah. The History, Literature, and Theology of the Johannine Community*, 45ff.

Matthew and John are the two most polemical Gospels for a very good reason – both arose in settings where the relationship with the larger Jewish community was still an important issue precisely because the Christian community had recently come out of that larger community. It may be in both cases they were thrust out of it (cf. Matt. 10:17 with John 16:2, 18:20).

It is also fair to say that if a case is going to be made for Gospels that arose out of or more likely *for* a "school" setting, the First and Fourth Gospels are the best candidates.[6] I think Matthew and probably also John are Gospels written for Jewish Christian teachers who have been and are being trained in a school setting where sapiential thinking and Wisdom literature are important formative influences. Even without a detailed argument, in view of the Jewish milieu out of which Matthew and John seem to have arisen it is possible to say with C. K. Barrett that,

> [t]here is thus an inherent probability that the early history of Christianity would manifest social formations recognizable as *schools* and *conventicles*, and there is a measure of confirmation of this in the fact that the gospels present a clear picture of Jesus as a teacher, addressed in conventional terms as Rabbi (e.g. Mark 9:5) and surrounded by a group of *mathetai*, who were divided into an outer ill-defined company, and an inner group selected out of the outer (Mark 3:13f.) very conscious of itself and of those who do not belong to it (Mark 4:11).[7]

Nowhere is Jesus more clearly presented as a teacher with learners (which is what *mathetes* means), than in Matthew's and John's Gospels. It is no accident that the term disciple (*mathetes*, "learner"), which occurs *only* in the first five books of the New Testament, occurs much more frequently in Matthew and John than in Mark or Luke (Matthew, seventy-three times; John, seventy-eight; Mark, forty-six; Luke–Acts, sixty-five combined, only thirty-seven in the Gospel).[8] It is also no accident that in both Matthew and John discipleship is defined as keeping Jesus' commands or words (*tereo* plus the *entell* root; cf. Matt. 18:19 with John 14:14, and Matt. 28:18–20 with John 14:15–26, 15:10).[9]

---

[6] For example, compare K. Stendahl, *The School of St. Matthew and its Use of the Old Testament* with R. A. Culpepper, *The Johannine School*. O. Cullmann, *The Johannine Circle*; R. E. Brown, *The Community of the Beloved Disciple*, 99ff. I am not advocating that these Gospels were written by a committee. I do think that the individuals who originated them wrote in and for not merely a community but probably for a "school," i.e., a group of disciples who had committed themselves to careful and ongoing study, transmission, and interpretation of the Jesus tradition, as a means of training to be teachers and/or community leaders.

[7] C. K. Barrett, "School, Conventicle, and Church in the New Testament," in *Wissenschaft und Kirche. Festschrift für Eduard Lohse*, 101.

[8] Culpepper, *Johannine School*, 270–71.

[9] U. Luz, "The Disciples in the Gospel according to Matthew," in *The Interpretation of Matthew*, 113, is astonished by this parallel, but should not have been.

Furthermore, when discipleship is explicated as entailing bearing fruit and loving one's neighbors: "John comes into very close theological proximity with Matthew who describes the disciple as the one who does God's will (12.46ff). For him too the love command is the content of God's will and... bearing fruit is important for distinguishing between genuine and counterfeit Christianity" (cf. Matt. 12:46ff; 7:15ff; 21:43; to John 13:35; 15:2–8).[10] In these two Gospels as well one finds the most actual teaching material. While I am not prepared to argue that these two Gospels are school products in the sense of Gospels produced in the main *by* groups, I do think they were written *for* early Christian pedagogical purposes, probably *for* school settings, and were edited accordingly.[11]

Scholars have long puzzled over why the Fourth Gospel is so different from the Synoptics, particularly in what it relates of Jesus' teaching. If one considers this difficult question in the light of sapiential pedagogical considerations the following conjecture commends itself. Matthew *primarily* intends to present what he views as the public teaching of Jesus and its explication;[12] John primarily presents what was appropriately used as "in house" explanations of the public teaching as well as some of the private teaching of Jesus meant first for the inner circle alone.[13] In the former case Jesus' public teaching takes the form of parables, aphorisms, riddles, beatitudes and other sapiential forms. In the latter case Jesus' teaching primarily takes the form of Wisdom discourses not unlike those found in Proverbs 8 or Sirach 24. In other words, Matthew primarily presents Wisdom for Christian teachers to use with outsiders or *new* converts; John presents Wisdom for those who need *further* instruction in the school of Christ.

---

[10] Luz, "Disciples," 118. On the same page he draws the right conclusion that these similarities are to be accounted for not by "literary dependence; more likely [by] a theological continuation by John and Matthew of related traditions." But if there is no literary dependence what is it that accounts for these similarities? I would suggest that both evangelists are depicting discipleship in a sapiential mode, reading the Jesus tradition in light of the sapiential material about discipleship to a sage in Proverbs, Ecclesiastes, Sirach, and the Wisdom of Solomon.

[11] The Fourth Gospel clearly evidences an editor and community looking back on and presenting earlier Johannine traditions; cf. John 19:35; 21:24–25 and the use of the phrase "the beloved disciple" which surely is a phrase coined by followers of that disciple, not by the disciple himself.

[12] The word primarily is important because the teaching is directed to the disciples from the first, though the crowd is also supposed to overhear (Matt. 5:1–2). From Matthew 13 if not Matthew 11, on there is more and more focus on teaching the disciples, which in some cases means private exposition and explanation of things like parables and Jesus' identity, which the public do not get the benefit of (cf. Matt. 11:25–27; 13:51–52; 16:13–20). Nevertheless, it should not be ignored that once again in Matthew 23 *both* the crowds and the disciples are addressed.

[13] I am not here raising or trying to answer the thorny historical questions about an an actual pre-Easter *Sitz im Leben* of some of Jesus' teaching in the Fourth Gospel, but merely saying how the evangelist seems to have viewed the matter.

The disciples in John are portrayed as typical, fulfilling the proper roles of a great Jewish teacher's followers by spending time with him (3:22), calling him rabbi (1:38, 49; 4:31; 9:2; 11:8), buying food for him (4:8, 31), and baptizing for him (4:2).[14] "Membership in the Johannine community... involved learning, remembering, obeying, and studying both the traditions about Jesus' words and signs and scriptures."[15] With the possible omission of the word signs, the very same thing can very likely be said about Matthew's community.

Probably a similar conclusion should be drawn about how the evangelists view themselves as well. Both the First and Fourth Evangelists should probably be seen as tradents: "Matthew" redacting Mark, Q, and M material; "John" editing a christological hymn, a signs source, some discourses, and a passion narrative. Each of these evangelists are very likely attempting to write an episodic *bios* of Jesus, in the mold of the ancient Greco–Roman "Lives".[16] As Plutarch reminds us (*Alex.* 1:1–2), there is a difference between a *bios* and a *historia*. The former uses historical data, but selectively because the main interest is in portraying in a portrait of words and deeds the historical *character* of an historical person who is seen as an *example*. The latter focuses more on important events, their historical consequences and the like. The difference here is one of intent in using the data, for clearly Plutarch's *Lives* contain a considerable amount of historical narrative.[17] The Gospels, somewhat like the *Lives*, are aimed at changing or improving the life and practices of their hearers. In short, they are written to inculcate or nurture both a certain kind of faith but also a certain kind of faithful living. To that end, a high degree of teaching material with a parenetic thrust is presented.

One among many clues that both Matthew and John are presenting their stories in sapiential fashion is the high incidence of the use of Father language for God, or Father–Son language. In Matthew Father is used of God some forty-two times; in John God is referred to as Father no fewer than 115 times. This is compared to only five times in Mark (none before Mark 8:38), and only fifteen times in Luke, some of which come from Q in any case. Perhaps even more

---

[14] R. A. Culpepper, *Anatomy of the Fourth Gospel*, 116.

[15] Culpepper, *Johannine School*, 271. The "we" in John 21:24 is those learners who have received the testimony of the Beloved Disciple about Jesus and the Jesus tradition. Someone among them must have been the final editor of the Fourth Gospel, but it should be noted that both this verse and John 19:35 must be taken seriously. Whoever the Fourth Evangelist was, he believed he was faithfully presenting another person's testimony about Jesus, not his own. Like the First Evangelist he should be seen primarily as an editor of his sources, not the author of them. Cf. M. Hengel, *The Johannine Question*, 94ff.

[16] I argued for this conclusion in the first chapter of my doctoral dissertation "Women in the Gospels and Acts", but the case has been more strongly made by a definitive study by R. A. Burridge, *What are the Gospels? A Comparison with Graeco–Roman Biography*, 191ff. All attempts to categorize the Gospels as novels, or simply as fiction, will have to reckon with this study which makes clear the family resemblance between the Gospels and other ancient *bioi*.

[17] G. Paul, "Symposia and Deipna in Plutarch's *Lives* and in other Historical Writings," in *Dining in a Classical Context*, 157.

significant is the fact that in both Matthew and John the use of the term Father for God is closely connected with an understanding of both Jesus as *the* Son of God, and the disciples as sons of God. That is, theology, Christology, and discipleship are linked through the Father language. In John this means "by believing that Jesus is from God, the believer is able to know God as Father."[18] To put it another way, knowing Jesus' origins and his destiny leads to both knowing who Jesus is and knowing God as Father. In Matthew as well it is true that one comes to know the Father only through the Father being revealed by and through the Son (Matt. 11:27b).

These two Gospels have the highest Christology of the canonical four, for they have grown out of and draw on the wealth of early Jewish Christian Wisdom thinking about God and Jesus in order to talk about the relationship of the Father and the royal Son, or about God and Wisdom. Both are deeply committed to presenting what they view as sufficiently exalted pictures of Jesus in their biographies. An adequate study and comparison of the Christologies of the First and Fourth Gospels would show that Matt. 11:27–28 is no anomalous non–Matthean meteorite fallen from a Johannine sky,[19] but rather evidence that when evangelists deeply steeped in Wisdom thinking came to reflect on Jesus, it was possible for them to come to very similar christological formulations. Matt. 11:27–28 may then be said to be a brief expression of a way of thinking that is expounded and expanded upon more fully in the Fourth Gospel. These two Gospels, though in many ways different, nevertheless show in the critical areas of how they reflect on Jesus, his teaching, and on his disciples that they both share a strong family resemblance, being deeply indebted to Wisdom. Matthew and John are different sons but they come from the same mother.

The flow of the narrative in both the First and the Fourth Gospels comes to a turning point which centers on the issue of whether the audience is going to accept or reject Jesus' teaching. Matthew 13 is that crucial turning point in the narrative where the ministry of Jesus turns to focus more exclusively on his disciples, having been rejected by the larger Jewish audience (cf. Matthew 11–12). Hence, though Jesus had said that he and even his disciples were sent only to Israel (cf. 10:5–6; 15:24, – though the latter is spoken by Jesus as he is in fact in the middle of helping a foreigner in a foreign place), in Matthew 13 Jesus speaks of his Jewish audience as being blind, deaf and without understanding (13:13). Accordingly, he will only speak to them in parables, while the disciples alone can now be addressed as the true people of God and given even the understanding of parables.[20] This same sort of pattern is seen in John as well,

---

[18] Culpepper, *Anatomy*, 114. The modern attempt to create a "Sophiaology" out of the biblical data faces severe difficulties not least because Wisdom ideas and Jesus as Wisdom are so closely linked in the New Testament to the Fatherhood of God.

[19] The importance of the terms Father and Son for describing the relationship of God and Jesus in Matthew's Gospel is well known. This saying simply clarifies what is implied elsewhere in this Gospel.

[20] J. D. Kingsbury, *The Parables of Jesus in Matthew 13*, 130–31.

where opposition builds up, there is a falling away of some (John 6:66ff) and thereafter Jesus primarily addresses his own disciples. It appears likely that the function of this sort of plot development is to explain to both of these respective Christian communities how it was that Jesus came to be rejected by most of his own people (cf. John 1:11–12 as a summary of the Johannine plot), only being accepted by a few disciples, and how the Christian community came to have a more universalistic focus than the ministry of Jesus had, at least in the main. It also serves to place a premium on Jesus' Wisdom instructions to his disciples.

A lot can also be learned by studying how a Gospel ends. Both Matthew and John end with stories about doubt and faith amongst the disciples and wish to point their communities forward beyond Easter, giving them direction after the resurrection appearances. O. Michel puts it this way:

> It seems to me that Matthew and John are confronted by quite similar problems in the question of certainty about Easter. Neither underestimates the old Easter stories but both point beyond these into the future. Neither Matthew nor the fourth evangelist wants to deprive the *horama* ("vision") of its significance within the tradition; it remains an important aspect of the Easter story....The problem of "doubt" is touched on in both Gospels. In Matthew the message of the Risen One and obedience to this word is the way doubt is overcome. In John the hearer is referred to the understanding inherent in faith itself; it can and may dispense with seeing. For Matthew the word of the Risen One contains the way to master doubt about the truth of the message and the reality of the Risen One.[21]

The above has been offered simply to begin to stimulate the reader into an initial contemplation of the similarities between the First and Fourth Gospels; it is not intended as a definitive argument. What follows, however, is a more detailed presentation meant to substantiate the indebtedness of these Gospels to Wisdom thinking and material, which will at least indirectly substantiate the suggestions made above.

MATTHEW – A WORD TO THE WISE

DESCRIBING THE SCRIBE AND HIS STUDENTS

It is the majority opinion that the Gospel of Matthew was written by a Jewish Christian and for an audience the majority of which was probably also Jewish Christian.[22] It appears to some scholars from the emphasis on polemics against

---

[21] O. Michel, "The Conclusion of Matthew's Gospel," in *The Interpretation of Matthew*, 33.

[22] Cf. e.g. the chart in Davies and Allison, *Matthew*, Vol. 1, 10–11; U. Luz, *Matthew 1–7*, 77–78.

the scribes and Pharisees (cf. Matthew 23), that "the community seems to stand within the broader Jewish community despite a bitter polemic with the parent group."[23] To the contrary, I would suggest that G. N. Stanton is right when he says that Matt. 21:43 must be taken seriously (cf. also 23:37–38; 27:25).[24] Matthew writes believing that his is a Gospel for a new people to whom the kingdom has been given, in contrast to the old people from whom it has now been taken away.[25] This is even more evidently the case in the Fourth Gospel, where one of the major themes is about Jesus replacing the major institutions of early Judaism with himself as temple, as offerer of grace, truth or new wine, as the substance of Passover and the like. But as is always the case with the splitting off of a religious sect from a parent group, much of the parent group's thought and methods continue to be used by the sect.

There was a great urgency in early Christianity to legitimate itself as offering the true interpretation of Jesus, Judaism, Torah and related matters. To this end early Jewish Christians set up schools or school–like settings where teachings of and about Jesus as well as the new interpretations of Torah were reflected on and passed on to a generation of Christians who had not been in contact with the historical Jesus or involved with his earthly ministry.

Schools in early Judaism were set up to conserve and convey a precious religious heritage and it is surely likely that this was also the primary purpose, at least during the period when almost all Christians were Jews, of early Christian schools as well. After an extensive study of ancient schools A. Culpepper concludes:

> [A] sense of tradition characterizes the schools and is manifested in their communal meals, worship, veneration of their founders, preservation of the founder's teachings and writings, collection and transmission of biographical traditions, and adherence to taboos and procedures regarding admission and maintenance of membership in the school. Similarities and differences can also be observed regarding what it meant to be a student or disciple. The schools can be viewed as falling along a line at one end of which the primary concern of the adherent is learning and acquiring knowledge and at the other extreme it is devotion to, imitation of, the teacher. Between the extremes one finds many blends of the two emphases, and probably in no case does either appear devoid of the other.... The distinguishing activities of the schools were teaching, learning, studying, and writing.... Evidence of preoccupation with teaching or study can, therefore be

[23] C. Deutsch, "Wisdom in Matthew: Transformation of a Symbol," 14.

[24] Stanton, *Gospel for a New People*, 146ff.

[25] On the break with the synagogue in Matthew's community cf. S. H. Brooks, *Matthew's Community. The Evidence of his Special Sayings Material*, 117f.; J. D. Kingsbury, *Matthew as Story*, 127: "Still, if the real readers were living in close proximity to a strong Jewish community, they are not to be thought of as a 'splinter group' that was nevertheless a member of the Jewish league of synagogues. The place of the real readers was no longer within Judaism but outside it."

used as an indication that a given community was a school or that a writing which reflects such concerns was produced within a school.[26]

He then goes on to conclude, rightly in my judgment, that both Matthew and John are Gospels produced in and probably for a school setting, as is evidenced by the preoccupation with the sort of things Culpepper stresses characterized schools. The stress in both works on veneration of the founder of the community, transmission of his teaching, admissions or defining rituals (baptism, foot washing), making boundaries evident by augmenting a clear sense of "we" versus "they" (cf. in Matthew "their synagogues", in John "the Jews"), and conveying certain biographical details about the founder's life, is notable. Minear has also rightly pointed out that the need for a *written* Gospel would be felt by the teachers and leaders of a Christian community much more strongly than by the members of the community in general, for whom *hearing* the Jesus tradition would normally suffice.[27]

The rather conservative editorial work of Matthew on Mark, and probably also on Q[28] reminds one that the First Evangelist very likely saw himself as primarily an editor or redactor, not an author. Stanton puts it well when he says, "Matthew is creative but not innovative; he is commited to the traditions at his disposal, but he endeavours to elucidate them for his own community.... The expansions... [one] observes are not the work of a Christian prophet but of an 'exegete'."[29] A better way to put it would be to say that Matthew is a scribe, writing for other Jewish Christian scribes, showing how to use the Gospel story to teach new converts.[30] This does not mean he was not creative in the way he handled the Jesus tradition, but it does mean he was conscious of trying to pass along traditions in a school setting, traditions that he felt needed to be remembered. That is, he acted like the ancient scribes and sages – conveying to his pupils the wisdom he had inherited, learned, or gained by revelation.[31]

In order to present Jesus as a sage and even as Wisdom the First Evangelist carefully constructs his Gospel out of three primary sources: Mark, Q, and M, using his material so that carefully arranged and edited collections of words and deeds do the job of portraying the character of the main subject of the Gospel – Jesus. This indirect method of portraiture was characteristic of ancient Greco–Roman biographies which also concentrate on words and deeds

[26] Culpepper, *Johannine School*, 253–55.

[27] Minear, *Matthew: The Teacher's Gospel*, 9.

[28] Cf. above. pp. 211ff.

[29] Stanton, *Gospel*, 344–45.

[30] This explanation is to be preferred to the view that the First Evangelist was a former rabbi, as it avoids the problems of anachronism. On this older view, cf. E. von Dobschütz, "Matthew as Rabbi and Catechist," in *The Interpretation of Matthew*, 19–29.

[31] It is impossible to say how conservative or liberal the Fourth Evangelist was in his editing, as there is really nothing comparable elsewhere in the Jesus tradition to much of his material, for example the "I am" discourses.

and often more on the former than the latter, especially if the person being written about was a notable teacher.[32] I would suggest that a person deeply steeped in Jewish sapiential material would be the most likely among Jews to be open to using such Hellenistic and Roman forms precisely because Wisdom material had always in principle maintained an openness to international Wisdom, which in due course entailed Hellenistic influences on the authors of Sirach and the Wisdom of Solomon, to mention but two examples. The effects of Hellenistic forms on Jewish Wisdom literature can already be seen in Sirach 44–50.[33] The use of the Greco–Roman biographical form would simply be one more example of how international forms and material could be appropriated for essentially Jewish, or in this case Jewish Christian, sapiential purposes.

A close examination of key pieces of Matthean editorial work shows not only the pedagogical orientation of this Gospel, but also the type of pedagogy the first evangelist had in mind. To begin with, it is striking in the First Gospel that while disciples repeatedly address Jesus as Lord (cf. e.g. 8:21, 25; 14:28; 16:22), when the Jewish leaders or a stranger addresses Jesus it is usually as rabbi or teacher (cf. 8:19; 12:38; 19:16; 22:16, 24, 36). Even more revealing is the fact that only Judas among the Twelve, once he is prepared to betray Jesus, calls Jesus rabbi (cf. 26:25, 49). What this shows is that in the First Evangelist's view it is *inadequate* simply to call Jesus *a* rabbi or teacher. It is not, however, *inaccurate*. Indeed, in the crucial passage in Matt. 23:8–10 Jesus makes plain that he alone is *the* teacher of the disciples, and that they should not assume the label of "rabbi" or call any merely earthly teacher father, because they have a heavenly Father. The Markan and Lukan parallels have nothing similar to this (cf. Mark 12:38–40; Luke 20:45–47), making clear this is a special concern of the First Evangelist. In Matt. 26:17–19 Jesus calls himself "*ho didaskalos*" with the assumption that both his immediate hearers and the more remote one who is to be approached about an animal knows who *the* teacher is (i.e. the assumption is that those who hear the message are disciples). The passage in Matt. 23:8–10 is offered to remind Matthew's present audience that they also are not rabbis or teachers (so also Matt. 10:24–25; cf. below). Rather, they are to think of themselves as the Evangelist thinks of himself – as a scribe, an interpreter of the teachings of *the* teacher, the sage Jesus.[34]

The end of the so–called Sermon on the Mount makes clear that the First Evangelist wishes to distinguish between Jesus the sage, who teaches as one

---

[32] Burridge, *What are the Gospels*, 166ff. According to Burridge, in Lucian's *Demonax*, 60% of the work is devoted to anecdotes and sayings, while in Philostratus' *Apollonius of Tyana* 68.8% is devoted to dialogues and travels.

[33] Cf. pp. 76ff. above.

[34] Kingsbury, *Matthew as Story*, 65–66. He takes a less nuanced view than offered here (cf. his 127). E. Schweizer, *The Good News According to Matthew*, 315, is nearer the mark in saying of the Christian scribes, "Such a teacher of the Law is of course no longer a 'rabbi' i.e. a great one, but rather a 'disciple' in the Kingdom of heaven, i.e. one who remains a 'learner'... throughout his life (cf. 23:10)."

who has independent authority, and "*their scribes*" (7:29). The point here is twofold: (1) Jesus is not merely a scribe; and (2) the problem is not with scribes *per se* but *their scribes*, i.e. non–Christian Jewish ones who associate with the Pharisees.

It cannot be stressed enough that the First Evangelist wishes to give Jesus' task of teaching pride of place, as in due course he will do when the commissioning of the disciples is discussed. For example, in the summary passages in 4:23, 9:35 and 11:1 Matthew cites teaching *ahead* of preaching and healing as the chief task of Jesus. This is especially significant when one notes that in his Markan source at Mark 1:39 there is no mention of teaching, there is no parallel to Matt. 9:35, and in the Lukan parallel to Matt. 11:1 instead of *didaskein* one finds *panta ta remata autou* (Luke 7:1). When one asks what the content of this teaching is in Matthew, the answer is that Wisdom material has an overwhelming predominance. Jesus offers beatitudes, aphorisms, parables, wisdom discourses. In short, Jesus is to be seen as a Jewish sage.

Many scholars have rightly thought that there is a clue to how the First Evangelist saw himself in Matt. 13:52 – "therefore every scribe who has been trained for the kingdom of heaven is like the master of a household who brings out of his treasure what is new and what is old."[35] I would suggest that this uniquely Matthean saying tells us as much about the audience for whom this Gospel was intended as about the author. Matthew is one scribe showing other Jewish Christian scribes the proper content and form of their teaching before they are sent out to make further disciples chiefly by teaching (cf. Matt. 28:19–20).[36]

There is, however, a right way and a wrong way to evaluate what Matthew means by a scribe. By scribe, he does not mean what is meant in later rabbinic writings, i.e., one who is chiefly if not exclusively an interpreter of Torah, both written and oral.[37] Nor will it do simply to collapse the categories of prophet, sage and scribe although clearly there is some overlap.[38] Matt. 23:34

---

[35] M. D. Goulder, *Midrash and Lection in Matthew*, 3–27; Colpe, *Matthew*, 124ff.; D. E. Orton, *The Understanding Scribe. Matthew and the Apocalyptic Ideal*, 165ff. It has even been suggested that the name *Matthaios* is alluded to in Matt. 13.52 in the use of the word *matheteutheis*, but this is probably pushing things too far.

[36] U. Luz, *Das Evangelium nach Mätthaus 2.(Mt 8–17)*, 364, is quite right that *grammateus* does not refer to all the disciples but a specific group of them. He is also right that the Christian use here is also not a technical one for someone who is just a Torah scholar. On what is meant by new and old, cf. 364–65.

[37] *Pace* Goulder, *Midrash and Lection*, 3ff. Goulder's anachronistic evaluation has been rightly criticized by Orton, *The Understanding Scribe*, 137ff.

[38] Orton, *Understanding Scribe*, 165ff. is guilty of this at points. Cf. the discussion above pp. 4ff. on the relationship of scribes, sages, and counsellors of the king. Some sages were undoubtedly also scribes and vice versa. In Sirach and the Wisdom of Solomon one sees the sage assuming some of the functions of a prophet, because of the reception of what they take to be new revelation.

demonstrates that Matthew can and does distinguish these three groups.[39] Rather, Matthew sees himself and his charges as sapiential scribes of the sort described in Sir. 39.1–3: "He seeks out the wisdom of all the ancients, and is concerned with prophecies; he preserves the sayings of the famous and penetrates the subtleties of parables; he seeks out the hidden meanings of proverbs and is at home with the obscurity of parables."[40] All of this requires: (1) the opportunity of leisure (only the one who has little business can become wise, Sir. 38:24); and (2) in all probability a school setting (thus Ben Sira urges "Draw near to me, you who are uneducated, and lodge in the house of instruction," Sir. 51:23). It is the chief job of the sapiential scribe to be an interpreter of the earlier Wisdom, not just in Torah or in the Wisdom books, but also in this case the Wisdom in the teachings of Jesus. As Orton has rightly pointed out, it is not an accident that Matt. 13:52 immediately follows a series of parables, and probably should in itself be seen as a *mashal*. The inner circle of disciples are presented here as those who understand Jesus' parables, that is, even his more enigmatic wisdom teaching.[41]

Understanding Matthew's view of his own task as well as that of his charges also in part depends on evaluating the negative things the First Evangelist has to say about the scribes associated with the chief antagonists in the story – the Pharisees. As Orton has shown it is neither true that Matthew polemicizes against all scribes, nor true that he confuses scribes and Pharisees.[42]

> On the contrary, Matthew displays a consistent regard for the scribes which strongly suggests he has a clear notion of who scribes are: he seeks to exonerate them from strident opposition to Jesus by characterizing scribes who do so as unrepresentative of scribes *per se*, hence always linking *opposing* scribes with known opponents of Jesus, especially Pharisees, or qualifying them as only "some of" the scribes; he portrays them positively by removing suggestions that they "tempt" Jesus and by making them courteous learners and genuine enquirers; he is aware that the scribes carry a genuine authority; he shows they are treated with respect by Jesus; only the Pharisaic scribes, who culpably distort the honoured picture of the scribe by their hypocrisy and false leadership, bear the full brunt of Jesus' criticism. We conclude that everything points to Matthew's having a positive and firm concept of the scribes.[43]

---

[39] Cf. the parallel in Luke 11:49 where Luke has "prophets and apostles". The Matthean formulation surely tells us something about the evangelist's interest in and ability to distinguish these groups.

[40] This passage especially helps one to understand the logic of Matthew 13 where parables are presented, understanding is affirmed, and the task of the scribe is described.

[41] Orton, *The Understanding Scribe*, 151ff.

[42] Ibid., 18ff.

[43] Ibid., 37.

The scribe who is a follower of Jesus has as his task to bring out of his treasure box or storeroom something new and old (Matt. 13:51). This verse must be compared to one closely similar in language in Matt. 12:35: "the good person out of his good treasure brings forth good, and the evil person out of his evil treasure brings forth evil." In both cases the person is producing something that she or he already has stored away.[44] In the case of Matt. 13:52 this means that whether the scribe is offering new or old teaching it is teaching he brings forth out of his reserves. In short, it is not teaching produced *de novo* upon request, but things already learned or known and produced at the appropriate occasion.[45] Probably, though one cannot be certain, it is important that the word "new" precedes the word "old" here. This suggests the scribe may be called upon to interpret the new revelation of Jesus or the old one in Torah, but the former takes precedence in the Christian community.[46]

This conclusion is supported by the observation that this Gospel, though it very often draws on and quotes the Old Testament, even more often offers the new teaching of Jesus or the new interpretation of Torah by Jesus. The Jewish Christian scribe will be well grounded in both the Jesus tradition and Torah but the former is given precedent and provides guidance for how to interpret the latter. This Gospel is a demonstration of how the evangelist suggests one should go about accomplishing the scribal tasks mentioned in Matt. 13:52.

It is important to stress that the evangelist does not allude to himself or even to his charges as sages *per se*, but rather as scribes. This is because he wishes to portray Jesus as the sage, the teacher, the one who creatively originated the sacred tradition, while he and his understudies are mainly called upon to understand, interpret, pass on, and apply the traditions they have received. This requires, especially in regard to the hermeneutical task, a great deal of creative work, but it is likely that this evangelist, had he been asked, would have repudiated the suggestion that he was to any significant degree creating sayings of Jesus *de novo*. It was not, or at least not in the main, the job of the scribe to create the sacred tradition, but to interpret and apply it, expanding and expounding or adopting and adapting it to new settings.

There are two other passages of mainly M material that reveal quite a lot about Matthew's purposes and aims in producing this Gospel, Matt. 16:17ff. and Matt. 28:18ff. I have dealt with the former passage at some length elsewhere, and concluded that the reference to binding and loosing is probably

---

[44] Kingsbury, *Parables of Jesus*, 131.

[45] *Pace* Orton, *The Understanding Scribe*, 152ff.

[46] A. T. Lincoln, "Matthew – A Story for Teachers?" in *The Bible in Three Dimensions*, 108. The argument of J. Gnilka, *Das Matthäusevangelium I.Teil* (Freiburg: Herder, 1986), 511 that Matthew by "old" means Jesus' teaching, and by "new" the spirit–filled interpretation of it is not convincing. In Matthew 5–7 alone there is too much allusion to and reaffirmation of the Law to allow this conclusion.

redactional.[47] In view of the Jewish parallels, its meaning seems to have to do with making decisions and giving commands on what one is *bound* to do and what one is *free* to do. That is, Peter the representative disciple is given the task, based on the teaching he has received from Jesus, of interpreting that tradition so as to explain what is and is not permitted in terms of behavior. This is deliberately meant to be a contrast with the teaching of the scribes and Pharisees because in their missionary teaching they are said not to allow people to go into the Kingdom of Heaven (Matt. 23:13, 15).[48] G. Bornkamm puts it this way: "apparently, Peter's 'binding and loosing' authority refers primarily to teaching authority.... The authority of Peter thus refers to the teaching of Jesus entrusted to him as being valid and obligatory for the whole Church on earth, and according to which the sentences will be passed in heaven, that is, in the last judgment."[49] In short, he is commissioned to be a scribe with authority to bind and loose.[50] This provides the climax of the first main part of Matthew's narrative.[51]

Matt. 28:18–20 is on any showing a critical portion of the First Gospel. This text has been prepared for throughout the Gospel. Nowhere in Mark are the disciples commanded to teach, though there is evidence that they have done so (Mark 6:30). By contrast, in Matthew, teaching is not only the preoccupation of Jesus (5:2), so that it becomes evident that Jesus sets out to teach and preach and heals only as people come to him with a request or a need, but right from the first discourse Jesus expects his disciples to teach and instructs them on the do's and don'ts involved (cf. 5:19). The point of mentioning the righteousness of scribes and Pharisees in Matt. 5:20 is because they are the rival teachers, and Jesus' scribes must manifest more exemplary behavior and teaching than they do.[52] Again in Matt. 10:24–25a in the first commissioning scene, a passage not paralleled elsewhere, a disciple is said not to be above the teacher (again *ho didaskalos*), but called to be like his teacher. All of this prepares one for the scene in Matt. 28:18–20.

---

[47] Witherington, *Jesus, Paul and the End of the World*, 86–94.

[48] Lincoln, "Matthew," 110. Lincoln, however, tries to argue that the disciples are only promised the role of teaching during the ministry but are not given nor do they take up such a role till after the Great Commission. This fails to make sense of Matt. 10:19, 24, 27.

[49] G. Bornkamm, "The Authority to Bind and Loose in the Church in Matthew's Gospel," in *The Interpretation of Matthew*, 85–97, here 93.

[50] Matt. 18:15–20 does not seem to be completely parallel here, though it is often argued that in this passage the community is given what was earlier bestowed on Peter. The subject in this segment of Matthew 18 is witnesses and apparently binding agreements (cf. vv 18–19). Cf. M. J. Suggs, *Wisdom, Christology, and Law in Matthew's Gospel*, 121: "Matt. 23:13 (cf. Luke 11:52!) reinforces what the language of 16:19 itself confirms, namely that to Peter are committed what are essentially scribal functions."

[51] Lincoln, "Matthew," 106ff.; Kingsbury, *Matthew as Story*, 38, 76.

[52] Note the connections between being wise and righteous in Wisdom pp. 1 and elsewhere in the late sapiential corpus; cf above.

B. J. Hubbard, in an important but neglected study, shows how Matt. 28:16–20 sums up various of the major themes of Matthew's Gospel, particularly the tasks of obeying commandments and teaching, two of the major tasks of Jesus' "learners."[53] Thus at crucial junctures in the story – in the first discourse, in the first commissioning of the disciples, at the occasion at Caesarea Philippi, at the crucial turning point in the narrative at the close of Matthew 13,[54] and in the conclusion – both Jesus and the disciples are portrayed as teachers, though the latter are dependent on the former both for the commission and the content of their tasks. In the Great Commission the "learners" are sent out to initiate more people (presumably predominantly Gentiles, *ta ethne*) into the community of Jesus, and make them learners like themselves. They are to accomplish this: (1) by teaching their audience what Jesus had previously taught and commanded the first disciples (hence the transmission of the traditions is mandated and given divine sanction); and (2) by means of the ongoing strengthening and authorizing presence of Jesus in and with his community (cf. Matt. 1:23; Matt. 18:20).

It is an interesting fact that neither the First nor the Fourth Evangelist show much interest in church hierarchy or structure, and in this regard are quite unlike the usual picture painted of "early Catholicism". Matthew hardly uses the term apostle; *mathetes* is the definitive way he characterizes Jesus' followers. John, while he does not use the additional term *grammateus* as Matthew does, also in the main characterizes Jesus' followers as "learners". Is this lack of apparent structure because in both communities there was a recognized dependence on the living presence of Christ in the midst of the disciples, perhaps conveyed through the Holy Spirit, to provide guidance at points where neither Torah nor the words of Jesus spoke or were clear, or where Jesus' words needed further interpretation and application (cf. Matt. 10:19–20; John 14:15)? Or is it because scribes or evangelists do not have the authority of an apostle, and so authority is perceived to be word–centered rather than person–centered after the apostolic era? Whatever the answer to this question, both of these Gospels need to be seen in light of the above discussion, and this means they need to be read with minds that have already been conditioned to think in sapiential ways. It is hoped that the all too cursory sketches that follow will make clear how fruitful interpreting these two Gospels in light of earlier sapiential material and wisdom ways of thinking can be.

THE FIRST GOSPEL: DAVID'S SON AND LORD, SOLOMON'S SUPERIOR

Among the various attempts to characterize what is distinctive about Matthew's portrayal of Jesus, certainly one of the most popular is the attempt to

[53] B. J. Hubbard, *The Matthean Redaction of a Primitive Apostolic Commissioning: an Exegesis of Matthew 28.16–20*, 89–90.

[54] Kingsbury, *Parables of Jesus*, 130ff.

argue that Jesus is portrayed as a new Moses, giving five new discourses, the first even from a mount! Without totally discounting this idea, I would like to suggest that it is not a major motif in this Gospel.[55] Not only is Jesus never said to be Moses-like, but in the series of comparisons in which the evangelist speaks of something greater than the temple or Jonah or Solomon being here present (12:6, 41, 42) there is no hint of an interest in Moses.[56] And if it is true that the "antitheses clarify the relationship of Jesus to Moses,"[57] then one must conclude that the author seems as interested, if not more interested, in how Jesus is *unlike* Moses in what he says about adultery, murder, divorce, oaths and the like, as in ways he is like him. Moses did not ban oath taking, all killing, and the like!

Furthermore, if Matthew 1 is primarily about how Jesus can be called Son of David and Matthew 2 about how he can be called Son of God,[58] then there seems at most to be a secondary interest in the comparison with Moses, even in Matt. 2:13ff. On closer inspection, Jesus is being compared not to Moses in this material but to Israel (2:13–15). It is Jesus as *Son* taking on the role of *Israel* (not Moses) that God is calling forth from Egypt. Even in the endangered child motif there are major differences (Jesus' family flees to Egypt, Moses' parents try to send him up the Nile and away from Egyptian civilization). Moses is not a Son of David nor a Son of God, and these are the two primary christological *titles* (along with Son of Man) on which the First Evangelist places stress. One may also query whether there are five or in fact six discourses, for one must do something with Matthew 23.

My point is simply this, that the Jesus as Moses figure motif is a minor one at best in this Gospel, and one is better served by looking elsewhere to discover Matthew's distinctive contributions to the portrayal of Jesus. Rather, Matthew makes his most distinctive contribution by showing how Jesus is: (1) a messianic Son of David like unto but greater than Solomon; (2) Wisdom, and (3) the Son of God whose characteristics of intimacy with the Father are modelled in part on the way Wisdom and the Father are described in earlier sapiential literature.[59]

---

[55] Hubbard, *Matthean Redaction*, 94: " Although Matthew was aware of and *alluded* to the idea that Jesus' prototype was Moses... he does not strongly emphasize it. Rather he depicts Jesus not as Moses who has come as Messiah, but as Messiah, Son of Man, Emmanuel who has absorbed the Mosaic function." I would add, and as Wisdom. D. R. Bauer, *The Structure of Matthew's Gospel*, 129ff. points out how well integrated into their contexts the five discourses are, so that it is difficult to tell where various of them begin, and how Matthew makes no theological capital out of there being five discourses. Five was a number into which various sorts of Jewish literature were divided, for instance, not just the Pentateuch but also the Psalms, the Megilloth, and the Pirke Aboth.

[56] On Matthew's use of the rhetorical strategy of *sunkrisis*, cf. Stanton, *Gospel*, 77–79.

[57] Stanton, *Gospel*, 80.

[58] R. E. Brown, *The Birth of the Messiah*, 133ff.

[59] It is a flaw, in an otherwise helpful work, that J. D. Kingsbury seeks to make the Son of God title so central in Matthew that it swallows up or incorporates all other titles. Matthew's Christology is considerably more complex than this. Cf. Kingsbury, *Matthew: Structure, Christology, Kingdom*, 40–103.

There have been a variety of previous attempts to show that Matthew's Gospel is deeply indebted to late Jewish Wisdom material. The efforts of M. J. Suggs and more recently of C. Deutsch are notable in this regard.[60] But in both cases their work can be and has been subjected to the criticism of making too much out of too few Matthean pericopes.[61] I intend to remedy this complaint, not by dwelling once again on the "purple passages" already well trod by Suggs and Deutsch, but by showing through a general sketch of the Gospel how Matthew presents the story of Jesus in a sapiential fashion throughout much if not all his work, and intends for his audience to read it that way.[62]

In this study there has been ample attention paid to the fact that Jewish Wisdom literature was almost always attributed to Solomon. It appears that if one wanted to indicate that what one was saying or writing amounted to Wisdom, Solomon would be brought into the picture as author or inspiration one way or another. What then happens when an early Jewish Christian wishes to portray Jesus as like Solomon but even greater, being the very embodiment of Wisdom? How would he go about it? I would suggest that he would go about it much as the First Evangelist has done not only stressing that Jesus is *the* son of David (eleven times over against only four in Mark and Luke and none in John), but making clear that Jesus was not just another sage or teacher, but *the* teacher – Wisdom.

Wisdom is seen as *the* teacher in numerous sapiential texts. As early as Proverbs 1 we are told that she cries out in the streets, summoning people, in particular the simple, to the city gate for her teaching (vv 20–33). What she offers is knowledge (v 29), counsel (v 30), and reproof (v 30). Proverbs 8 likewise speaks of her instruction (vv 10, 33). She is the one by whom kings reign and make just decrees (vv. 15–16). In Sir. 4:24 Wisdom and education are paralleled, and a bit earlier in the same chapter one hears: "Wisdom teaches her children and gives help to those who seek her.... Whoever holds her fast inherits glory" (vv 11, 13). In Wis. 6:14 she is again said to be sitting in the city gate like a sage prepared to teach those who will come to her, and it is said, "the beginning of wisdom is the most sincere desire for instruction" (v 17). Wisdom is to be sought because she is "an initiate in the knowledge of God" (8:4).

---

[60] Suggs, *Wisdom, Christology, and Law*; C. Deutsch, *Hidden Wisdom and the Easy Yoke. Wisdom, Torah, and Discipleship in Matthew 11.25–30*; Deutsch, "Wisdom in Matthew."

[61] Various of M. D. Johnson's criticisms are telling; cf. his "Reflections on a Wisdom Approach to Matthew's Christology,", 44–64. I agree that in Matthew 11 and 23 the First Evangelist is taking over material from Q where there seems already to have been a Wisdom Christology. If the case only rested on this material it would remain weak. Nevertheless, it must not be underestimated that Matthew does *use* such Q material, and surely he endorses that which he chooses to use.

[62] Particular attention needs to be paid to what Matthew says about the disciples, since it appears that Matthew's audience is supposed to see themselves, for better and for worse, in Jesus' first "learners." On the implied reader and the reader's correspondence with figures in Matthew's story, cf. D. B. Howell, *Matthew's Inclusive Story. A Study in the Narrative Rhetoric of the First Gospel*, 205ff.

> And if anyone loves righteousness, her labors are virtues; for she teaches self–control and prudence, justice and courage... she knows the things of old and infers the things to come; she understands turns of speech and the solution to riddles; she had foreknowledge of signs and wonders and the outcome of seasons (8:7–8).

This role Wisdom has of being *the* teacher, which is seen throughout the Jewish sapiential corpus, is in Matthew's Gospel assigned to Jesus himself, which in part explains how Matthew can portray Jesus as both sage and Wisdom. It is possible to argue that, "when one views the narrative as a whole, what is primary and most pervasive in the portrayal of its central character is not a particular title but his role as teacher."[63] But in calling Jesus *the* Teacher, a sapiential Christology is very likely implied.[64]

The Wisdom of Solomon portrays the great king exhorting other kings to seek wisdom and righteousness, relating his own experiences with Wisdom, and showing how wisdom has guided God's people through the ages. The scribe who gathered and edited the traditions found in the First Gospel did so with the portrait of Solomon and Wisdom found in sapiential literature (especially Wisdom of Solomon) in mind. He set out to show that Jesus was *the* Son of David, like unto but wiser even than Solomon because Jesus was Wisdom in the flesh. There is thus a major stress on showing Jesus as the perfect king manifesting all the qualities of self–control, prudence, good judgment, wise speech, and righteousness expected of a Solomonic royal figure. As Wisdom he must instruct his people. As Wisdom he would come and present himself to God's folk but like Wisdom be rejected and returned from whence Wisdom came. This roughly is the set of ideas the evangelist derived from his wisdom sources. With these general considerations out of the way it is time to examine how he set about demonstrating that Jesus was the ultimate Solomonic king, being the very embodiment of Wisdom.

---

[63] Lincoln, "Matthew," 122, perhaps overstates matters a bit because the portrayal as a teacher and the portrayal as Son of David, Son of God and the like are not either/or propositions. It is as Wisdom that Jesus beckons people to take up his yoke and learn from him (11:29).

[64] Deutsch, "Wisdom in Matthew," 19. How one reads Matt. 23:34 is important. It is significant that the term *didaskalos* is not used there, though the term *sophos*, sage, is. One must ask what the frame of reference is for this utterance. Are we meant to see this as being purely about the future, and thus Matthew's community, or as in the Lukan parallel is Jesus speaking as Wisdom in the past? I would suggest the latter, since there are other hints in the Gospel where Jesus implies his pre–existence (cf. Matt. 22:41ff.), and since the immediate context is about what Israel did to prophets in the past (cf. vv 31 and 35, noting particularly that the scope of murders is the A to Z of Old Testament figures ending with Zechariah, no Christian disciples are mentioned or alluded to). This saying, therefore, is speaking about Israel's past bad behavior towards sages and scribes, which continues into the present even into Matthew's community. In other words, while the saying is speaking to Matthew's audience since the persecution of God's mouthpieces continues, there is not a clear implication of Matthew intending to call Christian disciples sages, and in any case *didaskalos* is not used here. Cf. Luke 11:49.

The Gospel begins with the announcement that it will present Jesus the Messiah, the Son of David, and it starts where one ought to start with a king, with his royal pedigree. While the pedigree has some surprises in it, this is not unexpected since it was also true of Solomon as well. So intent is the evangelist on making clear that Jesus is seen as son of David, that he even stresses that Joseph is son of David (1:20), even though Joseph is not portrayed as Jesus' physical father.

Kings were often said to have miraculous births in antiquity, and Jesus is no different. Not only is Jesus born of a virgin but the reader is told that he is to be called Emmanuel, God with us (1:23, cf. the throne names in Isa. 9:6). The royal character of Jesus as Son of David will be reaffirmed from time to time, the evangelist judiciously sprinkling the title Son of David throughout the account. It is found especially at crucial junctures in the story and particularly as the story draws to a climax, which in view of its nature required that more stress be placed on the reality of Christ's royalty even though he was crucified (cf. 9:27; 12:23; 15:22; 20:30–31; 21:9, 15; 22:42, 45). Keep in mind that the precise phrase "the Son of David" is not attested before *Psalms of Solomon* 17:23. Using this title of Jesus reflects a late sapiential, not an Old Testamental, way of putting things.[65] Calling Jesus Son of David provokes hostility on the part of Jesus' opponents in Matthew. It appears, as Stanton suggests, that Matthew is exercised to put forward the idea of Jesus as Son of David, and show what sort of Son of David he was, in the face of Jewish opposition to this claim made by Matthew's community.[66]

Kings were often thought to embody the divine presence, but perhaps more is implied by the name Emmanuel, namely that God in some form is personally present with God's people in the person of Jesus. The form this personal presence takes will be defined later in the story when we are told at Matt. 11:19 that Wisdom, i.e. Jesus is vindicated by her deeds, and again at Matt. 13:42 the reminder comes that something even greater than Solomon is here.

But if Jesus is the great king, the Son of David, the one like but greater than Solomon, then one would expect: (1) that there would be signs in the heavens announcing his coming; (2) that he would be visited by a king's counselors or seers; and (3) that he would be involved in power struggles with other so–called great kings. This is precisely what one finds in Matthew 2. The birth of Jesus is signalled by a great star; he is visited by seers or astrologers who were the counselors of wise kings; and he is presented with gifts fit for a king.[67]

---

[65] Witherington, *Christology of Jesus*, 189.

[66] Stanton, *Gospel for a New People*, 181; Brooks, *Matthew's Community*, 121.

[67] It is interesting that Luke also seems to be intent on stressing the royal character of Jesus and his birth. In Wis. 7:4 Solomon says of his birth, "I was nursed with care in swaddling cloths. For no king has had a different beginning of existence; there is for all one entrance into life and one way out." Cf. Luke 2:7.

Finally, he is the subject of a plot by evil King Herod and forced to flee the country. The trip to Egypt was said to fulfill the Scripture, "Out of Egypt, I have called my Son." Kings, of course, were called God's sons (cf. 2 Sam. 7:14; Psalm 2).

Great kings were foretold by prophets, and when kings traveled anywhere they had criers going before them annoucing their coming and preparing the way. This is the role John the Baptist takes in the first Gospel. Not only is he said to fulfill the Isaianic scripture about preparing the way of the Lord (Isa. 40:3), but he speaks of the greater one coming after him in a way that diminishes his own status and exalts that of Jesus (Matt. 3:11). Later in the drama John is said to have heard about the messianic deeds of Jesus (11:2) and sends his own messengers to ask if Jesus truly is the one to come. Jesus then recites his deeds and in a statement paralleling 11:2 says that Wisdom is vindicated by her deeds.

Jewish kings, like most ancient kings, must be anointed before they may speak or act as royal ones. The ceremony of anointing is told in Matt. 3:13–17. There is first the rite of purification and then the anointment by God's very Spirit. Several aspects of this story have specific resonances with the Wisdom of Solomon even beyond the resonances of the Q version of the story.[68] First, it was the duty of all kings to "fulfill all righteousness". Notice how Wis. 1:1ff. begins: "Love righteousness, you rulers of earth, think of the Lord in goodness and seek him with sincerity of heart, because he is found by those who do not put him to the test, and manifests himself to those who do not distrust him... because wisdom will not enter a deceitful soul, or dwell in a body enslaved to sin.... For wisdom is a kindly spirit..." For the author of the Wisdom of Solomon, receiving the Spirit means receiving wisdom.

Jesus, in order to be seen to be a righteous king, submits to the rite of purification and is publicly anointed by God for office, and then publicly proclaimed to be God's royal Son.[69] The Matthean version of the announcement makes clear that Jesus has undergone a public investiture like a king and so the announcement of who has been invested with the Spirit is made to the onlooking crowd rather than to Jesus: "This is my son." This should be compared to the similar announcement to the inner circle of the disciples on the Mount of Transfiguration in Matt. 17:1–8, noting particularly how Matthew adds the phrase "with whom I am well pleased" at 17:5 to make clear the parallels. The new element in Matthew 17 that goes beyond Matthew 3 is that one is told his face "shone like the sun and his clothes became dazzling white". To the reader who knew Wisdom of Solomon this description in Matthew 17 is reminiscent of the description of Wisdom in Wis. 7:26, 29: "for she is a reflection of eternal light, a spotless mirror of the working of God, and an image

---

[68] On which cf. above.

[69] Notice how Matthew has altered the Markan text from "you are" to "this is," making it a public event (cf. Mark 1:11 to Matt. 3:17).

of his goodness.... She is more beautiful than the sun, and excels every constellation of the stars." Jesus as the ultimate royal one, the Son of David and of God, manifests the very properties of Wisdom.

Immediately after the discussion in Wisdom 1 cited above one hears about the king being immediately being put to the test:
Some ungodly ones say:

> "Let us lie in wait for the righteous man, because he is inconvenient to us and opposes our actions... He professes to have knowledge of God, and calls himself a child of God... he calls the last end of the righteous happy, and boasts that God is his father. Let us see if his words are true, and let us test what will happen at the end of his life; for if the righteous man is God's child, he will help him, and will deliver him from his adversaries. Let us test him with insult and torture him, so that we may find out how gentle he is, and make trial of his forbearance. Let us condemn him to a shameful death..." Thus they reasoned but they were led astray... through the devil's envy death entered the world... (2:12ff., excerpts)

In all the Synoptics there are two tests of Jesus, one just prior to the beginning of his ministry and one at the end involving both Gethsemane and then the following out of God's will even unto death on the cross. The final test is not over till Christ expires. The first part of the above quote illuminates the story in Matthew 4 while the latter part sheds light on Matthew 26–27. Jesus is being tested as the righteous king, the true Son of God that he is, like Solomon and others before him. He resists by relying on the word of God to answer the temptations.

When one gets to the beginning of the ministry account at Matt. 4:12ff. another quote from Isaiah, this time from 9:1–2, is cited. The knowledgeable Jewish Christian hearer of this Gospel will know that the verses cited are part of a longer laudatory passage about the coming of the great Davidic king who will be called Wonderful Counselor, Mighty God and other throne names and then it is said, "His authority shall grow continually, and there shall be endless peace for the throne of David and his kingdom" (Isa. 9:6–7). Thus when Jesus goes forth preaching and teaching he is meant to be seen as a king going forth bringing righteousness and justice to the land, by means of reforming words and deeds.

While Jesus' initial words echo those of the Baptist (cf. Matt. 3:2 — 4:17) it is well to remember at this juncture that Wisdom offers a similar admonition crying out in the streets, "Give heed to my reproof, I will pour out my thoughts to you; I will make my words known to you" (Prov. 1:20, 23). This connection is important because what immediately follows (Matt. 4:17) is first the calling of the learners (*disciples*) like Wisdom's calling of the simple (Prov. 1:22), and then the offering of the teaching.

It is not necessary here to go over in detail the sapiential character of the Sermon on the Mount, which would be better called the Teaching on the Mount (cf. Matt. 5:1).[70] Suffice it to say that it includes various sorts of sapiential utterances such as beatitudes; metaphors meant to inculcate good works (5:16); the upholding of Torah and its commandments as an expression of Wisdom and righteousness (cf. Sirach 24); practical teaching on self–control in regard to both anger and sexual aggression; prohibition of oaths and revenge; exhortations to love of enemies, to almsgiving, prayer, and fasting; instructions on wealth, health, loyalties; nature wisdom meant to inculcate a less anxious lifestyle; prohibition of judging others, of profanation; exhortations to seek the right thing from God, obey the golden rule, follow the narrow path, avoid false teachers; and to maintain integrity in one's words and deeds.[71]

When one surveys this list one is immediately struck by how both the list of topics and indeed much of the substance of this discourse follows the standing topics discussed in Proverbs 2ff. after the introduction of Wisdom herself. There is discussion about the narrow path (cf. Prov. 2:8ff with Matt. 7:13–14); exhortation to keep the commandments (cf. Prov. 3:1 with Matt. 5:17–20); a call to honor God in one's dealings with material goods (cf. Prov. 3:19 with Matt. 6:19–21). There are beatitudes (cf. Prov. 1:13 with Matt. 5:3ff.); a call to acknowledge God's wisdom in nature (cf. Prov. 3:19–20 with Matt. 6:25ff.); warnings against sexual impurity (cf. Prov. 5.1ff to Matt. 5:27–32); exhortations to guard one's speech (cf. Prov. 6:1–2 with Matt. 5:33–37); exhortations to deeds (cf. Prov. 6:4ff. with Matt. 5:16) and more parallels could be cited.

Critical here is the overall impact of the discourse. First, with some exceptions (the words against wealth or any oath taking, love of enemies, no divorce), basically what one has in the Sermon on the Mount is *conventional Wisdom*, prefaced by eschatologically oriented beatitudes. Jesus is offering the sort of teaching offered by a father to his child (or perhaps a sage to his pupils),[72] the sort of wisdom that the editor of Proverbs believed that Wisdom conveyed to her followers. Secondly, the sequence in Proverbs of (a) the introduction of Solomon's name (1:1), (b) the introduction of Wisdom and her call to repentance; followed by (c) the actual sapiential teachings (and then in Proverbs 10ff. by a host of proverbs), has marked parallels in Matthew 1–7. One should especially note how the discourse ends in Matt. 7:24ff. with the parable about the "wise man". The one who hears and follows the teaching in this discourse will become just such a person, but notice that Matthew carefully avoids the use of *sophos* here lest it be thought that the disciples too could be sages like Jesus. Rather they can become *andri phronimo*, as opposed to what in Proverbs

[70] On the use of the mountain motif, particularly as a place of teaching, cf. T. L. Donaldson, *Jesus on the Mountain. A Study in Matthean Theology*, 111ff. He is right to say that if Matthew had wanted to stress the Mosaic connections he would very likely have been more explicit. On the distinction between preaching and teaching in Matthew, cf. Luz, *Matthew 1–7*, 206–08.

[71] Brooks, *Matthew's Community*, 113, is right to point out that the construction of the discourses is by Matthew himself, pulling various traditions together.

[72] Cf. above pp. 175ff.

is seen as the stereotypical example to avoid – the fool (*andri moro*). The discourse thus closes with a clear allusion to the major categories of people discussed in Proverbs.

The evangelist then is trying to portray Jesus as the king greater than Solomon and, beyond even that as Wisdom offering her teaching. Thus the reader will not be jolted when shortly after this Jesus is identified as Wisdom. This identification has been being prepared for all along in this Gospel. It may be important to point out that Jesus conveys Wisdom only *after* having received the Holy Spirit. The evangelist stands in the tradition of late prophetic sages. He not only uses the Old Testament in sapiential ways (as Paul also did) but also believes in revelatory wisdom given from God to Jesus and through Jesus to his followers.

On first inspection the collection of miracle stories found in Matthew 8–9 might be thought not to fit in with the portrait of Jesus as a greater Solomon and/or Wisdom. This is forgetting the evidence that before and during the first century A.D., Jews associated Solomon, Son of David, with miracles and in particular cures and exorcisms.[73] Josephus *Ant.* 8:45 is representative in saying: "God granted him knowledge of the art used against demons... He also composed incantations by which illnesses are relieved." He then proceeds to recount an incident which he personally observed of an exorcism using "a ring which had under its seal one of the roots prescribed by Solomon..." and "speaking Solomon's name and reciting the incantations which he had composed" (8:46–47). Josephus is by no means alone in putting forward this idea about Solomon during and after the New Testament era (cf. *Apocalypse of Adam* 7:3–16, Solomon controls an army of demons; Pseudo–Philo. *Liber ant. bib.* 60; cf. 11QPsAp; *B. T. Git.* 68a).[74]

It is crucial to point out that once one gets beyond the birth narratives, in every instance prior to the final entry of Jesus into Jerusalem the phrase "Son of David" arises in the context where healing is requested (cf. 9:27; 12:23; 15:22; 20:30–31). This is a special Matthean interest, only found once in the common ministry material in Matthew's Markan source (cf. Matt. 20:30–31 to Mark 10:46–47). Here then one find a special editorial thrust of the First Evangelist and the message is clear – Jesus like Solomon is a healer, therefore he should be appealed to using the Solomonic title, Son of David, when one wants healing or even exorcism (cf. Matt. 15:22).

Matthew 10 offers the second and missionary discourse. These are specific instructions for Jesus' disciples or learners as they are sent out to participate in his ministry. They are to go to Israel alone, proclaim the good news, and heal the sick. What is especially telling about this material are its

[73] Witherington, *Christology of Jesus*, 156, 189.

[74] Cf. now D. C. Duling, "The Eleazar Miracle and Solomon's Magical Wisdom in Flavius' Josephus's *Antiquitates Judaicae* 8. 42–49," 14ff, and G. Theissen, *The Gospels in Context*. 103.

conclusions which suggest that the disciples, like their master, are to be seen as prophets and righteous men (Matt. 10:41). Now it must be remembered that in the Wisdom of Solomon it is Wisdom that instructs people in how to be righteous, and passes into holy souls "and makes them friends of God and prophets" (Wis. 7:27; cf. Sir. 24:33). Thus, this commissioning speech can be seen as the sending out of wandering prophetic righteous ones by Wisdom. This view is confirmed by the way Matthew handles the Q material in Matt. 23:34/Luke 11:49. Luke, who does not clearly identify Jesus with Wisdom, has this saying as an utterance of "the Wisdom of God" which is surely its original form. Matthew has altered it to an "I" saying because he believes in and is portraying Jesus as Wisdom. It is Jesus who sent and sends out prophets, sages, and scribes because Jesus is Wisdom who gives them the words and deeds to do what they are commissioned to do. As M. J. Suggs long ago stressed it is a mistake to assume that the Wisdom material in Matthew exhibits "erratic outcroppings on the relatively smooth landscape of the Gospel."[75] Rather, there is a consistent, sustained attempt to present Jesus as a Solomonic and even as a Wisdom figure.

Matthew 11 is a crucial chapter for any evaluation of the intent of the evangelist. Having already presented Jesus as the Solomonic king who acts as Wisdom by his words and deeds and in the way he commissions and sends out his learners, it was time to take stock and make clear what the implications of the first ten chapters of the Gospel were. Thus it is that the great prophet John, who is said to be not only a prophet, but even more importantly the one who prepares the way for the great king, is presented as asking who Jesus really is. Jesus' response is in effect that John should evaluate his deeds and words. Verses 4–5 should be compared with the reference to deeds in both 11:2 and 11:19. Wisdom is vindicated by her deeds.[76] In his response Jesus manifests the character of Wisdom in at least two places: (1) in the beatitude in v 6 ("Blessed is anyone who finds no *skandalon* in me");[77] and (2) in the comparison in vv. 16–17. In both places the implication is that there have been various peoples who have in fact found Jesus scandalous. The root of the scandal is in part his choice to associate with the least, last and lost.

Several things here parallel what is said of Wisdom in the sapiential literature: (1) Prov. 1:24–25 speaks of Wisdom being refused, not heeded; (2) Wisdom in Prov. 1:22–23 seems to address and associate with an unlikely audience, the simple, the scoffers, and the fools; (3) again at Wisdom's feast in Prov. 9:1–6 it is an unlikely, indeed scandalous, bunch she invites to dinner, the simple, those without sense, the immature. This is the proverbial counterpart

---

[75] Suggs, *Wisdom, Christology, and Law*, 32.

[76] On the use of *sophos/sophia* language in Matthew cf. W. Schenk, *Die Sprache des Matthäus. Die Text–Konstituenten in ihren makro–und mikrostrukturellen Relationen*, 432.

[77] Noting that Jesus says *in me*, not merely "in my teaching." This is because Jesus is speaking as more than just another sage.

to Jesus' being the friend of sinners and society's despised. Again the intent of the evangelist is made clearer when one reads these traditions in the light of the larger Wisdom corpus.[78]

Then in Matt. 11:20–24 there are a series of woes on cities which have rejected Jesus' powerful *deeds* (cf. vv 21, 23), the very means by which Wisdom is said to be vindicated. This in turn is followed by the critical saying in Matt. 11:25–27 which makes clear that Jesus offers revelatory wisdom which is hidden from the wise and intelligent and revealed to infants. Here the evangelist or his source draws on another sapiential text in which Daniel the sage is praising God for the revelatory wisdom he has received. Compare the following:[79]

and Daniel blessed the God of heaven. Blessed be the name of God he gives wisdom to the wise, and knowledge to those who have understanding. He reveals deep and hidden things; To you oh God of my fathers I give thanks and praise, for you have given me wisdom and power, and have now revealed to us what the king ordered. (Dan. 2:19–23 excerpts)	I thank you Father, Lord of heaven and earth because you have hidden these things from the wise and the intelligent and have revealed them to the infants... All things have been handed over to me...to reveal him. (Matt.11:25–27 excerpts)

The royal Son, who is the true sage, is the only one who can reveal the heavenly Father. The above texts are notable not only for their similarities but also for their salient difference – Daniel says that Wisdom has been given to the wise, Jesus by contrast says just the opposite. Here one can find a hint of a counter-order approach to Wisdom. Wisdom, since it is revelatory and not gained by

[78] I endorse in general the presentation of Suggs and Deutsch of the material in Matthew 11 and there is no need to belabor it here. Suggs, however, wrongly equates Wisdom and Torah and then proceeds to claim Jesus is presented as Wisdom–Torah. This is to read Matthew in the light of later Jewish sapiential discussions, not earlier ones (rightly, Deutsch, *Easy Yoke*, 134). Rather, Jesus fulfills the latter and embodies the former, for Torah is but one expression of Wisdom, and Jesus' new teaching often goes beyond mere adaptation or interpretation of Torah. Deutsch is nearer the mark in saying Jesus displaces Torah as the central referent for Matthew's community (*Easy Yoke*, 143). In my judgment Suggs is right in being cautious about Philo as background for this material in Matthew: "Philo stands outside – or better, beyond – the stream important for understanding Q and Matthew. Philo offers a goal toward which the development is moving, not an example of the central stream of wisdom and apocalyptic material which flowed into the primitive church" (*Wisdom, Christology, and Law*, 101, n. 4).

[79] Orton, *The Understanding Scribe*, 146ff., though he makes nothing of this parallel.

study, can be given to anyone. In the Matthean context the saying clearly implies that Wisdom has been withheld from the Pharisees and sages, and instead given to Jesus' followers who are alternately called the little ones, the babes, the learners in this Gospel. The content of this Wisdom is both the identity of the Son and the knowledge of the Father which only the Son can convey. This is the Matthean version of "The Father loves the Son and reveals to him all that he is doing" (John 5:20) and "No one comes to the Father but by me. If you know me you will know my Father also" (John 14:7).[80]

The invitation to hear and heed the royal Son comes immediately in 11:28–30 where the words about Wisdom found in Sir. 6:23ff and Sir. 51:26ff become the words of Jesus speaking as Wisdom. The yoke saying is important for a wide variety of reasons, but especially because it makes clear that it is Jesus as Wisdom offering *his* yoke, not any previous yoke that is in view. The material in Matt. 5:17–20 indicated clearly enough that both the law and the prophets in some sense were still binding on the audience until all is fulfilled, but it is not said that Jesus' yoke either equals or replaces these authorities. Rather, Torah is seen as *a* paramount expression of Wisdom, but not the only one.[81] In the larger context of the Gospel it can be seen that Torah is but a part of Jesus' larger teaching and so Jesus himself is being presented as like the scribes described in Matt. 13:52. i.e., as one who offers both conventional wisdom and new wisdom. The evangelist is not interested in some simplistic replacement theology, for Wisdom is bigger than Torah. Torah, Jesus' adaptation and interpretation of Torah, *and* the new teaching of Jesus can both be affirmed as treasuries of Wisdom.

It may even be that Matthew saw Jesus, being Wisdom, as the source of both Torah and the new Wisdom. This could be the implication of Matt. 23:34 which follows the discussion about David's pre–existent messianic Lord in 22:41–43, but perhaps this is pushing things too far. The character of this Gospel is seen clearly in Matt. 13:52, involving as it does both old Wisdom, but also some glimpses of the counter–order Wisdom of Jesus that turns the world upside down (as is hinted in 11:4–6,19).

The implications of Matt. 11:28–30 have been ably summed up by C. Deutsch:

> It is not contradictory to state that Matt. 11:28–30 presents Jesus as both Sage and Wisdom. For the sage of Sir. 51:13–20 has certain characteristics in common with Wisdom: the sage makes an invitation, as does Wisdom (51:23; 24:19; Prov. 8:4–11; 9:4–6); like Wisdom the sage has a house to which he invites disciples (51:23; 14:24–27; Prov. 9:1–2; 14:1 [cf. Matt. 13:1, 36]; like Wisdom the sage promises a reward

[80] On the closeness of Matthew to John throughout this section, cf. G. Maier, *Matthäus–Evangelium 1. Teil* (Neuhausen–Stuttgart: Hänsler Verlag, 1979), 393ff.
[81] *Pace* Deutsch, "Wisdom in Matthew," 38.

(Sir. 51:28; 24:18–21; Prov. 8:11; 9:5 [cf. Matt. 6:6, 33; 10:42]; and like Wisdom he is a teacher (Sir. 51:23; 4:11).[82]

The theme of new Wisdom, or Wisdom that goes beyond and sometimes perhaps even against the old Wisdom (or at least makes it obsolescent), is seen in the sabbath controversy in Matt. 12:1–8. Deutsch says Jesus is presented as sage here because he is seen interpreting *halachah* in order to justify otherwise unjustifiable actions.[83]

Especially important is the additional information found in the Matthean form of the tradition in v 6: "I tell you, something greater than the temple is here." For an early Jew or Jewish Christian, this surely would have been seen as a reference to God's very presence, a presence which is rejected, for the following verse speaks of the audience having condemned the guiltless, i.e., Jesus. Jesus then is seen to manifest the very presence of God or God's spirit (or Shekinah) that was thought to inhabit the Holy of Holies (so too 12:28, 31, 32). This again comports with the very close association of Wisdom and Spirit in the late sapiential material, but also with the expectation that a righteous ruler like unto Solomon will indeed be guiltless and will offer mercy and expect mercy from his people (cf. Wis. 1:1ff.). Matthew makes the relationship between Jesus and the Spirit he relies on clear in 12:28, where he changes what was very likely the original phrase taken from Exodus "by the finger of God" to "by the Spirit of God".[84] But this comports with the stress on showing Jesus to be a Solomon figure, casting out demons by the Spirit of God.

There are many who will bear witness against those who reject Jesus as Wisdom, and the ultimate witness will be the queen of Sheba who heard the very wisdom of Solomon and was amazed. The climactic words of the saying in 12:42 are "because she came from the ends of the earth to listen to the wisdom of Solomon, and see, something greater than Solomon is here." Luke also has this Q saying but Matthew enhances its importance by placing the Solomon example last, so as to end with the saying about the greater than Solomon. Notice that the saying does not merely suggest "the greater than Solomon's wisdom", but something greater than Solomon himself, namely Wisdom in the person of the royal one Jesus.[85]

---

[82] Deutsch, *Easy Yoke*, 131. The attempts to dismiss or minimize the Wisdom connections of this pericope by Stanton, *Gospel*, 366–71 are unconvincing not least because they fail to come to grips with the larger Wisdom context of the saying, in particular the first part of Matthew 11.

[83] Deutsch, "Wisdom in Matthew," 37.

[84] Witherington, *Christology of Jesus*, 201ff.

[85] I take it that the term *pleion*, though it is neuter, at least in the Matthean use of the term refers to Jesus himself as 12:6 and the parallel between 12.41–42 suggest. Surely Jesus is being compared to Jonah in the former case, and Solomon in the latter. Cf. Allison and Davies, *Matthew*, Vol. 2, 358–59.

Chapter 13, the so–called third discourse, relates a collection of narrative *meshalim*, further evidence that Jesus is Wisdom speaking and speaking in Wisdom form. The question of the understanding of the disciples is a crucial one in a Gospel that places emphasis on the teaching of Jesus. In Matthew 13, at the climactic point just before the saying about the scribe, Jesus asks his learners if they have understood all he has just said which involves both several parables and his explanation not only of a particular parable but also of why he speaks in parables to the public. Their response is an unequivocal Yes.

In view of various other characterizations of the disciples in this Gospel, including the peculiarly Matthean one that they are *oligo pistoi*, which is found both before and *after* Matt. 13:51 (cf. 6:30 (and par., Luke 12:28); 8:26; 14:31; 16:8; 17:20, always of the disciples), what emerges is that Matthew has softened Mark's portrayal of the disciples as totally lacking at various points in faith and understanding. They have some faith and they have some understanding, but clearly in both cases it is inadequate. They are, in short, still learners.

In the light of the conclusion of this Gospel where the disciples desert Jesus, and after the resurrection some still doubt (28:16), it seems clear that Matthew wants to stress that for the disciples the process of growing in faith and understanding is one that continues and must continue after Easter. Matthew's own audience of learners and scribes is meant to see aspects of themselves in these disciples who are in the process of becoming full–fledged disciples.

It is notable that one finds this same sort of portrayal of the disciples in the Fourth Gospel as well. The disciples in John believe and understand some things but inadequately. In particular they are constantly understanding Jesus at one level when in fact he is intending a deeper and more symbolic meaning. They are portrayed as lacking "wisdom", because had they known their sapiential literature they would have understood that Jesus' portrayal of himself as bread, water, life, light and the like had deeper spiritual meanings, for he is portraying himself as Wisdom, or at least as the one who truly gives what Wisdom is said to provide in the sapiential literature. I have argued elsewhere that one finds in John a crescendo not only of the miraculous but of less and less inadequate confessions of who Jesus is, climaxing not in John 11:17ff. but in Thomas' confession in John 20:28, as the followers become more adequate disciples.[86]

I would suggest that the reason for this correspondence between these two Gospels is because they have both adopted a sapiential model of pedagogy, which assumes that growth in learning and faith are in fact possible, even if they are dependent on revelation for the necessary increase in wisdom at times. These evangelists share the conviction that Christian disciples must grow in knowledge as well as in grace, and they have adopted the portrayal of

[86] Witherington, *Women in the Earliest Churches*, 177ff.

sage and disciple and a sapiential view of the educational process to their own respective ends. The disciples can understand; they are capable of receiving and understanding revelation.[87] It is thus not surprising that in Matthew not only does Jesus say that the disciples have been given the mysteries of the kingdom of heaven (13:11), and they respond that they understand (13:52), but the representative disciple, Peter, is portrayed as having received and at least partly understood the revelation of Jesus' identity (Matt. 16:17).

By combining the need for both revelation with further explication, both Matthew and John are able to forge a bond between the two kinds of Wisdom – hidden wisdom which can only be known through revelation, and wisdom derived from careful study of material from some given source whether it be creation, previous sapiential teaching, Torah, or other sources. In both Gospels Jesus himself is an example of hidden Wisdom; he is Wisdom incognito unless he reveals himself, but equally in both Gospels his teaching is a mixture of revelatory and investigatory Wisdom. In the Fourth Gospel revelatory Wisdom eclipses all other sorts by a great degree, whereas in Matthew the sorts of Wisdom presented are a mixture of both kinds, at least in the *public* teaching of Jesus up to Matthew 13, and in some cases even beyond it.

The conclusion of Matthew 13 finds Jesus back in his home town teaching and the first words out of the home folks' mouths are: "Where did this man get this wisdom and these deeds of power?" (v. 54). The problem here seems to be rather like the problem in John – the interlocutors cannot see beyond Jesus' merely human origins. They do not see that a greater than Solomon, even Wisdom in human guise, is here, and this is presumably because this hidden fact has not been revealed to them as it has to the disciples.[88] Those who do not know that Jesus is Wisdom incognito will not know where he gets his wisdom, power, authority. He is one who teaches "as one having [innate] authority, and not as their scribes" (Matt. 7:29), which distinguishes Jesus not only from his rivals, but also from his own scribes and disciples.

The road to full understanding is a difficult one. Initial revelation is not enough; further teaching is required. This becomes apparent in a text like Matt. 16.5–12 where it is only after *further* instruction that the disciples understand that they must beware of the teaching of the Pharisees and Sadducees, which is to say their "wisdom".[89] Likewise in the Fourth Gospel it is assumed that further instruction is necessary to be led into all truth. The initial revelation seen in Christ is necessary, but until the other paraclete comes and leads the disciples into all truth after the resurrection all will not yet be clear (cf. John 16:12ff; 20:9ff).[90] In both Gospels Jesus is the definitive teacher, the definitive

[87] Stanton, *Gospel*, 165ff.
[88] Noting that *sophia* here is used of Jesus; contrast Matt. 7:24 of the disciples.
[89] Kingsbury, *Matthew as Story*, 112.
[90] Christological understanding of the Scriptures also comes after the resurrection.

sage and the "disciples" remain just that, learners, even after the resurrection.[91] They will be called upon not only to continue to learn but even to teach and make further learners, but in neither Gospel are the disciples called teachers.

Beginning in Matthew 14 and continuing on into the passion narrative, Jesus will be increasingly portrayed as a teacher at odds with the teaching authorities of his day, not primarily because of the miracles he performs, but because of his teaching. The First Evangelist perceives this to be the main bone of contention between Jesus and his adversaries. Thus, for instance, in Matt. 15:1ff the Pharisees and scribes complain that Jesus' disciples break the tradition of the elders, to which Jesus replies not just that his interlocutors are hypocrites in such accusations but that in fact nothing that goes into a person makes them unclean. In short, increasingly Jesus offers a counter–order Wisdom that is at odds not just with the tradition of the elders about washing hands and the like, but even with the Old Testament laws about clean and unclean foods. The Pharisees and scribes are said to be guides or teachers not planted by the heavenly Father, in contrast to Jesus. Their bread must not be eaten for it has bad yeast in it.

Besides the rising tide of opposition to Jesus as teacher there is also an increase in revelation to the disciples in several forms: (1) Jesus finally reveals that it is his destiny to go up to Jerusalem and die and rise again after a short period of time, something the disciples cannot and do not understand prior to Easter; (2) Jesus' identity is at least partly revealed to Peter; (3) the transfiguration provides further confirmation to the leaders among the disciples that Jesus is God's royal Son. Despite all of this the disciples still do not fully understand.

Here again the rationale and need for further teaching of the sort that Matthew is providing and training his scribes to provide is made clear. Revelation is apparently not enough; further instruction as in Matt. 16:5–12 is also required. Thus even after the great revelations in Matthew 16 and 17, there is need for further teaching discourses in Matthew 18–25 which include a variety of parables as well as other sorts of teaching. The large bulk of the teaching material here too is sapiential in character which again drives home the point that Jesus is being likened to Solomon, not Moses. Jesus is *the* teacher because he offers even greater Wisdom than Solomon, and indeed because he is Wisdom, as Matthew 11 makes clear, doing the deeds of Wisdom. In both word and even in deed (particularly the healing of the blind) he is seen to be like but greater than Solomon, and so Solomon's title of being *the* Son of David devolves upon Jesus. It is no accident that this title closes the pre–Passion

---

[91] It is important to stress again that in John, as in Matthew, Jesus is *the* teacher, as opposed to the blind guides currently leading the Jews. In John the emphasis is on the fact that he is the one who has come from God and must return to God, which is to say Jesus is not only sage, but Wisdom (cf. John 1:38; 3:2; 11:28, *ho didaskalos*; 13:13–14, *ho didaskalos kai ho kurios*; 20:16–17). It is a title he may be addressed by both before and after the resurrection.

narrative ministry section of the Gospel in Matt. 20:29–34, and opens the passion narrative itself in Matthew 21. It is a particular stress of this evangelist.

Again it is the teaching which primarily prompts the questions about Jesus. In Matt. 21:23ff. the chief priest and elders come and interrupt Jesus' teaching and ask what authority he has to do such things as teach in the temple. Jesus, typically answering a question with a question, alludes back to the baptism and witness of John, and presumably to his own baptism. This seems to suggest that his authorization comes from the royal anointing he received there and the public testimony given by God (through John?). That is, Jesus is God's royal Son anointed and authorized in advance for his ministry. He is the Son of David, not only because he is a healing figure like unto Solomon (cf. Matt. 20:29ff), but also because he has come into Jerusalem as a royal figure and been proclaimed as such (Matt. 21:9). He is the one who comes in the name of the Lord.[92]

It is, however, at the close of Matthew 22 that one finally learns that it is not enough to say merely that the messiah is Son of David. To be sure there have been suggestions in this direction already in Matthew 2 and certainly again in Matthew 16. But here Jesus makes evident that proclaiming him Son of David is only part of the truth. He is also David's Lord. If Jesus is by implication claiming to be David's Lord then he must be seen in more transcendent categories than either just sage, or teacher, or even Solomonic Son of David. In this Gospel two ascriptions, besides the term Lord itself which seems to be more a description of a functional role than a title here, may fit such a claim: Son of God and Wisdom. It is at this juncture that a text like 2 Sam. 7:12ff comes into play, for it is necessary to ask. What is the connection in the evangelist's mind *between* these various titles?[93]

In 2 Samuel 7 David is promised: (1) the establishment of his kingdom through (2) an offspring who will build God a house; (3) "I will be a father to him and he shall be a son to me." This promise is made in regard to Solomon. I would suggest that when one reads this text and couples with it the understanding of the importance of Solomon witnessed to in the sapiential literature one finds here all the major elements of Matthew's Christology. Like Solomon Jesus is Son of David, only greater. Like Solomon Jesus is a royal son to God, indeed the royal Son of God, who is his Father (remembering the high incidence of Father language used of God in this Gospel). Like Solomon Jesus is the very embodiment of Wisdom; indeed, he is greater than Solomon for

---

[92] It is notable that up to Matthew 21, except in Matthew 1, the title Son of David is used in a healing context, but when one gets to the climax of the story, it once again assumes the fuller significance that Matthew 1 suggested that it had. Jesus is *the* Son of David, like but even eclipsing Solomon both in sapiential words and even in deeds.

[93] I do not deal here with the title Son of Man, as it would take too much space to show how its use in this Gospel is indebted not only to Daniel but the *Similitudes of Enoch*, where Wisdom and Son of Man come together. Witherington, *Christology of Jesus*, 233ff.

transcendent claims are made by Jesus of even being David's Lord, or as it is put in Matthew 11, God's Wisdom.

Finally, there is the matter of the house of God. The claim by Jesus that something greater than the temple is here has already been noted.[94] Jesus is going to go on to say, speaking as Wisdom in Matt. 23:38, that the house of God is left desolate to Jerusalem, because they have not welcomed Jesus as he was welcomed by some when he entered the city (cf. Matt. 21:9 — Matt. 23:39). The point is that they have not received him as the Son of David as they should have done. The threat that the house will be left desolate is a threat that God's presence, his Shekinah glory, is being withdrawn (cf. Ezekiel 10).

At the beginning and end of this Gospel it is plain that Jesus is being portrayed as Emmanuel, God with his people. It is relevant to point out that the same sort of claims are made about Wisdom, for she is "all–powerful, overseeing all, and penetrating through all spirits... an emanation of the glory of the Almighty... she reaches from one end of the earth to the other, and she orders all things well" (Wis. 7:23ff). She is "a kindly spirit" to which the author then adds "because the spirit of the Lord has filled the world, and that which holds all things together knows what is said." When in *1 Enoch* 42 she withdraws from earth, earth is bereft of God's presence.

Thus in Matthew Jesus is the manifestation of the presence of God on earth, and the description of him in 17:2 has prepared the reader for the conclusion of Matt. 23:37ff. Jesus as Wisdom promises to leave the house desolate because Jerusalem would not be gathered under his wings. Not incidently this is given immediately prior to the prediction of the destruction of the temple in Matthew 24 in the final portion of the final teaching discourse. How is this all connected with the promises about Solomon in 2 Samuel 7? I would offer the following conjecture.

In the First Evangelist's mind, Jesus is greater than Solomon in regard not only to sonship, or healing, or manifesting wise teaching, but also to the matter of God's house and, one might add, in inheriting a kingdom. While Solomon did build a house for God, Jesus is the presence that must fill that house or else it is desolate. All of the discourse in Matthew 23 has been given in the temple (cf. 24:1) by the one who is the manifestation of God's very presence, the human embodiment of God's very Wisdom, the one who, when he leaves the temple, leaves it bereft and ripe for destruction.[95] Henceforth, the presence of God is to be found neither on Gerizim nor on Zion but in the midst of true believers everywhere (cf. Matt. 18:20; 28:20).[96]

---

[94] Cf. the more explicit claim in John 2:19–22 that Jesus' body is the temple.

[95] E. Haenchen, "Matthäus 23," 38–63.

[96] The parallels here with John are again striking; cf. John 2 and 4:21ff. True worship must be Jesus-centered not temple or Torah-centered.

Thus, the First Evangelist masterfully ties together his chief christological ideas in Matthew 21–23, showing how Solomon's greater son is not merely Son of David, not merely a sage or teacher greater than Solomon, but even David's Lord, the very presence of God in the temple, God's Wisdom who longed to gather his people but was rejected. Deutsch puts it well when she says: "In Sir. 24:8–12 Wisdom–Torah came to dwell in the Temple [or Tabernacle]. Here in Matt. 23:37–39 we are told Wisdom will leave the Temple because Wisdom has been rejected."[97] In addition I would add that not just Sirach 24 but also 2 Samuel 7 as seen through a sapiential filter provides the key to understanding how Matthew relates his key christological ideas.

The final major denunciation of the scribes and Pharisees including the famous woes come in Matthew 23 at which point the reader is led to make a choice between two sorts of teachers and teachings. It is stressed that Jesus says to both the crowds and perhaps in particular the disciples that they are all just that and they should not allow themselves to be called rabbi or *kathegetes* (teacher, 23:8–10), for they have only one teacher – Jesus. The implication of this statement in view of what has preceded it both in Matthew 21 and even as far back as Matthew 11 and 13 is not only that Jesus is *the* teacher as the one greater than Solomon, as Wisdom come from God, as the Davidic Messiah, but also that the disciples are and must remain learners and in some cases may become scribes. This exclusive pedagogical Christology has implications for ecclesiology in Matthew's community. When one is always to be seen as a learner or scribe at most, then servant leadership is the only viable sort a human being can offer in such a community, there is no room for asking for positions of honor or greatness (cf. Matt. 20:20–28).

It is not necessary to go over the further teaching of Jesus in Matthew 24–25 which climaxes with the two key parables of the wise and foolish virgins and the talents. Both parables are meant to warn Jesus' disciples, in this case Matthew's scribes, to get on with the task at hand using what God has given them, all the while being prepared for what is yet to come. Lincoln has put his finger on the way the discourses function and work in the flow of the narrative when he says:

> Although they seem to disrupt the flow of the narrative and to have little to do with advancing the action, the five teaching discourses were in fact all the time preparing the disciples to be authoritative teachers of all that Jesus commanded them, the climactic commissioning to which the narrative builds up in its major two–part movement (cf. 16:17–19, 28:16–20).[98]

---

[97] Deutsch, "Wisdom in Matthew," 45.
[98] Lincoln, "Matthew – a Story for Teachers?" 115.

As I have pointed out, however, the sort of teacher the disciples are prepared to be are scribes, they do not become the equivalent of Jesus *the* teacher.

The conclusion of the passion narrative in Matthew 26–27 makes clear how the pronouncements of Jesus as Wisdom had in fact been sagacious and come true – he was indeed rejected, but was vindicated by God, worshipped by both female and male disciples (cf. Matt. 28:9, 19) and promised to go on being their Wisdom, that is, the living presence of God with them which continues to instruct them through the teaching already given by the historical Jesus and summarized in this Gospel. This Gospel is, as Minear and other have argued, the teacher's Gospel in the sense that it was meant for Jewish Christian teachers.[99] But in a much greater sense it is also *the teacher's* Gospel. For Matthew, that teacher was a nonpareil, the only one who truly deserved the title of teacher, for he was at once sage and Wisdom offering both conventional and counter order wisdom, David's Son and Lord, like Solomon but greater, royal Son of God and even the manifestation of God's presence on earth. It is hard to imagine a Christology higher than one that begins with a person who is Emmanuel and ends with the proclamation that he has been given *all* authority in heaven and earth to empower and send out his disciples for the task of replication. This Christology, and the vision of teaching, learning, and community that derives from it owes much to Jewish Wisdom literature, especially late Jewish Wisdom thinking. The yoke that Matthew beckons his scribes to take up is at once the yoke of Jesus' Wisdom, and the yoke of Jesus as Wisdom.[100]

JOHN: THE FIRST AND LAST WORD

THE BELOVED LEARNER AND CO.

Here is not the place to give a detailed discussion of the origins of the Fourth Gospel, which are complex on any showing. With most scholars I would argue that it is an independent witness to the Jesus tradition and does not draw on the Synoptic Gospels, though clearly it shares various traditions with them. It seems unlikely that the Beloved Disciple wrote the Gospel of John in its present form, not only because it hardly seems plausible that he would have gone around calling *himself* the Beloved Disciple, especially in view of John 13 and the example of humility held out for the disciple to follow. This is a likely conclusion also because of verses like John 19:35 and especially John 21:24.

There is, however, nothing preventing the Beloved Disciple from being a real person who passed on the Jesus tradition to his community, interpreting

[99] Minear, *Matthew – the Teacher's Gospel*, 2–10.

[100] Noting that Matt. 11:28–30 says "learn *apo eme*" which may be taken to mean "learn from me", but it also may mean learn about me. The second clause of 11:29 suggests the latter is the primary focus for first Jesus' character is spoken of, and then what he bestows rest, shalom.

it for them, so that the Fourth Gospel may be in some large measure as John 21:24 suggests, his testimony. It must be admitted that the character of the Gospel suggests that if some of this material goes back to an actual follower of Jesus during his earthly ministry, that follower was Judean, and not the Galilean John the son of Zebedee. Had the latter been the originator of this Gospel one would have expected more on the Galilean ministry, and especially more of the stories found in the Synoptics which involve the sons of Zebedee. The lateness with which the Beloved Disciple makes his appearance in this Gospel also suggests a Judean disciple who may have been with Jesus towards the close of his ministry, and perhaps also during the earlier visits of Jesus to Jerusalem during the festivals. What concerns me at this juncture is the use that the anonymous Fourth Evangelist made of the testimony of the Beloved Disciple and his other sources such as the Logos hymn.

In view of the lack of interest in "scribes" in this Gospel it seems best to conclude that this Gospel, while probably put together *in* and *for* a school setting (perhaps as an attempt to help disciples further grasp the significance of Jesus) was not written, as Matthew was, specifically for Jewish Christian scribes. It seems to have been written in an environment where there was a school which included several teachers all deeply indebted to the Beloved Disciple's legacy. G. R. Beasley–Murray's judicious assessment seems correct:

> As an authority figure to which the Johannine communities looked, the Beloved Disciple appears to have had a group of teachers about him. The existence of a Johannine literature alongside the Gospel, including the three epistles and the book of Revelation, points to a group of teachers having a common center of loyalty, with a diversity not too great to be contained within a unity.[101]

It also appears that the Fourth Gospel was written expecting the audience to recognize the sapiential overtones of the book, and in particular the way the hymn in John 1 conditions and prepares for all that follows. When one couples this with the knowledge of Jewish festivals and customs that the audience seems presumed to know about, it seems unlikely that John was writing solely or mainly for Gentiles. I believe the author had a Diaspora Jewish Christian audience in view, though there are sufficient Gentiles about who do not know Semitic languages and customs. Thus the evangelist is required to make parenthetical explanations here and there of some matters (cf. 4:9; 9:7; 19:17; 20:16).

---

[101] The school setting nicely explains the family resemblance of the whole Johannine corpus without requiring one to argue that one person wrote all five canonical Johannine documents, which in view of the major differences of style and grammar between the Book of Revelation and the other Johannine literature seems unlikely. Cf. Hengel, *Johannine Question*, 74ff; Culpepper, *Johannine School*, 261ff; G. R. Beasley–Murray, *John* (Waco: Word, 1987), lxxiv.

Most importantly, the reader or hearer reads or listens to this Gospel knowing something the disciples and other interlocutors in the story did not know prior to Easter – that Jesus is the incarnate Logos. This is meant to inform how one reads the story as a whole. Knowing the pilgrimage of Wisdom which has come down from above and returns there, is the key to understanding who Jesus is in this Gospel.[102] In light of these observations, let us turn to the story of Wisdom's pilgrimage as told in the Fourth Gospel.[103]

THE LAST GOSPEL: THE GRAVITY OF THE WORD

The discussion of the Wisdom influences on the Fourth Gospel normally begins and all too often ends with the discussion of the Logos Hymn in John 1. This is a mistake, especially if the Logos Hymn strongly shapes the way the story of Jesus is told thereafter.[104] It is not necessary to rehearse what I have already said on the Wisdom character of the Logos hymn, but it may prove useful to add to the voice of M. D. Hooker that of C. H. Dodd to reaffirm the main point:

> The evangelist does not, like some Gnostics, set out to communicate an account of the origin of the universe, as a way to that knowledge of God which is eternal life, and then fit Christ into the scheme. he says, in effect, "let us assume that the

[102] Cf. the chart in R. Kysar, *John, the Maverick Gospel*, 29–30. Unfortunately, the recent thesis by M. Scott, now published as *Sophia and the Johannine Jesus*, arrived after this study had been completed and was going to press and so I am not now able to interact with it fully. While in various ways it supports the thesis of this part of the present chapter there are several points where his judgment seems to have gone awry. First, he is quite wrong that in the Wisdom of Solomon Wisdom "is not pictured as dependent upon or subordinate to Yahweh, but is quite simply a feminine replacement for the traditional expression of God" (62, cf. 242). He wishes to support the arguments of Fiorenza, Johnson and others that Wisdom is a feminine expression of God *in toto* not merely of an attribute of God. It is quite clear from Wis. 8:2–5 that Wisdom is portrayed not as God, but as someone whom God loves and who lives *with* God; in short, they are distinguishable even in the Wisdom of Solomon. Secondly, the idea that the Prologue is about Wisdom becoming incarnate *in* Jesus (cf. 243) is not correct. The Logos is said to become incarnate *as* Jesus, that is, we are not talking about two distinguishable entities here but two stages in the career of one being. Thirdly, it seems unlikely, if Scott is right when he says that the Fourth Evangelist is going to great lengths to portray Jesus as *Sophia*, that the explanation that the term *Logos* is used simply because of Jesus' maleness is equally correct (244). As we have pointed out Jesus' maleness did not stop the First Evangelist from calling Jesus *Sophia*. It is because the Fourth Evangelist sees Jesus as the incarnate Word, in comparison with Torah being the Word, that he uses the term *logos*, for *sophia* does not equally well convey this idea. The usage is for conceptual not gender reasons. Again in the Fourth Gospel we are dealing with the portrayal of Jesus as Wisdom, to be sure, but the point is *transferral*. All that the early Jews or others sought in Wisdom and her benefits, the Fourth Evangelist now maintains can be found in Jesus.

[103] On all the above issues the standard commentaries should be compared, especially Barrett, *The Gospel According to John* (London: SPCK, 1978), 100f; E. Haenchen, *John 1* (Philadelphia: Fortress, 1984), 2ff; Beasley–Murray, *John*, lxviff.

[104] cf. p. 282ff. above.

> cosmos exhibits a divine meaning which constitutes its reality. I will tell you what that meaning is: it was embedded in the life of Jesus, which I will now describe."... the Prologue is an account of the life of Jesus under the form of a description of the eternal Logos in its relations with the world and with man, and the rest of the gospel an account of the Logos under the form of the record of the life of Jesus; and the proposition *ho logos sarx egeneto* binds the two together...[105]

Dodd then says he will set out to show how the whole Gospel is determined by the idea conveyed by "and the *logos* took on human flesh."[106] I would say it is determined by a variety of things, including the Jesus tradition itself, but that the whole prologue and the Wisdom trajectory it evokes of one who came down and must go back up into heaven again shapes the whole considerably, as will now be shown by some telling examples.[107]

The language of "before" and "after" as well as the language of "above" and "below," "descending and ascending" in the Fourth Gospel should be given close scrutiny. Such language is found already in the testimony of the Baptist especially in 1:30 where it is said that Jesus in some sense comes before John and is thus above John in rank. Such an idea is not found in the Synoptic parallels at this point. John then elaborates on this in 3:31 by saying that the one who comes from above is above all.

There is next an elliptical reference to angels "ascending and descending" on the Son of Man (1:51). Jesus *is* the juncture between earth and heaven, the one through whom the two realms are linked. In John 3:2, Nicodemus admits that Jesus is a teacher who comes from God, but of course the remark is ironic for he has said more than he realizes. He is not merely a teacher but that which must be taught – the Word that comes from God. The birth that comes through Jesus is a birth from above (*anothen*, vv 3, 7), he is the only one who has both descended from heaven and ascended into it as Son of Man (v 13).[108]

One also finds in 3:14 the first presentation of the theme that the Son must be lifted up (on the cross) in order that salvation may come. In John's theology the cross is the first step on Jesus' way back to heaven and therefore the moment at which he begins to be glorified, the moment at which his decisive hour has

---

[105] C. H. Dodd, *The Interpretation of the Fourth Gospel*, 285.

[106] It is strange that in the exposition that follows in Dodd's influential study, he does not pay much attention to the hints given in the Prologue that the Gospel should be exegeted in light of the Wisdom corpus.

[107] Culpepper, *Anatomy*, 226 is right that John sets limits on Christian Logos speculation by giving the Logos a narrative interpretation in the form of casting Jesus as the Logos even during his ministry. It is very likely true that the relationship of Jesus and the Word, or Jesus and Wisdom was a matter of significant discussion in the Johannine community and thus the evangelist felt it necessary to provide parameters for that discussion.

[108] It may be that the addition "who is in heaven" found in some MSS is original, in which case the whole sentence should be seen as the evangelist's parenthetical remark to his audience for whom the ascending as well as the descending is in the past. Cf. Barrett, *John*, 213.

come. What this passage and the rest of John 3 shows is that the Fourth Evangelist's theology of the Son of Man is first conditioned by the Wisdom path, perhaps especially in the light of *1 Enoch* 70:2, 71:1 where Enoch ascends and is identified with the Son of Man and *1 Enoch* 42 where Wisdom descends to earth and then returns to heaven rejected. This is important because it has been indicated in various places throughout the *Similitudes* that their subject matter is in fact Wisdom (cf. 46:3; 48:1–2, 7; 49:1–3; 51:3).[109] Secondly, John's theology of the cross is affected by how he views the path – dying on the cross is the first stage of being lifted up (cf. also John 8:28). Thirdly, even the larger theology of Jesus as God's beloved Son and God the Son (cf. the NRSV on John 1:18), who is begotten, not made, is affected for it is as the Son, that the Logos was sent into the world, as 3:16–17 make clear.

As E. Käsemann said, Jesus bestrides the Johannine earthly stage like a God.[110] In such circumstances it is not surprising that John should attribute divine qualities, especially those associated with Wisdom such as light and life, to Jesus throughout the Gospel (cf. here 3:19 and below on these Wisdom characteristics).[111] What is surprising is how at the same time John is able to portray Jesus not only as truly human (experiencing hunger, thirst, weariness) but as subordinant to and depending on the Father such that "My food is to do the will of him who sent me and to complete this work" (4:34), or "the Son can do nothing on his own, but only what he sees the Father doing" (5:19). Jesus is the Father's *Shaliach*, his agent on earth, along with the other things John wishes to say about him. He has been sent to earth for a specific purpose, to complete works given him by the Father (5:36–38, 6:29).

It is not just that Jesus has come from God in heaven, for that could be said of angels as well, but that he has been sent on the mission of redemption with both a special character and a special relationship with the Father; he is the only one who has actually *seen* the Father (6:46). As such this equips him to speak for the Father, and indeed to give the teaching which is from God (7:16–17).

There is an equal insistence about his return to heaven, often in terms of the Son of Man language such as is found in John 6:62: "what if you were to see the Son of Man ascending to where he was before?" If understanding in this Gospel amounts to knowing where Jesus came from and where he is going, then misunderstanding normally manifests itself in having a false conception of where Jesus has come from and is going. For example: (1) in 7:25 the people of Jerusalem say they know where Jesus is from, but they do not know his ultimate origins; (2) in 8:41 it is implied that Jesus came from a woman who bore him out of wedlock while his opponents are true and legitimate sons of Abraham (to this Jesus counters that he precedes Abraham, indeed he simply

[109] H. R. Moeller, "Wisdom Motifs and John's Gospel," 95.

[110] E. Käsemann, *The Testament of Jesus: a Study of the Gospel of John in Light of Chapter 17*, 8–9.

[111] A. Feuillet, *Johannine Studies*, 53ff.

exists, 8:58); (3) in 8:48 it is asked if he is not from Samaria; and 4) in 18.5ff. the opponents stress they are looking for Jesus from Nazareth. The errors about who Jesus is come from not knowing his ultimate origins, which is to say, not knowing he is the Logos, the Son sent from God, the Son of man who descends and ascends.

In 7:35 the puzzlement over who Jesus is comes from not knowing where he is going. The Pharisees show their lack of understanding by conjecturing that he intends to go to the Diaspora among the Greeks and teach the Greeks, when he says he is going somewhere they cannot follow. A variety of further examples could be cited, including the fact that Mary Magdalene in John 20 misunderstands the divine nature of Jesus (calling him only *Rabbouni*) precisely because she is trying to renew earthly relationships with Jesus and has not understood that Jesus must ascend so he can have a new form of relationship with all of his disciples. It is also telling that the way Jesus chooses to reveal who he truly is to the disciples through Mary is by having her say that he is ascending to his and their Father, his and their God (20:16–17). It is only when she understands his pilgrimage that she is able to proclaim, "I have seen the (risen) Lord."[112]

The above is only a very cursory sketch of the use of the language about coming from and going to heaven, but enough has been said to warrant the conclusion that the Fourth Evangelist makes understanding that Jesus is the one who has come from and returns to heaven a, if not *the*, key to understanding his identity in this Gospel.[113] In short, proper christological understanding requires a knowledge of the path traced by Wisdom now seen in the person of Jesus, the incarnation of God's Word/Wisdom.

Inasmuch as John 20 was very likely the original conclusion of this Gospel, it appears that the original plot of the Gospel itself is shaped by the sapiential path: (1) the Word pre–exists and comes to earth; (2) the Word takes on flesh and dwells among human beings teaching, healing, and acting so as to save the world; (3) the Word is lifted up on the cross and vindicated through the resurrection and finally, after both these events, returns to the Father and sends the Spirit as his surrogate. The initial plan of the plot was announced in 1:11–14; he came to earth, took on flesh, was rejected by his own but accepted by a few followers. These latter he empowered to become children of God.[114]

---

[112] Witherington, *Women in the Earliest Churches*, 177ff.

[113] Culpepper, *Anatomy*, 33–34, calls this perspective on Jesus which author and audience share in the light of the Logos hymn stereoscopic: "The gospel narrative therefore portrays Jesus as the one who continued the creative work of the divine *logos* by creating eyes for the man born blind, restoring the dead to life, and breathing life into spiritless disciples. The narrator also knows that Jesus will be exalted to the Father so he prepares the reader to understand Jesus' death as exaltation rather than humiliation. These entrance and exit points... condition the Johannine narrator's stereoscopic view of the ministry of Jesus." This is as much as to admit that the presentation of the ministry is thoroughly conditioned by the Logos hymn.

[114] On the plot of this Gospel, cf. Culpepper, *Anatomy*, 83ff.

The story ends, appropriately enough, with the risen one (incarnate and now glorified Word/Wisdom) speaking a Wisdom saying, a beatitude, "Blessed are those who have not seen, and yet come to believe." Hearing, believing, understanding are what disciples are to do. Seeing is not required for full faith. This is only what one would expect when the object of faith is the *Word* or *Wisdom*. In effect the evangelist says to his audience, Let the one who has ears to hear about and believe in Wisdom and Wisdom's pilgrimage do so.

Once one recognizes that the Logos hymn sets the interpretive agenda for the Gospel, it is important for the author to show Jesus revealing indirectly at various points that he is the pre–existent Logos. Culpepper aptly sums up this post–creation but pre–incarnational work of the Logos as follows:

> During the historical past, the history of Israel, he came into the world and enlightened those who had eyes to see him (1:9). Moses and the prophets wrote about him (1:45; 5:46), and Abraham saw his "day" (8:56). Isaiah, presumably in the heavenly vision (Isaiah 6), saw "his glory" (12:41). No one actually saw him, just as no one was able to see God (1:18; 6:46), but there is little doubt that for John the *logos* was the inspiration of the prophets and Jesus was the fulfillment to which they pointed.[115]

What is most intriguing about all this, is that in Wisdom 10–19 similar sorts of roles are predicated of Wisdom. She was present in the wilderness and provided water from the rock (11:4); she sustained Israel with manna (16:26); she rescued various righteous men including Lot and Joseph (10:6ff); she aided Abraham (10:5); she entered Moses allowing him to perform wonders and signs (10:16) and gave him the gift of prophecy (11:1 cf. 7:27). The Johannine Jesus understands himself to be the Word or Wisdom who had aided God's people throughout all previous generations.[116]

There are a variety of other aspects of the Fourth Gospel that seem to reflect an indebtedness to sapiential material. For example the "I am" discourses come readily to mind. Earlier in this study it has been mentioned that it is possible that the characterization and speeches of Wisdom, particularly in the Wisdom of Solomon, may have owed something to the Isis aretologies in which Isis speaks in the first person.[117] It has also been conjectured that this is the case with the "I am" discourses as well.[118] I would suggest that if there is such an influence in the "I am" discourses in John it has come to this Gospel by way of the influence of sapiential material on the Fourth Evangelist and not directly.

---

[115] Culpepper, *Anatomy*, 106.

[116] Painter, *Quest for the Messiah*, 256ff.

[117] Cf. above pp. 108ff.

[118] Cf. e.g. R. E. Brown, *The Gospel according to John I–XII* (Garden City: Doubleday, 1966), 534ff.

In the seven key "I am" sayings Jesus is characterized variously as living bread, light of the world, the door, life, and the authentic vine (cf. 6:35, 51; 8:12; 10:7, 9, 11, 14; 11:25; 14:6; 15:1, 5). *All* of these things are said at one point or another to come from or characterize personified Wisdom. Thus, for instance, in Prov. 8:38 Wisdom says, "he who finds me finds life and obtains favor from the Lord." In Wis. 7:26 she is said to be a reflection of eternal light. The characterization of Jesus as vine should be compared to the characterization of Wisdom in Sir. 24:17ff where it says, "Like the vine I bud forth delights, and my blossoms become glorious and abundant fruit. Come to me you who desire me, and eat your fill of my fruits... those who eat of me will hunger for more and those who drink of me will thirst for more." This passage from Sirach also seems to inform John 4:4: "Everyone who drinks of this water will be thirsty again, but those who drink of the water that I will give them will never be thirsty. The water I will give them will become in them a spring of water gushing up to eternal life."[119] Perhaps also one may compare "I am the bread of life. Whoever comes to me will never be hungry, and whoever believes in me will never be thirsty" (6:35). The latter text is also close to Prov. 9:5 where Wisdom beckons "Come eat of my bread, and drink of the wine I have mixed. Lay aside immaturity and live and walk in the way of insight." Wisdom is said to be a tree of life in Prov. 3:18 and in the immediately preceding verse there is a discussion of her ways and paths. The disciple is meant to see following her as a way to life and peace. Whether or not the absolute "*ego eimi*" in 8:58 owes anything to Wisdom material, the "I am" sayings with predicates certainly seem to.

The "I am" sayings are linked to discourses which expand and expound on the basic saying, and in view of the above one may say that these discourses owe something to Wisdom not merely in form but also in content. The use of food and drink metaphors to refer to deeper spiritual sustenance is characteristic of both these sources. The point in the Wisdom corpus is that all one truly longs for and needs can be found in Wisdom, and the Fourth Evangelist is trying to make the same point about Jesus.[120]

The "I am" discourses are also linked with the sign narratives which are clustered in the first half of the Fourth Gospel. These sign narratives are in a variety of ways different from the tales of "mighty works" in the Synoptics, and scholars have offered many explanations of the difference. Perhaps the most convincing explanation of at least the Johannine approach was offered by G. Ziener in two much neglected articles.[121] The author of Wisdom of Solomon

[119] Despite the different way of putting it, both texts seem to be saying basically the same thing. The point in John is that once one partakes of the living water one will not thirst for anything else and this is probably the point in Sirach as well. Cf. Beasley–Murray, *John*, 60–61.

[120] R. Bultmann, *The Gospel of John. A Commentary*, trans. G. R. Beasley–Murray (Oxford: B. Blackwell, 1971), 218ff.

[121] G. Ziener, "Weisheitbuch and Johannesevangelium," 37–60.

treats the serpents in the desert as a sign or symbol of something else. In fact, he sees all of the wonders performed by God as the Israelites left Egypt and wandered in the wilderness as symbols of salvation (*sumbolon soterias*) for God's people (Wis. 16:6). Like John he thinks of a miracle as a *semeion* (Wis. 10:16). Ziener shows how in his conception of Jesus' signs the Fourth Evangelist is drawing on the presentation of God's miracles for Israel, not simply in Exodus but in the retelling of those stories found in the historical review section of Wisdom 11–18.[122] What the author of Wisdom of Solomon says about God's Word could just as easily have been said by John of Jesus with little alteration: "For the one who turned toward it was saved, not by the thing which was beheld, but by you the Savior of all.... For neither herb nor poultice cured them, but it was your Word, O Lord, that heals all people. For you have power over life and death; you lead mortals down to the gates of Hades and back again" (Wis. 16:7, 12ff).

That what the author of Wisdom of Solomon attributes to Wisdom or God's personified Word (e.g. water from the rock in the desert 11:1–4) is in John attributed to Jesus, can also be seen in several further examples. For instance, in Wis. 16:20–26 the author discusses how "without toil you supplied them from heaven with bread ready to eat." This in itself appears to be just another discussion of the Exodus wonders until one arrives at the punchline in v 26: "so that your children whom you loved, O Lord might learn that it is not the production of crops that feeds humankind but that your Word sustains those who trust you."[123] This is the same sort of point the Fourth Evangelist is driving at in the discourse in John 6: "Do not work for the food that perishes, but for the food that endures for eternal life which the Son of Man will give you" (6:27). In both cases the wonder is seen to point to a larger verity outside itself which is much more important.

In Wisdom 18 the author discusses the miracle of light even at night that God provided for the Israelites as they left Egypt, but again his interest lies in the fact that "their enemies deserved to be deprived of light and imprisoned in darkness, those who had kept your children imprisoned through whom the imperishable light of the Law was to be given to the world" (18:4). This should be compared to the symbolic treatment of Jesus as "the light of the world in John 9 but which is presaged in the saying, "Whoever follows me will never walk in darkness but have the light of life" (John 8:12). The two levels of discussion about physical and spiritual sight and insight and physical and spiritual blindness are meant to make much the same point as is made in

---

[122] His argument that the sequence of signs in John follows the sequence in Wisdom 11ff. is not fully convincing but cf. Ziener, "Weisheitbuch," 405.

[123] Bearing in mind that in the light of Wis. 9:1–2 that Word and Wisdom seem to be basically two ways to speak of the same thing in this book. Just as Wisdom is personified or even hypostasized in Wisdom 7, so also in Wis. 18:15 one hears "your all–powerful Word leaped from heaven from the royal throne, into the midst of the land that was doomed, a stern warrior carrying the sharp sword of your authentic command." Cf. Heb. 4:12.

Wisdom 18, especially in regard to the fact that Jesus says not merely that his followers are being given light but also that his opponents are being deprived of light (John 9:39, "I came into this world for judgment so that those who do not see may see, and those who do see may be deprived of light").

The two level discussion of wonders in both John and the Wisdom of Solomon is made possible because both authors have a theology of eternal life and its negative counterpart. This theology, in the *way* it is expressed, reflects the use of sapiential language to cope with an idea that very likely does not appear in the Wisdom corpus before the Wisdom of Solomon – the idea of a positive afterlife.[124]

Thus, for the author of the Wisdom of Solomon, as for the Fourth Evangelist, physical death is not the end of the story. In Wis. 3:1–2 the author stresses, "but the souls of the righteous are in the hand of God, and no torment will ever touch them. In the eyes of the foolish they seem to have died...but they are at peace... their hope is full of immortality." This statement about only appearing to have died is similar to the discussion in John 11 when Jesus insists that Lazarus is sleeping. This is because death in the hands of the God of life is not necessarily the end. The author of the Wisdom of Solomon is in fact willing to say that God did not make death (1:13); it entered the world through the devil's envy (2:24) and only the devil's followers truly experience it.[125] It was God's intention that human beings were created for "incorruption", being made in the "image of his eternity" (Wis. 2:23). By contrast with the wicked "the righteous live forever" (5:15).

Not only in what he says about death and eternal life, but also in the role he allots to the devil in such matters the Fourth Evangelist seems very close to the author of the Wisdom of Solomon. For example, John 8:44 (where the devil is said to be the father of the wicked and to be "a murderer from the beginning... [he] does not stand in the truth") could just as easily have been said by the earlier sage. In the mind of both authors it was not the intention of God to condemn the world, even the fallen world, but rather to save it (cf. Wisdom 2–3 to John 3:16–21).

As Moeller says, with Jesus in John as with Wisdom in the Wisdom corpus but especially in the Wisdom of Solomon, one's destiny, whether life or death, hangs on whether one accepts or rejects Jesus or Wisdom.[126] The coming of Wisdom causes a division amongst human beings – some seek and find (cf. Prov. 8:17; Sir. 6:27; Wis. 6:12), others to their cost do not seek and regret it too late (Prov. 1:28). "The same language in John describes the effect of Jesus upon men [sic] (7:34; 8:21; 13:33)."[127]

---

[124] But cf. Job 19.

[125] J. E. Bruns, "Some Reflections on Coheleth and John," 414–16, has rightly pointed out how John's conception that physical life and death do not provide meaning for human existence seems to owe something to Qoheleth's discussion of these matters.

[126] Moeller, "Wisdom Motifs," 95.

[127] Brown, *John I–XII*, cxxiv.

Because the author of the Wisdom of Solomon equated Wisdom with God's Spirit and John seems to be drawing on his work, or perhaps sharing common late Wisdom material,[128] it is not surprising that the Fourth Evangelist sometimes uses this material to characterize not just Jesus but also the other Paraclete which he will send (cf. especially John 14:16–17, 26–27 with Wis. 1:6ff.; 6:17ff.; 7:7–14, 22–29; 9:17–18). John's pneumatology as well as his Christology owe something to the sapiential corpus.

This is also true of John's soteriology, as Dodd points out.[129]

> The need for a birth from above which is discussed in John 3, seems to owe something to the discussion in Wis. 7:14ff. where Wisdom is said to be the one who, coming down from above passes into human souls renewing all things and makes them friends of God and even prophets.

A bit later in John 3:14 the puzzling remark about Moses lifing up the serpent in the wilderness is made, and it is likened to the at of salvation provided on the cross by the Son. What is the connection? Dodd rightly points to Wis. 16:6 where "readers of the LXX however would remember that the serpent was, in the words of the Book of Wisdom *sumbolon soterian* (Wis. 16:6); it signigied the means by whih men [sic] passed from death to life".[130]

The point to be made here is that the Gospel of John makes a great deal more sense when read in light of the sapiential literature, and in view of the numerous similarities it has with it, it is hard to doubt that the evangelist intended it to be read that way.

The Fourth Gospel speaks of salvation in a way (usually as life or eternal life) and to a degree that is not characteristic of the Synoptics, but it is certainly reminiscent of the Wisdom of Solomon, where not only is immortality the reward for seeking and finding or receiving Wisdom, but it is also said "Who has learned your counsel unless you have given Wisdom and sent your holy Spirit from on high? And thus the paths of those on earth were set right, and people were taught what pleases you, and were saved by Wisdom" (Wis. 9:17–18). It is striking too that John's theology of the penetration of believers by Christ, so that he will dwell in them (14:23) seems to echo the idea found in Wis. 7:24, 27 that salvation amounts to Wisdom penetrating and indwelling human beings.

There are also points in Jesus' teaching where he seems to speak as Wisdom. For example when he says to his disciples, "If you love me you will keep my commandments" (14:15), one cannot help but hear an echo of Wis.

---

[128] Ziener, "Weisheitbuch," 60, finally concludes that both authors are drawing on a common late Wisdom tradition.

[129] Dodd, *Interpretation*, 281–82, 306.

[130] Dodd, *Interpretation*, 306.

6:18, "and love of Wisdom is the keeping of her laws, and giving heed to her laws is assurance of immortality." To this one should add the fact that John 13–17 seems to characterize Jesus as a sage or as Wisdom conveying his legacy of wisdom to his "learners" in private which is in many ways reminiscent of what one finds in Ben Sira and what he conveys in his house of instruction to his charges (cf. Sir. 51:23ff.). This suggestion will cause no surprise if one goes back and reviews the section at the beginning of this chapter which showed the similarities of Matthew and John in their treatment of things like teachers and learners and pedagogy.

Again, when Jesus gives his private teaching to his disciples and closes it in John 16–17, it appears he is speaking as Wisdom for the echoes of Sir. 4:11–13 are hard to miss. Compare the following:

Wisdom teaches (Heb.)/exalts (Gk.) her children	(cf. John 14–16)
and gives help to those who seek her.	(cf. John 14:16ff.)
Whoever loves her loves life, and	(cf. John 14:15)
those who seek her from early morning	
are filled with joy.	(cf. John 15:11)
Whoever holds her fast inherits glory,	(cf. John 17:22)
and the Lord blesses the place she enters...	
the Lord loves those who love her.	(cf. John 17:26)

It is also telling that in John the disciples are called Jesus' little children (13:33) just as they are said to be Wisdom's children (Sir. 4:11; 6:18 and earlier in Prov. 8:32–33).[131]

There is a great deal more that could be said when one begins to compare John's Gospel to the Wisdom corpus, especially the late Wisdom material, but the above must suffice for now. It has been pointed out that in: (1) the Logos hymn; (2) in the V-shaped plot of the Gospel; (3) the "I am" sayings and discourses; (4) the conception and character of the signs; (5) the use of Father language and teacher–learner language; and (6) various aspects of Christology, soteriology, and pneumatology this Gospel reflects a notable similarity to late Wisdom material, especially the Wisdom of Solomon. What the author of the Wisdom of Solomon says about Wisdom/Word, John says either about Jesus or in one place about the Paraclete he will send. This Advocate is so closely connected to Jesus that it is called "*another*" Paraclete, just as Wisdom, Word, and Spirit are very closely intertwined in the Wisdom of Solomon.

The Fourth Evangelist has been deeply affected by the Wisdom corpus and draws on it in his presentation of Jesus. The elements listed above encompass most of the primary things that distinguish the Fourth Gospel from

[131] Brown, *John I–XII*, cxxiii.

the Synoptics, and so it is perhaps not too much to say that a primary cause of the major differences between the Fourth Gospel and the Synoptics is the *way* the evangelist draws on Wisdom material to shape the source material that he *does not* share with the Synoptics, and even some of the common material.[132]

The Fourth Evangelist is intent on conveying the deeper significance of Jesus, the deeper Wisdom, the sort that learners can only understand after considerable time in school. By contrast, Matthew focuses on the kind of Wisdom Jesus conveyed in public such as parables and on the beginnings of private Wisdom instruction that Jesus gave his disciples about parables and the like. Both draw extensively on the Wisdom corpus to achieve their aims, but the level of their respective audiences differ and so the instruction differs. Both are concerned to show how Jesus continues to be *the* teacher for all believers whether they are novice disciples, mature Christians, or even scribes. Both, among other things, wish to present Jesus as God's Wisdom, God's Word. For Matthew revelation and then further instruction leads to illumination about who Jesus is and therefore also about who his learners are and what they ought to be. For John, understanding the pilgrimage of Wisdom, the whence and whither of the Logos, is the key to understanding who Jesus is.

The final aim of both Gospels is that in the end disciples, both female and male, would be led to worship Jesus (cf. Matt. 28:9, 17; John 20:17, 28) recognizing the divine one as he truly is, whether one calls him Emmanuel, Lord and God, the great I Am, Word, or Wisdom. This in the end is the aim of the pedagogical pilgrimage the disciple is taken on when she or he undertakes to hear and heed the Alpha or Omega of Wisdom's Gospels, Matthew or John.

---

[132] On John's use of the sources, cf. R. T. Fortna, *The Fourth Gospel and its Predecessor*, 1ff.

9

Final Reflections on Wisdom's Journey

It is neither possible nor needful to rehearse here all of the conclusions drawn in the individual chapters of this study. Certain lasting impressions and implications deserve brief mention, however. First, the Wisdom literature found in the Scriptures has many shades and hues. It is not easily brought under one or even a few simple rubrics. It can encompass many literary forms from proverbs to parables to beatitudes to discourses, and its subject matter can vary considerably as well. In general, its primary concern is with everyday life, how to live well and wisely.

The many-faceted quality of Wisdom literature explains why in this study the chapters vary considerably. There is not one *main* idea or leitmotif that is being traced throughout this work. Rather, this study shows the variety of ways biblical Wisdom thought and literature developed in the thousand year period between 900 B.C. and A.D. 100. The intent was to expose the reader to the scope and richness of the sapiential material, and when the study turned to the New Testament, to show how extensive the impact of Wisdom thinking and material was on the Christian canon. The reader must judge whether or not a sapiential reading of the material presented in chapters 4–8 sheds new light on the data.

D. Georgi, in the appendix to his major study on Paul's Corinthian opponents, argues that these opponents were part of a larger universalistic Jewish Wisdom movement that reached out to Gentiles as well as Jews throughout the Mediterranean crescent.[1]

[1] D. Georgi, *The Opponents of Paul in Corinth*, 337ff. This new appendix was added when the English edition was prepared.

He states, "Jewish Apologists took the practical consequences of the universal aspects of Jewish wisdom... [using the same] dialectic between universalism and particularity as the Hellenistic culture around them had."[2] Thus, Judaism, even before the first century A.D., was already part of a larger pluralistic world culture and was a major contributor to it. Georgi traces the origins of this combination of Judaism and Hellenism to Sirach, the Wisdom of Solomon, and Philo. As a result of this study it would appear clear that early Jewish Christianity was *also* part of this larger movement as well, drawing on the same Jewish sources, but presenting them in a way that comported with a unique christological focus on Jesus. Both Jesus and his opponents, Paul and his opponents, early Judaism and early Jewish Christianity were drawing on and presenting models of a sapiential world view for their respective and potential audiences. I would suggest that this was at least in part a response to an even larger Hellenistic wisdom milieu involving Cynics, Stoics, and the revival of sophistic rhetoric in the first century A.D.[3]

It seems clear that the Wisdom literature has a definite pedagogical intent and suggests certain kinds of pedagogical methods and models. By this I mean that the sages were mainly interested in shaping human behavior and doing so through the art of persuasion rather than by means of demand, though commandments are not lacking in the Wisdom corpus. Wisdom literature is inherently metaphorical, using images, analogies (even extended ones in the form of narrative *meshalim*) and often humor to shape human conduct. There is an inherent indirection and also hyperbole in this form of instruction which requires of the hearer that they listen well, ruminate on what is said, and be able to interpret metaphorical speech. Dramatic and memorable images, often of extremes of good or evil, are conjured up to make a lasting impression on the hearer about some crucial subject. Such language is not meant to be taken literally, but it certainly wishes to be taken seriously and to be heeded.

It is also appropriate to talk about a significant shift in the way sapiential material was handled once a vital positive concept of the afterlife became

---

[2] Georgi, 400.

[3] I shall argue this case more fully in my socio-rhetorical commentary, 1994 on 1 and 2 Corinthians entitled *Conflict and Community in Corinth* (Grand Rapids: Eerdmans). For now it is germane to point out that various classics scholars have noted that what mainly distinguishes the approach to life in the Mediterranean crescent in the Hellenistic and Roman periods from the approach in the earlier classical period is "a rise of asceticism, of mysticism, in a sense of pessimism; a loss of self-confidence, of hope in this life and of faith in normal human effort; a despair of patient inquiry, a cry for infallible revelation; an indifference to the welfare of the state, a conversion of the soul to God... " (G. Murray, *Five Stages of Greek Religion*, 155; cf. E. R. Dodds, *Pagan and Christian in an Age of Anxiety* , 1ff.). This judgment is only partially correct, as R. MacMullen and others have made clear, but it suggests that Judaism and Christianity both participated in a larger cultural movement that had an increasing focus on the individual and his or her welfare and salvation. The older wisdom that focused on the good of the state or the tribe was undergoing considerable challenge from a variety of "wisdoms" in the Imperial age.

factored in the discussion. Whether through an otherworldly perspective (e.g. in the Wisdom of Solomon) or a more eschatological perspective (e.g. in the teaching of Jesus or Paul), the important act–consequence idea is transposed into a new key. If not all wrongs need to be righted in *this* age or lifetime, then the usual conventional criteria by which ancient Jewish sages evaluated whether a person was living wisely or well in accord with the fear of God can often be allowed to fall by the wayside. I would point to four consequences of this: (1) the rise of the idea of the pious poor or even the pious but sickly person (e.g. a Lazarus, or a Paul); (2) increased stress on the dangers of wealth, and discussion of the wicked wealthy who have their reward in this lifetime (cf. the parable of the rich man and Lazarus); (3) the offering of a positive counter order wisdom which already in this age produces at least a soteriological reversal of fortunes; and (4) "The finality and eternity of the coming age limits and relativizes all contemporary human experience and institutions, all [human] knowledge and wisdom. All social institutions are profoundly temporal" (cf. 1 Cor. 7:29–31).[4] When a sage came to believe such things, his or her wisdom was often of a counter order sort and involved a serious critique, not a baptism of the status quo, unlike some of the earlier Jewish wisdom.

The protest of Old Testament scholars that the Wisdom corpus, at least until the last twenty years, has been much neglected is warranted. While Old Testament scholarship has now gone some way to make up for lost time, New Testament scholars have only just scratched the surface of the possible benefits that come from reading the New Testament in light of the Jewish Wisdom corpus and assessing the extent and nature of its influence. I have attempted in this study to provide a bridge in this study so that those whose basic provenance is New Testament studies have a taste of the Old Testament discussion, especially as it bears on New Testament studies. I am well aware that I have not done full justice to the material in the Hebrew Scriptures, but it is needful that scholars in differing disciplines spend more time sharing insights and discussing matters of common interest, especially when the subject is Wisdom literature. If this study causes some cross-disciplinary discussions or teases some of the audience into active thought, to borrow a phrase from C. H. Dodd, it will have achieved one of its main aims.

As the path of the development of Wisdom literature has been traced, an increasing particularism, and one may even say historicism, has been noted. By this I mean that in Jewish Wisdom material there was an increasing tendency to find the locus of Wisdom in Torah. From Ben Sira on, with the probable exception of Jesus' teaching, this Torah-centric approach is evident in all Jewish sapiential literature to one degree or another (cf. e.g. Baruch), although the author of the Wisdom of Solomon does sometimes seem to operate with a broader conception of Wisdom that included identifying it with God's Spirit. When Jesus and then his followers drew on the Wisdom traditions they too

[4] D. A. Fraser and T. Campolo, *Sociology through the Eyes of Faith*, 184.

continued this trend towards particularism, only in their context this meant that Wisdom was associated with and sometimes identified with Jesus himself. This trend towards particularism, the attempt to find a particular historical person or thing that could be said to be *the* locus of Wisdom on earth, is one of the most salient features that arises from a careful study of biblical Wisdom literature. From the point of view of canonical theology this suggests that the modern attempt to replace Torah or Jesus as the locus of Wisdom with something or someone else, particularly if one is talking about something ahistorical, would be a violation of the intended path of biblical Wisdom material.

Another important result of this study is that it definitely appears to be the late sapiential material, in particular Sirach and the Wisdom of Solomon (and less frequently Philo), that can be said to have most deeply influenced the sources and authors of the New Testament documents. This influence is not minimal and cannot be confined to a few critical passages such as Matt. 11:25-30. The earliest Christians were all Jews, and many of them seem to have been steeped in this sort of literature.

If I were to guess why it is that the *late* Wisdom material, rather than Proverbs, Job, or Ecclesiastes, most affects the New Testament material, I would suggest it is because *all* the New Testament writers operate with a theology of the afterlife, and this strongly affects how one views such matters as the act–consequence schema. All of them also operate with an eschatological point of view to one degree or another. Furthermore, after Ben Sira, all the Wisdom literature or Wisdom influenced apocalyptic literature was written for a minority group struggling to maintain its identity in the face of problems and even persecution. Thus Wisdom of Solomon or the parables of *Enoch*, and to a lesser degree Ben Sira, exhibited in various ways a world view more akin to that held by Jesus or the early Christians than Proverbs does. I suspect this made the late sapiential material more useful for the Jesus movement to appropriate than the earlier material.

It is also true that both the late Jewish sapiential material and the New Testament were written during a period of time when Wisdom, prophetic, and apocalyptic ways of thinking, speaking, and writing had cross-fertilized leading to a variety of permutations and combinations. The old form-critical categories of either Wisdom or prophetic, or either Wisdom or apocalyptic, must not be too rigidly applied to the Jewish or Christian literature at the turn of the era. Wisdom may not have been the mother of apocalyptic, much less of prophecy, but already by the time Daniel was written there were various forms of arranged marriages between the two.

Though there is a tendency to draw on late and often counter-order sorts of Wisdom material in the New Testament, there are more than trace amounts of the older conventional Wisdom material in the New Testament, going back all the way to the sort of material found in Proverbs. I have pointed out that, especially in James and to a lesser degree in Matthew, the older sort of Wisdom surfaces once more. This stands at a certain distance from what seems to have most characterized the words of Jesus, namely a counter-order Wisdom which was already presaged in Ecclesiastes. This latter sort of Wisdom, rather than providing support for conventional norms and values, often turned them on their heads. Jesus words about reversal both in the present and in the future for the least, the last, and the lost fall into this category, as does Paul's proclamation of the scandal of the cross which goes against all common sense notions of what God's wisdom might be for a world gone wrong. In short, New Testament writers and those whose words they drew on appropriated a variety of different sorts of Wisdom ideas and traditions, some more traditional, some more controversial. Both conventional and counter-order Wisdom traditions are found in both the Hebrew Scriptures and the New Testament.

The issue of the Hellenization of Judaism and Jewish Christianity is an important one for anyone who wishes to study Wisdom literature. It is not a matter of *whether* early Judaism or Jewish Christianity was Hellenized but rather to what degree and in what way. It must be stressed that arguments that support the conclusion that early Judaism was partially Hellenized do not necessarily provide any support for conclusions like: (1) even ordinary first century A.D. Palestinian Jews were more influenced by Greek thought than by various forms of Jewish thought; (2) Jesus mainly spoke Greek; or (3) Jesus was more like a Cynic than like Qoheleth or Ben Sira or the Teacher of Righteousness.

A careful study of Jesus' words and deeds, in particular his parables and aphorisms, reveals a family resemblance to other early *Jewish* literature but only minimal similarity to the Cynic corpus, much of which post-dates Jesus in any case. Jesus should be viewed in the main as a prophetic sage offering primarily counter-order Wisdom. If one accepts this view, it accounts for the character of a great deal of the Jesus tradition. This role as sage must not be narrowly defined so that eschatological and prophetical ideas and forms are thought to be necessarily inauthentic, for as I have been at pains to point out, sapiential, prophetical, and eschatological material cross-fertilized long before Jesus' day. This is not to say that Jesus did not to some degree feel the effects of Hellenization, but Hellenization is one thing, a Cynic Jesus quite another. A wandering Cynic was not Jesus' spiritual or theological father.

What arguments about the partial Hellenization of early Judaism even in Palestine *do* show is that in view of the character of late Jewish Wisdom material it is impossible to argue that the Christology reflected, for instance, in the christological hymns is a Christology that *must* have developed late in the first century A.D., outside Palestine and in a predominantly non-Jewish environment. I would suggest that most if not all the Christology found in the christological hymns, in Q, in Matthew, and to a great degree in Paul as well, developed first in Jewish Christianity in Palestine within the first twenty years after Jesus' death. This initial surge of creative thinking about Jesus, seeing him through the eyes of Jewish Wisdom material, was sparked by Jesus' own appropriation of those traditions.

More controversial was the suggestion that Jesus presented himself as Wisdom. In view of the fact that a variety of Jesus traditions in a variety of Gospel and non-Gospel sources make such a suggestion, it seems likely that he did so. Also, if one may judge the correctness of an idea by its ability to explain a variety of other puzzling things, the supposition that Jesus presented himself as Wisdom should be accepted.

This theory would explain to a great degree why Q, the christological hymns, and the First and Fourth Gospels take the form they do, offering not merely christological material but sapiential christological material. The high Christologies found in these sources, and also in Paul, require an adequate explanation. These Wisdom Christologies very likely go back at the very least to the early Jewish Christians who created the christological hymns. Thus, one must ask which is more likely, that an anonymous Jewish Christian or group of Jewish Christians somewhere in the 30s or 40s A.D. came up with this christological modification of Jewish monotheism, or that Jesus himself, in the way he presented himself suggested such a revolutionary notion, and then his disciples teased out the implications of this seminal idea? Since most scholars are willing to agree that Jesus was in various ways creative in his teaching and self-presentation it is surely both easier and more convincing to predicate the "Jesus as Wisdom" idea of a known creative force than an unknown one. When one arrives at the Prologue to John's Gospel one is not looking at an example of *creatio ex nihilo*. I would argue that it is simply the further development of a sapiential way of looking at Jesus that ultimately goes back to Jesus the sage himself.

To those weary of oppressively patriarchal religion one can say that Wisdom as a personified attribute of God and God's creation does indeed have a feminine face in various places in the Scriptures which should not be ignored or minimized. If the biblical authors are indeed trying to tell us that God is the most personal of all beings and that all human beings are created in God's image, then the presentation of qualities or traits of God that are *like* human female as well as male traits should be expected. There is, however, a difference between a metaphor or simile and an identity statement, as well as between a personification and a person.

To the extent that Wisdom Christology in the canon focuses on Jesus who was a male human being, and in particular on Jesus in his relationship to a God that he and his disciples called Father (a name which seems especially to have grown out of *sapiential* ways of looking at and addressing God), it will remain difficult if not impossible to use this material to construct certain kinds of sophiaologies without violating the historical integrity of the material and the intent of its creators. The data seems to provide warrants for analogies (God or Jesus is like a woman in this or that way), but not for female identity statements (i.e. God is a woman, God is a Goddess).

There is more explicit use of the Wisdom personification or hypostasization in the pre-Christian Wisdom material than in the New Testament, and it is more than doubtful whether any of the Jewish authors would have wanted to have conveyed the idea that God was a female, anymore than they were arguing for the idea that God was a male. God, in their view, was not a created being at all, but rather a creator of all.

Furthermore, when a New Testament author called Jesus Wisdom it is unlikely that he or she was trying to say anything about Jesus' human gender, the issue is rather about his divine character or at least his having this divine attribute. If one wishes to maintain that Wisdom refers *solely* to an aspect of what Christians call Jesus' divine nature, the use of the pronoun "she" as a metaphorical equivalent to Wisdom is not problematic. It can be argued, however, that at least from a traditional Christian point of view, this amounts to a kind of theological bifurcation that early Christian writers and the creators of the major creeds were trying to avoid. These early Christians realized that *identity* statements about *Jesus* in the New Testament are predicated of him as a person, and are not neatly parceled out to one nature or another. From this viewpoint, if one proceeds to use the pronoun "she" of Jesus as Wisdom, one would seem to many to be denying the form that Jesus' humanity actually took, or denying that it matters what form his humanity took, or at the very least confusing the issue. I would stress that one must beware of making a gender issue out of material that was not intentionally making gender claims.

Some contemporary sophialogies would seem to be at odds with the kind of incarnational thinking found in the Christological hymns especially in John 1, for they suggest a docetic Christ, a Christ whose particular historical human form is irrelevant.[5] This approach also involves the problem of deliberate anachronism, which is a serious problem when one is dealing with the faith of Jews or Christians, faiths strongly grounded in history. Some will argue that it *might* be more fruitful for those wishing to construct a sophialogy to pursue the associations found in the Wisdom of Solomon, where the Spirit and Wisdom are identified or closely associated.[6] It is too early to tell whether this approach will bear fruit.

Though this pilgrimage through biblical Wisdom is now at an end, the pilgrimage of Wisdom continues. It is hoped that this study will have advanced the understanding of that pilgrimage in some measure. If it sets someone else on the trail of Wisdom, trying to track down Wisdom, I will be content.

---

[5] This impression is especially created by the evident willingness to substitute "she" for "he" in the stories about Jesus in the Gospels. Among other things, this move does not respect the historical givenness of the text. Cf. Now my article "Three Modern Facts of Wisdom" 96–122.

[6] This approach too would not be entirely without problems for Trinitarian theology. Potentially it would set up a triad of God as father, Spirit as mother, and Jesus as son, in short, a heavenly family. Then indeed it would seem we have imported into the deity a gendered character to *all three* members of the Trinity, and a gendered way of viewing the interrelationships within the Trinity (e.g. the Spirit becomes mother of Jesus, something not even Luke 1:35 suggests). This would surely be at odds with the argument, by some feminists as well as others, that God is spirit, which is to say, God is an *a-sexual being*. Thus, this approach seems to create as many problems as it solves.

Bibliography

Most standard English commentaries and reference works such as grammars are not included in this bibliography. The standard JBL abbreviations for journals are used.

CHAPTER 1: BEGINNING THE JOURNEY

Albright, W. F. "Some Canaanite–Phoenician Sources of Hebrew Wisdom," in *Wisdom and the Ancient Near East*, ed. M. Noth and D. T. Winston (Leiden: E. J. Brill, 1955), 1–45.

Alt, A. "Zur Literarischen Analyse der Weisheit des Amenemope," in *Wisdom in Israel and the Ancient Near East*, ed. M. Noth and D. W. Thomas (Leiden: E. J. Brill, 1960), 16–25.

Amsler, S. "La sagesse de la femme," in *La Sagesse de l'Ancien Testament*, ed. M. Gilbert (Leuven University Press, 1979), 112–16.

Brueggemann, W. "The Social Significance of Solomon as a Patron of Wisdom," in *The Sage in Israel and the Ancient Near East*, ed. J. G. Gammie and L. G. Perdue (Winona Lake: Eisenbrauns, 1990), 126–32.

Bryce, G. E. *A Legacy of Wisdom. The Egyptian Contribution to the Wisdom of Israel* (Lewisburg: Bucknell University Press, 1979).

Camp, C. "The Female Sage in the Biblical Wisdom Literature," in *The Sage in Israel and the Ancient Near East*, ed. J. G. Gammie and L. G. Perdue (Winona Lake: Eisenbrauns, 1990), 185–204.

——*Wisdom and the Feminine in the Book of Proverbs* (Sheffield: JSOT Press, 1985).

——"Woman Wisdom as Root Metaphor: A Theological Consideration" in *The Listening Heart. Essays in Wisdom and the Psalms in Honor of R.E. Murphy*, ed. K. G. Hoglund, *et al.* (Sheffield: JSOT Press, 1987), 45–76.

Childs, B. S. *Introduction to the Old Testament as Scripture* (Philadelphia: Fortress, 1979).

Clements, R. E. *Wisdom for a Changing World. Wisdom in Old Testament Theology* (Berkeley: Bibal Press, 1990).

Clifford, R. J. "Proverbs IX: A Suggested Ugaritic Parallel," *VT* 25 (1975), 298–306.

Collins, J. J. "Proverbial Wisdom and the Yahwist Vision," in *Gnomic Wisdom*, ed. J. D. Crossan (Chico, CA: Scholars' Press, 1980), 1–18.

Conzelmann, H. "Die Mutter der Weisheit," in *Zeit und Geschichte. Festschrift für R. Bultmann* 2, ed. E. Dinkler (Tübingen: J.C.B. Mohr, 1964), 225–34.

Craigie, P. "Wisdom Literature," *Baker Encyclopedia*, Vol. 2, 2149.

Cranford, J. "Wisdom Personified," *Bib IL* 15 (4, 1989), 37–39.

Crenshaw, J. L. "The Acquisition of Knowledge in Israelite Wisdom Literature" *Word and World* (7, 1987), 245–52.

——*Ecclesiastes* (Philadelphia: Westminster Press, 1987).

——"Education in Ancient Israel," *JBL* 104 (1985), 601–615.

——*Old Testament Wisdom. An Introduction* (Atlanta: John Knox, 1981).

——"The Sage in Proverbs," in *The Sage in Israel and the Ancient Near East* (Winona Lake: Eisenbrauns, 1990), 205–216.

——"The Wisdom Literature," *The Hebrew Bible and its Modern Interpreters*, eds. D. A. Knight and G. M. Tucker (Philadelphia: Fortress, 1985), 378.

Crüsemann, F. "The Unchangeable World: The `Crisis of Wisdom' in Koheleth," in *God of the Lowly. Socio–Historical Interpretations of the Bible*, ed. W. Schottroff and W. Stegemann (Maryknoll: Orbis Books, 1984), 57–77.

Farmer, K. A. *Proverbs and Ecclesiastes. Who Knows what is Good?* (Grand Rapids: Eerdmans, 1991).

Fontaine, C. *Traditional Sayings in the Old Testament. A Contextual Study* (Sheffield: Almond Press, 1982).

Fox, M. V. "Aging and Death in Qohelet 12," *JSOT* 42 (1988), 55–77.

——"Frame–Narrative and Composition in the Book of Qohelet," *HUCA* 48 (1968), 83–106.

——"The Meaning of *Hebel* for Qohelet," *JBL* 105 (1986), 409–27.

——*Qoheleth and his Contradictions* (Sheffield: Almond Press, 1989).

——"Qohelet's Epistemology," *HUCA* 58 (1987), 37–55.

Gammie, J. G. "Stoicism and Anti–Stoicism in Qoheleth," *Hebrew Annual Review* 9 (1985), 169–87.

Gemser, B. *Sprüche Salomos* (Tübingen: J. C. B. Mohr, 1963).

Gese, H. *Lehre und Wirchlichkeit in der alten Weisheit* (Tübingen: J. C. B. Mohr, 1958).

Gilbert, M. "Le Discours de la Sagesse en Proverbes 8," in *La Sagesse de l'Ancien Testament*, ed. M. Gilbert (Gembloux: Leuven U. Press, 1979), 202–218.

Ginsberg, H. L. "The Structure and Contents of the Book of Qohelet," in *Wisdom in Israel and in the Ancient Near East*, ed. M. Noth and D. W. Thomas (Leiden: E. J. Brill, 1960), 138–49.

Gordis, R. "The Social Background of Wisdom Literature," *HUCA* 18 (1944), 77–118.

Heaton, E. W. *Solomon's New Men. The Emergence of Ancient Israel as a National State* (New York: Pica Press, 1974).

Hengel, M. *Judaism and Hellenism I.* (Philadelphia: Fortress, 1974).

Heschel, A. J. *The Prophets* (New York: Harper and Row, 1962).

Jamieson–Drake, D. W. *Scribes and Schools in Monarchic Judah. A Socio–Archeological Approach* (Sheffield: Almond Press, 1991).

Johnson, E. A. "Jesus the Wisdom of God. A Biblical Basis for a Non–Androcentric Christology," *ETL* 61 (1985), 261–94.

Kayatz, C. *Studien zu Proverbien 1–9* (Neukirchen: Neukirchen Verlag, 1966).

Kidner, D. A. *The Wisdom of Proverbs, Job, and Ecclesiastes* (Downer's Grove: IV Press, 1985).

——*Proverbs* (Downer's Grove: I-V Press, 1967).

Kitchen, K. A. "Some Egyptian Background to the OT," *Tyndale House Bulletin* 5–6 (1960), 4ff.

Lang, B. *Frau Weisheit. Deutung einer biblischer Gestalt* (Düsseldorf: Patmos Verlag, 1975).

——*Die weisheitliche Lehrrede. Eine Untersuchung von Spruche 1–7* (Stuttgart: KBW Verlag, 1972).

——*Wisdom and the Book of Proverbs. A Hebrew Goddess Redefined* (New York: Pilgrim Press, 1986).

Laumann, M. "Qoheleth and Time," *The Bible Today* 27 (1989), 305–10.

Leeuwen, R. C. van "Liminality and Worldview in Proverbs 1–9," in *Semeia* 50: *Parenesis: Act and Form*, ed. L. G. Perdue and J. G. Gammie (Atlanta: Scholars Press, 1990), 111–44.

Loader, J. A. *Polar Opposites in the Book of Qohelet* (Berlin: W. de Gruyter, 1979).

Loretz, O. *Qohelet und der Alte Orient* (Freiburg: Herder, 1964).

Mack, B. *Logos und Sophia. Untersuchungen zur Weisheitstheologie im hellenistischen Judentum* (Göttingen: Vandehoeck and Ruprecht, 1973).

——"Wisdom, Myth and Mythology," *INT* 24 (1970), 46–60.

Malina, B. *The New Testament World; Insights from Cultural Anthropology* (Atlanta: John Knox Press, 1981).

Marcus, R. "On Biblical Hypostases of Wisdom," *HUCA* 23 (1950–51), 157–71.

McKane, W. *Proverbs* (Philadelphia: Westminster, 1977).

Murphy, R. E. "The Faith of Qoheleth," *Word and World* 7 (1987), 253–260.

——"The Faces of Wisdom in the Book of Proverbs," in *Mélanges bibliques et orientaux en l'honneur de M. Henri Cazelles*, ed. A. Caquot and M. Delcor (Neukirchen: Nuekirchen Verlag, 1981), 337–45.

——*The Forms of Old Testament Literature. Vol. XIII Wisdom Literature* (Grand Rapids: Eerdmans, 1981).

——"Qoheleth's Quarrel with the Fathers," in *From Faith to Faith. Essays for D. Miller*, ed. D. Y. Hadidian (Pittsburgh: Pickwick Press, 1979), 235–45.

——"The Sage in Ecclesiastes and Qoheleth the Sage," in *The Sage in Israel and the Ancient Near East*. ed. J. G. Gammie and L. G. Perdue (Winona Lake: Eisenbrauns, 1990), 263–71.

——*The Tree of Life* (New York: Doubleday, 1990).

——"Wisdom's Song: Proverbs 1:20–33," *CBQ* 48 (1986), 456–460.

Plöger, O. *Sprüche Salomos (Proverbia)* (Neukirchen: Neukirchen Verlag, 1984).

Pury, A. de "Sagesse et Revelation dans l'Ancien Testament," *RTP* 27 (1977), 1–50.

Rad, G. von *Old Testament Theology* I (New York: Harper and Row, 1965).

——*Wisdom in Israel* (Nashville: Abingdon Press, 1988 rep.).

Ringgren, H. *Word and Wisdom. Studies in the Hypostatization of Divine Qualities and Functions in the Ancient Near East* (Lund: Ohlssons, 1947).

Robinson, H. Wheeler, *Inspiration and Revelation in the Old Testament* (New York: Oxford U. Press, 1946).

Schoors, A. "The Pronouns in Qoheleth," *Hebrew Studies* 30 (1989), 71–87.

Scott, R. B. Y. "Solomon and the Beginnings of Wisdom in Israel," in *Wisdom in Israel and the Ancient Near East*, ed. M. North and D. W. Thomas (Leiden: E. J. Brill, 1960), 262–79.

——*The Way of Wisdom in the Old Testament* (New York: Collier, 1971).

Shupak, N. "The *Sitz im Leben* of Proverbs in the Light of a Comparison of Biblical and Egyptian Wisdom," *RB* 94 (1987), 98–117.

Thompson, J. M. *The Form and Function of Proverbs in Ancient Israel* (Paris: Mouton, 1974).

Walton, J. H. *Ancient Israelite Literature in its Cultural Context* (Grand Rapids: Eerdmans, 1989).

Whybray, R. N. *Ecclesiastes* (Grand Rapids: Eerdmans, 1989).

——*The Intellectual Tradition in the Old Testament* (Berlin: Walter de Gruyter, 1974).

——"The Sage in the Israelite Royal Court," in *The Sage in Israel and the Ancient Near East*, ed. J. G. Gammie and L. G. Perdue (Winona Lake: Eisenbrauns, 1990), 133–40.

——*Wealth and Poverty in the Book of Proverbs* (Sheffield: JSOT Press, 1990).

Williams, J. G. *Those Who Ponder Proverbs* (Sheffield: Almond Press, 1981).

Wilson, F. M. "Sacred or Profane? The Yahwistic Redaction of Proverbs Reconsidered," in *The Listening Heart. Essays in Wisdom and the Psalms in Honour of R. E. Murphy*, ed. K. G. Hoglund, *et al.* (Sheffield: JSOT Press, 1987), 313–34.

Witherington, B., III, *Women in the Ministry of Jesus* (Cambridge University Press, 1984).

Wright, A. "The Riddle of the Sphinx: The Structure of the Book of Qoheleth," *CBQ* 30 (1968), 313–34.

——"The Riddle of the Sphinx Revisited: Numerical Patterns in the Book of Qoheleth," *CBQ* 42 (1980), 38–51.

CHAPTER 2: WISDOM AT A TURNING POINT

Beauchamp, P. "Épouser la Sagesse – ou n'épouser qu'elle? Une énigme du Livre de la Sagesse," in *La Sagesse de l'Ancien Testament*, ed. M. Gilbert (Leuven University Press, 1979), 347–369.

——"Le salut corporel des justes et la conclusion du livre de la Sagesse," *Bib* 45 (1964), 491–526

Beentjes, P. C. "Full Wisdom is Fear of the Lord," *Est Bib* 47 (1989), 27–45.

Blenkinsopp, J. *Wisdom and Law in the Old Testament* (Oxford University Press, 1983).

Boccaccini, G. *Middle Judaism. Jewish Thought 300 B.C.E. to 200 C.E.* (Minneapolis: Fortress, 1991).

Cadbury, H. J. "The Grandson of Ben Sira," *HTR* 46 (1955), 219–25.

Crenshaw, J. L. "The Problem of Theodicy in Sirach: on Human Bondage," *JBL* 94 (1975), 47–64.

Di Lella, A. A. "Conservative and Progressive Theology: Ben Sira and Wisdom," *CBQ* 28 (1966), 139–54.

Gammie, J. G. "The Sage in Sirach" in *The Sage in Israel and the Ancient Near East*, ed. J. G. Gammie and L. G. Perdue (Winona Lake: Eisenbrauns, 1990), 355–71.

Gilbert, M. "The Book of Ben Sira; Implications for Jewish and Christian Traditions," in *Jewish Civilization in the Hellenistic–Roman Period*, ed. S. Talmon (Philadelphia: Trinity Press Int., 1991), 81–91.

——"L'Éloge de la Sagesse, (Siracide 24)," *RTL* 5 (1974), 326–48.

Grelot, P. "L'Eschatologie de la Sagesse et les Apocalypses Juives," in *A la Recontre de Dieu. Memorial Albert Gelin* (Le Puy: Xavier Mappus, 1961), 165–78.

Hamp, V. "Zukunft und Jenseits im Buche Sirach," in *AT Studien, Festschrift Nötscher* (Bonn: Hanstein, 1950), 86–97.

Kloppenborg, J. S. "Isis and Sophia in the Book of Wisdom," *HTR* 75.1 (1982), 57–84.

Larcher, C. *Études sur le Livre de la Sagesse* (Paris: Gabalda Press, 1969).

Lee, T. R. *Studies in the Form of Sirach 44–50* (Atlanta: Scholars' Press, 1986).

Lefkowitz M. R. and M. B. Fant, *Women in Greece and Rome* (Baltimore: John Hopkins University Press, 1982).

Levison, J. "Is Eve to Blame? A Contextual Analysis of Sir. 25.24," *CBQ* 47 (1985), 617–23.

Mack, B. L. *Wisdom and the Hebrew Epic* (University of Chicago Press, 1985).

——"Wisdom makes a Difference: Alternatives to Messianic Configurations," in *Judaism and their Messiahs at the Turn of the Christian Era*, ed. J. Neusner, *et al.* (Cambridge University Press, 1987), 15–48.

Marböck, J. *Weisheit im Wandel* (Bonn: Hanstein Verlag, 1971).

Marcus, R. "On Biblical Hypostases of Wisdom," *HUCA* 23 (1953), 157–71.

Martin, J. D. "Ben Sira – a Child of His Time," in *A Word in Season. Essays in*

Honour of William McKane, eds. J. D. Martin and P. R. Davies (Sheffield: JSOT Press, 1986), 143–61.

Middendorp, T. *Die Stellung Jesu Ben Siras zwischen Judentum und Hellenismus* (Leiden: E.J. Brill, 1973).

Murphy, R. E. "To Know Your Might is the Root of Immortality (Wis. 15.3)," *CBQ* 25 (1963), 88–93.

Nelson, M. D. *The Syriac Version of the Wisdom of Ben Sira compared to the Greek and Hebrew Materials* (Atlanta: Scholars' Press, 1988).

Orlinsky, H. "Some Terms in the Prologue to ben Sira and the Hebrew Canon," *JBL* 110 (3, 1991), 483–490.

Pautrel, R. "Ben Sira et le Stoicisme," *Recherches de Science Religieuse* 51 (1963), 535–49.

Places, E. de "Le Livre de la Sagesse et les influences grecques," *Bib* 50 (1969), 536–42.

Reese, J. M. *Hellenistic Influence on the Book of Wisdom and its Consequences* (Rome: Pontifical Institute Press, 1970).

——"Plan and Structure in the Book of Wisdom," *CBQ* 27 (1965), 391–99.

Rickenbacher, O. *Weisheit Perikopen bei Ben Sira* (Göttingen: Vandenhoeck and Ruprecht, 1973).

Roth, W. "On the Gnomic–Discursive Wisdom of Jesus ben Sirach," *Semeia* 17, *Gnomic Wisdom* (Chico, CA: Scholars Press, 1980), 59–79.

Sanders, E. P. *Paul and Palestinian Judaism* (London: SCM, 1977).

Sanders, J. T. *Ben Sira and Demotic Wisdom* (Chico, CA: Scholars' Press, 1983).

——"Ben Sira's Ethics of Caution," *HUCA* 50 (1979), 73–106.

Schnabel, E. J. *Law and Wisdom from Ben Sira to Paul* (Tübingen: J. C. B. Mohr, 1985).

Segal, M. Z. *Seper Ben Sira' Hasalem* (Jerusalem: Bialik Foundation, 1972).

Sheppard, G. T. *Wisdom as a Hermeneutical Construct* (New York: De Gruyter, 1980).

Skehan, P. W. "Structures in Poems on Wisdom: Proverbs 8 and Sirach 24," *CBQ* 41 (1979), 365–79.

——and A. A. Di Lella, *The Wisdom of Ben Sira* (New York: Doubleday, 1987).

Smend, R. *Die Weisheit des Jesus Sirach. Hebräisch und Deutsch* (Berlin: Georg Reimer, 1906).

Suggs, M. J. *Wisdom, Christology, and Law in Matthew's Gospel* (Cambridge: Harvard University Press, 1970).

——"Wisdom of Solomon 2:10–51.: A Homily Based on the Fourth Servant Song," *JBL* 76 (1957), 26–33.

Trenchard, W. C. *Ben Sira's View of Women: a Literary Analysis* (Chico, CA: Scholars' Press, 1982).

Winston, D. "The Sage as Mystic in the Wisdom of Solomon," in *The Sage in Israel and the Ancient Near East*, ed. J. G. Gammie and L. G. Perdue (Winona Lake: Eisenbrauns, 1990), 383–97.

——*The Wisdom of Solomon* (Garden City: Doubleday, 1979).

Witherington, B., III, *Women and the Genesis of Christianity* (Cambridge University Press), 1990.
——*Jesus, Paul, and the End of the World* (Grand Rapids: I-V Press, 1992).
——*The Christology of Jesus* (Minneapolis: Fortress, 1990).
Wright, A. W. "The Structure of Wisdom 11–19," *CBQ* 27 (1965), 28–34.
Zimmermann, F. "The Book of Wisdom: Its Language and Character," *Jewish Quarterly Review* 57 (1966), 1–27, 101–35.

CHAPTER 3: HOKMAH MEETS SOPHIA

Batey, R. A. *Jesus and the Forgotten City* (Grand Rapids: Baker Book House, 1991).
Charlesworth, J. H. ed. *Jesus' Jewishness. Exploring the Place of Jesus in Early Judaism* (New York: Crossroad, 1991).
Crossan, J. D. *The Historical Jesus. The Life of a Mediterranean Jewish Peasant* (San Francisco: Harper, 1991).
Downing, F. G. *Christ and the Cynics: Jesus and Other Radicals in First Century Traditions* (Sheffield: JSOT Press, 1988).
——*Jesus and the Threat of Freedom* (London: SCM, 1987).
Feldmann, L. H. "How Much Hellenism in Jewish Palestine?" *HUCA* 57 (1986), 83–111.
Ferguson, E. *Backgrounds of Early Christianity* (Grand Rapids: Eerdmans, 1987).
Freyne, S. *Galilee, Jesus and the Gospels* (Philadelphia: Fortress, 1988).
Hengel, M. *The Hellenization of Judea in the First Century after Christ* (Philadelphia: Trinity, 1989).
Horsley, G. H. R. *New Documents Illustrating Early Christianity* (North Ryde, Aus: Macquarie University, 1984).
Jaeger, W. *Early Christianity and Greek Paideia* (New York: Oxford University Press, 1961).
Mack, B. *A Myth of Innocence* (Philadelphia: Fortress, 1988).
Malherbe, A. *The Cynic Epistles* (Missoula: Scholars Press, 1977).
Meier, J. P. *A Marginal Jew. Rethinking the Historical Jesus*, Vol. I (New York: Doubleday, 1991).
Nock, A. D. *Conversion* (Oxford University Press, 1933).
Overman J. A. "Deciphering the Origins of Christianity" in *Int.* 44:2 (1990), 193–95.
Peters, F. E. *The Harvest of Hellenism. A History of the Near East from Alexander the Great to the Triumph of Christianity* (New York: Simon and Schuster, 1970).
Robbins, V. K. *Jesus the Teacher, a Socio–Rhetorical Interpretation of Mark* (Philadelphia: Fortress, 1984).
Scott, B. B. "Jesus as Sage: an Innovating Voice in Common Wisdom," *The Sage in Israel and the Ancient Near East*, ed. J. G. Gammie and L. G. Perdue (Winona Lake: Eisenbrauns, 1990), 399–415.

Segal, A. F. "The Cost of Proselytism and Conversion," *SBL 1988 Seminar Papers* (Atlanta: Scholars' Press, 1988), 336–69.

Stowers, S. K. *The Diatribe and Paul's Letter to the Romans* (Chico, CA: Scholars Press, 1981).

Witherington, B. III, "On the Road with Mary Magdalene, Joanna, Susanna, and other disciples: Luke 8.1–3," *ZNW* 70 (3–4, 1979), 242–48.

CHAPTER 4: WISDOM IN PERSON

Achtemeir, P. "*Omne Verbum Sonat*: The New Testament and the Oral Environment of Late Western Antiquity," *JBL* 109.1 (1990), 3–27.

Allison, D. and W. D. Davies, *The Gospel According to Saint Matthew*, 2 Vols. (Edinburgh: T&T Clark, 1991).

Aune, D. "Oral Tradition and the Aphorisms of Jesus," *Jesus and the Oral Gospel*, ed. H. Wansborough (Sheffield: Sheffield Press, 1991), 242–58.

Bacchiocchi, S. "Matthew 11.28–30: Jesus' Rest and the Sabbath," *Andrews Sem. Studies* 22 (1984), 289–316.

Bailey, J. L. and L. D. Van der Broek, *Literary Forms in the New Testament* (Louisville: Westminster/John Knox, 1992).

Baird, J. A. *Discovering the Power of the Gospel* (Akron: Hampshire Books, 1989).

Beardslee, W. A. "Saving One's Life by Losing It," *JAAR* 47 (1979), 57–72.

Best, E. "Uncomfortable Words: VII. The Camel and the Needle's Eye (Mk 10.25)," *ET* 82 (1970–71), 83–89.

Betz, H. D. "The Logion of the Easy Yoke and of Rest (Matt. 11.28–30)," *JBL* 86 (1967), 10–24.

Blomberg, C. L. *Interpreting the Parables* (Downer's Grove: I–V Press, 1990).

Borg, M. *Conflict, Holiness, and Politics in the Teaching of Jesus* (New York: Edwin Mellen, 1984).

Boring, M. E. *The Continuing Voice of Jesus' Christian Prophecy and the Gospel Tradition* (Louisville: Westminster, 1991).

Boucher, M. I. *The Parables* (Wilmington: Michael Glazier, 1983).

Brooke, G. "The Feast of New Wine and the Question of Fasting," *ET* 95 (1983–84), 175–76.

Brosend , W. F. "The Recovery of Allegory," (Ph.D. Thesis: University of Chicago, 1992).

Brown, R. E. *New Testament Essays* (Garden City: Image Books, 1968).

Brown, S. "Reader Response: Demythologizing the Text," *NTS* 34 (1988), 232–37.

Buchler, A. "Learning and Teaching in the Open Air in Palestine," *JQR* 4 (1913–14), 485–91.

Bultmann, R. *De Geschichte der Synoptishen Tradition* (Göttingen: Vandenhoeck and Ruprecht, 8th edn. 1967; ET New York: 1963).

Burney, C. F. *The Poetry of Our Lord* (Oxford: Clarendon Press, 1925).

Carlston, C. E. "Proverbs, Maxims, and the Historical Jesus," *JBL* (1980), 87–105.

Catchpole, D. "The Beginning of Q," *NTS* 38 (2, 1992), 205–221.

Crenshaw, J. L. "Riddle," *IDB Sup* (Nashville: Abingdon, 1976), 749–50.

Crossan, J. D. *Cliffs of Fall: Paradox and Polylvalence in the Parables of Jesus* (New York: Seabury Press, 1980).

——*A Fragile Craft: The Work of Amos N. Wilder* (Missoula: Scholars Press, 1981).

——*In Fragments. The Aphorisms of Jesus* (San Francisco: Harper & Row, 1983).

——"Parable and Example in the Teaching of Jesus," *Semeia* 14 (1974), 63–104.

——"The Servant Parables of Jesus," *Semeia* 1 (1974), 17–55.

Curtis, W. A. "The Parable of the Laborers (Matt. xx.1–16)," *ET* 38 (1926–27), 5–10.

Daube, D. "Public Pronouncement and Private Explanation in the Gospels," *ET* 57 (1945–46), 175–77.

Davies, W. D. *The Setting of the Sermon on the Mount* (Cambridge University Press, 1964).

Derrett, J. D. M. "A Camel through the Eye of a Needle," *NTS* 32 (1986), 465–70.

——*Studies in the New Testament*, Vol. 1 (Leiden: E. J. Brill, 1977).

——"Law in the New Testament: Fresh Light on the Parable of the Good Samaritan," *NTS* 10 (1964), 22–37.

——*Historical Tradition in the Fourth Gospel* (Cambridge University Press, 1963).

——*The Parables of the Kingdom* (New York: Scribners, 1963).

Donahue, J. R. *The Gospel in Parables* (Philadelphia: Fortress, 1980).

Drury, J. *The Parables in the Gospels* (New York: Crossroad, 1989).

Dupont, J. *Les beatitudes*, 3 vols. (Louvain: Nauwelaerts, 1958, 1969, 1973).

——"Beatitudes egytiennes," *Bib* 47 (1966), 185–222.

——"Vin Vieux, Vin Nouveau (Luc 5,39)," *CBQ* 25 (1963), 286–304.

Feldman, A. *The Parables and Similes of the Rabbis. Agricultural and Pastoral* (Cambridge University Press, 1927).

Flusser, D. "Do You Prefer New Wine?" *Immanuel* 9 (1979), 26–31.

Funk, R. W. "The Old Testament in Parable: A Study of Luke 10.25–37," *Encounter* 26 (1965), 251–67.

——*et al., The Parables of Jesus* (Sonoma: Polebridge Press, 1988).

Gerhardsson, B. "If We Do not Cut the Parables out of their Frames," *NTS* 37 (1991), 321–335.

——"The Narrative Meshalim in the Synoptic Gospels," *NTS* 34 (1988), 339–63.

Gryglewicz, F. "The Gospel of the Overworked Workers," *CBQ* 19 (1957), 190–98.

Guelich, R. *Mark. 1.1, 8.26* (Waco: Word, 1989).

——*The Sermon on the Mount. A Foundation for Understanding* (Waco: Word, 1982).

Hirsch, E. D. *Validity in Interpretation* (New Haven: Yale University Press, 1967).

Hultgren, A. J. *Jesus and His Adversaries: The Form and Function of the Conflict Stories in the Synoptic Tradition* (Minneapolis: Augsburg, 1979).

Hunter, A. M. "Crux Criticorum – Matt. XI.25–30 – A Re-Appraisal," *NTS* 8 (1961–62), 241–49.

Iser, W. *The Act of Reading: A Theory of Aesthetic Response* (Baltimore: Johns Hopkins University Press, 1978).

Jeremias, J. *The Parables of Jesus* (New York: Harper and Row, 1963).

Jeremias, J. *Unknown Sayings of Jesus* (London: SCM, 1957).

Jülicher, A. *Die Gleichnisreden Jesu.* Vol. 1 (Darmstadt: Wissenschaftliche Buchgesellschaft, 1963).

Keck, L. E. *A Future for the Historical Jesus* (Nashville: Abingdon, 1971).

Kee, A. "The Old Coat and the New Wine," *NovT* 12 (1970), 13–21.

Kermode, F. *The Genesis of Secrecy: On the Interpretation of Narrative* (Cambridge: Harvard University Press, 1979).

Kloppenborg, J. S. *The Formation of Q* (Philadelphia: Fortress, 1987).

——*Q Parallels* (Sonoma: Polebridge Press, 1986).

Köbert, R. "Kamel und Schiffstau: zu Markus 10.25 (Par.) und Koran 7,40/38," *Bib* 53 (1972), 229–33.

Lakeoff, G. and M. Johnson, *Metaphors We Live By* (University of Chicago Press, 1980).

Lane, W. L. *The Gospel According to Mark* (Grand Rapids: Eerdmans, 1974).

Lauterbach, J. Z. "Ancient Jewish Allegorists," *JQR* 1 (1910–11), 301–33.

Lentricchia, F. *After the New Criticism* (University of Chicago Press, 1980).

Luz, U. *Matthew 1–7* (Minneapolis: Augsburg, 1989).

MacArthur, H. K. and R. M. Johnston, *They Also Taught in Parables* (Grand Rapids: Zondervan, 1990).

Mack, B. *Rhetoric and the New Testament* (Minneapolis: Fortress, 1990).

McEleney, N. "The Beatitudes of the Sermon on the Mount/Plain," *CBQ* 43 (1981), 1–13.

Maher, M. "`Take my Yoke upon You' (Matt. XI.29)," *NTS* 22 (1975–76), 97–103.

Marshall, I. H. *The Gospel of Luke* (Exeter: Paternoster Press, 1978).

Michaelis, C. "Die `p'-Alliteration der Subjektsworte der ersten 4 Seligpreisungen in Mt. V.3–6 und ihre Bedeutung für den Aufbau der Seligpreisungen bei Mt., Lk. und in Q," *NovT* 10 (1968), 148–61.

Motte, A. R. "La Structure du Logion de Matthieu," *RB* 88 (1981), 226–233.

Nolland, J. *Luke 1 — 9.20* (Waco: Word, 1989), 305–07.

Perdue, L. G. "The Wisdom Sayings of Jesus," *Forum* 2 (1986), 3–35.

Perkins, P. *Jesus as Teacher* (Cambridge University Press, 1990).

Pesch, R. *Markusevangelium*, 2 vols. (Freiberg: Herder, 1976).

Piper, R. *Wisdom in the Q Tradition: The Aphoristic Teaching of Jesus* (Cambridge University Press, 1989).

Ramaroson, L. "Comme `Le Bon Samaritain', ne chercher qu'a aimer (Lc. 10,29–37)," *Bib* 56 (1975), 533–36.

Rebell, W. "'Sein Leben verlieren' (Mark 8.35 parr.) also Strukturmoment vorund nachosterlichen Glaubens," *NTS* 35 (1989), 202–18.

Ricoeur, P. "Biblical Hermeneutics," *Semeia* 4 (1975), 29–148.

——*Interpretation Theory: Discourse and the Surplus of Meaning* (Fort Worth: Texas Christian University Press, 1976).

Riesner, R. *Jesus als Lehrer* (Tübingen: J. C. B. Mohr, 1984).

——"Jesus as Preacher and Teacher," in *Jesus and the Oral Gospel*, ed. H. Wansborough (Sheffield: Sheffield Press, 1991), 185–210.

Ru, G. de "Reward in the Teaching of Jesus," *NovT* 8 (1966), 202–22.

Schneiders, S. M. *The Revelatory Text* (San Francisco: Harper, 1991).

Schweizer, E. *The Good News According to Mark* (Atlanta: John Knox Press, 1970).

Scott, B. B. *Hear Then the Parable. A Commentary on the Parables of Jesus* (Minneapolis: Fortress, 1989).

Sellin, G. "Lukas als Gelichniserzähler: Die Erzählung vom barmherzigen Samariter (Luke 10, 25–37)," *ZNW* 66 (1975), 19–60.

Stein, R. H. *An Introduction to the Parables of Jesus* (Philadelphia: Westminster, 1981).

Talmon, S. "Oral Transmission and Written Transmission, or the Heard and Seen Word in Judaism of the Second Temple Period," in *Jesus and the Oral Gospel*, ed. H. Wansborough (Sheffield: Sheffield Press, 1991), 121–58.

Tannehill, R. C. "Reading it Whole: The Function of Mark 8.34–35 in Mark's Story," *QR* (1982), 67–78.

Taylor, V. *The Gospel According to St Mark* (New York: St Martin's Press, 1966).

Tolbert, M.A. *Perspectives on the Parables* (Philadelphia: Fortress, 1979).

——*Sowing the Gospel* (Minneapolis: Fortress, 1989).

Tuckett, C. M. "The Present Son of Man," *JSNT* 14 (1982), 58–81.

Vaage, L. E. "Q and the Historical Jesus," *Forum* 5.2 (1989), 159–76.

Vermes, G. "The Jesus Notice of Josephus Re-Examined," *JJS* 38 (1987), 2–10.

Wailes, S. L. *Medieval Allegories of Jesus' Parables* (Berkeley: University of California Press, 1987).

Waller, E. "The Parable of the Leaven: Sectarian Teaching and the Inclusion of Women," *USQR* 35 (1979–80), 99–109.

Westermann, C. *The Parables of Jesus in the Light of the Old Testament* (Minneapolis: Fortress, 1990).

Wilder, A. N. *The Bible and the Literary Critic* (Minneapolis: Fortress, 1991).

——*Jesus' Parables and the War of Myths. Essays on Imagination in the Scriptures* (Philadelphia: Fortress, 1982).

Witherington, B., III "Women and their Roles in The Gospels and Ats" (Ph.D. Thesis: University of Durham, 1981).

Young, B. H. *Jesus and his Jewish Parables* (New York: Paulist Press, 1989).

Young F. and D. F. Ford, *Meaning and Truth in 2 Corinthians* (Grand Rapids: Eerdmans, 1988).

Ziesler, J. A. "The Removal of the Bridegroom: A Note on Mark II. 18–22 and Parallels," *NTS* 19 (1972–73), 190–94.

CHAPTER 5: WISDOM'S LEGACY

Adamson, J. B. "An Inductive Approach to the Epistle of James," (unpublished Ph.D. Thesis, University of Cambridge, 1954).

——*The Epistle of James* (Grand Rapids: Eerdmans, 1976).

Baasland, E. "Der Jacobusbrief als Neutestamentliche Weisheitsschrift," *Studia Theologica* 36 (2, 1982), 119–39.

Bauckham, R. *Jude and the Relatives of Jesus in the Early Church* (Edinburgh: T&T Clark, 1990).

——"Pseudo–Apostolic Letters," *JBL* 107 (1988), 469–494.

Beardslee, W. A. "The Wisdom Tradition and the Synoptic Gospels," *JAAR* 35 (1967), 231–40.

Bertrand, D. "Le fond de l'epreuve. Epitre de Jacques 1,12–18," *Christus* 30 (1983), 212–218.

Bruce, F. F. *Peter, Stephen, James, and John* (Grand Rapids: Eerdmans, 1979).

Carlston, C. E. "Wisdom and Eschatology," *Logia*, 101–19.

Childs, B. S. *The New Testament as Canon. An Introduction* (Philadelphia: Fortress, 1984).

Christ, F. *Jesus Sophia. Die Sophia Christologie bei den Synoptiken* (Zürich: Zwingli Verlag, 1970).

Conzelmann, H. *The Theology of Saint Luke* (London: Faber, 1960).

Davids, P. H. "The Epistle of James in Modern Debate," in *ANRW* II.25.5, ed. W. Haase (Berlin: W. De Gruyter, 1987), 3621–3645.

Dibelius, M. *James* (Philadelphia: Fortress, 1976).

Edwards, R. A. "Matthew's Use of Q in Chapter Eleven," *Logia*, 257–75.

——*A Theology of Q* (Philadelphia: Fortress, 1976).

Fitzmyer, J. A. "The Priority of Mark and the `Q' source in Luke," *Perspective* 11 (1970), 131–70.

Fleddermann, H. "The End of Q," *SBL Seminar Papers* (1990), 1–10.

Haenchen, E. *Der Weg Jesu*, 2nd ed. (Berlin: De Gruyter, 1968).

Hahn, F. "Die christologische Begründung urchristlicher Paränese," *ZNW* 78 (1981), 90–99.

Hartin, P. J. *James and the Q Sayings of Jesus* (Sheffield: Sheffield Press, 1991).

Hengel, M. "Der Jakobusbrief als antipaulinische Polemik," in *Tradition and Interpretation in the New Testament*, eds. G. F. Hawthorne and O. Betz (Grand Rapids: Eerdmans, 1987), 248–78.

Hill, C. C. *Hebrew and Hellenists. Reappraising Division in the Early Church* (Minneapolis: Fortress, 1992).

Horsley, R. A. "Questions about Redactional Strata and Social Relations Reflected in Q," *SBL Seminar Papers* (1989), 186–203.

Jacobson, A. D. "The Literary Unity of Q," *JBL* 101 (1982), 365–89.

——*Wisdom Christology in Q* (Ann Arbor: Univ. Microfilms, 1978).

Kee, H. C. *Christian Origins in Sociologial Perspective: Methods and Resources* (Philadelphia: Westminster, 1980).

Kirk, J. A. "The Meaning of Wisdom in James: Examination of a Hypothesis," *NTS* 16 (1969), 24–38.

Kloppenborg, J. "Wisdom Christology in Q," *Lavel Théologique et Philosophie* 34 (1978), 129–47.

——"The Formation of Q Revisited: A Response to Richard Horsley," *SBL Seminar Papers (1989)*, 204–15.

——*et al., Q, Thomas Reader* (Sonoma: Polebridge Press, 1990).

Koester, H. *Ancient Christian Gospels* (Philadelphia: Trinity, 1990).

Lührmann, D. *Die redaktion der Logienquelle* (Neukirchen–Vluyn: Neukirchen Verlag, 1969).

MacGorman, J. W. "Introducing the Book of James," *SW Journ. Theo.* 12 (1969), 9–22.

Martin, R. P. *James* (Waco: Word, 1988).

Maston, T. B. "Ethical Dimensions of James," *SWJ. Theo.* 12 (1969), 23–39.

Neirynck, F. "Recent Developments in the Study of Q," *Logia. Les Paroles de Jesus–The sayings of Jesus. Memorial Joseph Coppens*, ed. J. Delobel (Leuven University Press, 1982), 29–75.

Obermüller, R. "Hermeneutische Themen im Jakobusbrief," *Biblica* 53 (1972), 234–44.

Perdue, L. G. "Parenesis and the Epistle of James," *ZNW* 72 (1981), 241–56.

——"The Wisdom Sayings of Jesus," *Forum* 2 (3, 1986), 3–35.

Polag, A "The Text of Q," in I. Havener, *Q. The Sayings of Jesus* (Wilmington: M. Glazier, 1987).

Polhill, J. B. "The Life–Situation of the Book of James," *Rev. Exp.* 66 (1969), 369–78.

Robinson, J. M. "Early Collections of Jesus's Sayings," *Logia*, 389–94.

——"Jesus as Sophos and Sophia: Wisdom Tradition and the Gospels," *Aspects of Wisdom in Judaism and Early Christianity*, ed. R. L. Wilken (South Bend: University of Notre Dame Press, 1975), 1–16.

——"*Logoi Sophon*: On the Gattung of Q," in *Trajectories through Early Christianity* (Philadelphia: Fortress, 1971), 71–113.

Saldarini, A.J. *Pharisees, Scribes, and Sadducees* (Wilmington: M. Glazier, 1988).

Schulz, S. *Q. Die Spruchquelle der Evangelisten* (Zürich: Theologischer Verlag, 1972).

Shepherd, M. H. "The Epistle of James and the Gospel of Matthew," *JBL* 75 (1956), 40–51.

Snodgrass, K. "The Gospel of Thomas; a Secondary Gospel," *Second Century* 7 (1989–90), 19–38.

Steck, O. H. *Israel und das gewaltsame Geschick der Propheten* (Neukirchen–Vluyn: Neukirchen Verlag, 1967).

Suggs, M. J. *Wisdom, Christology, and Law in Matthew's Gospel* (Cambridge: Harvard University Press, 1970).

Taylor, V. *New Testament Essays* (Grand Rapids: Eerdmans, 1972).

Theissen, G. *The Gospels in Context. Social and Political History in the Synoptic Tradition* (Edinburgh: T&T Clark, 1992).

Tuckett, C. M. "A Cynic Q?" *Bib* 70 (1989), 349–76, here 371–72.
——"The Present Son of Man," *JSNT* 14 (1982), 58–81.
——"Thomas and the Synoptics," *NovT* 30 (1988), 132–57.
Turner, N. "The Style of the Epistle of James," in *MHT IV, A Grammar of New Testament Greek* (Edinburgh: T&T Clark, 1976, 114–20).
Witherington, B. III "Principles for Interpreting the Gospels and Acts," *ATS* 19 (1987), 35–70.

CHAPTER 6: SINGING WISDOM'S PRAISE

Ashton, J. "The Transformation of Wisdom. A Study of the Prologue of John's Gospel," *NTS* 32 (2, 1986), 161–86.
Altridge, H. W. *Hebrews* (Philadelphia: Fortress, 1989).
Balchin, J. F. "Colossians 1:15–20: an Early Christological Hymn? The Arguments from Style," *Vox Evangelica* 15 (1985), 65–94.
Barrett, C. K. *The Gospel According to John* (London: SPCK, 1978, 2nd rev. ed.).
Bultmann, R. "Der Religionsgeschitliche Hintergrund des Prologs zum Johannes–Evangelium," in *Eucharisterion Festschrift für H. Gunkel*, Vol. 2 (Göttingen: Vandehoeck and Ruprecht, 1923), 3–26.
Cerfaux, L. "L'hymne au Christ – Serviteur de Dieu (Phil. 2:6–11 = Is. 52:13 — 53:12), *Miscellanea Historica in honorem A. de Meyer*, Vol. I (Louvain University Press, 1946), 117–30.
Cranfield, C. E. B. "Some Comments on Professor J. D. G. Dunn's *Christology in the Making* with Special Reference to the Evidence of the Epistle to the Romans," in *The Glory of Christ in the New Testament*, eds. L. D. Hurst and N. T. Wright (Oxford: Clarendon Press, 1987), 267–80.
Dalton, W. J. *Christ's Proclamation to the Spirits. A Study of 1 Peter 3:18 — 4:6* (Rome: Pontifical Biblical Institute, 1965).
Deutsch, C. "Wisdom in Matthew: Transformation of a Symbol," *NovT.* 32 (1990), 13–46.
Dunn, J. D. G. *Christology in the Making* (Philadelphia: Westminster Press, 1980).
——"Was Christianity a Monotheistic Faith from the Beginning?" *SJT* 35 (4, 1982), 303–36.
Forester, W. *Gnosis. A Selection of Gnostic Texts.* Vol. 1 (Oxford: Clarendon Press, 1972).
Frankowski, J. "Early Christian Hymns Recorded in the New Testament. A Reconsideration of the Question in Light of Heb 1.3," *BZ* 27 (1983), 183–94.
Freed, E. D. "Theological Prelude and the Prologue of John's Gospel," *SJT* 32 (1979), 257–69.
Georgi, D. "Der vorPaulinische Hymnus Phil 2,6–11," in *Zeit und Geschichte Dankesgabe an R. Bultmann zum 80 Geburtstag*, ed. E. Dinkler (Tübingen: J.C.B. Mohr, 1964), 263–93.

Gese, H. *Essays on Biblical Theology* (Minneapolis: Augsburg, 1981).
Glasson, T. F. "Col. 1.18, 15 and Sirach 24," *NovT* 11 (1969), 154–56.
——"Two Notes on the Philippians Hymn (II.6–11)," *NTS* 27 (1974), 133–38.
Gundry, R. H. "The Form, Meaning and Background of the Hymn quoted in 1 Timothy 3.16," in *Apostolic History and the Gospel* (Grand Rapids: Eerdmans Publishing Co., 1970), 203–22.
Hammerton–Kelly, R. G. *Pre–existence, Wisdom, and the Son of Man* (Cambridge University Press, 1973).
Hengel, M. "Hymns and Christology," in *Between Jesus and Paul. Studies in the Earliest History of Christianity* (Philadelphia: Fortress, 1983), 78–96.
——"Psalm 110 und die Erhöhung des Auferstandenen zur Rechten Gottes," in *Anfänge der Christologie*, eds. C. Breytenbach and H. Paulsen (Göttingen: Vandenhoeck and Ruprecht, 1991), 43–73.
——*The Son of God* (Philadelphia: Fortress, 1976).
Holladay, C. R. "New Testament Christology: Some Considerations of Method," *NovT* 25 (1983), 257–78.
Hooker, M. D. "The Johannine Prologue and the Messianic Secret," *NTS* 21 (1974), 40–58.
Hoover, R. W. "The Harpagmos Enigma: a Philological Solution," *HTR* 64 (1971), 95–119.
Howard, G. "Phil. 2.6–11 and the Human Christ," *CBQ* 40 (1978), 368–87.
Hughes, G. *Hebrews and Hermeneutics* (Cambridge University Press, 1979).
Humphrey, H. M. "Jesus as Wisdom in Mark," *BTB* 19 (1989), 48–53.
Hurst, L. D. "The Christology of Hebrews 1 and 2," in *The Glory of Christ in the New Testament. Studies in Christology*, eds. L. D. Hurst and N. T. Wright (Oxford: Clarendon Press, 1987), 151–64.
Hurtado, L. W. *One God, One Lord. Early Christian Devotion and Ancient Jewish Monotheism* (Philadelphia: Fortress, 1988).
——"Jesus as Lordly Example in Philippians 2.5–11," *From Jesus to Paul. Studies in Honour of F. W. Beare*, ed. P. Richardson and J. C. Hurd (Waterloo: Wilfrid Laurier University Press, 1984), 113–26.
Jeremias, J. "Zum Logos–Problem," *ZNW* 59 (1968), 82–85.
——"Zu Phil. 2.7," *NovT* 6 (1963), 182–88.
Jeremias, J. *The Servant of God* (Naperville: Allenson, 1957).
——*Die Briefe an Timotheus und Titus. Der Brief an der Hebräer* (Göttingen: Vandenhoek and Ruprecht, 1963).
Jervell, J. *Imago Dei. Gen. 1.26f im Spätjudentum, in der Gnosis und in den paulinischen Briefen* (Göttingen: Vandenhoeck and Ruprecht, 1960).
Käsemann, E. *The Wandering People of God. An Investigation of the Letter to the Hebrews* (Minneapolis: Augsburg, 1984).
Kelly, J. N. D. *A Commentary on the Pastoral Epistles* (London: A&C Black, 1963).
Lane, W. L. *Hebrews 1–8* (Waco: Word, 1991).
Lightfoot, J. B. *St Paul's Epistle to the Philippians* (London: Macmillan, 1898).

Mackinnon, D. M. "Review of Dunn's *Christology in the Making*", *SJT* 35 (4, 1982), 362–64.

MacMullen, R. *Paganism in the Roman Empire* (New Haven: Yale University Press, 1981).

Marshall, I. H. "Incarnational Christology in the New Testament," in *Christ the Lord. Studies in Christology Presented to Donald Guthrie*, ed. H. H. Rowdon (Downer's Grove: I–V Press, 1982), 1–16.

——*Carmen Christi: Philippians 2.5–11* (Grand Rapids: Eerdmans, 1983).

——"Some Reflections on New Testament Hymns," in *Christ the Lord. Studies Presented to Donald Guthrie*, ed. H. H. Rowden (Leicester: I-V Press, 1982), 37–49.

Meier, J. P. "Structure and Theology in Heb. 1.1–4," *Bib* 66 (2, 1985), 168–89.

Minear, P. S. "'We Don't Know Where...' John 20:2," *IN T* 30 (1976), 125–39.

Moule, C. F. D. "Further Reflexions on Phil. 2.5–11," in *Apostolic History and the Gospel*, eds. W. W. Gasque and R. P. Martin (Exeter: Pater Noster, 1970), 264–76.

——"Review of Dunn's *Christology*" *JTS* n.s. 33 (1982), 259–63.

Murphy O'Connor, J. "Christological Anthropology in Phil. 2.6–11," *RB* 83 (1976), 25–50.

Norden, E. *Agnostos Theos*. (Darmstadt: Wissenschaftliche Buchgesellschaft, 1956).

O'Brien, P. T. *Colossians, Philemon* (Waco: Word, 1982).

O'Neill, J. C. "The Source of Christology in Colossians," *NTS* 26 (1979), 87–100.

Painter, J. "Christology and the History of the Johannine Community in the Prologue of the Fourth Gospel," *NTS* 30 (1984), 460–74.

Pearson, B. A. "Hellenistic–Jewish Wisdom Speculation and Paul," in *Aspects of Wisdom in Judaism and Early Christianity*, ed. R. L. Wilken (South Bend: University of Notre Dame Press, 1975, 43–66.

Robinson, D. W. B. "The Literary Structure of Hebrews 1:1–4," *AJBA* 2 (1972), 178–86.

Sanders, J. A. "The Psalms Scroll of Qumran Cave 11," *Discoveries in the Judean Desert Journal* 4 (1965), 91–92.

Sanders, J. T. "Dissenting Deities and Philippians 2.1–11," *JBL* 88 (1969), 279–90.

——*The New Testament Christological Hymns* (Cambridge University Press, 1971).

Schnackenburg, R. *The Gospel According to St John*, Vol. I (London: Burns and Oates, 1968).

Schüssler Fiorenza, E. "Wisdom Mythology and the Christological Hymns of the New Testament," in *Aspects of Wisdom in Judaism and Early Christianity*, ed. R. L. Wilken (South Bend: University of Notre Dame Press, 1975), 17–41.

——*In Memory of Her: A Feminist Theologial Reconstruction of Christian Origins* (London: SCM Press, 1983).

Schweizer, E. "The Church as the Missionary Body of Christ," *NTS* 8 (1, 1961), 1–11.

——"Die Kirche als Leib Christi im dem paulinischen Antilegomena," *THLZ* 86 (1961), col. 241–56.

——"Paul's Christology and Gnosticism," in *Paul and Paulinism. Essays in Honour of C. K. Barrett*, ed. M. D. Hooker and S. G. Wilson (London: SPCK, 1982), 115–23.

——Stanley, D. "The Theme of the Servant of Yahweh," *CBQ* 16 (1954), 385–425.

Strecker, G. "Redaktion und Tradition im Christushymnus Phil. 2.6–11," *ZNW* 55 (1964), 63–78.

Wanamaker, C. A. "Phil. 2.6–11: Son of God or Adamic Christology?" *NTS* 33 (1987), 179–93.

Wilson, S. G. *Luke and the Pastoral Epistles* (London: SPCK, 1979).

Wink, W. "The Hymn of the Cosmic Christ," in *The Conversation Continues. Studies in Paul and John in Honor of J.L. Martyn* (Nashville: Abingdon Press, 1990), 235–44.

Witherington, B. III, *Jesus, Paul and the End of the World* (Downer's Grove; I-V Press, 1992).

Wright, N. T. *The Climax of the Covenant. Christ and the Law in Pauline Theology* (Edinburgh: T&T Clark, 1991).

CHAPTER 7: PAUL THE APOSTLE

Bailey, K. E. "Recovering the Poetic Structure of 1 Cor. 1.17 — 2.2," *NovT* 17 (1975), 265–96.

Barrett, C. K. "Christianity at Corinth," in *Essays on Paul* (Philadelphia: Westminster, 1982), 1–27.

Bassler, J. M. *Divine Impartiality* (Chico, CA: Scholars Press, 1982).

Bender, W. "Bemerkung zur Übersetzung von 1 Korinther 1.30," *ZNW* 71 (1980), 263–68.

Botte, D. B. "La Sagesse et les Origines de la Christologie," *RSPT* 21 (1932), 54–67.

Bouzard, W.C. "The Theology of Wisdom in Romans 1 and 2," *Word and World* 7.3 (1987), 281–91.

Brown, R. E. *The Semitic Background of the Term 'Mystery' in the New Testament* (Philadelphia: Fortress, 1968).

Charlesworth, J. H. "Jewish Hymns, Odes, and Prayers (ca. 167 B.C.E. – 135 C.E.)," in *Early Judaism and its Modern Interpreters*, eds. R. A. Kraft and G. W. E. Nickelsburg (Philadelphia: Fortress, 1986), 411–36.

Davies, J. A. *Wisdom and the Spirit. An Investigation of 1 Corinthians 1.18 – 3.20 against the Background of Jewish Sapiential Traditions in the Greco–Roman Period* (Lanham: University Press of America, 1984).

Deichgräber, R. *Gotteshymnus und Christushymnus in der frühen Christenheit* (Göttingen: Vandenhoeck and Ruprecht, 1967).

Dunn, J. D. G. *Romans 1–8* (Waco: Word, 1988).

Ellis, E. E. "Wisdom and Knowledge in 1 Cor.," in his *Prophecy and Hermeneutics in Early Christianity* (Tübingen: J.C.B. Mohr, 1978), 46–62.

Feuillet, A. *Le Christ Sagesse de Dieu. D'apres les Epitres Pauliniennes* (Paris: Gabalda Press, 1966).

Fiore, B. "'Covert Allusion' in 1 Corinthians 1–4," *CBQ* 47 (1985), 85–102.

Georgi, D. *Die Geschichte der Kollekte des Paulus für Jerusalem* (Hamburg: Herbert Reich, 1965).

——*Weisheit Salamos* (Gütersloh: Güterlohs Verlagshaus Gerd Mohn, 1980).

Goulder, M. D. "*Sophia* in 1 Corinthians," *NTS* 37 (1991), 516–34.

Grant, R. M. "The Wisdom of the Corinthians," in *The Joy of Study*, ed. S. E. Johnson (New York: Macmillan and Co., 1951), 51–55.

Grech, P. "Christological Motivations in Pauline Ethics," in *Paul de Tarse*, ed. L. de Lorenzi (Rome: Abbey of St. Paul, 1979), 541–58.

Hays, R. B. *Echoes of Scripture in the Letters of Paul* (New Haven: Yale University Press, 1989).

Hooker, M. D. *From Adam to Christ. Essays on Paul* (Cambridge University Press, 1990).

Horsley, R. A. "The Background of the Confessional Formula in 1 Kor. 8.6," *ZNW* 69 (1978), 130–35.

Horsley, R. "Gnosis in Corinth: 1 Corinthians 8.1–6," *NTS* 27 (1980), 32–51.

——"Wisdom of Word and Words of Wisdom in Corinth," *CBQ* 39 (1977), 224–39.

Johnson, E. E. *The Function of Apocalyptic and Wisdom Traditions in Romans 9–11* (Atlanta: Scholars' Press, 1989).

——"The Wisdom of God as Apocalyptic Power," in *Faith and History. Essays in Honor of P. W. Meyer* (Atlanta: Scholars' Press, 1990), 137–48.

Lampe, P. "Theological Wisdom and the `Word about the Cross'. The Rhetorical Scheme in 1 Corinthians 1–4," *Int* 44.2 (1990), 117–31.

Lang, F. *Die Briefe an die Korinther* (Göttingen: Vandenhoeck and Ruprecht, 1986).

Lim, T. H. "Not in Persuasive Words of Wisdom but in the Demonstration of the Spirit and Power," *NovT* 2 (1987), 137–49.

Mitchell, M. M. *Paul and the Rhetoric of Reconciliation* (Tübingen: J. C. B. Mohr, 1991).

Murphy O'Connor, J. "I Cor. VIII.6: Cosmology or Soteriology?" *RB* 85 (1978), 253–67.

Polhill, J. B. "The Wisdom of God and Factionalism: 1 Cor. 1–4," *Rev Exp* 80 (1983), 325–39.

Reese, J. M. "Paul Proclaims the Wisdom of the Cross: Scandal and Foolishness," *BTB* 9 (1979), 147–53.

Richardson, P. "The Thunderbolt in Q and the Wise Man in Corinth," in *From Jesus to Paul. Studies in Honour of F. W. Beare*, eds. Richardson and J. C. Hurd (Waterloo: Wilfrid Laurier University Press, 1984), 91–11.

Romaniuk, C. "Le Livre de la Sagesse dans le Nouveau Testament," *NTS* (1967–68), 498–514.

Roon, A. van "The Relationship Between Christ and the Wisdom of God According to Paul," *NovT* 16 (1974), 207–39.

Rylaarsdam, J. C. *Revelation in Jewish Wisdom Literature* (Chicago University Press, 1946.)

Schweizer, E. "Paul's Christology and Gnosticism," in *Paul and Paulinism, Essays in Honour of C. K. Barrett*, ed. M. D. Hooker and S. G. Wilson (London: SPCK, 1982), 115–23.

Scroggs, R. "Paul – *Sophos and Pneumatikos*," *NTS* 14 (1967–68), 33–55.

Sellin, G. "Das `Geheimnis' der Weisheit und das Rätsel der `Christuspartei' (zu 1 Kor. 1–4)," *ZNW* 73 (1982), 69–96.

Stadelmann, H. *Ben Sira als Schriftgelehrter* (Tübingen: J. C. B. Mohr, 1980).

Stowers, S. K. *The Diatribe and Paul's Letter to the Romans* (Chico, CA: Scholars Press, 1981).

Stuhlmacher, P. "The Hermeneutical Significance of 1 Cor. 2:6–16," in *Tradition and Interpretation in the NT. Essays in Honor of E. E. Ellis for his 60th Birthday*, ed. G. Hawthorne and O. Betz (Tübingen: J. C. B. Mohr, 1987), 328–43.

Suggs, M. J. "`The Word is Near to You.' Rom. 10:6–10 within the Purpose of the Letter," in *Christian History and Interpretation: Studies Presented to John Knox*, ed. R. Farmer, *et al.* (Cambridge University Press, 1967), 289–312.

Theissen, G. *Psychological Aspects of Pauline Theology* (Philadelphia: Fortress, 1987).

Tomson, P. J. *Paul and the Jewish Law* (Minneapolis: Fortress Press, 1990).

Wilckens, U. "Zu 1 Kor. 2.1–16," in *Theologia Crucis–Signum Crucis, Festschrift für E. Dinkler*, ed. C. Anderson *et al.* (Tübingen: J. C. B. Mohr, 1979), 501–37.

——*Weisheit und Torheit* (Tübingen: J. C. B. Mohr, 1959).

Williams, J. G. "Neither Here nor There, Between Wisdom and Apocalyptic in Jesus' Kingdom Sayings," *Forum* 5.2 (1979), 7–30.

Wilson, R. McL., "Gnosis at Corinth," in *Paul and Paulinism. Essays in Honour of C.K. Barrett*, eds. M. D. Hooker and S. G. Wilson (London: SPCK, 1982), 112–14.

Witherington, B. III, "The Influence of Galatians on Hebrews," *NTS* 37 (1991), 146–52.

——*Jesus, Paul, and the End of the World* (Grand Rapids: I-V Press, 1992).

Wuellner, W. "Greek Rhetoric and Pauline Argumentation," in *Early Christian Literature and the Classical Intellectual Tradition. In Honorem R. M. Grant*, ed. W. R. Schodel and R. L. Wilken (Paris: Editions Beauchesne, 1979), 177–88.

CHAPTER 8: THE GOSPELS OF WISDOM

Barrett, C. K. "School, Conventicle, and Church in the New Testament," in *Wissenschaft und Kirche. Festschrift für Eduard Lohse*, ed. K. Aland and S. Meurer (Bielefeld: Luther Verlag, 1989), 96–110.

Bauer, D. R. *The Structure of Matthew's Gospel* (Sheffield: Almond Press, 1988).

Bornkamm, G. "The Authority to Bind and Loose in the Church in Matthew's

Gospel," in *The Interpretation of Matthew*, ed. G. N. Stanton (London: SPCK, 1983), 85–97.
Brooks, S. H. *Matthew's Community. The Evidence of his Special Sayings Material* (Sheffield: JSOT Press, 1987).
Brown, R. E. *The Birth of the Messiah* (Garden City: Doubleday, 1977).
——*The Community of the Beloved Disciple* (London: G. Chapman, 1979).
Bruns, J. E. "Some Reflections on Coheleth and John," *CBQ* 25 (1963), 414–16.
Burridge, R. A. *What are the Gospels? A Comparison with Graeco–Roman Biography* (Cambridge University Press, 1992).
Colpe, O. L. *Matthew: A Scribe Trained for the Kingdom of Heaven* (Washington: Catholic Biblical Association, 1976).
Cullmann, O. *The Johannine Circle* (London: SCM Press, 1976).
Culpepper, R. A. *Anatomy of the Fourth Gospel* (Philadelphia: Fortress Press, 1983).
——*The Johannine School* (Missoula: Scholars Press, 1975).
Deutsch, C. *Hidden Wisdom and the Easy Yoke. Wisdom, Torah, and Discipleship in Matthew 11.25–30* (Sheffield: JSOT Press, 1987).
——"Wisdom in Matthew: Transformation of a Symbol," *NovT* 32.1 (1990), 13–47.
Dobschütz, E. von "Matthew as Rabbi and Canohechist," in *The Interpretation of Matthew*, (London: SPCK, 1983), 19–29.
Dodd, C. H. *The Interpretation of the Fourth Gospel* (Cambridge University Press, 1958).
Donaldson, T. L. *Jesus on the Mountain. A Study in Matthean Theology* (Sheffield: JSOT Press, 1985).
Duling, D. C. "The Eleazar Miracle and Solomon's Magical Wisdom in Flavius' Josephus's *Antiquitates Judaicae* 8. 42–49," *HTR* 78 (1985), 1–26.
Feuillet, A. *Johannine Studies* (New York: Alba House, 1965).
Fortna, R. T. *The Fourth Gospel and its Predecessor* (Edinburgh: T&T Clark, 1988).
France, R. T. *Matthew – Evangelist and Teacher* (Exeter: Pater Noster Press, 1989).
Goulder, M. D. *Midrash and Lection in Matthew* (London: SPCK, 1974).
Haenchen, E. "Matthäus 23," *ZTK* 48 (1951), 38–63.
Hare, D. R. A. *Jewish Persecution of Christians* (Cambridge University Press, 1967).
Hengel, M. *The Johannine Question* (London: SPCK, 1989).
Howell, D. B. *Matthew's Inclusive Story. A Study in the Narrative Rhetoric of the First Gospel* (Sheffield: JSOT Press, 1990).
Hubbard, B. J. *The Matthean Redaction of a Primitive Apostolic Commissioning: an Exegesis of Matthew 28.16–20* (Missoula: Scholars Press, 1974).
Johnson, M. D. "Reflections on a Wisdom Approach to Matthew's Christology," *CBQ* 36 (1974), 44–64.
Käsemann, E. *The Testament of Jesus: a Study of the Gospel of John in Light of Chapter 17* (Philadelphia: Fortress, 1968).
Kingsbury, J. D. *Matthew as Story* (Philadelphia: Fortress, 1986).
——*Matthew: Structure, Christology, Kingdom* (Philadelphia: Fortress, 1975).
——*The Parables of Jesus in Matthew 13*. London: SPCK, 1969).
Kysar, R. *John the Maverick Gospel* (Atlanta: John Knox, 1976).
Lincoln, A. T. "Matthew – A Story for Teachers?" in *The Bible in Three*

Dimensions, ed. D. J. A. Clines, *et al.* (Sheffield: JSOT Press, 1990), 103–25.
Luz, U. "The Disciples in the Gospel according to Matthew," in *The Interpretation of Matthew*, ed. G. N. Stanton (London: SPCK, 1983), 98–128.
——*Das Evangelium nach Mäthaus 2 (Mt. 8–17)* (Zurich: Benziger Verlag, 1990).
——*Matthew 1–7* (Minneapolis: Augsburg, 1985).
Michel, O. "The Conclusion of Matthew's Gospel," in *The Interpretation of Matthew*, ed. G. N. Stanton (London: SPCK, 1983), 30–41.
Minear, P. *Matthew: The Teacher's Gospel* (New York: Pilgrim Press, 1982).
Moeller, H. R. "Wisdom Motifs and John's Gospel," *Bul ETS* 6 (1963), 92–100.
Orton, D. E. *The Understanding Scribe. Matthew and the Apocalyptic Ideal* (Sheffield Academic Press, 1989).
Painter, J. *The Quest for the Messiah. The History, Literature, and Theology of the Johannine Community.* (Edinburgh: T&T Clark, 1991).
Paul, G. "Symposia and Deipna in Plutarch's *Lives* and in other Historical Writings," in *Dining in a Classical Context*, ed. W. J. Slater (Ann Arbor: University of Michigan Press, 1991), 157–69.
Schenk, W. *Die Sprache des Matthäus. Die Text–Konstituenten in ihren makro–und mikrostrukturellen Relationen* (Göttingen: Vandenhoeck and Ruprecht, 1987).
Scott, M. *Sophia and the Johannine Jesus* (Sheffield: JSOT Press, 1992).
Stanton, G. N. *A Gospel for a New People. Studies in Matthew* (Edinburgh: T&T Clark, 1992).
Stendahl, K. *The School of St. Matthew and its Use of the Old Testament* (Lund: Gleerup, 1967), 2nd ed.
Suggs, M. J. *Wisdom, Christology, and Law in Matthew's Gospel* (Cambridge: Harvard U. Press, 1970).
Ziener, G. "Weisheitbuch and Johannesevangelium," *Biblica* 38 (1957), 396–418, and 39 (1958), 37–60.

CHAPTER 9: FINAL REFLECTIONS ON WISDOM'S JOURNEY

Dodds, E. R. *Pagan and Christian in an Age of Anxiety* (Cambridge University Press, 1965).
Fraser, D. A. and T. Campolo, *Sociology through the Eyes of Faith* (San Francisco: Harper Collins, 1992).
Witherington, B. III "Three Modern Faces of Wisdom" *ATS* 25 (1993), 96–122.

Scripture Index

APOCRYPHAL/DEUTERCANONICAL BOOKS